D0203423

Addiction

Addiction

A Reference Encyclopedia

Howard Padwa and Jacob Cunningham

A B C  C L I O

Santa Barbara, California • Denver, Colorado • Oxford, England

Copyright 2010 by ABC-CLIO, LLC

Library of Congress Cataloging-in-Publication Data

Padwa, Howard.
    Addiction : a reference encyclopedia / by Howard Padwa and Jacob Cunningham.
       p. cm.
    Includes bibliographical references and index.
    ISBN 978–1–59884–229–6 (hc. : alk. paper) — ISBN 978–1–59884–230–2 (ebook)
1. Drug addiction—United States—Handbooks, manuals, etc. 2. Alcoholism—United States—
Handbooks, manuals, etc. 3. Substance abuse—Treatment—United States—Handbooks,
manuals, etc. 4. Drug abuse—Government policy—United States—Handbooks, manuals, etc. I.
Cunningham, Jacob. II. Title.
HV5825.P26 2010
616.8600973—dc22   2009045777

14 13 12 11 10   2 3 4 5

This book is also available on the World Wide Web as an eBook.
Visit www.abc-clio.com for details.

ABC-CLIO, LLC
130 Cremona Drive, P.O. Box 1911
Santa Barbara, California 93116-1911

This book is printed on acid-free paper ∞

Manufactured in the United States of America

Contents

List of Entries

About This Book

Addiction: A Reference Encyclopedia is designed to be a handy reference guide that is accessible to a wide reading audience. The book is divided into three main sections. The first part is a reference essay on the science behind the major addictions, with a focus on the neurochemistry that underlies addiction. This essay also provides a brief historical overview of many of the addictions. The book's second section consists of alphabetically organized entries on individuals, events, organizations, and developments in the study of addiction, with a focus on government attempts to control the use of addictive substances and the major figures and groups in the history of addiction in the United States. The third and final section is a selection of primary source documents, designed to give readers greater insight into some of the key developments in the history of addiction. In addition, there is a final section with suggestions for further reading for those interested in learning more about various aspects of addiction and its history in the United States.

Acknowledgments

Howard Padwa and Jacob Cunningham would like to thank Holly Heinzer, Lauren Thomas, and Kim Kennedy-White at ABC-CLIO for helping usher them through the process of producing this book. They would also like to thank all of their friends and family for their love and support throughout the writing of this book. In particular, Howard would like to thank the lovely Joy Moini, and Jacob would like to thank the newest member of his family—Libby Buchanan.

Reference Essay
Addiction: A Scientific and Historical Overview

I. WHAT IS ADDICTION?

According to *Webster's College Dictionary*, addiction is defined as a "dependence or commitment to a habit, practice, or habit-forming substance to the extent that its cessation causes trauma" (Random House, 16). Generally, when people think of addiction, they think of addiction to psychoactive substances or psychoactive drugs—chemicals that act on the central nervous system (CNS), and induce feelings of pleasure or well-being. If used for a prolonged period of time, these substances can cause individuals to become physically dependent, as their bodies require a steady flow of them to function normally. Once individuals are using a psychoactive substance in this manner, they are addicted, and cannot stop using without experiencing extreme physical or psychological discomfort.

Though addiction has traditionally been seen as a phenomenon that could be caused only by psychoactive substances, research in the last thirty years has shown that individuals can also suffer from the symptoms of addiction when it comes to habits and activities as well. Excessive eating, gambling, Internet use, shopping, sex, and steroid use can generate problems similar to those caused by psychoactive substances such as alcohol, cocaine, or heroin. Though scientists are still working to find out what makes these behaviors addictive, research has shown some commonalities between the neurochemical reactions that these behaviors cause and the effects that psychoactive drugs have in the CNS. But what unites addiction to chemicals and addiction to behaviors is not so much the chemical mechanisms behind them, but rather their effects on addicts' behaviors. Addiction to substances and addiction to behaviors share what researchers term "the three C's":

1. Compulsive Use: People who are addicted to a substance or a behavior have an irresistible impulse to ingest the addictive substance or engage in the addictive behavior. They have repetitive and ritualized patterns of use or behavior, and sometimes hear voices encouraging them to continue taking the addictive substance or engaging in the addictive behavior.

2. Loss of Control: Addicts cannot limit or resist their urges to take addictive substances or engage in addictive behaviors. Even if they want to stop, the impulse to take the addictive substance or engage in the addictive behavior overwhelms addicts' willpower, and they are unable to quit without help from others.

3. Continued Use Despite Adverse Consequences: Despite the fact that continuing to use the addictive substance or engage in the addictive behavior may cause them shame, financial problems, legal troubles, and do irreparable damage to their friendships and family relationships, addicts are unable to quit.

The following section will discuss the first class of addictions—addiction to psychoactive substances—that are prevalent in the United States. The third and final section in this essay will address some of the most common behavioral addictions.

II. ADDICTIVE AND PSYCHOACTIVE SUBSTANCES

How Do Psychoactive Substances Work? What Makes Them Addictive?

Psychoactive drugs affect the way that people feel by altering the normal functioning of the CNS, which consists of the brain and the spinal cord. The CNS is the control center for the body, governing both conscious activity (thoughts, moods), and unconscious activity (the beating of the heart, the breathing of the lungs). The CNS is composed of a series of neurons—cells that conduct information through electrical impulses—and works by releasing neurotransmitters—chemicals that are given off by transmitter cells at the end of one neuron and picked up by receptor cells at the end of another. When released into the space between two neurons, neurotransmitters stimulate and bind to receptor cells, much like a key would fit a lock, or the way two puzzle pieces would fit together. Psychoactive drugs act by either chemically stimulating or inhibiting the production, release, or reception of these neurotransmitters within the CNS. In particular they alter the functioning of neurotransmitters within the mesolimbic dopaminergic reward pathway (more commonly known as the reward/reinforcement center), a part of the brain that instinctively leads human beings to repeat actions that are pleasurable or necessary for survival. By acting on neurotransmitters within the reward/reinforcement center, psychoactive substances can trigger feelings of satiation and pleasure that the human brain is hardwired to crave, and ultimately, they can be too strong to resist. For some individuals, certain drugs can have such a powerful impact on the reward/reinforcement center that they will make replicating their psychoactive effects a priority over everything else in their lives—even basic necessities for survival such as food and water. This can cause intense craving for these substances, which in turn, leads to addiction.

A drug's psychoactive effects will depend on its chemical actions on specific neurotransmitters. If, for example, a drug increases the production of a neurotransmitter that communicates feelings of pleasure, the drug will enhance the user's sense of well-being. Or, on the other hand, a drug could limit the production of neurotransmitters that communicate unenjoyable sensations, leading the user to feel less pain or discomfort. Some drugs are so structurally similar to certain neurotransmitters that they can bind to receptors that are tied to the communication of specific sensations or feelings. If a drug has a chemical composition that is similar to that of a neurotransmitter that communicates pleasurable feelings, for example, it will bind to the receptors that are designed to receive those neurotransmitters, and create artificial sensations of contentment or satisfaction. Some other drugs work by delaying the metabolism of neurotransmitters, or by altering the neuron's ability to store them, thus creating either an overabundance or shortage of neurotransmitters. In all of these cases, what gives drugs their ability to affect feeling is not anything foreign that they introduce into the body; instead, it is their artificial affect on chemicals that the body naturally produces in the CNS that gives them their psychoactive powers.

Some of the major neurotransmitters affected by psychoactive drugs include:

- Acetylcholine—a neurotransmitter that controls body temperature, skeletal muscle movement, memory, learning, and the expression of emotions.

- Dopamine—a neurotransmitter that controls fine skeletal movement and is associated with the control of emotions.

- Endorphins—neurotransmitters that are involved in the regulation of pain, the mitigation of stress, and other physiological functions.

- Epinephrine (adrenaline) and norepinephrine (noradrenaline)—neurotransmitters that give energy and affect feelings of motivation, hunger, confidence, and alertness. They also control mood and perceptions of pleasure.

- Gamma-aminobutyric acid (GABA)—a neurotransmitter that controls inhibitions, impulses, muscle relaxation, and arousal.

- Serotonin—a neurotransmitter that can affect energy and mood.

When a person takes a psychoactive drug, it reaches the CNS and the reward/reinforcement center after it has been absorbed into the bloodstream. It is at this point that the person who takes a drug will feel its psychoactive effects. Even though many drugs that are often abused (alcohol, opiates) actually make some people feel physically sick when they first take them, the enjoyable psychological sensations these substances create by stimulating chemical activity in the reward/reinforcement center counterbalance their negative side effects for many individuals. Yet despite these positive feelings drugs can create, they also have their downside. Sometimes this can happen when a person consumes too much of a drug, leading to such an overproduction or overstimulation of neurotransmitters that it creates feelings that are no longer pleasurable. If a person takes too much of a drug that stimulates epinephrine, for example, feelings of elation and euphoria can quickly evolve into irritability, anxiety, and violent behavior. What is more, the body can become accustomed to the unnaturally high or low levels of certain neurotransmitters once individuals consume a drug for a long period of time, and their minds adapt to feel that the artificially high or low amount of neurotransmitters produced by drugs are necessary to feel healthy. At this point, they may need the drug to function normally, and if forced to go without their drug of choice, they experience withdrawal symptoms. When drug users experience withdrawal, they tend to experience sensations that were the opposite of those the drug gave them. For example, people coming down from a drug like cocaine, which gives a surge of energy, will feel lethargic and depressed. To alleviate these feelings and regain the artificial high they were experiencing when they were under the influence of cocaine, users' natural inclination is to take more of the drug so they can regain that fleeting surge of energy and well-being. Soon, people can become trapped in this cycle of highs and lows, and this is when they can begin using drugs with increasing regularity. Taking a drug repeatedly in a short amount of time can have a reinforcing effect, as both the body and mind come to believe that they need the drug to feel satisfied, healthy, or "normal." Depending on the drug, as well as the individual, this can lead to the development of a tolerance to a drug, as well as physical and psychological dependence, or addiction.

Tolerance develops when the body requires more and more of a psychoactive drug to achieve the same effect that a small dose used to have. For example, people can become drunk with just two beers the first time they drink alcohol, but once they have started drinking regularly, it may take them five or six beers to feel the same level of intoxication. Tolerance to some drugs is caused by changes in the way that receptors work after a drug has been used consistently for a long period of time. For some drugs, tolerance occurs due to changes in metabolism and liver activity, as the body begins to adapt and process the drugs quicker than it did before. Other substances can create tolerance by exhausting the body's natural supply of neurotransmitters, as the artificial overproduction of these chemicals eventually leaves the body unable to release them as easily as it once did. As an individual develops a tolerance to a drug's effects, it takes more and more of a drug to have the psychoactive effects that a small dose once had.

In some cases, tolerance can lead to dependence, meaning that drug takers can no longer function normally—physically or psychologically—without their drug of choice. A telling sign of psychological or physical dependence is if individuals experience withdrawal symptoms, becoming either sick or anxious if they have to go too long without their drug of choice. Sometimes this occurs because the body becomes so accustomed to having a drug that it no longer is able to perform its regular functions without it. When people are dependent on opiates or alcohol, for example, they can become violently ill if forced to go without them for an extended period of time. In extreme cases where people are highly dependent on drugs, they can suffer seizures, enter comas, and even die from withdrawal symptoms. When individuals are dependant on a drug, they will continue using it in order to continue feeling its positive effects and avoid withdrawal symptoms, even if excessive use is causing problems in other areas of their lives. Often, withdrawal effects are so severe that they create symptoms similar to those experienced by individuals with serious mental illness. With some drugs, like MDMA, the effects are more subtle, but still present, as regular users may not become sick without their drugs, but they report not being able to experience pleasure without being under the influence. In these cases, users may not be physically addicted to a drug, but they may be psychologically dependent on it.

Beyond the neurochemical processes that underlie chemical dependence, environmental factors can play an important role in addiction, as social and cultural factors can either inhibit or encourage individuals to try, and continue using, psychoactive substances. What is more, researchers have also argued that individuals' psychological makeup may predispose some people to become addicted, as they are more likely to turn to psychoactive substances to deal with emotional problems, or to cope with traumas or other social or family problems. According to many psychological theories, people turn to addictive substances and behaviors as defense mechanisms to deal with these issues. Models of behaviorist psychology hold that addiction develops as a learned behavior that is reinforced over time, creating cravings and urges independent of the neurochemical processes that lead people to repeat addictive behaviors. Heredity has also been shown to play a role in addiction, as studies have demonstrated that levels of certain enzymes and neurotransmitters, which are passed down genetically, influence the likelihood of developing addiction, both to psychoactive substances and to behaviors such as playing video games, eating, and gambling. The National Institute on Alcohol Abuse and Alcoholism and the National Institute on Drug Abuse are funding research to further explore the links between genetics and addiction. In addition, individuals with mental illness are more likely to become addicted to psychoactive substances than those who are not; similarly, people diagnosed with depression and anxiety disorders are more likely than others to develop addictions to alcohol or other drugs, as are people with Attention Deficit Disorder (ADD) or personality disorders.

There are several treatment options available for addicts trying to quit using psychoactive substances, though the chances of success are still rather slim. Twelve-step groups modeled on the program of Alcoholics Anonymous work by using mutual support and a spiritual process that tries to address the underlying psychological and emotional causes of substance abuse to help addicts stop using and stay sober. Therapeutic strategies and medicines borrowed from psychiatry and psychology also help individuals stop using drugs. In addition, there are some medicines that can help individuals quit, either by easing the pain that addicts experience when they stop using drugs, causing reactions that make addicts sick any time they use drugs, or by altering neurobiological processes that give drugs their psychoactive powers, thus blocking the pleasant effects that users are accustomed to experiencing when they take drugs. Generally, it is not enough to use just one of these methods, and studies have shown that addicts have the best chance of quitting and staying sober if they do several of these interventions in tandem with one another. Despite these treatment options, the chances of addicts remaining drug-free after treatment are only 20%, and researchers are continuing to look for a more reliable and lasting cure for addiction to psychoactive substances.

Since many psychoactive substances are used recreationally, it can be difficult to determine if individuals' drug use is merely a habit that they choose not to stop, or if they are addicted. Though it does not have any official definition of addiction, the American Psychiatric Association (APA) has guidelines for determining if an individual is dependent on a substance or not. According to the APA, people can be classified as dependent is if they meet three or more of the following seven criteria over a twelve-month period:

1. They develop a tolerance, marked by a need for increased amounts of a substance to feel intoxicated, or if use of the same amount of the substance does not have the same effects it used to.

2. They suffer from withdrawal symptoms when forced to go without the substance.

3. The substance is taken in larger amounts or over a longer period of time than the individual originally intended.

4. They want to cut down or control their use of a substance, but they cannot.

5. They spend a great deal of time trying to obtain the substance, using the substance, or recovering from intoxication with the substance.

6. They give up or cut back on social, work-related, or recreational activities because of their substance use.

7. They continue using a substance even though they know that it is causing them problems.

According to these criteria, 10.3 million Americans over the age of twelve—nearly 5% of the population—were dependent on drugs or alcohol in 1999.

The remainder of this section will give a brief scientific overview of each of the major addictive substances that are common in the United States today, with a focus on the neurochemical processes that underlie the addictions. For the addictive substances that are particularly prevalent today, this section will also include a brief summary of their history in Europe and the United States.

The Major Addictive Substances in the United States Today

Alcohol

Scientific Overview

Alcohol is one of the most commonly used psychoactive substances in the world, and it is one of the first to be used by human beings. Part of the reason that alcohol use is so widespread is because the form of it that we consume recreationally—ethyl alcohol—is produced naturally when the sugars in certain foods ferment. Alcohol is formed when yeast that is in the air begins feeding on the sugars in overripe fruits, vegetables, and grains, creating a chemical reaction that produces carbon dioxide and ethyl alcohol. Most people consume alcohol in the form of beer (which comes from the fermentation of grains), wine (which comes from the fermentation of fruit), or liquors, which are stronger, more potent beverages that are made by distilling fruits, vegetables, grains, wine, or beer. Most beers in the United States contain about

4 to 6% alcohol, while wines have about 12 to 14% alcohol, and liquors can have anywhere from 25 to 95% alcohol. There are other forms of alcohol, such as methyl alcohol, isopropyl alcohol, and butyl alcohol, but they are used in industrial processes and as chemicals in consumer products, not consumed in beverages.

Whereas many other psychoactive drugs act on just a few chemicals in the brain, alcohol's effects are much more widespread—it affects many neurotransmitters and receptors, and alters chemistry in the parts of the brain that control reasoning, judgment, mood, and emotions. Some of the key CNS chemicals it acts on include serotonin, dopamine, endorphins, GABA, and neurotransmitter receptors that affect reaction time, memory, movement, and psychological inhibitions. In low to moderate doses, alcohol lowers inhibitions, increases self-confidence, promotes sociability, relaxes, sedates, and reduces tension. Its ability to lower inhibitions is particularly notable, as it tends to multiply whatever feelings or mood the drinker was experiencing before they started drinking: If people are feeling happy when they drink, those feelings will usually be multiplied, and if they are sad, angry, or lonely, alcohol will generally bring them down into a state of depression, anger, and even violence. In higher doses (2 ounces of alcohol for females, 2.5 ounces of alcohol for males), the initial relaxation and lowered inhibitions can become exaggerated, leading people under the influence of the drug to feel confused, suffer from poor judgment, and become extremely emotional. Alcohol's ability to make emotions stronger while lowering inhibitions makes people more likely to take risks they would not normally take, leading them to engage in risky behaviors like being more sexually promiscuous than usual, or driving even though they are too intoxicated to safely control a vehicle. Beyond these effects on the brain, alcohol, when consumed in high doses, also begins to have strong physical effects, such as lowering blood pressure and slowing reflexes. The drug's effects lead people who are heavily intoxicated with alcohol to slur their speech, lose their balance, and become confused. In heavier doses, it can also cause "blackouts" or "brownouts"—periods of time in which a person seems to be awake and conscious, but afterwards does not remember anything that happened. In addition, excessive use can lead to hangovers—withdrawal episodes marked by nausea, headaches, extreme thirst, dizziness, moodiness, and depression—once all the alcohol is metabolized and released by the body.

When people begin drinking regularly, they can start to develop both a physical and a psychological tolerance to alcohol. Over time, the livers of heavy drinkers adapt and begin processing alcohol more quickly, while brain neurons become more resistant to the effects of the drug and require more and more alcohol to create feelings of intoxication. After a few months of steady and intense drinking, people can begin to suffer more severe withdrawal symptoms that go beyond ordinary hangovers. Major withdrawal symptoms include hallucinations and delirium tremens—an uncontrollable shaking of the whole body that can last up to ten days. To alleviate these unpleasant and potentially dangerous withdrawal symptoms, the natural impulse of heavy drinkers is to consume more alcohol to make them stop. This just makes their tolerance and physical dependence on the drug even stronger, however, and leads to a cycle of drunkenness and withdrawal symptoms that is the hallmark of alcohol addiction, or alcoholism.

The longer alcoholics continue to drink, the more likely it becomes they will do serious damage to their minds and bodies. If used excessively for a prolonged period of time, alcohol can cause liver disease, since heavy consumption of the drug overworks the organ and destroys liver cells. In addition, chronic and heavy alcohol use can cause stomach inflammation, intestinal bleeding, ulcers, cardiovascular disease, and damage to both nerve and brain cells. Alcoholism can have negative effects on mental health, leading to memory problems, hallucinations, paranoia, depression, insomnia, and anxiety. Though the majority of people who consume alcohol do not use it so much that they run into these particular problems, it is estimated that those who drink heavily for an extended period of time can die fifteen years earlier than the rest of the population because of alcohol-related complications. If blood-alcohol levels become too high, the physical slowing of central nervous system functions can lead to respiratory problems, cardiac failure, comas, and even death.

In addition to these consequences for the individual, alcoholism is also a major social problem since the behavior of alcoholics has a great effect on those around them, and use of the drug is so widespread; between the violence, absenteeism from work, drunk driving accidents, and neglect of family members and loved ones caused by excessive alcohol use, the negative consequences of the drug's abuse causes untold harm to millions every year. In 2004, researchers estimated that 12 to 14 million people in the United States had a drinking problem, and that the combined cost of problems related to alcohol abuse was $184 billion, or an average of $638 per man, woman, and child in the country.

Though the majority of people who use alcohol do not become addicted, those who do face a very difficult task when they decide to stop drinking. The severity of withdrawal symptoms makes it very difficult to quit, as does the fact that alcohol is often used socially. If individuals spend most of their leisure time at a local bar or drinking with friends, it is hard for them to find something to fill the gap left in their lives when they stop using alcohol. To attenuate the physical effects of alcohol withdrawal and help alcoholics stop drinking, there are several drugs, including naltrexone, acamprosate, ondanestron, benzodiazepines, and anti-depressants. In addition, another drug that has been used in the treatment of alcoholism has been disulfiram (also known as "Antabuse"), which works by changing the way the body metabolizes alcohol, creating unpleasant effects including nausea, headaches, and breathing difficulties whenever someone taking the drug drinks alcohol. By making people sick even when they consume small amounts of alcohol, Antabuse can help alcoholics stop drinking, though in some cases the impulse to use alcohol is so strong that alcoholics will continue drinking even while taking it. Behavioral approaches towards the treatment of alcoholism have been proven effective, with peer pressure, urging from loved ones, and teaching coping skills that can help chronic drinkers avoid drinking all helping alcoholics control their drinking problems. One of the most popular methods for helping alcoholics recover is the twelve-step model of Alcoholics Anonymous, which combines mutual support, introspection, and spiritual healing to help people overcome the temptation to drink. Though there is some evidence that each of these approaches towards treating alcoholism can help, none of them have proven universally effective, or able to help all alcoholics. Generally, a combination of these interventions is believed to be the best way to help alcoholics overcome their drinking problems.

A Brief History of Alcohol

Alcohol use dates back thousands of years, and ancient civilizations recognized both the pleasant effects alcohol had, as well as the potential dangers it could pose. From its beginnings, alcohol has played an important role in many Judeo-Christian and European traditions, from the use of wine in Jewish and Christian religious ceremonies to the Ancient Greeks' celebrations devoted to Dionysus, their god of wine. In the Middle Ages and the early-modern period, alcohol was a regular part of the European diet, especially because drinking the unsanitary water of the times could be dangerous since it often spread disease. Alcohol was also widely used as a medicine that could alleviate pain and anxiety, and over time it became associated with social events like fairs and carnivals. The rituals that evolved around alcohol consumption —activities like toasting and buying a round of drinks for friends—helped cement alcohol's symbolic place as a beverage of friendship and camaraderie in Europe. Yet from the time human beings began using alcohol, many recognized the problems it could cause. The Book of Deuteronomy in the Old Testament warned against drunkenness, and many in Europe disliked the drug because of the tendency of peasants and the working poor to drink to excess, arguing that drinking made the lower classes neglect their families, become lazy, and behave violently. For centuries, critics assumed that people who drank excessively did so by choice, and that alcoholism was a sin of excess, a moral failing on the part of the drinker rather than a physical or psychological addiction that drinkers were powerless to stop. The potential problems associated with excessive drinking became clearer when the process of distillation, which allowed for the production of beverages with much higher alcohol contents, became prevalent in the late-fifteenth century. With the large-scale commercialization of beer, wine, and distilled liquors in the late-eighteenth and early-nineteenth centuries, drinking became increasingly common in industrialized countries.

Views on alcoholism began to change in the late-eighteenth century when Benjamin Rush, an American surgeon, argued that chronic drinkers were victims of a disease, and unable to stop drinking even if they wanted to. Rush recommended building special asylums where alcoholics could sober up, and stay until they were cured of their compulsion to drink. This theory was further advanced with the work of Swedish physician Magnus Huss, who in 1849 coined the term "alcoholism" to describe the problems, both physical and mental, that excessive alcohol use could cause. In the nineteenth century, however, most continued to think of alcoholism as a moral problem, rather than a medical one. As early as 1808, people in the United States began creating organizations devoted to temperance (the moderate use of alcohol) and abstinence. In the nineteenth century, mutual aid societies designed to help alcoholics overcome their problems developed across the country, as did special institutions for problem drinkers. Alcohol also had its advocates as well, however, since drinking was a popular pastime, taxes on alcohol provided a great source of income for both state and federal governments, and the business of producing and distributing alcohol was a profitable one. Though some state and local governments did take steps to limit the availability of alcohol, drinking remained prevalent in most of the United States. In 1920, opponents of alcohol achieved one of their major goals with the passage of the Eighteenth Amendment, which prohibited the manufacture and sale of beverages with an alcohol content greater than 0.5%. In some respects, alcohol prohibition was a success, as it led to decreases in alcohol-related diseases, as well as a fall in rates of domestic violence, violent crime, and public disorders related to alcohol. The downside of prohibition, however, was that many people disregarded the law, either producing illicit alcohol on their own or resorting to a black market for alcohol that emerged in the 1920s. In 1933, prohibition was repealed, but there are still controls over who can consume alcohol. Under the 1984 National Minimum Drinking Age Act, the federal government effectively prohibits states from allowing individuals under the age of twenty-one to purchase alcohol.

After World War II, the disease concept of alcoholism gained ground, and in 1970, the government formally recognized alcohol abuse and alcoholism as a major public health problem with the passage of the Hughes Act, which formed the National Institute on Alcohol Abuse and Alcoholism to research alcohol and its potential dangers. In addition, several organizations have developed to spread awareness about the dangers of drunk driving, in particular Mothers Against Drunk Driving (MADD) and Students Against Destructive Decisions (SADD). Twelve-step programs for people who are friends or relatives of alcoholics, such as Al-Anon and Alateen, have also grown in recent years.

Amphetamines

Scientific Overview

Amphetamines are synthetic chemicals, meaning that they are made in laboratories and not found anywhere in nature. While these drugs are commonly used in medicines designed to help people with allergies, behavioral problems, trouble staying awake, and weight-control issues, they can become highly addictive when abused. In the last thirty years, illegal forms of amphetamines have become popular as the government has issued tighter controls over the use of the drugs in medications. The illegal forms of amphetamine have many street names, including "speed," "ice," "crank," "crystal meth," and "ya ba." Though they can be taken in pill form, amphetamines are often crushed up and snorted, smoked, or injected.

Amphetamines work by increasing the levels of epinephrine, norepinephrine, and dopamine released by the body. In addition to blocking their reabsorption into the body, amphetamines also hinder the metabolism of these neurotransmitters, meaning that their effects last much longer than other stimulant drugs, such as cocaine. As a result, people feeling the effects of amphetamines can experience increases in heart rate, higher body temperature, rapid breathing, higher blood pressure, more energy, and diminished hunger. Mentally, the drugs produce a sense of euphoria and well-being, and they also make the body release other neurotransmitters that are similar to those released during sex, making users feel an added pleasure while under the influence of the drug. The excess energy experienced by amphetamine users makes them go on binges in which they use the drug continuously and stay up for days at a time—an experience that while pleasurable, places tremendous strain on the body. Users begin feeling the psychoactive effects of amphet-amines immediately if they smoke or inject the drugs, in as little as three minutes if they snort them, and in fifteen minutes if they swallow them. Amphetamines' effects can last anywhere from four to six hours. The ups of amphetamines are often counteracted by dev-astating downs, with users becoming irritable, paranoid, anxious, and confused once they use the drugs for a prolonged period of time. Amphetamines can also make users more aggressive and overconfident, and more likely to act violently. Excessive amphetamine use can make users psychotic, and it can even cause symptoms that are very similar to those experienced by people with mental illnesses such as schizophrenia. Sometimes, a dose as small as 55 milligrams can cause mental problems, though they are rarely perma-nent. In addition, if people take too high a dose of amphetamines, they could suffer from an overdose, which could lead to convulsions, a stroke, an overly rapid heartbeat, and col-lapse. Generally, the damages and side effects caused by amphetamine abuse wear off after about a week. Yet if used for a longer period of time, the drugs can cause more permanent damage.

If used responsibly and in moderation, however, amphetamines—particularly the ones included in legally prepared medications that are taken by mouth—do not neces-sarily cause these problems. While the use of amphetamines is not necessarily healthy, the drug usually only causes major problems when taken regularly for stimulation or for recreational purposes. The problem is that many people who get into trouble with amphetamines do so by initially using the drugs in their legal and prescribed forms, and then quickly becoming dependent on them. Though illegally produced amphet-amines account for a large part of the amphetamine addiction problem today, the majority of the cases of amphetamine abuse over the last fifty years has started with people who took the drugs in legally manufactured forms.

Amphetamines are addictive because once people use the drugs for a long time, their bodies become reliant on them to produce dopamine and norephinephrine. At this point, it becomes very difficult for users to experience pleasure without amphetamines, and they are likely to start taking higher doses of the drugs at shorter intervals. Regular amphetamine users develop a high tolerance to the drug, and if used consistently for a long time, the drugs can cause sleep deprivation, malnutrition, strokes, and damage to the heart muscle. Once addicted to amphetamines, people experience severe with-drawal symptoms including depression, anxiety, fatigue, and an intense craving for the drugs if forced to go without them. Extended use of amphetamines can also dam-age nerve cells and cause permanent changes in the brain, leading to problems that continue even after the user has stopped taking amphetamines. The most effective treatments for amphetamine addiction are behavioral, as currently there are no drugs that can help ease the process of getting off of amphetamines, though clinical research has shown that some FDA-approved drugs can help reduce the high that people expe-rience when they take amphetamines. Other interventions that have been proven effec-tive in the treatment of amphetamine addiction are participation in twelve-step programs, behavioral therapy, family support, and encouragement to participate in nondrug related activities. In particular, researchers have found that "contingency management" treatments—in which addicts are given tangible rewards for staying clean—are effective in helping amphetamine addicts kick the habit.

A Brief History of Amphetamines

Amphetamines were first synthesized in the late-nineteenth century, when scientists were trying to produce ephedrine, a natural plant extract that was used to treat asthma. Its stimulant effects, however, were not recognized at the time. Though not identical to ephedrine, scientists began to find the drugs useful in the 1930s, when they determined that they could be effective as decongestants in nasal inhalers that were used by people suffering from asthma and hay fever. Soon, doctors began recommending them for the treatment of narcolepsy, epilepsy, Parkinson's disease, seasickness, obesity, depression, and behavior disorders in children. In addition to the original amphetamines, a series of related chemicals were developed over the course of the twentieth century. In 1919 Japanese scientists developed methylamphetamine (also known as methadrine, desoxyn, or methamphetamine), a drug that was four times as strong as the original amphetamine. In the 1930s, Tufts University researcher Abraham Myerson found that the drugs had a positive effect on mood, and advocated their use for the treatment of depression. During World War II, governments on both sides of the conflict used the drug for military purposes, including it in soldiers' rations in hopes that the drugs would make them march longer and fight more aggressively, and help pilots remain alert when they were on extended missions. In the 1950s, a Swiss company began producing methylamphetamine under the trade name of Ritalin, a drug which is still used today to treat children suffering from ADD and Attention Deficit Hyperactivity Disorder (ADHD). In the 1950s and 1960s, companies recognized that the drug also worked to make people less hungry, and began marketing them aggressively. The over-prescription of amphetamines, combined with their increased popularity in the drug culture of the late 1960s, made amphetamine addiction more prevalent. Even though some scientists were warning that amphetamines could be addictive as early as the 1930s, the U.S. government did not take action to institute tighter controls over them until the 1960s. Amphetamines became controlled substances under the Drug Abuse Control Amendments of 1965, and they were classified as Schedule II drugs under the Comprehensive Drug Abuse Prevention and Control Act of 1970. This meant that they could now only be used for medical purposes. Today they are still used to treat ADD and hyperactivity in children, narcolepsy, and sometimes to help people lose weight.

Once amphetamines became more tightly controlled and difficult to obtain through medical channels, underground chemists started to produce various forms of illegal amphetamines for recreational use. In the 1980s, people began manufacturing two forms of methamphetamine—"crank" (methamphetamine sulfate) and "crystal meth" (methamphetamine hydrochloride) by mixing together commonly available chemical products and compounds. In the early 1990s, a new form of methamphetamine known as "ice" became popular on the black market. Ice has less of the physical side effects that other amphetamines have on the heart and lungs, but greater mental effects, making users more paranoid and likely to hallucinate than other amphetamines do. Since it does not act as powerfully on the body, users tend to take larger amounts of "ice," and consequently, they are more likely to overdose on it than they are other kinds of amphetamines. According to the U.S. Drug Enforcement Administration (DEA), there are over 300 different methods that illicit producers use to make methamphetamines for the black market. Many of these methods for manufacturing amphetamines involve combining pseudoephedrine, a chemical found in cold medicines and decongestants, with highly toxic chemicals and products like battery acid, paint thinner, lead acetate, acetone, hydrochloric acid, and drain cleaner. The fact that such dangerous chemicals are included in illicitly manufactured amphetamines can make the drugs even more harmful for the people who consume them. Biker gangs used to be heavily involved in the manufacture and distribution if illicit amphetamines, through in recent years Mexican gangs have taken over the production, smuggling, and distribution of the drugs on the illicit market. In the last few years, "ya ba," an amphetamine produced in Southeast Asia, has become increasingly prevalent on the U.S. black market as well. According to the U.S. government's National Institute on Drug Abuse, 4.3% of the population that is over 12 years old has used methamphetamines at least once, though rates of use among youth have actually been decreasing in recent years. Overall, however, more people have had to visit emergency rooms because of problems associated with methamphetamine use in recent years, and by 2004 it accounted for 8% of the admissions into addiction treatment centers (compared to just 1% in 1992).

Caffeine

Scientific Overview

Caffeine is the most widely consumed psychoactive substance in the world. It is found in the beans, leaves, and fruits of over sixty plants, and is in many of the foods, drinks, and medicines we consume on a regular basis, including coffee, tea, soft drinks, and chocolate. According to some studies, 85% of the people in the United States consume significant amounts of caffeine on a daily basis.

Caffeine works by blocking the body's release of adenosine, a chemical that the brain releases to tell nerve cells to stop releasing the neurotransmitters dopamine, epinephrine, and serotonin. As with most drugs, the effects of caffeine vary depending on how it is used, what other drugs are taken with it, and how fast the body can metabolize it. The drug is often used as a medicine, either as a bronchodilator for people with breathing problems, as a pain medication, or to counteract sudden drops in blood pressure. Many over-the-counter medicines—especially decongestants, pain relievers, and medicines that help people stay awake—have caffeine as one of their main active ingredients. More commonly, however, people use caffeine as a stimulant drug since it can temporarily increase alertness, make them less tired, and help them think more clearly. About 100 milligrams of caffeine is enough to have these effects, and people often consume enough caffeine to experience them on a daily basis. A cup of percolated coffee, for example, has 100 milligrams of caffeine, while instant coffee has 75 milligrams, and a cup of tea can have anywhere from 10 to 100 milligrams. A can of soda usually has about 40 to 50 milligrams of caffeine, while so-called "energy drinks" have about 80 milligrams. A piece of chocolate can have anywhere from 24 milligrams (milk chocolate) to 140 milligrams (baking chocolate). While the body is able to metabolize some of the drug, people can start to experience negative side effects if they consume more than 200 milligrams in a day. People who consume too much caffeine can experience anxiety, insomnia, stomach problems, high blood pressure, and feel nervous, while extremely high levels can cause heart palpitations, muscle twitches, and vomiting. According to some research, long-term consumption of high levels of caffeine can increase the risk of heart disease, ulcers, diabetes, and liver problems. Yet because caffeine is so prevalent in everyday products, many people quickly develop a physical dependence on the drug, especially if they consume over 500 milligrams per day. Once someone is dependent on caffeine, they can suffer withdrawal symptoms that include headaches, sleeplessness, depression, nausea, and irritability if they do not get their usual amount of the drug. These withdrawal symptoms generally last thirty-six to seventy-two hours, and disappear if the person takes a dose of caffeine in some form.

Treatment for caffeine addiction is still relatively new, and according to addiction experts, it is still unclear what works best to help people get over their caffeine habits. Often, people with caffeine addiction can use the so-called "step-down" approach, gradually reducing their caffeine intake over time, though some people find it easier to "go cold turkey"—just quit using the drug altogether at once. Support groups, therapy, and counseling are also helpful for people who are dependent on caffeine and trying to quit.

A Brief History of Caffeine

Humans have consumed caffeine in various forms since the Stone Age, when people found that chewing on the seeds, bark, and leaves of certain plans helped ease fatigue, make them more aware, and better their mood. The first written record of people drinking brews made from tea leaves date back to the year 35 A.D., when it was consumed in China, and the beverage became popular in Europe and North America at the end of the sixteenth century. Coffee was first cultivated in Ethiopia around 650 A.D., and its use spread to the Arab world by the thirteenth century and over to Europe in the fifteenth century. In Africa, people have been using another caffeinated plant, the kola nut, for centuries, though its use did not become popular in Europe and the United States until the late 1800s, when people began combining it with carbonated liquids to create what we now know as "cola." In Central America, people had been consuming the caffeinated beans of the cacao tree since 600 B.C., though its use did not become widespread in Europe until the nineteenth century when it was sold in chocolate bars made from cacao. The caffeine alkaloid was first isolated from coffee in 1819 by German chemist Friedlieb Ferdinand Runge. Another German scientist, Hermann Emil Fischer, was the first to figure out the structure of the caffeine molecule and create it artificially. In the nineteenth century, when European and North American scientists began studying addiction in greater detail, many considered coffee, tea, and other caffeinated beverages to be just as potentially dangerous to the health of users as other drugs like opium and cocaine. While still recognized as addictive today, caffeine is not considered as dangerous a drug if consumed in moderate amounts. Even though it is habit-forming and some studies link its heavy use with anxiety and depression, caffeine is not subject to tight controls the same way that many other psychoactive drugs are. According to the U.S. Food and Drug Administration, caffeine is a "safe food substance," not a dangerous drug.

Cannabis and Its Derivatives

Scientific Overview

Human beings have been using the leaves of the hemp plant (also known as cannabis or marijuana), which probably originated in China or Central Asia, for a variety of purposes for at least 10,000 years. There are many uses for the plant, as its fibers can be used to produce rope and cloth, its seeds are edible, it contains an oil that can be used as a fuel, and it also contains active ingredients that have been used as medicines throughout history. Even today, some recommend using marijuana to alleviate pain, and as a medicine for the treatment of certain forms of glaucoma and muscular sclerosis. Of the 420 chemicals in the cannabis plant, over sixty of them, called cannabinoids, are believed to have some psychoactive properties. The main psychoactive ingredient in cannabis is the chemical delta-9-tetrahydrocannabinol (THC), which makes up somewhere between 1 and 3% of the cannabis leaf as it grows in nature. Illegal growers, however, have adopted new techniques for growing the plant to enhance its psychoactive effects, and much of the marijuana available on the black market today has THC concentrations as high as 15%. The resin of the cannabis plant, known as hashish, has the highest levels of THC, though most of the marijuana used in the United States today comes from the less potent leaves, buds, and stems of the plant. The drug is usually smoked, though it can be eaten if added to food. Most users, however, prefer to smoke cannabis since it takes longer to feel the psychoactive effects of the drug if it is eaten, and consuming the drug orally increases the likelihood that the drug will have unpleasant effects.

It was not until the 1990s that scientists discovered which neurotransmitters the THC chemical acts on, finding that it works by affecting the receptors for the neurotransmitter anandamide, and increasing the production of norepinephrine and dopamine. Compared to many other psychoactive substances, the effects that people feel when under the influence of cannabis are relatively mild. The main sensations produced by marijuana include euphoria, a slightly altered sense of sight and sound, and a distortion of the sense of time. The main reason marijuana users use the drug is to gain the overall sense of pleasure, calm, and relaxation that it produces, especially in small doses. When used in social settings, the initial feelings brought on by marijuana—euphoria, talkativeness, and sometimes uncontrollable laughter—are similar to the initial effects of alcohol. In doses of about 2.5 milligrams, the changes in perception become more intense, with users experiencing decreases in feelings of tension and depression, a disrupted short-term memory, increased drowsiness, hallucinations, flashbacks, and a sense of being mentally separated from the outside world. For individuals unaccustomed to these effects, this can lead to anxiety and paranoia, though regular users grow to find the experience a pleasant one. These mental effects are accompanied by physical feelings of relaxation and sedation, the attenuation of physical pain, bloodshot eyes, diminished muscular coordination, increased feelings of hunger and thirst, and nausea. Within an hour of use, the effects of marijuana begin to diminish, and generally dissipate within four to six hours. The high induced by the drug lasts longer when it is eaten than when it is smoked, though it also takes much longer to take effect.

Users develop a tolerance to marijuana relatively quickly, and the drug can remain in the bodies of chronic users for up to three months after they last smoked it. The withdrawal symptoms experienced by marijuana users, however, are relatively mild when compared to most other addictive drugs. Part of the reason withdrawal symptoms from marijuana are minimal is that the THC chemical remains in the brain for a long period after the drug was last used, and it sometimes takes weeks for chronic users to start feeling any unpleasant side effects when they stop taking the drug. Some people report never feeling any withdrawal symptoms when they stop using it, though studies show that in the long-run, most regular users can experience a variety of symptoms, including anger, irritability, depression, an inability to concentrate, trouble sleeping, and a craving to start using marijuana again. Nonetheless, the side effects of marijuana withdrawal are not nearly as severe as those caused by withdrawal from nicotine, alcohol, opiates, or other commonly abused drugs. Many individuals who first try the drug casually do wind up becoming habitual users, even if they do not suffer from extreme and immediate withdrawal symptoms when they stop. Most of the negative consequences of chronic cannabis use are physical, with regular users developing respiratory problems (largely because the drug is smoked), and some studies have shown that prolonged use can have negative effects on the immune system and cognitive functioning, while impairing short-term memory, attention span, and motivation. Other studies have also found a correlation between cannabis use and the development of psychotic disorders, though scientists have not found any causal link between marijuana and mental illness. For people who are unable to stop using marijuana, the most popular treatment options include interventions such as cognitive behavioral therapy, and twelve-step support groups. Scientists are also working to develop medicines that can help people stop using marijuana, though these efforts are yet to yield any effective cure for cannabis dependence.

A Brief History of Cannabis and Its Derivatives

While humans have used cannabis as a food and a fiber for thousands of years, they have also been aware of its psychedelic effects since antiquity, with ancient Chinese, Indians, and Romans all writing of the drug' psychoactive effects. Over the centuries, it was widely used as a medicine for headaches, mania, insomnia, venereal disease, tuberculosis, dysentery, asthma, and as a painkiller during childbirth among other things. The practice of smoking the drug for its psychoactive effects evolved into a pastime in India, the Middle East, and Africa, and eventually spread to Europe and North America in the nineteenth century. French soldiers who served in Egypt and Algeria brought the practice of using of the drug for its psychoactive effects back to Europe, and by the mid-nineteenth century it became a fashion among a group of high-class poets in Paris. The drug was mentioned in seminal works of French literature from the era, most notably Alexandre Dumas' *Count of Monte Cristo*. In the United States, some writers, most notably Fitz Hugh Ludlow, also experimented with cannabis. In addition, French physician Joseph Moreau de Tours experimented with cannabis in hopes that it could give him insight into the experience of the mentally ill, and possibly offer a cure for their afflictions. In the United States, cannabis was a common plant (even George Washington grew it on his plantation), though it was cultivated more for use as a fiber than anything else.

The practice of using cannabis recreationally probably came over to the United States with slaves, who brought it with them from Africa, and then with migrant laborers who came to the United States from Latin America during World War I. The association of the drug with minorities who, according to some of the racist beliefs of the time, were amoral and dangerous, spawned opposition to the drug, as did some early-twentieth century research that argued it was potentially just as harmful as alcohol and opium. With the passage of the Pure Food and Drug Act of 1906, cannabis became less prevalent in common medical preparations, though it was not subject to the same tight controls as other drugs, such as opiates, under the 1914 Harrison Narcotics Act.

In the years after World War I, commentators, doctors, and legislators began pushing for tighter controls over the drug, and calls for legislation increased when fear of Mexican immigrants grew during the Great Depression. Authorities in Washington, while acknowledging that marijuana use was endemic and potentially problematic in southern and western states, believed that it could be more effectively regulated by state governments than by the Federal Bureau of Narcotics. Political pressure to institute federal controls, however, grew in the 1930s, and in 1937 the federal government took action with the passage of the Marihuana Tax Act, which gave the Treasury Department the power to regulate cannabis. But despite these controls, marijuana use exploded in the 1960s when the drug became a favorite of hippies and others in the counterculture. Largely in response to the spread of cannabis use, the federal government passed the Comprehensive Drug Abuse Prevention and Control Act of 1970, which raised the penalties for growing, importing, exporting, and dealing the drug to up to ten years in prison, while making possession of the drug punishable by up to two years in jail. In 1972, the National Organization for the Reform of Marijuana Laws (NORML) petitioned the government to reclassify the drug and lighten the restrictions on it. After years of legal wrangling, NORML finally got the DEA to hear its case in 1987, and the judge in the case agreed that the drug should be reclassified so it could be used as a medicine. In spite of the recommendation, the DEA refused to reclassify the drug, and in federal law, it remains a Schedule I drug—the most highly controlled class of drug—to this day.

Beginning in the 1970s, many states took action to either decriminalize possession of marijuana or to allow for it to be used as a medicine, though the legal status of these statutes remains in limbo. While states can pass whatever laws they want concerning marijuana, federal law, which still classifies it as a highly controlled substance, technically trumps state laws when there is a conflict between the two. As a result, the fate of medical marijuana laws and state efforts to decriminalize the drug remain up in the air. Meanwhile, recreational use remains prevalent in the United States today, with some 14.8 million people in the United States reporting using the drug in the last month in a National Survey on Drug Use and Health conducted in 2006. Marijuana use continues to remain common amongst the young, as over 63.3% of the people who tried the drug for the first time were under eighteen. In 2007, 14.2% of eighth graders reported trying marijuana at least once, while over 40% of high school seniors have used the drug at some point in their lives.

Coca and Its Derivatives

Scientific Overview

The coca leaf comes from a shrub that grows in South America, and has been cultivated there for thousands of years. The leaf of the coca plant contains fourteen different drugs, most notably cocaine. In its pure form, coca contains only 0.5% cocaine, and does not cause many of the problems that cocaine does since the other components of the plant neutralize the effects of the drug. Once isolated from the coca plant, cocaine looks like a fine white powder. The drug is usually snorted, and rarely it is dissolved in water and then injected. In the 1980s, a new form of cocaine became popular when drug dealers began dissolving cocaine and then heating it to create crystals that could be smoked. The cocaine crystals that emerge from this process are often referred to as "crack" because of the crackling sound they make when they are smoked.

Cocaine works by causing the release of the neurotransmitters norephinephrine, epinephrine, and dopamine and then slowing their reabsorption into the body, meaning the people who take the drug not only produce these neurotransmitters at a faster rate, but experience their effects more powerfully. As a result, people who are under the influence of cocaine experience feeling of euphoria, confidence, excessive energy, hyperstimulation, reduced fatigue, increased sexual desire, and alertness. Physically, the drug causes hyperactivity, restlessness, a higher temperature, and increases in blood pressure and heart rate. While these mental and physical effects can be pleasant, they can also be dangerous. When under the influence of cocaine, people's inhibitions are lowered, while their emotions become more sensitive than usual. As a result, people are more likely to behave aggressively, fight, or do other things when they are high on cocaine that they would not normally do. If cocaine is snorted, these effects last about fifteen to thirty minutes, while the drug wears off much more quickly if it is smoked (five to ten minutes). When the pleasant mental effects of the drug dissipate, users become tired and depressed, and suffer a malaise that, depending on the individual, can last hours, days, or even weeks. To regain the exhilaration they experienced when under the influence of the drug, some cocaine users will begin using the drug regularly, taking larger doses in shorter and shorter intervals, and soon they can become addicted. Even if regular cocaine users abstain from the drug for an extended amount of time, it is difficult for them to stay off it. About a week after cocaine users stop taking the drug, they are likely to start feeling cravings for cocaine as their energy level drops, it becomes difficult to feel pleasure from activities or friends, and a severe episode of depression begins. At this point, it becomes very difficult to stay away from the drug.

Excessive cocaine use can cause overdoses, due either to the strong stimulation that the drug causes, or to the depression that follows the cocaine high. Death from cocaine overdoses can occur due to seizures, hypertension, or stroke, while some people enter comas when they are coming down from cocaine. Beyond the problems associated with overdoses, cocaine has other serious side effects. Long-term cocaine use can lead to neurological problems that make users feel like there are little bugs crawling under their skin. Some people suffer from gastrointestinal problems after prolonged cocaine use, while others develop psychotic symptoms and other mental problems caused by dramatically altered dopamine levels. To make matters worse, because the drug is usually obtained illegally, cocaine is often adulterated or "cut" with other substances to make drug users think they are buying more of the drug than they actually are. On average, the cocaine sold on the street is only 60% actual cocaine, as it is usually mixed with other white powders such as baby laxatives, lactose, aspirin, sugar, flour, or baking soda. Since it is unclear what else people are ingesting when they take cocaine, the drug can cause all sorts of other unforeseen complications.

For people suffering from cocaine addiction, there are several common forms of treatment. Behavioral interventions focus on teaching addicts to break old habits, not spending time with old friends who use cocaine, and identifying and avoiding "triggers" that make addicts want to go back to the drug. Other treatments focus on teaching people strategies they can use to resist emotions and urges that make them want to take cocaine, and there are organizations like Cocaine Anonymous and Narcotics Anonymous that use twelve-step programs to help cocaine addicts stop taking the drug and stay clean.

A Brief History of Coca and Its Derivatives

The people of South America have traditionally chewed coca leaves to gain a mild stimulant effect, using the drug for social and religious occasions, to lessen hunger, and increase endurance, for centuries. In the late 1800s, people in Europe and North America began using coca leaves as an ingredient in many tonics and wines, including Coca Cola (a cocaine-free extract is in the soda that is available on the market today). In 1861, German scientist Albert Nieman isolated cocaine from the other chemicals in the coca leaf in a white crystalline form. The pure cocaine Nieman isolated was 200 times as strong as the coca leaf found in nature. In the 1880s, Austrian physician Karl Koller discovered that the drug could be used as an anesthetic for minor surgery, and soon doctors began recommending it to patients who were suffering from everything from depression and stomach problems to asthma, alcoholism, and morphine addiction. Though some in the scientific community (including the famous psychologist Sigmund Freud) believed that cocaine was a wonder-drug that could cure a wide variety of ailments, many physicians began to notice its habit-forming qualities in the 1880s. What made it particularly addictive, they observed, was that the drug's effects were very rapid, and that the high dissipated quickly, leaving the user eager to take the drug nearly nonstop. Nonetheless, pharmaceutical companies based in Germany, the United States, and Britain began producing the drug in large amounts around the same time, and the drug became a key ingredient in many popular remedies for hay fever and sinus pains. In the 1890s, the drug made its way into the underworld, and became popular among many prostitutes, gamblers, and petty criminals, as well as doctors. Around the same time, social reformers and commentators became alarmed at the seemingly "immoral" use of the drug. At the turn of the twentieth century, many druggists began refusing to sell narcotics to these so-called "unrespectable" and "criminal classes," and soon the drug became highly regulated in many countries. This was especially the case in the United States, as racists and alarmists began claiming that its use made African Americans behave violently, causing even more fear of the drug. In 1914, the Harrison Narcotics Act placed the drug under tight federal controls, and soon it started to circulate on the black market like other tightly controlled drugs such as morphine and heroin.

Cocaine use—both legally in medical preparations and illegally—diminished in the 1930s, and by the 1950s many in the law enforcement community did not consider its use particularly widespread or problematic. The drug's popularity surged once again in the 1970s, especially after more severe restrictions on amphetamines took effect and law enforcement shifted its focus to cracking down on the traffic in other drugs such as marijuana and heroin. By the mid-1970s, a booming cocaine business grew in Colombia, where clandestine manufacturers and traffickers began producing the drug and smuggling it into the United States, where it was illicitly sold to urban youths, party-goers in discos and nightclubs, and other recreational users. By the early 1980s, Colombian traffickers established a stronghold in Miami, which became the base of their U.S. operations. By the mid-1980s and through the 1990s, these Columbian cartels grew so powerful that they became a serious problem not only for drug enforcement agents in the United States, but also for the government in Colombia, and they soon spread their operations into Peru, Bolivia, and Venezuela. In the 1980s, crack use also became prevalent, particularly in poor urban communities in the United States. By the late 1990s, rates of cocaine use began to decrease in some areas, but many public health experts fear this was because drug users had switched over to methamphetamines. According to a survey conducted by the National Survey on Drug Use and Health in 2005, about 2.4% of youths between the ages of twelve and seventeen used cocaine at least once in the previous year, while a total of 2 million people in the United States reported being current cocaine users. In 2007, the federal government seized over 96,000 kilograms of illegal cocaine. Today, cocaine is a Schedule II controlled substance, meaning it is only legal for use in surgery as a local anesthetic.

Opiates and Opioids

Scientific Overview

Opiates are chemicals that are derived from opium, a drug that is processed from unripe seed pods of the *Papaver somniferum* poppy plant. While there are over twenty-five alkaloids in opium, two of them, morphine (which makes up 10 to 20% of opium) and codeine (.07 to 2.5%) are the most prevalent psychoactive chemicals in the drug. In the last 200 years, scientists have created other, sometimes more powerful, substances that are either derived from the chemicals in opium, such as heroin, hydrocodone, oxycodone, and hydromorphone, or are opioids—completely synthetic drugs such as meperidine, methadone, and propoxyphene, which have similar effects. While opium and its derivatives have been used as medicines since antiquity, the last few centuries have seen an increase in the recreational use of, and addiction to, these substances. Today, heroin is the most prevalent opiate on the black market, though addiction to opiates that are prescribed (such as oxycodone) has become increasingly common in recent years. Depending on their form, opiates and opioids can be swallowed, smoked, snorted, or injected.

Opiates and opioids get their psychoactive effects by acting on three major neurotransmitter receptors in the brain, creating sensations of pleasure and increasing the release of GABA, dopamine, serotonin, and endorphins while limiting the release of norepinephrine. These drugs are chemically similar to the chemicals that the body naturally produces to limit feelings of pain, thus making the drugs extremely effective painkillers. When feeling the psychoactive effects of opiates and opioids, individuals experience positive changes in mood, euphoria, a sense of relaxation, and clouded mental functioning since the drugs tend to slow CNS activity. In higher doses, they can cause drowsiness, confusion, slurred speech, and hallucinations. Often, people who have taken high doses of the drugs will nod off into a dream-filled sleep for a few minutes. Opiates and opioids have strong physical side effects, including decreased blood pressure, droopy eyelids, insensitivity to light, itching, nausea, and constipation. When people first take these drugs, they usually experience nausea due to the artificial stimulations of neurons, though the feelings of pleasure that opiates and opioids produce are enough to make many people enjoy the experience nonetheless. For individuals who inject opiates such as heroin intravenously, the physical changes that occur when the drug takes effect on the body are pleasant and exciting, as they report the sensation of a "rush" of feeling in the lower abdomen and a warm flushing of the skin. In higher doses, the physical effects of opiates and opioids can cause serious physical problems such as comas, and they can slow down the respiratory system to the point that individuals can stop breathing. These are the most common causes of overdose deaths. Long-term use of opiates and opioids can cause physical problems, including heart problems, anemia, bone and joint infections, and pneumonia. Many of the most serious physical consequences of regular opiate use, however, come from the way the drugs are used—particularly by those who inject them. Unsanitary needles and excessive injecting can cause abscesses and skin and muscle infections, and the sharing of used needles often leads to infection with diseases such as hepatitis and HIV/AIDS. In addition, individuals who use these drugs habitually often experience a host of physical problems due to self-neglect, as well as psychiatric symptoms of depression and anxiety.

Opiates and opioids are highly addictive, and tolerance to the drugs can develop in a matter of days. Individuals who use these drugs for pain relief quickly need to begin upping their dosage in order to achieve the same painkilling effects, while those who use opiates and opioids for their psychoactive effects have to take more and more of the drugs to achieve the euphoria and other pleasant sensations they produce. The physical withdrawal symptoms can be extreme, and the desire to avoid them is a major reason that people can so easily become addicted to them. In addition to a craving for more drugs and feelings of anxiety, individuals who are undergoing withdrawal from opiates and opioids experience uncontrollable yawning and perspiration, runny noses, teary eyes, goose bumps, tremors, hot and cold flashes, aches, loss of appetite, insomnia, increased blood pressure, heavy breathing, diarrhea, stomach pain, and vomiting. The best way to alleviate these unpleasant symptoms is to take a fresh dose of opiates or opioids, thus increasing tolerance and making withdrawal even more difficult when users next come down from the drugs.

Though these withdrawal symptoms generally subside within two or three days, they are extraordinarily difficult to endure, and addicts will go to great lengths—even lying or stealing—to get more drugs and avoid these negative side effects. Some addicts become psychologically addicted to the drug, as they seek out its pleasant effects, though many report that they do not continue using opiates and opioids for long periods of time in order to get high; instead, they continue using them because the negative side effects of withdrawal are so painful.

Though getting off of opiates and opioids is difficult, there are many treatment options available for addicts. One approach is to wean addicts off of them, gradually decreasing their dose of drugs each day in order to minimize withdrawal symptoms. Another is to orally give methadone, an opioid that helps addicts avoid withdrawal symptoms, but does not produce the psychoactive effects that other forms of opiates and opioids can generate. This method, known as methadone maintenance, helps individuals who are addicted to more dangerous forms of opiate use (like heroin injection) stop using the drugs they used to, but critics argue that this treatment is little more than trading addiction to one drug (heroin) for addiction to another (methadone). Other drugs, such as buprenorphine and naltrexone, can also be used to treat addicts by blocking the psychoactive neurochemical effects of opiates and opioids. Most researchers agree, however, that medical interventions are just the first step in treating addiction to opiates and opioids, and that a combination of therapy, support, and participation in twelve-step groups like Narcotics Anonymous increases addicts' chances of avoiding relapse.

A Brief History of Opiates and Opioids

Until the twentieth century, opium was considered one of the most powerful and effective medicines known to man, renowned for its ability to dull pain, ward off illnesses, and produce pleasure. It was commonly used in India and China for centuries before becoming popular in Europe during the Renaissance, when Swiss researcher Paracelsus created a tonic called laudanum—a mixture of opium, alcohol, and spices —that was used to treat dysentery, diarrhea, coughs, and to alleviate physical pain. Scientists in France and Britain later came up with alternative recipes for laudanum, and its popularity spread throughout Europe in the seventeenth and eighteenth centuries. Opium soon became a key ingredient in many folk remedies for ordinary aches and pains, and also in medicines mothers would give their children to help them get to sleep. In the nineteenth century, many European poets and writers—such as Britain's Thomas De Quincey and France's Charles Baudelaire—began describing the drug's powerful psychoactive effects, leading to increased interest in its potential use as a recreational drug. Observers in Europe did, however, see the potential harm the opium habit could have when they traveled to parts of the Middle East and Asia, where the practice of opium smoking was more popular. Around the same time, scientists in Europe created powerful medicines that came from opium, with the discovery of morphine in 1805, codeine in 1832, and the creation of heroin, which was derived from morphine, in 1874. These new drugs—morphine in particular—were incredibly powerful, and doctors began prescribing them to patients liberally. By the 1870s, medical researchers in both North America and Europe began observing that many of their patients who took morphine became addicted to it, and began calling for greater precautions to be taken when the drug was used. Nonetheless, the drug remained popular, as did ordinary over-the-counter medicines that had opium among their main ingredients.

In the United States, morphine addiction became prevalent after soldiers in the Civil War began using the drug to ease the pain of wounds incurred on the battlefield. Around the same time, the practice of opium smoking became increasingly popular among Chinese migrant workers in the Western United States. Around the turn of the twentieth century, a series of legal controls over opium and its derivatives took effect: in response to fear of the Chinese immigrants who used opium, several states began passing ordinances against opium smoking; the 1906 Pure Food and Drug Act required proper labeling of medicines, leading many manufacturers to drop opium from their products; in 1909, the United States organized an international conference to tackle the opium problem in Asia; in 1914, the federal government instituted tight controls over opium and its derivatives with the passage of the Harrison Narcotics Act; and in the 1920s, the League of Nations took the lead in an international campaign to stamp out opiate addiction across the globe. Though these efforts, together with advances in medical knowledge about the dangers of opiates, helped reduce levels of addiction, the problem still remained prevalent, and a black market for the drugs emerged in the 1920s. In World War II, economic restrictions on international commerce helped reduce drug smuggling in the United States, but heroin use started to increase again in the 1950s and 1960s. In addition, new synthetic opioids were discovered, and spawned a new wave of addiction.

Today, one of the most commonly abused opiates is heroin, which is grown overseas and then smuggled into the United States. According to the 2006 National Survey on Drug Use and Health, there were 338,000 heroin users in the United States, and in 2007, 1.5% of high school seniors reported having tried the drug. In addition, addiction to prescription opiates has become increasingly problematic in recent years, and from 1999 to 2002, accidental deaths from substances such as hydrochodone, oxycodone, and methadone jumped 91%.

Tobacco

Scientific Overview

Tobacco is a plant that belongs to the same family that includes tomatoes, belladonna, and petunias, and most of the tobacco available on the commercial market today comes from a mild, broad-leafed variety of the plant called *Nicotiana tabacum*. While the leaves of tobacco can be crushed up and snorted, sucked, or chewed, most of the tobacco used in the United States is smoked and inhaled into the lungs, either in cigars or cigarettes. Though smoking is the most prevalent form of tobacco use, smokeless tobacco remains popular as well, particularly in the form of moist snuff, powder snuff, and loose-leaf tobacco, which can be consumed in a variety of ways. Moist snuff is used by sticking it in the mouth, next to the gums, where nicotine is then absorbed into the capillaries in the mouth. Powder snuff is generally consumed either by sniffing, rubbing on the gums, or chewing, while loose leaf tobacco is used by stuffing larger sections of tobacco leaves into the mouth and chewing them so that the juices of the tobacco leaf can be absorbed into the system. What gives tobacco its stimulant effect is the chemical nicotine, which in nature makes up between 2% and 5% of the leaves.

Though one of the most addictive substances known to man (it is harder to quit smoking than it is to stop using opiates or alcohol), the physical and mental effects of nicotine are less intense than the sensations caused by other drugs. When chewed or sucked, it takes about five to eight minutes for the effects of nicotine to reach the brain, while smoking and inhaling the drug gets it to the brain much faster, usually between five and eight seconds. The average cigarette contains about ten milligrams of nicotine, though only one to three milligrams of that nicotine are delivered to the lungs when smoked; chewing tobacco delivers more nicotine to the body (4.5 milligrams per chew), while a pinch of snuff delivers 3.6 milligrams. This makes the effects of smokeless tobacco slightly more intense than those of cigarettes. Nicotine acts as a stimulant by disrupting the natural balance between several neurotransmitters—endorphins, epinephrine, acetylcholine, and dopamine. By affecting acetylcholine, it increases the heart rate, blood pressure, memory, learning, mental activity, and aggression. The epinephrine that nicotine causes to be released creates a surge of energy, leading to a rise in glucose levels in the blood, as well as a higher heart rate, increased blood pressure, and more rapid respiration. In addition to these physiological effects, the drug also suppresses appetite and increases the body's metabolism, and the average regular smoker weighs between six and nine pounds less than nonsmokers. The drug also enhances the body's release of dopamine, a neurotransmitter that makes users feel satisfied and calm. Thus while it creates a feeling of calm and satisfaction on the one hand, nicotine is also a very strong stimulant on the other. The stimulant effects of nicotine, particularly the release of dopamine, are usually short-lived, lasting only a few minutes. To maintain the sense of satisfaction triggered by dopamine, people who use tobacco naturally want to take additional doses of the drug. This is a major reason that the drug is highly addictive.

While most of these effects come from the nicotine in tobacco, other chemicals present in tobacco smoke can be addictive as well. In particular, acetaldehyde is known by researchers to contribute to the addictiveness of tobacco. When the effects of the drug wear off, tobacco users become irritable, have trouble sleeping, have increased appetites, and experience headaches and fatigue. A fresh dose of tobacco relieves these symptoms, thus making the substance very habit forming, and regular tobacco users try to maintain a steady level of the drug in their bloodstream. Consequently, many people who try tobacco become regular users. According to studies, 23% of the people who try tobacco wind up using the drug daily, compared to just 11% of people who try alcohol. On average, a heavy smoker will consume between thirty and forty cigarettes a day, which translates to over 10,000 cigarettes per year. Even knowledge of the potentially harmful effects of smoking is not enough to get many smokers to quit, as 80% of them know their habit can cause cancer, but nonetheless continue to smoke. Within a few weeks after people stop using tobacco, the withdrawal symptoms can subside, though the craving can remain present for a long time after their last cigarette or cigar.

Beyond the pharmacological effects of the drug that make it so addictive, tobacco is also highly habit forming because of the social and cultural contexts in which it is used. Many people become used not only to tobacco itself, but also to the ritual of having a cigarette after a meal or with a beer, or to taking cigarette breaks from work. Some believe that the act of smoking is rebellious or cool, or that it makes them seem sexually attractive. Chewing tobacco is also reinforced by the context in which it is used, as athletes (particularly baseball players) become accustomed to using the drug while they play sports. Given the drug's tendency to speed up metabolism and make users lose weight, some people continue using it for fear that they will gain weight when they quit. These factors encourage people to continue using tobacco even if they do not find the experience pleasurable when they first try it, and once they use the drug enough, they become used to its negative side effects. In fact, this is the case with many tobacco users, who experience coughing, dizziness, headaches, and nausea the first time they try the drug.

What makes tobacco particularly harmful is the way in which it is usually used—smoking. The smoke in tobacco has about 4,000 chemicals other than nicotine, many of which are created by chemical processes that occur when the leaf is burned. A lot of these chemicals are ones we would not normally ingest. To name a few, tobacco smoke contains cadmium (an ingredient found in oil paint), hydrogen cyanide (a key ingredient found in the poison used in gas chambers), vinyl chloride (an ingredient in garbage bags), benzene (a chemical used in rubber cement), and arsenic (an active ingredient in rat poison). These chemicals cause many side effects independent of the adverse effects of nicotine itself, giving smokers yellow teeth, breathing problems, headaches, nausea, and feelings of "pins and needles" in the hands and feet. Together with these unpleasant effects, tobacco smoke can cause a host of serious physical problems for regular smokers. Smoking can accelerate the hardening and blocking of arteries (the major cause of heart attacks) and trigger irregular heartbeats. Smokers also have much higher rates of lung diseases like emphysema and chronic bronchitis, and people who smoke are twelve to twenty-two times as likely to develop lung cancer as those who do not. Approximately 392,000 people in the United States die prematurely because of the effects of smoking every year, and studies estimate that smoking can shorten life spans by about fourteen years. Even tobacco users who do not smoke can experience serious health issues that result from regularly chewing the substance, ranging from dental problems to cancers of the mouth and throat.

According to the Center for Disease Control (CDC), there are three effective methods for quitting tobacco use. One is to use a nicotine patch (which is placed on the arm), and another is the chewing of a nicotine gum. Both of these products deliver nicotine into the body, but without the harmful side effects caused by smoking. This helps tobacco users maintain a level of nicotine in their system, but get out of the habit of smoking. Slowly, nicotine users who employ a patch or gum can lower the amount of nicotine that they ingest in order to minimize withdrawal symptoms and make the process as painless as possible. Together with these methods, encouragement and support from friends and family helps tobacco users quit, as do learning strategies on how to handle stress and resist the urge to go back to tobacco.

A Brief History of Tobacco

Humans have been using tobacco for centuries, particularly in Central and South America. Some of the first European explorers to come to the Western Hemisphere, including Christopher Columbus, reported seeing Native Americans use tobacco for its stimulating and sedative qualities, and also as a medicine to treat headaches, snake bites, and stomach pains. They soon brought the drug back to Europe, and by the 1600s, its cultivation and use had spread across Europe, and into Russia, Asia, and Africa. Though the most common form of tobacco use was smoking it out of a pipe, chewing tobacco and snuff became more popular in Europe and the North American colonies in the eighteenth century. Though some political and religious leaders tried to ban the practice of smoking, such prohibitions proved useless, as tobacco users began smuggling the drug and using it in secret, and laws banning the drug eventually fell by the wayside. Soon, instead of banning the drug, many governments began to use tobacco as a source of revenue by taxing it. Tobacco became a mainstay in some economies, especially those of the British colonies in North America, where plantations in what later became the Southern United States made tremendous profits growing and trading the drug. In the early-twentieth century, changes in technology and marketing helped the tobacco industry reach new heights. With the creation of the cigarette rolling machine in 1881 by U.S. inventor James Bonsack, and the beginning of mass production of cigarettes, smoking tobacco became cheaper and easier than before. The creation of a new, milder type of tobacco leaf also helped make tobacco use more popular, as it enabled smokers to use the drug more, but without feeling the negative side effects of smoking as quickly. Shrewd marketing techniques employed by the cigarette industry also helped make smoking more popular than ever before. During World War I and World War II, for example, tobacco companies supplied cheap (and sometimes free) cigarettes to soldiers in order to get them to start smoking in hopes that they would continue the habit when they returned home from battle. In the 1920s, they also began targeting women and youths with their advertising, portraying smoking as glamorous, fashionable, and even as a good way to lose weight. Though some states tried banning smoking, legislation against cigarettes was repealed by the 1920s, and in the 1930s, both the federal and state governments benefited greatly from the taxes they could impose on cigarettes, using them as much-needed sources of revenue during the Great Depression. Though some health experts began warning of the health risks related to tobacco use as early as the 1940s, the tobacco industry tried to minimize these concerns. Around the same time, cigarette companies began working to lower the amounts of tar and other harmful substances in their products, and they also started putting filters on cigarettes in order to convince consumers that their specific brands were less harmful than others. Despite these marketing ploys, however, the scientific evidence against the health hazards caused by tobacco use became clear in 1964 with the publication of a Surgeon General's report, which concluded that smoking caused lung and throat cancers, as well as chronic bronchitis. From 1967 through 2000, the Surgeon General published twenty-four more reports on smoking, and over the course of this period, a public health campaign to discourage people from smoking developed.

Beginning in the 1950s, smokers also began suing tobacco companies for negligence, arguing that through their advertising and public relations campaigns, the tobacco industry misled them by minimizing the real health risks involved in using their products. Plaintiffs in these cases argued that the tobacco industry was at least partially responsible for the smoking-related health complications smokers developed. In the 1990s, judges began to rule against the tobacco industry in some of these lawsuits, and as a result, tobacco companies have been forced to pay billions of dollars to smokers and their families, donate large sums of money to research into smoking-related diseases, and become subject to tighter regulations in their advertising and lobbying activities. All of these developments, together with anti-smoking campaigns from governmental agencies and public health advocates, have led to an overall decrease in tobacco use in the United States. In 2001, an estimated 56.3 million people had smoked tobacco in the previous month, while some 7.3 million people used smokeless tobacco regularly. About five times as many people, some 35.4 million people in the United States, smoked cigarettes daily in 2001. These figures, while still significant, mark a drastic drop from rates of tobacco use in the past. For example, in 1965, 51% of the people in the United States reported having used cigarettes in the previous month, a number that dropped to just 24.9% in 2001.

Other Prevalent Psychoactive Substances in the United States

In addition to the substances discussed in the previous section, there are many other substances—some of them subject to tight legal controls, some of them completely unregulated—that people in the United States often use to experience psychoactive effects. Though some of these substances (sedative-hypnotics in particular) can cause physical dependence, many of them are not physically addictive. They can, however, be psychologically addictive, and some of them can also cause severe physical damage when used regularly.

Inhalants

Inhalants are a group of substances that, even though they are intended for other uses, can produce psychoactive effects when consumed. Many glues, adhesives, aerosol propellants (like those used in cans of deodorant), fire extinguishers, cleaning products, paints, paint thinners, fuels, nail polish removers, and gasolines contain substances such as toluene, trichlorethylene, benzene, hexane, and methanol, which if inhaled, can cause intoxication, as well as serious brain damage. These chemicals have similar effects to those of chemicals such as ether, nitrous oxide, and chloroform, which were developed for use in medicine and as anesthetics.

When used for their psychoactive properties, these substances can be either sniffed through the nose, sucked from a rag, placed in a bag and then inhaled, inhaled from a balloon, or sprayed directly into the mouth. Within minutes, inhalants begin to have their psychoactive effects, affecting levels of the neurotransmitters dopamine, glutamate, and GABA. When they take hold, inhalants create feelings of giddiness, dizziness, light-headedness, floating sensations, hallucinations, and drowsiness. Though these effects are pleasant for many people who abuse inhalants, there are also many negative side effects associated with their use. While intoxicated, people under the influence of inhalants can experience headaches, eye irritation, sensitivity to light, ringing in the ears, coughing fits, nausea, and diarrhea, and sometimes they pass out. About an hour after an individual takes inhalants, these effects subside, and there are no significant withdrawal symptoms when a person's CNS functioning returns to normal. With some inhalants, nitrous oxide in particular, psychoactive effects can take hold and dissipate much quicker, with people feeling the effects of the drug within seconds after taking it, and returning to a normal psychological state in just a few minutes. Scientists have not observed individuals who use inhalants regularly develop any tolerance to the drugs, though users who enjoy the experience are prone to start abusing them regularly.

Inhalants can cause damage with one-time use, though the negative consequences of their abuse become more manifest the more an individual uses them. If used regularly, the toxic chemicals that give inhalants their effects on the CNS can take their toll on both body and mind. Toluene, for example, causes cognitive impairment, and problems with vision, the lungs, and the kidneys. Severe intoxication with benzene can cause heart problems, paralysis, and unconsciousness, and some studies have shown long-term exposure to the drug may increase the risk for leukemia. Hexane and methanol use can also lead to significant cognitive impairments. Generally, these negative effects dissipate, though repeated use of inhalants can lead to a greater risk of permanent damage. Long-term use of inhalants has been shown to lead to problems with the heart, liver, kidneys, lungs and stomach, as well as lasting brain damage that can cause trouble walking, hearing loss, thought disorders, and psychosis.

Since the chemicals that give inhalants their psychoactive properties are so common, it is difficult to pinpoint when people began using them for psychoactive purposes. Some historians believe that the Ancient Greeks and Jews inhaled gaseous substances for their psychoactive effects, and there is evidence that people in the Mediterranean, Africa, and North America have done the same for centuries. In 1730, German physician Frederick Hoffmann discovered anodyne, an anesthetic that was a liquid form of ether, and it was sometimes used as an intoxicant. In 1776, English scientist Joseph Priestly discovered nitrous oxide, or "laughing gas," and in 1831, scientists developed chloroform. All of these substances, while useful as anesthetics and in medicine, were known for their psychoactive properties. In the early-twentieth century, inhalant use became more popular with the greater availability of gasoline and chloroform. Use increased during World War II, and in the 1960s, it became widespread with the fad of inhaling model airplane glue. In the 1990s, nitrous oxide made a resurgence in the rave and party scenes. Today, researchers believe that most people who use inhalants start in their early to mid-teens, mainly because the substances are so easily available. Most teenagers who use inhalants generally stop after a year or two, though some continue using them for up to fifteen years. In many parts of the world inhalants are among the most widely used psychoactive substances by adolescents, with the United States having one of the highest rates of use. In 2003, 16% of eighth graders, 13% of tenth graders, and 11% of high school seniors reported having used inhalants. Researchers estimate that the use of inhalants causes between 700 and 1,200 deaths per year in the United States.

Khat

Khat is a plant that comes from the Middle East and East Africa that has stimulant effects. While the drug has been used in the Arab world as far back as the thirteenth century, its use has become increasingly common in countries like Somalia and Yemen in recent years. When the leaves and stems of khat are chewed, or the crushed into a tea that can be drunk, the plant's main psychoactive ingredient, cathinone, can have a stimulant effect. The substance creates a mild sense of euphoria, and makes people who use it talkative, hyperactive, and aggressive, and it can also enhance self-esteem. Excessive use of the drug can cause physical exhaustion, irritability, and make people behave violently, and in some cases it can cause hallucinations or lead to over-dose deaths. For people who become addicted to khat, the withdrawal symptoms are similar to those experienced by amphetamine addicts. Though the drug is more popular in other parts of the world, it is becoming increasingly prevalent in U.S. cities that have large East African and Middle Eastern immigrant populations. In the 1950s, the U.S. pharmaceutical industry figured out how to create a synthetic version of cathinone known as methcathinone, though it was never mass produced due to harmful side effects. Some illegal drug makers, however, have started to manufacture methcathinone synthetically in drug labs similar to those that produce methamphetamines, producing it in forms that are taken orally, injected, or smoked. Methcathinone is much more intense than khat, both in its effects and addictiveness. Studies have shown that long-term methcathinone use can lead to problems with dopamine production, as well as complications in the nervous and muscular systems. According to U.S. drug enforcement officials, khat and methcathinone are becoming increasingly popular, especially among teenagers and young adults. Khat, however, is not a controlled substance under federal law in the United States.

Psychedelics

Psychedelics are a family of drugs that dramatically alter users' perceptions, and create illusions, delusions, or hallucinations. While many drugs (particularly cannabis) can have psychedelic properties, the main classes of psychedelics are indole psychedelics, phenylalkylamines, anticholinergics, and others that are in a class of their own—including ketamine, PCP, and salvia. These drugs get their powers by interfering with dopamine, norepinephrine, acetylcholine, anandamine, and serotonin in particular. It is believed that their effects on serotonin give these drugs their psychedelic properties, though researchers have yet to figure out the exact neurochemical effects they have on the CNS. According the 2006 National Survey on Drug Use and Health, 23 million people in the United States have used LSD, peyote, psilocybin, or PCP at some point in their life, with about 1.1 million people reporting that they had used them for the first time in the past year. Use of MDMA (more commonly known as "ecstasy") was also prevalent, with 528,000 people in the United States reporting having used the drug within the previous month. In 2006, the number of people who used MDMA for the first time increased by over 30% from the previous year.

Of the indole psychedelics, one of the most notable is lysergic acid diethylamide (LSD). LSD is a semi-synthetic form of *Claviceps purpurea*, a fungus that grows naturally on rye and other cereals. LSD is usually chewed or swallowed, and its effects begin between fifteen minutes and an hour after ingestion. Physically, LSD has effects somewhat similar to those caused by amphetamines, as it increases blood pressure while also making people who take it sweat and become dizzy. These effects are minor, however, when compared to the mental changes it produces. Initially, LSD enhances stimulus reception, while also altering senses of perception. Some users also report experiencing synesthesia, a crossover mixing of senses in which colors, shapes, and sounds seemingly merge. After this initial stage of enhanced and distorted perceptions, cognitive processes speed up, and many users believe that the thoughts and ideas they have during this period are insightful, philosophical, or even magical. Though these insights may seem profound to people under the influence of the drug, LSD makes it very difficult to communicate, and people who are experiencing an LSD high are often unable to express themselves verbally. While many individuals report enjoying LSD, the experience can be unpleasant and even frightening for some users. People who take the drug without others around to keep them calm can feel extreme emotions, ranging from anxiety and paranoia to delusions of grandeur. These effects wear off after about six to eight hours. Tolerance to LSD develops quickly, though once an individual stops using the drug for a few days, it dissipates, and there are few known physical withdrawal symptoms. Users report being mentally and emotionally exhausted the day after they use the drug, but the withdrawal symptoms are not a major cause of addiction. Dependence on LSD, when it does develop, is more psychological or emotional than anything else. Individuals who have bad experiences with LSD can sometimes develop depression, and they can also suffer from mental flashbacks of their LSD experiences even years later. Somewhere between 24% and 64% of individuals who have used LSD regularly experience flashbacks later in life.

LSD's psychedelic potential was first discovered by Swiss chemist Albert Hoffman, who accidentally ingested a small amount of the drug while working in his laboratory in 1943. After Hoffman published work describing the drug's effects, scientists began researching to see if the drug could be used as a therapy for treating mental illness or alcoholism, and it was even marketed as a drug to help individuals undergoing psychotherapy in the 1950s. The U.S. government also tried to put the drug to use, conducting experiments to see if the CIA could use it as a mind-control drug. In the 1960s, Harvard psychologists Timothy Leary and Richard Alpers became strong public advocates of the drug, arguing that it was an invaluable tool for spiritual exploration. Over the course of the 1960s, LSD became a popular drug in the counterculture, and it became illegal in the United States in 1966. LSD was classified a Schedule I drug under the Comprehensive Drug Abuse Prevention and Control Act of 1970, and despite its illegal status, it became increasingly popular among youths in the 1990s. Most of the LSD available on the black market today is produced in illicit labs in the Western United States.

In addition to LSD, there are many other indole psychedelics that are used recreationally in the United States today. The seeds of the morning glory plant, for example, are sometimes used since they have psychedelic effects similar to LSD. Other chemicals that are found in nature include dimethyltryptamine (DMT) and yage, drugs that come from plants in South America. Among the most prevalent of the other indole psychedelics are psilocybin and psilocin, chemicals that naturally occur in about seventy-five species of mushrooms. When these mushrooms are eaten, they initially cause nausea before having psychedelic effects that include changes in perception and an altered sense of consciousness. These effects peak about ninety minutes after the mushrooms are eaten, and wear off in about six hours. Though the psychedelic effects of these mushrooms have been known for centuries, it was not until 1956 that scientists discovered that psilocybin and psilocin were the active ingredients that gave them their psychoactive powers. Psilocybin and psilocin are Schedule I drugs under the Comprehensive Drug Abuse Prevention and Control Act of 1970.

Phenylalkylamine psychedelics are drugs that are chemically related to amphetamines and adrenaline, but have dramatically different psychoactive effects. One of the more popular phenylalkylamine psychedelics is mescaline, a chemical found in two species of cactus—Peyote and San Pedro. These cacti can either be eaten or boiled and then drunk as a tea, and a synthetic form of mescaline can be swallowed in capsules. The effects of mescaline are similar to those of LSD, but tend to give users more colorful visions and induce more hallucinations. Individuals who take mescaline feel these psychoactive effects for approximately twelve hours. Mescaline has been used ritually by people in Mexico for thousands of years, and its use became prevalent in religious ceremonies of some Native Americans in the United States in the twentieth century. Scientists first isolated mescaline from cacti in the 1890s, and in the twentieth century, some artists and philosophers experimented with the drug. It became popular in the counterculture of the 1960s, and has been available on the black market since then. Though regulated under the 1970 Comprehensive Drug Abuse Prevention and Control Act, many individuals have claimed that the drug should be legal for use in religious ceremonies. In 1990, however, the Supreme Court ruled that its use was not protected by the Constitution in *Employment Division v. Smith*. Since then, though, some exceptions have been made for the drug to be used in certain religious rituals.

The most common phenylalkylamine psychedelic that is used today is methylene dioxymethamphetamine (MDMA). The drug is usually swallowed, though it can also be snorted or injected. Within thirty minutes, individuals who take MDMA begin to feel the drug's effects on dopamine, serotonin, and nerve cells, creating altered sensory perceptions and feelings of happiness, peace, pleasure, increased self-esteem, and empathy for others. Physically, MDMA has effects similar to those of amphetamines, as it speeds up the heartbeat and respiration, while also causing sweating, hyperactivity, and a clenching of the jaw. In high doses, MDMA can cause increases in blood pressure and anxiety, and in some users it can cause seizures. After about five hours, the effects of the drug dissipate. Although users can develop a tolerance to MDMA's psychoactive effects, there is no evidence of physical addiction to the drug, but many users can become psychologically or emotionally dependent on it. It is clear, however, that the drug does have some potentially serious side effects after it is used. For one, MDMA stimulates the release of so much serotonin that it can take the body up to a week to produce more and restore normal levels of the neurotransmitter. The lack of serotonin can make individuals lethargic and depressed in the days after they use MDMA. What is more, there is scientific evidence that MDMA can do permanent damage to nerve cells.

MDMA was first synthesized by German scientists in 1912 in hopes that it could be used as an appetite suppressant, though it did not garner much attention until the 1950s, when scientists with the U.S. Army began experimenting with it as a drug that could be used for brainwashing. In the 1970s and 1980s, some psychologists saw therapeutic potential in the drug, since it seemed to help individuals who took it gain insights into emotions and memories that they had suppressed. After people began to use the drug recreationally, the government began investigating it, and in 1988 it was classified a Schedule I drug. In the 1990s and 2000s, the drug became increasingly popular in dance clubs and at raves featuring electronic trance and techno music. Today, most of the MDMA in the United States is smuggled in from Europe, though there are some illegal labs that manufacture it as well.

Anticholinergic psychedelics are found in plants such as belladonna, henbane, mandrake, datura, jimsonweed, and thornapple. They get their psychedelic effects by blocking receptors of the neurotransmitter acetylcholine. Physically, these drugs increase heart rate and raise body temperatures, while mentally they can create hallucinations. Heavy use of these drugs can induce a deep sleep that can last for up to two days. The plants are still used ritually by tribes in Mexico and Africa today, and synthesized forms of the drug are used to treat Parkinson's disease and help people with mental illness overcome the negative side effects of other medications they take. Most of these drugs that are used for recreational purposes today are diverted from their legal medical sources, though jimsonweed grows naturally in the United States.

In addition to the indole, phenylalkylamine, and anticholinergic psychedelics, there are other psychedelics that are used recreationally in the United States today. One of them, ketamine, commonly known as "Special K," is a drug that is meant for use as an anesthetic, an animal tranquilizer, or for the treatment of alcoholism, but is sometimes used recreationally as well. The drug is usually snorted, though sometimes it is smoked, swallowed, or injected. A dose of 200 milligrams is usually enough to produce a mellow and hazy intoxication, marked by a feeling of being separated from one's body, dizziness, and poor muscular coordination. In higher doses, the drug can cause hallucinations or delirium. The effects of ketamine generally last for about an hour, though aftereffects may linger for up to a day after the drug is used. Ketamine is currently a Schedule III drug, meaning that it is only legally available with a medical prescription. A stronger relative of ketamine is phencyclidine hydrochloride (PCP), a drug that creates similar sensations, but less likely to cause hallucinations. PCP is more potent than ketamine, however, and more likely to make users forgetful, aggressive, or violent. PCP overdoses can cause comas, convulsions, seizures, and kidney failure, and sometimes users do not remember what happened when they were under the influence of the drug. PCP's effects generally last about forty-eight hours, though the effects can linger for a couple of days. Even though it originated as a medicine for both humans and animals in the 1950s, the manufacture of PCP is no longer legal, and most of the PCP on the black market today is made in illegal laboratories. Another strong psychedelic that has become increasingly popular in recent years is salvia, a plant that has effects similar to those of ketamine and PCP. When salvia is smoked, users begin to experience dreamlike hallucinations, delirium, and out-of-body experiences. The salvia high is a brief one, rarely lasting more than ten minutes.

Though scientists are unsure how salvia acts on the brain, its psychedelic effects are much stronger than those of LSD. Despite its strength, salvia is currently classified as an herb, and not a drug, in the United States, though government officials are now considering reclassifying it as a controlled substance.

Sedative-Hypnotics

Sedative-hypnotics are a group of synthetic substances that have effects that are similar to alcohol—they lower inhibitions, slow down physiological functions, and create a generalized feeling of sedation. Most of them act on the neurotransmitters GABA, serotonin, and dopamine, and they also induce sleep. There are three major types of sedative-hypnotics—benzodiazepines, barbiturates, and other drugs.

Benzodiazepines gain their psychoactive powers by increasing the ability of receptors to pick up the neurotransmitter GABA, while also upping levels of dopamine and serotonin, which together gives the drugs a calming effect on users. Generally, these drugs are prescribed as medicines for individuals suffering from psychological disorders, and also to help people while they go through withdrawal from other addictive drugs such as alcohol. Since the drugs are very soothing, however, it is easy for people who begin taking them under a doctor's supervision to start using them regularly, and eventually start taking more than they are prescribed. Overdoses of benzodiazepines can be severe, leading to a host of symptoms ranging from drowsiness and breathing problems to unconsciousness, comas, and even death. Individuals who use benzodiazepines for an extended period of time can develop a tolerance as their livers become more efficient in processing the drugs, and if used heavily for a long period of time, they can develop a physical and mental dependence on the drugs similar to alcohol dependence. For someone who is addicted, withdrawal from benzodiazepines can be very difficult, marked first by anxiety, and followed by a variety of physical symptoms including twitches, vomiting, yawning, hypertension, and dizziness. In some cases, people undergoing withdrawal from benzodiazepines can even hallucinate, have seizures, or temporarily lose their senses of sight, hearing, and smell. Despite these dangers, benzodiazepines are generally considered safe if used with caution. They were originally developed in the 1950s, though from their beginnings, some of them (Valium, in particular) became widely abused since doctors underestimated their addictive potential. Most of the benzodiazepines available today come from legal medical sources, though there is an illicit market for the drugs as well. Today, some of the most common benzodiazepines are alprazolam, diazepam, clonazepam, and triazolam, which are used to treat anxiety and insomnia.

Barbiturates are a class of drugs that, even more than benzodiazepines, bear strong resemblances to alcohol. They mainly act on GABA neurotransmitters, and lower inhibitions, anxiety, and feelings of restlessness. However, the visible effects of barbiturates are not always calming, as they tend to exaggerate the preexisting mood of users rather than simply sedating them. If an individual is angry when they take barbiturates, they are prone to become violent, while if an individual is relaxed when they take the drugs, they are more likely to fall asleep. There are three different types of barbiturates, each of which has a different potential for recreational use, abuse, or addiction. Long-acting barbiturates such as phenobarbital have effects that last between twelve and twenty-four hours, and they are usually prescribed for the treatment of neurological conditions such as epilepsy. These drugs usually have minimal psychoactive effects, and are not likely to be abused. There are also barbiturates like penthonal, which are generally used as anesthetics, and usually make people who take them unconscious very quickly. Since their action is so quick, most individuals do not even feel any psychoactive effects from these drugs, and it is rare for anyone to use them habitually. The third class of barbiturates, which has effects that last from four to six hours, however, is more likely to be addictive. These drugs, which are meant to help people get to sleep, also induce feelings of calm and sedation, and can be habit-forming. Tolerance to barbiturates develops when the liver begins to metabolize them quicker, and when nerve cells become less sensitive to their effects. If individuals take heavy doses of barbiturates for a month, they are likely to develop withdrawal symptoms that include anxiety, nausea, sweating, cramps, or convulsions six to eight hours after the last dose. These symptoms tend to last two or three days. In the decades after chemists created the first barbiturate medicine in 1903, the drugs were used for the treatment of anxiety disorders, and barbiturate addiction became widespread in the United States in the 1950s, 1960s, and 1970s. Barbiturates' potential for abuse, together with the more recent development of safer medicines to treat anxiety and insomnia, have made the drugs rare in medical practice today.

Some other prominent sedative-hypnotics include gamma hydroxybutyrate (GHB), a drug that was first used to help people with sleeping problems in the 1960s. While scientists know that it is chemically similar to GABA and that it lowers dopamine levels, it is still unclear how it acts on neurotransmitters in the CNS. The drug is usually drunk after it is dissolved in water or alcohol. In small doses, it creates feelings of relaxation, while higher doses can lead to slowing of the heartbeat and breathing, trouble speaking, and problems with balance, coordination, and speech. Overdoses can cause nausea, depression, hallucinations, seizures, and even comas. Tolerance to GHB develops quickly, and the withdrawal symptoms include insomnia and anxiety. In addition to GHB, some other sedative-hypnotics that are prevalent in the United States today include gamma butyrolactone (GBL), methaqualone (often referred to as "Quaaludes"), and zolpidem.

III. ADDICTIVE BEHAVIORS

While the term "addiction" has traditionally been used to describe the phenomena of physical and psychological dependence on psychoactive substances, research in the last thirty years has broadened the scope of what is understood to be "addictive." Behaviors such as gambling, eating, having sex, shopping, or using the Internet—which cause little problems for most people—can become as habitual and out of control as the use of psychoactive substances for some individuals. Consequently, some addiction researchers have begun to classify these behaviors as potentially addictive, even though scientists are only now starting to learn how they act on neurotransmitters.

Though knowledge of the neurotransmitter activity that causes behavioral addictions is still rudimentary, it is clear that individuals with behavioral addictions share several things in common with people who have addictions to psychoactive substances—they engage in the addictive behavior compulsively, they are unable to stop the addictive behavior, and they continue it despite knowledge that it has negative consequences. Just as alcoholics will drink compulsively, uncontrollably, and even though they know their drinking has negative consequences, people who are addicted to the Internet will continue going online even though they know it could have disastrous consequences for themselves and their loved ones. Behavioral addictions are also similar to addictions to psychoactive substances in that they are hard to break, that individuals who stop their addictive behaviors are likely to relapse, that the problem gets progressively worse over time, that individuals become preoccupied with the activity, that they regularly use the behavior as a way to escape other problems in their lives, and that they often deny that they are addicted even when they have reached a point that their lives become unmanageable.

In the past, behavioral addictions have been classified as psychiatric problems that are different from addiction. While the APA classifies dependence to chemical substances under one category, behavioral addictions are broken up into several different ones. In its diagnostic manual, the APA classifies gambling addiction as an "impulse control disorder," one that is in the same family as other behaviors like compulsive stealing or the setting of fires. Food addiction and compulsive overeating are considered their own category of problems, as is sexual addiction. Yet recent research has shown that there are some strong affinities between certain behavioral addictions and addictive drugs. First of all, individuals suffering from addiction to behaviors display the same "three C's" that mark addiction to psychoactive substances—a compulsion to engage in the behavior, a loss of control over their behavior, and continued engagement in the behavior in spite of adverse consequences. What is more, the sensations that keep individuals who are addicted to behaviors such as gambling or overeating are similar to those that make individuals continue to use psychoactive substances. The adrenaline rush experienced by compulsive gamblers, for example, has often been described as similar to the highs that cocaine and amphetamines can produce. Furthermore, studies have shown that individuals who are addicted to psychoactive substances are more likely to become victims of behavioral addictions as well. There is, for example, a high correlation between food addiction and alcoholism, and between gambling addiction and excessive use of alcohol and tobacco. Also, individuals who are able to overcome addictions to psychoactive substances sometimes replace their chemical addictions with behavioral ones, using food, sex, or gambling to gain the feelings they once got from drugs or alcohol. The inverse can also be true; research has shown, for example, that many recovering sex addicts, once cured of their addiction to sex, become heavy amphetamine users. These correlations indicate that there is a connection between addictive behaviors and addiction to psychoactive chemicals, since the same individuals who abuse drugs also became addicted to certain behaviors, and often for the same reasons. Studies have also shown that some of the factors that predispose individuals to becoming addicted to psychoactive substances—genetics, a past trauma, or being a victim of physical or emotional abuse—also make them more likely to become addicted to certain behaviors.

Beyond these signs that some compulsive behaviors may be more like "addictions" than scientists have previously recognized, recent research has indicated that the neurochemistry underlying behavioral addictions may be similar to that of addiction to psychoactive substances. Studies have shown, for example, that individuals receiving medicines that increase dopamine levels (just as many psychoactive drugs do) tend to develop compulsive or addictive behaviors when it comes to eating, gambling, shopping, and having sex. GABA has also been shown to play a role in both substance abuse disorders and compulsive behaviors, as does serotonin. Individuals who are compulsive gamblers also have disproportionately high levels of endorphins in their system, as do opiate addicts and alcoholics. Furthermore, recent research has shown that the same parts of the brain that make individuals use psychoactive substances habitually also encourage habitual engagement in addictive behaviors. In addition, similar cultural and social factors that predispose individuals to become addicted to psychoactive substances also make them more likely to engage in addictive behaviors. The theories that behavioral addictions and substance addictions have a good deal in common are also supported by the fact that some of the most effective treatments for substance addictions are also effective in the treatment of behavioral addictions. Naltrexone, for example, has been shown to help individuals with gambling problems and sex addictions, while SSRIs (drugs that act on the neurotransmitter serotonin), in combination with counseling, and twelve-step recovery groups are among the best options available to individuals suffering from behavioral addictions, just as they are for people who are physically dependent on psychoactive substances.

The remainder of this section will give a brief overview of the main behaviors that researchers believe can be addictive, as well as a historical overview of how the understandings of these addictions has evolved over time. As in the preceding section about psychoactive substances, the discussion of addiction in this section will focus mainly on neurochemical understandings of addictive behaviors.

Food-Related Addiction

Scientific Overview

Since eating is an essential human activity, it is counterintuitive, and somewhat controversial, to classify it as an "addictive" behavior. Yet for some individuals, eating can become out of control, and take on a character that has more in common with an addiction than it does with the regular intake of calories and nutrients. Individuals with eating disorders—those who either eat too much, or those who eat too much and then intentionally purge it from their system—experience some of the same neurochemical processes in their brains as individuals who are addicted to psychoactive substances. In particular, recent studies have shown that fatty and sugary foods can create changes in dopamine and acetylcholine levels in the brain, particularly when consumed in excess. For individuals who consume them in large amounts, there can be unpleasant withdrawal symptoms that are similar to, thought not as extreme as, withdrawal from psychoactive substances such as opiates. Other studies have shown that food also acts on serotonin and GABA in ways similar to psychoactive drugs for individuals with food addictions. What is more, these eating disorders share the three main behavioral traits that unite all addictions—they are compulsive, they are out of control, and individuals suffering from them continue their behaviors even though they know it can have negative consequences. The major difference between food addictions and addiction to psychoactive substances is that food reaches the brain through a relatively slow ingestion process, whereas psychoactive drugs activate the brain's rewards system more directly. Most of the individuals who fall victim to food-related addictions are adolescent females who are overly concerned with their body image and pleasing others.

There are two major classes of food addiction—bulimia nervosa, and binge-eating disorder. Individuals with bulimia nervosa eat large amounts of food in a two-hour period (a practice known as binging), and then use unnatural methods—such as forcing themselves to vomit, or taking laxatives—to purge the food from their system. Others may undertake other measures to compensate for their overeating, such as excessively exercising or fasting for periods in between binges. Many of the health consequences of bulimia nervosa are related to malnutrition, as people with the disorder are prone to develop heart problems due to a lack of electrolytes in their system. Bulimia nervosa also has psychological effects including loneliness, isolation, irritability, and depression. In addition, the disorder causes a host of problems due to the purging process. Excessive vomiting can cause dental problems, and it places great stress on the stomach, esophagus, and throat, putting individuals with prolonged cases of bulimia nervosa at higher risk of ulcers and throat cancer. Researchers believe that social pressures, particularly to be thin, are among the main causes of bulimia nervosa. There is also some evidence that there are neurochemical factors that make the binge-and-purge cycle a self-reinforcing and addicting one, as the binging process increases dopamine levels, while the purging process can cause an increase in endorphins. About 1% of females in the United States develop bulimia nervosa at some point during their adolescence or young adulthood. Bulimia nervosa is generally treated with a team approach, with a doctor advising victims on how to cope with the medical problems that it causes, nutritionists providing help with diet and eating habits, psychotherapists providing emotional support and counseling to help change eating behaviors, and sometimes psychiatrists, who may administer anti-depressants to help counter the psychiatric effects of the condition.

The second class of food-related addiction is binge-eating disorder, which is also commonly referred to as compulsive overeating. Binge-eating disorder is marked by repeated episodes of binge eating, but without the purging process that follows in bulimia nervosa. Binge-eating disorder is much more common than bulimia nervosa, affecting over 6% of the U.S. population. For binge eaters, food is not merely a source of nutrition—it is also a drug that has psychological effects, something that they turn to in response to their emotions. Some foods can activate the reinforcement-reward system in the brain, causing pleasure when they are ingested in large amounts, while also blocking out unwanted emotions. In particular, binge eaters overeat when they are anxious, since food naturally has a calming effect on the body. When people eat in this manner, they can lose control over how much they eat, how quickly they eat, or what they eat, and in extreme cases they only stop when they are physically unable to eat anymore. Binge-eating can have serious physical effects, as it can cause obesity, which in turn can lead to high cholesterol, diabetes, high blood pressure, and heart disease. Moreover, obesity can cause mental distress, leading to irritability, anxiety, depression and low-self esteem—feelings that can sometimes be forgotten with a fresh eating binge, thus creating a vicious cycle of binging and feeling ashamed of it. Though binge-eaters often try dieting, and can achieve some success with it, 90% of the people who go on diets return to their original weight within two years. Thus to treat binge eating, practitioners recommend that binge-eaters address both the physical and psychological causes that lead them to overeat. Generally, this involves a combination of one-on-one counseling, psychiatric treatment, cognitive behavioral therapy, and at times treatment with anti-depressants. There are also self-help groups for compulsive eaters, such as Overeaters Anonymous (OA), a twelve-step group modeled on the program of Alcoholics Anonymous. Since it is impossible to stop eating altogether, OA encourages abstinence from compulsive overeating, usually with the use of dietary guidelines that can help keep the temptation to overeat in check. A potential problem with OA, however, is that it may create a fear that normal eating habits are unhealthy, and lead binge-eaters towards more serious problems, such as bulimia nervosa, or anorexia nervosa (a condition in which individuals starve themselves).

A Brief History of Food-Related Addictions

Scientists have become increasingly interested in food-related addictions in the past fifty years since they have become more prevalent in the United States. Long before then, however, researchers began formulating hypotheses about what caused eating disorders. Sigmund Freud, the famous Austrian psychoanalyst, believed that eating disorders were manifestations of unconscious sexual conflicts within the psyche. This theory remained prevalent until the 1960s and 1970s, when therapists seeing individuals with eating disorders found that such understandings were neither applicable, nor particularly helpful, with many of their patients. One of them, Hilde Bruch, came up with an alternative hypothesis, arguing that individuals with eating disorders were suffering from feelings of powerlessness, and that by dramatically altering their eating habits, they sought to gain control. By guiding them in an exploration of the underlying insecurities that drove eating disorders, Bruch believed that she could help patients overcome their food-related problems. Other psychoanalysts in the 1970s also postulated that addictive behaviors related to food were manifestations of deeper emotional problems. Beyond therapy, the most common medications given to individuals who compulsively ate were diet pills, many of which had amphetamines as their active ingredients. By the 2000s, however, pharmacological advances led to the discovery of more effective and safer treatments, as anti-depressants, appetite suppressants, and hormones have all been shown to help individuals control their eating habits.

Beginning in the mid-1980s, some researchers began to argue that bulimia nervosa and binge-eating had addictive properties. By the early 2000s, they began to identify connections between overeating and neurotransmitters in the brain, as well as the links between endorphins and bulimia nervosa. It has only been in the last few years, however, that the term "addiction" has been applied to food-related disorders, and in 2008, Yale University hosted the first academic conference devoted to the topic of food addiction. Recently, researchers at Yale also developed the first diagnostic tool for identifying food addictions, combining tools that researchers used to test for unhealthy eating habits with scales that practitioners have used to screen for other behavioral addictions.

Gambling Addiction

Scientific Overview

Gambling—playing games of chance where money or other items of value can be lost—is increasingly popular in the United States. Some of the more prevalent forms of gambling include playing games at casinos, purchasing lottery tickets, playing cards, or betting on sporting events. Gambling is a common pastime in the United States, as some 60 to 80% of adults have gambled in the last year, and the gambling industry has grown tenfold in the last thirty years. Thirty-seven states have lotteries, which earn a total of about $17 billion annually, while casinos make over $30 billion a year in gambling, and Internet gambling has been growing at an astonishing rate, doubling every year from 1997 through 2001, at which point it exceeded $2 billion a year. By 1998, people in the United States spent more money on gambling than baseball, going to the movies, and trips to Disneyland combined. Despite its prevalence, most gambling is not problematic, though given its increasing popularity, researchers estimate that some 15 million people in the United States display some signs of gambling addiction, and that 5 to 7% of the individuals who gamble are at risk for developing an addiction.

While there are no hard and fast definitions of what separates gambling "addiction" from nonproblem gambling, there are several tests that clinicians use to decide if an individual's gambling habit is an addiction or merely a pastime. While it can be an enjoyable hobby for most people, most experts agree that it can become addictive if it begins to interfere in other areas of the gambler's life. When trying to determine if gambling is causing such problems, clinicians use questionnaires to see how much gambling is (or is not) affecting individuals. According to the APA, individuals are problem gamblers if they meet five of the following criteria, but are not suffering from a manic episode:

1. They are preoccupied with gambling.
2. They need to gamble with increasing amounts of money to achieve the desired level of excitement.
3. They have repeatedly tried to stop gambling, but without success.
4. They become restless or irritable when they try to stop or cut down on their gambling.
5. They gamble to escape problems or relieve a bad mood.

6. They continue playing in order to earn back money they lost gambling.

7. They jeopardize or lose significant relationships, a job, or career opportunities because of their gambling.

8. They rely on money from others when their financial situation deteriorates because of their gambling.

According to researchers, there are two major "types" of gamblers—action gamblers and escape gamblers. Action gamblers are individuals who receive a rush from gambling and are attracted to the behavior by the excitement that it gives them. These individuals are more likely to play games that require some degree of skill and are highly interactive, like blackjack or craps. Escape gamblers, on the other hand, gamble excessively to tune out and forget about their worries. These individuals are more likely to engage in more passive forms of gambling, such as slot machines. For both action and escape gamblers, there are generally four phases in the development of their addiction. First, there is the winning phase; this is the initiation phase of gambling addiction, as gamblers begin playing recreationally and find the feeling of winning satisfactory. For individuals who develop gambling addiction, there is usually a big win during this initial phase, thus fueling the craving to gamble more. Gradually, as they begin to devote more money and time to gambling, the behavior can become addictive. The second step in the evolution of gambling addiction is the losing phase; at this point, gamblers start losing the money they initially gained, and sometimes may wind up losing more than they won. Then they try to recoup their losses by gambling more. It is at this point that gambling can become problematic and out of control, as gamblers will begin neglecting other important things in their life—friends, family, work—to keep playing. Gamblers can start to experience depression, irritability, and begin lying about their habits, since more gambling seems to be the only way to gain emotional satisfaction. If they continue gambling in this manner, gambling addicts may enter a third phase—the desperation phase. At this point, gamblers may lose their jobs, borrow money, or turn to criminal activities like stealing or drug dealing in order to get money to gamble. In extreme cases, some gambling addicts will reach a fourth and final phase—the giving-up phase. At this point, gamblers may realize that they have no chance of winning back the money they have lost, but they want to continue playing anyway since they are addicted to the behavior. When they win, gamblers in this phase may feel elation, though if they lose, they can suffer from depression and panic attacks, or have suicidal thoughts. According to studies, approximately 20% of gambling addicts may attempt suicide once they reach this point.

Though scientists are just now starting to understand what makes gambling addictive, recent studies have shown that gambling addiction works in ways similar to addiction to psychoactive substances—by acting on neurotransmitters in the brain. In particular, they have found that gambling stimulates activity in the reward-reinforcement center, and triggers the release of the neurotransmitter dopamine, just as many psychoactive substances do. In addition, studies have shown that gambling, by triggering excitement with potential financial rewards, may cause the release of the neurotransmitter serotonin. By increasing the levels of neurotransmitters that affect energy, emotions, and mood, gambling may have neurochemical affinities with some psychoactive substances, which also can become addictive because of their ability to alter levels of these neurotransmitters.

Further evidence that gambling addiction may have neurochemical bases has come from studies on the treatment of gambling addiction, as researchers have tried using the same drugs that are used to treat individuals who are addicted to psychoactive substances to treat gambling addicts. Drugs that act on receptors in the brain have been shown to be effective in reducing gambling urges, as have other drugs that act on the neurotransmitters acetylcholine and endorphins. In addition, cognitive behavioral therapy, psychoeducational programs, and psychoanalytic treatment have been shown to help gambling addicts overcome their addictions, just as they have individuals with substance addictions. Though there are few studies on their effectiveness, twelve-step groups may also help gambling addicts stop their self-destructive behavior. In 1957, Gamblers Anonymous (GA), a twelve-step group similar to Alcoholics Anonymous, began providing mutual support for individuals with gambling problems, and today the group helps many gambling addicts stop gambling without the use of any drugs or formal therapy. In 1971, the first inpatient treatment unit for gambling addiction was established at the Brecksville, Ohio Veterans Administration Hospital by Dr. Robert L. Custer.

A Brief History of Gambling Addiction

Gambling is a pastime with ancient roots, as historical records indicate that individuals in the Chinese, Babylonian, and Etruscan civilizations all engaged in games of chance for money or material things as far back as 3000 B.C. The indigenous populations of the Western Hemisphere also engaged in forms of gambling, as is borne out by the fact that they used objects similar to dice, lottery balls, and playing cards. Gaming became increasingly popular in Europe in the early-modern period, as the governments of Italy and the Netherlands began having state-sponsored lotteries in the sixteenth century. Non-state-sponsored betting was prominent as well, as dice games, card games, and cockfighting were all popular forms of entertainment. All of these pastimes came over to the Americas with European settlers during the colonial era. Colonial governments instituted lotteries to raise money when tax revenues were small, and states used lotteries to raise money for the construction of schools, colleges, and churches after gaining independence from Britain. In the nineteenth century, however, moral opposition to gambling grew, especially as alternative means of raising money (taxes in particular) were implemented by state governments. Early opponents of gambling claimed that the practice was an immoral vice, that relying on chance to earn money could compromise individuals' work ethic, and that it could lead individuals with poor self-control to ruin. Members of the medical community agreed with this last point, arguing that some individuals could not control their gambling due to personality disorders, and that if allowed to continue, they would resort to criminal activities to support their gambling habits. Though they recognized that problem gamblers sometimes had no control over their actions, both religious reformers and psychologists agreed that while they were sick, gambling addicts were also indulging in an immoral vice.

Despite the moral condemnations of problem gambling, many problem gamblers began to recognize that they suffered from a disease—and were not simply satisfying an appetite for vice—in the 1950s. In 1957, Gamblers Anonymous (GA) was founded in Los Angeles. The early founders of GA recognized that they were not gambling for fun, but that they had an "obsession" that was extremely difficult to overcome and causing them untold misery. Gamblers were not alone in recognizing that they were suffering from a condition that was more like a disease (such as alcoholism) than a vice that they indulged in for pleasure. In the 1960s and 1970s, the work of psychiatrist Robert L. Custer gave medical merit to the theory that gambling was indeed uncontrollable for some individuals. Whereas uncontrolled gambling was previously considered a vice, Custer observed that many individuals with gambling problems had remorse; though they continued to gamble, they did not necessarily want to, and they recognized that their gambling had negative consequences both for them and those around them. In 1972, Custer co-founded the National Council on Problem Gambling, an organization devoted to advocating for individuals suffering from gambling problems. The plight of individuals suffering from gambling addiction gained great notoriety in 1976 when Henry Lesieur published *The Chase*, a book that told the stories of pathological gamblers from their own point of view. Considered the first sociological study of problem gambling, *The Chase* helped give the problem, once dismissed as a vice, a human face, and spawned interest in both researching, and helping cure, gambling addiction.

In 1980, thanks in large part to Custer's research, pathological gambling was classified as a "disorder" of its own in the American Psychiatric Association's 1980 Diagnostic and Statistical Manual of Mental Disorders (DSM III). Inclusion in the DSM III marked a significant shift in the way that compulsive gambling was viewed, as it was no longer just a vice—it was also a clinical disorder, or a disease. In the revised edition of DSM III, which came out in 1987, further descriptions of pathological gambling were published, laying out diagnostic criteria that showed compulsive gambling had a good deal in common with other addictions. In 1994, the new edition of the DSM (DSM IV) went a step further, laying out characteristics of pathological gambling, including the progressive nature of the disorder, asserting that problem gamblers could suffer from withdrawal when they stop gambling, and recognizing that in spite of themselves, they could jeopardize their family relationships and resort to illegal activity. Today, gambling problems are recognized as legitimate psychiatric disorders.

In 1997, Congress appointed the National Gambling Impact Study Commission to examine the consequences, both social and economic, of gambling in the United States. The Commission found that gambling is growing more prevalent in the United States with the proliferation of racetracks, lotteries, casinos, and Internet gaming. According to polls, this is not necessarily a bad thing; since gambling does produce economic activity, it is a good way to raise state revenues without increasing taxes, and it is enjoyed responsibly by the majority of gamblers. However, the Commission also found that the social costs of gambling are great, especially because with its spread, there has also been an increase in problem gambling and gambling addiction, particularly among adolescents. The rise in problem gambling, the Commission estimated, could cost society approximately $5 billion per year, a number that while significant, still paled in comparison to the social cost of alcohol abuse ($166 billion per year) and heart disease ($125 billion per year). The Commission noted that despite the risks involved with problem gambling, understanding of gambling was still minimal, and it called for further research. Notably, it recommended that the Substance Abuse and Mental Health Services Administration expand its scope of study to include problem gambling in its surveys on drug abuse, a sign that the federal government now considered gambling to be an addiction and a mental health problem, on par with other addictions.

Internet Addictions

Though it has only been in widespread use since the early 1990s, researchers have found that the Internet has potential to be addictive. A 1999 survey found that almost 6% of the individuals who used the Internet did so compulsively, and a more recent study found that 11% of college students identified themselves as addicted. According to the Center for Internet Addiction Recovery, an individual is addicted to the Internet if any compulsive behavior involving the Internet interferes with normal functioning, and causes stress on the addicts, as well as their family, friends, and loved ones. Using this definition of Internet addiction, the Center for Internet Addiction Recovery estimates that between 5 and 10% of the people in the United States suffer from some form of the disorder.

While most people use the Internet daily with little problem, using the Internet becomes the top priority in the lives of addicts. Since researchers have only begun to explore Internet addiction in the last ten years, there are no official diagnostic criteria or behavioral patterns that define the disorder. However, researchers have found that some signs of Internet addiction include compulsive use, a preoccupation with being online, lying or hiding the extent or nature of online behavior, and an inability to stop using the Internet. In some cases, addicts go online to alter their mood, similar to the way that individuals who are addicted to psychoactive substances may turn to drugs or alcohol when they are feeling depressed or irritated. What is more, many individuals feel like they need to use the Internet regularly to feel normal, a sensation that according to researchers, is similar to the phenomena of tolerance and withdrawal that are hallmarks of addiction to psychoactive substances. Another sign that Internet addiction may be similar to other addictions is that over half of the individuals suffering from the disorder also reported addictions to drugs, alcohol, smoking, or sex. Thus the Internet may trigger the reward-reinforcement center in the brain in ways similar to those that psychoactive substances and other addictive behaviors do. Though scientists have yet to uncover the neurochemical bases that lie behind Internet addiction, these trends make the Internet, according to researchers, as potentially addictive as other behaviors or drugs.

On average, an Internet addict will spend thirty-eight hours per week online. According to Kimberly S. Young, a pioneer in the field of Internet addiction, there are several criteria that can be used to determine if an individual is suffering from Internet addiction. Individuals can be classified as "addicted" to the Internet if they are preoccupied with the Internet even when not online, if they feel the need to spend increasing amounts of time online to achieve satisfaction, if they have tried to cut down on Internet use but been unsuccessful, if they feel depressed or irritable when cutting down on Internet use, if they jeopardize personal relationships or their job because of their Internet use, and if they use the Internet as a way of escaping problems or relieving feelings of anxiety or depression. Given that the Internet has only been in widespread use for fifteen years, science's understanding of Internet addiction is just beginning to take shape, and researchers continue to work to come up with more precise definitions of Internet addiction, as well as a better understanding of what causes it and makes it so hard to break.

One of the most prevalent forms of Internet addiction, particularly among youths, is addiction to online gaming. Researchers believe that individuals begin gaming compulsively to compensate for other things that are lacking in their lives, and are drawn to it since it simulates social contact, but with a degree of anonymity that attracts individuals who may be anxious in social situations. In particular, Massively Multiplayer Online Role Playing Games (MMORPGs) offer individuals the opportunity to express themselves in ways that they may not in real life, and the gratification they get from this form of interaction may underlie what keeps them coming back to the Internet compulsively. MMORPGs in particular may draw people into Internet addiction since the games have no end, and they provide a never-ending series of tasks and goals, thus allowing users to gain feelings of power and status when they succeed. Studies have shown that because of these factors, individuals who play MMORPGs are more likely than others to develop Internet addictions. On-Line Gamers Anonymous (OLGA), an online group based on the twelve-step model of Alcoholics Anonymous, has a screening tool to help individuals determine if their MMORPG playing is problematic or not. According to OLGA, an individual may be addicted to online gaming if most of the people they know are people they play games with, if they are preoccupied with gaming even when engaged in other activities, if they feel a rush of euphoria when playing, and if they ever confuse their real life personality with their character's identity in the MMORPG. Once addicted to MMORPGs, individuals may suffer from depression, anger, anxiety, fear, sadness, and loneliness when they are not gaming. In some extreme cases, MMORPG addicts who can no longer play their game may even become violent or suicidal. For individuals suffering from online gaming addiction, OLGA offers mutual support in online chatrooms and message boards on its Web site, and in face-to-face meetings.

Most other forms of Internet addiction are related to other behavioral addictions, as individuals use the anonymity and easy access that the Internet offers to engage in other compulsive behaviors. One of the most common is addiction to cybersex, a new and increasingly prevalent form of sex addiction. Researchers estimate that 20% of Internet addicts engage in online sexual activity, and many of these individuals had never displayed any signs or symptoms of sex addiction before engaging in cybersex. What makes cybersex appealing is the anonymity of it, as well as the fact that individuals can conceal their age, marital status, race, job, and aspects of their personality that they believe may make it difficult for them to find sexual partners offline. Online gambling is also a prevalent behavior for Internet addicts, particularly for youths who may be too young to enter a casino to gamble legally, but who can conceal their identity and play online. Like more traditional gambling addicts, people addicted to online gambling tend to hide their behaviors and feel a need to bet increasing amounts of money to gain emotional satisfaction from the experience. Shopping addiction also has an analogue on the Internet, as increasing numbers of shopping addicts do their buying online since it is both easier and more anonymous than going to a store. According to the Center for Internet Addiction, a distinct type of online shopping addiction is addiction to online auctioning sites, where individuals shop by placing bids on items posted for sale. Winning bids for items on these sites stimulates a rush similar to winning a gamble. In more serious cases, individuals will place bids on items they do not need or cannot afford just so they can experience the sensation of winning an auction. At times, individuals will bankrupt themselves, and even steal from friends and loved ones, in order to continue participating in online auction forums.

Research has shown that as with many behavioral addictions, cognitive behavioral therapy provides the most effective way to treat Internet addictions, as do self-help and twelve-step groups. Hospitals and clinics have developed programs that specialize in treating Internet addiction, and in extreme cases, individuals suffering from Internet addiction may benefit from treatment at inpatient recovery centers.

Sex Addiction

Scientific Overview

Sex addiction is marked by an uncontrollable impulse to have sex or engage in sexual behaviors. Some of the behaviors that are hallmarks of sexual addiction—masturbation, the use of pornography, attending strip or sex clubs—are normal in moderation, but can become addictive for people who are hypersexual (have no control over and excessively engage in sexual activities). The uncontrollable drive to engage in sexual behavior can also lead some sex addicts to illegal activities, such as soliciting prostitutes, sexual harassment, sexual abuse, exhibitionism, molestation, and rape. Researchers believe that sex addiction is initially driven by individuals' desires to cope with anxiety, stress, or the feeling of loneliness. Since sexual activity naturally causes the release of pleasure-giving neurotransmitters such as dopamine and endorphins, individuals who engage in sexual behavior too much may become accustomed to having high levels of these neurotransmitters in their system. Then to regain the "high" that sexual activity produces, sex addicts continue to engage in more sexual behaviors, leading to a cycle of highs and lows similar to those produced by addiction to psychoactive substances. To increase the sensations produced by sexual activity, sex addicts will begin engaging in risky sexual behavior—having affairs, having sex with strangers in public places, or even committing rape. Once they are addicted, sex addicts gain little enjoyment from their behavior, usually regretting it, feeling shame, self-hatred, and despair over the money they waste or the dangers of acquiring a sexually transmitted disease that they expose themselves to. According to some studies, between 3 and 6% of the U.S. adult population suffers from sex addiction. The vast majority of these sex addicts are men.

There are five distinct phases in sex addiction. The first, the initiation phase, is when unusually intense sexual observations or experiences arouse the individual, and sex takes on the role that psychoactive drugs sometimes do by providing a way to escape from or cope with life's problems. Second, the establishment phase is when individuals act out on their sexual desires, creating an addictive cycle where they engage in sexual behavior, and then feel ashamed about it, leading them to engage in the behavior once again so they can regain the high they experienced during the sexual act. Third is the escalation phase, as over time the addictive sexual behavior becomes more frequent, intense, and risky, and individuals lose complete control over their sexual impulses. Next comes the de-escalation phase, which only occurs for some sex addicts. During this phase, they may cut back on their sexual behaviors, but substitute for it with other behaviors such as drinking or using drugs. Finally, in severe cases, sex addicts may reach an acute phase, where they are constantly preoccupied with their sexual activities to the point that they become alienated from both family and friends. Research has found that while the progression from the initiation phase to the acute phase used to take years, it can now take place in a matter of weeks thanks to the anonymity and easy access offered by the Internet.

The APA does not officially recognize sex as addictive, though it classifies many behaviors that sex addicts engage in as sexual disorders. Among the most common are exhibitionism (an intense desire to expose one's genitals to an unsuspecting stranger), fetishism (a period of intense sexual fantasies involving the use of nonliving objects), frotteurism (rubbing up against nonconsenting persons), pedophilia (a desire to engage in sexual relations with a prepubescent child), sexual sadism (a desire to engage in sexual activities that involve the suffering of others), sexual masochism (a desire to engage in sexual activities that involve being humiliated), transvestic fetishism (a desire to engage in sexual activities that involve cross-dressing), and voyeurism (a desire to observe unsuspecting people who are naked or involved in sexual activities). All of these behaviors, according to researchers, may be symptoms of a broader problem of sexual addiction. Yet even acts that society deems psychologically normal (sex with multiple partners, masturbation), can be signs of sex addiction if they are performed in unhealthy ways, particularly if sexual activity becomes the main preoccupation in an individual's life. If the sexual behavior does not agree with the person's values, is unsafe, is dishonest, or involves coercion, it may also be a sign that an individual is not engaging in sexual behavior out of desire, but rather because he or she feels an innate need to. As with other addictive behaviors, individuals can cross the line from being sexually active in a healthy way into sexual addiction if they lose control over their sexual activity, continue to engage in it despite negative consequences, and develop an obsession or preoccupation with their sexual exploits. The key to determining if individuals are sex addicts or not, therefore, lies not in the frequency of how often they engage in the behaviors, but rather the consequences of it. If sexual behaviors compromise individuals' health, relationships, career, or legal status, yet are unable to stop, researchers may classify them as sex addicts.

In a 1991 survey of nearly 1,000 sex addicts, researcher Patrick Carnes identified ten common characteristics among them. First, they had an obsessive sexual fantasy life, marked by excessive reading of romance novels, or spending time on the Internet looking at sexually explicit material. Secondly, many became aroused by sex that was seductive, with arousal depending on the sexual encounter being seen as a "conquest." Third, individuals with sex addiction were prone to be more easily aroused by visual images of sex. Fourth, they tended to enjoy exhibitionist sex, where they became aroused by exposing themselves to others and seeing reactions of shock or interest from viewers. Fifth, they tended to engage in anonymous sex—sex with unknown persons, often in public places like restrooms or parks. Sixth, many sex addicts gained arousal from prostitution, as the act of paying for sex became linked with sexual excitement. Seventh, they had a tendency to "trade sex," gaining arousal by using sex to control others, effectively using sex as leverage. Eighth, they gained arousal from intrusive sex or by violating other people's personal boundaries—rubbing up against them without their permission, for example. Ninth, some sex addicts enjoyed "pain exchange sex," which involved the doling out or receiving of physical pain or humiliation to enhance sexual pleasure. Tenth, some sex addicts reported enjoying exploitative sex, where arousal was enhanced by using force or power to coerce an unwilling partner into sexual activity.

Beyond the feelings of powerlessness, shame, and loss of control that sex addiction causes its victims, it also can have very tangible repercussions. Since they are so eager to engage in sexual activity, sex addicts are less likely to take the necessary precautions to have safe sex, and will often have unprotected sex. This can lead to the acquisition of HIV and other sexually transmitted diseases, as well as unplanned pregnancies. What is more, when sex addicts' impulses become severe, they may lead them to behave in ways that could lead to them getting fired for sexual harassment or arrested for illegal or coercive sexual activities, and they can suffer great financial costs due to the money they spend feeding the addiction, particularly if they go to prostitutes.

Treatment for sex addiction usually involves a combination of counseling and participation in twelve-step groups such as Sexaholics Anonymous and Sex and Love Addicts Anonymous, which are both modeled on the program of Alcoholics Anonymous. These groups, Sexaholics Anonymous in particular, have many critics, since they define sexual behaviors that may in fact not be pathological (such as sex before marriage) as problematic. Beyond support therapy and support groups, researchers are also beginning to work on developing drugs that may help limit sexual urges by acting on the neurotransmitters in the brain that are connected to sex. Drugs that block acetylcholine, for example, may interfere with males' abilities to get an erection or have an orgasm, and others that block serotonin may also be useful in the treatment of sexual addictions.

A Brief History of Sex Addiction

Scientists have believed that some individuals (particularly women) could develop sexual addictions as far back as Ancient Greece. In the nineteenth century, researchers started calling this disorder nymphomania, though they only applied this term to female sex addicts. Nymphomania was never clearly defined at this time, as doctors used it to explain a wide array of behaviors, ranging from women giving fetching glances to men, to women sexually attacking them. Most theories of nymphomania had physical underpinnings, as medical theorists believed that nervous disorders, brain inflammations, spinal lesions, genital problems, and even misshapen heads could cause the disorder.

In the nineteenth century, scientists also began to diagnose male sex addiction as a disorder called satyriasis, though they thought it was not as severe as nymphomania. As was the case with nymphomania, scientists had a variety of theories concerning the causes of satyriasis, ranging from genital inflammations to lesions of the spinal cord, brain tumors, opium use, lack of sex, or too much sex. In extreme cases of nymphomania and satyriasis, doctors would sometimes use castration in hopes of curing the disorder and eliminating the patient's sexual appetites. In the early-twentieth century, progressives and reformers often referred to these individuals as "hypersexuals" who threatened public morals and decency, and they often tried to institutionalize them so they could be treated by psychiatrists. When attitudes towards sexuality changed in the 1960s, however, concern public concern about nymphomaniacs, satyriasists, and hypersexuals began to wane.

In the 1970s and 1980s, when concerns about other behavioral addictions emerged, theories of sexual addiction started to surface. Recognizing their own sexual behaviors as addictions, sex addicts began organizing self-help groups, such as Sex and Love Addicts Anonymous, in 1977. One of the first books to identify sexual addiction as a disorder was Patrick Carnes's 1983 book *The Sexual Addiction*, which brought the condition into the spotlight for both the scientific community and the community at large. The idea of sex addiction, while still being studied by scientists, has grabbed the attention of the mainstream media, as magazines, talk show hosts, and even television evangelical preachers have run features on some of the spectacular and salacious exploits of some sex addicts. Not only do they report on sex addiction, but many television hosts try to bring sex addicts on to their shows to explain their dilemmas and repent. According to many critics, this phenomenon is not driven by a desire to help the sex addict, but rather by a desire to drive up ratings with titillating tales of what sex addicts did when in the grips of their addictions. With public interest, however, treatment options also developed, with the first inpatient program for sexual addicts opening in Minneapolis in 1985.

Shopping Addiction

Scientific Overview

Like eating and having sex, shopping is a normal behavior, and in fact an essential one in any capitalist society. However, some individuals can become obsessed with the act of buying material goods, to the point that it can dominate their lives and become an addiction. Researchers maintain that there are three different types of shopping—functional shopping (the acquisition of goods and services that are necessary), emotional-social shopping (shopping as an act that creates enjoyment and fosters social interaction), and identity-related shopping (buying things so that individuals can self-improve, or move closer to becoming their ideal self). Emotional-social and identity-related shoppers are prone to develop shopping addictions, since they use the act of looking for and buying goods to help compensate for other things that are lacking, either in their social lives or in their self-esteem. For these individuals, it is not just the act of purchasing, but also the process of shopping that provides satisfaction. Studies suggest that these individuals are also prone to other addictions or mental illnesses, leading researchers to speculate that the neurotransmitters dopamine, serotonin, and endorphins are somehow involved in shopping addiction. More than a quarter of shopping addicts have histories of alcohol abuse, drug abuse, gambling addiction, or eating disorders, and many suffer from other mental problems such as anxiety, depression, obsessive-compulsive disorder, or impulse control disorder as well. Studies have shown that the majority of shopping addicts are women, and that the disorder usually begins in the late teens or early twenties. A 1992 study found that 8% of the adults in the United States were compulsive buyers, though among youth, the rates were nearly twice as high.

For most individuals, shopping can be a fun and relaxing leisure activity. But for emotional-social shoppers and identity-related shoppers, however, it creates a sense of excitement, or a "buzz" akin to that experienced by gambling addicts or some drug addicts when they first begin developing an addiction. Shoppers may experience withdrawal symptoms that are both physical and psychological when they stop shopping. This leads them to shop some more in order to regain the feeling of euphoria that they once had, and initiates a cycle of shopping highs and nonshopping lows, which eventually develops into a shopping addiction. According to researchers, shopping becomes an addiction when it becomes excessive—when individuals spend a disproportionate amount of their time shopping, and when they buy more than they can afford. For some individuals, the urge to buy things becomes irresistible, even if it leads to problems in their personal, social, and professional lives. Regardless of how much time they can spend shopping or what they can afford, shopping addicts continue shopping in spite of its adverse effects on their lives.

According to researchers, there are three core characteristics that distinguish shopping addiction from ordinary shopping behavior. First, shopping addicts have an irresistible impulse to buy, and spend all the money they have even if they do not need anything. They report feeling both excitement and satisfaction when they shop, even if they regret their purchases or feel guilty about overspending when they get home. Often, shopping addicts suffer from anxiety and depression, and buying and spending become ways to mask or be distracted from these feelings. Secondly, shopping addicts have no control over their shopping, often leading them to purchase items they cannot afford and do not need. At times they do not want to purchase anything, they feel a need to shop, even if it means sacrificing time that should be spent working, or with friends and family. Third, they continue this behavior despite adverse consequences. Shopping addicts may find themselves racking up tremendous amounts of debt on credit cards, and in extreme cases, they may become bankrupt. They also spend so much time shopping, or thinking about shopping, that it becomes difficult for them to concentrate on affairs at home or at work. The loss of money and time that shopping addiction causes leads shopping addicts to suffer from distress, anxiety, and depression over their loss of control.

For individuals suffering from shopping addiction, individual therapy, and group therapy are all useful in helping address the underlying causes of shopping addiction. Self-help groups modeled on the twelve-step approach of Alcoholics Anonymous, such as Debtors Anonymous (DA), have also been shown to help cure the addiction. DA considers debt a disease like alcoholism, though it recognizes that it is impossible to abstain from shopping the way that Alcoholics Anonymous recommends members stop drinking. Instead, DA aims to cure shopping addiction by encouraging members to only shop within their means, thus avoiding debt and the problems associated with it. Certain medicines, particularly anti-depressants, have also been shown to help shopping addicts resist the craving to shop, and help alleviate withdrawal symptoms when they cut back on their shopping behavior.

A Brief History of Shopping Addiction

As early as the nineteenth century, medical researchers recognized that some individuals were unable to stop shopping, terming the disorder "oniomania," and psychiatrists in the early-twentieth century recognized it as an impulse disorder, akin to kleptomania (a compulsion to steal) and pyromania (a compulsion to set fires). Kleptomania captured the attention of many researchers in the late-nineteenth and early-twentieth centuries much more than shopping addiction did. In the early 1990s, scientists in the United States, Canada, Britain, Germany, France, and Brazil all began studying shopping addiction once again.

Steroids Addiction

Scientific Overview

Always looking to gain a competitive edge, athletes often turn to substances to help enhance their performance on the field. Sometimes, they will use therapeutic drugs, such as painkillers, anesthetics, muscle-relaxants, and anti-inflammatory drugs so they can compete at the highest level even when injured or suffering from muscle pains. Others, however, use ergogenic drugs—more commonly referred to as performance-enhancing drugs—to gain a competitive edge. Most of these drugs are banned by sports-governing bodies such as the International Olympic Committee and the National Collegiate Athletic Association, and professional sports bodies such as Major League Baseball and the National Football League are starting to crack down on the use of these substances. Stimulant drugs such as ephedra, and hormones, such as human growth hormone (HGH), androstenedione, dehydroepiandrosterone (DHEA), and erythropoietin help enhance athletic performance by increasing energy levels and supplementing the hormone levels in the body to increase strength and endurance. One of the most damaging, and potentially addictive, performance enhancing drugs is the class of substances known as anabolic-androgenic steroids (AAS). While in the 1950s and 1960s, use of these substances appeared to be limited to highly trained athletes, they became increasingly popular in the 1970s and 1980s, so that by 1989, some 1 million people in the United States were obtaining AAS on the black market. About one-quarter of this population was in high school.

AAS are the most abused performance-enhancing drugs today. They are derived from the male hormone testosterone and then synthesized in order to increase body weight and muscle strength while also making users feel more aggressive and confident. Athletes are not alone in their use of AAS, as many young males turn to them to enhance their personal appearance. The benefits of AAS, however, are short-lived, as they tend to weaken bones, make users more prone to tendon injuries, and also cause cancer and sexual problems. Long-term use of AAS leads to a suppression of the body's natural production of testosterone, meaning that when they stop using, male users may develop some feminine characteristics, such as larger breasts. What is more, heavy use by males can lead to a shrinking of the testicles, sometimes to the point that they retract back into the body.

Beyond these negative physical side effects, AAS also have emotional and mental effects that make them potentially addictive. Just as is the case with drugs such as cocaine and amphetamines, the initial confidence AAS give can quickly morph into aggressiveness, emotional instability, rage, and at times can lead to depression or psychosis. What is more, the emotional effects of AAS make them reinforcing, as about one-third of users feel a sense of euphoria when they first start using them. Once this euphoria vanishes and is replaced by the negative mental effects of AAS, many users naturally start taking more AAS to chase away the negative emotions and replace them with the euphoria that they experienced when they first started using the drugs. Research has shown that individuals who use AAS regularly fit many of the criteria psychiatrists use to determine if an individual is addicted to a substance—users take them over longer periods of time than they first planned, they often try to stop taking them without success, they spend substantial amounts of time obtaining or using them, they continue to use despite knowledge of the problems they can cause, they suffer from withdrawal symptoms, and withdrawal symptoms are often relieved by a fresh dose of AAS. Furthermore, recent studies have suggested that anabolic steroids can be as addictive as other psychoactive drugs.

A Brief History of Steroid Addiction

Scientists in the nineteenth century began making connections between testosterone, growth, and behavior, and they perfected the extraction procedure to produce a highly purified and active preparation of the hormone in the 1930s. The German military recognized its ability to make troops stronger and more aggressive, and gave them to some soldiers during World War II. Around the same time, testosterone was used to treat individuals suffering from mental disorders, hypertension, and artery disease.

In the 1950s, Russian athletes used testosterone to enhance their performance in competition, and later that decade U.S. doctor John B. Ziegler first synthesized anabolic steroids, combining testosterone with other hormones and chemicals. Ziegler's steroid went by the trade name Dianabol, and was soon followed by other testosterone preparations such as Ultandren, Nivelar, Adroyd, Durabolin, and Stanozol. By the 1960s, athletes in the United States began using the drugs to enhance their performance in competition; weightlifters used them in order to enhance body strength, body builders used them to increase their muscle size, shape, and definition, and participants in track and field events such as the shot put and javelin used them to give themselves more strength so they could throw farther. By the 1980s, sprinters and swimmers were using them as well, since they helped sustain training at a high intensity level, and over a longer period of time. At the same time, their use proliferated to nonathletes as well, as pharmaceutical companies began selling them for medical use, but most of them were diverted by the black market for sale to individuals who used them to enhance their personal appearance and physique.

In the mid-1990s, officials with the Food Drug Administration began taking notice of the trend, and started to crack down since selling AAS without a medical prescription constituted a violation of the 1938 Food, Drug and Cosmetic Act. In the 1990s, the extent of the problem in professional sports became well-publicized with revelations that several record-holding track and field stars and baseball players had used AAS. Today, major sports organizations are starting to take measures so that their athletes do not use AAS, and the government has begun sponsoring public health campaigns to discourage youth from using them.

REFERENCES

American Psychiatric Association. 1994. *Diagnostic Criteria from DSM-IV.* Washington, D.C.: American Psychiatric Association.

Assael, Shaun. 2007. *Steroid Nation: Juiced Home Run Totals, Anti-aging Miracles, and a Hercules in Every High School: The Secret History of America's True Drug Addiction.* New York: ESPN Books.

Avena, Nicole. 2007. "Examining the Addictive-Like Properties of Binge Eating Using an Animal Model of Sugar Dependence." *Experimental and Clinical Psychopharmacology.* 15, no. 5: 481–491.

Black, Donald W. "A Review of Compulsive Buying Disorder." *World Psychiatry.* 6, no. 1: 14–18.

Blocker, Jack S. and Cheryl Krasnick Warsh, eds. 1997. *The Changing Face of Food and Drink: Substance, Imagery, and Behavior.* Ottawa: Social History Inc.

Brandt, Allan M. 2007. *The Cigarette Century: The Rise, Fall, and Deadly Persistence of the Product That Defined America.* New York: Basic Books.

Brewer, Judson A. and Marc N. Potenza. 2008. "The Neurobiology and Genetics of Impulse Control Disorders: Relationships to Drug Addictions." *Biochemical Pharmacology.* 75: 63–75.

Byun, Sookeun, Celestino Ruffini, Juline E. Mills, Alecia C. Douglas, Mamadou Niang, Svetlana Stepchenkova, Seul Ki Lee, et al. 2008. "Internet Addiction: Metasynthesis of 1996–2006 Quantitative Research." *CyberPsychology & Behavior.* 12: 1–5.

Carson-Dewitt, Rosalyn, ed. 2001. *Encyclopedia of Drugs, Alcohol & Addictive Behavior. Second Edition.* New York: Macmillan Reference USA.

Center for Counseling & Health Resources, Inc. 2009. "Gambling Statistics." [Online article; retrieved 1/31/09] www.overcominggambling.com/facts.html#Statistics.

Center for Internet Addiction and Recovery. 2009. "Cybersex/Cyberporn Addiction." [Online article; retrieved 2/6/09] http://www.netaddiction.com/cybersexual_addiction.htm.

Center for Internet Addiction and Recovery. 2009. "eBay Addiction." [Online article; retrieved 2/6/09] www.netaddiction.com/resources/ebay_addiction.html.

Center for Internet Addiction and Recovery. 2009. "Online Gambling Addiction." [Online article; retrieved 2/6/09] http://www.netaddiction.com/resources/online_gambling _addiction.html.

Center for Internet Addiction and Recovery. 2009. "What Is Internet Addiction?" [Online article; retrieved 2/6/09] www.netaddiction.com/whatis.htm.

Colantuoini, C., J. Schwenker, J. McCarthy, P. Rada, B. Ladenheim, J.-L. Cadet, G. J. Schwartz, T. H. Moran, and B. G. Hoebel. 2001. "Excessive Sugar Intake Alters Binding to Dopamine and Mu-opioid Receptors in the Brain." *Neuroreport.* 12, no. 16: 3549–3552.

Coombs, Robert Holman, ed. 2004. *Handbook of Addictive Disorders: A Practical Guide to Diagnosis and Treatment.* Hoboken, NJ: John Wiley & Sons, Inc.

Corwin, Rebecca L. and Patricia S. Grigson. 2009. "Symposium Overview. Food Addiction: Fact or Fiction?" *Journal of Nutrition.* 139: 1S–3S.

Crothers, Thomas D. 1902. *Morphinism and Narcomanias from Other Drugs.* Philadelphia: W.B. Saunders & Company.

Drewnowski, Adam, Dean D. Krahn, Mark A. Demitrack, Karen Nairn, and Blake A. Gosnell. 1995. "Naloxone, an Opiate Blocker, Reduces the Consumption of Sweet High-Fat Foods in Obese and Lean Female Binge Eaters." *American Journal of Clinical Nutrition.* 61: 1206–1212.

Eisele, Joe. 2007. "Balancing Body and Mind in Treatment: Centers See Biochemical Repair as a Needed Element for Success." *Addiction Professional.* January–February.

Gamblers Anonymous. 2009. "History." [Online article; retrieved 1/31/09] http://www .gamblersanonymous.org/history.html.

Gamblers Anonymous, 2009. "Twenty Questions." [Online article; retrieved 1/31/09] www.gamblersanonymous.org/20questions.html.

Gearhardt, Ashley N., William R. Corbin, Kelly D. Brownell. 2009. "Preliminary Validation of the Yale Food Addiction Scale." *Appetite.* doi:10.1016/j.appet.2008.12.003 (in press)

Giladi, Nir, Nina Weitzman, Shaul Schreiber, Herzel Shabati, and Chava Peretz. 2007. "New Onset Heightened Interest or Drive for Gambling, Shopping, Eating, or Sexual Activity in Patients with Parkinson's Disease: The Role of Dopamine Agonist Treatment and Age at Motor Symptoms Onset." *Journal of Psychopharmacology.* 21, no. 5: 501–506.

Goodman, Aviel. 2008. "Neurobiology of Addiction: An Integrative Review." *Biochemical Pharmacology.* 75: 266–322.

Groneman, Carol. 2000. *Nymphomania: A History.* New York: W.W. Norton & Company.

Gwinnell, Esther, and Christine Adamec. 2006. *The Encyclopedia of Addictions and Addictive Behaviors.* New York Facts on File.

Hewitt, Brenda G. "The Creation of the National Institute on Alcohol Abuse and Alcoholism: Responding to America's Alcohol Problem." [Online article; retrieved 11/01/08] www.niaaa.nih.gov/AboutNIAAA/OrganizationalInformation/History.htm.

Hirschfelder, Arlene B. 1999. *Encyclopedia of Smoking and Tobacco.* Phoenix: Oryx Press.

Iancu, Iulian, Katherine Lowengrub, Yael Dembinsky, Moshe Kotler, and Pinhas N. Dannon. 2008. "Pathological Gambling: An Update on Neuropathophysiology and Pharmacotherapy." *CNS Drugs.* 22, no. 2: 123–138.

Inaba, Darryl S. and William E. Cohen. 2000. *Uppers, Downers, All Arounders: Physical and Mental Effects of Psychoactive Drugs.* Medford, OR: CNS Publications.

Kashkin, K. B. and H. D. Kleber. 1989. "Hooked on Hormones? An Anabolic Steroid Addiction Hypothesis." *Journal of the American Medical Association*. 262, no. 22: 3166–3170.

Koob, George F. 2006. "The Neurobiology of Addiction: A Neuroadaptational View Relevant for Diagnosis." *Addiction*. 101, Suppl. no. 1: 23–30.

Kreek, Mary Jeanne, David A. Nielsen, Eduardo R. Butelman, and K. Steven LaForge. 2005. "Genetic Influences on Impulsivity, Risk Taking, Stress Responsivity and Vulnerability to Drug Abuse and Addiction." *Nature Neuroscience*. 8, no. 11: 1450–1457.

Lende, Daniel H. and Euclid O. Smith. 2002. "Evolution Meets Biopsychosociality: An Analysis of Addictive Behavior." *Addiction*. 97: 447–458.

Lin, Geraldine C. and Lynda Erinoff, eds. 1990. *Anabolic Steroid Abuse*. Rockville, MD: National Institute on Drug Abuse.

Merish, Lori. 1996. "Engendering Naturalism: Narrative Form and Commodity Spectacle in U.S. Naturalist Fiction." *NOVEL: A Forum on Fiction*. 29, no. 3: 319–345.

Mohn, Amy R., Wei-Dong Yao, and Marc G. Caron. 2004. "Genetic and Genomic Approaches to Reward and Addiction." *Neuropharmacology*. 47, Supplement 1: 101–110.

National Gambling Impact Study Commission. 1999. *Final Report*.

National Institute on Drug Abuse. 2009. "Study Information for the NIDA Genetics Consortium." [Online article; retrieved 04/01/09] http://zork.wustl.edu/nida/study _descriptions/link.htm.

National Institute on Drug Abuse. 2008. *InfoFacts: Hallucinogens—LSD, Peyote, Psiolocybin, and PCP*. [Online article; retrieved 11/1/08] www.nida.nih.gov/Infofacts/hallucinogens .html.

National Institute on Drug Abuse. 2008. *InfoFacts: Heroin*. [Online article; retrieved 11/1/08] www.nida.nih.gov/Infofacts/heroin.html.

National Institute on Drug Abuse. 2008. *InfoFacts: Marijuana*. [Online article; retrieved 11/1/08] www.nida.nih.gov/Infofacts/marijuana.html.

National Institute on Drug Abuse. 2008. *InfoFacts: MDMA (Ecstasy)*. [Online article; retrieved 11/1/08] www.nida.nih.gov/Infofacts/ecstasy.html.

National Institute on Drug Abuse. 2008. *InfoFacts: Methamphetamine*. [Online article; retrieved 11/1/08] www.nida.nih.gov/Infofacts/methamphetamine.html.

National Institute on Drug Abuse. 2007. *InfoFacts: Khat*. [Online article; retrieved 11/1/08] www.nida.nih.gov/Infofacts/khat.html.

Online Gamers Anonymous. "A Screening Tool for Excessive Gamers." [Online article; retrieved 02/06/09] http://www.olganon.org/?q=self_tests_on_gaming_addiction.

Online Gamers Anonymous. "Withdrawal Symptoms." [Online article, retrieved 2/6/09] www.olganon.org/?q=game_addiction_withdrawal_symptoms.

Parrot, Andrew, Alun Morinan, Mark Moss, and Andrew Scholey. 2004. *Understanding Drugs and Behaviour*. West Sussex, United Kingdom: John Wiley & Sons, Ltd.

Pelchat, Marcia Levin. 2009. "Food Addiction in Humans." *Journal of Nutrition*. 139: 1S–3S.

Phillips, K. M. and Barry Reay. 2002. *Sexualities in History: A Reader*. Great Britain: Routledge.

Random House Webster's College Dictionary. 1996. New York: Random House.

Rasmussen, Nicolas. 2008. *On Speed: The Many Lives of Amphetamine*. New York: New York University Press.

Ray, Oakley and Charles Ksir. 1993. *Drugs, Society & Human Behavior*. St. Louis: Mosby.

Schuckit, Marc Alan. 2006. *Drug Abuse and Alcohol Abuse: A Clinical Guide to Diagnosis and Treatment*. New York: Springer.

Sournia, Jean-Charles. 1990. *A History of Alcoholism*. Trans. by Nick Hindley and Gareth Stanton. Oxford: Basil Blackwell.

Taylor, William N. 1991. *Macho Medicine: A History of the Anabolic Steroid Epidemic*. Jefferson, NC: McFarland & Company, Inc.

Thombs, Dennis L. 2006. *Introduction to Addictive Behaviors*. Third Edition. New York: Guilford Press.

Uhl, George R. 2004. "Molecular Genetic Underpinnings of Human Substance Abuse Vulnerability: Likely Contributions to Understanding Addiction as a Mnemonic Process." *Neuropharmacology*. 47, Supplement 1: 140–147.

U.S. Drug Enforcement Administration. "Cocaine." [Online article; retrieved 11/1/08] www.usdoj.gov/dea/concern/cocaine.html.

Weil, Andrew T. and Winifred Rosen. 1993. *From Chocolate to Morphine: Everything You Need to Know about Mind-Altering Drugs*. Boston: Houghton Mifflin Company.

White, William L. 1998. *Slaying the Dragon: The History of Addiction Treatment and Recovery in America*. Bloomington, IL: Chestnut Health Systems.

Wood, Ruth I. 2006. "Anabolic Steroids: A Fatal Attraction?" *Journal of Neuroendocrinology*. 18, no. 3: 227–8.

Young, Kimberly S. 2007. "Cognitive Behavior Therapy with Internet Addicts: Treatment Outcomes and Implications." *CyberPsychology & Behavior*. 10, no. 5: 671–679.

AL-ANON

Al-Anon is a mutual aid group for relatives and friends of alcoholics. Formally separate from, but born out of, Alcoholics Anonymous (AA) in the 1940s, Al-Anon similarly follows AA's famous Twelve Steps and Twelve Traditions in an attempt to help relatives deal with alcoholism, which it considers a family disease. Apolitical, nondenominational, and volunteer-based, Al-Anon grew out of the informal gathering of family members with alcoholic loved ones into an international organization with tens of thousands of local chapters.

The creation of Al-Anon is inextricably intertwined with the history of AA, which began in 1935 with the encounter of two alcoholics who formed a mutual aid society based upon members standing in front of the group to make personal declarations or tell their stories. Over time, AA developed a Twelve-Step Program and Twelve Traditions as guiding components, but in general it has remained an open organization predicated on abstinence, avoiding advancing hard and fast answers to alcoholism and recovery, and organizing into local mutual-support groups. While helpful for many alcoholics, AA did not, at least at first, offer much for their families and loved ones. In AA's first years, spouses and relatives of AA members often waited together for their alcoholic loved ones to finish their mutual aid meetings. These moments together led to the realization that alcohol had a profound impact not just upon the alcoholics in their families, but upon their own lives as well. Discussions about their experiences with alcohol and alcoholics, which often took place in ad hoc locations such as church kitchens, led to the creation of informal family groups that gathered to share their members' experiences and provide mutual support and encouragement. Some of the earliest of these group meetings took place in Long Beach, California, Chicago, Richmond, Austin, and Toronto in the mid-1940s. A group in Rochester, NY was among the first to adapt the Twelve Steps for use by the husbands and wives of alcoholics, and formal groups for family members of alcoholics began to spread across the country by the end of the decade.

The growth of group meetings for relatives of AA members represented a bit of a problem for AA itself. While AA was not unsupportive of this development, it was not eager to admit family members of alcoholics into AA proper, and it continued to define itself as an organization strictly dedicated to, and comprised of, alcoholics. To provide family members and friends of alcoholics a place to share their experiences, the AA Board of Trustees took the names of interested family members and listed them at General Services so that they might meet on their own, independently of AA. By 1948, approximately 90 unofficial groups had applied for listing within AA's official directory, signaling the demand for either an institutional change to allow for family members to attend AA meetings, or for the creation of an AA-like group for family members of alcoholics. Soon thereafter, a Clearing House Committee of relatives of AA members in the New York City area was formed. It initially met in a member's home before moving into what was known as the Old 24th Street AA Club House. From that location, and with the help of Lois, the wife of AA cofounder Bill W., the Clearing House Committee recruited volunteers, answered the questions of interested individuals, created a Family Group leaflet, and undertook a survey of all known groups that met to provide support for relatives of AA members. As a result of this poll, in 1951 they adopted the name of Al-Anon Family Groups. The use of "Al-Anon," rather than "AA," in their official name

signaled their organizational independence from AA. Yet the mission of the new group was intimately tied to that of AA. When Al-Anon began, the group's publicly stated goals were to foster cooperation and understanding of the AA program in the home, to help members live by the Twelve Steps and grow spiritually along with their alcoholic loved ones, and to welcome and give comfort to families of new AA members. In 1951, Al-Anon adopted, with only minor alterations, AA's Twelve Steps, and the Al-Anon Family Group Headquarters, Inc. (as it was incorporated in 1954) similarly approved the Twelve Concepts in 1970. Much like AA, Al-Anon grew in large part thanks to articles about it in major publications such as *Time* and *Life*, and being featured on television programs during the 1950s. This exposure, together with the growth of AA itself, helped Al-Anon grow exponentially in the mid-twentieth century, as the group exploded from a small organization of just 145 registered groups in 1951 to 500 in 1954 and 1,500 in 1963.

Officially, Al-Anon is autonomous from AA, but the Sixth Tradition of Al-Anon states that there should always be cooperation between the two organizations. In this regard, the relationship between AA and Al-Anon is akin to that between AA and Narcotics Anonymous. Weekly Al-Anon meetings resemble those that take place amongst AA members, with Al-Anon members gathering in support of one another's difficulties in dealing with alcoholic relatives. The meetings are guided by the Twelve Steps and Twelve Traditions of AA, with Al-Anon members importantly abiding by the First Step, which involves relatives of alcoholics admitting that they, too, are powerless over alcohol. This is not a profession of

Al-Anon members' own alcoholism, but rather a recognition that alcohol can have a powerful impact on the whole family, with its effects not limited to the alcoholic alone. Thus believing alcoholism to be a kind of family disease, the group considers the Twelve Steps an important recovery tool that should not be limited to those with drinking problems.

With the conception that an individual's alcoholism is a family disease that can make relatives sick, Al-Anon tries to get its members to focus on their own issues rather than those of their alcoholic relatives. Particular attention is paid to the emotional complications that result from being unable to bring about their loved ones' sobriety, and another common issue worked on in Al-Anon meetings is the sense of shame, inadequacy, or personal failure that can emerge when AA meetings help the relative achieve an abstinence from alcohol that family members were unable to bring about in spite of their best efforts. Keeping with its emphasis that alcoholism is a family disease, Al-Anon is allied with Alateen, a similar mutual aid group for children and teens with alcoholic relatives or friends. Alateen began in 1957 when a teenager, whose father was in AA and whose mother was in Al-Anon, founded a kind of teen version of Al-Anon that has grown to around 3,500 worldwide groups today. Al-Anon Family Group Headquarters, Inc. officially coordinates Alateen, and most local Alateen groups are sponsored by a local Al-Anon member.

Including Alateen gatherings, Al-Anon claims to currently hold 24,000 meetings spread across 115 countries. Al-Anon also maintains a Web site, http://www.al-anon.alateen.org, which connects members and provides information to prospective members. Al-Anon's monthly magazine, *The Forum*, is available from the Web site, as are additional Al-Anon publications.

(See also **Alateen**; **Alcoholics Anonymous (AA)**; **Narcotics Anonymous (NA)**; **Alcohol Mutual Aid Societies**)

References

Al-Anon. 1992. *Al-Anon Faces Alcoholism*. New York: Al-Anon Family Group Headquarters, Inc.

Al-Anon. 1995. *How Al-Anon Works for Families and Friends of Alcoholics*. Virginia Beach, VA: Al-Anon Family Groups.

Al-Anon. 1997. *Paths to Recovery: Al-Anon's Steps, Traditions, and Concepts*. Virginia Beach, VA: Al-Anon Family Groups.

Carson-Dewitt, Rosalyn, ed. 2001. *Encyclopedia of Drugs, Alcohol & Addictive Behavior. Second Edition*. New York: Macmillan Reference USA.

Galanter, Marc, ed. 1989. *Recent Developments in Alcoholism: Volume Seven—Treatment Research*. New York: Springer.

White, William L. 1998. *Slaying the Dragon: The History of Addiction Treatment and Recovery in America*. Bloomington, IL: Chestnut Health Systems.

ALATEEN

Alateen is a mutual aid group for children and teenagers with alcoholic relatives or friends. Created in 1957 in California by a teenager whose father was in Alcoholics Anonymous (AA) and whose mother was in Al-Anon, Alateen is a version of Al-Anon designed for the children of families with an alcoholic member. It is coordinated by Al-Anon Family Group Headquarters, Inc., and it currently claims to have around 3,500 groups worldwide.

The origins of Alateen are to be found in Al-Anon, which itself emerged out of AA. AA began with the encounter of two alcoholics in 1935 who formed a mutual aid society based upon members standing in front of the group to make personal declarations or tell their life stories. Over time, AA developed a Twelve-Step Program and Twelve Traditions as guiding components, and became composed of local mutual support groups instead of a top-heavy, national bureaucracy. Alateen's immediate forbearer, Al-Anon, grew out of the shared plight of spouses and relatives of AA members who, in the early years of AA's development, often waited together for their alcoholic loved ones to finish their mutual aid meetings. These moments together led to the realization that alcohol had a profound impact not just upon the alcoholics in their families, but upon their own lives as well. Discussions about their experiences with alcohol and alcoholics led to the creation of informal family groups that gathered to share their members' experiences and provide mutual support and encouragement. This eventually led to the official founding of Al-Anon Family Groups in 1951. In what would become the basis for Alateen meetings, weekly Al-Anon meetings used the Twelve Steps and Twelve Traditions to help relatives of AA members cope with the broader impact of their loved ones' alcoholism. Al-Anon members worked at focusing on their own issues rather than those of their alcoholic relatives, and particular attention was paid to the emotional complications that resulted from being unable to bring about their loved ones' sobriety. Another issue commonly worked on in Al-Anon meetings (as well as in later Alateen gatherings) was the sense of shame, inadequacy, or personal failure that could emerge when AA meetings helped relatives achieve an abstinence from alcohol that alcoholics' family members themselves were unable to bring about.

While Alanon was helpful for many family members of alcoholics, some children of AA members felt that the group did not meet their needs. To address these shortcomings, a seventeen-year old son of an AA member in California founded a new organization—Alateen—in 1957. In order to bring together other teens with relatives attending AA or Al-Anon meetings, the anonymous teenager, with his mother's support, envisioned Alateen as a group that could serve as a teen version of Al-Anon, focusing on the needs of family members of alcoholics who were between twelve and twenty years old. The initial group was comprised of the founding young man and five other teens, and it met in a room downstairs from the room in which their parents met. The idea of a group for young adults caught on quickly, as by 1963, there were over 200 Alateen groups, and the group continued to grow when it was featured in national publications such as *Time* and *Seventeen*. Today, Alateen has developed into an organization with thousands of groups meeting worldwide.

Despite this impressive growth, Alateen is not an independent organization, and it is officially coordinated by Al-Anon Family Group Headquarters. Al-Anon's influence extends to the local level as well, with an active, adult member of Al-Anon required to serve as the sponsor of Alateen weekly meetings. Similarly, Alateen members' personal sponsors can come from the ranks of Al-Anon, though they are also free to have a sponsor who comes within Alateen. Weekly Alateen meetings operate very much like Al-Anon meetings. Importantly, Alateen meetings feature members abiding by Al-Anon's First Step, which involves admitting a powerlessness over alcoholism. By declaring an inability to control or cure a relative's alcoholism, Alateen members are encouraged to focus on their own well-being regardless of whether the loved one's drinking stops or not. They are likewise taught to emotionally detach themselves from the drinker's problems while continuing to love the person. Alateen does slightly alter AA's and Al-Anon's Twelfth Step, which is modified to state the organization's goal of carrying their message to other youths with alcoholic relatives or friends.

Alateen maintains a Web site, http://www.al-anon.alateen.org/alateen.html, containing information about Alateen meetings and published Alateen material. Alateen's newsletter, *Alateen Talk*, is also available from the Web site.

(See also **Alcohol Mutual Aid Societies**; **Alcoholics Anonymous (AA)**; **Al-Anon**; **Narcotics Anonymous (NA)**)

References

"About Alateen." [Online article, retrieved 05/16/09] http://www.al-anon.alateen.org/alaabout.html.

Al-Anon. 1973. *Alateen—Hope for Children of Alcoholics*. New York: Al-Anon Family Groups.

Al-Anon. 1991. *Youth and the Alcoholic Parent*. New York: Al-Anon Family Groups.

Carson-Dewitt, Rosalyn, ed. 2001. *Encyclopedia of Drugs, Alcohol & Addictive Behavior. Second Edition*. New York: Macmillan Reference USA.

"Twelve Traditions of Alateen." [Online article, retrieved 05/16/09] http://www.al-anon.alateen.org/alatraditions.html.

White, William L. 1998. *Slaying the Dragon: The History of Addiction Treatment and Recovery in America*. Bloomington, IL: Chestnut Health Systems.

ALCOHOL BOOTLEGGING AND SMUGGLING

Bootlegging and smuggling, the acts of illegally producing and transporting alcohol, became nationwide phenomena after the implementation of national prohibition as federal law in 1920. Despite the efforts of the Prohibition Unit, which was created to enforce the Volstead Act, bootleggers and smugglers found means of providing Americans with the alcoholic beverages they still craved. In some cases, bootleggers and smugglers became popular figures as a result of crimes that fascinated those members of the public who were opposed to the Eighteenth Amendment, which was repealed in 1933.

When the Volstead Act, and thereby national prohibition, became federal law on January 20, 1920, alcohol did not disappear from American life. Despite a ban on most alcoholic beverages, there was still a considerable demand for drink that was catered to by bootleggers and smugglers. The illegal beverages they provided could be clandestinely bought in places like drugstores, barbershops, and hotels, but the most popular place to purchase and consume this alcohol was the speakeasy—a kind of underground bar that emerged during national prohibition.

The most successful and famous speakeasies served those affluent members of society who longed for a drink despite the illegality and high price of alcohol. Cocktails, in particular, became features of the speakeasy experience, as prohibition generally had the unintended consequence of elevating consumption rates for hard alcohol. Speakeasies themselves flourished, especially in places like New York City, which effectively abandoned its enforcement of prohibition after 1924. Evidencing the great thirst that existed for illegal liquor, New York's police commissioner estimated that there were 32,000 speakeasies operating within the city in 1929. Such a figure was over twice as great as the number of legal drinking establishments that existed in the city before prohibition.

The Prohibition Unit—the federal agency created in 1920 in order to enforce national prohibition and the Volstead Act—was largely unsuccessful in policing speakeasies and stopping the bootlegging and smuggling of alcohol. This result was surprising to those in power who reasoned that enforcement would not be an enormous task because, after all, enough Americans supported national prohibition to pass a constitutional amendment. The mistaken belief that a modestly endowed Prohibition Unit would be sufficient to police the liquor ban thus gave enterprising bootleggers and smugglers, who risked a first-offense fine of $1,000 and six months in jail, ample opportunity to devise means of providing Americans with illicit alcohol. One particularly effective method of smuggling alcohol was to bribe agents within the Prohibition Unit. This practice was so common that within the first six years of prohibition, one out of every twelve agents of the Prohibition Unit was fired for acts of corruption such as taking bribes or conspiring to sell illegal liquor.

The underfunding of the Prohibition Unit, which in part led to so much corruption within its ranks, also meant that the agency as a whole could not afford to protect the nation's lengthy borders from extensive and sophisticated smuggling efforts like the one devised by the infamous Bill McCoy. His first smuggling ventures involved loading his ship in the Caribbean with cases of liquor and simply sneaking his cargo back to American docks. But what distinguished McCoy from other smugglers engaging in similar activities, however, was his origination of "Rum Row," which referred to the lining up of alcohol-carrying ships just beyond American waters. These boats were within the safety of international waters, but close enough to the American shore that other boats could sail out to meet them and purchase high-quality liquor. This novel set up was so successful that, after upgrading ships, McCoy's boat was described as a high-end "floating liquor store." And consumer demand was particularly strong because McCoy's goods were noted for being undiluted and unadulterated, unlike much bootleg liquor in America, which could be downright dangerous to consume. As a result, the term "the real McCoy" was born to describe the quality of McCoy's smuggled liquor, which was brought to shore in the boats of customers who were generally successful in outracing and evading the thinly stretched Coast Guard patrols. In fact, the setup was so difficult for the Coast Guard to combat that Rum Rows sprang up across the Atlantic seaboard, with outposts along every state and nearly every city from Maine to Florida. Similar Rum Rows existed in the Gulf of Mexico and along the Pacific. McCoy's signature business model, which quickly brought him a great deal of wealth and fame before his arrest in 1923, helps explain why the Prohibition

Unit admitted that in 1925 it had stopped just 5% of the liquor being smuggled into the United States.

The bootlegging of alcohol inside of the country was tough to halt as well. Beyond the challenges involved in finding illegal stills and permanently shutting down bootlegging operations, the Prohibition Unit had difficulties prosecuting violators of the Volstead Act. With national prohibition growing increasingly unpopular, the court system often became jammed with alcohol-related cases. For example, in southern Alabama, the center of moonshine production, as high as 90% of all cases in the system resulted from alleged violations of the Volstead Act. And with the general public becoming increasingly resentful of national prohibition, some prosecutors found juries to be quite sympathetic to bootleggers and smugglers and consequently reluctant to convict. Heightened penalties for violations of the Volstead Act were introduced in 1929 in an attempt to curb bootlegging and smuggling, but these modifications were ineffective in creating greater compliance with the law.

Ultimately, the extensive bootlegging and smuggling efforts that persisted throughout national prohibition spoke to the public's dissatisfaction with the Volstead Act. The occasional championing of notorious smugglers also reflected a substantial opposition to the government's ban on the commercial manufacture and sale of liquor. With the passage of the Twenty-First Amendment in 1933, alcohol became legal and effectively ended drinking Americans' reliance upon, and fascination with, alcohol bootleggers and smugglers.

(See also **McCoy, Bill**; **Prohibition Unit**; **Speakeasies**; **Volstead Act (18th Amendment)**))

References

Burns, Eric. 2004. *The Spirits of America: A Social History of America*. Philadelphia: Temple University Press.

Clark, Norman H. 1976. *Deliver Us from Evil: An Interpretation of American Prohibition*. New York: W. W. Norton Company.

Lender, Mark Edward and James Kirby Martin. 1982. *Drinking in America: A History*. New York: The Free Press.

Pegram, Thomas P. 1998. *Battling Demon Rum: The Struggle for a Dry America, 1800–1933*. Chicago: Ivan R. Dee.

ALCOHOL MUTUAL AID SOCIETIES

Abstinence-based mutual aid societies, which are comprised of individuals with drinking problems who seek to curb alcohol use and abuse, first emerged amongst Native American tribes in the eighteenth century, though later in the century, Non-Native Americans developed their own mutual aid societies. By the nineteenth century, alcohol mutual aid societies had multiplied in number and orientation, only to fade away in the early-twentieth century. Today, groups like Alcoholics Anonymous (AA) have taken up the mantle of alcohol mutual aid societies.

Alcohol mutual aid societies originated with "recovery circles," the cultural revival efforts of various Native American leaders in the mid-eighteenth century. Perhaps most prominent amongst a number of Native American "seers," the Delaware Prophet (Neolin) articulated a mission of religious and cultural revitalization that could only be achieved by abstaining from alcohol and returning to native traditions. The Delaware Prophet, along with other important Native prophetic leaders, used the story of his own recovery from alcohol abuse to demonstrate how a Native American community could recapture its vitality if it abstained from alcohol, which was believed to be an instrument of foreign oppression and exploitation.

About a century after the emergence of Native American recovery circles, alcohol mutual aid societies became prominent among Non-Native American communities. The first significant temperance organization of this type was the Washingtonian movement (or the Washingtonians). Founded in 1840 by six Baltimore drinkers, the Washingtonians differed from previous temperance figures in that they were not led by teetotalers, elites, or religious figures. Instead, the Washingtonians, comprised of lower-middle and working class alcoholics, democratized temperance activity. They also succeeded in gaining members where other temperance figures had failed, in large part because they focused on saving individual alcoholics rather than advocating greater social reform and pushing for tighter legal restrictions on alcohol. The Washingtonians blossomed into a national organization as a result of large rallies and powerful orators, but the group's lifeblood was the weekly meeting of local Washingtonian societies, which stressed support, encouragement, advice, and solidarity. At these regular gatherings, members often told sobering tales about the harmful effects that alcohol had on their lives, the benefits of their newfound sobriety, and the importance of remaining free of drink. When members relapsed into drinking, other members would rally around in support, providing the emotional, financial, and medical support to help

them through the crisis. In this regard, Washingtonian methods prefigured the techniques that would later be employed by twentieth-century alcohol mutual aid societies like Alcoholics Anonymous.

When, in the late 1840s, the Washingtonians disappeared as a result of irreparable divisions over issues of membership, religious ties, political aims, as well as the general difficulty of members remaining sober, fraternal temperance societies like the Sons of Temperance, the Order of Good Templars, the Independent Order of Rechabites, the Order of the Friends of Temperance, and the Independent Order of Good Samaritans rose in prominence. These groups generally opened their doors to anyone who signed a pledge of abstinence and met other membership requirements, but they eventually declined in importance as a result of divided views on the direction these alcohol mutual aid societies should take—to focus on rehabilitating the alcoholics, or to work towards legally prohibiting alcohol.

Ribbon Reform Clubs originated in the early 1870s and represented a new wave in the history of alcohol mutual aid groups. The Royal Ribbon Reform Club, the Blue Ribbon Reform Club, and the Red Ribbon Reform Club sought to avoid the divisions that befell previous alcohol mutual aid societies by banning political discussions at all group events. In general, members were expected to meet regularly for mutual support, engage in rescue work for the sake of other alcoholics, and sign pledges of abstinence. In addition, members wore, on their lapels, ribbons (in the color of their particular reform club), both as a symbol of their fight against alcohol abuse and so that members could find one another while traveling.

Another significant alcohol mutual aid society was the Keeley Clubs, a group organized by recovering alcoholics affiliated with Leslie Keeley's institutes for inebriates, which extended across the country beginning in the mid-1890s. Keeley argued that alcoholism was a disease, and that, consequently, through a combination of his (pharmacologically spurious) injections, behavior modification techniques, and a supportive therapeutic environment, alcoholics could be cured. Keeley Clubs employed morning meetings filled with speeches, discussions, and mutual support. Keeley Clubs, like most of the alcohol mutual aid societies and treatment institutions of the nineteenth century, slid towards obsolescence in the early-twentieth century.

Alcohol mutual aid societies reemerged in the 1930s with the founding of AA. From its first meeting—the encounter of two alcoholics in 1935—until today, AA has been centered on members standing in front of the group to make personal declarations or tell their life stories. Over time, AA developed a Twelve-Step Program and Twelve Traditions as guiding components, but in general it has remained an open organization predicated on abstinence, avoiding advancing hard and fast answers to alcoholism and recovery, and organizing into local mutual support groups instead of a top-heavy, national bureaucracy. In AA, advice is thus offered not by professionals, but rather via other alcoholic members who relate stories of their own experiences as a means of suggesting to others how they might best deal with their own alcoholism.

As a result of these approaches, AA has grown into the world's largest alcohol recovery group and most successful alcohol mutual aid society. In recent decades, mutual aid groups like Al-Anon and Alateen have borrowed aspects of AA's model to fashion alternative alcohol mutual aid societies for relatives of alcoholics. Another recent alcohol mutual aid society, LifeRing, has diverged significantly from AA's model by eliminating AA's spiritual components and empowering individuals, in a secular manner, to take the lead in their fights against addiction.

(See also **Alcoholics Anonymous (AA)**; **Al-Anon**; **Alateen**; **Keeley, Leslie E.**; **LifeRing**; **Recovery Circles**; **Ribbon Reform Clubs**; **Washingtonians**)

References

Blocker, Jr., Jack S., David M. Fahey, and Ian R. Tyrrell, eds. 2003. *Alcohol and Temperance in Modern History: An International Encyclopedia*. Santa Barbara, CA: ABC-CLIO.

Kurtz, Ernest. 1979. *Not—God: A History of Alcoholics Anonymous*. Center City, MN: Hazelden Educational Services.

Lender, Mark Edward and James Kirby Martin. 1982. *Drinking in America: A History*. New York: The Free Press.

O'Brien, Suzanne J. Crawford, ed. 2008. *Religion and Healing in Native America: Pathways for Renewal*. Westport, CT: Praeger.

Pegram, Thomas P. 1998. *Battling Demon Rum: The Struggle for a Dry America, 1800–1933*. Chicago: Ivan R. Dee.

ALCOHOLICS ANONYMOUS (AA)

Alcoholics Anonymous (AA) is the largest alcohol recovery group in the world, with the sole requirement for membership being the desire to stop drinking. AA is an international organization, but its central unit is local meetings in which members share their stories of alcoholism and recovery as a means of helping other members either become or remain sober.

Alcoholics Anonymous (AA) began in 1935 with "Bill W.," a temporarily sober alcoholic, seeking the support of an alcoholic surgeon, "Dr. Bob," in Akron, Ohio. With the meeting of these two men, AA was effectively founded. Bill W. (1895–1971) and Dr. Bob (1879–1950) initially met through the efforts of a local Oxford Group network. The Oxford Group began in 1921 under the name of "The First Century Christian Movement" as a network of groups whose meetings featured participants standing up and publicly confessing their shortcomings. Members would also proselytize to new recruits by talking about salvation through the Oxford Group, which was founded on a Protestant ideology that espoused surrendering one's self and one's pride to God, accepting divine guidance, recovering through a process of spiritual growth, and a belief in the ability of individuals to reform and improve themselves without the aid of clergy. Some members who had alcohol problems strove to achieve sobriety via their involvement with the Oxford Group, but the organization was not exclusively devoted to the aid and rehabilitation of alcoholics.

Bill W., a traveling stock-market analyst based out of New York, came to the Oxford Group through the proselytizing efforts of a friend who hoped to save him from his drinking habit. After a spiritual awakening in 1934, Bill W. headed to Akron with the idea of using the Oxford Group as a means of saving other alcoholics. Bill W.'s meeting with Dr. Bob constituted the first meeting of the nascent AA. The Oxford Group was

displeased, however, with meetings exclusively held for alcoholics, and by 1939 the breakaway group officially took the title "Alcoholics Anonymous." This name was derived from the practice of members referring to themselves as "a nameless bunch of drunks."

Reflecting their origins within the Oxford Group, AA meetings, from the beginning, featured members standing in front of the group to make personal declarations or tell their life stories. And though AA published a guide in 1939 that would come to be known as "The Big Book," it remained an open organization that avoided advancing hard and fast answers to alcoholism and recovery. It put forth a generic and unscientific notion of members being "allergic" to alcohol, thus suggesting the need for total abstinence. And AA essentially remained an organization of local mutual-support groups instead of a top-heavy, national bureaucracy. Advice was thus offered not by professionals, but rather via other alcoholic members who related stories of their own experiences as a means of suggesting to others how they might best deal with alcoholism.

What united AA groups was their now famous, "twelve-step" model for recovery from alcoholism, which was laid out in the Big Book. The steps for individuals who want to work the AA program are:

1. Admitting that they are powerless over alcohol and that their lives have become unmanageable.

2. Coming to believe that a power greater than themselves could restore sanity to their lives.

3. Deciding to turn their wills and lives over to the care of God,

however they understand him (their personal "higher power").

4. Making a moral inventory of themselves.

5. Admitting to their higher power, themselves, and to other people the exact nature of their wrongs.

6. Being ready to have their higher power remove these defects of character.

7. Asking the higher power to remove their shortcomings.

8. Making a list of all persons they have harmed, and becoming willing to make amends to them.

9. Making amends to such people wherever possible, unless doing so would cause harm to them or to others.

10. Continuing to take personal inventory and admitting when they are wrong.

11. Through prayer and meditation, working to improve conscious contact with their higher power.

12. Having had a spiritual awakening through these steps, trying to carry the message to other alcoholics, and to practice these principles in all aspects of their daily lives.

During World War II, AA started publication of *The AA Grapevine*, a journal which began as a way of keeping in touch with servicemen abroad, but became, and continues to be to this day, a means of addressing and encouraging alcoholics of various backgrounds and attachments to alcohol to attend AA meetings. It featured members testifying to their personal experiences with alcohol and recovery, and it also included discussions of the effects of drugs other than alcohol. Thanks in large part to this publication, AA had 12,986 members spread across 556 local groups by the end

of the war. In 1950, the group culled member correspondence to create its "Twelve Traditions of Alcoholics Anonymous"—a series of basic guidelines for structuring AA groups, including calls for anonymity, unity, acceptance of a broadly defined higher power, economic self-sufficiency, and being apolitical. The publication of the Twelve Traditions spurred a new, dramatic growth in AA as an organization, as by the end of that year, membership exceeded 96,000, and more than 3,500 local groups were in existence. The fact that "a desire to stop drinking" was the only requirement for membership within AA allowed local groups great freedom to deal as they saw fit with the issues specifically facing its local members, further increasing AA's significance within American life. And with endorsements ranging from the likes of President Eisenhower to advice columnist Dear Abby, AA became the predominant self-help organization for alcoholics in the country during the 1950s.

Though AA had long worked to encourage alcoholics to stop drinking, as the middle of the twentieth century progressed, AA became more involved in institutional efforts to help alcoholics. Members helped create AA "farms," "retreats," and "Twelve-Step houses," many of which enjoyed the support of the National Council on Alcoholism. The "Minnesota Model," a chemical dependency treatment that is most often associated with the Hazelden Institute but has become one of the primary methods of treatment in the United States, employs AA's Twelve Steps. Through these efforts and others, AA membership grew from 311,450 in 1970 to 907,575 in 1980. By 1990, AA counted around 2 million members—a precipitous increase from its initial group of Bill W. and Dr. Bob in 1935.

With this veritable explosion in membership numbers also came an increasing diversification of AA in terms of its programs and members. Some local groups moved away from AA's original emphasis on God and spirituality and towards a more secularized version of AA. Similarly, local meetings have become more specialized in recent years, with some meeting groups limited to specific demographics. For example, there are now AA groups organized by gender, age, language, sexual orientation, and co-occurring problems.

AA's diversification is paralleled by the emergence of other treatment and recovery groups that offer alcoholic-related support. For instance, Al-Anon (which was founded by Bill W.'s wife, Lois Wilson) and Alateen are voluntary organizations that cater to the spouses and children of alcoholics, respectively. Other alternatives to AA include Women for Sobriety, Rational Recovery, Moderation Management, and LifeRing. Additionally, the success of AA's twelve-step approach to alcohol abuse spawned twelve-step programs for other addiction problems. Prominent examples include Gamblers Anonymous, Narcotics Anonymous, Cocaine Anonymous, and Sexaholics Anonymous.

(See also **Al-Anon**; **Alateen**; **Alcohol Mutual Aid Societies**; **Hazelden Foundation**; **Gamblers Anonymous (GA)**; **LifeRing**; **Narcotics Anonymous (NA)**; **Washingtonians**)

References

Alcoholics Anonymous. 2001. *Alcoholics Anonymous: The Story of How Many Thousands of Men and Women Have Recovered from Alcoholism*. New York: Alcoholics Anonymous World Services, Inc.

Blocker, Jr., Jack S., David M. Fahey, and Ian R. Tyrrell, eds. 2003. *Alcohol and Temperance in Modern History: An International Encyclopedia*. Santa Barbara, CA: ABC-CLIO.

Edwards, Griffith. 2000. *Alcohol: The Ambiguous Molecule*. London: Penguin Books.

Kurtz, Ernest. 1979. *Not—God: A History of Alcoholics Anonymous*. Center City, MN: Hazelden Educational Services.

Mendelson, Jack H. and Nancy K. Mello. 1985. *Alcohol: Use and Abuse in America*. Boston: Little, Brown and Company.

White, William L. 1998. *Slaying The Dragon: The History of Addiction Treatment and Recovery in America*. Bloomington, IL: Chesnut Health Systems.

AMERICAN ASSOCIATION FOR THE STUDY AND CURE OF INEBRIETY (AASCI)

The American Association for the Study and Cure of Inebriety (AASCI), which was founded in 1870, broke new ground as an organization dedicated to the study of alcohol and drug addiction. The AASCI, which was comprised of doctors, reformers, and superintendents of inebriety treatment centers, was a pioneer in casting alcoholism and drug addiction not as moral failings on the part of the individual, but rather as medically treatable conditions. This view, as well as the AASCI itself, began to fall out of favor as the prohibitionist cause gained steam around the turn of the century, but the AASCI's ideas took on a new life elsewhere with the passage of the Twenty-First Amendment and the repeal of prohibition in 1933.

The AASCI began in 1870 under the name of the American Association for the Cure of Inebriates. The group had three main purposes—to facilitate the exchange of information among professionals in the fields of alcoholism and addiction treatment, to provide political advocacy for legislation to establish and support the work of inebriate asylums, and to publish a professional journal and treatises on addiction treatment. The AASCI was founded by Dr. Joseph Parrish, who served as the medical director and chair of the board of directors of the Pennsylvania Inebriate Asylum in Media, Pennsylvania. Much of the association's leadership consisted of leading professionals within the world of late-nineteenth-century inebriety treatment.

For example, one of the group's leading members, Dr. Nathan S. Davis, was not only involved with AASCI, but also helped found the American Medical Association and the Chicago Washingtonian Home, a facility dedicated to the treatment of alcoholics. In his work with the Washingtonians, Davis helped advance the belief that individuals could overcome alcoholism through moral example, testimonials, and support groups. Another of the AASCI's leading members, Dr. Thomas Crothers, contributed to the organization's understanding of alcoholism as a medically treatable condition. Crothers was a physician who devoted much of his professional life towards treating inebriety and gaining recognition of it as a disease. In doing so, he went beyond traditional moral conceptions of alcohol abuse and furthered existing theories about alcoholism being an illness (and not a sin) by giving the concept of inebriety greater scientific footing. Over many years working at inebriate asylums, Crothers gathered a body of evidence that he felt validated his disease conception of alcohol

addiction. When he joined the AASCI in 1873, Crothers worked to popularize his notion of alcoholism as the longtime editor of the AASCI's *Quarterly Journal of Inebriety.* Under Crothers' editorship, the *Quarterly Journal of Inebriety* attracted contributions from many of the most innovative medical theorists of the nineteenth century, such as neurologist George M. Beard. The AASCI worked to keep controversial papers and articles that were mere advertisements for certain facilities or doctors out of its journal, thus using it as a tool to further the professional credibility of the study of inebriety. The AASCI had some success with this, as by 1891, over 2,000 physicians across the country subscribed to the *Quarterly Journal of Inebriety.*

The leaders of the AASCI challenged conventional thinking about alcohol abuse by arguing that inebriety was a disease, and not a moral failing. Given that it was a disease, they believed that the best way to help alcoholics was to give them medical treatment. With this claim, the AASCI differed from other contemporary conceptions of drunkenness, which often viewed inebriety as a vice or a moral failing. Though these more moralistic ideas were actually held by some AASCI members in the early days of the organization, the idea that inebriety was a disease that could be passed down hereditarily, warranted medical attention, and required treatment nevertheless became the main line of thinking for the organization.

Though most AASCI members believed that inebriety was a disease, the group's publications put forward many different theories about what kind of disease alcoholism was. Some within the AASCI believed that anyone who became drunk could be classified as an "inebriate," while other AASCI members argued that drinkers were diseased only when they chronically turned to alcohol. Despite these inconsistencies, the AASCI helped popularize some key concepts about inebriety. For example, the AASCI often published articles that discussed "chronic poisoning," a term invoked to describe the physiological basis of opium abuse. Similarly, Beard was influential within the AASCI with his definition of alcoholism as a form of neurasthenia, a neurological disorder that many nineteenth-century physicians believed was responsible for a variety of physical and mental illnesses.

Notwithstanding the diversity of theories about inebriety within its membership ranks, the AASCI grew from its initial coalition of all six inebriety institutions that existed in 1870 into an organization of thirty-two inebriety facilities by 1878. The organization's rapid growth spoke to the popularity of the AASCI's theories about inebriety, and as its influence grew, more and more physicians and alcohol reform organizations began to adopt the group's medical understanding of inebriety as a disease. But by 1904, the AASCI had receded in prominence to the point of being united with the American Medical Temperance Association (AMTA), another organization that was founded by Davis. After it joined forces with the AMTA, the organization changed its name, becoming the American Medical Society for the Study of Alcohol and Other Narcotics. Though Crothers continued to defend the AASCI's work and wanted to further the understanding of inebriety as a medical problem, proponents of alcohol prohibition eventually came to dominate the organization. Consequently, the *Quarterly Journal of Inebriety* ceased publication in 1914, and the AASCI faded into obscurity. The AASCI may have existed until the 1920s, but if so, it must have been as a faint shadow of its former self.

(See also **Crothers, Thomas Davison**; **Washingtonians**)

References

Blocker, Jr., Jack S., David M. Fahey, and Ian R. Tyrrell, eds. 2003. *Alcohol and Temperance in Modern History: An International Encyclopedia*. Santa Barbara, CA: ABC-CLIO.

Edwards, Griffith. 2000. *Alcohol: The Ambiguous Molecule*. London: Penguin Books.

Lender, Mark Edward and James Kirby Martin. 1982. *Drinking in America: A History*. New York: The Free Press.

Murdock, Catherine Gilbert. 1998. *Domesticating Drink: Women, Men, and Alcohol in America, 1870–1940*. Baltimore: The Johns Hopkins University Press.

White, William L. 1998. *Slaying the Dragon: The History of Addiction Treatment and Recovery in America*. Bloomington, IL: Chestnut Health Systems.

AMERICAN SOCIETY OF ADDICTION MEDICINE (ASAM)

The American Society of Addiction Medicine (ASAM) is a nonprofit organization made up of physicians who treat patients with addiction problems. ASAM's mission is to increase access to, and improve the quality of, addiction treatment, educate health care providers and physicians on addiction, support research and prevention of addiction, promote the role of the physician in the care of addicted patients, and to establish addiction medicine as a specialty within the medical field.

ASAM's roots date back to the 1950s, when physician Ruth Fox worked to establish the New York City Medical Committee on Alcoholism, a group of physicians interested in the study of alcoholism and its treatment that met at the New York Academy of Medicine. The Medical Committee met regularly, and in 1954 it convened its first scientific meeting and established the New York City Medical Society on Alcoholism, with Dr. Fox as its president. In 1967, this group changed its name to the American Medical Society on Alcoholism (AMSA). In the early 1980s, the organization incorporated similar groups, such as the American Academy of Addictionology and the California Society for the Treatment of Alcoholism and Other Drug Dependencies, into its membership. In 1986, AMSA began offering a national certification examination for doctors in the field of addiction medicine. The organization achieved one of its major goals—to get addiction treatment recognized as a subfield within medicine—in 1988, when it was approved and given membership by the House of Delegates of the American Medical Association. To reflect its interest in all addictions, not just alcoholism, the society changed its name to the American Society of Addiction Medicine (ASAM), in 1989. In 1990, ASAM achieved a major success when the American Medical Association gave addiction medicine a separate code as a self-designated specialty, officially recognizing addiction as a specialty within the medical field. In the 1990s, ASAM continued its work in establishing addictionology as a subfield within medicine,

coming up with a set of guidelines for training programs in addiction medicine in 1990, and publishing editions of its *Principles of Addiction Medicine*, a reference guide that documented the scientific and clinical foundations of addictionology, in 1994, 1998, and 2003. More recently, ASAM established its Medical Specialty Action Group in order to further the group's goal of establishing addiction medicine as a primary specialty within the medical field, and develop standards for training on addictive disorders for use in residency training programs.

Today, ASAM continues to advocate for addiction medicine to be recognized as a medical disorder by physicians, health insurers, health care organizations, and policymakers. By partnering with government and private-sector organizations, the group sponsors programs and creates educational materials to help physicians, health professionals, and government officials understand both the medical and societal aspects of substance abuse. Through its publications, *ASAM News*, *Journal of Addiction Medicine*, *Principles of Addiction Medicine*, and *ASAM Patient Placement Criteria*, the organization disseminates information about addiction and its treatment. The group is also a strong advocate for addiction treatment, pushing for addiction medicine specialists to be paid by insurance companies the same way that other medical specialists are, and also working to secure funding to study the efficacy of different addiction treatments.

More information on ASAM and its activities are available at the group's Web site: http://www.asam.org/.

(See also **Reference Essay**)

References

American Society of Addiction Medicine. "ASAM Historical Timeline." [Online article retrieved 05/14/09] http://www.asam.org/Timelines.html.

American Society of Addiction Medicine. "ASAM Mission." [Online article retrieved 05/14/09] http://www.asam.org/about.html.

American Society of Addiction Medicine. "The American Society of Addiction Medicine Strategic Plan 2006–2010." [Online article retrieved 05/14/09] http://www.asam.org/CMS/images/PDF/General/Strategic%20Plan.pdf California Society of Addiction Medicine. "About CSAM." [Online article retrieved 05/14/09] http://www.csam-asam.org/about_csam.vp.html.

Carson-Dewitt, Rosalyn, ed. 2001. *Encyclopedia of Drugs, Alcohol & Addictive Behavior. Second Edition.* New York: Macmillan Reference USA.

AMERICAN TEMPERANCE SOCIETY (ATS)

The American Temperance Society (ATS) was the first national temperance organization in the United States. Buoyed by a Protestant revival and led by media-savvy directors, the ATS grew into an organization of approximately 1.5 million Americans by 1835. Though it did not operate as a prohibitionist organization, the ATS was significant in helping pave the way to national prohibition, as the temperance organization's initial notions of moderate drinking being acceptable eventually gave way to the ideal of complete abstinence from alcohol.

The origins of the ATS are to be found in an 1826 state convention brought together by Boston reverend Justin Edwards. At this assembly, Massachusetts clergymen took the lead in establishing a group they named the American Society for the Promotion of Temperance. This new organization differed from its closest predecessor, the Massachusetts Society for the Suppression of Intemperance (MSSI), which was founded in 1813 by elite figures in the state, and whose main tactics in combating intemperance were to pressure local officials to lock up public drunks and advocate restricting licenses for the sale of liquor. Since the elitist MSSI did not believe in prohibition, they favored the idea of suppressing intemperance by means of allowing only the most upstanding local citizens to possess alcohol sales licenses. The American Society for the Promotion of Temperance, whose name was abbreviated to the American Temperance Society in 1827, articulated very different notions of temperance and how to go about achieving it nationally.

The ATS' innovations as a temperance organization were multiple. Unlike the MSSI and other previous temperance groups, the ATS cast their opposition to intemperance in religious terms, often invoking a divine inspiration for their efforts. Similarly, the ATS utilized missionary tactics to convert the drinker to temperance. Since fourteen of sixteen directors of the American Temperance Society were members of the American Tract Society, the group used many of the American Tract Society's propaganda tactics, distributing millions of temperance pamphlets throughout the country. These temperance tracts built upon the writings of temperance advocates like Dr. Benjamin Rush by utilizing (sometimes spurious) statistics to emphasize the broad threat that they believed drunkenness posed to the vitality of the nation. Another new ATS development was the uncompromising nature of their stance on temperance. Instead of working towards moderate consumption as the ideal, the ATS fixed complete abstinence from distilled drinks as the definition of temperance.

The structure that the ATS took as an organization also represented a new stage in the development of temperance activity in the United States. The ATS was significant since it was the first national temperance organization, but just as importantly, it also granted local chapters a great deal of initiative and power. As a result, unlike its more centralized predecessor, the MSSI, the ATS functioned as a fairly democratic institution with a broad public membership base spread across the country. Money, tracts, and speakers flowed from the national body to its local chapters, while the local associations were responsible for the work of rallying their particular communities to temperance in specialized ways. Thus the strength of the national temperance organization emerged from the diversity of its local specialization, as it had vibrant local branches that catered to temperance-minded African Americans, artisans, business groups, or women. Women, in particular, played an important role in the ATS, which became one of the first American voluntary organizations of any type to attract large numbers of women to its ranks. Women were especially active in spreading petitions and fundraising for local temperance societies. Though men remained the leaders of the ATS, women often outnumbered men in the rank and file of the organization.

In the mid-1830s, the ATS changed both its stance on alcohol and the nature of the organization itself. By 1835, the ATS had approximately 1.5 million members spread across some 8,000 auxiliaries; their ranks thus constituted about 12% of the nation's free population. Despite these impressive numbers, the ATS concluded that a new approach to temperance was needed to win the national fight against alcohol. As such, in 1836 the ATS adopted teetotalism and reorganized itself as the American Temperance Union. The teetotal pledge differed from other pledges since the teetotaler pledged to give up all alcohol, and not just distilled spirits. Fermented drinks such as wine, cider, and beer were thus no longer acceptable beverages for the newly defined temperate person, who viewed wine as equally dangerous as whiskey. With this embrace of teetotalism, the ATS changed not only its name, but also its constituency. Members who preferred to abstain simply from distilled spirits found themselves at often harsh odds with teetotalling members, and some tepid supporters of the ATS withdrew their assistance. The end result of the ATS' reorganization into the American Temperance Union was the radicalization of mainstream temperance agitation and political activity, which would gain momentum in the late-nineteenth and early-twentieth centuries.

(See also **Prohibition Party**; **Rush, Benjamin**; **Woman's Christian Temperance Union (WCTU)**))

References

Blocker, Jr., Jack S., David M. Fahey, and Ian R. Tyrrell, eds. 2003. *Alcohol and Temperance in Modern History: An International Encyclopedia*. Santa Barbara, CA: ABC-CLIO.

Lender, Mark Edward and James Kirby Martin. 1982. *Drinking in America: A History*. New York: The Free Press.

Mendelson, Jack H. and Nancy K. Mello. 1985. *Alcohol: Use and Abuse in America*. Boston: Little, Brown and Company.

Rorabaugh, William J. 1979. *The Alcoholic Republic: An American Tradition*. New York: Oxford University Press.

Tyrell, Ian R. 1979. *Sobering Up: From Temperance to Prohibition in Antebellum America, 1800–1860*. Westport, CT: Greenwood Press.

ANSLINGER, HARRY J.

Harry J. Anslinger was one of the most influential figures in U.S. drug control policy during the twentieth century. He was the first head of the Federal Bureau of Narcotics, and kept the position from 1930 through 1962. For the duration of his tenure, Anslinger advocated for the tough treatment of addicts and traffickers, and he also was a very public decrier of the dangers of habit-forming drugs and an outspoken critic of the maintenance treatment of addicts.

Henry Jacob Anslinger was born in Altoona, Pennsylvania in 1892, and he became involved with law enforcement by compiling statistics and investigating arson cases. When the United States entered World War I in 1917, Anslinger was in the Ordinance Division of the War Department, where he worked as an overseer of government contracts. He was then sent to Holland to work for the State Department, and when the war concluded he remained in Europe, where he gathered intelligence on Russia and drug smuggling from Germany to the United States. He was then transferred to Venezuela and the Bahamas, where he worked in intelligence gathering on rum smuggling in the Caribbean. There, he enjoyed his first major professional success, as he persuaded the British to establish a certificate system that would make it possible to keep records of all ship movements. Officials in the Treasury Department were impressed by this, and he was soon appointed the chief of the Foreign Control Section of the Prohibition Unit. In 1929, he was appointed Assistant Commissioner of Prohibition. Though it was becoming clear that alcohol prohibition was not working as he rose through the ranks of the Prohibition Unit, Anslinger remained an enthusiastic supporter of the cause, recommending that the United States try to limit alcohol smuggling through international agreements and by empowering the Justice Department, rather than the Treasury Department, to oversee enforcement. He also recommended expanding the gamut of the Volstead Act to make illegal purchase of alcohol a crime with severe punishment. By toughening the law, he reasoned, people would be discouraged from temptations to break it.

When Levi G. Nutt was compelled to resign from his post as the head of the Narcotic Division of the Prohibition Unit in 1930, Anslinger was named his replacement, and within a few months, he became the head of the Narcotic Division's successor—the Federal Bureau of Narcotics (FBN). As the nation's chief enforcer of narcotics control laws, Anslinger bought many of the attitudes he had during his work at the Prohibition Bureau—that high fines and mandatory prison sentences would be effective deterrents—to the task of narcotics control. However, he was also shrewd enough to adapt some of the lessons learned from the failure of alcohol prohibition to his campaigns against narcotics. Most importantly, he learned that an overly zealous enforcement campaign against widely used substances was doomed to failure, especially because federal judges were likely to let off ordinary citizens brought up on trifling charges. Taking this into consideration, Anslinger made an effort to bring drug law offenders to local courts, where judges were more likely to mete out punishment. He also instructed agents not to focus their enforcement efforts on individuals who were suffering from illness, or became addicted while ill, but rather to crack down on recreational users, who were seen as more delinquent than sick. Anslinger also tried to keep the FBN's activities limited to drugs that were widely considered dangerous—opiates and cocaine—and he resisted suggestions that the FBN tackle other, more common addictive substances such as barbiturates and amphetamines. Another lesson Anslinger took from prohibition was that citizens groups, such as the Anti-Saloon League and the Woman's Christian Temperance Union, were valuable allies in lobbying for both the passage and enforcement of tougher restrictions on habit-forming substances. Taking this into consideration, the FBN under Anslinger worked with citizens groups to help spread the word concerning habit-forming drugs and the dangers they could pose. He also allowed for supplies of narcotics to be available at times when the nation needed them, as he did when he provided assurances that there were adequate supplies of morphine for medical use during World War II. To help with public relations, Anslinger also discouraged his agents from focusing on local druggists and doctors, instead encouraging them to crack down on the individuals who were less likely to gain public sympathy—smugglers and racketeers. Anslinger believed that together

with the imprisonment and forced cure of addicts in the Public Health Service Narcotic Hospitals, attacking large-scale traffickers would be the most effective way to handle the drug menace.

Though he wanted to maintain a low profile in some areas, Anslinger nonetheless became a very outspoken advocate of tighter controls. In the 1930s, Anslinger organized a propaganda campaign against the dangers of narcotics to drum up support for the Uniform State Narcotic Act of 1932. In spite of reluctance to complicate matters by policing a drug that was not included in the Harrison Narcotics Act, Anslinger came to play a critical role in adding a new substance—marijuana—to the list of federally controlled substances by supporting and helping push through the 1937 Marihuana Tax Act. As with the Uniform State Narcotic Act, Anslinger oversaw a rigorous campaign against marijuana to scare the public into supporting legislation aimed at the drug. Leading the way with an article titled "Marihuana—Assassin of Youth" that he published in 1937, Anslinger helped cement public fears about narcotics by telling tales of young people committing suicide, indulging in sexually deviant behavior, thieving, or becoming murderous when under the influence of drugs. Anslinger contributed to anti-drug sentiment by making accusations (sometimes accurate, sometimes not) that enemies of the United States—such as the Mafia, the Japanese during World War II, and Communist countries—were involved in drug trafficking, thus making a connection between narcotics use and national security concerns. He was particularly vigilant on this point when it came to the Chinese Communists, as he repeatedly argued before both Congress and the press that the Chinese government was smuggling heroin into the United States in order to weaken the population so they could invade. When lobbying for the FBN to receive more funding from Congress, Anslinger continually repeated the dangers that drugs posed to youth and national security to make his case. In addition to linking narcotics with enemies of the United States, Anslinger also argued that all the drugs controlled by the FBN, ranging from marijuana to heroin, were equally dangerous, and that the government needed to crack down on both users and dealers in order to prevent the drug epidemic from spreading. Thanks in large part to Anslinger's propaganda, attitudes towards both narcotics and narcotics users hardened between the 1930s and 1960s, as conceptions of addicts being criminals, rather than victims of a disease, became dominant in the United States.

After World War II, Anslinger feared that smuggling would rise with the renormalization of global commerce, so he supported the creation of mandatory minimum sentences for drug offenders to discourage trafficking, a provision that became law in 1951 with the passage of the Boggs Act. When concern over the resurgence of heroin on American streets emerged in the 1950s, he argued that tougher laws and more effective enforcement, above all else, would be the solution to the problem. Anslinger's line of argument held sway in Congress, and his vision of a tougher control regime was partially realized with the passage of the 1956 Narcotic Control Act. Anslinger was also a staunch opponent of outpatient maintenance treatments for addicts, as he claimed that such arrangements merely facilitated and spread addiction, rather than curing it. He also argued that maintenance was inappropriate, especially after World War II, since he believed that most addicts were criminals anyway, and as such, undeserving of care. He often publicly debated Lawrence Kolb, who had become critical of the FBN's anti-maintenance policies, during the 1950s. In 1961, he co-authored a book, *The Murderers: The Story of the Narcotic Gangs*, to make the case that tougher enforcement was necessary since drug smuggling was being carried out by some very powerful organizations—the Mafia and the Communists. Sometimes Anslinger used more unsavory methods to try to disprove his critics. For example, he tried to silence Alfred Lindesmith, an outspoken critic of the FBN, by supporting the writing of works that would have undermined Lindesmith's research and his faculty position at the University of Indiana. In addition to Lindesmith, Anslinger also worked to undermine the credibility of researchers such as Marie Nyswander and Vincent Dole, who argued that addicts should not be treated as criminals, and advocated the use of methadone treatments for opiate addicts.

Anslinger retired from the FBN in 1962, and then served two years as the U.S. representative to the United Nations Narcotics Commission. He passed away at the age of 83, in 1975.

(See also **Anti-Saloon League (ASL)**; **Boggs Act**; **Dole, Vincent**; **Federal Bureau of Narcotics (FBN)**; **Harrison Narcotics Act**; **Kolb, Lawrence**; **Lindesmith, Alfred R.**; **Narcotic Control Act**; **Nutt, Levi G.**; **Nyswander, Marie**; **Marihuana Tax Act**; **Primary Source Documents**; **Prohibition Unit**; **Public Health Service Narcotic Hospitals**; **Woman's Christian Temperance Union (WCTU)**)

References

Acker, Caroline Jean. 2002. *Creating the American Junkie: Addiction Research in the Classic Era of Narcotic Control.* Baltimore: Johns Hopkins University Press.

Acker, Caroline Jean and Sarah W. Tracy, eds. 2004. *Altering American Consciousness: The History of Alcohol and Drug Use in the United States, 1800–2000.* Amherst, MA: University of Massachusetts Press.

Anslinger, Harry J and Will Oursler. 1961. *The Murderers: The Story of the Narcotic Gangs.* New York: Farrar, Straus and Cudhay.

Belenko, Steven R., ed. 2000. *Drugs and Drug Policy in America: A Documentary History.* Westport, CT: Greenwood Press.

Courtwright, David T. 2001. *Dark Paradise: A History of Opiate Addiction in America.* Cambridge, MA: Harvard University Press.

Davenport-Hines, Richard. 2001. *The Pursuit of Oblivion: A Global History of Narcotics, 1500–2000.* London: Weidenfeld & Nicolson.

Krebs, Albin. 1975. "Harry J. Anslinger Dies at 83; Hard-Hitting Foe of Narcotics." *New York Times.* (November 18): 40.

Musto, David F. 1987. *The American Disease: Origins of Narcotic Control.* Expanded Edition. New York: Oxford University Press.

ANTI-DRUG ABUSE ACTS

The Anti-Drug Abuse Acts were two pieces of federal legislation that toughened federal drug laws in the United States in the 1980s. Emphasizing law enforcement and social control as key elements in the fight against drug abuse in the United States, the Acts marked a return to the punitive approaches towards drug abuse and drug trafficking that had taken place in the 1950s with the Boggs Act and the Narcotic Control Act.

In the 1980s, drug abuse became a major social issue. Media coverage on drug abuse increased dramatically, especially with the rise of cocaine use and the widespread use of a new form of cocaine—crack—in America's inner cities. Beginning in late 1984, the news media began reporting on the use of crack cocaine in poor neighborhoods of Los Angeles, and on the harmful effects it had on the health of youths who used the drug. By 1986, newspapers, magazines, and television news programs ran stories focusing on the dangers of the drug, spurring calls for the government to take more rigorous action against crack and those who dealt it. The cocaine-related deaths of college basketball star Len Bias and football player Don Rogers brought the dangers of the drug into clearer relief. The rise in news coverage of the drug, not surprisingly, led increasing numbers of people to believe that it posed a grave social menace, and between 1985 and 1989, the number of Americans who believed that drugs posed the most serious problem in the United States rose from just 2% to 38%. Against the background of President Ronald Reagan's War on Drugs, which had begun in the early 1980s, these concerns fueled public fears of crack and cocaine, so that by the middle of the decade, illicit drugs rose to the top of the social policy agenda. In September of 1986, Reagan gave a television address where he called for "zero tolerance" policies towards not only dealers, but also users, of illicit drugs. Consequently, drug abuse became a key issue in the 1986 Congressional elections, and many politicians supported tougher measures against drug abuse and trafficking, either to gain votes, or to show that they were not "soft on drugs.'' On October 27, 1986, this political pressure culminated in the passage of the Anti-Drug Abuse Act of 1986.

The stated purpose of the Act was to encourage foreign cooperation in eradicating drug crops, halt the international drug traffic, improve the enforcement of federal drug laws, provide strong federal leadership, establish effective drug abuse prevention and education programs, and expand federal support for drug treatment and rehabilitation centers. The actual focus of the Act, however, leaned heavily towards the law enforcement side of drug control. The minimum sentence for selling or possessing large amounts of drugs (a kilogram or more of heroin, 1,000 kilograms of marijuana, five kilograms of cocaine) rose to ten years with no maximum, meaning that major dealers could be sentenced to life in prison. If anyone suffered injury or death due to the sales of narcotics, the minimum penalty rose to twenty years. The fines for these offenses were also extremely harsh, as drug law offenders could be fined up to $4 million, and if dealers were working as part of a drug ring, the financial penalty could be up to $10 million. The penalties for repeat offenses of these provisions were doubled. The law also stipulated that there could be no possibility of probation or suspended sentences for these offenders. The Act also allowed for the doubling of penalties for individuals who used minors to sell or distribute drugs, and increased penalties for selling drugs to minors and pregnant women. While extremely tough on dealers, the penalties for possession of small amounts of drugs for personal use were not as harsh. The maximum punishment for possession was one year in prison and a $5,000 fine, and double that for repeat offenders. In these cases, the courts had

the right to place individuals on probation. If individuals already had two prior convictions for possession, they faced a minimum of ninety days in prison, but no more than three years.

Aside from stiffening penalties, the Act also authorized the federal government to issue grants to states for law enforcement programs and programs aimed at disrupting the drug trade. It also allowed for increased funding for international efforts to crack down on the global drug traffic. In addition to these provisions that were designed to help limit the availability of drugs, there were also sections of the Act that aimed at preventing demand for illicit drugs. One section of the Act authorized the creation of a presidential media commission on alcohol and drug abuse to organize media campaigns that spread public awareness about the dangers of drug abuse. It also called for a presidential conference, the White House Conference for a Drug-Free America, which issued its final report in 1988. The report highlighted the dangers that drugs posed to the United States, giving support to the harsh enforcement provisions of the Anti-Drug Abuse Act. Overall, of the $1.7 billion in additional money set aside for anti-drug efforts by the 1986 Act, 86% of it went towards law enforcement efforts. Not surprisingly, the mandatory minimum sentences imposed by the Act led the U.S. prison population to increase dramatically, as it almost doubled between 1980 and 1988.

In spite of the measures of the 1986 Act, politicians, the media, and the general public remained heavily concerned about the dangers drug addiction posed to the American public. Even though there were tougher penalties for dealing, many Americans continued to use cocaine, crack, heroin, and marijuana. Instead of shifting course away from the punitive approach, which clearly had its shortcomings, Congress enacted another tough law, the Anti-Drug Abuse Act of 1988, in October of that year. The Act increased many penalties, and allowed for the death penalty in murder cases that involved drug-trafficking organizations. It also created a special offense that targeted crack cocaine, allowing for possession of small amounts of the drug to be punishable by sentences of a minimum of five years, and a maximum of twenty. In addition to these measures, the 1988 Act also made some innovations. Most importantly, it authorized the creation of the Office of National Drug Control Policy to coordinate federal anti-drug efforts. The 1988 Act also had more provisions allowing for treatment, as it mandated that half of the $2.8 billion it allocated be spent on programs aimed at decreasing demand, such as educational and treatment programs. Due to budget problems, however, only $500 million of the $2.8 billion that was designated by the legislation was actually spent.

Though provisions of the 1988 Act called for spending to reduce demand for narcotics, the Anti-Drug Abuse Acts of 1986 and 1988 marked a new height in the federal government's law-and-order campaign against narcotics use. Supported by both the media and the political establishment, these laws had tremendous consequences for drug dealers and users, as they toughened the punishments for both dealing and possessing controlled substances. Soon after the laws were enacted, many critics began to question the wisdom of using such draconian methods to address the drug problem. In response to the tremendous

amounts of money spent on enforcing drug laws and the growing number of people put in prison because of them, some prominent commentators started to call for the legalization of narcotics, arguing that the damages caused by the campaign against drugs seemed to be greater than the damages caused by the drugs themselves.

(See also **Crack Epidemic**; **Drug Addiction and Public Policy**; **Drug Policy Alliance Network**; **Office of National Drug Control Policy (ONDCP)**; **Reagan, Ronald and Nancy**)

References

Belenko, Steven R., ed. 2000. *Drugs and Drug Policy in America: A Documentary History*. Westport, CT: Greenwood Press.

Chepesiuk, Ron. 1999. *The War on Drugs: An International Encyclopedia*. Santa Barbara, CA: ABC-CLIO.

"H.R. 5854." [Online information retrieved 04.17/09] http://thomas.loc.gov/cgi-bin/bdquery/z?d099:HR05484:@@@L&summ2=m&.

Huggins, Laura E., ed. 2005. *Drug War Deadlock: The Policy Battle Continues*. Stanford, CA: Hoover Institution Press.

Musto, David F., ed. 2002. *Drugs in America: A Documentary History*. New York: New York University Press.

ANTI-SALOON LEAGUE (ASL)

The Anti-Saloon League (ASL) was a prominent national temperance organization that played a central role in bringing about national prohibition in 1920. Organized as a highly efficient, nonpartisan lobby backed by powerful industrialists and religious figures, it pressured politicians into passing the Volstead Act, which it also played a key role in writing and pushing through Congress.

Founded in 1893, the ASL emerged out of a local Ohio temperance society and became a national temperance organization that tried to generate mass support for measures that would have prohibited alcohol and at the same time pressured politicians into passing them. To do this, the ASL constructed itself as a highly professional and organized group dedicated to the single issue of temperance. Unlike other advocates of prohibition who formed their own, separate political parties, the ASL operated within the two-party political system, believing that success would be more difficult to achieve if they tried to advocate for prohibition from outside of the political establishment. Consequently, the ASL supported any candidate, whether Republican or Democrat, who was willing to back its temperance measures. The result was the creation of a powerful, nonpartisan political pressure group that played a vital role in bringing about national prohibition.

The ASL was created by Howard H. Russell, a Congregationalist minister who, during his years as a divinity student at Oberlin College in the mid-1880s, worked to increase enforcement of local saloon laws. After graduating and preaching elsewhere, Russell returned to Oberlin in 1893, and in that year founded the Ohio Anti-Saloon League. In doing so, Russell enjoyed the support of Ohio Methodist institutions, and to help run this new league, he hired Wayne Wheeler, who would later become the General Counsel and chief

Washington lobbyist for the Anti-Saloon League of America, and the author of the Volstead Act.

The ASL's program was marked by practical political compromise and piecemeal progress, not a desire to institute national prohibition all at once. As a result, the ASL focused its efforts on local-option elections, which gave voters the choice of whether saloons should be licensed or not. This flexibility enabled the ASL to concentrate its campaigning on winnable elections, thus effectively extending prohibition, piece by piece, to parts of Ohio that had resisted going fully dry. Similarly, the ASL worked to elect local and state politicians sympathetic to prohibition so as to ultimately build a coalition of politicians and voters willing to draft and pass a constitutional amendment legislating national prohibition.

Local successes based on this tactic of nonpartisan political pressuring quickly translated into national momentum, and in 1895 the Ohio Anti-Saloon League merged with other temperance associations to form the American Anti-Saloon League, which was renamed the Anti-Saloon League of America in 1905. By 1907 the ASL operated in forty-three states and territories and had 300,000 subscriptions to its monthly journal, *The American Issue*. The ASL's publishing influence was even more expansive by 1909, when it became the primary publisher of temperance literature in the nation.

The success of the ASL on a national level resulted from many innovations it brought to the temperance movement. Temperance work had previously been tied to Protestantism, but with the emergence of the ASL, this partnership was strengthened to a far greater degree. Russell's work as a minister was but one component of this collaboration between temperance advocates and Protestants, for the overwhelming majority of ASL officials were also ordained ministers or active laymen. Through their efforts, the pulpit effectively became a springboard for the ASL and its temperance activities. The ASL's deep connections with religious figures even extended into significant partnerships with prominent Catholics. Progressive "social gospel" priests often gave their public support to the ASL, and a number of priests even held state or national league offices. The ASL did not, however, limit itself to working within the religious community, as it also developed an impressive list of major financial donors from the industrial world. Millionaires such as Andrew Carnegie, Pierre du Pont, Henry Ford, and John D. Rockefeller, among others, contributed large sums of money to the ASL. Though the bulk of the ASL's budget came from individual donations of less than $100 a year, the support of such notables gave the ASL an extremely impressive capital base and cachet within the temperance world. Perhaps the most integral ingredient for the ASL's success was its highly efficient bureaucratic organization. Somewhat based upon a business model of vertical integration, the ASL was driven by a central leadership committee comprised of paid, skilled, and well-educated clergymen and professionals. These leaders developed national campaigns, disseminated temperance literature, sent orators across the country, recruited volunteers, drafted legislation, and lobbied politicians.

The figure most responsible for running this highly influential political pressure machine was Wheeler, ASL founder Rev. Russell's protégé. Wheeler was so representative of the ASL's tenacious and calculating approach that the League's critics often dubbed its political pressure "Wheelerism." A lawyer by trade, Wheeler became general counsel of the national league in 1916, and his power only became more pronounced in the years immediately thereafter. Applying his namesake brand of political pressure with great acumen after the passage of the 1913 Webb-Kenyon Act, which forbade the shipment of liquor from wet into dry areas, Wheeler became a powerful voice for national prohibition within Washington political circles. Working with fellow ASL leader Ernest Hurst Cherrington, Wheeler drafted the Prohibition Amendment and subsequently composed a major part of the bill that enabled its enforcement—the Volstead Act.

Though Prohibition was undoubtedly the victory the ASL had long been working towards, the passage of the Eighteenth Amendment and the Volstead Act also sowed the seeds of discord that would eventually divide the organization. While Cherrington and the majority of the ASL wanted to shift their attention towards education now that liquor had been prohibited, Wheeler and a minority of ASL members argued that the league's focus should be on improving enforcement of national prohibition. The result was a decidedly weakened organization that, coupled with the growing withdrawal of church support over the course of the 1920's, led to an ASL that could wield only a fraction of the tremendous power it once possessed. The one great instance where the ASL's past glory was evident occurred with the 1928 presidential election, when the group lent its support to the Republican Party and its candidate Herbert Hoover. Hoover's subsequent victory demonstrated the impact the ASL could still have, but it spelled the end of its highly successful nonpartisan political pressure program. With the repeal of prohibition, the ASL was further marginalized, though it hung on for a number of years before reconstituting itself multiple times. It has lived on as the American Council on Alcohol Problems since 1964.

(See also **Hobson, Richmond Pearson**; **Prohibition Party**; **Volstead Act (18th Amendment)**; **Webb-Kenyon Act**; **Woman's Christian Temperance Union (WCTU)**)

References

Blocker, Jr., Jack S., David M. Fahey, and Ian R. Tyrrell, eds. 2003. *Alcohol and Temperance in Modern History: An International Encyclopedia.* Santa Barbara, CA: ABC-CLIO.

Lender, Mark Edward and James Kirby Martin. 1982. *Drinking in America: A History.* New York: The Free Press.

Mendelson, Jack H. and Nancy K Mello. 1985. *Alcohol: Use and Abuse in America.* Boston: Little, Brown and Company.

Pegram, Thomas P. 1998. *Battling Demon Rum: The Struggle for a Dry America, 1800–1933.* Chicago: Ivan R. Dee.

ASSOCIATION AGAINST THE PROHIBITION AMENDMENT (AAPA)

The Association Against the Prohibition Amendment (AAPA) was a highly influential lobby and national organization that worked towards the repeal of the Eighteenth Amendment of the U.S. Constitution, which had instituted alcohol prohibition. With the backing of influential political, financial, and corporate figures, the AAPA played an important role in shaping and organizing the popular and political will behind the passage of the Twenty-First Amendment, which repealed Prohibition on December 5, 1933.

Founded in 1918 by William H. Stayton, the AAPA was the first wet citizens' lobby of any great stature in the United States. Working in Washington, D.C. for the Navy League of the United States during the first discussions of the nascent Eighteenth Amendment, Stayton created an organization of people committed to challenging National Prohibition even before the federal ban on alcohol went into effect in 1920. Early on, Stayton opposed the Eighteenth Amendment on the grounds that it increased his taxes, spoiled his investments, and harmed the U.S. economy since it prevented the international trade of valuable alcohol exports. As disregard for Prohibition increased over the years, Stayton railed against prohibition, arguing that it was a symptom of a wider problem—the fanatical desire of reformers to meddle in the affairs others and regulate the details of their lives. In general, Stayton and the AAPA viewed the prohibition of alcohol as the federal government overstepping its bounds by controlling the individual decisions of U.S. citizens. Though many disliked the Eighteenth Amendment for these, and other, reasons, Stayton attracted few followers in the early years of the AAPA. By 1921, despite widespread defiance of Prohibition, the AAPA could only count around 100,000 members of its national organization, which was not nearly enough to overturn the Eighteenth Amendment. Financially, too, the AAPA was hardly primed to repeal the Eighteenth Amendment in 1921, as its treasury was mostly financed by Stayton himself up to that point.

As the 1920s progressed, however, more Americans disgruntled with Prohibition joined the AAPA, in large part because it was essentially the only group of its kind. By 1926, the AAPA's national membership rose to 726,000, with members concentrated in New York, Ohio, Illinois, and California. As significant as the spike in membership numbers was the prestige of some of the newer members of the AAPA. As the alliance's momentum grew, the AAPA attracted men of great prominence to its cause. Some notable members included: author Irvin S. Cobb, ex-New York Mayor Seth Low, railroad tycoon Stuyvesant Fish, chemical giants Irene and Pierre Du Pont, publisher Charles Scribner, financier John J. Raskob, and civic leader and philanthropist Marshall Field III. Pierre Du Pont joined, he said, because he believed the Prohibition movement had erred in failing to distinguish between the moderate use of alcohol and drinking to excess. Many new members joined, however, because they were persuaded by the AAPA's argument that since so many citizens defied the increasingly unpopular Eighteenth Amendment, the federal government was breeding a dangerous disrespect for the U.S. Constitution by trying to enforce an unenforceable law.

During the Great Depression, the AAPA pushed an economic argument against the Eighteenth Amendment. With many Americans financially scuffling, the AAPA argued that Prohibition was an unneeded economic burden upon the country. The AAPA claimed that enforcing Prohibition cost taxpayers over $300 million, and that a ban on alcohol amounted to $11 billion in lost tax revenues by 1931. And with unemployment at high levels, the AAPA argued that

Prohibition cost the nation untold numbers of jobs in brewing, distilling, bottling, shipping, retail sales, and service. In essence, the AAPA suggested that repealing the Eighteenth Amendment could help America out of the Great Depression.

The AAPA took this message, and others, to politicians and laypeople in a grassroots campaign to create a constitutional amendment that would repeal Prohibition. The AAPA subsidized research studies that illustrated the failure of Prohibition, and they published these findings in newspapers and magazines. On the political front, they supported every wet politician, regardless of the candidate's party. However, the AAPA ultimately found greater political support from the Democratic Party, when in 1928, AAPA leader John J. Raskob was selected Democratic national chairman by the party's candidate for president, Alfred Emanuel Smith, himself an opponent of Prohibition. Smith lost the presidential election to Herbert Hoover, a supporter of Prohibition, but four years later, the AAPA convinced the Democratic Party to make repealing the Eighteenth Amendment a part of the party's platform. Thus, when Franklin D. Roosevelt, the Democratic Party's subsequent presidential candidate, won the election, the AAPA's position gained the highest possible political backing.

In additional to having the next president on their side, the AAPA also reaped the rewards of their years of political lobbying when Congress approved a bill to end Prohibition even before Roosevelt entered the White House. In each house, the Seventy-Second Congress passed a constitutional amendment to repeal the Eighteenth

Amendment. In the subsequent drive for the amendment's ratification at state conventions, AAPA members played significant roles. 73% of voters nationwide advocated repealing the Eighteenth Amendment, and amongst the thirty-seven state conventions held in 1933, only South Carolina preferred maintaining Prohibition. On December 5, 1933, the Twenty-First Amendment was ratified, ending both Prohibition and the AAPA, which disbanded that very evening with a celebratory dinner in New York City's Waldorf-Astoria Hotel.

(See also **Volstead Act (18th Amendment)**; **Women's Organization for National Prohibition Reform (WONPR)**)

References

Barr, Andrew. 1999. *Drink: A Social History of America*. New York: Carroll & Graf Publishers, Inc.

Blocker, Jr., Jack S., David M. Fahey, and Ian R. Tyrrell, eds. 2003. *Alcohol and Temperance in Modern History: An International Encyclopedia*. Santa Barbara, CA: ABC-CLIO.

Burns, Eric. 2004. *The Spirits of America: A Social History of America*. Philadelphia: Temple University Press.

Kyvig, David E. 2000. *Repealing National Prohibition*. 2nd ed. Kent, OH: Kent State University Press.

Rose, Kenneth D. 1996. *American Women and the Repeal of Prohibition*. New York: New York University Press.

BETTY FORD CENTER

Founded in 1982, the Betty Ford Center is a hospital dedicated to the treatment of chemical dependency located in Rancho Mirage, California on the campus of the Eisenhower Medical Center. The Center is named after Betty Ford, the wife of former President Gerald Ford who was successfully treated for prescription drug and alcohol abuse and sought to create a center that emphasized the special needs of chemically dependent women. The Betty Ford Center sees drug dependencies as chronic progressive diseases that, if left untreated, can become fatal. While it encourages patients to take responsibility for their own well-being and recovery, it also features a family-treatment program that utilizes group therapy to treat family members who have been affected by a loved one's alcoholism or drug dependency.

The Betty Ford Center came into existence through the considerable efforts of the hospital's namesake former First Lady. Born Elizabeth Anne Bloomer in Chicago on April 8, 1918 and raised in Grand Rapids, Michigan, she became Betty Ford after marrying former President Gerald R. Ford on October 15, 1948. After Ford lost his re-election bid to Jimmy Carter in the 1976 election, the couple left the White House and moved to Rancho Mirage, California, the future home of the Betty Ford Center.

In 1978, Betty Ford left the couple's new home in Rancho Mirage and admitted herself, after a family intervention, to the Long Beach Naval Hospital for treatment of her prescription drug and alcohol use. The details of her chemical dependency are recounted in her 1978 autobiography, *The Times of My Life*, which included an unplanned chapter on her admittance to treatment in Long Beach. A second book, *Betty: A Glad Awakening*, detailed the successful treatment she received there, and after her release from the hospital, she became a vocal and prominent figure in public health campaigns to raise awareness of alcohol and drug dependency issues and their treatment.

As part of this new role in life, Ford began discussing with friends the need for a treatment center that would emphasize the special needs of women, whose chemical dependencies have typically been more hidden and neglected in comparison to those of men. These conversations came to a tangible fruition when, in 1982, Ford co-founded, along with her good friend, Ambassador Leonard Firestone, the nonprofit Betty Ford Center at the Eisenhower Medical Research Center. As a result of her considerable fundraising efforts on behalf of the institution, the Betty Ford Center has grown into a treatment facility of international renown. Soon, the facility treated over 33,000 people from all fifty states and more than thirty foreign countries.

Abiding by Ford's emphasis on the importance of treating chemically dependent women, the Betty Ford Center's eighty beds are always evenly divided between women and men. Likewise, the treatment programs offered at the Betty Ford Center are gender-specific. Male and female patients also reside in separate halls. Guided by the view that drug dependencies are chronic progressive diseases that can be fatal if left untreated, the Betty Ford Center offers a variety of programs intended to treat both patients and family members affected by their loved ones' alcoholism or drug use. An outpatient program permits patients to continue to reside at home and work in the local community while they are in treatment, while the inpatient program mandates that patients live in one of the on-campus residence halls. The inpatient program utilizes a twelve-step approach to recovery, and the cost of the program covers the attendance of one family member. The Betty Ford Center also offers a residential day treatment that likewise features a twelve-step program, but unlike in the inpatient program, patients live in sober, off-campus homes and only attend treatment during the day. A ninety-day program—which is geared towards chronic relapsers, patients with a prolonged detoxification period, and those with multiple prior treatments—is also available, as are five-day family programs, which offer support and education. There is also a children's program, which works with children ages seven through twelve who are not themselves addicted, but who have chemically dependent family members.

Leadership of the Betty Ford Center has been passed from the former First Lady to her daughter, Susan Ford Bales. Mrs. Ford, however, continues to live in Rancho Mirage and play an active role in the hospital's development.

(See also **Reference Essay**)

References

Betty Ford Center. "A Brief History of the Betty Ford Center." [Online information retrieved 05/20/09] http://www.bettyford center.org/welcome/ourhistory.php.

Betty Ford Center. "Alcohol and Drug Rehabilitation." [Online information retrieved 05/20/09] http://www.bettyfordcenter.org /programs/index.php.

Carson-Dewitt, Rosalyn, ed. 2001. *Encyclopedia of Drugs, Alcohol & Addictive Behavior. Second Edition*. New York: Macmillan Reference USA.

Gerald R. Ford Presidential Library and Museum. "Betty Ford Biography." [Online information retrieved 05/2/09] http://www.fordlibrarymuseum.gov/grf/ bbfbiop.asp.

White, William L. 1998. *Slaying the Dragon: The History of Addiction Treatment and Recovery in America*. Bloomington, IL: Chestnut Health Systems.

BISHOP, ERNEST S.

Dr. Ernest S. Bishop was a physician who became a staunch advocate for the maintenance treatment of opiate addicts in the 1910s and 1920s. Though the federal government moved towards harsher stances on the questions of addiction and addiction treatment at this time, Bishop believed that addiction was a physical disease caused by the body's production of antibodies. Consequently, he held that addicts should be treated as patients, not as criminals—a stance he maintained until his death in 1927.

Ernest Simons Bishop was born in Pawtucket, Rhode Island in 1876, earned his undergraduate degree at Brown University in 1899, and his M.D. from Cornell University in 1908. Upon completing medical school, Bishop worked as a resident at Bellevue Hospital in New York until 1912. At Bellevue, he was in charge of the alcoholic and prison wards, and it was there that he became particularly interested in the treatment of addiction.

Bishop argued that narcotic addiction resulted not from addicts' appetites for drugs, but rather from autoimmune processes that occurred in the body once an individual began using them. He began to elaborate these theories in medical journals in the early 1910s, and published them in a collection called *The Narcotic Drug Problem* in 1920. Inspired by the work of European researchers who studied the immune system, Bishop hypothesized that the body produced antitoxins in response to the introduction of opiates into the system, similar to the way that bacteria sparked the creation of certain antibodies. These antitoxins, he held, explained how addicts developed tolerance, since they were able to fight off the effects of relatively large doses of drugs. Once an individual had consumed enough opiates, he argued, the body would produce these antitoxins continuously. And if they were not neutralized by a dose of opiates, he maintained, these antitoxins would turn poisonous, thus causing the pain and discomfort that addicts experienced during withdrawal. Consequently, he concluded that addicts did not seek out drugs in ever-increasing doses for pleasure—rather, they did so in order to avoid the negative symptoms that would occur when antitoxins turned poisonous. More importantly, his thesis postulated that since opiates caused physical changes in the body, anyone could become addicted; it was a matter of physiology, not psychology, he argued, that created addiction.

Not surprisingly, Bishop became an outspoken opponent of policies that would have restrained physicians' rights to prescribe opiates as they saw fit, and he argued that even gradual reduction methods designed to wean addicts off of narcotics were unnecessarily cruel and barbaric. Instead, he advocated for the maintenance treatment of addicts on an outpatient basis. This marked a drastic departure from the way that most politicians, journalists, and even many doctors of his day, viewed addiction. Whereas most in the mainstream believed that addicts were simply indulgers in a vice and chose to engage in their drug-taking behavior, Bishop believed that most addicts were actually upright citizens, individuals who wanted to be cured, but were frustrated by failed attempts to quit using narcotics. Consequently, Bishop argued that doctors should treat addicts not with a specific regimen of drugs in hopes of achieving abstinence, but rather that they should treat each addict's case differently, just as they did with their other patients. These beliefs made him a critic of the federal government's attempts to stamp out addiction with repressive policies, and he vocally opposed the forced detoxification of addicts that was mandated by New York State's Boylan Act. Bishop also opposed the work of some fellow practitioners such as Charles B. Towns and Alexander Lambert, who used methods that rapidly, but painfully, withdrew narcotics from addicts.

In spite of Bishop's efforts, the scientific community refuted his antitoxin theory, and the federal government rejected his argument that maintenance treatment was the best way to handle the addiction problem. The 1919 Supreme Court decisions in *United States v. Doremus* and *Webb et al. v. United States* established that the Harrison Narcotics Act did outlaw the maintenance prescription of opiates to addicts, putting Bishop in the awkward position of rejecting a policy that was upheld by the highest court in the country. In late 1919, the Narcotic Division, which was charged with enforcing the provisions of the Harrison Act, sent out a questionnaire to physicians asking them their opinions on maintenance, and in particular, if they thought Bishop's antibody theory was valid; most refuted it, arguing instead that maintenance treatment was inadvisable and that addicts should undergo detoxification in inpatient institutions. Undeterred, Bishop continued to prescribe narcotics to addict patients, and in 1920 the Treasury Department indicted him for violating the Harrison Act. Critics claimed that the indictment was politically motivated, and that the government was trying to bully one of the most ardent critics of

anti-maintenance policies into silence. Nonetheless, the Justice Department kept Bishop under indictment for five years without bringing him to trial.

In 1925, the charges against Bishop were dropped when he fell ill, and he passed away in 1927.

(See also **Boylan Act**; **Harrison Narcotics Act**; **Primary Source Documents**; *United States v. Doremus* and *Webb et al. v. United States*)

References

Belenko, Steven R., ed. 2000. *Drugs and Drug Policy in America: A Documentary History*. Westport, CT: Greenwood Press.

Courtwright, David T. 2001. *Dark Paradise: A History of Opiate Addiction in America*. Cambridge, MA: Harvard University Press.

Holmes, F. R., ed. 1924. *Who's who in New York*. New York: Who's Who Publications.

Musto, David F. 1987. *The American Disease: Origins of Narcotics Control*. Expanded Edition. New York: Oxford University Press.

Musto, David F., ed. 2002. *Drugs in America: A Documentary History*. New York: New York University Press.

BOGGS ACT

The Boggs Act, passed in 1951, was the first piece of federal legislation to impose mandatory minimum sentences for drug offenses. Together with the Narcotic Control Act of 1956, it ushered in a new, harsher era of narcotics control in the United States. In addition to creating minimum sentences for drug dealers and users, the Act also had the unintended consequence of spawning criticism from the legal and medical communities, which began to advocate for the federal government to reconsider the punitive approach to handling the drug problem.

Strict enforcement of the Harrison Narcotics Act and Marihuana Tax Act by the Federal Bureau of Narcotics (FBN), coupled with Supreme Court decisions sanctioning tough anti-maintenance treatment approaches and the internment of addicts in Public Health Service Narcotic Hospitals, had seemingly stemmed the tide of addiction by the beginning of the 1940s. With the United States' entry into World War II in 1941, restrictions on commerce allowed the federal government to tighten controls and crack down on smuggling. Yet the apparent gains in the FBN's anti-narcotic campaign seemed to be easily lost, as rates of addiction reportedly rose in Black and Puerto Rican ghettos in northern cities after the war. Even more disconcerting was the revelation that rates of addiction were rising among teenagers in these areas, as use of both heroin and marijuana became more prevalent. Many feared that organized crime, and possibly the new communist government in China, were behind the increase in drug smuggling. To address the problem, officials in the FBN began pushing for mandatory minimum sentences in order to discourage the illicit drug trade and put the traffickers who were responsible for the uptick in illicit drug use behind bars.

In 1951, they got their wish when Louisiana Representative Hale Boggs introduced a new law that modified the 1922 Narcotic Import and Export Act. The law amended the Narcotic Import and Export Act by stipulating that any individual who knowingly imported or brought any opiates, cocaine, or marijuana into the United States, or anyone who knowingly received, concealed, bought, sold, transported, or conspired to traffic them, would be fined up to $2,000 and imprisoned for between two and five years. Repeat offenders were given even harsher treatment, with five to ten years becoming the punishment for second violations of the Act, and ten to twenty years the punishment for subsequent violations. The law also stipulated that repeat offenders could not be given suspended sentences or granted probation. These provisions stripped judges of the leeway to let individuals found guilty of drug trafficking get away with a slap on the wrist, as now they had no choice but to sentence them to prison time. By including the purchase and transportation of illegally trafficked drugs as offenses, the law also allowed for the prosecution of many users, who even though they may not have been involved in smuggling, were probably using drugs that had been illegally brought into the country. Thus even though the law's main target was smugglers, addicts could also become subject to the automatic sentencing protocols laid out in the Act.

In spite of the new regulations, it became clear within a few years that tougher enforcement did not have the desired effect of reducing rates of addiction in American cities. The excessively punitive nature of the Act also spurred two professions whose practice were profoundly affected by it—doctors and lawyers—to take action to oppose it. The American Bar Association responded by creating a special Committee on Narcotics in 1954, and in early 1955 it passed a resolution urging Congress to reconsider the Boggs Act and other aspects of federal drug control policy. The American Medical

Association also criticized the tough turn that federal drug policy had taken, leading the New York Academy of Medicine to investigate the efficacy of existing policies and study the possibility of developing more medically oriented approaches to the drug problem. In its report, issued in 1955, the New York Academy of Medicine recommended that the government begin treating addiction as a disease, and to allow doctors to give maintenance doses of narcotics to their addict patients. In spite of these pleas from powerful professional associations, the push towards harsher treatment of drug traffickers, dealers, and users continued in 1956 with the passage of the Narcotic Control Act.

(See also **Anslinger, Harry J.**; **Federal Bureau of Narcotics (FBN)**; **Harrison Narcotics Act**; **Marihuana Tax Act**; **Narcotic Control Act**; **Public Health Service Narcotic Hospitals**)

References

Belenko, Steven R., ed. 2000. *Drugs and Drug Policy in America: A Documentary History*. Westport, CT: Greenwood Press.

Musto, David F. 1987. *The American Disease: Origins of Narcotic Control*. Expanded Edition. New York: Oxford University Press.

Ryan, James G. and Leonard Shulp, eds. 2006. *Historical Dictionary of the 1940s*. Amherst, NY: M.E. Sharpe.

BOYLAN ACT

The Boylan Act, which was enacted by the New York State legislature in April of 1914, was one of the most rigorous and comprehensive attempts by a state to cut down on the open availability and use of opiates for nonmedical reasons before the passage of the Harrison Narcotics Act. The Boylan Act was particularly noteworthy because it had provisions that allowed for the forced cure of addicts in state institutions. Within a few years, however, authorities found that the Boylan Act had the unintended consequence of increasing the black market for narcotics, and it was overturned.

Beginning in 1910, there was increasing concern about the spread of cocaine and opiate use. In New York City in particular, there was growing pressure to do something to limit the availability of these habit-forming drugs. Charles B. Towns, a man who sold cures for drug addiction, became a staunch advocate of tighter narcotics control and joined forces with other social reformers to convince state senator John. J. Boylan to introduce a piece of anti-narcotic legislation in the legislature in 1913. It was passed in April of 1914, months before the first federal anti-narcotic law, the Harrison Act, made it through Congress.

The Boylan Act anticipated many of the provisions of the Harrison Act, as it established that pharmacists and druggists could only dispense opium and its derivatives with a written prescription from a physician. Furthermore, it required that prescriptions for opiates be written only after doctors performed a physical examination to establish the need for patients to use the drugs. Any prescription for more than four grains of morphine, thirty grains of opium, two grains of heroin, or six grains of codeine had to be verified by physicians over the telephone before pharmacists could dispense them. To limit the spread of morphine and heroin addiction, the Act also stipulated that only physicians, or pharmacists filling prescriptions written by physicians, could dispense syringes or hypodermic needles. If physicians were caught violating the law, their licenses could be revoked, and infractions of any provisions of the law were misdemeanor offenses.

The most groundbreaking provisions of the Boylan Act lay in its Section 249a, which allowed for the commitment of some addicts who broke the law to state, county, or city hospitals or other institutions for addiction treatment. For addicts who resisted treatment, there were provisions for their forcible transfer to institutions for vagrants. The state, therefore, had the legal power to force addicts to quit. According to Towns and other critics, however, the law was not strong enough, particularly since it did not allow for the commitment of addicts who received drugs from physicians. This meant that if addicts were getting provisions through medical channels, they could continue to indulge in their drug-taking behavior as much as they liked. What is more, there were no provisions limiting how much doctors could prescribe, thus leaving a loophole for physicians to give maintenance treatment to addicts, instead of compelling them to quit.

In spite of the conditions that allowed for the maintenance treatment of addicts, the general public viewed the Boylan Act as a ban on the habitual use of opiates and cocaine. Anxious addicts volunteered to be cured or wanted to be committed so that they would not run afoul of the law, and flooded hospitals and institutions. Stricter enforcement of narcotics control laws fed these fears, as the number of arrests for drug-related crimes in New York nearly quadrupled between 1913 and 1914. When the Harrison Act took effect in March of 1915, enforcement became even tighter, and many physicians stopped prescribing narcotics for fear of violating both state and federal laws. As the medical channels that allowed for addicts to acquire narcotics legally narrowed, a black market for the substances grew in New York, with many addicts frantically turning to street dealers to get the narcotics they needed. Ironically, in their efforts to limit addiction by placing tighter legal restrictions on supplies, the reformers who supported the Boylan Act increased the social costs of drug addiction, as more and more addicts either wound up in state institutions or turned to illegal sources for supplies of drugs.

In 1916, Towns began advocating for tighter regulations that would close the loophole that allowed for doctors to prescribe maintenance treatments of narcotics. This bill, also put forward by Boylan, would have set a three-week limit on the provision of narcotics to addicts on an outpatient basis, instituted a system in which addicts would have been forced to register with the state, and it called for health departments to take over incurable cases of addiction. Though the bill passed the New York State Senate, the State Assembly did not pass it, instead choosing to appoint a joint committee to examine the narcotics problem. The committee began its work in December of 1916, exploring the various treatments for addiction, and surveying medical professionals in hopes of finding a consensus on how best to tackle the drug problem. While many witnesses before the committee supported the proposed law's anti-maintenance stance, some prominent witnesses, such as physician Ernest S. Bishop, testified that maintenance treatment was medically acceptable and necessary, not a mere indulgence of addiction. Moreover, the committee found that the institutions in place to treat addicts were sorely lacking, and that attempts to treat addiction were generally ineffective.

The conclusions of the committee led to the 1917 passage of the Whitney Act, which asserted that physicians had the right to treat addicts as they saw fit, even if it meant giving maintenance prescriptions, provided that their ultimate goal was to wean addicts off of drugs. It also allowed for addicts found in violation of the law to be paroled to a physician for outpatient treatment, instead of being sent to an institution for detoxification. Justice officials were pleased, as the law cut the number of court cases for illegal possession of drugs in half since it allowed for addicts to go to their doctors—instead of street dealers—to get narcotics. In the course of the next two years, however, it became apparent that this approach to the drug problem had deficiencies as well, since some doctors and pharmacists took advantage of their privileged place under the law to dispense excessive amounts of narcotics for financial gain. Thus even when placed under the control of medical authorities, narcotics remained widely available and addiction continued to spread. This state of affairs strengthened the arguments of Towns and other opponents of outpatient maintenance treatments, as provisions meant to control how doctors and pharmacists dispensed narcotics on an outpatient basis were too difficult to enforce effectively. It was not until 1919, when the Supreme Court decisions in *United States v. Doremus* and *Webb et al. v. United States* banned maintenance prescriptions nationwide, that the questions surrounding maintenance and outpatient

treatment of addicts would be resolved, both in New York State, and throughout the country.

(See also **Bishop, Ernest S.**; **Harrison Narcotics Act**; **Towns, Charles B.**; *United States v. Doremus* **and** *Webb et al. v. United States*)

References

Belenko, Steven R., ed. 2000. *Drugs and Drug Policy in America: A Documentary History.* Westport, CT: Greenwood Press.

King, Rufus. 1972. *The Drug Hang-Up: America's Fifty-Year Folly.* Springfield, IL: Bannerstone House.

Musto, David F. 1987. *The American Disease: Origins of Narcotics Control.* Expanded Edition. New York: Oxford University Press.

BRENT, CHARLES HENRY

Charles Henry Brent was an Anglican Minister and Episcopal Bishop who became one of the world's leading advocates for international narcotics control in the early-twentieth century. Until his death in 1929, he remained one of the world's most outspoken leaders in the crusade against narcotics addiction.

Born in Canada in 1862, Brent began his career working as an assistant Anglican minister in a poor area of Boston before being appointed the Episcopal Bishop for the newly acquired U.S. territory in the Philippines in 1902. When his career in the Philippines began, Brent became involved in typical missionary activity, working to develop schools and hospitals while also trying to convert Filipinos to Christianity. In time, however, his main cause became the campaign against the opium habit. Even though opium was used as a medicine by many Filipinos, Brent, like many of his fellow American missionaries, believed that the habit was problematic because it seemingly harmed the health of the people who became addicted, and that it was immoral. As he became more passionate about opium, Brent also gained political influence, meeting with high-ranking officials in Washington on his annual trips home, and he became a leading voice in pushing for the United States to govern the Philippines both wisely and morally. He believed, as many missionaries and other Americans did at the time, that it was the duty of the United States to "civilize" the Filipinos and keep them from vices like gambling, prostitution, and opium.

Brent first became a major spokesperson in the anti-opium crusade in 1902, when he led a campaign against Philippine Governor (and later U.S. president) William Howard Taft in response to Taft's proposal to create a government-run opium monopoly in the territory. After Taft withdrew his proposal, he appointed Brent to join the Philippines Opium Committee, a group assigned with the task of researching the nature of the opium problem there. The committee recommended that the government should take over opium sales in the Philippines for a three-year period, gradually reduce the amount of opium it made available, and eventually prohibit the use of the drug except for medical purposes. Back in Washington, authorities called for more drastic measures, and by 1908 nonmedicinal opium use was banned in the Philippines.

Brent argued, however, that internal controls over opium distribution and use were not enough. The problem, he believed, was that no matter what the U.S. government did, the fact that opium was widely available in neighboring countries (particularly China) made it impossible for the United States' opium policy in the Philippines to be effective. Whatever the policy was in the Philippines, he feared, it was too easy for smugglers to bring the drug over from China undetected, meaning that it would remain widely available in spite of the United States' new opium control policy. Soon, Brent became among the leading supporters of a growing international effort to support China's efforts to check the flow of opium that made its way into China from India, Indochina, and other countries in Asia. In 1906, when the U.S. government began considering an international conference to address the opium question, Brent supported the idea. Taking advantage of good relationships he had with important political leaders such as Taft and President Theodore Roosevelt, Brent effectively lobbied for the convening of an international conference to discuss international opium control, which met at Shanghai in 1909.

Brent served as the president of the initial Shanghai meeting, and he chaired the United States' delegation at the 1911 International Opium Conference at The Hague. In the 1920s, once the principles of international narcotics control had been brought into effect by the Treaty of Versailles, Brent assumed a critical role in the League of Nations' efforts to organize and implement a global drug control regime. He represented the United States at the meeting of the League of Nations Advisory Board on narcotics control in 1923, and he also served as a U.S. delegate to the Second Geneva Conference in 1924, before passing away in 1929.

(See also **China and the Chinese; Hague Convention; League of Nations; Philippines; Shanghai Commission**)

References

Davenport-Hines, Richard. 2001. *The Pursuit of Oblivion: A Global History of Narcotics, 1500–2000.* London: Weidenfeld & Nicolson.

McAllister, William B. 2000. *Drug Diplomacy in the Twentieth Century.* London: Routledge.

Musto, David F. 1987. *The American Disease: Origins of Narcotics Control.* Expanded Edition. New York: Oxford University Press.

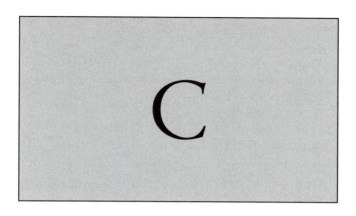

C

CARNES, PATRICK J.

Patrick J. Carnes is a psychologist and one of the pioneers of the study of sex addiction. Through his work as an author and a practitioner, he has brought attention to the previously misunderstood, and hardly discussed, problem of sex addiction.

Carnes graduated from St. John's University in Collegeville, Minnesota in 1966 before completing his master's degree at Brown University in 1969 and earning his doctorate in counselor education and organizational development from the University of Minnesota in 1980. During his training, and when he worked as a therapist for substance abusers and their families, Carnes noticed that addictive compulsivity took many forms other than alcohol and drug abuse—it also became manifest in addictions to overeating, gambling, sexuality, and buying. These experiences led him to design the sexual dependency unit at Golden Valley Health Center in Golden Valley, Minnesota, the first

inpatient unit for sexual addiction in the country. Since then, he has advised the development of treatment facilities for sexual addiction throughout the country. In 1996, Carnes became the clinical director for Sexual Disorder Services at The Meadows in Wickenburg, Arizona. He then moved to Pine Grove Behavioral Center in Hattiesburg, Mississippi in 2004, and he developed the Gentle Path Treatment Program there. He also founded the Certified Sex Addiction therapist program, a network of local, regional, and residential programs that specialize in the treatment of sex addiction. Carnes also currently serves as the co-editor of *Sexual Addiction and Compulsivity*, which is the official journal of the National Council of Sexual Addiction and Compulsivity.

Beyond his work as a therapist and director for sex addiction programs, Carnes has also written some of the pioneering works in the study of sex addiction. In early 1976 he wrote an extended paper, ''The Sex Offender:

His Addiction, His Family, His Beliefs," based on two years of experience running groups for sex offenders. This paper eventually evolved into one of the first books on sex addiction, his 1983 work *Out of the Shadows: Understanding Sexual Addiction*. In *Out of the Shadows*, Carnes laid out three different levels of sexually addictive behavior. Level one involved behaviors that are often regarded as normal, acceptable, or tolerable, such as masturbation or viewing pornography. Level two behaviors were illegal and regarded as nuisance crimes—such as exhibitionism, voyeurism, or obscene telephone calls. Level three behaviors were the most serious ones, as they were not only illegal, but also had grave consequences for the victim. Rape and incest fell into this third category. Beyond its classification system, *Out of the Shadows* was important since it brought the topic of sex addiction, which had previously been unrecognized and rarely discussed, out into the open. In his 1991 book *Don't Call It Love: Recovery from Sexual Addiction*, Carnes conducted an extensive survey of nearly 1,000 patients who had been admitted into inpatient treatment programs for sexual addiction problems. Based on his survey, Carnes determined ten different addictive sexual behavior patterns, ranging from fantasy sex to anonymous sex and paying for sex. He also co-wrote *In the Shadows of the Net: Breaking Free of Compulsive Online Sexual Behavior*, one of the first books to look in detail at cybersexual addictions.

Carnes currently works as the executive director for the Gentle Path Treatment Program for sexual addiction, located at Pine Grove Behavioral Center in Hattiesburg, Mississippi.

(See also **Reference Essay**)

References

"Biography: Dr. Patrick Carnes." [Online information retrieved 04/27/09] http://gentlepath.com/bio-carnes.php.

Carnes, Patrick. 2001. *Out of the Shadows: Understanding Sexual Addiction*. Third Edition. Center City, MN: Hazelden Publishing.

Coombs, Robert Holman, ed. 2004. *Handbook of Addictive Disorders: A Practical Guide to Diagnosis and Treatment*. Hoboken, NJ: John Wiley & Sons, Inc.

CENTER ON ADDICTION AND SUBSTANCE ABUSE (CASA)

The Center on Addiction and Substance Abuse (CASA) is a nonprofit organization dedicated to the study of all potentially addictive substances, and it works to combat their abuse. It is the only nation-wide organization that brings together individuals from all professional disciplines in order to better understand and prevent addiction.

CASA was founded in 1992 at Columbia University in New York City by Joseph A. Califano Jr., the former Secretary of Health, Education, and Welfare under President Jimmy Carter, and Dr. Herbert D. Kleber, former deputy director of the Office of National Drug Control Policy. In organizing CASA, Califano brought together a board of directors that included leaders from politics, industry, academia, advertising, and the media. In its early years, CASA received funding from the Robert Wood Johnson Foundation, as well as other foundations, private companies, and government bodies. Initially, CASA focused on providing analysis of the social and economic costs of both illegal and legal drug use. The group then moved on to begin creating national projects in the fields of drug and alcohol treatment and prevention. In 1992, it launched its CASASTART program, a collaboration between schools, law enforcement, and community organizations, that aims to help teenagers who are either at risk of starting to use, or are already using, alcohol and illicit drugs to avoid drug use and improve their level of academic performance. Early studies of CASASTART showed that the program helped decrease drug use, helped participating students advance in school, lowered violence, and decreased participants' susceptibility to peer pressures to become involved in drugs and crime. By 2001, there were seventeen CASASTART programs across the country. Another of its major projects was CASAWORKS FOR FAMILIES, a program designed to help mothers who were addicted to drugs and alcohol and on welfare become self-sufficient. The three-year project combined drug and alcohol treatment, literacy courses, and job training for participating women. The program was successful, helping participants stop using drugs and alcohol while more than doubling their rates of employment. In addition, CASA has published major reports on teenage substance abuse, drug use in prisons, substance abuse on college campuses, the relationship between drug use and sex, and on substance abuse among people with learning disabilities. CASA has also studied the connection between sports and substance abuse.

Today, CASA has a Policy and Research division that assesses the impact of substance abuse on the U.S. population, studies the links between substance abuse and other health and social problems, and makes recommendations to improve public policies on substance abuse. Its Health and Research division conducts studies to determine what addiction treatment strategies are most effective. In 2009, CASA merged with Join Together, a major provider of information, strategic planning assistance, and leadership development for community-based drug and alcohol programs. Through articles in the popular press and scientific journals, as well as press conferences and testimonies before governmental bodies, CASA continues to work to spread awareness of the social and economic costs of drug abuse, assess what prevention, treatment, and law enforcement strategies are most effective in combating substance abuse, and remove the stigma surrounding substance abuse so addicts can gain the hope they need to recover.

(See also **Office of National Drug Control Policy (ONDCP)**; **Partnership for a Drug Free America**)

References

Carson-Dewitt, Rosalyn, ed. 2001. *Encyclopedia of Drugs, Alcohol & Addictive Behavior. Second Edition*. New York: Macmillan Reference USA.

CASASTART. "About CASASTART." [Online information retrieved 05/11/09] http://casastart.org/content/AboutCASASTART.aspx.

National Center on Addiction and Substance Abuse at Columbia University. "About CASA." [Online information retrieved 05/11/09] http://www.casacolumbia.org/templates/AboutCASA.aspx?articleid=276&zoneid=1.

National Center on Addiction and Substance Abuse at Columbia University. "CASAWORKS for FAMILIES: A Promising Approach to Welfare Reform and Substance-Abusing Women." [Online information retrieved 05/11/09] http://www.casacolumbia.org/Absolutenm/articlefiles/CASAWORKS_for_Families_6_4_01.pdf.

National Center on Addiction and Substance Abuse at Columbia University. "Mission Statement." [Online information retrieved 05/11/09] http://www.casacolumbia.org/absolutenm/templates/AboutCASA.aspx?articleid=2&zoneid=1.

CHINA AND THE CHINESE

Both Chinese immigrants and the country of China itself played key roles in the development of U.S. drug policy in the early-twentieth century. Racism against Chinese immigrants gave political traction to the move towards domestic controls over narcotics, while a desire to help the Chinese government stamp out drug abuse on the Chinese mainland helped spur the push towards international drug control.

Within the United States, the opium habit came to be seen as a foreign and menacing tradition associated with Chinese immigrants in the late-nineteenth century. Chinese immigrants began coming to the United States in large numbers for the California gold rush of 1848, and many also came to work as laborers on the construction of the transcontinental railroad. Even though many of these immigrants had not used opium before they moved to the United States, a good number of them became accustomed to smoking opium during their rare days off once they immigrated. Purchasing the drug at local Chinese stores, in small mining towns, or from shopkeepers in San Francisco's Chinatown, many of these immigrants gradually developed opium habits as a way to escape from the hard lives they led as immigrant laborers in the Western United States. According to studies conducted by doctors in the late-nineteenth century, about 15% of the Chinese immigrants living in the United States smoked opium daily.

In the 1870s, two factors made the Chinese opium habit problematic in the minds of commentators in the United States. First of all, the opium habit began spreading beyond the narrow confines of the immigrant Chinese community at that time. Public smoking shops and opium dens open to both Whites and Chinese immigrants began popping up in Nevada, California, and major cities in the Midwest (Chicago, St. Louis), the South (New Orleans) and on the East Coast (New York). At first, most of the non-Chinese who attended opium dens were young people from the lower classes, many of them individuals who made livings in the seedy underworlds of gambling and prostitution. Soon, however, many began to fear that the habit was spreading to the middle and upper classes. They argued that if allowed to spread, opium could lead to both the physical and moral decline of youths from all classes and races.

Fear of the opium habit's spread dovetailed with another development that stirred anti-Chinese sentiment—economic depression. When the economy was hit by a severe downturn in the 1870s, many came to see Chinese immigrants as threatening since they were believed to take jobs from native-born workers. As economic troubles mixed with traditional racism and fear of foreigners, many began to suspect that

Chinese immigrants used opium as part of a wider conspiracy to harm the United States and its citizens; some speculated that they gave the drug to White women in exchange for sexual favors, while others argued that the drug was intimately tied to other deviant practices like prostitution and gambling that were believed to be common in the Chinatowns of U.S. cities. Some even speculated that the Chinese tried to poison Whites with the drug, spreading rumors that they mixed it with candy that they sold to children in hopes of getting them hooked. As early as 1875, some local governments in the Western United States were moved to pass legislation based on this anti-Chinese sentiment, and eleven states introduced legislation to crack down on the opium habit between 1877 and 1890. Anti-Chinese sentiment remained prevalent in the writings of anti-opium activists in the late-nineteenth and early-twentieth centuries, and it helped garner support for some of the first pieces of federal narcotics control legislation in the United States—the Smoking Opium Exclusion Act of 1909 and the Harrison Narcotics Act of 1914. The association of the opium habit with the Chinese continued well into the twentieth century. In the early years of narcotics control, both the general public and the authorities believed that the opium habit, and opium dens in particular, were problems associated with the Chinese, and as late as the 1950s drug control officials blamed China for the illicit importation of other opiates (like heroin) into the United States. Though there is still some connection between China and the opium problem in the United States today, much of the focus has shifted to organizations based in other parts of the world—other Asian countries and Latin America in

particular—that orchestrate the traffic of controlled substances into the United States.

While fears of Chinese immigrants helped push the move towards domestic narcotics control in the United States, concern over China and opium played an even bigger role when it came to the creation of an international drug control regime. The Chinese had been trying to limit the spread of the opium habit in their country since the 1700s, but with little success. The main reason was that other countries—European powers who had colonial holdings in Asia in particular—got rich off of the Chinese opium problem. The colonial governments of Britain, France, and Holland all had systems in which the authorities were in charge of growing and selling opium, much of which made its way to Chinese customers. The opium habit in China, therefore, was a major source of profit for the European colonial powers. Thus there was a tension between China's efforts to promote the health of its own citizens by limiting their opium use, and European financial interests. At times in the nineteenth century, the clash between Chinese public health goals and European economic motives led to armed conflict. The Chinese tried to stand up to the European powers when they refused to restrict the importation of opium into Chinese ports, leading to skirmishes that came to be known as the Opium Wars—the first lasting from 1839 to 1843, the second from 1856 to 1860. In both conflicts, the Chinese suffered bitter defeats, and they were forced to allow foreign opium into their country. By the late-nineteenth century, however, many European countries began to soften their stance and consider making changes to their opium policies, and the United States became a leading advocate for reforming the opium trade. Eventually, the desire to help the Chinese address their opium problem led to the convening of the first two international drug control conferences—at Shanghai in 1909 and The Hague in 1911. The agreement struck at The Hague eventually laid the groundwork for the international drug control regime that emerged after World War I.

(See also **Hague Convention**; **Harrison Narcotics Act**; **Shanghai Commission**; **Smoking Opium Exclusion Act**)

References

Bewley-Taylor, David R. 1999. *The United States and International Drug Control, 1909–1997*. London: Pinter.

Courtwright, David T. 2001. *Dark Paradise: A History of Opiate Addiction in America*. Cambridge, MA: Harvard University Press.

Davenport-Hines, Richard. 2001. *The Pursuit of Oblivion: A Global History of Narcotics, 1500–2000*. London: Weidenfeld & Nicolson.

McAllister, William B. 2000. *Drug Diplomacy in the Twentieth Century*. London: Routledge.

Morgan, H. Wayne. 1974. *Yesterday's Addicts: American Society and Drug Abuse, 1865–1920*. Norman, OK: University of Oklahoma Press.

Musto, David F. 1987. *The American Disease: Origins of Narcotics Control*. Expanded Edition. New York: Oxford University Press.

CIPOLLONE V. LIGGETT GROUP, INC. ET AL.

Cipollone v. Liggett Group, Inc. et al. was a landmark 1980s lawsuit that signaled a turning point in the history of litigation against the tobacco industry. Although the plaintiff ultimately failed to win any compensation after an appeals court set aside the verdict on a technicality, the case exposed a cache of industry documents that proved big tobacco was aware of the link between smoking and cancer. The case thus paved the way for successful class-action lawsuits and the Master Settlement Agreement.

Cipollone v. Liggett Group, Inc. et al. was filed by attorney Marc Edell on August 1, 1983. Edell had become familiar with pulmonary pathology as a result of previously defending an asbestos company in health litigation cases wherein the defendants claimed that workplace health risks resulted from smoking, rather than exposure to asbestos. Familiar with the risks of smoking and sensing that the tobacco industry was ripe for litigation, Edell came across Rose Cipollone, a fifty-eight-year-old woman from Little Ferry, New Jersey undergoing treatment for lung cancer. Shortly thereafter, Edell filed suit against three major tobacco companies—Liggett, Philip Morris, and Lorillard—on her behalf.

Rose Cipollone (nee DeFrancesco) began smoking Chesterfields at the age of sixteen, and despite her heavy-smoking father's fatal stroke (which her mother attributed to cigarettes) just two years earlier, she was smoking an estimated pack and a half of them per day within a couple of years of her first cigarette. Married and pregnant a few years later, Rose was urged by her husband, Antonio Cipollone, to quit smoking for the sake of the baby's health. During the trial, Rose stated that although she cut down on her smoking during the pregnancy, she found herself addicted and unable to quit. She also testified that in

1955 she switched from Chesterfields to L&Ms, a new Liggett and Myers filtered cigarette with a "Miracle Tip" that was billed as "Just What the Doctor Ordered." Cipollone's shift to the ostensibly safer and healthier L&Ms was typical of the times, as by 1958, around half of all smokers switched from unfiltered to filtered cigarettes, which debuted in the wake of a series of scientific reports in the 1950s that linked smoking to cancer. In 1968, Cipollone began smoking Virginia Slims, a new line manufactured by Philip Morris and advertised as the cigarette for modern, but still feminine, women. She then switched to Philip Morris' Parliament brand in 1972, in large part, she testified, because they claimed to diminish the level of tar a smoker ingested. Cipollone finally moved on to Lorillard's True cigarettes in 1974, reportedly at the behest of her doctor. True, which billed itself as being low in tar and nicotine, was suggested by the doctor, who reasoned that if Cipollone intended to continue smoking, it would be the healthiest brand for her. These brand changes, some of them undertaken with the intent of improving her health, did not prevent her from developing lung cancer in 1981, and she died from it at the age of 58 on October 21, 1984.

The suit that Edell filed on Cipollone's behalf in 1981 consisted of five allegations. Edell claimed that the tobacco industry had designed safer cigarettes but opted not to sell them, thus intentionally putting out a product they knew to be dangerous. The suit also alleged that, prior to federally mandated warning labels, tobacco companies had failed to adequately warn consumers about the risks of smoking that they themselves were aware of. Additionally,

Edell argued that cigarette advertising made untrue health claims that intended to contradict what was known about the dangers involved in smoking. Furthermore, Edell made the claim that the tobacco industry fraudulently misrepresented cigarettes' health effects. Lastly, the suit alleged that the tobacco industry had committed fraud by suppressing scientific findings that linked smoking to a variety of illnesses and diseases.

Despite the significant popular and scientific awareness of smoking's perils, Edell's chances of successful litigation were decidedly low. In fact, the tobacco industry had avoided paying even a single cent in damages in any of the approximately 300 lawsuits previously brought against it. Big tobacco's remarkable record of success was in large part the result of its decision that it would not deliberate over which cases it should it take to trial and which cases it should settle out of court; instead it would aggressively defend every claim in order to thwart the overwhelming majority of suits before they even reached trial. With a formidable legal team behind it, the tobacco industry utilized an approach that featured frequent delays, denials, and the filing of numerous (and often unjustified) preliminary legal motions. These actions ratcheted up the cost of litigation for the plaintiffs, so that few could ultimately afford the monetary cost of bringing suits to trial. In those rare instances, as was the case in *Cipollone*, in which a lawsuit reached the trial stage, the tobacco industry's two-fold defense was to roundly deny that smoking definitively caused cancer, and, just as importantly, to assert that since it had no knowledge of a link between their product and a serious disease, it had no responsibility to warn consumers about smoking's dangers.

What distinguished *Cipollone* from other similar cases that were stymied by big tobacco's effective legal defense strategy was Edell's acquisition of approximately 300,000 internal tobacco industry documents. Drawing upon his experience as a lawyer for asbestos companies, Edell gained access to a trove of documents that exposed exactly what the tobacco industry really knew about the dangers of smoking. One of the most significant revelations contained within these documents, which formed the basis of many future cases against big tobacco, was that industry scientists were aware of a significant link between smoking and cancer at least as far back as the mid-1940s. Additionally damaging to big tobacco were internal memos demonstrating industry executives' personal knowledge of the dangers of smoking. Equally revealing were memoranda and letters that illuminated how the Council for Tobacco Research (originally called the Tobacco Industry Research Committee), a tobacco industry-funded research center, worked towards discrediting research that linked smoking to cancer, suppressed unfavorable scientific findings, and prepared scientific witnesses for trials and congressional testimony dealing with the medical repercussions of smoking.

The tobacco industry's traditional argument that any illnesses Cipollone suffered were the result of her personal decision to smoke—and that therefore the defendants bore no responsibility for her death from lung cancer—was not nearly as persuasive when considered alongside these revealing industry documents. In fact, Edell used documents exposing the addictive nature of nicotine to argue that the tobacco industry actively worked to engineer and market cigarettes so that smokers who were concerned enough about the safety of smoking to consider quitting would continue smoking despite the serious health hazards.

In the end, the jury granted $400,000 in damages to Cipollone's widower, thus marking the first monetary award won against the tobacco industry. The trial was not a complete victory for Edell, however, as the jury ruled that Cipollone was principally responsible for her fatal lung cancer and that the tobacco industry was not guilty of conspiracy and fraud. The $400,000 was awarded solely on the jury's decision that Liggett contributed to Cipollone's death by not warning consumers, as it should have, of smoking's dangers prior to 1966—the year when the tobacco industry was required to place warning labels on cigarette packaging. And after both sides appealed the case, the verdict was thrown out in 1990 as a result of a technicality. Antonio Cipollone died shortly thereafter, and the family eventually decided not to continue the case.

While the tobacco industry ultimately avoided paying any damages in *Cipollone*, it hardly emerged from the suit unscathed. For one, its time-tested defense strategy was seriously imperiled by the jury's finding. More significantly, though, were the internal documents Edell acquired. These letters, memos, and research findings made it impossible for the industry to subsequently claim an ignorance of the link between smoking and cancer, and it opened up big tobacco to a wave of future litigation along the lines of the *Cipollone* case. And while the Cipollone family eventually chose to drop the case after years of litigation without winning so much as a single dollar for their efforts, other lawyers following the case saw the opportunity for class-action lawsuits that would pool the resources of smokers with similar claims and make it more difficult for the tobacco industry to wait out plaintiffs. *Cipollone* similarly laid the groundwork for state governments to begin suing tobacco companies in the 1990s for health insurance costs, and it likewise paved the way for the Master Settlement Agreement of 1998.

(See also **Master Settlement Agreement (MSA)**; **P. Lorillard**; **Primary Source Documents**; **Tobacco Industry Research Committee (TIRC)**))

References

Brandt, Allan M. 2007. *The Cigarette Century: The Rise, Fall, and Deadly Persistence of the Product That Defined America.* New York: Basic Books.

Cordry, Harold V. 2001. *Tobacco: A Reference Handbook.* Santa Barbara, CA: ABC-CLIO.

Goodman, Jordan, ed. 2005. *Tobacco in History and Culture: An Encyclopedia.* Detroit: Thomson Gale.

COMMITTEE ON DRUG ADDICTION

The Committee on Drug Addiction was an organization within the National Research Council devoted to the study of drug addiction. In its ten years of work, from 1928 through 1938, it strove to encourage pharmacological research into opiate addiction and sought to create an effective medical substitute for opiates that would not be addictive. Ultimately, however, the Committee's research failed to yield any discoveries on how to effectively substitute other chemicals for opiates in medical practice.

The Committee on Drug Addiction was the brainchild of Reid Hunt, a professor of pharmacology at Harvard University, and former member of the Treasury Department's Special Narcotic Committee. Hunt believed that pharmacological research in the United States was lacking, and that it was important for the country to become more involved in drug research. In particular, Hunt urged for research to discover non-habit forming opiates and anesthetics that could take the place of potentially addictive drugs such as opium and cocaine. In 1928, Hunt's vision was realized when the Bureau of Social Hygiene offered to transfer the scientific work of its Committee on Drug Addictions to a new body under the auspices of the National Research Council. That December, the National Research Council appointed a committee—the Committee on Drug Addiction—to oversee research on opiate addiction and the search for nonaddictive opiate substitutes. In 1932, the Bureau of Social Hygiene withdrew its funding for the Committee, and the Rockefeller Foundations stepped in to fund its research. The Committee on Drug Addiction focused not so much on the social aspects of drug addiction as it did on the pharmacology behind it, and finding pharmacological solutions for the problem.

One of the Committee on Drug Addiction's major activities involved research carried out by organic chemist Lyndon F. Small at the University of Virginia. The focus of Small's work was the effort to break down the morphine molecule and then reconstruct it in hopes of developing a new morphine derivative that, while pain-killing, would not be habit-forming. Others in Small's laboratory tried to synthetically create molecules similar to morphine. The Committee's pharmacological research was carried out at the University of Michigan, where compounds were tested for their addictiveness and therapeutic effectiveness. Compounds that seemed to hold promise in experiments at the Michigan laboratory were then tested on addicted inmates at the federal prison at Fort Leavenworth, Kansas, and at the Public Health Service Narcotic Hospital located in Kentucky.

In 1930, the Committee on Drug Addiction seemingly had a breakthrough with the discovery of a compound later named desomorphine. Small oversaw the synthesis of desomorphine, and initial animal tests at the Michigan laboratory showed that it had significant pain-killing powers, though tests in the mid-1930s revealed that it was indeed addictive. In the late 1930s, Small developed Metopon, a drug that was a mild success—it was less addictive than morphine, and its therapeutic use was limited to the treatment of chronic pain in cancer patients. Though it was less habit-forming than morphine, Metopon's painkilling powers were not as strong, meaning that the search for an effective morphine substitute would have to continue. Over the course of its eleven-year existence, the Committee experimented with several hundred morphine-related compounds, yet Metopon was the only one that was ever marketed.

The Committee on Drug Addiction formally came to an end in 1939, when the programs at the University of Virginia and University of Michigan were transferred to the Division of Chemotherapy at the National Institutes of Mental Health. The members of the National Research Council who had been running the research on drug addiction continued to serve within the National Institutes of Mental Health, though they did so as the Advisory Committee on Drug Addiction. The Advisory Committee was relatively inactive during World War II, but was reconstituted as the Committee on Drug Addiction and Narcotics in 1947.

(See also **Committee on Drug Addictions**; **Public Health Service Narcotic Hospitals**)

References

Acker, Caroline Jean. 2002. *Creating the American Junkie: Addiction Research in the Classic Era of Narcotic Control*. Baltimore: Johns Hopkins University Press.

The National Academies. 1969. "Committees on Drug Addiction, Drug Addiction (Advisory) and Drug Addiction & Narcotics, 1928–1965." [Online article accessed 03/08/09] http://www7.nationalacademies .org/archives/Committees_on_Drug_Addic tion.html.

COMMITTEE ON DRUG ADDICTIONS

The Committee on Drug Addictions was an umbrella organization that supported research in the field of narcotics addiction in the 1920s. Originally, it focused on medical approaches towards understanding and treating addiction, though by the end of the decade, it shifted towards advocating for a more law-and-order approach to the drug problem, pushing more for tighter controls on supplies of drugs and less for the treatment of addicts. This view ultimately shaped the direction of addiction policy in the United States until the 1960s.

The Committee on Drug Addictions was the brainchild of New York attorney Arthur D. Greenfield, who was interested in the problem of opiate addiction, and a vocal opponent of maintenance treatment. Leading addiction experts, such as Surgeon General Rupert Blue, Dr. Ernest S. Bishop, and Charles E. Terry all supported the creation of a body that could scientifically study the problems of addiction and addiction treatment. In 1921, John D. Rockefeller Jr. allocated $12,000 for the creation of this group— the Committee on Drug Addictions. Soon, the Bureau of Social Hygiene started providing the majority of funding for the Committee. The Committee had an impressive membership list, with representatives from the Bureau of Social Hygiene and the American Social Hygiene Association, the former chair of the New York City Parole Commission, and Terry among others. The intention of the committee was to lay down a definitive scientific groundwork that could guide future drug policy.

By 1924, the Committee developed a three-pronged approach to dealing with the addiction problem. First, it wanted to focus on education, particularly that of physicians, in order to teach them that over-prescription of opiates could be a major cause of addiction. Second, it advocated for sociological research that focused on the troubles caused by drug trafficking and the impact that the black market for narcotics had on addicts. Third, it called for what was termed "pure research," which included the study of how to limit supplies of opium to the world's scientific needs, studies on the causes of addiction, and psychological research on the effects that class,

personality, and the autoimmune system had on opiate addiction. In addition, the Committee researched the development of nonaddicting substances that could be substituted for morphine and help wean addicts off of the drug. In all of these arenas, the Committee did not lead the research, but rather served as a central coordinating body that gave financial support to, and summarized the work carried out by, other groups, such as the National Health Council, the American Social Hygiene Association, and the National Research Council.

In the 1920s, organizations working with the support of the Committee of Drug Addictions began studying various aspects of the drug problem in the United States. Terry led a series of surveys of physicians and pharmacists to try to determine how much opiates were medically necessary in the United States, in large part to provide data that could go to the League of Nations, which was trying to create a worldwide international opium control regime. The Committee also funded psychiatric, psychological, metabolic, and pharmacological studies on the effects opiates had on the body. In the late 1920s, the Committee funded a three-year study of physiological and psychological effects of addiction at Philadelphia General Hospital's narcotics ward, leading to the creation of the Philadelphia Committee for the Clinical Study of Opium Addiction. Among the Philadelphia Committee's most important findings was that withdrawal from morphine and heroin, while an extremely unpleasant experience, was not life-threatening. It also concluded that there were no major physiological differences that made addicts different from nonaddicts.

Another major accomplishment of the Committee on Drug Addictions was the

1928 publication of an exhaustive review of the scientific literature on addiction from the United States and Europe—*The Opium Problem*. Charles Terry and Mildred Pellens, who was also a member of the Committee on Drug Addictions, authored the encyclopedic work, which drew from over 4,000 different sources. The main theses of *The Opium Problem* were that addiction was a disease, that the implementation of the Harrison Narcotics Act and the ban on maintenance treatment worsened the plight of addicts, and that bans on the sale of opiates created a widespread, and well-organized, black market for narcotics. When it first came out, George McCoy, the director of the Public Health Service's Hygienic Laboratory, wanted to keep the work from being published, thinking it would do more harm than good to educate physicians about addiction since most addicts were, he claimed, of the criminal class. Ultimately, however, Terry and Pellens won the debate with McCoy, leading him to resign from the Committee.

In addition to its research, the Committee on Drug Addictions also became prominent in the policy realm. Committee member Lawrence B. Dunham, who had been a law enforcement official in New York, worked with the League of Nations Opium Advisory Committee, and he also advised Levi G. Nutt on federal drug legislation and helped him set quotas for raw opium imports. In the late 1920s, the Committee became more focused on the enforcement side of drug control, as both Dunham and Committee chair Katharine Bemet Davis believed that the best way to control the addiction problem would be to limit the world's supply of opium. Anticipating programs that would come to fruition later in the century, the Bureau of Social Hygiene funded a commission that explored the possibility of using crop-substitution programs in Persia—a major grower of opium poppies—to reduce the worldwide supply of narcotics. When Dunham became Chair of the Committee in 1928, it became even more devoted to a supply-side view of addition, with a focus on limiting drug production. Dunham maintained that drug addicts suffered from inherent personality defects, so the only way to keep them from becoming addicted was to keep drugs out of their hands. These beliefs ultimately became the most widely held views concerning addiction and addiction policy in the United States until the 1960s. They also alienated original members of the Committee, such as Terry, who remained an outspoken critic of the government's anti-maintenance stance and advocate for maintenance clinics.

As the Bureau of Social Hygiene realized the limitations of the Committee on Drug Addictions, it invited the Division of Medical Sciences of the National Research Council to assume responsibility over research into drug addiction. In December of 1928, the National Research Council appointed a new, separate entity—the Committee on Drug Addiction—that took on the role of conducting the scientific research that had been done by the Committee on Drug Addictions.

(See also **Bishop, Ernest S.**; **Committee on Drug Addiction**; **Harrison Narcotics Act**; **League of Nations**; **Nutt, Levi G.**; **Terry, Charles E.**)

References

Acker, Caroline Jean. 2002. *Creating the American Junkie: Addiction Research in the Classic Era of Narcotic Control*. Baltimore: Johns Hopkins University Press.

The National Academies. 1969. "Committees on Drug Addiction, Drug Addiction (Advisory) and Drug Addiction & Narcotics, 1928–1965." [Online article accessed 03/08/09] http://www7.nationalacademies.org/archives/Committees_on_Drug_Addiction.html.

Terry, Charles E. and Mildred Pellens. 1928. *The Opium Problem*. New York: Bureau of Social Hygiene.

COMPREHENSIVE DRUG ABUSE PREVENTION AND CONTROL ACT

The Comprehensive Drug Abuse Prevention and Control Act was a sweeping piece of federal legislation that brought all of the major pieces of federal drug legislation—from the 1914 Harrison Narcotics Act through the Drug Abuse Amendment Acts of 1965—under one law. Since it took effect in 1971, the Act has remained the basis of federal drug laws in the United States. Though its focus was, like the legislation that preceded it, on cracking down on drug law violators, the Act was also significant in that it followed up on the 1966 Narcotic Addict Rehabilitation Act by calling for the furthering of education to prevent drug abuse, research into narcotic addiction, and rehabilitation for addicted offenders.

Before 1970, there were several legal bases for federal drug control. The 1914 Harrison Act governed commerce and possession of opiates and cocaine, while the 1937 Marihuana Tax Act placed controls on marijuana. The penalties for trafficking and using these drugs were expanded dramatically in the 1950s, with the passage of the Boggs Act and the 1956 Narcotic Control Act. All of these laws were enforced by the Federal Bureau of Narcotics, which in 1968 was renamed the Bureau of Narcotics and Dangerous Drugs. The 1965 Drug Abuse Amendment Acts established that amphetamines, barbiturates, and hallucinogens could be controlled by the federal government, and the Food and Drug Administration was charged with enforcing regulations governing these substances. In spite of this slew of laws, however, recreational drug use seemed to proliferate throughout the 1960s, as drug use became a common pastime in the counterculture, and also prevalent among soldiers returning from the Vietnam War. In 1969, President Richard Nixon took notice of the problem, which he aimed to suppress through a ten-point program that included measures to cut down on the drug traffic and provide more education, research, and rehabilitation for addicts. In addition, Nixon recommended a comprehensive new law that would unite all of the existing principles of drug control in the United States under one legislative umbrella.

In its stages as a draft piece of legislation, the Act focused heavily on enforcement, as the Attorney General told Congress its main accomplishment would be to keep drugs off of American streets and launch a tougher enforcement program that would put major drug traffickers behind bars. Some lawmakers, however, wanted assurances that there would be provisions for drug education and rehabilitation in the law as well. The resulting law—the Comprehensive Drug Abuse Prevention and Control Act—reflected the interests that went into its drafting, as it focused heavily on the repression of illicit trafficking and dealing, while also including provisions for drug education to prevent youths from trying drugs, a section authorizing research on narcotic addiction, and a provision for the medical treatment of addicts.

Title I of the Act, covering Rehabilitation Programs Relating to Drug Abuse, focused on treatment and education. Section 1 of the Rehabilitation section authorized the government to make grants to state and local governments, and also for contracts with private organizations, to collect, prepare, and disseminate educational materials dealing with drug abuse. It also allocated funds to evaluate these programs. Section 3 of Title I authorized research into narcotic addiction, and protected the privacy of individuals involved in this research. In Section 4 of Title I, the Secretary of Health, Education, and Welfare was entitled to research what treatment methods could be used to help drug users overcome their addictions. The National Institute of Mental Health was subsequently directed to coordinate health and educational initiatives relating to drug addiction. In 1972, the Drug Abuse Office and Treatment Act further expanded prevention and treatment programs.

Title II of the Act, which would later become known as the Controlled Substances Act, divided drugs into five schedules, depending on their potential for abuse and their use in mainstream medical practice. Schedule I drugs were substances that the government believed had high potential for abuse, were not used in medical treatment in the United States, and were not believed to be safe, even when used under medical supervision. Among the drugs placed on this schedule were heroin, marijuana, and LSD. Schedule II drugs were drugs that while having a high potential for abuse,

also had accepted medical uses in the United States. Among the substances included on this schedule were cocaine and its derivatives, morphine, methadone, and amphetamines. Schedule III drugs such as barbiturates were substances that were believed to have less potential for abuse, and were considered acceptable for use in medical practice, while drugs on Schedule IV and V were considered to have even lower potential for abuse and were accepted in mainstream medical practice. Drugs on Schedules I and II were the most tightly regulated, as it became a violation to distribute these substances without a written order on a form distributed by the Attorney General. Copies of this form needed to be kept for two years, so that government officials could inspect them and closely monitor the transfer of these drugs. The penalties also were steepest for violations involving Schedule I and II drugs, as manufacture, distribution, and possession with an intent to sell these substances was punishable by up to fifteen years in prison and a fine of up to $25,000. For repeat offenders, these sentences could be doubled. The penalty for violations involving Schedule III drugs was up to five years in prison and a $15,000 fine, while for Schedule IV drugs the punishments could be up to three years in prison and a $10,000 fine, and for Schedule V drugs the maximum sentences were one year in prison and a fine of up to $5,000. The Act also allowed punishments of up to a year in prison and a fine of up to $5,000 for the possession of controlled substances, and the penalties for repeat possession offenses were doubled. The law did, however, give judges the option of putting individuals brought up on charges of possession on probation.

The Controlled Substances Act targeted large-scale drug traffickers in particular. While the Act did not impose mandatory minimum sentences on most offenders, it did call for a minimum of ten years in prison, and possibly a life sentence, for individuals found to be involved in large-scale drug trafficking, and it also allowed for a maximum fine of $100,000. For repeat offenders, these sentences were doubled. Individuals caught trying to import Schedule I and II drugs were also punished severely, with sentences of up to five years in prison and fines of up to $15,000. The Act also gave sweeping powers to law enforcement officials, allowing them to carry firearms, execute and serve search warrants, make arrests without warrants, seize property, and even break and enter premises in order to carry out investigations if they had a warrant from a judge.

Overall, the Comprehensive Drug Abuse Prevention and Control Act both unified and solidified prior trends in the federal approach to the drug problem. It kept and enhanced many of the repressive characteristics of earlier drug control measures such as the Boggs Act and the 1956 Narcotic Control Act with hefty sentences and fines for drug law violators, though it did rescind the use of the death penalty for heroin dealing that was a key provision of the Narcotic Control Act. At the same time, it also had some provisions in Title I that provided for treatment and allowed for education, and not just repression, to be used in the campaign against drug addiction. In this respect, it reflected some of the trends that began to take shape with the Narcotic Addict Rehabilitation Act of 1966.

(See also **Anti-Drug Abuse Acts**; **Boggs Act**; **Drug Abuse Control Amendments of 1965**; **Harrison Narcotics Act**; **Narcotic Addict Rehabilitation Act**; **Narcotic Control Act**)

References

Belenko, Steven R., ed. 2000. *Drugs and Drug Policy in America: A Documentary History.* Westport, CT: Greenwood Press.

Carson-Dewitt, Rosalyn, ed. 2001. *Encyclopedia of Drugs, Alcohol & Addictive Behavior. Second Edition.* New York: Macmillan Reference USA.

Chepesiuk, Ron. 1999. *The War on Drugs: An International Encyclopedia.* Santa Barbara, CA: ABC-CLIO.

King, Rufus. 1972. *The Drug Hang-Up: America's Fifty-Year Folly.* Springfield, IL: Bannerstone House.

Musto, David F., ed. 2002. *Drugs in America: A Documentary History.* New York: New York University Press.

COMPULSIVE OVEREATING MUTUAL AID GROUPS

Overeaters Anonymous (OA) and Weight Watchers International (WWI) are two of the most prominent groups designed to provide mutual aid and support for compulsive overeaters. Compulsive overeating is considered an impulse control disorder by some and a behavioral addiction by others, and some researchers have suggested similarities between it and other excessive behaviors such as compulsive spending and compulsive gambling. Regardless of how it is scientifically understood, OA treats compulsive overeaters with a twelve-step program adapted from Alcoholics Anonymous (AA), while WWI stresses behavior modification as a means of helping its members lose weight.

Explanations of the cause of overeating vary considerably, with many scholars suggesting that cultural forces play a significant role in shaping individuals' perceptions of the body and can lead to unhealthy obsessions about weight and food. Others see psychological commonalities amongst compulsive overeaters, leading some to conclude that binge eating is an addiction in which an individual overeats in an attempt to fill up a kind of emotional emptiness. Similarly, some scholars suggest that overeaters experience, following an episode of binge eating, feelings of guilt and self-disgust, which in turn spur a new round of eating. This cycle has been likened to psychological dependence or addiction.

OA, the first compulsive overeating mutual aid group, believes that obesity is the symptom of a disease it calls compulsive overeating, and it maintains that this illness can be controlled, but not cured. In this stance, and its concomitant belief that compulsive overeating is comprised of physical, emotional, and spiritual elements, OA falls squarely within the tradition of AA and other twelve-step groups. In fact, OA was established as a result of co-founder Rozanne S. attending a Gamblers Anonymous (GA) meeting in 1958 in support of a friend with a gambling problem. While listening to the group's stories of compulsive gambling, she concluded that the Twelve Steps, which originated with AA and had been adapted by GA, could similarly be applied to help herself and others deal with compulsive eating. The first OA meeting was held in Los Angeles, California on January 19, 1960, and the organization has since grown into an international organization with approximately 6,500 local groups that meet weekly in over seventy-five countries.

OA estimates that it currently has around 54,000 members worldwide.

In adopting AA's Twelve Steps and Twelve Traditions with only slight modifications, OA stresses the First Step, which involves members admitting their powerlessness over compulsive overeating. In stressing that their compulsive overeating is not a matter of willpower, OA members, as AA attendees do, invoke a vaguely defined "higher power" as an important influence. And like AA meetings, OA's weekly gatherings are founded on the principle of fellowship and the act of sharing stories. Notably absent from OA meetings, however, is an emphasis on dieting or weight loss. OA instead focuses on encouraging its members to seek self-understanding and emotional satisfaction through their relationships with others, and it believes that with more solid psychological and spiritual footing, members will develop a healthier relationship with food on their own terms. Consequently, up until recently, OA allowed members to define "abstinence" on their own. In 2009, though, the organization came to define abstinence as the action of refraining from compulsive eating and compulsive food behaviors.

Another important compulsive overeating mutual aid group, WWI, has instead taken the approach of focusing on weight loss. Rather than emphasizing spiritual and emotional well-being as OA's Twelve Steps do, WWI stresses behavior modification as a means of helping members manage their binge eating and maintain their diets. Among the mechanisms by which WWI tries to control compulsive overeating are ploys for distracting one's self, instituting delays on eating, and preparing snacks that require effort to chew. WWI also differs from OA in that it is an international company rather than a nonprofit organization. As such, there are fees for attending its meetings, and WWI employs professional nutritionists, physicians, and physiologists unlike OA. WWI sets diet challenges for its members and creates eating and exercising programs to help them achieve their weight loss goals. Many people find this framework more practical and conducive to weight loss than OA's focus on the emotional, psychological, and spiritual well-being of its members.

(See also **Alcoholics Anonymous (AA)**; **Gamblers Anonymous (GA)**)

References

Carson-Dewitt, Rosalyn, ed. 2001. *Encyclopedia of Drugs, Alcohol & Addictive Behavior. Second Edition.* New York: Macmillan Reference USA.

Weiner, Sydell. 1988. "The Addiction of Overeating: Self-Help Groups as Treatment Models." *Journal of Clinical Psychology.* 54, no. 2: 163–167.

CRACK EPIDEMIC

The most typical form of cocaine use in the 1970s and early 1980s was the snorting of cocaine powder, but the mid-1980s saw the emergence of a new form of cocaine use—crack smoking. Far cheaper than cocaine in its powder form, crack found a sizeable market in impoverished, inner-city neighborhoods in the 1980s. Some scholars, however, believe that the so-called "crack epidemic" of the period was more media exaggeration than social reality, resulting from misinformation about crack's addictiveness combined with crack's greater visibility amongst the lowest classes in urban ghettos.

Though controlled by federal drug laws since the early-twentieth century, cocaine re-emerged as a popular drug the 1970s, when its use by celebrities and musicians transformed it into a glamorous substance in many circles. The rise of Latin American drug trafficking organizations also played a significant role in the reemergence of cocaine in American life, as they smuggled it into the United States and distributed it on American streets on a large scale. Nonetheless, cocaine remained relatively expensive, costing between $80 and $100 per gram in the 1970s. Crack emerged in the mid-1980s as a more potent, low-cost alternative to powder cocaine. Underground chemists in Los Angeles first devised crack in the early 1980s by mixing cocaine with baking soda and boiling down the mixture into a smokeable rock form. The new form of cocaine was on the black market by late 1984 and it spread throughout lower-class neighborhoods of Los Angeles, Miami and New York City by the middle of the 1980s. Originally dubbed "cocaine-rock," the substance soon came to be known as "crack," getting its name from the cracking or crackling sound that is made when the substance is heated and smoked in glass pipes. Crack was more powerful than powdered cocaine, faster-acting (it got users high within seconds), and also significantly cheaper, costing just $5 to $10 per rock. Crack's potency and relative cheapness, authorities feared, could make the drug spread like wildfire. Street dealers stood to benefit from crack since its effects wore off quicker than cocaine, meaning that users would need to come back to buy more of the drug more regularly. Users, drug policymakers feared, would turn to crack instead of cocaine since it was relatively inexpensive and created a high that was more powerful.

The emergence of crack generated calls of alarm, as many claimed that the country was in the midst of a crack epidemic from the mid-1980s through the early 1990s. Members of the media, politicians, and public health officials alike contributed to a seeming consensus that crack represented the most dangerous drug ever created or known. Characterized as extremely destructive and almost instantaneously addictive, crack came to be seen as a kind of narcotic juggernaut that jeopardized the well-being of Americans of all stripes. Newspaper, magazine, and television reports spoke of crack's rapid spread beyond the ghettos of the big cities in which it originally appeared, and alarmed suburban and rural readers and viewers, who feared a crack epidemic that could cut across social, racial, and geographic lines. In particular, the media seized on the problem of "crack babies"—children who were born to crack-addicted mothers with serious health problems. Fear that crack use had reached epidemic proportions and had tremendous social costs became a driving force behind national drug policies in the 1980s, and Congress passed tough anti-drug legislation—the Anti-Drug Abuse Acts—largely in response to the dangers the drug seemingly posed to the American public.

Despite (or perhaps because of) this intense focus on the crack epidemic, the true place of crack in American life was obscured in the 1980s. Lost amidst the hubbub over crack was the fact that the drug was never widely used by Americans, and in further contradiction of

media reports about the instantaneous addictiveness of the drug, few people who tried crack continued using it. One reason that only a small percentage of people who smoked crack a first time opted to do it again is that the drug has a strong, almost overwhelming, impact. The repeated use of a drug of this strength and impact is generally limited to the small segment of the population that uses heroin heavily. As such, even amongst cocaine users, only a small percentage of them smoked crack heavily. National Institute on Drug Abuse (NIDA) surveys from the 1980s and 1990s confirm the relative rarity of crack use during the so-called crack epidemic. The NIDA-led National Household Survey on Drug Abuse of 1990 revealed that in the first years after crack's emergence, overall drug use, including that of cocaine and its derivatives, declined. The survey from the following year showed that the percentage of Americans between the ages of twelve and twenty-five who had ever tried cocaine and related drugs peaked in 1982—well before the appearance of crack—and continued to decline thereafter. NIDA's 1986 study measuring crack use amongst high school seniors found that 4.1% had tried crack at least once in the previous year, but as the crack scare continued, yearly surveys showed this figure dropped each subsequent year. Through the early 1990s, this number hovered around just 1.5%, clearly indicating that Americans were not using crack in epidemic proportions. An explanation for the disconnect between Americans' sense in the late 1980s and early 1990s that they were living in the midst of a crack epidemic and the reality that crack never truly threatened wide swaths of the population may lie in the fact that those most affected by crack were the impoverished, Blacks, and Latinos. Because they had little financial means of combating their addiction and a greater visibility in the nation's ghettos and barrios than middle-class cocaine users, crack users and addicts attracted media scrutiny and political attention disproportionate to the true level of crack use in the country. Racial prejudices, too, likely contributed to suburban and rural Americans' fears of a crack epidemic.

By 1990, a number of media reports emerged that called into question the phenomenon of a crack epidemic. These stories revealed that crack was not nearly as addictive as it had been built up to be, nor had it made significant inroads beyond inner-city neighborhoods. By the election year of 1992, fears of a crack epidemic had essentially come to an end. George H. W. Bush said little about illicit drugs during his re-election campaign, and the Clinton administration did not continue to address the drug problem in the same way as its Republican predecessors had done, so the concerns about crack began to fade by the mid-1990s.

(See also **Anti-Drug Abuse Acts**; **Drug Addiction and Public Policy**; **Drug Smuggling**; **National Institute on Drug Abuse (NIDA)**; **Reagan, Ronald and Nancy**)

References

Belenko, Steven R., ed. 2000. *Drugs and Drug Policy in America: A Documentary History*. Westport, CT: Greenwood Press.

Chepesiuk, Ron. 1999. *The War on Drugs: An International Encyclopedia*. Santa Barbara, CA: ABC-CLIO.

Erickson, Patricia G., Edward M. Adlaf, Reginald G. Smart, and Glenn F. Murray, eds. 1994. *The Steel Drug: Cocaine and Crack in Perspective*. New York: Lexington Books.

Reinarman, Craig and Harry G. Levine, eds. 1997. *Crack in America: Demon Drugs and Social Justice*. Berkeley, CA: University of California Press.

CROTHERS, THOMAS DAVISON

Dr. Thomas Davison Crothers was a nineteenth-century physician who devoted much of his professional life towards treating alcoholism and drug addiction and getting them to be recognized as diseases. Crothers went beyond traditional conceptions of substance abuse rooted in ideas of sinfulness and gluttony, and furthered existing theories about alcoholism and drug abuse constituting an illness by examining them within a scientific—rather than a moralistic—framework. Crothers worked to popularize his notions about substance abuse as the longtime editor of the American Association for the Study and Cure of Inebriety's (AASCI) *Quarterly Journal of Inebriety* and a contributing writer to various other scientific and medical publications. He also became a supporter of the Woman's Christian Temperance Union (WCTU) and their call for alcohol prohibition.

Thomas Davison Crothers was born on September 21, 1842 in West Charlton, New York, and he received his medical degree from Albany Medical College in 1865. He was a medical cadet at the Ira Harris Military College during the Civil War, and he practiced privately from 1866 to 1870 in West Galway, New York. After serving as assistant professor of the practice of medicine at his alma mater, Albany Medical College, from 1871 to

1874, Crothers began working on the medical staff of the nation's first inebriate asylum in Binghamton, New York. Crothers also established and headed a similar inebriate asylum, the Walnut Hill Asylum (later Walnut Lodge Hospital), in Hartford, Connecticut.

Over the course of his work in the early 1870s at these various institutions, Crothers began writing about the need to classify alcoholism and drug addiction as an illness—termed inebriety—rather than a moral failing. The idea that compulsive substance use constituted an illness had a number of adherents in the late-eighteenth and nineteenth centuries, but Crothers' work sought to give such a notion greater scientific footing. His writings emphasized that inebriety was a condition in which the body became physically and psychologically dependent upon alcohol, opiates, cocaine, or other substances. In order to function normally, he argued, the inebriate's bodies depended on continued consumption of the substance to which they were addicted. Dependence on alcohol and drugs, he maintained, had marked stages of development, including physical "cravings," an inability to stop consuming, the degeneration of nerve and brain cells, and, ultimately, insanity or death. He also hypothesized that the damage caused by excessive drinking or drug-taking could be passed on to future generations, as offspring of alcoholics and addicts were prone to develop substance abuse problems as well.

Crothers derived these ideas from his years of first-hand work with inebriates at asylums and hospitals in New York and Connecticut, and he popularized his findings through numerous publications that established his reputation as an international expert on inebriety and addiction. Crothers became a member of the AASCI in 1873, and he edited its *Quarterly Journal of Inebriety* (later the *Journal of Inebriety*) from 1876 to 1914. Crothers also penned numerous articles for other professional journals, such as the *Journal of the American Medical Association*, and some of his books include *Morphinism and Other Drug Diseases* (1892), *Inebriety* (1893), *Drug Habits and Their Treatment* (1901), *Morphinism and Its Treatment* (1902), *Morphinism and Narcomanias from Other Drugs* (1902), and *Clinical Study of Inebriety* (1911). He taught the first courses in the United States on inebriety as a disease at Albany Medical College and Vermont University in 1899. In addition, Crothers' disease conception of inebriety gained greater international cache via his involvement with the American Medical Temperance Association, the British Society for the Study of Inebriety, the Colonial and International Congress on Inebriety in London (1886), the International Temperance Congress in London (1897), the International Congress against the Abuse of Alcoholic Drinks in Paris (1899), and the Congress on Alcoholism in London (1909). Crothers also played a key role in spreading knowledge of the dangers of opiate and cocaine addiction, which had first been first written about by European researchers, in the United States.

Perhaps most importantly, Crothers brought his disease conception of inebriety to a more popular audience. In addition to his numerous contributions to scientific, medical, and professional journals, Crothers lectured at temperance gatherings, and also warned audiences about the dangers of habit-forming drugs other than alcohol. Many temperance advocates saw Crothers' work as a scientific validation of their own claims about the dangers of alcohol and other drugs such as opiates and cocaine. For his part, Crothers was pleased with the WCTU's "scientific temperance" educational programs to the point that he developed Scientific Temperance Instruction materials for use in public schools. Crothers' partnership with the WCTU was not exactly a perfect union though, as he was reluctant to accept a prohibitionist platform. He felt, instead, that medicine represented the best means of dealing with alcoholism and addiction. Ultimately, however, Crothers embraced prohibition as an effective preventative approach to combating alcoholism.

Crothers' main contribution to the history of inebriety lies not within the temperance movement, but rather with his decades-long fight to have inebriety understood and established as a medical disease. His medical claim that inebriates were sick and diseased, and in need of care, treatment, and restraint stood in contrast to the notion prevalent among temperance proponents that drunks and addicts were sinful and that their problems stemmed from moral failures. Many historians have written off his work as scientifically unsound, but in the late-nineteenth and early-twentieth centuries, there were few individuals in the field of inebriety who had as much experience working with patients as Crothers did. And regardless of contemporary historical and scientific skepticism of Crothers' conclusions, his work in classifying inebriety had an important influence upon later researchers, most notably E. Morton Jellinek. Crothers died on January 12, 1918 in Hartford, Connecticut.

(See also **American Association for the Study and Cure of Inebriety (AASCI)**; **Degeneration Theory**; **Jellinek, E. Morton**; **Primary Source Documents**; **Woman's Christian Temperance Union (WCTU)**))

References

Blocker, Jr., Jack S., David M. Fahey, and Ian R. Tyrrell, eds. 2003. *Alcohol and Temperance in Modern History: An International Encyclopedia*. Santa Barbara, CA: ABC-CLIO.

Courtwright, David T. 2001. *Dark Paradise: A History of Opiate Addiction in America*. Cambridge, MA: Harvard University Press.

Crothers, Thomas D. 1902. *Morphinism and Narcomanias from Other Drugs*. Philadelphia: W.B. Saunders & Company.

Lender, Mark Edward. 1984. *Dictionary of American Temperance Biography: From Temperance Reform to Alcohol Research, the 1600s to the 1980s*. Westport, CT: Greenwood Press.

Murdock, Catherine Gilbert. 1998. *Domesticating Drink: Women, Men, and Alcohol in America, 1870–1940*. Baltimore: Johns Hopkins University Press.

Musto, David. F. 1987. *The American Disease: Origins of Narcotics Control*. Expanded Edition. New York: Oxford University Press.

CUSTER, ROBERT L.

Dr. Robert L. Custer was one of the fathers of the modern understanding of gambling addiction, and a pioneering researcher in its treatment. Among his major accomplishments was the creation of the first inpatient program for the treatment of pathological gambling, and convincing the American Psychiatric Association to classify pathological gambling as a psychiatric disorder.

Robert L. Custer was born in Midland, Pennsylvania, in 1927. He attended Ohio State University for his undergraduate degree, went to medical school at Western Reserve University, and did his psychiatric training at the University of Missouri. In the 1950s, Custer and his wife began treating people with addictions. While working at the Veterans Administration hospital in Brecksville, Ohio, Custer set up the first treatment program for the treatment of gambling addiction in 1972, upon the request of members of Gamblers Anonymous (GA). That same year, he also co-founded the National Council on Problem Gaming. Experience working with compulsive gamblers helped Custer revolutionize the way treatment providers approached clients with gambling problems. Previous researchers who had studied gambling addiction used a Freudian approach to the problem, assuming that people gambled compulsively as a substitute for sex. Based on his experience working with problem gamblers, Custer rejected this thesis, instead arguing that problem gamblers played excessively for a different reason—to escape pain. Custer believed that pathological gambling was a disease, and pushed for it to be considered as such by the medical and psychiatric communities. In 1980, he accomplished his goal with the inclusion of compulsive gambling in the American Psychiatric Association's Diagnostic Statistical Manual of Mental and Nervous Disorders. Custer also took his advocacy beyond the medical community, serving as an expert witness in criminal trials, where his testimonies on pathological gambling helped establish legal precedents by urging for the compassionate treatment of pathological gamblers. In his 1985 book *When Luck Runs Out*, Custer told the stories of problem gamblers, helping bring public attention to the problem. Beyond telling their stories, *When Luck Runs Out* laid out the different personality types which are prone to develop gambling problems, ranging from the conscientious and hard-working to the aggressive and the insecure. Denial, according to Custer, was a key part of pathological gambling, as he observed that problem gamblers developed a belief they did not have a problem, as did their families.

In 1983, Custer organized Taylor Manor, a psychiatric center in Ellicott City, Maryland, to treat gambling addiction. Patients at the center received individual counseling, attended weekly group therapy sessions and GA meetings, and also got assistance arranging the repayment of their gambling debts. At Taylor Manor, Custer found that gambling addicts usually were not driven by a desire for money, as many theorists of compulsive gambling held they did, but rather by a fear of dying. Later in his career, Custer also contributed to some of the first studies looking at the role of neurotransmitters in gambling addiction. In 1987, he also established a treatment program for pathological gamblers at Charter Hospital in Las Vegas.

Custer continued to work in private practice until his death in 1990, at the age of sixty-three, from lung cancer.

(See also **Lesieur, Henry R.**; **Gamblers Anonymous (GA)**; **National Council on Problem Gaming (NCPG)**; **Reference Essay**)

References

Custer, Robert L. and Harry Milt. 1985. *When Luck Runs Out: Help for Compulsive*

Gamblers and Their Families. New York: Facts on File Publications.

Fowler, Glen. 1990. "Robert L. Custer, 63, Psychiatrist Who Led Treatment of Gamblers." *New York Times*. September 9, 42.

National Council on Problem Gaming. "About NCPG." [Online information retrieved 05/21/09] http://www.ncpgambling.org/i4a/pages/index.cfm?pageid=3285.

Roy, Alec, Byron Adinoff, Laurie Roehrich, Danuta Lamparski, Robert Custer, Valerie Lorenz, Maria Barbaccia, Alessandro Guidotti, Ermino Costa, and Markku Linnoila. 1988. "Pathological Gambling: A Psychobiological Study." *Archives of General Psychiatry*. 45, no. 4: 369–373.

Thompson, William N. 2001.*Gambling in America: An Encyclopedia of History, Issues, and Society*. Santa Barbara, CA: ABC-CLIO.

Weisbroat, Irwin. 1991. "A Tribute to Robert L. Custer, M.D." *Journal of Gambling Studies*. 7, no. 1: 3–4.

D

DAI, BINGHAM

Bingham Dai was, along with Alfred Lindesmith, one of the first sociologists to study opiate addiction as a social behavior, rather than a medical disease. His work helped bring a new social perspective to the way that researchers viewed addiction, ushering the study of opiate use out of the specialized realms of medicine and psychiatry, and initiating inquiries into the connections between opiate users and their social environments.

Bingham Dai was born in Futien, China, on August 22, 1899, and he completed his bachelor's degree at St. John's University in Shanghai in 1923. After teaching high school, Dai began to work with the Shanghai-based National Anti-Opium Association. The group sought to reduce the prevalence of addiction by educating people on the dangers of the drug, and pushing for prohibitive legislation against its use. The subject became more personal for Dai when he saw his uncle, who had worked with him on anti-opium campaigns, fall victim to

opiate addiction and die from complications related to it. This experience led Dai to believe that moral persuasion and legal sanctions alone were not enough to battle the problem of opiate addiction, and he sought to develop a more compassionate, understanding view of addiction that was free of the moral biases that colored the way most individuals—both in China and the United States—viewed the opium habit and opiate addicts. The Provincial Government of Futien sent Dai to the United States to study education and also to solicit prominent Americans to assist China in its battle against drug addiction. But when he came to the United States to study sociology at Yale and the University of Chicago, Dai sought not only to serve as an advocate for China's anti-opium organizations, but also to study the phenomenon of opiate addiction from a new perspective. At Yale, he wrote a proposal to study addiction as a sociological problem—one that reflected tensions in the way that individuals related to their social worlds—and not merely as a medical or psychiatric one. Since he believed that merely addressing addiction with law-and-order measures that restricted supplies would not suffice, Dai's proposal was met with skepticism from Lawrence Dunham at the Bureau of Social Hygiene when he solicited him for help with his work. Others, such as Walter Treadway of the Division of Mental Hygiene in the U.S. Public Health Service, were intrigued by his proposal, and soon Dai received permission from Federal Bureau of Narcotics chief Harry J. Anslinger to undertake a detailed study, based on arrest and conviction reports, of opiate addicts in Chicago.

Dai's study, *Opium Addiction in Chicago*, was published in 1937. Dai's focus in *Opium Addiction in Chicago* was not on compiling numbers or studying the way that addiction worked, but rather on the relationship between opiate users and their social environments. Dai found that Chicago addicts generally lived in areas of the city with low rents, high vacancy rates, and a high number of transient and homeless people. Due to their destitution and instability, these neighborhoods did not offer the sense of community or instill the social norms that were common in mainstream society. Consequently, Dai concluded that addiction was more likely to strike individuals who lived in areas where people lived by themselves and social control was minimal. Thus the social environment, Dai found, could be a key risk factor for addiction. To determine which individuals in these downtrodden areas were more likely to become addicted, Dai conducted interviews with addicts at local psychiatric hospitals and shelters. Using a psychoanalytic model, Dai unearthed childhood traumas, bad parenting, and other problems in addicts' pasts that predisposed them to addiction.

In addition to drawing conclusions based on what addicts told him, Dai also observed addicts' behavior, and concluded that many of them did not follow social norms. To alleviate the feelings of isolation and emotional pain that they experienced as outcasts, Dai concluded, many addicts sought refuge in opiates. Thus individuals who became addicts were socially maladjusted—a conclusion that gave backing to the theories of other addiction specialists such as Lawrence Kolb, who believed that addiction had fundamentally psychological underpinnings.

Dai's research did have one major shortcoming, as he only interviewed individuals who had either run afoul of the law or were in poverty—meaning that all of the people he surveyed were all socially outcast or deprived—so he did not get a picture of what opiate addiction was like for the well-to-do or those who had not been arrested for their drug use. Nonetheless, Dai's research was groundbreaking, as it was the first study that attempted to construct the addicts' social world as they experienced it, instead of simply describing it from an outsider's perspective. Furthermore, he showed that it was not necessarily due to individual shortcomings that people became addicted, but that the social environment could predispose people to opiate addiction. Addicts, therefore, were not always at fault for their disease—the society that put them in such a poor and precarious environment also shouldered some of the blame.

With *Opium Addiction in Chicago*, Dai pioneered a new way to understand addiction. Unlike law enforcement, which believed that addiction was a willful choice made by drug users, and unlike the medical establishment, which maintained that psychological problems facilitated addiction, Dai established that the social environment planted the psychological and anti-social seed out of which addiction could grow.

(See also **Anslinger, Harry J.**; **Committee on Drug Addictions**; **Kolb, Lawrence**; **Lindesmith, Alfred R.**)

References

Acker, Caroline Jean. 2002. *Creating the American Junkie: Addiction Research in the Classic Era of Narcotic Control*. Baltimore: Johns Hopkins University Press.

Chih-hsiang, Hoh, ed. 1933. *Who's Who in China: Biographies of Chinese. Supplement to the Fourth Edition*. Shanghai: China Weekly Review.

Dai, Bingham. 1970. *Opium Addiction in Chicago*. Montclair, NJ: Patterson Smith.

D.A.R.E. (DRUG ABUSE RESISTANCE EDUCATION)

D.A.R.E. (Drug Abuse Resistance Education) is a program designed to give youths the skills they need to avoid becoming involved in drugs, gangs, and violence, and it is one of the most widespread school-based substance abuse prevention programs in the country. Despite its prominence, D.A.R.E. has a number of detractors who question the effectiveness of the program, which lost federal funding in 2001.

D.A.R.E. began in 1983 as a partnership between the Los Angeles Police Department and the Los Angeles Unified School District intended to inculcate in fifth-graders information and skills for avoiding drugs and violence. The D.A.R.E. program lasted seventeen weeks, was taught by a personable police officer, and involved the students taking "no drug" pledges and participating in a culmination ceremony. Subsequent versions of the course were supplemented with D.A.R.E. t-shirts, pins, and bumper stickers, which contributed an enhanced visibility within schools and the community. Kids completing the course were taught various approaches to resist the allure of drugs, with classroom simulations giving students the opportunity to practice saying "no" and staving off peer pressure. D.A.R.E. also taught students about drug use and its consequences, thereby providing them with the information needed to make informed decisions about the place of drugs in their lives. Additionally, D.A.R.E. tried to generally cultivate high self-esteem in its students, thus signaling the program's belief that students who are happy with themselves, optimistic about the future, and confident that they can realize their potential would be less vulnerable to the many pressures to use drugs. Furthermore, D.A.R.E. sought to create positive relationships between young people and the law enforcement officers in their communities. The federal government soon took notice of the program, and it encouraged the expansion of D.A.R.E. across the country by allowing communities to spend federal money to create their own D.A.R.E. programs. D.A.R.E. thereafter grew to operate in 75 to 80% of the nation's school districts. It currently reaches around 30 million students in what it reports are over 300,000 classrooms in all fifty states. Millions of students in forty-three other countries will also go through the D.A.R.E. program.

The program that so many millions of young students have been a part of was, in its initial form, centered on the "Just Say No" mantra of the era, but it has undergone a series of revisions in the wake of studies that have called the effectiveness of its message into question. One of the first critiques of D.A.R.E. came in 1994 with the publication of the Research Triangle Institute's analysis of the program. Among the institute's findings was the determination that children who took D.A.R.E. were no more likely than children who did not go through the program to not try illicit drugs. In fact, the institute's report suggested that children's curiosity about some drugs actually increased as a result of learning about them through D.A.R.E. Detroit and other communities came to similar conclusions about D.A.R.E.'s ineffectiveness after doing their own analyses. The federal government took note of these findings, and in 2001 the Department of Education withdrew funding for D.A.R.E. A January 2003 General Accounting Office (GAO) report confirmed the soundness of the federal government's decision, as it concluded that six long-term evaluations done in the 1990s found no significant differences between the illicit drug use of fifth- and sixth-grade students who participated in D.A.R.E. and those who did not.

In response to these findings, D.A.R.E. revised its curriculum for seventh-graders. This modified version of D.A.R.E. revolves around challenging the myths that young people hold about drug use. It focuses on teaching youths about how drug use impairs brain functioning, and it strives to inculcate good decision-making skills in its students. Interactive, role-playing components are now more central to D.A.R.E. sessions, with police officers functioning less as instructors and more as coaches or facilitators. Early analysis of this new iteration of D.A.R.E.

indicates an increased effectiveness over the old program. D.A.R.E. now also has a K-12 curriculum, as well as after-school programs and additional community education projects.

(See also **Office of National Drug Control Policy (ONDCP)**; **Partnership For A Drug Free America**; **Reagan, Ronald and Nancy**)

References

D.A.R.E. "About D.A.R.E." [Online information retrieved 05/20/09] http://www.dare.com/home/about_dare.asp.

"GAO Literature Review Reiterates Ineffectiveness of Original D.A.R.E." 2003. *Alcoholism & Drug Abuse Weekly*. 15, no. 4 (January 27).

Retsinas, Joan. 2001. "Decision to cut off U.S. Aid to D.A.R.E. Hailed." *Providence Business News*. (March 12): 5B.

Rosenbaum, Dennis. 1998. "Assessing the Effects of School-Based Drug Education: A Six-Year Multilevel Analysis of Project D.A.R.E." *Journal of Research in Crime and Delinquency*. 35, no. 4: 381–412.

DEBTORS ANONYMOUS (DA)

Debtors Anonymous (DA) is a twelve-step program modeled after Alcoholics Anonymous (AA) that seeks to provide help to members suffering from what is it calls "compulsive debting"—a difficult-to-classify condition characterized by individuals' inability to control often excessive shopping or spending urges, which is also known as compulsive buying disorder. Founded by members of AA in 1971, DA views debting as a disease and pledges mutual support in members' attempts to become solvent. DA claims to have 500 local groups in the United States and at least a dozen other countries, and a distinct—but not separate—part of DA called Business Debtors Anonymous (BDA) focuses on DA members who are also business owners.

DA's origins can be traced back to 1968, when a group of AA members first held an independent meeting to discuss their problems with money. This small group initially called itself the Penny Pinchers, but they later dubbed themselves Capital Builders. Both names referred to its members' practice of making daily deposits of their funds into savings accounts. This practice was intended to help solve what they believed was their inability to save money, but as time passed, the group came to the conclusion that their true monetary problems centered on an inability to become solvent. The group also came to understand their debting as a disease, and consequently, by 1971, the group adopted the name of Debtors Anonymous and the Twelve Steps of AA. Though the pieces of DA had come together, the group of recovering AA members disbanded after two years of meetings. A reconstituted DA reemerged in 1976 with a small group that began weekly meetings at St. Stephen's Rectory in New York City. A second group was organized within the same year, and over the ensuing years, DA has grown into an organization comprised of over 500 local groups meeting in the United States and in at least a dozen other countries.

At local meetings, DA members convene and read the organization's preamble, which defines the group as a fellowship comprised of individuals who share their experiences, strength, and hope so that together they may solve their common problem—compulsive debting—and help others who suffer from it. The preamble further states that DA's primary purpose is to stop debting one day at a time. A local member will chair the meetings, which largely consist of members sharing stories of their experiences as compulsive debtors or shoppers. As DA is a nonprofit organization funded by its members' voluntary contributions, gatherings also involve taking a collection for the meeting's financial support. DA meetings may also involve the reading of the Twelve Steps—the recovery program adapted from AA in order to fit the needs not of alcoholics, but of compulsive debtors—or other DA literature such as the *Signs of Compulsive Debting* or the *Tools of DA*. Meetings also serve as occasions to encourage members to record all financial transactions down to every penny, and develop a spending plan, which is a list of all items or services a member intends to purchase. Members then review the list in order to determine whether the purchases are reasonable, thus encouraging the cultivation of healthier spending practices. In some cases, members will place in an envelope the amount of money needed for each section of expenses in the spending plan.

In addition to weekly meetings, DA also involves Pressure Relief Groups and Pressure Relief Meetings. Pressure Relief Groups are comprised of newer DA members who are still working to control their spending and two other recovering debtors who have been DA members for a while and who have successfully avoided incurring any unsecured debt for a minimum of 90 days. This Pressure Relief Group then meets in a series of Pressure Relief Meetings in which the newer members' financial situations are assessed in detail by the two veteran members, who help create an appropriate spending and action plan.

Beyond these meetings, compulsive debtors can avail themselves of the services of BDA, a distinct but not separate component of DA that focuses on the recovery of members who are business owners. At BDA meetings, members apply DA principles to running a business, with business-owning members helping one another identify behaviors that contribute to incurring unsecured debt. For instance, BDA meetings may revolve around members' stories detailing an ignorance of when bills were due, discussion of the confusion that members suffer from when trying to differentiate personal finances from business finances, the lack of a business plan, an ignorance of operating costs, or an undervaluing and under-pricing of goods and services. BDA members consequently teach one another how accumulating cash reserves and paying bills and employees on time can contribute to operating a debt-free business.

(See also **Alcoholics Anonymous (AA)**)

References

Black, Donald W. 2007. "Compulsive Buying Disorder: A Review of the Evidence." *CNS Spectrums*. 12, no. 2: 124–132.

Debtors Anonymous. "History of Debtors Anonymous." [Online article accessed 05/21/09] http://www.debtorsanonymous.org/about/history.htm.

Morenberg, Adam D. 2004. Governing Wayward Consumers: Self-Change and Recovery in Debtors Anonymous. Tampa, Florida: University of South Florida.

DEGENERATION THEORY

Degeneration was a scientific theory in the late-nineteenth and early-twentieth centuries that informed a good amount of thinking about addiction during the period. By prognosticating that addiction could be both a cause and a symptom of health and hereditary problems, degeneration made the habitual use of alcohol and psychoactive substances seem particularly problematic.

Researchers in both Europe and the United States elaborated degeneration theory in the nineteenth century. As early as the eighteenth century, theorists such as the French researcher George-Louis Leclerc, Comte de Buffon hypothesized that species could degenerate—become smaller, weaker, or sterile—over time. For Buffon, degeneration resulted from creatures living in environments that were not well suited to them. In the 1850s, French medical researcher Benedict Morel put forth the theory that degeneration was occurring in modern Europe, arguing that maladaptive behaviors—including criminal activities, alcoholism, and opiate abuse—could lead to changes that would be passed down to subsequent generations, which he believed would inherit physical and psychological problems from their ancestors. Abuse of alcohol or opium, Morel believed, had the power to cause unhealthy changes that could be passed down to future offspring, either in the form of alcoholism or opiate addiction, or other nervous or physical diseases. In time, such beliefs became common in the United States as well. Thomas Crothers, one of the leading researchers into addiction in the late-nineteenth and early-twentieth-century United States, for example, argued that the children of opium-takers were more likely to have opiate-addicted children, and that alcoholics were more likely to have alcoholic children. Even if addiction was not passed on, he argued, other problems would become manifest in the children of people who used psychoactive substances excessively, as the poisons of alcohol and opium would impair or alter cell function and growth in drug users, who in turn would pass on physical or mental problems to their children. Alcohol and drug abuse, therefore, not only affected the individuals who indulged in these substances, but also had the potential to doom future generations to a variety of problems. As these individuals with a tainted inheritance reproduced, the theory went, they in turn would have children who also had some sort of physical or psychological problem. As the numbers of alcoholics and drug abusers grew, therefore, so would the number of individuals who inherited problems caused by the misdeeds of preceding generations. Consequently, if left unchecked, alcohol and drug abuse had the potential to lead to the degeneration of not only the individual, but also of all humanity.

In the first half of the twentieth century, degeneration theory was debunked, mainly because it could never be proven. Scientists were unable to show the neurological damages caused by substance abuse, nor could they demonstrate that such damage could be passed on to future generations. More generally, scientists in Europe and North America abandoned the idea that traits acquired during one's lifetime could be passed on to one's offspring. The horrors inflicted by Nazi Germany, which were rooted in ideas similar to degeneration, gave the theory a bad name, and most scientists abandoned it altogether. Nonetheless, degeneration played a key role in the late 1800s and early 1900s, as it armed the opponents of alcohol and psychoactive drug use with a theory that supported their claims that indulgence in these substances could have disastrous consequences, not only for the individual, but also for all of mankind.

(See also **Crothers, Thomas Davison**; *United States v. Doremus* **and** *Webb et al. v. United States*)

References

Courtwright, David T. 2005. "Mr. ATOD's Wild Ride: What Do Alcohol, Tobacco, and Other Drugs Have in Common?" *The Social History of Alcohol and Drugs*. 20: 105–124.

Crothers, Thomas D. 1902. *Morphinism and Narcomanias from Other Drugs*. Philadelphia: W.B. Saunders & Company.

Pick, Daniel. 1989. *Faces of Degeneration: A European Disorder, c. 1848–c. 1918*. Cambridge, United Kingdom: Cambridge University Press.

DISULFIRAM

Disulfiram is the single most prescribed medication for the treatment of alcoholism. Unlike naltrexone, which is another medication sanctioned by the Food and Drug Administration for use in the treatment of alcoholism and which generally works by inhibiting the pleasure a drinker derives from alcohol, disulfiram deters drinking by generating nausea, dizziness, vomiting, and headaches if the patient consumes alcohol. For disulfiram to be most effective, it should be taken orally on a daily basis and combined with counseling treatment.

Disulfiram was developed in the 1940s after Danish researchers Erik Jacobsen and Jens Hald, who were experimenting with the chemical on worms, discovered that after they ingested small amounts of it, they experienced discomfort when they drank alcohol. Based on this accidental discovery, Jacobsen and Hald speculated that the chemical could be useful in the treatment of alcoholism, and in initial studies, they found that most alcoholics who ingested disulfiram were discouraged from drinking. By the later 1940s, the chemical began to be used as an adjunct in the treatment of alcoholism, usually under the trade name of Antabuse. In 1948, Dr. Ruth Fox began using it in the United States, and a review of Jacobsen and Hald's research introduced American physicians to the drug's potential for the treatment of alcoholism. When physicians in the United States began prescribing Antabuse, many patients complained about the drug's side effects, though these complaints usually resulted from the administration of overly high doses. Criminal justice systems then began exploring the use of the drug as an aid in the treatment and monitoring of alcoholic lawbreakers, and some jurisdictions made the drug a condition of probation or parole for some offenders. In the 1950s, French researchers developed Antabuse implants, which could be surgically inserted into the abdomen, and were effective for up to six months.

The chief mechanism by which disulfiram deters drinking is the disulfiram-ethanol reaction (DER), which occurs when a patient taking disulfiram drinks alcohol of any variety. Disulfiram causes a DER by blocking the activity of a number of the body's enzymes, and most importantly the enzyme aldehyde dehydrogenase (ALDH), which is instrumental in the liver's transformation of ethanol (alcohol) into acetate, carbon dioxide, and water. Without ALDH to break down ethanol in the body, acetaldehyde, one of the chemicals that causes hangovers, builds up in the blood and causes a DER. A patient on disulfiram who drinks alcohol and experiences a DER will consequently suffer something akin to an acute and severe hangover, with symptoms including flushing of the skin, dizziness, shortness of breath, mental confusion, nausea, vomiting, headaches, and an accelerated heart rate, with the severity of these conditions generally dependent on the levels of disulfiram and alcohol the patient has consumed. Though very rare, severe DERs can cause death. Additional side effects of disulfiram use may also include an increase in the absorption and toxicity of lead, as well as potential liver toxicity. The most common side effect, however, is drowsiness, and for this reason, most patients take disulfiram before going to bed. Inadvertent DERs can also occur as a result of patients on disulfiram innocently coming into contact with alcohol sources like fermented vinegar, mouthwash, aftershave lotion, cough syrup, or rubbing alcohol.

Because serious side effects can come from disulfiram, the medication is always administered by a doctor. A typical disulfiram regimen involves the patient taking the medication orally in tablet form on a daily basis, usually in doses of 250 to 500 milligrams. Doses in excess of 500 milligrams can be administered to patients who do not experience DERs if they drink after taking a typical dose of disulfiram, but elevated amounts of disulfiram in the body do increase the risk of serious side effects. Since the severity of disulfiram's DER and side effects depends upon the amount of alcohol a patient consumes while on the medication, physicians will only give disulfiram to patients they know to have abstained from alcohol for a minimum of twelve hours, though a window of forty-eight hours between the patient's last drink and the administering of disulfiram is more ideal.

An alternative way of administering disulfiram is by implanting it beneath the abdominal wall. The body does not absorb disulfiram very well when it is implanted, and this method generally leads to weaker and diminished DERs in patients who take a drink. It nonetheless remains a medical technique of some value because the overall effectiveness of disulfiram is primarily dependent on the patient regularly taking the medication. For alcoholics who lack a regular schedule that permits daily visits to a physician who can administer disulfiram, implantation is seen as a more dependable way of delivering a daily dose of the medication to the patient. Not surprisingly then, disulfiram has proven most effective in treating the alcoholism of patients who have regular obligations and timelines guiding their lives, as a tablet of physician-administered disulfiram can more dependably become a part of their daily routine.

(See also **Food and Drug Administration (FDA)**; **Naltrexone**; **Reference Essay**)

References

Carson-Dewitt, Rosalyn, ed. 2001. *Encyclopedia of Drugs, Alcohol & Addictive Behavior. Second Edition*. New York: Macmillan Reference USA.

Fuller, Richard K., et al. 1986. "Disulfiram Treatment of Alcoholism: A Veterans Administration Cooperative Study." *Journal of the American Medical Association*. 256, no. 11: 1449–1455.

White, William L. 1998. *Slaying the Dragon: The History of Addiction Treatment and Recovery in America*. Bloomington, IL: Chestnut Health Systems.

DOLE, VINCENT

Vincent Dole was a leading researcher into the science of addiction in the mid-twentieth century. He opposed the Federal Bureau of Narcotics' punitive approach towards the addiction problem, and he worked to find medical solutions to solve the problems caused by addiction. Most notably, along with his wife Marie Nyswander, he helped pioneer the use of methadone maintenance treatments for opiate addicts.

Vincent Paul Dole was born on May 18, 1913 in Chicago. He earned his bachelor's degree in mathematics from Stanford University in 1934, and a medical degree from Harvard in 1939. After serving as an intern at Massachusetts General Hospital in Boston, Dole became an assistant in kidney research at the Rockefeller Institute in New York City in 1941. After a stint as a lieutenant commander with the Naval Medical Research Unit during World War II, Dole was named an associate member of the Rockefeller Institute in 1947, and he was appointed a full member in 1951 before becoming a professor there in 1955.

In 1962, Dole was examining metabolic diseases while working on a study of obesity, and he found that some people craved food just as much as addicts craved drugs. Around the same time, Dole became aware of the enormity of the drug problem in New York City. This prompted him to become interested in the study of addiction, and he soon read one of the most recent works on individuals addicted to narcotics, Marie Nyswander's *The Drug Addict As Patient*. In 1964, he invited Nyswander to come work with him at the Rockefeller Institute to conduct research on the treatment of opiate addiction. At the time, heroin addiction and its social ramifications were major social and public health problems in New York City. However, there had been very little community-based research into the problem at the time, since most research was focused in the government's Public Health Service Narcotic Hospitals.

Given his background as a physician, Dole believed that addiction was a physiological problem caused by changes that occurred due to continuous administration of opiates. Methadone, he believed, could prevent withdrawal symptoms and stabilize the physiology of the addict since it was longer-acting than heroin. Together, Dole and Nyswander began testing the effectiveness of methadone substitution treatments for opiate addicts, administering it to addicts who had been using heroin for at least fourteen years. In their research, they found that 100 milligrams of methadone blocked the effects of 200 milligrams of heroin, but that addicts who took the drug did not experience many of the painful withdrawal symptoms that usually came on when they stopped using heroin. They found that methadone was so effective in attenuating the withdrawal symptoms associated with heroin use that many of their volunteers were able to redevelop interests in going back to school or work. Thus long-term methadone maintenance—legally stabilizing

heroin-addicted patients on a daily oral dose of methadone—held the promise of breaking the cycle of using heroin and engaging in criminal activity to support the habit. Consequently, methadone could decrease addicts' tendency to turn to the black market for drugs so they could avoid withdrawal symptoms, and increase the likelihood that they would reintegrate into society as law-abiding citizens. And since methadone was itself an opiate, it decreased the likelihood of relapse, which until then had been a major stumbling block in attempts to treat heroin addiction. In 1965, Dole and Nyswander published their findings in the *Journal of the American Medical Association*, and that same year, they also got married.

In spite of the promise of his research, Dole faced opposition from the Federal Bureau of Narcotics (FBN), which did not want doctors to have the authority to provide narcotics to addicts. Though the FBN tried to intimidate him into stopping his work, and spread rumors about him in order to discredit him, Dole was undeterred and continued his research into the potential benefits of methadone. Impressed by Dole and Nyswander's work, Ray Trussell, the commissioner of New York City hospitals, helped them established a research and demonstration project on methadone at Manhattan General Hospital. The project proved a success and garnered public attention, leading many in the scientific and drug policy communities to advocate for methadone maintenance as a viable medical option for the treatment of heroin addiction. By the early 1970s, methadone maintenance programs spread across the country, and eventually, overseas as well.

Dole passed away in 2006, at the age of 93, in New York City.

(See also **Federal Bureau of Narcotics (FBN)**; **Methadone**; **Nyswander, Marie**)

References

Acker, Caroline Jean. 2002. *Creating the American Junkie: Addiction Research in the Classic Era of Narcotic Control.* Baltimore: Johns Hopkins University Press.

Drug Policy Alliance Network. "Vincent P. Dole, 1913–2006." [Online article http://www.drugpolicy.org/news/080306dole.cfm accessed 05/03/09].

Edwards, Griffith. ed. 2002. *Addiction: Evolution of a Specialist Field.* Oxford, UK: Blackwell Science.

Hevesi, Dennis. 2006. "Vincent P. Dole, Methadone Researcher, Is Dead At 93." *The New York Times.* (August 3): B7.

DRUG ABUSE CONTROL AMENDMENTS OF 1965

The Drug Abuse Control Amendments of 1965 expanded the number of substances that were controlled by the federal government in the United States. Until the passage of the Amendments, many addictive substances, such as amphetamines, barbiturates, and psychedelics were not closely regulated, or subject to the same tight controls as opiates, cocaine, and cannabis were. The 1965 Drug Abuse Control Amendments changed this, helping set the stage for the range of controlled substances to be dramatically expanded with the Comprehensive Drug Abuse Prevention and Control Act of 1970.

In the 1950s, many in the federal government began to fear that certain substances—amphetamines and barbiturates in particular—were beginning to pose a public health risk. Amphetamines began to become more prevalent in the decades after World War II, particularly in the form of diet pills and other medicines sold to keep people awake. Use of barbiturates also became more widespread during this time, as they were key ingredients in medicines designed to control anxiety, such as Valium. In 1947, Massachusetts Representative Edith Rogers proposed a bill to bring barbiturates under federal control, in a law similar to the Harrison Narcotics Act. A few years later, Texas Representative Hale Boggs—the author of the 1951 Boggs Act—also proposed broadening the gamut of federally controlled substances to include barbiturates, though the Federal Bureau of Narcotics, which did not want the added responsibility of policing the use and distribution of more substances, opposed the idea, and the list of controlled substances was not expanded. Instead, the Food and Drug Administration (FDA) was empowered in 1951 to classify substances as being safe for self-administration or dangerous enough to require control by doctors and pharmacists. In October of 1955, the FDA began a campaign to stamp out the sale of stimulant drugs, including amphetamines, at gas stations and truck stops, and forty-three defendants in six states were brought up on charges.

In spite of the tightening of FDA rules governing amphetamines and barbiturates, use of these drugs continued to spread in the late 1950s. In 1955 and 1956, when Senator Price Daniel was investigating the nation's drug control policies, FDA officials warned of the dangers that barbiturates posed, claiming that they were just as dangerous, if not more so, than opiates. The mass media publicized some high-profile accidents and crimes linked to amphetamines and barbiturates, thus increasing the calls for the government to take action to control the substances. Like Harry J. Anslinger of the FBN had done in earlier decades to emphasize the need for tighter controls over narcotics, members of Congress, led by Senator Thomas Dodd, told spectacular stories about crimes, violence, and sexual deviance among youths who were under the influence of barbiturates and amphetamines. The push for tighter controls finally got the jumpstart it needed in 1962, when Senator Estes Kefauver began investigating the drug industry and the FDA. In 1962, the Kefauver Commission's findings led to the strengthening of the FDA's power to control drugs, and around the same time, the death of actress Marilyn Monroe from a barbiturate overdose increased public concern over the drugs. In 1964, Dodd introduced another piece of legislation, which he titled the Psychotoxic Drug Control Act, which would have empowered FDA inspectors to carry guns, make arrests, and seize contraband drugs. President Lyndon Johnson, however, was reluctant to empower another federal enforcement agency to enforce the nation's drug laws, though he did support the move to take action against amphetamine and barbiturate abuse. In one of his first messages as president, Johnson urged lawmakers to rush through a piece of legislation to institute tighter controls over the production and distribution of amphetamines, barbiturates, and other psychoactive drugs not covered under the Boggs Act and the Narcotic Control Act of 1956. Soon thereafter, a group of senators, including Senator Dodd, began

crafting a new piece of legislation to carry out the president's wish.

The proposal, titled the Drug Abuse Control Amendments of 1965, amended the 1938 Food, Drug, and Cosmetic Act, which had expanded the regulatory powers of the FDA. Instead of just targeting amphetamines and barbiturates, the legislation was more expansive, targeting all drugs that were depressant (containing barbiturates), stimulant (containing amphetamines), or hallucinogenic. The Amendments stipulated that individuals involved in the transfer of these drugs needed to register with the government and become subject to regular inspections. Possession of the drugs without a license or prescription was made a federal crime under the Amendments, though medical practitioners were exempt if they were using the drugs in the course of their professional practice. Though as rigorous as the laws controlling opiates, cocaine, and cannabis, the Drug Abuse Control Amendments were not as harsh when it came to punishment. The penalty for possession was a maximum of two years imprisonment and a $5,000 fine, and repeat offenders could face up to six years in prison and a fine of up to $15,000. The Amendments also increased the power of FDA officials to police drug trafficking, giving them the right to carry firearms, serve warrants, seize drugs, and in certain circumstances, even to make arrests without warrants. To gain the support of the pharmaceutical industry, which may have opposed the Amendments since they restricted access to some of its most popular drugs, it also included a provision that cracked down on the production of counterfeit drugs. The House Committee passed the proposal 402-0, and the Senate quickly followed suit. In July 1965, President Johnson signed the Amendments into law. Shortly after they were passed, fifteen substances, including LSD, mescaline, and peyote (except when being used for religious purposes), were added to the list of drugs controlled under the Amendments.

To help enforce the Amendments, the FDA borrowed officials with experience cracking down on drug trafficking from the FBN. The FDA, however, only needed to enforce the Amendments for a few years, as the drugs controlled under them were brought under the umbrella of substances governed by the Comprehensive Drug Abuse Prevention and Control Act in 1970.

(See also **Anslinger, Harry J.**; **Comprehensive Drug Abuse Prevention and Control Act**; **Federal Bureau of Narcotics (FBN)**; **Food and Drug Administration (FDA)**)

References

Belenko, Steven R., ed. 2000. *Drugs and Drug Policy in America: A Documentary History.* Westport, CT: Greenwood Press.

King, Rufus. 1972 *The Drug Hang Up: America's Fifty-Year Folly.* New York: W.W. Norton & Company.

Musto, David F. 1987. *The American Disease: Origins of Narcotic Control.* Expanded Edition. New York: Oxford University Press.

Musto, David F., ed. 2002. *Drugs in America: A Documentary History.* New York: New York University Press.

DRUG ADDICTION AND PUBLIC POLICY

Drug addiction poses difficult questions from a public policy perspective. On one hand, addiction can be treated as a disease to be eradicated, with the focus of public policy being the elimination of addictive behaviors. Yet nearly a century since the United States passed its first piece of federal drug control legislation, addiction remains prevalent, and some of the main effects of prohibitive policies have been to stimulate a black market for illicit drugs, and put a tremendous number of individuals involved in drug trafficking and drug use behind bars. The government could take a more hands-off approach to addiction, letting people use psychoactive substances and engage in addictive behaviors as they choose, even if it means that they will harm themselves and society. This approach, however, is also problematic—a fact that has been borne out by the tremendous public health and social costs that harmful psychoactive substances that are loosely regulated, such as alcohol and tobacco, have inflicted on American society. Given the shortcomings of tight controls over addictive substances, and the problems caused by control regimes that are too loose, addiction is a social problem that has no easy solutions. Consequently, addiction has spawned a good number of debates—both philosophical and practical—concerning how it should be treated by society. There are no clear answers to the social and public policy questions brought up by addiction, and according to some drug policy analysts, addiction is a problem that has no clear-cut "solution"—the best society can do is work to minimize the harm that addiction causes. This approach, however, also brings up as many questions as it answers. Most prominent among them: How exactly is society supposed to minimize the harms caused by drug addiction?

While most people agree that psychoactive drugs can cause harm to both individuals and society as a whole, a growing number of critics have begun to argue that the policies in place to restrict their use cause even more harm than the drugs themselves. The fact that the United States spends billions of dollars on drug control every year, but still has the worst drug problem of any industrialized nation, shows that perhaps the American approach to handling the drug problem has been less than ideal. Taking these considerations into account, many intellectuals have begun to argue for the decriminalization and/or legalization of marijuana, cocaine, and heroin, believing that if legal, these substances would do less harm than they currently do on the black market. There are two main lines of argument for a change in the United States' drug laws—one based on the collateral damage caused by the drug war, the other based on the public health crises caused by tight restrictions on narcotics.

The arguments for legalization are based not so much on the belief that drugs are good, but rather the understanding that the social harm they cause today comes largely from the fact that they are highly restricted. While tight controls over substances such as heroin or cocaine may keep them out of some people's hands, they also drive up their prices, leading users to steal to feed their habits. Thus while restrictive controls probably keep many individuals from using drugs, the rules that enforce them have the unintended consequence of instigating crime—theft by users seeking to feed their habits, and violent crime that results from street battles waged by cartels and street dealers. The potentially lucrative profits that the drug trade offers, especially for inner-city youths with few other opportunities for socioeconomic advancement, encourages participation in criminal activity instead of continuing school or seeking out legal work. According to studies, the potential for quick money offered by the illicit drug trade lures many youths into the drug trafficking underworld, and is partially responsible for high school dropout rates and low levels of employment in economically depressed areas. Furthermore, the fact that drug prices are so high has led highly organized and violent criminal syndicates to become involved in the trafficking and distribution of narcotics on America's streets. Even when the government was able to break up criminal organizations involved in the drug traffic in the 1970s, new homegrown and international syndicates quickly took their place, and the supply of drugs on American streets continued to grow in spite of the government's efforts to stamp out the traffic. The problems caused by these gangs, who sometimes engage in violent turf-battles, are enormous, and these groups are responsible for a good amount of the crime and random violence that takes place in the United States. If the profit motive were taken out of drug dealing, critics argue, these gangs would cease to exist, or at least cut back on their operations.

Beyond the criminal activity that occurs because of the limitations on drugs, another argument against the current control regime is that the punishments it metes out to drug-law offenders are too severe. Prisons in the United States are severely overcrowded, and a major reason for this is that so many drug-law offenders are behind bars. The number of drug-law offenders incarcerated in U.S. prisons increased eightfold between 1985 and the late 1990s, and three-quarters of the individuals locked up for drug-law violations are either Black or Hispanic. This has tremendous social costs, as it leads many individuals charged with drug-related crimes to have a criminal record early in life, meaning that even when they get out of prison, they have limited prospects of future education or employment. What is more, since drug addiction is such an expensive habit, many users spend all the money they can get on drugs and neglect other aspects of their health. Consequently, infectious diseases such as tuberculosis are particularly prevalent among the drug-using population.

Despite the fact that so many Americans lose their freedom because of anti-drug legislation, illicit drugs remain available and widely used by the people the drug laws hope to keep from using them—adolescents and young adults. In the late 1990s, over half of high school seniors reported having used an illicit drug at least once in their life—a sign that despite the efforts of law enforcement, dangerous drugs are still widely available to those who seek them out. What is more, drug enforcement is a costly enterprise, as by the mid-1990s, federal, state, and local governments spent some $35 billion per year on drug control, up from just $10 billion in the mid-1980s. The thrust of this spending is on enforcement, as three-quarters of drug control budgets go towards the apprehension, punishment, and incarceration of drug law offenders, while less than one-fifth of these budgets are devoted to the treatment of addiction. Critics also point out that an increasing proportion of drug-related arrests have been of individuals convicted of illegal possession, not sales. Between 1980 and 2006, the number of arrests for drug possession more than tripled, from 500,000

to over 1.5 million nationwide, and by 2007, 82.5% of all drug-related arrests were for possession, not manufacture or sale. Drug use was the most common reason for individuals to be arrested in 2007, with over 1.8 million people being brought up on drug-related charges nationwide.

Another argument for the legalization, or at least the loosening, of narcotics controls comes from the angle of health concerns. Since intravenous drugs such as heroin are illegal, users are often in dire need of a dose when they are able to procure them. Consequently, they take little care to practice safe hygiene when using these drugs, and they often use needles that have already been used by others. The sharing of needles by intravenous drug users is among the more prevalent ways that infectious diseases such as hepatitis and HIV-AIDS spread. In the mid-1990s, about 35% of new AIDS cases resulted from intravenous drug use, and in areas such as New York City, where the heroin addict population was particularly numerous, nearly half of intravenous drug users tested positive for HIV.

Despite all of these arguments for a reconsideration of the United States' drug policies, there are also powerful forces that advocate for the maintenance of the status quo. Chief among them is the political establishment. Though intellectuals, reformers, and a handful of lobbyists may put forward persuasive arguments as to why drug laws should be changed, few politicians want to take the risk of being seen as "soft on drugs." Voters, often concerned that either drugs or drug dealers may affect their lives or the well-being of their children, rarely elect candidates who advocate a reconsideration of the United States' drug policy. Even if candidates for public office explain that they want to reform drug laws in order to minimize the social harm that drugs cause, there is concern that softening the government's stance on narcotics would "send the wrong signal," and tacitly encourage drug use.

Furthermore, statistics show that despite the shortcomings of the American approach to drug control, limiting the availability of substances does have public health benefits. Comparisons of illicit drugs with substances such as alcohol and tobacco—which are legal, but still harmful—bear this out. Four times as many individuals in the United States suffered premature death due to alcohol than illegal drugs, and sixteen times as many premature deaths are attributable to tobacco. Despite the arguments of drug war critics that the current regime does not effectively limit the availability of illicit drugs, demographic data shows that overall, the use of controlled substances such as cocaine, heroin, and methamphetamines is declining. What is more, the restrictions that force these drugs on to the black market makes them more expensive; cocaine, for example, sold for more than the price of gold in the late 1990s. Thus while creating incentive for organized crime to become involved in the drug business, the current control regime has also made illicit drug use less prominent, simply because the drugs are too expensive for most people to procure regularly. Some critics point out that alcohol and tobacco cause greater overall harm to public health than substances that are controlled more tightly, and that therefore the legal controls over narcotics should be loosened. What they do not take into account, however, is that a major reason alcohol and tobacco cause significant damage is

because they are so widely available and so many people use them. If other drugs, such as cocaine or opiates, were as openly available as alcohol and tobacco, it is possible that they would cause even greater damage than they already do, since more people would use them.

In the last decade, policy options other than simple prohibition or legalization came to the fore in several states. According to some polls, over 60% of Americans considered drug abuse a problem that should be addressed primarily with counseling and treatment to help addicts overcome their afflictions, rather than using coercion and the criminal justice system to solve the problem. In 1996, for example, Arizona passed Proposition 200, which allowed for first- and second-time nonviolent drug-law offenders to receive treatment instead of incarceration. According to studies, the program saved the state $6.7 million in 1999, since drug treatment is less costly than imprisonment. In 2000, California passed Proposition 36, which allowed for some nonviolent drug offenders to receive community-based drug treatment instead of going to jail. Maryland also passed a treatment law that diverted many prisoners into drug treatment, and Washington, D.C. passed a similar measure in 2002. Other municipalities have passed "harm reduction" measures, such as methadone maintenance programs to help get addicts off of heroin, or needle exchange programs to prevent the spread of infectious diseases. In addition, the creation of Drug Courts, which allow for nonviolent drug-law offenders to participate in court-supervised community treatment instead of prison, have also proliferated throughout the country, and proven successful by helping addicts overcome their afflictions instead of punishing them for them. Though these alternatives have shown promise, they still have not been panaceas, as they have not "fixed" or "solved" the drug problem by any means. They have, however, opened the door for policymakers to consider new options on how to reduce the damages caused by drug addiction.

(See also **Drug Enforcement Administration (DEA)**; **Drug Courts**; **Drug Policy Alliance Network**; **Drug Smuggling**; **Reference Essay**)

References

Carson-Dewitt, Rosalyn, ed. 2001. *Encyclopedia of Drugs, Alcohol & Behavior. Second Edition.* New York: Macmillan Reference USA.

Chepesiuk, Ron. 1999. *The War on Drugs: An International Encyclopedia.* Santa Barbara, CA: ABC-CLIO.

Coombs, Robert Holman, ed. 2004. *Handbook of Addictive Disorders: A Practical Guide to Diagnosis and Treatment.* Hoboken, NJ: John Wiley & Sons, Inc.

Huggins, Laura E., ed. 2005. *Drug War Deadlock: The Policy Battle Continues.* Stanford, CA: Hoover Institution Press.

Klieman, Mark A. R. 1992. *Against Excess: Drug Policy for Results.* United States: Basic Books.

MacCoun, Robert J. and Peter Reuter. 2001. *Drug War Heresies: Learning from Other Vices, Times & Places.* Cambridge: Cambridge University Press.

U.S. Department of Justice: Bureau of Justice Statistics. 2009. "Drugs and Crime Facts." [Online article retrieved 02/26/09] http://www.ojp.usdoj.gov/bjs/dcf/enforce.htm#arrests.

West Huddleston III, C., Karen Freeman-Wilson, Douglas B. Marlowe, and Aaron Roussell. 2005. *Painting the Current Picture: A National Report Card on Drug Courts and Other Problem Solving Court Programs in the United States.* Bureau of Justice Assistance. [Online article retrieved 04/25/09] http://www.ndci.org/publications/10697_PaintPict_fnl4.pdf.

DRUG COURTS

Drug Courts are special judicial proceedings that are used as sentencing alternatives for nonviolent drug-law offenders. Instead of putting drug users in prison, drug courts allow for drug-law violators to be placed in community-based treatment programs that they are compelled to complete.

Drug Courts began in the late 1980s, when several states and local jurisdictions set them up to handle the increasing number of drug-related cases on court dockets, and address the problem of drug-law violators crowding prisons that resulted from tougher statutes against drug trafficking. At that time, Congress and state legislatures were responding to increased drug use with mandatory minimum sentences, and police were conducting rigorous campaigns that led to a large number of arrests. As a result of the emphasis on tougher enforcement, arrests for drug use skyrocketed, and court dockets became overcrowded, leaving judges little time to deal with more serious felony cases. Furthermore, the large number of drug-related incarcerations overwhelmed the capacity of local jails and state prisons in many jurisdictions. This problem was especially prevalent in Miami, which had become a major hub of the illicit drug traffic, as approximately 90% of felony defendants there had tested positive for illicit drugs. Seeing that arrests and punishments alone would not solve the drug problem, but simply overcrowd the criminal justice system, judicial and law enforcement officials in Miami decided to try providing treatment as an alternative to prosecution and incarceration for nonviolent drug-law offenders. Miami established the first Drug Court in the United States in 1989, allowing for felony drug law defendants to enter an intensive, community-based treatment and rehabilitation program under close judicial supervision. Within ten years, 471 other jurisdictions across the country had picked up on the Miami model and created their own Drug Court programs.

Drug Courts involve a collaboration of judicial, prosecution, defense, probation, law enforcement, treatment, mental health, and social services experts to provide an alternative to other interventions —namely putting drug users in prison— by identifying substance-abusing offenders and putting them in a program where under court monitoring, they undergo long-term treatment in the community. Individuals in Drug Court programs receive an intensive regimen of substance abuse and mental health treatment and case management services, and they are subject to regular drug testing and probation supervision while also reporting to regularly scheduled status hearings before a judge with expertise in dealing with Drug Court defendants. If individuals in Drug Court programs successfully complete their assigned treatment plan, charges can be either drastically reduced or dropped altogether.

Drug Courts are innovative in two major respects. First, they transform traditional judges assigned with enforcing the law into problem solvers, making them less concerned with violations of the law and more worried about the underlying reasons that people wind up in the judicial system. Bringing treatment alternatives into the judicial system, Drug Courts allow for judges to play a preventive role by addressing the problems that lead to illegal behaviors involving controlled substances. Secondly, Drug Courts develop innovative partnerships designed to deal with the needs of the criminal justice system in treating addicts by allowing for the judicial system to work with community treatment organizations. In so doing, they allow for addicts to be given treatment services by a team of providers, instead of placing the burden of rehabilitation on the criminal justice system.

Research has shown that by increasing direct supervision over drug law offenders, coordinating their access to public resources, and expediting the processing of cases, Drug Courts can help break the cycle of criminal behavior, substance abuse, and incarceration that many drug users fall into if jailed and then released into the community without much support. In 2005, the U.S. Government Accountability Office conducted a study proving that Drug Courts were effective, as individuals who went through the programs were less likely to be arrested or convicted in the future than those who did not. The study also found that Drug Courts not only helped the individuals who participated in the programs, but that they were also more cost effective than traditional sentencing since they saved the government the money it would cost to incarcerate drug law offenders.

By 2009, there were more than 2,140 Drug Courts in operation in the United States, and every state either has Drug Court programs, or is planning on creating them. Based on the success of Drug Court programs, many jurisdictions throughout the United States have created similar programs for individuals who come before the justice system but are also suffering from social problems, as the model has now been adapted to address the problems of the mentally ill, the homeless, prostitutes, and recently released inmates.

(See also **Anti-Drug Abuse Acts**; **Drug Addiction and Public Policy**; **Narcotic Addict Rehabilitation Act**)

References

Carson-Dewitt, Rosalyn, ed. 2001. *Encyclopedia of Drugs, Alcohol & Addictive Behavior. Second Edition.* New York: Macmillan Reference USA.

Chepesiuk, Ron. 1999. *The War on Drugs: An International Encyclopedia.* Santa Barbara, CA: ABC-CLIO.

Office of National Drug Control Policy. "Drug Courts." [Online article retrieved 04/25/09] http://www.whitehousedrug policy.gov/enforce/drugcourt.html.

Terry III, W. Clinton, ed. *The Early Drug Courts: Case Studies in Innovation.* Thousand Oaks, CA: SAGE Publications.

West Huddleston III, C., Karen Freeman-Wilson, Douglas B. Marlowe, and Aaron Roussell. 2005. *Painting the Current Picture: A National Report Card on Drug Courts and Other Problem Solving Court Programs in the United States.* Bureau of Justice Assistance. [Online article retrieved 04/25/09] http://www.ndci.org/ publications/10697_PaintPict_fnl4.pdf.

DRUG ENFORCEMENT ADMINISTRATION (DEA)

The Drug Enforcement Administration (DEA) is the federal agency assigned with enforcing controlled substances laws and regulations in the United States. Among the DEA's major responsibilities are the investigation and prosecution of major violators of the nation's drug laws, managing a national drug intelligence program in cooperation with federal, state, local, and foreign officials, seizing assets derived from or related to illicit drug trafficking, and corresponding with foreign governments and international bodies to coordinate transnational drug control efforts.

The DEA grew out of the reorganization of the nation's previously existing drug-law enforcement agencies in the late 1960s and early 1970s. The Federal Bureau of Narcotics within the Treasury Department had been in charge of drug-law enforcement from 1930 until 1968, when President Lyndon Johnson merged it with the Bureau of Drug Abuse Control within the Department of Health, Education, and Welfare to form a new agency, the Bureau of Narcotics and Dangerous Drugs (BNDD). Though the BNDD enjoyed some success in breaking up major drug-smuggling rings, concern over the increase in drug use in the late 1960s led the federal government to take action to further curtail drug use, most notably with the passage of the Comprehensive Drug Abuse Prevention and Control Act in 1970. Some drug enforcement efforts remained hampered, however, by bureaucratic divisions, particularly between the BNDD, the Customs Service, and other organizations within the Justice Department. In 1973, President Richard Nixon declared a "war on the drug menace" (Drug Enforcement Administration, 2008), and called for a reorganization of the nation's drug enforcement apparatus to become better coordinated in order to face what he believed was an increasingly organized and complex international drug traffic. In particular, Nixon wanted to respond to the development of cocaine processing in Latin America and heroin refining in Southeast Asia, both of which were believed to feed the illicit market in the United States. That year, he presented Reorganization Plan Number 2 to Congress, proposing the creation of a single federal agency to both consolidate and coordinate the government's drug control efforts. By Executive Order, Nixon created a new organization—the DEA—to coordinate all federal drug control efforts. Nixon's Executive Order empowered the Attorney General to coordinate all drug-law enforcement efforts among federal, state, and local authorities. In the early 1980s, the DEA began working under the FBI.

A major DEA responsibility is to develop and maintain a national narcotics intelligence system to collect and produce intelligence concerning drug trafficking, establish and maintain close working relationships with all agencies involved in drug-related intelligence gathering, and increase the efficiency of intelligence reporting and analysis. The DEA divides drug intelligence into three main categories—tactical, operational, and strategic. Tactical intelligence is designed to provide support to investigative efforts by identifying traffickers and their operations, operational intelligence is designed to provide analytical support to investigations, and strategic intelligence focuses on developing a more comprehensive understanding of the entire system by which illicit drugs are produced, smuggled, and distributed worldwide. The DEA's intelligence program has two major components—an Office of Intelligence at its national headquarters, and Regional Intelligence Units in field offices located throughout the world, which are designed to provide

a continuing flow of intelligence and facilitate the exchange of information between the agency and its field offices. Domestically, DEA agents collaborate with local law enforcement through its State and Local Task Force Program, which allows for the agency to exchange intelligence and expertise with state and local law enforcement. The DEA also has a strong international presence, as it maintains field offices in sixty-three countries. Overseas, DEA officers assist foreign drug enforcement agents in their undercover work and surveillance, and they provide their foreign counterparts with information concerning the drug trade. The DEA also conducts trainings for police in countries that host its agents at its training facilities in Quantico, Virginia, and on-site in host countries. In addition, the DEA helps coordinate transnational drug control efforts by participating in international forums on drug control that bring together drug law enforcement officials from throughout the world to share intelligence and develop strategies for cracking down on international drug traffic.

Today, the DEA is involved in virtually every aspect of the federal government's campaign against the drug traffic. It oversees the Department of Justice's Asset Forfeiture Program, which confiscates the money and property of major drug traffickers. The agency also has 106 aircraft that it deploys to gather intelligence concerning the growing of narcotics that may go to the illicit market, both domestically and abroad, and it also uses aircraft to track and crack down on smuggling operations. It oversees crop eradication programs domestically, and assists foreign governments with their own efforts to track down and destroy narcotics that are being grown for distribution on the illicit market. To assure that substances produced for medical purposes are not diverted to the black market, the DEA also has a program designed to investigate and crack down on organizations that sell legally produced drugs in violation of the Comprehensive Drug Abuse Prevention and Control Act. The DEA also has a laboratory, which it uses to test seized samples and build cases against major drug traffickers. Though the majority of its activities focus on limiting the activities of traffickers and drug dealers, the DEA also has agents assigned to serve as Demand Reduction Coordinators, who work with community coalitions, civic leaders, drug prevention organizations, treatment experts, and the general public in order to help educate the public on the dangers of illicit drug use.

Today, the DEA has approximately 5,235 special agents and an annual budget of more than $2.3 billion. Yet in spite of all of its efforts and resources, the DEA estimates that it only halts $1 billion worth of the $65 billion illegal drug trade each year.

More information on the DEA and its activities is available at its Web site: http://www.usdoj.gov/dea/.

(See also **Comprehensive Drug Abuse Prevention and Control Act**; **Drug Addiction and Public Policy**; **Federal Bureau of Narcotics (FBN)**; **United States International Drug Control Efforts**)

References

Chepesiuk, Ron. 1999. *The War on Drugs: An International Encyclopedia*. Santa Barbara, CA: ABC-CLIO.

Drug Enforcement Administration. 2008. "DEA History in Depth." [Online article accessed 04/18/09] http://www.usdoj.gov/dea/history.htm.

U.S. Department of Justice. 2009. "DEA Mission Statement." [Online article accessed 04/18/09] http://www.usdoj.gov/dea/agency/mission.htm.

U.S. Department of Justice. 2009. "Programs and Operations." [Online article accessed 04/18/09] http://www.usdoj.gov/dea/programs/progs.htm.

DRUG POLICY ALLIANCE NETWORK

The Drug Policy Alliance Network is one of America's leading organizations promoting changes in U.S. drug policy. The group maintains that policies grounded in science, concerns over health, and a respect for human rights should replace the current American drug control regime, which is rooted in largely punitive pieces of legislation, such as the of 1970 Comprehensive Drug Abuse Prevention and Control Act and the Anti-Drug Abuse Acts.

The Drug Policy Alliance Network was formed in 2000 when two organizations calling for drug policy reform—the Drug Policy Foundation, and the Lindesmith Center—merged. The Drug Policy Foundation was founded in 1987 by Arnold S. Trebach, a lawyer and professor at American University, and Kevin B. Zeese, an attorney who had worked with the National Organization for the Reform of Marijuana Laws (NORML) in the early 1980s. The group, based out of Washington, D.C., used debates and seminars on drug policy issues to promote discussion and reconsideration of the nation's drug laws. Among the major topics considered at Drug Policy Foundation meetings included the legalization and decriminalization of currently illegal substances such as marijuana and heroin, and finding ways to curb drug abuse while protecting individual rights, which they maintained were unjustly curtailed by the nation's law-and-order drug control regime. The foundation was also active in litigation concerning federal drug possession laws, and it had a grant program to support reform-minded research centers, needle exchange programs, and harm reduction groups. International financier George Soros was one of the foundation's biggest backers.

The Lindesmith Center, named for early critic of federal drug policy Alfred R. Lindesmith, was founded in 1994 by lawyer and professor Ethan Nadelmann in New York City. The Center, also funded by Soros, quickly emerged as a leading drug policy reform advocacy institute, dedicated to broadening debates on U.S. drug policy, and pushing for more harm reduction policies. To fulfill its mission of educating people interested in exploring drug policy, the Center had a library and information center, and it organized conferences and seminars that brought the media, government officials, and scholars together to discuss drug policy alternatives. In July of 2000, the Drug Policy Foundation and the Lindesmith Center merged to form the Drug Policy Alliance Network, in order to create a more powerful advocacy presence, both nationally and internationally, in their calls for drug policy reform.

Today, the Drug Policy Alliance Network continues to advocate drug policies that decrease the harms of both drug abuse and drug prohibition, and seeks solutions to the drug problem that promote safety while maintaining individual rights and liberties. The main premise of many of the Drug Policy Alliance Network's activities is that while drug abuse is problematic, attempts to combat the drug problem with zero-tolerance approaches that lead to the incarcerations of hundreds of thousands of Americans have even more disastrous results. The Network funds many projects, both nationally and at the state level. Among its more prominent programs are Safety First, a project that aims to spread information to parents and teens about psychoactive drugs and marijuana law reform projects, and it also has an Office of National Affairs in Washington that lobbies in order to promote programs that offer treatment instead of incarceration for nonviolent drug-law offenders. It also has state offices in California, New Mexico, New York, and New Jersey. On the state level, the Drug Policy Alliance Network and some of its member organizations have enjoyed significant success. Beginning in 1996 with California's Proposition 215, which modified state law to allow for the medical use of cannabis, the Drug Policy Alliance Network and its affiliated organizations have seen seven other states pass similar laws. In 2006, the Drug Policy Alliance Network helped push through needle exchange programs for intravenous drug users in New Jersey. Currently, the Drug Policy Alliance Network is organizing broad coalitions to eliminate state mandatory minimum sentencing laws in Alabama, New York, Maryland, and Wisconsin.

More information on the Drug Policy Alliance Network and its activities is available at their Web site: http://www.drugpolicy.org.

(See also **Anti-Drug Abuse Acts; Comprehensive Drug Abuse Prevention and Control Act; Drug Addiction and**

Public Policy; **Lindesmith, Alfred R.**; **National Organization for the Reform of Marijuana Laws (NORML)**))

References

Carson-Dewitt, Rosalyn, ed. 2001. *Encyclopedia of Drugs, Alcohol & Addictive Behavior. Second Edition*. New York: Macmillan Reference USA.

Chepesiuk, Ron. 1999. *The War on Drugs: An International Encyclopedia*. Santa Barbara, CA: ABC-CLIO.

Drug Policy Alliance Network. "About DPA Network." [Online articles accessed 04/23/09] http://www.drugpolicy.org/about/history/ and http://www.drugpolicy.org/about/.

DRUG SMUGGLING

As long as the United States has had laws strictly controlling the flow of drugs, there have been individuals and criminal organizations that have illicitly trafficked and sold them. For nearly a century, the government has sought to crack down on illicit drug operations, but in spite of these efforts, the black market for controlled substances has continued to flourish.

From the time that the United States passed the first federal law restricting the flow of drugs into the country with the Smoking Opium Exclusion Act in 1909, smugglers have found a way to undermine control efforts. Within months of the passage of the 1909 Act, smugglers on the West Coast began bringing opium into the country illegally, smuggling in opium that was hidden in the recesses of ships that transported ordinary consumer goods. The 1914 Harrison Narcotics Act, which placed restrictions on transfers of opiates and cocaine in the United States, had the unintended consequence of scaring doctors away from prescribing drugs to addicts legally. This led many to turn to the black market for supplies, especially after the Supreme Court ruled that the law forbade the prescription of maintenance doses of drugs to addicts in 1919. Even though the Geneva Opium Convention of 1925 closed many loopholes that had allowed for drugs that were legally purchased overseas to be smuggled internationally, the illicit drug traffic grew in the 1920s and 1930s, as organizations based in Europe, Latin America, and Asia worked to bring controlled substances into the United States. Often, traffickers would use diplomats as smugglers since they were less likely to be inspected when they entered the country. Before the 1970s, the biggest drug smuggling operation was the "French Connection," which began business in the 1930s and supplied more than 90% of the illicit heroin that made its way on to American streets until it was broken up. The French Connection was a collaboration between French criminal Jean Jehan and the Italian Mafia. The scheme worked by importing opium poppies from Turkey into southern France, where criminals ran laboratories that converted the opium into heroin. From there, French smugglers brought the drugs to the United States, and gave them to the Italian Mafia, which distributed them on the local level. The French Connection accelerated its activities in the years after World War II, producing and smuggling increasing amounts of heroin. By the early 1950s, rates of heroin addiction were on the rise in the United States, fed in large part by drugs manufactured and smuggled through the French Connection. The French Connection came to an end in the early 1970s when the United States convinced Turkey to stop growing opium, and the French police, in collaboration with U.S. drug-law enforcement agents, made a series of arrests that disrupted the operations of the drug ring. By the early 1980s, however, other smugglers began using French Connection networks, picking up where the syndicate left off by illegally importing massive amounts of heroin made from poppies grown in Iran, Pakistan, and Afghanistan into the United States.

With the dismantling of the French Connection, drug trafficking operations based in Latin America picked up as well. By the late 1970s, a syndicate led by Jaime Herrera-Nevares based out of Durango, Mexico had a $60 million per year heroin smuggling operation active in several American cities, and in the early 1980s, the group established connections in South America and began dealing in cocaine as well. A two-year investigation of the Herrera-Nevares ring culminated in the arrest of 120 traffickers in 1985, and the leaders of the gang were arrested in Mexico in 1988. The Black Tuna gang, a marijuana trafficking ring that brought illicit drugs from Colombia into the United States through Miami, smuggled at least 500 tons of marijuana into the country in the late 1970s. Around the same time, traffickers based out of Medellin, Colombia began smuggling tons of Colombian marijuana and cocaine into the United States, helping feed the growth of cocaine use in the early 1980s. The Medellin Cartel was violent, engaging in bombings, kidnappings, and killings in both Colombia and the United States in order to quell potential threats to its operations. It was also shrewd, masking its operations by becoming involved in the banking and import industries in the United States, and it even got high-ranking government officials, most notably Panamanian leader Manuel Noriega, to participate in its operations. The Medellin Cartel's dominance over the Colombia-based cocaine trade came to an end in 1993, when Colombian police killed the group's leader, Pablo Escobar. As had happened when the French Connection was dismantled, however, the decline of the Medellin Cartel did not mark the end of drug smuggling out of Colombia, as another organization, the Cali Cartel, quickly expanded to take over many of the drug trafficking operations that were once run out of Medellin. When leaders of the Cali Cartel were arrested in the 1990s, Mexican organizations emerged to fill the void, and like their predecessors in Colombia, they became involved in large-scale violence and corruption. Mexico-based groups such as the Amado Carrillo-Fuentes, Arellano-Felix Brothers, Juan-Garcia-Abrego, and the Miguel Caro-Quintero organizations have become involved in the smuggling of heroin, marijuana, cocaine, and amphetamines into the United States. In addition, Asian and African traffickers continue to bring heroin made from poppies grown in Southeast Asia into the United States, while MDMA is smuggled in from Europe and Israel. Terrorist organizations such as Al-Qaeda and rebel organizations such as Columbia's FARC are involved in drug trafficking as well. Domestic production of methamphetamines, marijuana, and hallucinogens also feeds a good portion of the illicit drug market in the United States today.

Despite rigorous enforcement efforts, the Drug Enforcement Administration estimates that it is only able to stop $1 billion worth of the $65 billion illicit drug trade each year. According to critics of American drug policy, the continued prevalence and efficiency of drug smuggling operations serves as proof that the war on drugs is an unwinnable one, and evidence that the government should try different approaches to the drug problem.

(See also **Drug Addiction and Public Policy**; **Drug Enforcement Administration (DEA)**; **Federal Bureau of Narcotics (FBN)**; **Primary Source Documents**; **Reference Essay**)

References

Campbell, Lindsay. 1909. "Foiling the Opium Smugglers." *The San Francisco Call*. January 23.

Chepesiuk, Ron. 1999. *The War on Drugs: An International Encyclopedia*. Santa Barbara, CA: ABC-CLIO.

Davenport-Hines, Richard. 2001. *The Pursuit of Oblivion: A Global History of Narcotics, 1500–2000*. London: Weidenfeld & Nicolson.

Drug Enforcement Administration. 2008. "DEA History in Depth." [Online article accessed 04/18/09] http://www.usdoj.gov/dea/history.htm.

Huggins, Laura E., ed. 2005. *Drug War Deadlock: The Policy Battle Continues*. Stanford, CA: Hoover Institution Press.

DRUGS AND THE COUNTERCULTURE

From the late 1950s through the early 1970s, the United States saw the emergence of a counterculture, a movement among youth that opposed the values of mainstream society. A key part of the counterculture's rebellion included the use of controlled psychoactive substances.

Though it had no official organization, the counterculture was a loosely connected but large community of people who, in the period roughly spanning from 1957 to 1973, opposed the mainstream culture and politics of the American establishment. The counterculture originated as a reaction against the conservative government and norms of the 1950s and in opposition to the segregation and discrimination against African Americans, and it was later galvanized by opposition to the United States' war in Vietnam, the call for women's rights, and a more general rejection of authority. The counterculture had its roots in the so-called "Beat generation" of the 1950s. Writers such as Jack Kerouac, Allen Ginsberg, and William S. Burroughs helped define the Beats as a group that rejected popular American concepts that equated success with manhood and capitalism, instead focusing on experience as the key to fulfillment. Psychoactive drugs were among the key tools that the Beats believed could be used in achieving novel and individualistic experiences, as they allowed for users to delve deeper into the unconscious and parts of the spirit that were not elements of mainstream culture. Kerouac, for example, used amphetamines while writing *The Subterraneans* and his iconic classic *On the Road*. Kerouac believed that amphetamines were valuable tools in the creative process, as they allowed for the creation of spontaneous prose, accelerating writing until it came as smoothly and naturally as thoughts, so it could be done on an unconscious level. Though Ginsberg did not use drugs regularly himself, his 1957 *Howl*, one of the most influential works of the counterculture, glorified the rebellious character of the drug user, as well as the visions of compassion and peace that could be achieved through the use of peyote.

In *Junkie*, Burroughs recounted his time as an opiate addict in the 1940s and 1950s, describing how he traveled freely and lived a lifestyle that could be a model for his fellow Beats. Burroughs' *Naked Lunch* also contained passages that framed drug use as a way to experience funny, frightening, and unreasonable excess, making it seem a chemical embodiment of rebellion against the constricting norms of mainstream society. Also experimenting with marijuana and cocaine, the Beats influenced the counterculture that emerged as a more general rejection of the mainstream.

In the 1960s, the counterculture evolved and grew in numbers, as increasing numbers of youths were mobilized by social issues and opposition to the Vietnam War. Among the main markers of the counterculture were opposition to materialism, the practice of free love, living in communes, going to rock festivals, and practicing Eastern Mysticism. Psychoactive drugs were key in many of these activities. Among the most famous countercultural figures who promoted the use of psychoactive drugs was Timothy Leary, a former Harvard professor who advocated for individuals to "tune in, turn on, and drop out" by taking LSD, and started a church called the League of Spiritual Discovery, which used LSD as a sacrament. In 1964, Ken Kesey and a group called the Merry Pranksters went on a famous cross-country trip aboard a psychedelically painted school bus, and took LSD throughout the journey. The exploits of Leary and Kesey became legendary within the counterculture, and inspired youths to experiment with psychoactive drugs—psychedelics in particular.

The use of drugs in the counterculture both hardened and softened the government's approach to handling addiction. On the one hand, it led to tighter controls, as drugs like LSD were made illegal, and a new, tougher control regime was instituted in 1970 largely in response to the rise of drug use among American youths in the counterculture. On the other hand, the spread of psychoactive drug use beyond the socioeconomic margins—to the children of the wealthy and veterans who joined the counterculture as part of their protest against the Vietnam War—made many Americans realize that drug problems could strike anyone, and spurred a move to provide more treatment options for addicts.

(See also **Comprehensive Drug Abuse Prevention and Control Act**; **Drug Abuse Control Amendments of 1965**; **Leary, Timothy**; **Narcotic Addict Rehabilitation Act**)

References

Boon, Marcus. 2002. *The Road of Excess: A History of Writers on Drugs*. Cambridge, MA: Harvard University Press.

Chepesiuk, Ron. 1999. *The War on Drugs: An International Encyclopedia*. Santa Barbara, CA: ABC-CLIO.

Davenport-Hines, Richard. 2001. *The Pursuit of Oblivion: A Global History of Narcotics, 1500–2000*. London: Weidenfeld & Nicolson.

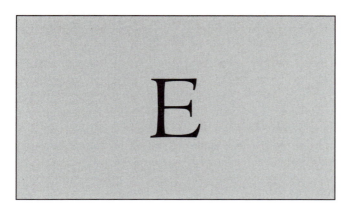

E

ENGLE V. R. J. REYNOLDS

Howard A. Engle, M.D., et al. v. R. J. Reynolds Tobacco et al., generally known as "the Engle case," was a class-action lawsuit filed in 1994 on behalf of all Floridians injured by, or addicted to, cigarettes. The Engle case was the first class-action suit against the tobacco industry that went to trial, the first class-action suit against the tobacco industry to go to verdict, and the longest trial in the history of civil litigation, and it also featured the largest figure for punitive damages ($145 billion) in legal history. These punitive damages were eventually overturned by the Florida Supreme Court, but the court still maintained the jury's verdict that the tobacco companies were responsible for smoking-related diseases.

Upon being filed in 1994 in Dade County, Florida, the Engle case stated an initial intent to sue the tobacco companies on behalf of addicted smokers throughout the country. This massive scope was diminished by the Third Circuit Court of Appeals, which ruled that the suit could only be brought in the name of Florida's smokers. Though limited to Floridians, the Engle case was still estimated to cover approximately 700,000 ill smokers in the state and their heirs.

The Engle case was filed by Stanley and Susan Rosenblatt, a Miami-based, husband-and-wife legal team that previously led another major class-action lawsuit against the tobacco industry. In *Broin v. Philip Morris*, the Rosenblatts filed suit on behalf of Norma Broin, an American Airlines flight attendant who had never smoked but still contracted lung cancer at an early age, and approximately 60,000 other nonsmoking flight attendants who sought roughly $5 billion in redress from big tobacco as a result of illnesses and injuries suffered from their exposure to secondhand smoke. Facing a difficult case, the tobacco companies avoided admitting to secondhand smoke's health risks to nonsmokers by settling, out of court, to the tune of a $349 million settlement, which consisted of $49 million for the Rosenblatts' fees and $300 million to fund a research center dedicated to smoking-related illnesses or diseases.

When the Rosenblatts filed the Engle case, therefore, they had experienced success in suing the tobacco industry, but they had not yet brought a class-action lawsuit against tobacco to trial. The Engle case would constitute the first class-action suit against the tobacco industry to make it to trial, and the judge presiding over it determined that it would be tried in three separate phases. The first stage of the Engle case concluded in July 1999, when the jury ruled that the tobacco companies were liable for punitive damages as a result of making a defective product that caused a variety of serious illnesses, including lung cancer. When the jury further concluded that the tobacco industry committed fraud, misrepresentation, and breach of warranties, it was clear that big tobacco's oft-repeated claim—that science had not proven a link between smoking and cancer—no longer held water with the American public.

The second and third phases of the Engle case dealt with determining the amount of money the plaintiffs should receive after the jury initially found the tobacco industry liable. After a very long process, the jury granted the plaintiffs approximately $145 billion in punitive damages, which constituted the largest punitive damages award in the nation's history by a very large margin. As a point of reference for this massive figure, the largest punitive damages awards prior to the Engle case came in the wake of the Exxon Valdez oil spill in Alaska. For that disaster, Exxon Corp. was found liable for $5 billion in damages. But the Engle case was history-making not just because of this extremely large payout, though, for the $145 billion was not awarded to the plaintiffs until July of 2000, thus making the case the longest trial in the history of civil litigation.

In response to this historic verdict, the tobacco companies argued that such a large monetary award could bankrupt the industry. The Florida State legislature consequently agreed to cap awards at $100 million per defendant. The tobacco companies ultimately paid even less than that to the plaintiffs, as in May 2003, the Third District Court of Appeals decertified the class-action suit and revoked the $145 billion award. The plaintiffs appealed to the Florida Supreme Court, which in July 2006 agreed with the Third District Court of Appeals, thus nullifying the punitive damages award.

The Florida Supreme Court did, however, determine that the findings of the jury in phase one of the lawsuit were valid and binding, and that individual plaintiffs could pursue litigation on those grounds. That meant that although big tobacco had avoided paying $145 billion in punitive award damages, the Engle case legally established the tobacco industry's liability for selling a defective, dangerous, and addictive product. As a result, the Engle case paved the way for individual suits against the tobacco industry that, unlike *Cipollone v. Liggett Group, Inc. et al.*, had good chances of successful litigation.

(See also **Cipollone v. Liggett Group, Inc. et al.**; **Secondhand Smoke**)

References

Brandt, Allan M. 2007. *The Cigarette Century: The Rise, Fall, and Deadly Persistence of the Product That Defined America*. New York: Basic Books.

Cordry, Harold V. 2001. *Tobacco: A Reference Handbook*. Santa Barbara, CA: ABC-CLIO.

Goodman, Jordan, ed. 2005. *Tobacco in History and Culture: An Encyclopedia*. Detroit: Thomson Gale.

FEDERAL BUREAU OF NARCOTICS (FBN)

The Federal Bureau of Narcotics (FBN) was the organization that oversaw the federal government's enforcement of the nation's narcotics laws from 1930 through 1968. Its creation in 1930 marked the first time that domestic and international narcotic control efforts were united under one agency. In its thirty-eight years of existence, the FBN was driven by the harsh, law-and-order approach of its long-time leader, Harry J. Anslinger, in its campaign against narcotics.

The idea of establishing a separate agency to oversee the federal government's narcotic control efforts came from Pennsylvania Representative Stephen G. Porter. As alcohol prohibition became increasingly unpopular over the course of the 1920s, Porter believed that narcotics prohibition could become more effective and less controversial if administered by a different agency. Charges of corruption within the Narcotic Division of the Prohibition Unit under Levi G.

Nutt also highlighted the need for a new administrative body to oversee drug control in the United States. The cumbersome nature of the Federal Narcotic Control Board, which had been established in 1922 to govern narcotic imports and exports, also necessitated a change to become more efficient. Porter believed that since a good amount of the narcotics that caused America's drug problem were being smuggled in from overseas, it was important for domestic and international efforts at drug control to be harmonized under one organizational umbrella. In 1930, Porter's vision was realized with the creation of the FBN, under the leadership of a narcotics commissioner, former Narcotic Division head Harry J. Anslinger. In addition to overseeing domestic efforts to control narcotics and enforce the provisions of the Harrison Narcotics Act and the Narcotic Drug Import and Export Act, the FBN also sent representatives to join the U.S. delegations at international drug control conferences. To help with efforts to detect and prevent drug smuggling, the

FBN had the power to assign agents to international ports and borders. The Federal Narcotics Control Board was dissolved, and its power to control imports and exports of narcotic drugs was transferred to the FBN. The head of the FBN was also authorized to advise individual states on their own drug policies and help them draft their own anti-drug laws.

Under Anslinger's leadership, the FBN was conservative at first, choosing its battles prudently in order to avoid running into many of the problems that had plagued officials charged with enforcing alcohol prohibition. For one, the FBN worked to limit the number of substances it was charged with controlling, since the more widespread the use of drugs it needed to control, the more difficult and unpopular enforcement would become. Therefore the FBN under Anslinger resisted calls to add substances such as barbiturates and amphetamines to the list of substances controlled under the Harrison Act, though it did become active in propaganda to limit marijuana use in the lead up to the passage of the 1937 Marihuana Tax Act. The FBN also knew that federal judges were less likely to convict individuals brought up on charges related to use and possession, so it made a concerted effort to bring drug law offenders to local courts where they were more likely to be given a sentence. FBN agents in the 1930s focused their enforcement efforts neither on individuals who used drugs because they were suffering from illness nor on individuals who had become addicted to drugs while using them as medicines; instead it cracked down on individuals it considered to be recreational users, and people involved in illicit trafficking and dealing. The main policy of the FBN was to cut off the illicit drug traffic at its source by

curbing the smuggling of illicit drugs into the United States, while also attacking the domestic trafficking of controlled substances.

In the early going, the FBN struggled, seeing its budget cut from $1.7 million to $1 million in its first three years of operations. The funding cuts hurt the FBN's ability to carry out enforcement activities, as in 1934 it was unable to catch any major smugglers. In 1935, the FBN was almost swallowed by an agency within the Treasury Department, and some in the government began to question if the FBN's policies on opiates were pushing opium smokers to harder forms of the drug like heroin. With the growing concern about marijuana in the mid-1930s, however, the FBN returned to prominence, helping lead the charge against the drug with a propaganda campaign that eventually led to the passage of the 1937 Marihuana Tax Act. By expanding the gamut of controlled substances, the Marihuana Tax Act gave the FBN more work to do, as from 1937 through 1942 it seized about 60,000 tons of marijuana and arrested about a thousand individuals per year for violating marijuana laws.

During World War II, smuggling and domestic addiction decreased, thanks in large part to the disruption of commerce and the cutting off of trafficking routes over the course of the conflict. When the war ended in 1945, FBN officials feared that when trade was reestablished, smuggling would resume, and that returning soldiers could come home addicted to narcotics they received on the battlefield or during their off-duty time in Europe and Asia. To deter use and smuggling, Anslinger advocated for mandatory minimum sentences for individuals convicted of violating drug laws, a wish that was granted with the passage of the Boggs Act in 1951. Not only did the Boggs Act serve as a deterrent for would-be users and dealers, but it also forced judges, some of whom had been reluctant to sentence drug-law violators to prison, to actually mete out prison sentences for drug-law offenders. To strike fear into Congress and get increases in its budget, the FBN, under Anslinger's leadership, also made strong allegations linking drug smuggling to Communist China, thus making the cause of narcotic control seem like one that not only dealt with addicts at home, but also with America's enemies abroad. In large part due to agitation from the FBN, a more severe set of federal drug laws took force in 1956 with the passage of the Narcotic Control Act. According to some critics, the FBN's activities helped accelerate the growth of the black market for narcotics, as by making them less available, it increased the profitability of smuggling and trafficking.

In the 1950s, rigid enforcement by the FBN led many in both the medical and legal professions to question the actions of the agency, criticizing FBN agents for intimidating physicians and suggesting that crime could be reduced by providing addicts with drugs instead of interning them in prisons or Public Health Service Narcotic Hospitals. The FBN responded with brochures aimed at discrediting its critics, and highlighting the dangerousness of outpatient maintenance treatment and other alternatives to its law-and-order approach to narcotics control. In some cases, the FBN went to extreme measures to silence its opponents. In the early 1960s, for example, the FBN tried to intimidate addiction researchers Marie Nyswander and Vincent Dole, who had pioneered the use of methadone treatment for weaning addicts off of opiates. When that failed, they resorted to spreading rumors about them, stealing their professional records, and spying on them.

When Anslinger retired in 1962, he was succeeded by Harry Giordano, a pharmacist, who was not as outspoken in his support of the FBN's harsh policies. Pressure to modify national drug policies from outside the agency also led to some major changes for the FBN. In 1963, a Presidential Commission on Narcotic and Drug Abuse issued a report recommending the relaxation of mandatory minimum sentences, the dismantling of the FBN, and the reallocation of its funding to the Departments of Justice, Health, Education, and Welfare. Scandals and allegations of corruption within the FBN increased pressures to dissolve the agency. In 1968, the FBN was transferred from the Treasury Department to the Justice Department, joined with the Bureau of Drug Abuse Control, and renamed the Bureau of Narcotics and Dangerous Drugs.

(See also **Anslinger, Harry J.**; **Dole, Vincent**; **Marihuana Tax Act**; **Nutt, Levi G.**; **Nyswander, Marie**; **Porter, Stephen G.**)

References

Belenko, Steven R., ed. 2000. *Drugs and Drug Policy in America*. Westport, CT: Greenwood Press.

Davenport-Hines, Richard. 2001. *The Pursuit of Oblivion: A Global History of Narcotics, 1500–2000*. London: Weidenfeld & Nicolson.

Musto, David F. 1987. *The American Disease: Origins of Narcotic Control*. Expanded Edition. New York: Oxford University Press.

FETAL ALCOHOL SYNDROME (FAS)

Fetal Alcohol Syndrome (FAS) is a pattern of behavioral, growth, and facial abnormalities that can occur in children born after prenatal exposure to alcohol. The term was first used clinically in 1973. Although the terms "fetal alcohol effects" (FAE) and "alcohol-related birth defects" (ARBD) have also been employed by scholars, scientists, and physicians in subsequent years, FAS is still used to refer to a set of symptoms that can include low birth weight, an undersized head, heart malformations, a cleft palate, and cognitive and behavioral anomalies and limitations, among many other things. It is estimated that FAS is the number one cause of mental retardation in the United States, with a rate of occurrence that may be anywhere between one birth per 750 and 1.95 births per 1,000.

People have been aware of the dangers of consuming alcohol while pregnant for centuries, but it was not until the gin epidemic of the 1750s—when gin, for the first time, became inexpensive and prevalent enough for large numbers of lower-income women to be able to purchase it —that a greater reckoning of the impact of a mother's drinking upon her child's health took place. Still, it would take over 200 years before science developed the term FAS to refer to the set of abnormalities resulting from prenatal exposure to alcohol, with Jones, Smith, Ulleland, and Streissguth's foundational article, "Pattern of Malformation in Offspring of Chronic Alcoholic Mothers after Prenatal Exposure to Alcohol," identifying the major traits of the syndrome in 1973. Soon after the term FAS was offered, the terms FAE and ARBD were introduced to describe individuals who

had some, but not all, of the components of FAS. As a result of these terminological developments, some diagnostic murkiness entered the field.

Though defining exactly what constitutes FAS is difficult and debatable, a picture of its symptoms can nonetheless be painted with a fairly fine brush. A child with FAS will likely experience growth deficiencies that can be manifest in the form of being underweight, shorter than normal, or possessing a small head size or circumference (microcephaly). Beyond these general growth deficiencies, a more particular set of physical problems is commonly associated with FAS, as afflicted children may have eye-slit fissures, hollow lower chests, permanently curved fingers, scoliosis, cleft lips or palates, the fusion of the radius and ulna at the elbow, heart defects, or kidney malformations. Cognitive and memory defects are also components of FAS, and common abnormalities of this type are developmental delays, hyperactivity, sleep disturbances, and difficulties understanding cause and effect.

It has been difficult for physicians and scientists to determine what exactly causes FAS or what a mother can safely do, beyond maintaining complete abstinence, to guarantee her child does not get FAS, but it is largely understood that the timing of a woman's drinking during pregnancy is a determining factor. For instance, consuming alcohol during the first trimester can lead to major physical abnormalities in the child (such as damage to various organs and facial anomalies), while drinking in the second trimester increases the chances of more subtle physical abnormalities and the mother undergoing a spontaneous abortion. The consumption of alcohol in the third trimester is associated with low birth weights and can lead to pre- and post-natal growth retardation. Central nervous system damage can occur as a result of drinking at any point in the pregnancy.

The only way to ensure that a child will not be born with FAS is for the mother to abstain from all drinking, but a pregnant mother who drinks will not necessarily damage the embryo. The level at which a mother's drinking becomes a risk factor in the appearance of FAS has been studied, and the minimum number of drinks consumed in the span of one occasion during pregnancy that has been found to cause FAS is five. More specifically, it has been shown that imbibing five drinks in the course of one night (even if that is all the drinking a mother does in one week) is more damaging to the fetus than consuming a single drink per night for five different nights over the span of one week. Even having five drinks on one occasion does not guarantee FAS will ensue, as relatively few of the 2 to 3% of pregnant women who drink at this level have children with FAS. This suggests that other factors in addition to alcohol consumption are at play in FAS.

Poverty, and the poor nutrition and high levels of stress that often come with it are widely seen as factors that make FAS more likely. Smoking, too, can contribute to FAS's appearance, as it, by itself, is capable of producing birth defects. A mother's smoking means less oxygen reaches cells that are critical for normal central nervous system development, and it can generate respiratory illnesses and a low birth weight, with some studies showing that the babies of smoking mothers weigh, on average, 200 grams less than the infants of nonsmoking mothers. Smoking thus seems to elevate the risk of FAS occurrence for mothers who also drink. Drugs—particularly those taken intravenously—similarly expose the fetus to a variety of risks, and maternal drug use is also associated with an increased risk of FAS occurrence for the children of pregnant women who consume alcohol.

Regardless of what exactly is necessary to cause the syndrome, FAS is estimated to be the single greatest cause of mental retardation in the United States. The numbers vary a bit, but somewhere between one out of 750 and 1.95 out of 1,000 babies born in the United States are considered to have FAS. This figure is about twice that of the overall rate of FAS in the industrialized world, which stands at 0.97 births per 1,000. In comparison with Europe, American FAS rates appear even higher, as only 0.08 births per 1,000 in Europe are considered to have FAS.

The high rates of FAS in the United States have generated a fairly substantial public awareness of the perils of drinking during pregnancy. Not only are most Americans generally cognizant that abstinence during pregnancy is the best means of preventing FAS, but all alcoholic beverages have labels that alert consumers to the fact that alcohol can cause birth defects. However, the drinking behavior of pregnant women, and particularly that of women who consume at particularly dangerous levels, seems to have changed little as a result of this knowledge. FAS thus remains a serious public health issue.

(See also **Reference Essay**)

References

Abel, Ernest L. 1998. *Fetal Alcohol Abuse Syndrome*. New York: Plenum Press.

Blocker, Jr., Jack S., David M. Fahey, and Ian R. Tyrrell, eds. 2003. *Alcohol and Temperance in Modern History: An International*

Encyclopedia. Santa Barbara, CA: ABC-CLIO.

Carson-Dewitt, Rosalyn, ed. 2001. *Encyclopedia of Drugs, Alcohol & Addictive Behavior. Second Edition.* New York: Macmillan Reference USA.

Jones, Kenneth L., David W. Smith, Christy N. Ulleland, and Ann Pytkowicz Streissguth. 1973. "Pattern of Malformation in Offspring of Chronic Alcoholic Mothers after Prenatal Exposure to Alcohol." *Lancet.* 301: 1267–1271.

FOOD AND DRUG ADMINISTRATION (FDA)

The Food and Drug Administration (FDA) is the federal agency charged with ensuring the safety and efficacy of ingredients and products. The primary focus of the FDA in its earliest years was upon food regulation, but the regulation of drugs like patent medicines, prescription-only drugs, and narcotics became a greater concern for the agency over the course of the ensuing decades. More recently, the FDA has taken an interest in regulating tobacco as well.

The FDA emerged from the development of other government agencies responsible for ensuring the public safety of consumer products. Originally called the Division of Chemistry, which was established in 1862, the group's name was changed to the Bureau of Chemistry in 1901. The Pure Food and Drug Act of 1906 gave the Bureau of Chemistry new powers, enabling it to regulate the interstate commerce in adulterated or mislabeled foods, enforce purity standards laid out in the U.S. Pharmacopoeia and National Formulary, and ban the making of false or misleading claims about foods and drugs. Under the leadership of Harvey Washington Wiley, the chief chemist of the Department of Agriculture, the Bureau of Chemistry enthusiastically enforced the law. Following Wiley's resignation in 1912, drug regulation became a greater concern for the agency, and seizures of mislabeled drugs escalated in the 1920s and 1930s. In 1927, its name was changed to the Food, Drug, and Insecticide Administration, and the nonregulatory research functions of the group were transferred to other government agencies. In July of 1930, the organization's name was changed again to its current title—the Food and Drug Administration.

The FDA's 1938 Food, Drug, and Cosmetic Act targeted a new generation of bogus product, tonics, and cures. Effectively replacing the somewhat outdated 1906 legislation, the new act not only brought cosmetics and medical devices under the purview of the agency, but also increased the agency's regulatory power over drugs. Under the terms of the new law, all drugs were required to be labeled with directions for safe usage, and manufacturers needed to prove to the FDA that their drugs were safe before they could be sold on the market. In a related move, the FDA established requirements for prescription-only (non-narcotic) drugs. Drug abuse became a central concern of the FDA in ensuing decades. In fact, between the 1940s and the 1960s, the illegal sale and abuse of amphetamines and barbiturates required more regulatory effort by the FDA than all other drug problems in the nation combined. Dealing with this level of drug abuse required the FDA to go well beyond its origins in a chemistry lab, as the agency's interdiction efforts sometimes involved the work of undercover inspectors. Congress, too, recognized the seriousness of the situation, and granted the FDA increased authority over drugs including amphetamines, barbiturates, and hallucinogens with the passage of the 1965 Drug Abuse Control Amendments. In 1940, the FDA was moved from the Department of Agriculture to the Federal Security Agency, and in 1953, it was transferred again, to the Department of Health, Education, and Welfare. The FDA was then transferred to the Public Health Service within the Department of Health, Education, and Welfare in 1968, before being transferred to its current home, within the Department of Health and Human Services.

The FDA became interested in the possibility of regulating tobacco in early 1994, and a letter from FDA commissioner David Kessler later that year made public the agency's view that such regulation could be warranted if cigarettes were viewed as nicotine-delivery devices. With the inside information of whistleblower Jeffrey Wigand, Kessler determined that the tobacco industry used nicotine as a drug, intentionally enhanced the addictive properties of cigarettes, and marketed their products to children. After receiving President Clinton's approval, Kessler invoked the Food, Drug, and Cosmetic Act in announcing that since cigarettes were essentially a drug-delivery system, the FDA would henceforth regulate all nicotine-containing products. The FDA's pronouncement also included resolutions regarding tobacco advertising and the sale of tobacco products to minors. For instance, tobacco advertisements in publications that children might read would only be allowed to appear in black and white, thus ostensibly making them less appealing to youths. In response to Kessler's announcement, the FDA was sued by the tobacco industry, which claimed that only Congress had the authority to regulate tobacco because cigarettes did not fit the Food, Drug, and Cosmetic Act's definition of a drug or drug-delivery device. The case ultimately wound up in the Supreme Court, which ruled, 5-4, that the FDA did not have the jurisdiction to regulate tobacco. In order for the FDA to gain regulatory control over tobacco, Congress needed to pass a law granting it authority, something that may finally happen in 2009 if the Family Smoking Prevention and Tobacco Control Act becomes law.

(See also **Drug Enforcement Administration (DEA)**; **Kessler, David**; **Primary Source Documents**; **Pure Food and Drug Act**; **Wigand, Jeffrey**; **Wiley, Harvey Washington**)

References

Blocker, Jr., Jack S., David M. Fahey, and Ian R. Tyrrell, eds. 2003. *Alcohol and Temperance in Modern History: An International Encyclopedia*. Santa Barbara, CA: ABC-CLIO.

Brandt, Allan M. 2007. *The Cigarette Century: The Rise, Fall, and Deadly Persistence of the Product That Defined America*. New York: Basic Books.

CNN.com. 2009. "House Passes Bill Giving FDA Power Over Tobacco Ads, Sales." [Online article retrieved 05/22/09] http://www.cnn.com/2009/POLITICS/04/02/tobacco.regulation/index.html.

Cordry, Harold V. 2001. *Tobacco: A Reference Handbook*. Santa Barbara, CA: ABC-CLIO.

Lender, Mark Edward. 1984. *Dictionary of American Temperance Biography: From Temperance Reform to Alcohol Research, the 1600s to the 1980s*. Westport, CT: Greenwood Press.

Swann, John P. "History of the FDA." [Online article retrieved 05/22/09] http://www.fda.gov/oc/history/historyoffda/default.htm.

GAMBLERS ANONYMOUS (GA)

Founded in 1957 in Los Angeles, California, Gamblers Anonymous (GA) is the United States' first mutual support organization for problem or compulsive gamblers. The organization was born out of the agreement between two Alcoholics Anonymous (AA) members to apply the Twelve Steps of AA to their gambling problems, and the group's initial meeting marked the first time that the addictive-disease model became the basis for recovery from gambling addiction. GA, which developed a screening questionnaire that was used for years by professionals to determine if an individual was a compulsive gambler, grew into an organization of approximately 1,000 local groups by 2005.

GA began with the January 1957 meeting, in Reno, Nevada, of two AA members who were being divorced by their wives on account of their gambling problems. The two men met regularly, avoided gambling, and determined that a twelve-step approach like the one used by AA to promote alcohol abstinence could be applied to individuals with gambling problems. They resolved to hold such a meeting when they returned to Los Angeles, and the first official GA meeting took place in that city on September 13, 1957.

Just as AA meetings revolve around the organization's stance that alcoholism is a disease, so too are GA meetings guided by its members' view that compulsive gambling is a progressive illness that can be arrested, but never fully cured. Similarly, GA members are encouraged to take a first step towards recovery by admitting a powerlessness over their addiction—in this case gambling. The rest of AA's Twelve Steps, including submitting to a personally defined "higher power," are adopted by GA, and a slightly modified version of AA's Twelve Traditions also figures prominently in GA.

One GA innovation, however, was the development of a questionnaire intended

155

to determine whether an individual was a compulsive gambler. The document, which consisted of twenty questions, assessed the respondent's gambling history, attitude toward gambling, and ways in which gambling had affected the individual's life. Questions included: Have you ever lost time from work or school on account of gambling? Has gambling ever made your home life unhappy? Have you felt remorse after gambling? Do you ever gamble to deal with financial difficulties? If you lose while gambling, do you feel the need to immediately win back your losses? Have you gambled beyond your last dollar? Have you borrowed to finance your gambling? Have you ever celebrated good news by gambling for a few hours? GA determined that most compulsive gamblers would answer affirmatively to at least seven of the twenty prompts, and professionals used the GA questionnaire as their primary means of determining whether an individual was a compulsive gambler up until 1980, when the mental health establishment began recognizing problem gambling as a psychiatric disorder, which they called pathological gambling.

In 1972, the Board of Trustees of GA in the New York City area took the step of asking their Spiritual Advisor, Monsignor Joseph A. Dunne, to create a Council on Compulsive Gambling, which would work to call national attention to the issue of compulsive gambling. GA could not establish such an organization itself and still remain true to its code of anonymity, but it nonetheless played a catalytic role in the foundation of what would become the National Council on Problem Gaming (NCPG), the nation's first organization dedicated to the issue of problem gaming.

In addition to spurring the creation of the NCPG, GA also generated a parallel organization, Gam-Anon. Just as Al-Anon was born out alcoholics' family members and loved ones desiring mutual support in dealing with the difficulties of having an alcoholic relative, so, too, was Gam-Anon created in New York to assist relatives and loved ones of compulsive gamblers. And just as Alateen was founded to help the children of alcoholic family members, Gam-A-Teen emerged to provide mutual aid and support to the children of compulsive gamblers.

(See also **Al-Anon**; **Alateen**; **Alcoholics Anonymous (AA)**; **Custer, Robert L.**; **National Council on Problem Gaming (NCPG)**)

References

Carson-Dewitt, Rosalyn, ed. 2001. *Encyclopedia of Drugs, Alcohol & Addictive Behavior. Second Edition.* New York: Macmillan Reference USA.

Dunne, Joseph A. 1985. "Increasing Public Awareness of Pathological Gambling Behavior: A History of the National Council on Compulsive Gaming." *Journal of Gambling Behavior.* 1, no. 1: 8–16.

Gam-Anon. "About Gam-Anon." [Online information retrieved 05/21/09] http://www.gam-anon.org/about.htm.

Gamblers Anonymous. 2009. "Gamblers Anonymous." [Online article; retrieved 1/31/09] http://www.gamblersanonymous.org/about.html.

Gamblers Anonymous. 2009. "History." [Online article; retrieved 1/31/09] http://www.gamblersanonymous.org/history.html.

Petry, Nancy M. 2005. "Gamblers Anonymous and Cognitive-Behavioral Therapies for Pathological Gamblers." *Journal of Gambling Studies.* 21, no. 1 (March): 27–33.

HAGUE CONVENTION

The second major international conference on opium control met at The Hague, in the Netherlands, in 1911. Though it took almost a decade for the agreements reached at The Hague to take effect, the conference was significant since it established the principles of international narcotics control that would shape drug policies across the globe until the 1960s.

Thirteen countries had met at Shanghai in 1909 in the first meeting that aimed to create a global narcotics control regime. Despite the agreement on general principles for drug control, however, few tangible results came from the Shanghai meeting since most of the major powers were unwilling to put their national drug industries at risk. Disappointed with the lack of decisive action at Shanghai, the United States began advocating for another international conference in the autumn of 1909. Though officials from many of the countries that participated in the Shanghai meeting were reluctant to participate in another conference, the United States, led by anti-opium reformer Hamilton Wright, continued to push for another conference, which eventually met at The Hague in December of 1911. Wright hoped to accomplish more with this conference than the vague and noncommittal agreements struck at Shanghai. Asking countries to take concrete steps and not just make promises, the United States hoped that the meeting would mark the beginning of a unified and global opium control regime.

The United States set the agenda for the conference, asking participants to consider an international scheme that would strictly regulate the production, manufacture and distribution of opiates, harmonize penal sanctions for drug law violations across the world, and grant reciprocal rights to search ships suspected of smuggling the drug. As they did at Shanghai, however, other nations balked at the costs such international regulations would have on their own commercial interests. Given the profitability of colonial opium manufactures and monopolies throughout Asia, many powers were unwilling to sacrifice such a significant source of revenue. Furthermore, countries feared that if they agreed to stop producing and shipping the drugs, others would step up their opiate operations so they could profit from the fact that other drug-producing nations were cutting back. The fact that two major players in the drug business—Turkey, which was a major producer of raw opium, and Switzerland, which was a principal manufacturer of morphine and heroin—were not at the conference made this fear all the more legitimate. There was also a rivalry between producing and manufacturing countries at the conference. Some participants argued that even if the opium-growing countries agreed to limit the amounts they sent to the Far East, states involved in the manufacture of opiate pharmaceuticals would take advantage, and flood the Asian market with other drugs such as morphine and heroin. Thus in order to institute effective control over the transport of opiates, any international agreement would have to meet two key prerequisites. First, it would need to have the signatures not only of nations who drafted the agreement, but also those of all countries involved in the opium trade. Otherwise, the opiate traffic would not be checked, but simply move to wherever it could operate without restriction. Secondly, such an agreement could not simply target raw opium, but would need to control the drug in its manufactured and synthetic forms as well.

Given the potential drawbacks of such strict regulations, the participants at the conference were not eager to commit themselves to the narcotic control effort wholeheartedly. Commercial concerns aside, there were other major stumbling blocks

that made the United States' goal of instituting strict and internationally uniform controls untenable. Some nations (France, Germany, Holland) were reluctant to sign an agreement that would require them to alter their national legislation, regulate their drug manufacturing industries, or allow foreign agents to search their ships; others (Britain and China) still did not agree with the U.S. delegation on how to distinguish medical from recreational drug use, thus complicating the task of defining what sort of opium use was acceptable and what was not. The agreement that emerged out of the conference in January of 1912, therefore, did little to create an effective drug control regime, as representatives only agreed to sign a convention that was both vague and noncommittal.

The Convention's biggest weakness lay in its provisions concerning ratification. To ease concerns that drug control would be ineffective unless all countries involved in the drug trade (and not just the ones present at the conference) were in agreement, the representatives at The Hague agreed that the protocols—indefinite though they were—would not take effect until the entire drug-producing world signed the Convention. Thus in Article 22, the Convention listed thirty-four countries that were not present at the conference but would need to sign the treaty in order for it to become operational. If all of the listed countries did not sign by the end of 1912, there was to be a second conference at The Hague to reconsider a new convention. This proved a major impediment to ratification. By the middle of 1913, twelve of the thirty-four countries had still not signed, among them a major opium producer (Turkey). At the follow-up meeting in July of 1913, a handful of countries announced that they would not ratify the treaty at the present time because attempts at control without the participation of all producing and manufacturing countries would be useless. Thus another deadline for universal ratification was set, this time for December 31, 1913. Though three more countries signed the agreement by the end of the year, nine nations had yet to ratify it, many of them opium-growing states in Southeastern Europe that were too preoccupied fighting wars to consider the treaty. A third such conference then met at The Hague in June of 1914, and called for all powers to sign by the end of the year. But before the ratification process could be completed, the beginning of World War I in August derailed it, and put the task of international drug control on the back-burner until the end of the conflict.

Despite its shortcomings and the fact that it did not take effect before the summer of 1914, the Hague Convention marked a broad step towards drug regulation by establishing a framework that would shape drug laws across the world. For one, it laid out scientific definitions of some of the major drugs that should be controlled—"raw opium" (coagulated juice obtained from the *Papaver somniferum* plant), "prepared" (i.e. smoking) opium (raw opium that is dissolved, boiled, roasted, and fermented), morphine (the alkaloid $C_{17}H_{19}NO_3$), heroin (diacetyl-morphine, $C_{21}H_{23}NO_5$), and cocaine ($C_{17}H_{21}NO_4$). In addition, the convention also specified that medical preparations that had these drugs as ingredients should be regulated, recommending that any medicines with more than 0.2% morphine, 0.1% heroin, or 0.1% cocaine become subject to government restrictions. In so doing, it set an internationally standardized scientific definition of what substances

were to be controlled, and at what levels. These standards would guide many countries as they began drafting their own drug control legislation over the next five years. Furthermore, in spite of its wishy-washy language and complicated ratification procedure, the Hague Convention set out what the major goals of drug control were to be—the limitation of exports and imports, tight regulations that restricted access to the drugs for anyone other than doctors and pharmacists, the repression of opium smoking, the proper labeling of narcotics, and a crackdown on smuggling. In the United States, The Hague agreement helped give momentum to the move towards domestic drug control, which resulted in the Harrison Narcotics Act in 1914. In addition, the provisions of The Hague treaty would also have significant repercussions after World War I. Article 273 of the Treaty of Versailles, which ended the war, forced many countries that had yet to sign The Hague agreement to implement the provisions it laid out. The principles of the Hague Convention also helped set the agenda when the international community met to reconsider the drug problem at the League of Nations in the 1920s.

(See also **Harrison Narcotics Act**; **League of Nations**; **Shanghai Commission**; **Wright, Hamilton**)

References

Bewley-Taylor, David R. 1999. *The United States and International Drug Control, 1909–1997*. London: Pinter.

Davenport-Hines, Richard. 2001. *The Pursuit of Oblivion: A Global History of Narcotics, 1500–2000*. London: Weidenfeld & Nicolson.

Lyons, F. S. L. 1963. *Internationalism in Europe, 1815–1914.* Leyden, Netherlands: A.W. Sythoff-Leyden.

McAllister, William B. 2000. *Drug Diplomacy in the Twentieth Century.* London: Routledge.

HARRISON NARCOTICS ACT

The Harrison Narcotics Act, which was passed in 1914 and took effect in 1915, marked the beginning of federal narcotics control in the United States, putting certain potentially addictive drugs into a separate legal category. Until the passage of the Comprehensive Drug Abuse Prevention and Control Act of 1970, it remained the overarching piece of federal drug policy legislation in the country.

Before the Harrison Narcotics Act, there were no federal laws governing commerce or use of narcotics other than the 1906 Pure Food and Drug Act, which required preparations, including narcotics, to be properly labeled, and the 1909 Smoking Opium Exclusion Act, which prohibited the importation of opium prepared for smoking into the United States. There were a handful of state laws and other local regulations governing drugs like morphine, opium, and cocaine, but the federal government did not have any overarching laws limiting the domestic trade and exchange of these drugs.

The move towards federal regulations covering narcotics began in the first decade of the twentieth century. Many reformers considered the use of narcotics to be immoral, and also used racist scare-tactics associating the use of certain drugs with minorities, claiming that opium was part of a Chinese effort to poison White Americans, or that cocaine made Blacks particularly violent. Some leaders in Washington also wanted the United States to pass a law controlling domestic drug use to prove to other countries participating in the Shanghai and Hague conferences on international drug control that the United States was sincere in its efforts to create a global drug control regime.

Hamilton Wright, a member of the U.S. delegation at these international conferences and leading proponent of stricter drug control, began working with members of Congress to draft a federal law controlling narcotics in 1909. Wright's proposed law would have controlled the sale and purchase of drugs through taxation and obligated vendors to register with the government, record all of their drug transactions, and most importantly, require them to have a special stamp issued by the federal government. By including provisions that would have punished anyone who was caught in possession of narcotics without a government stamp, Wright's plan would have made it possible for the federal government to decide who could, and who could not, sell and possess these drugs. First, Wright tried to persuade Illinois Congressman James R. Mann to introduce the bill, but Mann refused. Later, he convinced Vermont Congressman David Foster to introduce another such bill that would have put new controls over opiates, cocaine, chloral, and cannabis, but the bill was eventually defeated in 1911 due to opposition from the pharmaceutical industry.

Undeterred by these failures, Wright continued his efforts to get Congress to pass a federal drug control law. In 1912, when Wright returned from The Hague conference, he believed that the United States now had a moral and diplomatic obligation to conform to the guidelines laid out by the convention and pass stricter controls over the domestic trade in narcotics. He secured the agreement of New York Democrat Francis Burton Harrison to help get his anti-narcotics proposal approved by Congress. Harrison worked with Wright to assure his fellow representatives that the bill would not harm the interests of the medical or pharmaceutical professions, and consulted with these groups to gain their support. In 1913, a National Drug Trade Conference met in Washington to consider Wright's proposed bill. The pharmaceutical industry representatives and pharmacist organizations opposed the bill because it would have created an overly complex procedure for selling narcotics, and would have been too cumbersome in its record-keeping requirements. Several suggestions put forth by the National Drug Trade Conference made their way into the bill that Harrison eventually proposed; chloral and cannabis were dropped from the list of drugs to be restricted (leaving just opium, cocaine, their derivatives and salts), the amount of the proposed tax on sellers of the drugs was reduced, the recordkeeping requirements were simplified, and preparations containing small amounts of the controlled substances were exempted from the law. In June of 1913, the chairman of the conference signed a draft of the bill, and Harrison, now with the support of the medical and pharmaceutical professions, presented the bill in Congress that summer.

The bill Harrison proposed included many compromises with the professional interests that had opposed earlier versions of Wright's narcotics control bills, but still imposed strict rules governing the transfer and sale of many dangerous drugs. The bill required anyone who purchased narcotics to keep records of their purchases for up to two years so that government agents could inspect them to assure that the drugs were obtained legally; copies of orders for narcotics now had to be kept on file at local revenue offices; pharmacists could only sell preparations containing opium, cocaine, or their derivatives to people who presented a prescription issued by a physician, dentist, or surgeon registered under the Act; patent medicines containing more than very small amounts of morphine, cocaine, opium, and heroin could no longer be sold by mail order or in general stores; retail dealers and physicians who dispensed the drugs needed to have a tax stamp in order to sell the drugs; and everyone who sold narcotics had to be registered with the government. Congress passed the bill in late June. In the Senate, the Finance Committee made one significant change to the bill, allowing physicians to provide narcotics to patients by mail, and after some prolonged debates over the right of physicians to prescribe narcotics and what amount of heroin should be permitted in medicinal preparations, the bill was finally passed in December of 1914 and took effect in March of 1915. The Treasury Department, which issued the stamps allowing people to possess narcotics, was put in charge of administrating the law. Violations of the Act could be punished by a fine of up to $2,000 or up to five years in prison. Over five years after Wright's first proposal, the Harrison Act finally instituted national controls over the domestic traffic in opiates and cocaine.

Ultimately, the Harrison Act was an important first step, but not the ultimate end, of the legislative effort to institute a nationwide system of narcotics control in the United States. It restricted the freedom to sell narcotics by requiring revenue stamps, and benefited large pharmaceutical firms since it allowed for the prosecution of small, unregistered peddlers and patent-medicine salesmen. Yet it did not address the questions of addiction or recreational narcotics use. According to the Act, a medical professional could give prescriptions for drugs or distribute them "in the course of his professional practice" and in "good faith." While meant to prohibit the distribution of drugs to recreational users and addicts, it was unclear if it was within the scope of a doctor's "professional practice" to give drugs to an addict who needed them to avoid withdrawal symptoms. The ambiguities of the law would not be made clear until the Supreme Court set precedents in *Jin Fuey Moy v. United States* in 1916 and, in 1919, *United States v. Doremus* and *Webb et al. v. United States*. Building upon the legal edifice constructed by the Harrison Act, the United States would have a comprehensive narcotics control regime in place by the 1920s.

(See also **Pure Food and Drug Act**; **Smoking Opium Exclusion Act**; *Jin Fuey Moy v. United States*; *United States v. Doremus* and *Webb et al. v. United States*; **Wright, Hamilton**)

References

Belenko, Steven R., ed. 2000. *Drugs and Drug Policy in America: A Documentary History*. Westport, CT: Greenwood Press.

Courtwright, David T. 2001. *Dark Paradise: A History of Opiate Addiction in America*. Cambridge, MA: Harvard University Press.

Musto, David F. 1987. *The American Disease: Origins of Narcotics Control*. Expanded Edition. New York: Oxford University Press.

Musto, David F., ed. 2002. *Drugs in America: A Documentary History*. New York: New York University Press.

HAZELDEN FOUNDATION

The Hazelden Foundation stands as one of the nation's most renowned addiction treatment facilities. A nonprofit organization, the Hazelden Foundation utilizes a multidimensional approach to annually treating thousands of patients addicted to alcohol and other drugs in multiple locations across four states. Hazelden also serves as a major publisher of literature related to addiction and recovery, and the Hazelden Foundation includes research facilities and a graduate school in addiction studies.

The first Hazelden treatment facility was launched in Center City, Minnesota in 1948 as a small institution devoted to the care and rehabilitation of alcoholic priests and professionals. As such, much of the funding for the first Hazelden center came from local businesses and the local Catholic diocese, and in its early years, Hazelden stressed a simple approach to treating addicts. Residents at Hazelden were expected to make their beds, behave properly, talk with one another, and attend daily lectures on the Twelve Steps of Alcoholics Anonymous (AA).

Over time, however, the Hazelden approach took on other facets as it expanded. With the aid of greater financial contributions from donors and significant collaborations with other alcoholic treatment facilities in Minnesota, Hazelden began employing what would come to be called the "Minnesota Model." This model emphasized understanding alcoholism as a progressive disease that necessitated lifelong abstinence, and it advocated a different approach to treating alcoholics. Instead of shunning drunks as societal failures, Hazelden's Minnesota Model emphasized treating alcoholics with respect and put great importance on creating a mutually supportive environment for treating addicts. The Twelve Step approach continues to be a part of the Minnesota Model, but it has been supplemented by additional rehabilitation measures to form a multidimensional approach to addiction treatment. The result is a Hazelden more broadly developed than in its original form, and over the course of its history, more than 200,000 addicted individuals have been treated at Hazelden facilities.

In its second decade, Hazelden began a process of physical expansion. It opened a halfway house for men in 1953 and a treatment facility for women in 1956, and Hazelden geographically branched out by opening treatment centers in Chicago, Manhattan (NY), Newberg, Oregon, and multiple locations within Minnesota. Through these branches, Hazelden has also developed education and training programs. Hazelden's programs include a certificate program for chemical dependency counselors and a Graduate School of Addiction Studies, which opened in 1999. In addition, Hazelden offers a Pastoral Training Program and Professional-in-Residence and Physician-in-Residence programs. The Butler Center for Research is also a part of the Hazelden Foundation, and it seeks to improve recovery from addiction by conducting clinical research, collaborating with other research centers, and disseminating scientific findings. Through these expansions as an institution, Hazelden generally moved from a focus on providing treatment services to an emphasis on providing patients with recovery services that cover a wider range of problems beyond alcoholism. Thus, at Hazelden's Renewal Center, people suffering from depression, anxiety, posttraumatic stress disorder, gambling problems, and eating disorders are given recovery services.

Finally, Hazelden has a long tradition of publishing within the field of addiction and recovery literature. This began with purchasing the rights to the recovery meditation book *Twenty-Four Hours a Day*, which it published to great success; it has sold over 8 million copies to date. It has also published important texts like *Not-God: A History of Alcoholics Anonymous* and *Codependent No More*. Hazelden claims to have sold 2,649,955 publications in 2007 alone, and over the course of its history, it has distributed over 50 million publications.

(See also **Alcoholics Anonymous (AA)**)

References

Blocker, Jr., Jack S., David M. Fahey, and Ian R. Tyrrell, eds. 2003. *Alcohol and Temperance in Modern History: An International Encyclopedia*. Santa Barbara, CA: ABC-CLIO.

Hazelden. "Hazelden Touches the Lives of People Everyday." [Online article retrieved 11/12/2008.] http://www.hazelden.org/web/public/whatishazelden.page.

HILL & KNOWLTON

Hill & Knowlton is one of the most influential public relations firms in the United States, and from 1953 to 1968 it represented the tobacco industry. The CEOs of major tobacco companies, in a rare moment of cooperation, hired the firm in the midst of a growing wave of reports linking smoking to cancer, and one of Hill & Knowlton's biggest maneuvers was to create the Tobacco Industry Research Committee (TIRC), an agency that worked to cast doubt about the pernicious health effects of smoking.

Hill & Knowlton was the nation's premier public relations firm when it was hired by the tobacco industry in 1953. It had reached this summit as a result of working with top executives of major businesses in the steel, oil, and aircraft industries since the 1930s. The firm's president, John W. Hill, who had quit smoking due to health concerns in the early 1940s, ironically used his considerable public relations know-how to distort or undermine a growing amount of scientific data emerging in the 1950s that linked smoking to cancer and other illnesses.

When the CEOs of the major tobacco companies held a rare meeting at the Plaza Hotel in New York City on December 14, 1953, they did so in order to craft a coordinated, long-term response to widely read and repercussive reports such as the 1952 piece "Cancer by the Carton," which appeared in *Reader's Digest*. Similar articles that brought recent scientific findings regarding smoking and cancer to a mainstream audience, like those that appeared in *Ladies Home Journal*, *The New Republic*, *Consumer Reports*, and *The Nation*, generated a significant drop in the nation's level of cigarette consumption and led to roughly 40% of the public believing that smoking caused lung cancer. It was thus with the recognition that a new approach was necessary in order to ensure the survival of the cigarette industry that the tobacco companies hired Hill & Knowlton to stem the scientific and popular tide amassing against smoking.

One of Hill's biggest undertakings was to have the tobacco companies agree to create the Tobacco Industry Research Committee (TIRC) in 1954. The industry initially floated titles such as "The Committee of Public Information" and "The Cigarette Information Committee," but Hill argued that "Research" needed to be in the name in order to lend the institution a greater air of scientific legitimacy. Minutes from the Plaza Hotel meeting detail the tobacco industry's promise to Hill that they could supply Hill & Knowlton with authoritative scientific material that would refute the health charges being leveled against cigarettes. And according to Philip Hilts, the author and *New York Times* reporter who broke a number of stories about the tobacco industry based on uncovered internal documents, Hill warned tobacco executives that they would need to drop the approach of scientific denial if cigarettes were proved to be dangerous to smokers' health.

Hill & Knowlton's first major public relations move with the newly created TIRC was to publish a full-page advertisement that ran under the headline, "A Frank Statement to Cigarette Smokers." This January 4, 1954 piece, which appeared in 448 newspapers in 258 American cities and is estimated to have reached 43 million readers, announced the creation of the TIRC as an institution dedicated to supporting scientific research into tobacco's health effects. The advertisement, which took the form of a letter from big tobacco to the general public, included the statement that the tobacco industry accepted its obligation to people's health as a basic responsibility, which it claimed was paramount to any other business consideration. The tobacco industry further stated that it believed its products were not harmful to one's health, claimed it had cooperated with scientists and public health officials, and promised to always cooperate with them in the future. In essence, the "Frank Statement" that Hill & Knowlton crafted presented the tobacco industry as allied with science, despite the fact that the TIRC was actually formed in order distort, undermine, and discredit the growing chorus of scientific reports that linked smoking to cancer and other illnesses.

To give a face of respectability to what was fundamentally an industry-supported entity, Hill & Knowlton hired the noted geneticist Clarence Cook "C.C." Little to serve as the TIRC's scientific director. Little was an avowed skeptic of the link between smoking and cancer, and he consistently advanced the notion that such a connection was controversial and far from certain. As such, many of the studies that Little promoted while at the helm of the TIRC stressed the role of heredity in cancer, thereby articulating a potential uncertainty regarding smoking as a carcinogenic act. While many scientists felt the findings published by Little to be essentially compromised by the tobacco industry's sponsorship, Hill & Knowlton's TIRC was nonetheless generally successful in its efforts to change what was a growing scientific consensus around cigarettes' pernicious health effects in 1953 into a fairly broad public and scientific debate by 1960. Hill & Knowlton's public

relations coup thus amounted to effectively transforming science, which represented a grave threat to big tobacco's future success, into an industry tool that could convince concerned consumers to continue, or even begin, smoking.

In addition to launching the influential TIRC (which was renamed the Council for Tobacco Research in 1964), Hill & Knowlton maintained uncertainty and controversy over the health effects of cigarettes with a sustained effort to shape the ways various media outlets discussed and reported the topic. For one, Hill & Knowlton created the Tobacco Institute, a Washington-based lobby that would present, in a unified voice, the tobacco industry's views to the public and Congress. In addition, Hill & Knowlton kept files on scientific experts in order to be able to quickly launch attacks on the credibility of their findings, and it also maintained close contact with important writers and press editors so as to keep the tobacco industry's views present in the media alongside negative reports about smoking. By actively courting media figures, Hill & Knowlton was able to advance the notion that science's link between smoking and cancer was debatable and deserving of "balanced" coverage.

Hill & Knowlton also made a concerted effort to shape the medical profession's attitude toward smoking. One component of this agenda was the distribution of the periodical *Tobacco and Health* to doctors and dentists at no cost. With a circulation of over 500,000 and its basic message being that the link between smoking and cancer was uncertain, *Tobacco and Health* helped prevent the medical establishment from universally concluding that smoking was unhealthy.

Hill & Knowlton's overall efforts were successful in stabilizing a tobacco industry that was imperiled by a wave of scientific findings in the early 1950s that linked smoking to cancer. Their public relations moves moreover had the effect of boosting per capita consumption of cigarettes to their highest levels ever by 1961. But by the late 1960s, however, even Hill & Knowlton's strategies for creating scientific uncertainty were ineffective, as studies overwhelmingly demonstrated the severe health hazards of smoking. With the tobacco industry's legal concerns taking priority over public relations as a result of these repercussive scientific findings, Hill & Knowlton resigned from the Tobacco Institute in 1968, thus ending a long and influential partnership between the public relations firm and the tobacco industry.

(See also **Tobacco Industry Research Committee (TIRC)**; **Tobacco Institute**)

References

Brandt, Allan M. 2007. *The Cigarette Century: The Rise, Fall, and Deadly Persistence of the Product That Defined America.* New York: Basic Books.

Burns, Eric. 2007. *The Smoke of the Gods: A Social History of Tobacco.* Philadelphia: Temple University Press.

Cordry, Harold V. 2001. *Tobacco: A Reference Handbook.* Santa Barbara, CA: ABC-CLIO.

Goodman, Jordan, ed. 2005. *Tobacco in History and Culture: An Encyclopedia.* Detroit: Thomson Gale.

Parker-Pope, Tara. 2001. *Cigarettes: Anatomy of an Industry from Seed to Smoke.* New York: The New Press.

HOBSON, RICHMOND PEARSON

Richmond Pearson Hobson was a member of the U.S. House of Representatives who, in 1913, put forth the Hobson Resolution, a national prohibition bill. Hobson's legislation failed to pass, but he continued to prominently work alongside the Anti-Saloon League (ASL) in efforts to oppose alcohol. Later in his career, he devoted himself to the campaign against opiates, cocaine, and cannabis.

Hobson was born on August 17, 1870 in Greensboro, Alabama and domestically educated at Southern University and the U.S. Naval Academy. Hobson continued his studies abroad in Paris, and upon returning to the United States, he attended Washington and Jefferson College. He found employment on various naval construction projects, including as an assistant constructor in the Navy Department's Bureau of Construction and Repair in Washington, D.C. and an instructor in naval construction in Annapolis, Maryland. Hobson achieved naval fame despite never having a regular ship command as a result of his experience as a sailor during the Spanish-American War. In 1898, while serving on the USS *New York* off the coast of Cuba, Hobson either volunteered for, or was given the assignment of, sinking the *Merrimac* in order to block the channel of Santiago Harbor, and thus the mobility of the Spanish fleet. Despite failing to sink the *Merrimac* within the channel and subsequently being taken prisoner, Hobson nonetheless became a national hero for his efforts upon his release on July 6, 1898. Though rather delayed, Congress awarded Hobson with the

Medal of Honor in 1933 for his brave actions.

After retiring from the navy in 1903, Hobson returned to his native Alabama and began a speaking tour against alcohol. As a representative of the ASL, Hobson delivered a popular, hour-long speech, entitled "The Great Destroyer," in a nationwide tour that made him one of the most significant personalities in the prohibition movement. On the strength of his war record and zealous devotion to the prohibitionist cause, Hobson was elected to Congress in 1906. He would serve four consecutive terms before leaving the position in 1915, and during his time in the House of Representatives he introduced over twenty bills to prohibit alcohol. His first attempt at legislating a ban on alcohol was in 1911, but his most ambitious bill, which he proposed in 1913, aimed to add a prohibition amendment to the U.S. Constitution. Termed the Hobson Resolution, Hobson's bill specifically proposed to prohibit the sale and manufacture, but not the use of, intoxicating beverages. Texas Congressman Morris Sheppard introduced a similar bill in the Senate in concert with Hobson's proposal, but it, like the Hobson Resolution, failed to garner the two-thirds majority necessary to amend the constitution. The Hobson Resolution, however, was supported in the House by a small majority, 197 to 190.

ASL officials took this majority in the House as a sign that they might achieve their goal of legal prohibition by focusing their efforts on supporting dry Congressmen in the upcoming 1914 elections. As a result of ASL efforts, the Senate was decidedly dry after the 1914 elections, but the House did not have enough of a prohibitionist contingent to extend, to a two-thirds proportion, the small majority that had initially supported the Hobson Resolution. With the 1916 elections, however, the ASL elected the congressional majority they needed to make national prohibition a reality in the nation's near future. By that time, though, Hobson had been voted out of office. He failed in his 1914 re-election bid, in large part because of the unpopular tenor of his anti-alcohol message and his seemingly single-minded obsession with prohibition as a Congressman. As such, some of his fellow Congressmen dubbed him a "national nuisance." Similarly, his claim that 5 million Americans were slaves of the "Great Liquor Trust" rankled many voters in his Alabama district.

His 1911 book, *The Great Destroyer*, though, remained one of the most popular books within the prohibitionist movement. The book's success put forward traditional arguments about alcohol's destructive consequences, but Hobson added a scientific rationale for his push for national prohibition. He argued that booze was a poison that eroded the brain's uppermost tissue, which was the most recently evolved area. As a result, he concluded that every time a person drank, a decline in willpower resulted. Moreover, with willpower weakened, drinkers would have their moral senses erode, err in their recognition of right and wrong, and have a diminished consciousness of God, brotherly love, and self-sacrifice. Hobson attempted to further buttress the scientific rationale behind his call for prohibition with a racist argument, telling the House of Representatives that was considering the Hobson Resolution in 1914 that liquor would make African Americans brutes and cause them to commit unnatural crimes. He admitted that alcohol would have the same effect on Whites, but because Whites were, he claimed, further evolved, it would take a longer time for alcohol to reduce Whites to the same level.

Upon leaving Congress in 1914, Hobson continued his fight against the nation's addictions. He lectured for the ASL until 1922, and he organized the American Alcohol Education Association, the International Narcotic Educational Association, the World Conference on Narcotic Education, and the World Narcotic Defense Association. With these groups, Hobson expanded the target of his propaganda to include narcotics, which he believed posed just as great a threat as alcohol. An ardent publicist in the crusade against narcotics, Hobson used school textbooks, radio programs, and testimony in Congress to spread word of the dangers posed by habit-forming drugs. Some, including the American Medical Association, believed that Hobson's claims concerning drugs were exaggerations, but he nonetheless remained one of the United States' most active agitators for tighter narcotics control in the 1920s. Hobson was particularly outspoken on heroin, which he claimed caused crime and violence. Often, Hobson blamed the drug problem in the United States on other countries, claiming that the United States was a victim of poor narcotics control in foreign nations, which he believed flooded the United States with cocaine, opiates, and cannabis. This helped Hobson solidify the already-established association of narcotics with foreigners and minorities, using racism and jingoism to mobilize anti-narcotic sentiment just as he had done in his campaigns against alcohol.

Throughout his work on narcotics, Hobson did not always spread accurate information, but his work was important since it helped contribute to the popular perception of drug use as a dangerous and loathsome activity. He continued his work into the 1930s, organizing events to increase pressure on Congress to pass the Marihuana Tax Act in 1937. Shortly thereafter, he passed away in New York City, on March 16, 1937.

(See also **Anti-Saloon League (ASL)**; **Marihuana Tax Act**; **Volstead Act (18th Amendment)**))

References

Barr, Andrew. 1999. *Drink: A Social History of America*. New York: Carroll & Graf Publishers, Inc.

Blocker, Jr., Jack S., David M. Fahey, and Ian R. Tyrrell, eds. 2003. *Alcohol and Temperance in Modern History: An International Encyclopedia*. Santa Barbara, CA: ABC-CLIO.

Clark, Norman H. 1976. *Deliver Us from Evil: An Interpretation of American Prohibition*. New York: W. W. Norton Company.

Lender, Mark Edward. 1984. *Dictionary of American Temperance Biography: From Temperance Reform to Alcohol Research, the 1600s to the 1980s*. Westport, CT: Greenwood Press.

Mendelson, Jack H. and Nancy K. Mello. 1985. *Alcohol: Use and Abuse in America*. Boston: Little, Brown and Company.

Musto, David F. 1987. *The American Disease: Origins of Narcotic Control*. Expanded Edition. New York: Oxford University Press.

Pegram, Thomas P. 1998. *Battling Demon Rum: The Struggle for a Dry America, 1800–1933*. Chicago: Ivan R. Dee.

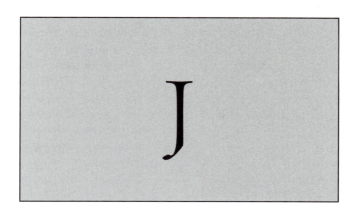

JACOBS, DURAND F.

Durand F. Jacobs is a researcher who helped pioneer the study of gambling addiction, and the field of behavioral addiction in general. Among Jacobs' chief accomplishments was the elaboration of his "General Theory of Addictions," which helped add a new dimension to the way that addictionologists and researchers viewed addictive behaviors and addictions to psychoactive substances.

Durand F. Jacobs was instrumental in establishing the first inpatient treatment program for compulsive gamblers in 1972. He worked as the Chief of the Psychology Service at the Jerry L. Pettis Memorial Veterans Hospital, in Loma Linda, California from 1977 through 1990, and he has also held positions teaching psychiatry at Loma Linda University School of Medicine, and at the Fuller Graduate School of Psychology in Pasadena, California. He was President of the California State Psychological Association in 1989, and the Vice President of the National Council on Problem Gaming in 1995.

From the 1940s through the 1980s, many researchers examined each type of addiction as a separate phenomenon, and attempted to develop different ways of explaining how each type of addiction functioned. Alcoholism, drug addiction, gambling addiction, and other behavioral addictions were all considered distinct disorders with different causes. Based on observations of members of self-help groups such as Alcoholics Anonymous, Gamblers Anonymous, and Overeaters Anonymous, however, Jacobs saw a pattern, and postulated that these diverse addictions had more in common than was first thought. In a series of articles he published in the 1980s, Jacobs elaborated his "General Theory of Addictions," which sought to unite the experiences of individuals who are addicted to psychoactive substances and those of individuals who are addicted to behaviors.

Jacobs identified two types of individuals who are predisposed to addiction.

The first type included people with what he termed "unipolar physiological resting states" (Jacobs 1989, 38)—people who are either chronically depressed or excited. This state of being either under-aroused or over-aroused, he argued, predisposed individuals to respond to only a small window of stress-reducing activities, including addictive substances and behaviors. The second group of individuals predisposed to addiction consisted of those with psychological problems rooted in past family, developmental, and interpersonal experiences that created feelings of inferiority or rejection later in life. For these individuals, Jacobs hypothesized that addictive patterns of behavior—both those involving psychoactive substances and those that do not—have a quality that allows individuals to escape from their emotional pain and experience, and help them feel important, successful, and powerful. Addictive behaviors, for both types of individuals, created what Jacobs termed a "dissociative-like state" (Jacobs 1989, 39), as they allowed individuals to feel an altered state of identity. Entering this dissociative-like state, Jacobs hypothesized, was the goal and outcome of all addictive behaviors.

Jacobs used his theory to predict that only a small segment of the general population was at risk for addiction, since both sets of predisposing factors—a unipolar physiological resting state, and psychological problems—were necessary for addictive behaviors to be maintained over long periods of time. In addition, Jacobs hypothesized that addictive behaviors need to take place in an environment that was conducive to addiction—one that allowed individuals to experience pleasurable effects from their addictive experiences. Though a series of preconditions were necessary for addiction, according to Jacobs, addictive patterns of behavior could manifest themselves in a variety of ways, ranging from overindulgence in substances such as food, alcohol, or psychoactive drugs, to excessive engagement in activities like gambling, sex, shopping, working, and even fire-setting. All of these behaviors, for certain individuals in the right circumstances, he maintained, could serve as defenses against physical and psychic pain. In studies, Jacobs' theory that a "dissociative-like state" was common in all of these behaviors were borne out, as gambling addicts, alcoholics, and chronic overeaters all reported entering a "trance-like"—or dissociative-like—state. Thus from this point of view, addictive behaviors were not simply results of neurochemical triggers or processes within the brain, but rather purposeful activities individuals pursued to achieve an altered state of identity. Beyond the neurochemistry and physiology, therefore, addiction also had a fundamentally psychological component.

By emphasizing the role of motivations and psychology in addiction, Jacobs' work has helped keep addiction scientists from focusing too narrowly on the physiological and neurochemical sides of addiction. While not refuting the neurochemical understanding of addiction, Jacobs' theories have complemented them, and made room for alternate understandings of addiction to help guide the diagnosis, treatment, and prevention of the disease.

(See also **Custer, Robert L.**; **Lesieur, Henry R.**; **Primary Source Documents**)

References

"Biography of Durand F. Jacobs Ph.D."
[Online information accessed 03/28/09]
http://www.snsus.org/pdf/biography-durand
_f_jacobs.pdf.

Jacobs, Durand F. 1989. "A General Theory
of Addictions: Rationale for and Evidence
Supporting a New Approach for Understanding and Treating Addictive Behaviors." In Howard J. Shaffer, Sharon A.
Stein, Blasé Gambino, and Thomas N.
Cummings, eds. *Compuslive Gambling:
Theory, Research, and Practice*. Lexington, MA: Lexington Books.

JELLINEK, E. MORTON

E. Morton Jellinek was perhaps the most
influential proponent of the disease conception of alcoholism. Jellinek famously
argued that there were five varieties (or
"species") of alcoholism and that there
was a progression of "phases" that went
from psychological to physical addiction.
While Jellinek made this claim as a temporary hypothesis, his ideas enjoyed a
long life in part because of his important
posts within the community of alcohol
researchers, including as associate editor
of the *Quarterly Journal of Studies on
Alcohol* and one of the founders of the
nation's first outpatient clinics for the
treatment of alcoholics.

Elvin Morton Jellinek was born on
August 15, 1890 in New York City,
though he was raised in Hungary and
educated at a number of European
schools. He spent time as a student at
the Universities of Berlin, Grenoble, and
possibly Tegucigalpa (Honduras), eventually earning (according to Jellinek, but
not the university's records) a Master of
Education degree from the University of
Leipzig in 1914. He left Hungary in the
1920s and worked as a biostatistician in
Sierra Leone from 1920 through 1925,
and in Honduras for the United Fruit
Company from 1925 until 1930. Jellinek
spent most of the 1930s as director of
the Biometric Laboratory at the Memorial Foundation for Neuroendocrine
Research at Worcester State Hospital in
Massachusetts. He began his research on
alcohol in 1939 with the Research Council on Problems of Alcohol in New York,
and from 1940 to 1950, Jellinek continued his research at the Laboratory of
Applied Psychology at Yale University.
While at Yale, Jellinek also served as
the first director of the Section of Studies
on Alcohol, helped found the Summer
School of Alcohol Studies, and became
associate editor of the *Quarterly Journal
of Studies on Alcohol*.

Jellinek is perhaps most noteworthy for
his work towards popularizing, and giving
scientific backing to, the idea that alcoholism is a treatable disease. Jellinek developed this notion first at Yale, where he
published his work on the drinking habits
of different societies and "the Jellinek
estimation formula," which aimed to give
an approximate count of the number of
alcoholics in a particular population.
Additionally, through his post as associate
editor of the *Quarterly Journal of Studies
on Alcohol*, Jellinek helped legitimize the
academic study of alcohol and its consumption by effectively linking it to more
entrenched and respected scholarly disciplines such as epidemiology. His academic theories about alcohol and
drinking also had concrete applications,
for Jellinek was instrumental in creating
the Yale Plan Clinics, which were the first
American outpatient clinics for the treatment of alcoholics.

Jellinek's disease concept of alcoholism certainly had its antecedents. In the

mid-nineteenth century, the Swedish physician Magnus Huss coined the term "alcoholism" and provided a scientific classification of it as a disease. In addition, in America during the last quarter of the nineteenth century, Thomas Crothers argued that inebriates should not be viewed as moral failures, but rather as sick individuals afflicted by a damaging disease. Toward this end, Crothers highlighted the element of addiction within inebriety.

Jellinek went further than his precursors, however, through studies that enabled him to identify five varieties (or what he termed "species") of alcoholism. "Alpha" and "beta" alcoholics, he claimed, did not fit the disease model, for they were simply psychologically dependent upon drink. "Epsilon" alcoholics, too, were not diseased, and their affliction was characterized by unpredictable and sporadic drinking binges. Since their periodic drinking failed to evidence increasing physiological dependence upon alcohol, epsilon alcoholics did not meet the criteria for the disease model of alcoholism. "Gamma" and "delta" alcoholics, however, experienced various states of physical addiction and thus qualified as diseased drinkers. In Jellinek's model, gamma and delta alcoholisms were characterized by increasing physiological adaptation to alcohol, changes in cell metabolism, symptoms of withdrawal, physical or psychological "cravings" for drink, and a "loss of control" over alcohol consumption. The difference between the two diseased types of alcoholism revolved around what would happen when each type of alcoholic went without alcohol. Gamma alcoholics, Jellinek argued, were able to abstain from drink without experiencing withdrawal symptoms.

Delta alcoholics, on the other hand, were unable to stop drinking for any length of time without feeling the effects of withdrawal, thus leading them to continue consuming alcohol nonstop. Hence, there was a progression of "phases" in alcoholism that led from psychological to physical addiction.

Though Jellinek admitted that his rubric for understanding alcoholism was only a hypothesis, his theories nonetheless became the bedrock principles of modern research into alcoholism. His disease conception of alcoholism became entrenched in part because of his influential positions as an editor of the *Quarterly Journal of Studies on Alcohol* and compiler of the *Classified Abstract Archive of the Alcohol Literature*. His magnum opus, *The Disease Concept of Alcoholism*, published in 1960, helped cement his unparalleled position within the world of alcohol research. Another key part of Jellinek's legacy was his relationship with Alcoholics Anonymous (AA). Jellinek was one of the first in his profession to seize upon the group's value—both to alcoholics and alcohol researchers. In fact, the study from which Jellinek's theory of "phases" in alcoholism emerged was generated from data he collected from AA members.

After leaving Yale in 1950, Jellinek continued his work on alcoholism at a number of postings. He was employed by the Texas Addiction Research Foundation, the University of Toronto, and Stanford University. While working with the World Health Organization, he helped create the World Health Organization Committee on Alcoholism, and he also aided in the establishment of the National Council on Alcoholism. Jellinek died at his desk on October 22, 1963 in Palo Alto, California.

(See also **Alcoholics Anonymous (AA)**; **Crothers, Thomas Davison**)

References

Blocker, Jr., Jack S., David M. Fahey, and Ian R. Tyrrell, eds. 2003. *Alcohol and Temperance in Modern History: An International Encyclopedia*. Santa Barbara, CA: ABC-CLIO.

Edwards, Griffith. 2000. *Alcohol: The Ambiguous Molecule*. London: Penguin Books.

Lender, Mark Edward. 1984. *Dictionary of American Temperance Biography: From Temperance Reform to Alcohol Research, the 1600s to the 1980s*. Westport, CT: Greenwood Press.

Sournia, Jean-Charles. 1990. *A History of Alcoholism*. Trans. by Nick Hindley and Gareth Stanton. Oxford: Basil Blackwell.

White, William L. 1998. *Slaying the Dragon: The History of Addiction Treatment and Recovery in America*. Bloomington, IL: Chestnut Health Systems.

JIN FUEY MOY V. UNITED STATES

The 1915 Supreme Court case *Jin Fuey Moy v. United States* was the first test of the constitutionality of the 1914 Harrison Narcotics Act, which was the first sweeping federal legislation controlling the sale and traffic of narcotics in the United States. The case marked a setback for the Treasury Department, which was charged with enforcing the provisions of the Harrison Act.

According to the Act, people needed to have a stamp issued by the government if they were going to have narcotics in their possession. One exception, however, was for patients who received the drugs after getting a prescription from their physician. The law stipulated that these medical professionals could only prescribe narcotics "in good faith" and "in the course of...professional practice"—wording that was designed to prevent them from giving out prescriptions to recreational users or addicts. The law, however, was ambiguous on some key questions: What did "good faith" mean? If doctors believed that addiction was a disease and that addicts needed narcotics as medicines, could they provide care to their patients by giving them the drugs they craved? Was it within the scope of a doctor's "professional practice" to give drugs to addicts, or could that be considered something that fell outside the scope of "legitimate" medical treatment? According to law enforcement officials with the Treasury Department, the Harrison Act should have forbidden physicians from prescribing narcotics for the sole purpose of maintenance—allowing addicts to continue taking drugs and avoid withdrawal symptoms. In the months after the Harrison Act went into effect, the government indicted many doctors and pharmacists, as well as addicts who received prescriptions for narcotics, charging that they were acting in "conspiracy" to violate the law.

In December of 1915, a case addressing these questions was argued before the Supreme Court. The case involved Jin Fuey Moy, a Pittsburgh doctor, who prescribed morphine to an addict named Willie Martin. The government claimed that Moy did not prescribe the drug for "medical" purposes, but rather to feed Martin's addiction. Since such a prescription was not, according to the government, issued in "good faith," and because Martin did not have one of the revenue stamps that were required for him to have morphine in his possession, Martin's possession of drugs was illegal, and he was therefore guilty of violating the stipulations of the Harrison Act. The district judge who heard the case, however, disagreed. He claimed that since Martin only consumed drugs, and did not import, export, or sell them, he did not break the law. Merely having the drug in his possession, therefore, was no proof that he had violated the Act. When it ruled on the case in June of 1916, the Supreme Court agreed, writing that since it was a revenue act administered by the Treasury Department, the Harrison Act only governed commerce in narcotics, not their possession. Moreover, if the law was to be interpreted as the government had wanted, the Supreme Court wrote in its opinion, the law would target more citizens than it was intended to by making possession of narcotics a punishable offense. Since the Harrison Act was a revenue law that merely regulated the transfer of drugs, and not their use, the Court concluded, the government overstepped its bounds in its prosecution of Martin and Moy.

The Treasury Department, which was responsible for enforcing the provisions of the Harrison Act, was furious with the decision. They complained that the ruling would make it virtually impossible to control narcotics effectively since it would become very difficult to bring cases against addicts, recreational drug users, and the doctors and physicians who supplied them with drugs for non-medical purposes. The ruling invalidated the convictions of many people who had been found guilty of violating the Harrison Act, and federal officials wanted to find a way to make it so anyone found in possession of narcotics without a revenue stamp or legitimate prescription could be prosecuted. The Treasury Department got what it wanted a few years later in 1919, when the Supreme Court made landmark rulings in *Webb et al. v. United States* and *United States v. Doremus*, allowing for a stricter interpretation of the Harrison Act. Jin Fuey Moy was brought up on charges of violating the Harrison Act again in 1920, and this time, in light of the precedent established in the *Webb* decision, he was found guilty.

(See also **Harrison Narcotics Act**; **Special Narcotic Committee**; *United States v. Doremus* and *Webb et al. v. United States*)

References

Belenko, Steven R., ed. 2000. *Drugs and Drug Policy in America: A Documentary History*. Westport, CT: Greenwood Press.

Jin Fuey Moy v. United States. 241 U.S. 394 (1916).

Musto, David F. 1987. *The American Disease: Origins of Narcotics Control*. Expanded Edition. New York: Oxford University Press.

KEELEY, LESLIE E.

Dr. Leslie E. Keeley rose to fame in the late-nineteenth century as a result of his patented "Double Chloride of Gold" cure for inebriety (which was also known as the "Bi-Chloride of Gold" or "Keeley Cure"), and though it had no scientific value as a medical cure, Keeley became a millionaire. In addition to devising this medicinal approach, Keeley popularized his treatment method of combating alcoholism and drug addiction with the establishment of Keeley Institutes across the United States and, to a lesser extent, internationally. The last Keeley Institute closed in 1966, but Keeley remains a significant figure in the history of addiction treatment for his view that inebriety was a curable disease, and for programs in Keeley Institutes that anticipated aversion therapy and Alcoholics Anonymous (AA).

Leslie Enraught Keeley was born in Ireland in 1832, and immigrated to the United States in his youth before graduating from Rush Medical College of Chicago. Though this institution was named after Benjamin Rush, an early American opponent of the consumption of distilled sprits, Keeley did not follow Rush's stance on alcohol to a tee. Instead of following that strain of Rush's thought that argued inebriety was in part a moral decision made by the drinker, Keeley developed Rush's other main idea—that drunkards suffered from a physical dependence upon alcohol that necessitated the development of a cure. Rush's techniques for curing the drinker's dependence upon alcohol generally revolved around housing such an individual in a sanitarium and enforcing abstinence. Keeley, too, utilized the notion of inebriate houses, but added a chemical concoction, his so-called "Double Chloride of Gold" cure, to his treatment method.

With the help of associate John Oughton, Keeley initially experimented with a pill containing chloride of gold and sodium. When this pill proved nearly fatal, the duo developed a liquid solution probably consisting of atropine, strychnine, and arsenic that alcoholic patients would have injected four times per day over a three-to-four week period (opium addicts would stay on the regimen for slightly longer). In 1879, Keeley opened his first institution in Dwight, Illinois, to provide a place where patients could stay while receiving his treatment. Keeley also developed cures for opium and tobacco users, as well as for individuals suffering from nervous disorders, but the Double Chloride of Gold treatment for drunkenness was his most popular product. An extensive advertising campaign and mail-order product line, which provided consumers with two bottles of the Double Chloride of Gold cure for $9.00, proved extremely profitable, as did the licensing of Keeley Institute franchises throughout the United States. By 1900, every state had at least one Keeley Institute, and some states used public funds to subsidize the treatment of indigent alcoholics at the institutions. For patients who roomed in a Keeley Institute sanitarium, the cost was between $100 and $200 for a four-week stay. Patients were required, however, to get their meals elsewhere, since Keeley argued that he wanted them to have free access to as much whiskey as they desired. In contrast to confinement in an institution, this treatment method was thus geared towards helping patients retain a sense of their independence and liberty despite their thirst for alcohol.

This stance was popularized through Keeley's writings about the essential curability of inebriety. In publications such as "The Non-Heredity of Inebriety" (1890) and "Drunkenness: A Curable Disease" (1892), Keeley cautioned society against damning alcohol abusers. Instead of writing them off, Keeley argued that with proper treatment—not punishment or legislation—drunkards could be cured, and thus reformed into productive members of society. This claim stood in opposition to temperance movement ideas of the time, and Keeley generally articulated a nonjudgmental approach to alcohol abuse that consequently appealed to a broad segment of inebriates.

In addition to Double Chloride of Gold injections, the Keeley Cure's appeal rested upon the incorporation of behavior modification techniques and a supportive therapeutic environment. Keeley claimed that patients would remain permanently sober if they followed the guidelines laid out in the pamphlet, "To the Keeley Graduate." If individuals abstained from drink, tobacco, caffeine, and narcotics, exercised regularly, ate a healthy diet, and established appropriate friendships, including with fellow patients, Keeley argued that his graduates would be fully cured of their addictions and lead normal lives. Towards this end, in 1891, Dwight patients organized Bi-Chloride of Gold Clubs, which met each morning for speeches, discussions, and mutual support. These clubs, which numbered fifty within a year, foreshadowed the later development of AA. When AA began to spread in the 1940s, Keeley Institutes were involved, and the location in Dwight was affiliated with AA and hosted AA meetings.

The Keeley Institute also anticipated aversion therapy techniques to treat alcohol abuse. In addition to the hypodermic injections and tonics that constituted the bulk of the Double Chloride of Gold cure, particularly severe patients who struggled to find success under the normal treatment were given whiskey and shots of strychnine and apomorphine. Apomorphine acted as an emetic, and its combination with strychnine and whiskey thus constituted an early form of aversion therapy, something that would be tried with disulfiram and other treatments later in the twentieth century.

Scientists and the medical establishment were not universally supportive, however, of Keeley's Double Chloride of Gold cure. Dr. Thomas Crothers, a physician and influential editor of the *Quarterly Journal of Inebriety* who claimed that inebriates were diseased, dismissed Keeley's cure as quackery by describing the use of gold as lacking any therapeutic value whatsoever. Pharmacology never recognized Double Chloride of Gold, and Keeley never revealed its formula or the research upon which he devised the substance.

In general, the critiques of the medical establishment, compounded by the failures of ex-patients to remain abstinent, spelled the beginning of the end for Keeley Institutes. By the time of Keeley's death in 1900, however, an estimated 400,000 patients had been treated by Keeley Institutes and the Keeley Cure. Keeley's assistant and partner, James Oughton, and Oughton's son, James H. Oughton, took control of the institutes after Keeley's passing. The institute in Dwight closed in 1966.

(See also **Alcoholics Anonymous (AA)**; **Crothers, Thomas Davison**; **Disulfiram**; **Rush, Benjamin**)

References

Lender, Mark Edward. 1984. *Dictionary of American Temperance Biography: From Temperance Reform to Alcohol Research, the 1600s to the 1980s*. Westport, CT: Greenwood Press.

Lender, Mark Edward and James Kirby Martin. 1982. *Drinking in America: A History*. New York: The Free Press.

Morgan. H. Wayne. 1981. *Drugs in America: A Social History, 1800–1980*. Syracuse, NY: Syracuse University Press.

Murdock, Catherine Gilbert. 1998. *Domesticating Drink: Women, Men, and Alcohol in America, 1870–1940*. Baltimore: The Johns Hopkins University Press.

White, William L. 1998. *Slaying the Dragon: The History of Addiction Treatment and Recovery in America*. Bloomington, IL: Chestnut Health Systems.

KESSLER, DAVID

David Kessler is a pediatrician, lawyer, and administrator who served as the commissioner of the Food and Drug Administration (FDA) from 1990 to 1997. Under his leadership, the FDA boldly asserted its jurisdiction over tobacco, though the Supreme Court later ruled that the FDA did not have the authority to regulate cigarettes.

Kessler was born on May 13, 1951 in New York City, and he graduated from Amherst College in 1973. He subsequently earned an M.D. degree from Harvard in 1979, as well as a law degree from the University of Chicago in 1978. Kessler then worked as a consultant to Republican Senator Orrin Hatch of Utah, specifically working on, among other things, the regulation of tobacco and cigarettes. In 1990, Kessler was appointed to be the commissioner of the FDA by President George H. W. Bush.

In early 1994, Kessler began investigating the possibility of the FDA regulating tobacco. His decision to look into bringing tobacco under the agency's authority may very well have been related to the recent airing of ABC's newsmagazine *Day One*, which tackled the topic of the tobacco industry with the help of an informant from

R. J. Reynolds who went by the name of "Deep Cough." With the insider information "Deep Cough" provided, *Day One* detailed how the tobacco industry added nicotine to cigarettes in order to keep smokers addicted to its products. A later episode of *Day One* highlighted another element of the tobacco industry's manipulation of cigarettes by focusing on cigarette additives, which included thirteen substances banned in food by the FDA.

Before the airing of *Day One*'s final segment, which made an argument for the cigarette simply being a delivery device for the use of nicotine, Kessler had already sent a letter to the Coalition on Smoking OR Health that stated his interest in potentially restricting nicotine or even banning cigarettes that contained nicotine. Kessler's letter noted the difficulties that would be involved in regulating nicotine, particularly with regard to satisfying both Congress, which is responsible for the Food, Drug, and Cosmetic Act, and the nation's 40 million smokers. Kessler clearly understood that bringing tobacco under the regulatory authority of the FDA would not be easily achieved.

Key to Kessler's initiative was Jeffrey Wigand, a whistleblower who first visited Kessler's FDA office on May 18, 1994. Known initially only by his code name of "Research," Wigand (who was later portrayed by Russell Crowe in the lead role of the popular film *The Insider*) was in charge of research at, and a top-level executive for, Brown & Williamson (B&W) until he became uncomfortable with what he was doing for the tobacco company. Upon objecting to B&W's continued inclusion of coumarin, which tests showed to cause liver cancer in mice, in pipe tobacco, Wigand was fired.

Despite signing a confidentiality agreement upon leaving B&W, Wigand nonetheless came to Kessler with inside information on how his former employer manipulated nicotine levels in its cigarettes and specifically targeted youths as potential smokers. And as B&W's former head of research, Wigand had intimate knowledge of the thousands of ingredients and additives that went into cigarettes, could explain the chemical details of cigarette smoke, and revealed the ammonia-based compounds used by tobacco companies to manipulate nicotine levels in cigarettes. Armed with this insider information regarding the ways in which the tobacco industry used nicotine as a drug, intentionally enhanced the addictive properties of cigarettes, and marketed their products to children, Kessler received President Bill Clinton's approval to try and bring tobacco under the regulatory authority of the FDA.

In August of 1996, Kessler boldly announced that the FDA would regulate all nicotine-containing products as medical devices since the nicotine in cigarettes was a drug, and cigarettes themselves essentially constituted a drug-delivery system. He furthermore stated that the FDA would curb youth access to tobacco products and restrict tobacco advertising directed towards children. Specifically, Kessler sought to prohibit tobacco purchases by anyone under the age of eighteen, ban cigarette vending machines, end the practice of giving away free sample packs, drive tobacco billboards away from schools and playgrounds, and force all tobacco advertising to be printed in black and white and text-only form. And to convince Americans that the FDA should be in the business of regulating tobacco in the ways he outlined, Kessler drew upon internal industry documents and Wigand's inside information to demonstrate the tobacco companies' sustained efforts to boost nicotine levels in cigarettes and thereby make smoking more addictive.

In response to these new FDA rules regarding tobacco, the industry filed a suit claiming that only Congress had the authority to regulate tobacco. Their suit also claimed that cigarettes could not be regulated by the FDA because cigarettes did not fit the Food, Drug, and Cosmetic Act's definition of a drug or drug-delivery device. The court initially ruled that the FDA could legally impose labeling requirements on, and restrict access to, tobacco. But it also determined that the FDA could not restrict advertising to youths. Both sides appealed this mixed verdict, and in June 1998 the appeals court struck down the FDA's rules. In December 1999, the case made its way to the Supreme Court, which, in a 5-4 ruling in March 2000, determined that the FDA did not have the jurisdiction to regulate tobacco. Though it admitted the great impact tobacco has upon public health, the Supreme Court essentially ruled that only Congress—not the FDA —could establish jurisdiction over tobacco. Though Kessler wound up just one Supreme Court Justice away from bringing tobacco under the regulatory authority of the FDA, his bold maneuvering amounted to little in the end. Kessler had little to no hope of persuading Republicans, whose candidates received 80% of the tobacco industry's political funding, to pass legislation that would grant the FDA jurisdiction over tobacco. In order for the FDA to gain regulatory control over tobacco, Congress needed to pass a law granting it authority, something that may finally happen in 2009 if the Family Smoking Prevention and Tobacco Control Act becomes law.

Since his work on tobacco, Kessler has also published research on the problems associated with overeating, describing how fat, salt, and sugar alter brain chemistry. Kessler is currently a professor of Pediatrics and Epidemiology and Biostatistics at the University of California, San Francisco.

(See also **Food and Drug Administration (FDA)**; **Primary Source Documents**; **Reference Essay**)

References

Brandt, Allan M. 2007. *The Cigarette Century: The Rise, Fall, and Deadly Persistence of the Product That Defined America*. New York: Basic Books.

Campaign for Tobacco-Free Kids. 2009. "FDA Authority Over Tobacco." [Online article accessed 05/10/09] http://www .tobaccofreekids.org/reports/fda/.

Cordry, Harold V. 2001. *Tobacco: A Reference Handbook*. Santa Barbara, CA: ABC-CLIO.

Goodman, Jordan, ed. 2005. *Tobacco in History and Culture: An Encyclopedia*. Detroit: Thomson Gale.

Kessler, David A. 2009. *The End of Overeating: Taking Control of the Insatiable American Appetite*. New York: Rodale Books.

KOLB, LAWRENCE

Lawrence Kolb was one of the leading figures in the study of drug addiction in the United States during the twentieth century. Early in his career, he became familiar with addiction while working for the Public Health Service, and he put forth influential theories that divided addicts into six distinct subcategories. Later in his career, he became an outspoken critic of Harry J. Anslinger of the Federal Bureau of Narcotics (FBN), and others who advocated treating addiction as a law-and-order problem instead of a medical one.

Lawrence Kolb was born in Galloway, Maryland in 1881, and graduated from medical school at the University of Maryland in 1908. After a year working as a resident at University Hospital in Baltimore, he moved to New York, where he conducted mental tests on immigrants at Ellis Island. In 1919 he moved to Wisconsin to organize a hospital for the treatment of patients suffering from nervous conditions, and remained there until 1923, when he was assigned by the Public Health Service to conduct research on narcotics addiction. In one of his first assignments, his task was to work on a team that had to estimate how many opiate addicts there were in the United States, and after extensive study, he concluded that there were approximately 100,000 narcotic addicts in the country. He then led another study on addiction, interviewing about 200 addicts in prisons and hospitals to learn more about the condition, and particularly, who was susceptible to it.

Based on his research, Kolb published numerous articles in medical journals in the 1920s. One of his key accomplishments was his disproving of the antitoxin thesis of addiction, which had been put forward by addiction specialists such as Ernest S. Bishop. More importantly, Kolb elaborated a theory that there were six types of addicts. The first type consisted of individuals who were psychologically healthy, and had become addicted after they started taking drugs for medical reasons, usually under the guidance of a trained physician. The second type of addict, Kolb believed, was the individual suffering from what he termed "psychopathic diathesis," the third type was the psychopath, the fourth type was the inebriate who alternated between alcohol and opium, the fifth type was the individual with neuroses, and the sixth type was the individual with mental disorders. Kolb maintained that for these last five types of addicts, drug-taking was fundamentally different than it was for those who became addicted when they began taking narcotics as prescribed by a physician. Whereas the first type of addict felt little pleasure from opiates— only relief from pain—Kolb held that the other five types found opiates extremely pleasurable since they were sensitive to their euphoric effects. Kolb believed that opiates also served a psychological purpose for users, as the drugs helped alleviate feelings of inadequacy, serving as a psychic crutch that enabled individuals with nervous, mental, or emotional disorders to feel healthy. The reason that these addicts were prone to relapse, he hypothesized, was that feelings of inadequacy would return when they stopped using opiates.

Kolb's theories on addiction informed his views on addiction policy in the 1910s and 1920s. He maintained that most individuals who had become addicted to narcotics when a doctor prescribed them had done so before 1915, when the Harrison Narcotics Act placed limits on narcotics and made doctors less likely to prescribe them. Many of these individuals, he believed, were able to quit taking opiates, and had little incentive to continue using since they did not find them pleasurable. Moreover, by the mid-1920s, he believed this type of addict was exceedingly rare. Instead, he believed that the majority of addicts in the 1920s were the pleasure-seeking types who used the drugs to overcome preexisting nervous, mental, or emotional problems. The problems that most addicts had, he maintained, were not caused by drugs, but they became manifest in the form of addiction when they started using narcotics. If individuals with mental, emotional, and nervous problems had access to opiates, he argued, deficiencies in their character and mental makeup that could otherwise remain hidden would come out in the form of drug addiction. Thus a tight system of control to keep narcotics out of these individuals' hands, he reasoned, was appropriate. Kolb also supported the government's anti-maintenance stance, though he was in favor of giving opiates to individuals who needed them to alleviate physical pain.

Nonetheless, Kolb maintained that opiates were still less dangerous than other substances such as cocaine and alcohol, which he believed were more prone to cause social disruption and criminal activity. He also became an outspoken critic of propagandists such as Richmond Pearson Hobson, who depicted all addicts as criminals and claimed that addiction was becoming a more widespread and serious social problem. Also, when the federal government began considering the construction of special institutions to treat addicts, Kolb did not support the idea. He maintained that addiction was not nearly as widespread as others suggested, and that individuals who used narcotics to overcome deficiencies in their nervous, mental, or emotional makeup would, in order to cope with their problems, return to the habit even after they were cured of addiction.

After spending time working in Europe and Missouri in the late 1920s and early 1930s, Kolb was appointed medical director of the Public Health Service Narcotic Hospital in Lexington, Kentucky—an institution where addicts were interned and forced to undergo treatment for addiction, and where research into possible cures for addiction was carried out. Kolb was an odd choice for the job, given that he did not believe special institutions dedicated to the cure of addicts were desirable or necessary. Yet once he was appointed, Kolb oversaw the construction and furnishing of the institution, and also planned out the treatment regimen for residents there. When he first took charge of the Lexington Hospital, Kolb opposed the physical layout of the building, which was originally designed to be more of a prison than a hospital. Kolb viewed the Narcotic Hospital as an alternative to prison for addicts, so as much as possible, he worked to house addicts outside of cell blocks. When the Lexington facility opened in July of 1935, Kolb was actively involved in setting up procedures and overseeing the activities of inmates, and he remained the chief medical officer there until 1938.

Beginning in the late 1930s, Kolb expanded his work beyond the narrow field of addiction treatment, and advocated for the creation of a national institute dedicated to research on mental health—a vision that was realized in 1949 with the creation of the National Institute of Mental Health. After he retired from the Public Health Service in 1944, Kolb served as deputy director of mental health for California, and he also served as the assistant superintendent of the State Hospital at Norristown, Pennsylvania. Kolb also remained active in the addiction field. In 1956, he began to support experimental plans for maintenance treatment of addicts proposed by the New York Academy of Medicine, and he became a fierce opponent of severe federal laws against the use of opiates, marijuana, and cocaine in the early 1950s. As he grew older, and government approaches towards the drug problem became tougher, Kolb became more critical of punitive strategies towards the treatment of drug addiction. In the 1950s he had public debates with former FBN head Harry J. Ansligner on the subject, and in 1962 he published a book, *Drug Addiction: A Medical Problem*, which argued that addicts should be treated more like patients and less like criminals. He made his views even more public when he testified before Congress in 1965. In one of his last official acts before his death, he served on the American Medical Association's methadone maintenance evaluation committee, a group that reported favorably on the possibility of treating opiate addiction with methadone substitution therapies. Kolb passed away in 1972.

(See also **Anslinger, Harry J.**; **Bishop, Ernest S.**; **Hobson, Richmond Pearson**; **Methadone**; **Public Health Service Narcotic Hospitals**)

References

Acker, Caroline Jean. 2002. *Creating the American Junkie: Addiction Research in the Classic Era of Narcotic Control*. Baltimore: Johns Hopkins University Press.

Courtwright, David T. 2001. *Dark Paradise: A History of Opiate Addiction in America*. Cambridge: Harvard University Press.

"Lawrence Kolb, Psychiatrist, 91." 1972. *New York Times*. (November 19): 80.

Musto, David F. 1987. *The American Disease: Origins of Narcotics Control*. Expanded Edition. New York: Oxford University Press.

LEAGUE OF NATIONS

The League of Nations was an intergovernmental organization that emerged after World War I in order to provide nations a way to settle their differences peacefully, and also to foster international cooperation in dealing with global issues. The League came into existence in January of 1919, and it continued to function until the outbreak of World War II in 1939. One of the global issues the League tackled in its twenty years of existence was the question of narcotics control, and in a series of conferences in the 1920s and 1930s, it set up a global narcotics control regime that would form the basis of the more comprehensive international control system that emerged after World War II.

Before World War I, there had been international conferences at Shanghai and The Hague to consider the international drug problem. In spite of the agreements struck at these conferences, there were many forces that made countries resist ratifying the Hague Convention. Nations with pharmaceutical industries that manufactured narcotic preparations were reluctant to force their constituents to limit drug production. Those with colonies that produced opium, and made a profit by selling it both to colonial subjects and overseas, were equally reluctant to make economic sacrifices for the sake of international drug control efforts. Tough economic conditions, both during World War I and in its aftermath, made these countries particularly resistant to the idea of limiting their commerce in narcotics. Thus even though an agreement was reached at the Hague, it did not take effect until after World War I since not enough countries had signed the treaty. In particular, two major drug-producing countries —Germany, which had a large pharmaceutical industry involved in the production of narcotics, and Turkey, which was a major opium grower—had not yet ratified the Convention before the outbreak of war. Both Germany and Turkey were on the losing side of World War I, however, and the victorious countries—the United States, Britain, and China in particular—insisted that ratification of the Hague Convention be a condition of the peace. Article 273 of the Treaty of Versailles, which ended World War I in 1919, compelled the defeated countries to ratify the Hague Convention and implement its provisions. With the Hague Convention now operational, the League of Nations assumed control over the execution of the agreement. Until its dissolution, the League became the central organ for international drug control.

In 1920, the League created the Advisory Committee on Traffic in Opium and Other Dangerous Drugs to advise the organization on matters concerning narcotics trafficking and addiction. At the first conference to address the international narcotics problem in November of 1924, negotiations were derailed by squabbles between the British and Japanese representatives, Chinese objections that the League wanted to meddle in its internal affairs, and the fact that colonial powers were reluctant to ratify any provisions that would have forced them to cut down on opium smoking in their colonial possessions. At a second conference later that year, countries objected to proposals by the United States that they thought were too ambitious and unenforceable. Displeased with the reluctance of other nations to adopt more enthusiastic control measures, the U.S. delegation at the Conference withdrew, but an agreement, the Geneva Opium Convention, was finally signed in 1925. The 1925 agreement provided for the creation of a Permanent Central Board within the League of Nations to track the international trade in narcotics, collect statistics concerning the growth, manufacture, and trade of drugs, and gather intelligence on international smuggling. The Convention also created

a system of import certificates, which stipulated that governments could not allow narcotics to be sent abroad unless they were provided with a certificate from the authorities in the destination country assuring that they were aware that narcotics were being sent, and affirming that they would be used only for medical or scientific purposes. In addition, the Convention also included provisions for the enhancement of domestic drug control measures, restrictions on the trade in coca and marijuana, and controls on manufactured drugs. It also established procedures so new drugs could be added to the list of controlled substances in the future. If a member state did not adhere to the rules set out at the 1925 Conference, the Permanent Central Board had the power to call for an international boycott of narcotic imports and exports to and from that country. The 1925 Convention marked a significant step in the move towards international narcotics control by bringing about the regularization and surveillance of narcotic production and exchange, though it was only somewhat effective; governments that wanted to ignore the provisions of the Convention were able to continue importing and exporting narcotics to and from nations that did not sign the treaty. Given that some major opium and coca producing countries did not become parties to the agreement, this meant that both states and smugglers could still freely purchase narcotics without reporting to the League. Moreover, the Convention did not place any limits on the agricultural or pharmaceutical production of narcotics, meaning that while the League could track the amounts of narcotics being produced by signatory nations, it had no power to limit them.

Over the course of the 1920s, the League took a further step by trying to estimate the total amount of opiates that were necessary for use in medicine worldwide, in hopes of then restricting production to those levels so no drugs would be available for diversion to the black market. In 1931, the Convention for Limiting the Manufacture and Regulating the Distribution of Narcotic Drugs was ratified. This Convention called for the limitation of narcotic drug production to the worlds' medical and scientific needs, in hopes that countries would limit their production of narcotics, thus cutting off supplies that could go to the illicit drug traffic. A new organization—the League's Drug Supervisory Body—was established to collect statistics concerning how much each country needed, based on estimates that were annually submitted by the nations that signed the treaty. The Supervisory Body then set limits on how much each growing or manufacturing country would be allowed to produce and import each year. Signatory countries were also required to submit statistics on all narcotic imports and exports that they made. If there were inconsistencies between a country's allotment for drug production and importation and how much they actually produced or imported, The Permanent Central Board maintained the power to call for a boycott of narcotic imports and exports to that nation. Though effective in some respects, the 1931 Convention also had its deficiencies, as it was difficult for many nations to estimate what their medical and scientific "needs" for narcotics were, and some countries also had trouble tracking their narcotic production, imports, and exports systematically. These shortcomings aside, the 1931 Convention marked a

critical step towards realizing and implementing a comprehensive international system for controlling narcotics—something that negotiators had been trying to do since they first met at Shanghai in 1909.

The League's subsequent efforts to step up international narcotics control efforts fell short. In large part, this was due to the unraveling of the League itself, as the rise of totalitarian governments in Germany and Japan made efforts at international cooperation more difficult. Moreover, enforcement was difficult, as narcotics manufacturers from Europe moved their factories to countries in the developing world, where surveillance was not as tight and their activities were not as likely to come to the attention of the League. What is more, cultivation of opium in Asia and coca in Latin America continued unabated, meaning that supplies of illicit drugs remained abundant. Furthermore, the boycotts of countries that violated the rules of the 1925 and 1931 Conventions were generally ineffective, since producing countries could simply start sending their narcotics to nations that had not signed the treaties. To address these concerns, the League held a conference in 1936, and the resulting agreement—the Convention for the Suppression of the Illicit Traffic in Dangerous Drugs—came into force in 1939. This Convention set up central offices for the supervision and coordination of efforts to suppress drug smuggling. By the time this Convention took effect, however, efforts at international cooperation were crumbling due the rise of fascism and the beginning of World War II.

Nonetheless, the work of the League of Nations in the 1920s and 1930s marked a key step towards the creation of a comprehensive global narcotics control regime, and laid the groundwork for international narcotics controls that would be adopted by the United Nations after World War II.

(See also **Shanghai Commission**; **Hague Convention**; **United Nations**)

References

Bewley-Taylor, David R. 1999. *The United States and International Drug Control, 1909–1997*. London: Pinter.

McAllister, William B. 2000. *Drug Diplomacy in the Twentieth Century*. London: Routledge.

Renborg, Bertil A. 1943. *International Drug Control: A Study of International Administration by and through the League of Nations*. Washington, D.C.: Carnegie Endowment for International Peace.

Renborg, Bertil A. 1957. "International Control of Narcotics" *Law and Contemporary Problems*. 2, no. 2: 86–112.

LEARY, TIMOTHY

Timothy Leary was a major figure in the 1960s counterculture who advocated the use of psychoactive drugs, LSD in particular. Once a professor at Harvard University, Leary ran afoul of the law, but he continued to advocate drug use even after his views cost him his job and his freedom. He remained a proponent of psychoactive drug use until his death in 1996.

Timothy Francis Leary was born on October 22, 1920 in Springfield, Massachusetts. He attended Holy Cross College, West Point, and the University of Alabama, having disciplinary problems at each of them. His problems following rules, however, did not stifle his academic career, and he received his doctorate in psychology from the University of California, Berkeley in 1950. Though a student of the discipline, Leary believed that conventional psychotherapy was ineffective, and during his time at Berkeley he began experimenting with group therapy and transactional analysis theory, which later became more popular in psychological practice. He taught at Berkeley and was the director of psychological research at the Kaiser Foundation Hospital in Oakland from 1955 until 1958, and in 1959 he joined the faculty at Harvard. In spite of his professional success, Leary went through a difficult emotional time at this point in his life, as his wife had committed suicide and he was left to raise his son and daughter on his own.

Leary's path to academic achievement was put off track in 1960, when on a trip to Mexico he consumed psychedelic drugs—in this case, psilocybin—for the first time. Leary found the psilocybin experience to be a transcendental one, and when he returned to Harvard, he began introducing his fellow researchers to the drug, which at the time, was legally available for psychiatric research. Beyond his colleagues, Leary also administered the drug to prison inmates and divinity students. In 1962, he proposed using LSD in experiments, and when revelations came out that he had shared the drug with undergraduate students, he was fired in 1963. Undeterred, Leary continued to be an outspoken proponent of LSD, and he moved to a country estate in Millbrook, New York, which was supposed to be a center for drug research. In reality, the Millbrook estate turned out to be more of a hippie commune, a center where guests took psychoactive drugs and meditated. Leary's legal troubles continued when he was arrested and convicted on marijuana charges in Texas, and his house in Millbrook was raided by law enforcement. Despite these problems, the counterculture of the 1960s provided a ready audience for Leary's message, most famously summed up by his call for people to "tune in, turn on, and drop out"—to tune in and turn on to the magical world of the psychedelic, and drop out of mainstream society. In the 1960s, he experimented with psilocybin with leading countercultural figures such as Allen Ginsberg, Jack Kerouac, and William S. Burroughs. He also wrote several books, such as *High Priest* and *Politics of Ecstasy*, where he encouraged readers to explore psychedelic drugs. In 1967, he founded the League of Spiritual Discovery, a quasi-religious group that used LSD as its sacrament, arguing that the hallucinations produced by the drug expanded consciousness in a way that was so profound it was transcendent. Leary also toured the country with a traveling light-and-sound show that he used to expound the virtues of psychedelic drugs, and by the end of the decade, he was a celebrity—adored by the counterculture and those who wanted to undertake psychedelic journeys with LSD, and reviled by law enforcement and others who were horrified by his message, fearful that it would inspire youths across the country to try psychoactive drugs.

Though he had disavowed politics in the 1960s, Leary announced that he was going to run for governor of California in 1970. His campaign was stymied, though, when he was convicted on a marijuana charge and sentenced to ten years in prison, which he served in San Luis Obispo, California. Leary escaped from prison by climbing up a rooftop and telephone pole and crossing over the prison's barbed wire before dropping onto a nearby highway. From there, he fled first to Algeria and then to Afghanistan, where he was again arrested and deported back to the United States in 1973. In all, however, Leary served just forty-two months in prison, as California Governor Edmund G. Brown Jr. ordered his release in 1976. Leary spent the next two decades of his life living in Beverly Hills, and giving lectures on college campuses across the country. While he continued to advocate experimentation with drugs, Leary also became the leader of the futurist movement, which looked at trends in the future and technology. He also dabbled in virtual reality, designed computer games, and started a software company. Later in his life, he became fascinated by death, and in 1995, when he learned that he had an inoperable cancer, he responded by saying he was thrilled with the prospect of dying. In 1996, he passed away due to prostate cancer at the age of seventy-five.

(See also **Drugs and the Counterculture**)

References

Chepesiuk, Ron. 1999. *The War on Drugs: An International Encyclopedia*. Santa Barbara, CA: ABC-CLIO.

Davenport-Hines, Richard. 2001. *The Pursuit of Oblivion: A Global History of Narcotics, 1500–2000*. London: Weidenfeld & Nicolson.

Mansnerus, Laura. 1996. "Timothy Leary, Pied Piper of Psychedelic 60's, Dies at 75" *New York Times*. (June 1): 1 and 12.

LESIEUR, HENRY

Henry Lesieur is a gambling addiction specialist in Rhode Island, and one of the pioneering researchers in the study of gambling addiction. Most notably, in his 1977 book *The Chase*, Lesieur put a human face on the problem by telling the stories of problem gamblers to a wide audience.

Henry Lesieur learned about problem gambling when he was a teenager working at a gas station near a horse track. During his time there, he heard stories from the people who bet on horseracing, and became interested in problem gambling. As a graduate student at the University of Massachusetts, Amherst, he continued talking to gamblers, both among the student body and the members of Gamblers Anonymous. He turned the information gleaned from these discussions into his master's thesis, and eventually published them in a book—*The Chase*—in 1976. In *The Chase*, Lesieur conducted a detailed study of fifty-three problem gamblers, interviewing each individual for between one and eight hours. Providing such an in-depth understanding of the experiences and psychologies of gambling addicts, *The Chase* was one of the first works to tell the story of problem gamblers from their own perspective. *The Chase* highlighted that the main problem facing gambling addicts was that they did not quit playing when they were ahead. The thrill of previous winnings, he found, kept them coming back for more, just as many narcotic addicts become addicted after a pleasant first experience with drugs. When gamblers started losing, however, continuing to gamble was no longer a matter of reliving a previous success; instead, it became about "the chase"—trying to make up for losses by winning them back with further gambling. Lesieur also found that gamblers became engrossed in the action and excitement of gambling,

to the point that they neglected other areas of their life, and that they would rationalize their losses in order to justify continued gambling. Eventually, gambling behavior would spiral out of control, Lesieur found, as gamblers would turn to others—family, co-workers, and friends—to help finance their habits. In extreme cases, gamblers could become bookmakers themselves, or turn to crime to get money to gamble.

After the publication of *The Chase*, Lesieur began working in the department of criminology at St. John's University in New York City, and he later continued his work researching and treating gambling addiction at Lifespan Hospital in Rhode Island. Among his most notable contributions to the study of gambling problems was the development of the South Oaks Gambling Screen (SOGS), which he created along with Sheila Blume in 1987 to identify possible gambling addicts. The SOGS is currently used by practitioners on six continents and has been translated into more than thirty-five languages. He has also conducted research on pathological gambling among youths, and participated in studies looking at the neurochemistry of gambling addictions. Lesieur also founded the *Journal of Gambling Studies* and served as its editor for twelve years. Today, he treats pathological gamblers, their spouses, and their parents in the Rhode Island Gambling Treatment Program.

(See also **Custer, Robert L.**; **Gamblers Anonymous (GA)**)

References

Comings, D. E., R. J. Rosenthal, H. R. Lesieur, L. J. Rugle, D. Muhleman, C. Chiu, G. Diets, and R. Gade. 1996.

"A Study of the Dopamine D2 Receptor Gene in Pathological Gambling." *Pharmacogenetics.* 6, no. 3: 223–234.

"Henry R. Lesieur, PsyD, PhD, NCGC." *Rhode Island Hospital.* [Online information accessed 04/26/09] http://www.lifespan.org/rih/services/mentalhealth/gambling/staff/lesieur.htm.

Lesieur, Henry R. *The Chase: Career of the Compulsive Gambler.* New York: Anchor Press.

Thompson, William N. 2001. *Gambling in America: An Encyclopedia of History, Issues, and Society.* Santa Barbara, CA: ABC-CLIO.

LIFERING

LifeRing, which is also sometimes referred to as LifeRing Secular Recovery, is a nonprofit, mutual aid organization that offers a nonspiritual alternative to Alcoholics Anonymous (AA) and other twelve-step abstinence programs. Unlike AA, which involves members admitting a powerlessness over alcohol and submitting to a personally defined "higher power" as important steps on the road to their recovery, LifeRing strives, in a secular manner, to empower individuals to take the lead in their fights against addiction. LifeRing, which split from Secular Organizations for Sobriety (SOS) in 1997 and officially incorporated itself in 1999, has meetings in the United States, Canada, and Europe.

LifeRing's history can be traced back to another nonspiritual addiction recovery group, SOS, which began when James Christopher, an alcoholic looking for help, became uncomfortable with AA's invocation of spirituality and a higher power as central components of overcoming addiction and maintaining sobriety. After publishing a well-received article, "Sobriety Without Superstition," Christopher decided to form a secular, self-help organization for recovering alcoholics. SOS's first meeting took place in November 1986 in North Hollywood, California.

SOS remains an active secular recovery organization with meetings in every state across the country, but in 1997, a number of SOS members split off and formed a separate faction, which officially incorporated itself as LifeRing in 1999. Since its founding, LifeRing has, like SOS, provided its members with a secular program for addiction recovery. LifeRing's approach is typified by its belief that within each member is an addict self and sober self that struggle with one another for dominance within the recovering person.

LifeRing's central tenet is the "Three-S" philosophy. The first "S" in this philosophy refers to sobriety, which LifeRing defines as the complete abstention from alcohol or addictive drugs at all times. The second "S" refers to secularity, as LifeRing eschews the spiritual elements, such as the submission to a higher power, that famously characterize AA and numerous other twelve-step programs. Secularity does not, however, mean that all LifeRing members are atheists; instead, LifeRing's notion of secularity revolves around the inclusion of addicts of all faiths with the understanding that an individual's recovery, regardless of his or her religious background, can be achieved through human, rather than divine, intervention. The third "S" in LifeRing's philosophy is self-help, which foregrounds another difference between it and twelve-step programs. Whereas the AA and Narcotics Anonymous (NA) programs are predicated on alcoholics and addicts admitting their powerlessness over addictive substances, LifeRing focuses on individual motivation and effort as the keys to its members overcoming their addictions and achieving sobriety.

LifeRing meetings are consequently run in a different fashion than those of AAs or NAs. As a secular group, LifeRing meetings do not, of course, begin with any prayers, but LifeRing meetings are also distinctive from AA's in their lack of formal sponsorship. Members of LifeRing are encouraged to empower themselves, and this empowerment can take on a variety of forms, as LifeRing believes that individual members should be free to incorporate any ideas and approaches they find useful to their recovery. This can include adopting elements of the AA approach to sobriety, and a survey LifeRing undertook of its own members affirms the prevalence of this approach; the survey indicated that 55% of LifeRing members reported continued participation in twelve-step groups. Of those LifeRing members participating in multiple mutual aid recovery groups, 44% considered LifeRing the most important group for their recovery, while 30% reported that they held LifeRing and twelve-step programs to be of equal importance. The fact that LifeRing meetings often take place on the same treatment premises that twelve-step groups use further highlights the openness of LifeRing's approach to promoting individualized recovery.

The LifeRing survey also provided information about the organization's demographic makeup. The average member is forty-eight years old, and 81% of members describe themselves as White. 81% of LifeRing members have some level of college experience, and 58% of the organization's members are men. Religiously, LifeRing members run the gamut of affiliations, with 31% reporting a background in Protestantism, 25% from Catholicism, and 4% from Judaism. 16% of members described themselves as something "other," and 24% claimed to have no religious background. Despite coming from a variety of religious backgrounds, 82% of LifeRing members reported having little or no religious participation within the last year. About 75% of the organization's members, however, did report having prior contact with a twelve-step program before joining LifeRing.

LifeRing puts out a number of publications, including, *How Was Your Week?*, the organization's main handbook, and *Recovery By Choice*, a workbook featuring exercises and worksheets intended to assist members in crafting a personalized recovery program. These books, as well as additional information about LifeRing meetings, can be found at the organization's Web site, http://www.unhooked.com.

(See also **Alcoholics Anonymous (AA)**; **Narcotics Anonymous (NA)**)

References

LifeRing. "About LifeRing." [Online information accessed 05/21/09] http://www.unhooked.com/lifering.org/index.htm.

Save Our Selves. "An Overview of SOS: A self-empowerment approach to recovery." [Online information accessed 05/21/09] http://www.sossobriety.org/overview.htm.

Save Our Selves. "The SOS Story." [Online information accessed 05/21/09] http://www.sossobriety.org/james%20christopher.htm.

White, William L., and Nicolaus, Martin. "Styles of Secular Recovery." 2005. *Counselor.* (August): 58–60.

LINDESMITH, ALFRED R.

Alfred R. Lindesmith was a professor of sociology at Indiana University who was one of the first academics to study opiate addiction from a sociological perspective. His work led him to become an outspoken critic of federal drug policies in the middle of the twentieth century, as he advocated for addicts to be treated more like individuals suffering from a disease, rather than criminals.

Alfred Ray Lindesmith was born in Clinton Falls, Minnesota on August 3, 1905. He graduated from Carleton College in Minnesota in 1927, getting a bachelor's degree in education, and he earned a master's degree in English from Columbia University Teacher's College in 1929. After working at Central State Teacher's College in Wisconsin, he went on to earn his doctorate in sociology at the University of Chicago in 1937, and he then took a position as a professor at the University of Indiana. It was during his time at Chicago that Lindesmith took an interest in addiction and drug policy, as he made connections with Ben Reitman, a doctor who specialized in the treatment of drug addiction. Through Reitman, Lindesmith made contacts with a Chicago thief, con artist, and drug addict named Broadway Jones, who provided him with an entrée into the drug scene and social world of Chicago's opiate addicts. In his dissertation, *The Nature of Opiate Addiction*, Lindesmith interviewed more than sixty addicts, and he also conferred with fellow graduate student Bingham Dai, who was writing his dissertation on the sociology of addiction as well. In his dissertation, Lindesmith found that withdrawal from opiate use was agonizing, that addicts continued to use opiates in order to avoid withdrawal symptoms (and not for pleasure), that they

developed a self-concept based on their drug use, that they were of normal intelligence, that they were not violent or sexually deviant, that they were spread evenly among races and classes, that addiction was a mental phenomenon, and perhaps most importantly, that most addicts did not feel that tight drug control laws could stop illicit drug dealing.

When Lindesmith published his findings in a series of journal articles in the 1940s, the Federal Bureau of Narcotics (FBN) was displeased, since his conclusions directly contradicted the assumptions that lay behind federal drug control policy. Possibly in hopes of discrediting him, FBN agents worked to sabotage Lindesmith's career at Indiana University before he could get tenure. Undeterred, Lindesmith continued his studies, and in 1947 he published them in his first book, *Opiate Addiction*. He soon became a public critic of the FBN and its policies, and the FBN responded by convincing conservative judges and intellectuals to write articles that dismissed Lindesmith's work in hopes of silencing him and his criticism of the federal approach to drug control. The federal authorities even went so far as to consider planting narcotics in Lindesmith's home so they could "prove" he was a drug addict and debunk his theories, even though he never used drugs illegally or advocated their use. Few of Lindesmith's fellow professors or intellectuals supported him either, though many criticized and dismissed his work. By the mid-1950s, Lindesmith ceased publishing in scholarly journals, and concentrated on advocating for changes in the nation's narcotics laws in more public forums. He published articles in such popular publications as *The Nation, The Saturday Review,* and *The New York*

Times, and he also expressed his views in testimonies before Congress.

After the passage of the Boggs Act and the Narcotic Control Act of 1956 stiffened federal penalties against drug users and dealers, powerful organizations such as the American Bar Association and the American Medical Association began to echo Lindesmith's criticisms of the federal government's approach to the drug problem. This led to the publication of Lindesmith's final, and most important book, *The Addict and the Law*, in 1965. In *The Addict and the Law*, Lindesmith argued that the Harrison Narcotics Act, which was the basis of federal anti-drug legislation at the time, was not intended to serve as a basis for prohibitive policies against drug use, and that the FBN purposefully misinterpreted it in order to make political and budgetary gains. The Boggs Act and the Narcotic Control Act, he argued, were continuations of the flawed logic of drug prohibition. Continuing to wage battle against drug use by stiffening penalties and tightening enforcement were useless, he maintained, since previous efforts to control opiates had not succeeded in reducing rates of addiction, but instead had the opposite effect of enticing people to become involved in drug trafficking due to the increased prices of illegal drugs caused by tight enforcement. Instead of trying to crack down on drug supplies by using the police and the criminal justice system, Lindesmith argued that the government should adopt a drug policy like Britain's, which allowed for the provision of small amounts of drugs to addicts living in the community. Anticipating future developments that would take place in the 1980s,

Lindesmith warned that if the government continued with its policies of repression against drug dealers and users, the prison population would explode in the United States. Though *The Addict and the Law* did not have a substantial effect on public policy, it was groundbreaking in that it helped plant an intellectual seed that would spur debates over drug policy for decades to come.

Lindesmith retired from Indiana University in 1975, though he remained active in his calls for drug policy reform, speaking to civic organizations, community groups, and charitable foundations. He passed away in February of 1991, though his legacy was carried on in 1994 when an advocacy organization dedicated to drug law reform—the Lindesmith Center—was named for him.

(See also **Dai, Bingham**; **Drug Policy Alliance Network**; **Federal Bureau of Narcotics (FBN)**; **Primary Source Documents**)

References

Chepesiuk, Ron. 1999. *The War on Drugs: An International Encyclopedia*. Santa Barbara, CA: ABC-CLIO.

Keys, David Patrick and John F. Galliher. 2000. *Confronting the Drug Control Establishment: Alfred Lindesmith as a Public Intellectual*. Albany: State University of New York Press.

Lindesmith, Alfred R. 1947. *Opiate Addiction*. Bloomington, IN: Principia Press, Inc.

Lindesmith, Alfred R. 1965. *The Addict and the Law*. Bloomington, IN: Indiana University Press.

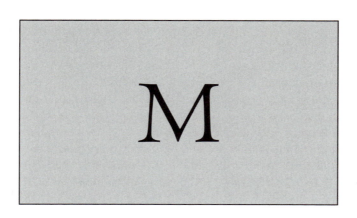

MARIHUANA COMMISSION

The Marihuana Commission was a federal commission that studied the public policy questions posed by marijuana in the early 1970s. Though it found that the drug did not pose significant dangers, and recommended its decriminalization, the federal government disregarded its findings, and continued to treat marijuana as a dangerous drug under the 1970 Comprehensive Drug Abuse Prevention and Control Act.

Until the 1960s, marijuana use was relatively rare in the United States, generally limited to drug-using subcultures in the inner cities and rural areas. This began to change in the 1960s, as the practice of smoking marijuana became increasingly popular with the emergence of the counterculture. Though use of the drug rose, it nonetheless remained illegal and subject to criminal penalties under the 1937 Marihuana Tax Act, and later under the 1970 Comprehensive Drug Abuse Prevention and Control Act.

As the number of arrests for marijuana-related offenses grew, so did calls for the government to reconsider the actual effects of marijuana and the wisdom of having such tight controls over it. The 1970 Comprehensive Drug Abuse Prevention and Control Act created an opening for authorities to consider these questions by empowering Congress to establish a National Commission on Marihuana and Drug Abuse to undertake a study on marijuana. The Commission had thirteen members—four members of Congress, and nine appointed by President Richard Nixon. The Commission studied scientific literature on marijuana use and its effects, and also sponsored a national study on patterns of marijuana use, public attitudes towards the drug, and the enforcement of marijuana laws. In 1972, it published its first report, "Marihuana: A Signal of Misunderstanding."

In its report, the Commission estimated that even though use of the drug was widespread among the adult population, about half of the individuals who tried marijuana only experimented with it out of curiosity, and did not use it regularly. The Commission found that most of the individuals who used the drug more than once did so only occasionally —generally less than once a week—and only for recreational purposes, not because they were addicted. Only 2% of the population that used marijuana used it daily. Based on its research, the Commission concluded that there was little danger or physical or psychological harm coming from occasional use, and that since most marijuana users did not indulge in the drug regularly, it did not constitute a major threat to public health. Furthermore, the Commission found that the drug caused neither physical dependence nor criminal behavior, thus making it but a minor nuisance—not a major threat—from a public safety perspective. Taking these findings into account, the Commission recommended that possession of one ounce of marijuana or less should be decriminalized, though it advised that the cultivation and distribution of the drug for commercial purposes should continue to be limited. While advising that marijuana use should be discouraged, the Commission counseled against using the criminal justice system as a weapon in the campaign against the drug. Even though he had personally appointed most of the Commission's members, President Nixon dismissed the report and did not propose the changes in national drug policy that the Commission had recommended.

Even though it did not have the support of the President, several prominent organizations, including the American Bar Association, the National Education Association, the National Council of Churches, the American Public Health Association, and the governing board of the American Medical Association endorsed the decriminalization of marijuana in subsequent years. The report also helped garner support for the National Organization for the Reform of Marijuana Laws, an advocacy group that pushes for a reconsideration of the nation's marijuana control regime. In 1973, Oregon decriminalized possession of small amounts of marijuana, and ten other states stopped incarcerating individuals caught possessing the drug. Political support for decriminalization began to decrease in the mid-1970s, however, especially after national statistics began to show that marijuana use was on the rise among high school students.

(See also **Comprehensive Drug Abuse Prevention and Control Act**; **Drugs and the Counterculture**; **Marihuana Tax Act**; **National Organization for the Reform of Marijuana Laws (NORML)**)

References

Carson-Dewitt, Rosalyn, ed. 2001. *Encyclopedia of Drugs, Alcohol & Addictive Behavior. Second Edition*. New York: Macmillan Reference USA.

National Commission on Marihuana and Drug Use. 1972. *Marihuana: A Signal of Misunderstanding*. Washington, D.C.: U.S. Government Printing Office.

MARIHUANA TAX ACT

The Marihuana Tax Act was a piece of 1937 legislation that effectively outlawed the recreational use of marijuana in the United States. Like the Harrison Narcotics Act did for opiates and cocaine, the Marihuana Tax Act did not directly ban the use of cannabis, but regulated it so tightly that its use was effectively made illegal.

Until 1937, cannabis was regulated by the 1906 Pure Food and Drug Act, which required that cannabis and preparations containing the drug be labeled as such when sold to the public. In the years leading up to the passage of the Harrison Act, many reformers wanted to include cannabis on the list of controlled substances, along with opiates and cocaine, but given that the drug was used mainly in plasters, veterinary medicine, and medical preparations that were not intoxicating, it was left off the list of drugs controlled by the Act. In addition, it was not universally accepted that cannabis was a habit-forming drug at the time, and many witnesses before the House Ways and Means Committee charged with considering the Harrison Act denied that it had addictive qualities.

In the following decades, however, attitudes towards the drug began to change. Popular association of the drug with Mexicans in the 1910s and 1920s made the substance seem foreign and menacing to many in the United States. This trend became more prevalent in the 1930s, as Mexicans competed for jobs with Whites in the Western United States during the Great Depression, fueling jingoism against Mexicans and their cultural practices. In 1925, the League of Nations added cannabis to the list of substances controlled by international narcotics control agreements, thus increasing the pressure to regulate it domestically. Furthermore, rumors that the drug made individuals go on murderous rampages and commit crimes led some to believe that the drug was just as dangerous as the more tightly regulated drugs. In 1929, when the Public Health Service Narcotic Hospitals were established, provisions were made for the institutions to treat individuals addicted

to cannabis—a sign that increasing numbers of lawmakers in Washington, D.C. believed the drug was dangerous and habit-forming. What is more, some states, such as Louisiana, New Mexico, and Colorado passed state laws against marijuana in the 1920s. In spite of these changes, however, federal drug enforcement officials were reluctant to add another substance to the list of drugs it was charged with controlling, since they already had their hands full trying to control the smuggling and use of opiates and cocaine. Nonetheless, pressure continued to mount, especially after a presenter at the 1934 meeting of the American Psychiatric Association claimed that rates of cannabis use in southern states were as high as 25%, and that the drug had a tendency to cause homosexual behavior.

As pressure to crack down on cannabis use began to mount in the early 1930s, the initial response of officials with the Federal Bureau of Narcotics (FBN) was to minimize the problem, and encourage states to enact laws and enforce them if they wanted to address it. The FBN at first believed that marijuana was not nearly as menacing as heroin, doubted the constitutionality of proposed federal laws for marijuana control, and feared that marijuana laws would be difficult to enforce since cannabis plants—unlike opium poppies and coca leaves—could be grown so easily on U.S. soil. Eventually, however, the combination of pressure from local police forces in the southwestern parts of the country, coupled with appeals from governors and the Secretary of the Treasury, convinced FBN leader Harry J. Anslinger to lead the legislative charge against marijuana in the mid-1930s. To garner public support for anti-marijuana legislation, Anslinger led a public relations onslaught against the drug, writing articles decrying its dangers such as "Marihuana: Assassin of Youth," which appeared in *American Magazine* in July of 1937. In spite of opposition from some medical authorities who testified before Congress during the deliberations concerning the necessity of marijuana control, a new bill controlling the drug—the Marihuana Tax Act—became law in October of 1937.

Like the Harrison Act, the Marihuana Tax Act did not ban the use or sale of the drug. Instead, it regulated it, by requiring a stamp from the Treasury Department in order to sell the drug. Prices for the marijuana tax stamps varied, from $1 per year for producers of the drug and medical professionals, to $5 for individuals who were not medical professionals, and $24 for importers and manufacturers of the drug. In addition, all marijuana transfers were taxed $1 per ounce. The Act also had provisions that anyone who grew, transported, prescribed, or sold the drug needed to register with the federal government to pay the tax, but since the drug was illegal in most states, registration would have made individuals subject to prosecution for violating state laws. In addition, the federal government refused to give any of the tax stamps necessary to sell the drug legally, thus making commerce in the drug effectively impossible. Violators of the law—anyone who possessed marijuana without a tax stamp—were subject to a fine of up to $2,000 and up to five years in prison. Though the law allowed for the use of marijuana as a medicine, such exceptions were rarely made, and as a result of the Act, medical preparations that included marijuana were pulled from the market by 1939.

In the first five years the law was in place, it was enforced rigorously by federal officials, as they destroyed about 60,000 tons of marijuana and an average of about 1,000 individuals per year were arrested for violating the law. In 1950, the constitutionality of the Act was challenged in *United States v. Sanchez et al.*, when a District Court ruled that the Act was so severe that it imposed a penalty for the transfer of marijuana—not a tax —and that it was therefore unconstitutional. The Supreme Court, however, upheld the constitutionality of the Act, concluding that it was legal even though it imposed severe regulations on the drug and discouraged and deterred the sale, possession, and use of cannabis.

Like the Harrison Act, the Marihuana Tax Act was, while technically a revenue-raising measure, a piece of legislation that effectively outlawed the sale and possession of drugs. As a result of the Act, marijuana came to be treated similarly to other controlled substances, such as opiates and cocaine. It was not until the 1960s and 1970s that attitudes and approaches towards marijuana would begin to change.

(See also **Anslinger, Harry J.**; **Federal Bureau of Narcotics (FBN)**; **Harrison Narcotics Act**; **Pure Food and Drug Act**)

References

Belenko, Steven R., ed. 2000. *Drugs and Drug Policy in America: A Documentary History.* Westport, CT: Greenwood Press.

Chepesiuk, Ron. 1999. *The War on Drugs: An International Encyclopedia.* Santa Barbara, CA: ABC-CLIO.

Davenport-Hines, Richard. 2001. *The Pursuit of Oblivion: A Global History of*

Narcotics, 1500–2000. London: Weidenfeld & Nicolson.

Earlywine, Mitch. 2002. *Understanding Marijuana: A New Look at the Scientific Evidence*. Oxford: Oxford University Press.

Musto, David F. 1987. *The American Disease: Origins of Narcotic Control*. Expanded Edition. New York: Oxford University Press.

MASTER SETTLEMENT AGREEMENT (MSA)

Struck in response to a wave of state suits against big tobacco, the Master Settlement Agreement (MSA) was a 1998 deal between the attorneys general of forty-six states and the tobacco industry. The MSA halted the states' suits and prohibited most forms of future litigation against tobacco companies, who, in exchange, agreed to pay states billions of dollars towards the cost of caring for smoking-related illnesses and to fund anti-smoking programs. While the MSA has had the effect of reducing smoking levels, many feel the details of the MSA enabled the tobacco industry to get the better end of this landmark deal.

The MSA took shape in the wake of the failure of a similar pact—the Global Settlement Agreement (GSA)—between big tobacco and a number of attorneys general. Announced on June 20, 1997, the GSA called for tobacco companies to pay $365.5 billion over the following twenty-five years in order to cover the states' medical costs for smoking-related illnesses and fund smoking cessation programs. Under the terms of the GSA, the tobacco industry also agreed to accept stronger warning labels on its products and assented to new and greater restrictions on the ways it advertised and

promoted them. In exchange for these moves, the tobacco companies would be protected from the class-action lawsuits that had begun to seriously threaten the industry's future viability. In addition, the states would prohibit punitive damage awards being granted on account of past industry misconduct. Though the GSA was announced, it would not be legally binding without the passage of a Congressional act to authorize it. Debated vigorously by public health figures, attorneys, and industry lobbyists, as well as congressional figures on both sides of the aisle, the GSA proved to be a difficult sell. Despite the attempts of Senator John McCain (R-Arizona) to modify the GSA so as to gain more congressional backers for the bill, the GSA was not ratified, essentially leaving the attorneys general and the tobacco companies back where they began.

Since the government proved unable to pass the GSA, when the tobacco companies and attorneys general returned to the negotiating table, the tobacco industry presented a diminished version of the GSA that was called the MSA. Unlike its predecessor, the MSA went into effect immediately after being announced on November 16, 1998 because it dropped all elements of the GSA that would have required congressional approval. Consequently, Food and Drug Administration regulation of tobacco was not a part of the MSA, nor were new regulations regarding stronger label warnings and stricter public smoking bans.

The MSA was also quickly accepted in large part because of the way the agreement was proffered. Only eight attorneys general were present at the negotiations that shaped the MSA, and they, in turn, offered all states the opportunity to sign on—but with only seven days to decide. Ultimately, forty-six states decided to accept the money guaranteed by the MSA rather than take the route of continued litigation and the financial uncertainty and legal risks that would come with it. Mississippi, Florida, Texas, and Minnesota were not part of the MSA, as they separately reached agreements with the tobacco companies.

Under the regulations of the MSA, the four major tobacco companies—Philip Morris USA, R. J. Reynolds Tobacco Company, Brown & Williamson Tobacco Corporation, and Lorillard Tobacco Company—agreed to pay $206 billion to the remaining forty-six states over a period of twenty-five years. (Forty smaller tobacco companies later joined the agreement.) The tobacco companies additionally consented to fund a national foundation dedicated to public health and reducing smoking. This foundation could not be like the industry-led Tobacco Institute Research Committee/ Council for Tobacco Research or the Tobacco Institute, which had tried to obscure evidence that smoking was dangerous, and were disbanded under the terms of the MSA. The tobacco companies also agreed to operate with greater transparency. This meant that industry records and research would be opened up to examination, and industry documents—many of which exposed decades of corporate fraud, prevarications, and full knowledge of the health threats that smoking posed—were to be posted on publicly accessible, user-friendly Web sites.

More noticeable to the general public, the tobacco companies assented to drastic changes in the ways in which they could advertise and market their products. In general, they agreed to stop targeting youths. One component of this was a prohibition on the use of cartoon characters, such as Joe Camel, in their advertisements. Youth access to free samples was also prohibited, as was all outdoor advertising. The sale of merchandise bearing tobacco brand names was banned, and the MSA also restricted sponsorship by brand names. Proof-of-purchase gifts were prohibited, and the minimum size for a pack of cigarettes was set at twenty.

While these changes certainly altered the face and practices of the tobacco industry, many were unhappy with the MSA. Critics of the MSA argued that the advertising restrictions were not tight enough, as the agreement did not have any provision banning the use of human figures (such as the Marlboro Man) in tobacco advertising. Many officials and public health advocates believe that the $206 billion the tobacco companies agreed to pay is not enough to cover the true costs of caring for patients with tobacco-related illnesses. Moreover, under the MSA, though individual and class-action suits could still be brought against tobacco companies, states, who have to bear the biggest brunt of health care costs, forwent their right to future litigation. As such, many feel that in signing on to the MSA, the states, whose insurance programs will have to bear the monetary burden of dealing with smoking-related sicknesses, made a financially imprudent decision when considered in the long term.

In the short term, too, the MSA has not proven to be as financially helpful in reducing smoking and its public health effects as many states had believed it would. In a number of cases, tobacco industry funds went towards balancing state budgets rather than directly into anti-tobacco programs. Though the Centers for Disease Control and Prevention recommended that a minimum of 20% of MSA funds should be funneled to such programs, only about 4% of these funds made it to their intended destination. And because the tobacco industry's continued financial contributions to the MSA depended on the stability and profitability of tobacco companies, cash-strapped state governments, who prior to the MSA had been opponents of the industry in many a courtroom, oddly became invested in the financial well-being of big tobacco. That the states and the tobacco industry had become strange bedfellows as a result of the MSA became apparent in Illinois, when a jury there returned a $10.1 billion verdict in a class-action lawsuit against Philip Morris, and in response, thirty attorneys general filed an amicus brief telling the court that if the tobacco giant went bankrupt, there would be dire financial consequences for the states that had become dependent on its financial contributions.

These financial contributions, it turns out, have not been as sizeable as expected. Because of a tax within the MSA that caused cigarette prices to rise, the big tobacco companies lost some of their market share to cheaper, no-frills cigarette manufacturers. This triggered a provision within the MSA that permitted the tobacco companies, on account of lost revenues, to reduce their annual payments. The financial impact of this was far from trifling, as Philip Morris, for example, in 2006 said it expected to withhold $1.2 billion from its annual payments on account of its reduced market share. States were not the only ones who financially suffered on account of missing out on these payments, as institutions involved in anti-smoking efforts quickly found themselves without vital funds. For example, payments to the Public Education fund ceased in 2003 as a result of market share changes, and the American Legacy Foundation, which runs the "Truth" anti-smoking campaign, also received its last payment from the tobacco industry that year.

For all its shortcomings, the MSA did, however, significantly reduce smoking levels in the United States. Youth smoking levels, in particular, are at their lowest point in almost thirty years, and in general, tobacco sales fell by more than 20%, putting them to their lowest level since 1950. The MSA's impact upon the tobacco industry and smoking in America has thus been mixed.

(See also **P. Lorillard**; **Tobacco Industry Research Committee (TIRC)**; **Tobacco Institute**)

References

Brandt, Allan M. 2007. *The Cigarette Century: The Rise, Fall, and Deadly Persistence of the Product That Defined America*. New York: Basic Books.

Cordry, Harold V. 2001. *Tobacco: A Reference Handbook*. Santa Barbara, CA: ABC-CLIO.

Goodman, Jordan, ed. 2005. *Tobacco in History and Culture: An Encyclopedia*. Detroit: Thomson Gale.

MCCOY, BILL

Bill McCoy was one of the nation's most notorious liquor smugglers during national prohibition. Launching a famous smuggling operation that utilized a row of ships off the U.S. coastline, McCoy gained a reputation for importing high-quality, unadulterated liquor, which was referred to as "the real McCoy." He was arrested for violating the Volstead Act, and upon his release, did not return to rum running.

William McCoy was born in Syracuse, New York in 1877 and served in the U.S. Navy. After his service, Bill, along with his brother, Ben, developed a successful business building yachts and speedboats in Florida, often for rich and powerful Americans like Andrew Carnegie, John Wannamaker, and members of the Vanderbilt family. The onset of the Great Depression, however, hurt McCoy's financial standing and likely drew him into a new enterprise—smuggling.

Smuggling also appealed to McCoy for reasons beyond the wealth that could be made by engaging in it during hard economic times. Though McCoy was not a drinker, he personally opposed national prohibition because of what he saw as its oppressive character. Likening the Eighteenth Amendment to the Stamp Act and the Fugitive Slave Law, McCoy claimed that prohibition ran counter to his notion of American freedoms. Similarly, McCoy cast himself in the mold of the nation's founding fathers, who, he said, would patriotically defy the laws that they resented. In particular, McCoy modeled his role as a smuggler after John Hancock, who, in addition to being the first signer of the Declaration of Independence, proudly defied British embargoes by smuggling liquor (and other items) into the colonies and encouraged others to do the same. As a result, McCoy deemed that Hancock might stand as the patron saint of rumrunners.

McCoy's first smuggling efforts involved loading his ship in the Caribbean with cases of liquor and sneaking his cargo back to American docks. But what distinguished McCoy from other smugglers engaging in similar activities, however, was his origination of "Rum Row," which referred to the lining up of alcohol-carrying ships just beyond American waters. These boats were within the safety of international waters, but close enough to the American shore that other boats could sail out to meet them and purchase high-quality liquor. This novel setup was so successful that, after upgrading ships, McCoy's boat was described as a high-end, floating liquor store. And consumer demand was particularly high because McCoy's goods were noted for being undiluted and unadulterated, unlike much bootleg liquor in America, which could be downright dangerous to consume. As a result, the term "the real McCoy" was born to describe the quality of McCoy's Rum Row liquor.

Once purchasing their alcohol and returning to their own speed boats, McCoy's patrons were generally successful in outracing Coast Guard patrols to the shore. In fact, the setup was so difficult for the Coast Guard to combat that Rum Rows sprang up across the Atlantic seaboard, with outposts along every state and nearly every city from Maine to Florida. Similar Rum Rows existed in the Gulf of Mexico and along the Pacific. McCoy's signature business model, which brought him a great deal of wealth very quickly, was highly successful.

But while other smugglers continued to operate under this setup, McCoy was actually captured by the government fairly early on. In 1923, he pleaded guilty to violating the Volstead Act and served less than one year of time in a low-security federal prison in Atlanta. Upon his release, McCoy did not return to the smuggling business and instead became a realtor. In the following years,

Rum Rows devolved into more violent operations, and the Coast Guard more effectively policed the nation's shores. Though he was only a part of the business for a relatively short period of time, Bill McCoy was perhaps America's most notorious smuggler. He died in 1948.

(See also **Alcohol Bootlegging and Smuggling**; **Volstead Act (18th Amendment)**).

References

Burns, Eric. 2004. *The Spirits of America: A Social History of America*. Philadelphia: Temple University Press.

Lender, Mark Edward and James Kirby Martin. 1982. *Drinking in America: A History*. New York: The Free Press.

METHADONE

Methadone is a synthetic opiate used to treat opiate addiction. Though the use of methadone treatments has its drawbacks, it is still one of the most effective tools that addiction scientists have to help ease addicts off of illicit opiates such as heroin.

The German pharmaceutical company IG Farbenindustrie first developed methadone as a synthetic opiate when the country's supplies of drugs shipped from overseas were cut off during World War II. After the war, the pharmaceutical company Lilly took over its production, and named the drug Dolophine. Scientists at the Addiction Research Center in Lexington, Kentucky began experimenting with the drug as a potential cure for opiate addiction, but had mixed results. They put addicts on high doses and then abruptly withdrew the drug, leading the patients to suffer extended withdrawal pains akin to those they experienced when coming off of heroin. Nonetheless, in the 1950s methadone gradually began to replace morphine and codeine as the main drug used to help heroin addicts detoxify.

In the early 1960s, researchers Vincent Dole and Marie Nyswander at Rockefeller University in New York City began experimenting with the drug as a substitution treatment to wean heroin addicts off of street drugs. Dole and Nyswander tested the drug on hardened addicts—individuals who had been addicted to opiates for at least fourteen years. They gave addicts participating in their study large daily doses of methadone that was dissolved and mixed with orange juice as they came off of heroin. They found that methadone blocked many of the effects of heroin withdrawal. Once an addict was on methadone, doses of heroin could be reduced progressively, and eventually stopped within a few weeks. Dole and Nyswander concluded that methadone was a particularly effective treatment since it did not have the same psychoactive effects as heroin, and it did not make users as sedated or tranquilized. Moreover, they found that patients on methadone began to gain a sense of hope, as they started to take better care of themselves and sought out work. While patients participating in their study began on locked wards, Dole and Nyswander soon realized that such security measures were unnecessary with methadone, and as participants in their study improved, they let them leave the hospital each day to work part-time jobs. These successes gave Dole and Nyswander hope that methadone could help heroin addicts recover and lead relatively normal lives in mainstream society. In 1965, they published their findings in the *Journal of the American Medical*

Association, and they also set up a similar program at Beth Israel hospital in New York City.

The Federal Bureau of Narcotics (FBN), which was in charge of enforcing the nation's drug laws at the time, initially opposed the work of Dole and Nyswander, since they did not want to give doctors the authority to prescribe any opiates or opioids—even methadone—to addicts. FBN officials tried to intimidate Dole into stopping his research, but in spite of their efforts, addiction specialists began to take notice of the promise that methadone held. In 1968, Dole and Nyswander convened the first National Methadone Conference, and by the end of the 1960s, the National Institute of Mental Health funded methadone maintenance projects in Chicago, New Haven, and Philadelphia. Nonetheless, methadone continued to have its opponents, both from traditional treatment communities and from Black militant groups such as the Black Panthers, who believed that it was part of a conspiracy to keep young Black males addicted to drugs. By the early 1970s, however, methadone became more widely accepted, as the federal government encouraged the spread of methadone maintenance programs, and the newly founded National Institute on Drug Abuse also endorsed it. By 1973, there were approximately 400 methadone programs running across the United States.

Even though methadone maintenance treatment became more widespread in the 1970s, it remained controversial. Many in the addiction treatment community wanted patients on methadone to eventually be weaned off of the drug, though Dole and Nyswander maintained that once on methadone, individuals needed to continue taking it for life.

Though some found that other drugs, such as the hypertension drug clonidine, could help people on methadone stop using it, most researchers found that it was extremely difficult to get individuals off of methadone once they started taking it. Concerns about methadone being diverted to the black market, and children taking the drug, also emerged in the 1970s. In the 1980s, when attitudes towards drug abuse hardened, the federal government placed limits on how much federal funding for drug programs could be used for methadone, leading many programs to be cut. When anti-drug sentiment reached its zenith under President Ronald Reagan, many in the federal government opposed it as an overly "soft" response to the drug problem. Studies in the 1980s, however, found that methadone was effective not only in treating addiction itself, but also in addressing the public health problem of HIV/AIDS, since it got heroin users to stop injecting drugs intravenously and sharing needles—a practice that spread the disease. In the 1990s, the federal government began to support methadone maintenance as an important tool in the battle against drug addiction, and by 2000, there were nearly 150,000 individuals on methadone maintenance treatments in the United States.

The use of methadone treatments is somewhat controversial in the addiction community since addicts are prone to develop dependency on the drug, meaning that it represents a simple exchange of addiction to one drug (heroin) for addiction to another (methadone). In fact, less than 20% of individuals who go on methadone are able to stop taking it. According to its supporters, it is a preferred treatment since it effectively stabilizes addicts as they go off of street drugs, helps attenuate withdrawal symptoms, and provides them with a safe, legal environment where they can receive services that help them overcome their addiction to illegal drugs. Consequently, their argument goes, methadone holds the promise of allowing addicts to lead normal and productive lives, instead of dooming them to the cycle of highs and lows, as well as the need to take recourse to the black market for drugs, that are the hallmarks of heroin addiction.

(See also **Dole, Vincent**; **Nyswander, Marie**; **Public Health Service Narcotic Hospitals**; **Reference Essay**)

References

Carson-Dewitt, Rosalyn, ed. 2001. *Encyclopedia of Drugs, Alcohol & Addictive Behavior. Second Edition.* New York: Macmillan Reference USA.

Chepesiuk, Ron. 1999. *The War on Drugs: An International Encyclopedia.* Santa Barbara, CA: ABC-CLIO.

Davenport-Hines, Richard. 2001. *The Pursuit of Oblivion: A Global History of Narcotics, 1500–2000.* London: Weidenfeld & Nicolson.

Edwards, Griffith. ed. 2002. *Addiction: Evolution of a Specialist Field.* Oxford, UK: Blackwell Science.

Musto, David F., ed. 2002. *One Hundred Years of Heroin.* Westport, CT: Auburn House.

MOTHERS AGAINST DRUNK DRIVING (MADD)

Mothers Against Drunk Driving (MADD) is a nonprofit organization whose mission is to stop drunk driving, support the victims affected by it, and prevent underage drinking. To these ends, MADD has grown from a handful of mothers dedicated to fighting drunk driving into the nation's most prominent grassroots anti-drunk driving organization.

MADD was founded by Candy Lightner in May 1980 following her daughter's death as a result of a hit-and-run incident involving a drunk driver. Thirteen-year-old Cari Lightner was walking on the sidewalk to a church carnival in Fair Oaks, California when she was struck from behind by a repeat drunk driving offender. In fact, the driver, who had a blood-alcohol content of 0.20 at the time of the incident, had a number of prior convictions from drunk driving, including one just two days before killing Cari Lightner. He was out on bail at the time of the fatal crash, for which he received a sentence of two years. Enraged by the leniency of the punishment, a resolute Candy Lightner incorporated MADD in September of that year in order to empower victims of drunk driving in their fight to prevent incidents such as the one that took the life of her daughter.

Originally called Mothers Against Drunk Drivers, Lightner's MADD initially attempted to prod the government to pass new, tougher DUI (Driving Under the Influence) legislation. Though the death toll caused by drunk driving was significant in the late 1970s and early 1980s, public awareness of it was limited, and the punishments given to offenders were generally light. As a result, MADD's early efforts failed to generate legislative change. But Lightner and other members of her small, though quickly growing, organization aroused enough media attention to bring about the creation of a California Governor's Task Force on Drinking-Driving. MADD's fight against drunk driving quickly went well beyond California, as Lightner joined forces with Cindy Lamb, a woman whose five-month-old daughter became the nation's youngest paraplegic as a result of a drunk-driving crash, and who had launched a chapter of MADD in Maryland. Lightner and Lamb, the most public faces of MADD, came together at a repercussive press conference on Capitol Hill on October 1, 1980, resoundingly placing MADD at the center of a new, national, grassroots movement to fight drunk driving.

Cindy Lightner's passionate advocacy and tragic personal history helped distinguish MADD amongst other anti-drunk driving groups, such as RID (Remove Intoxicated Drivers) and SADD (Students Against Destructive Decisions; originally known as Students Against Driving Drunk). While these two organizations certainly played a role in heightening awareness of the serious consequences of drunk driving, it was Lightner and MADD who were most instrumental in giving a voice to drunk driving's victims. In fact, by 1982, when MADD proclaimed itself the voice of the victim, it had grown into a national organization with 100 chapters. In the following year, Lightner helped put a face on drunk-driving victimhood when NBC produced and aired a made-for-television movie called *MADD: The Candy Lightner Story*. The film generated additional awareness of MADD and its efforts, as a national poll taken a month after the program's airing showed that 84% of Americans knew of MADD. Building upon its newfound prominence in the public eye, MADD grew into a national organization comprised of some 320 chapters in 1985.

MADD parlayed this organizational growth into legislative change on the federal level in the early 1980s. For example, in 1982 the Presidential Commission on Drunk Driving was formed. In the same year, a bill giving states federal highway funds for anti-drunk driving efforts was enacted, and in 1984 the National Minimum Drinking Age Act was passed, effectively persuading states—by the federal government threatening to withhold federal highway funds—to set twenty-one as the minimum age for legally purchasing and publicly possessing alcohol. Prior to 1984, only twelve states had twenty-one as the minimum drinking age.

As MADD grew into *the* group of and for drunk-driving victims, it underwent a slight modification of the organization's name—from Mothers Against Drunk Drivers to Mothers Against Drunk Driving. The name change was intended to reflect the group's opposition to the crime of drunk driving, rather than towards the individuals who commit it. This stance is reflected in MADD's advocacy for Victim Impact Panels (VIP), which allow victims of drunk driving incidents a forum for discussing their experiences with first- and second-time DWI offenders. In addition to mentally and emotionally helping victims, MADD believes these VIPs reduce the rate of recidivism amongst participating DWI offenders.

In the 1990s, MADD changed its mission statement to accentuate its aim of preventing underage alcohol use. Reflecting this new organizational focus, in 1996 MADD began lobbying for a "Zero Tolerance" policy that would declare any measurable amount of alcohol in the system of a driver under the age of twenty-one to be illegal. Similarly, by declaring alcohol to be the nation's top drug problem affecting youth, MADD has called upon the Office of National Drug Policy to set aside a portion of its drug education funds for alcohol education. MADD has also attempted to curb incidents of teenage drunk driving by raising arguments that are not always directly related to the issue of drinking and driving. For instance, MADD has sponsored a series of public service announcements that linked teenage alcohol consumption to sexually transmitted diseases, obesity, date rape, and a reduced life span. More conventionally, MADD has called upon the alcoholic beverage industry to cease any advertising campaigns, such as those that employ cartoon characters, athletes, or celebrities, that may hold a particular appeal to young people.

For drivers who are of legal drinking age, MADD has engaged in a variety of programs to help cultivate more responsible alcohol consumption. The "designated driver"—an individual who is selected in advance of a group's drinking to remain sober and be responsible for the transportation of those who do consume alcohol—is a lasting concept that MADD has done much to popularize. MADD also promotes awareness of the perils of drunk driving through public service announcements in the run-up to holidays, when drinking and driving is more prevalent.

(See also **National Minimum Drinking Age Act**; **Students Against Destructive Decisions (SADD)**)

References

Blocker, Jr., Jack S., David M. Fahey, and Ian R. Tyrrell, eds. 2003. *Alcohol and Temperance in Modern History: An International Encyclopedia.* Santa Barbara, CA: ABC-CLIO.

Laurence, Michael D., John R. Snortum, and Franklin E. Zimring, eds. 1988. *Social Control of the Drinking Driver.* Chicago: University of Chicago Press.

Ross, H. Laurence. 1992. *Confronting Drunk Driving: A Social Policy for Saving Lives.* New Haven, CT: Yale University Press.

NALTREXONE

Naltrexone, which also goes under the trademarked name of Revia or Vivitrol, is an opioid antagonist that was developed in order to treat opiate addiction, but it has also been used to reduce the incidence of relapse among alcoholics. Taken orally, naltrexone was first synthesized in 1965 as a medication capable of reversing most effects of morphine-like drugs, and in the early 1990s it was discovered to possibly reduce an individual's craving for alcohol. Recent studies suggest that naltrexone may also be effective in treating compulsive shopping disorder, eating disorders, and addiction to cigarettes.

Naltrexone's origins can be traced back to the early 1960s and William Martin and Abraham Walker at the U.S. Addiction Research Center, where the two suggested that opioid antagonists might be effective in the treatment of opiate addicts. Since opioid antagonists would block the pleasurable effects of morphine-like drugs, they reasoned that

opiate addicts would have little incentive to continue using if administered an opioid antagonist. The next step in developing such a drug occurred in 1965 when H. Blumberg and H. B. Dayton successfully synthesized naltrexone, and study of the drug's efficacy took place as a result of the Special Action Office for Drug Abuse Prevention's call for nonaddictive antagonist drugs to be used in the treatment of heroin addiction.

Naltrexone is structurally similar to other opioid antagonists like oxymorphone and naloxone, but distinct from them in important ways that get at naltrexone's particular abilities to treat opiate addiction and alcoholism. Unlike oxymorphone, which is a strong painkiller, naltrexone is not an analgesic. And unlike naloxone, which is typically used in emergency situations of opioid overdose, naltrexone is generally used for longer-term recovery from opiate addiction (though it, too, is capable of reversing the effects of an opioid overdose.) Contributing to its particular usefulness in the long-term treatment of opiate addicts is the fact that naltrexone can be taken orally and lasts at least 24 hours, which is considerably longer than other opioid antagonists. As such, naltrexone can be effective in treating opiate addicts throughout the process of detoxification, and not just in overdose situations.

In a number of studies, naltrexone has proven to be extremely effective in combating opiate addiction. Five-year success rates as high as 95% have been reported, signaling naltrexone's tremendous efficacy when administered in particular situations and to particular subject groups. In general, it seems that recovering opiate addicts with fairly stable lives are more receptive to naltrexone programs—which require weekly doses of around 350 milligrams, with some patients taking 50 milligrams per day and others swallowing a 150-milligram pill every third day—than street addicts who typically altogether refuse to begin a naltrexone regimen or discontinue one shortly after starting. Naltrexone cannot be given to a patient who is still physically dependent on opiates, as ingesting it will cause withdrawal symptoms such as diarrhea, abdominal cramps, a runny nose, goose bumps, and muscle, joint, and bone pain. In order to avoid inducing withdrawal, naltrexone should be administered to patients only after seven to ten days have been allotted for physical dependence to run its course.

In addition to its ability to counteract the effects of opiates, researchers in the early 1990s discovered that naltrexone was also effective in diminishing the rate of relapse in alcoholics. It seems that naltrexone reduces alcoholics' craving for alcohol, though it does not appear to induce greater numbers of alcoholics to become completely abstinent from drinking. The Food and Drug Administration approved naltrexone for use in treating alcoholism in 1995, making it an alternative to disulfiram for those looking for medicinal assistance in controlling their drinking. More recent research suggests that naltrexone may also be effective in helping individuals stop smoking, control overeating, and curb compulsive shopping.

(See also **Disulfiram**; **Food and Drug Administration (FDA)**; **Public Health Service Narcotic Hospitals**; **Reference Essay**)

References

Black, Donald W. 2007. "Compulsive Buying Disorder: A Review of the Evidence." *CNS Spectrum.* 12, no. 2: 124–132.

Carson-Dewitt, Rosalyn, ed. 2001. *Encyclopedia of Drugs, Alcohol & Addictive Behavior. Second Edition.* New York: Macmillan Reference USA.

O'Brien, Charles P., Laura A. Volpicelli, and Joseph R. Volpicelli. 1992. "Naltrexone in the Treatment of Alcoholism: A Clinical Review." *Alcohol.* 13, no. 1: 35–39.

O'Malley, Stephanie S., Adam J. Jaffe, Grace Chang, Richard S. Schottenfeld, Roger E. Meyer, and Bruce Rounsaville. 1992. "Naltrexone and Coping Skills Therapy for Alcohol Dependence." *Archives of General Psychiatry.* 49: 881–887.

NARCOTIC ADDICT REHABILITATION ACT

The Narcotic Addict Rehabilitation Act was a piece of 1966 legislation that allowed for the civil commitment of addicts before they went to trial or faced sentencing. It was among the first pieces of federal legislation that provided a treatment alternative, instead of prison sentences and fines, for drug law offenders. As such, it represented a revolutionary step in the way that legal authorities in the United States handled addiction, as instead of just punishing it, the Narcotic Addict Rehabilitation Act also provided a means for curing addiction.

From the 1930s through the 1950s, drug control policies in the United States had become increasingly stringent. Though there were Public Health Service Narcotic Hospitals that were designed in part to treat addicts, these hospitals had a largely punitive component, as residents stayed in cellblocks with barred windows that made the institutions resemble prisons more than hospitals. While the one treatment option available to most addicts was rather punitive, so was the approach that federal law enforcement officials took towards drug use and dealing. The Federal Bureau of Narcotics (FBN), under the leadership of hardliner Harry J. Anslinger, was merciless in its prosecution of not only dealers, but also addicts, when enforcing the Harrison Narcotics Act and the Narcotic Import and Export Act. New pieces of legislation in the 1950s—the 1951 Boggs Act and the 1956 Narcotic Control Act—stiffened penalties for not only drug traffickers and dealers, but also for addicts, and instituted mandatory minimums for drug law violations while also stipulating that some violations of the nation's narcotics control legislation could be punishable by death. Partially in response to the draconian punishments allowed under the Boggs Act and the Narcotic Control Act, many in the medical community, as well as lawyers and certain sectors of the mainstream media, began to protest against the government's approach to the drug problem, arguing that in addition to punishing those who supplied drugs, it also had a responsibility

to both treat and rehabilitate addicts. The fact that rates of drug abuse rose dramatically in the early 1960s in spite of the tougher law enforcement approach gave fodder to these criticisms, as long prison sentences alone did not seem to quash drug addiction, but counter-intuitively, seemed to contribute to its spread.

In 1962, President John F. Kennedy convened a White House Conference on Drug Abuse, and by 1963 it had evolved into a Presidential Commission on Narcotic and Drug Abuse. In its first report, issued in 1963, the Commission recommended the relaxation of mandatory minimum sentences, increases in appropriations for research on drug addiction, and the redistribution of funds from the FBN to the departments of Justice, Education, and Welfare. Furthermore, it allowed for local governments to receive federal aid to establish treatment centers, meaning that addicts would now have places to go for treatment legally without having to enter a Public Health Service Narcotic Hospital. While states such as New York and California took advantage of these initiatives to create experimental programs for the outpatient treatment of addicts, the federal government still sought to create treatment alternatives for drug law offenders throughout the country. The result was the 1966 Narcotic Addict Rehabilitation Act (NARA). NARA stipulated that individuals charged with or convicted of breaking federal laws who were addicted, and likely to be rehabilitated through treatment, could be civilly committed to treatment so that they could restore their health and return to society as upstanding citizens. If individuals were convicted of an offense, NARA allowed them to submit to physical examinations to determine if they were addicted or not. If the exams showed that lawbreakers were addicts, NARA then allowed for them to be given mandatory treatment in an institution for up to three years instead of going to prison. If individuals were found guilty of committing a federal offense, the mandatory stay in treatment could be longer. In addition, NARA also made provisions for addicts who did not commit crimes—but still wanted to be cured—to volunteer for civil commitment and treatment so that they could be rehabilitated and resume normal lives. Significantly, NARA empowered the Surgeon General to enter into contract agreements with any public or private agency to examine and treat addicts, so only a fraction of the individuals who entered treatment under the auspices of the Act wound up receiving treatment in the Public Health Service Narcotic Hospitals. NARA not only allowed for local treatment centers to take on the task of rehabilitating addicts, but it also gave state and local governments financial assistance for their creation, maintenance, and functioning, providing them with $15 million—more than double the entire budget of the FBN. Federally funded treatment, therefore, was no longer limited to the Public Health Service Narcotic Hospitals, but could be carried out at any number of treatment centers that began to pop up throughout the country. By 1971, NARA had funded the creation of fifty community-based drug treatment programs.

In the first two years NARA was in operation, many of the addicts who came before judges were not found to be suitable for treatment, and instead given jail sentences. In addition, many NARA patients were noncompliant, and did not complete treatment successfully. Studies in the early 1970s showed that the NARA program had mixed results, as high numbers of former NARA patients went back to using drugs upon completion of the program, though not as many of them wound up falling back into full-blown addiction.

Even though studies showed that the program had mixed success, it was nonetheless significant for several reasons. First, it created an option for judges to put addicts who came before them in rehabilitative programs instead of prison, an option that would resurface in the 1990s with the emergence of Drug Courts. Secondly, by funding state and local treatment programs, NARA led to the drying up of the addict populations that had once filled the Public Health Service Hospitals in Fort Worth, Texas and Lexington, Kentucky, and not surprisingly, these institutions were closed within a decade of its enactment. Most importantly, however, NARA represented a landmark in the way that the federal government handled the drug problem. For the first time since the creation of the Public Health Service Narcotic Hospitals in the 1930s, NARA added a therapeutic and rehabilitative piece to federal drug policy, providing a much-needed counterbalance to the practices of the FBN, which had tried to solve the drug problem by simply arresting and incarcerating traffickers and dealers without taking much care for another major aspect of the drug problem—the fact that there were addicts who, by going uncured, provided a lucrative market for the dealers the FBN was tracking. By taking a major step to address the question of demand for drugs, and not just cracking down on supplies, NARA marked a turning point in the way that the federal government would address the drug problem from the mid-1960s onward.

(See also **Boggs Act**; **Drug Courts**; **Federal Bureau of Narcotics (FBN)**; **Narcotic Control Act**; **Public Health Service Narcotic Hospitals**)

References

Belenko, Steven R., ed. 2000. *Drugs and Drug Policy in America: A Documentary History.* Westport, CT: Greenwood Press.

Martin, William R. and Harris Isbell, eds. 1978. *Drug Addiction and the U.S. Public Health Service.* Rockville, MD: National Institute on Drug Abuse.

Musto, David F. 1987. *The American Disease: Origins of Narcotic Control.* Expanded Edition. New York: Oxford University Press.

Musto, David F., ed. 2002. *Drugs in America: A Documentary History.* New York: New York University Press.

White, William L. 1998. *Slaying the Dragon: The History of Addiction Treatment and Recovery in America.* Bloomington, IL: Chestnut Health Systems.

NARCOTIC CLINICS

As the federal government began instituting narcotic control measures in the 1910s, many state and local governments responded by establishing maintenance clinics—places where addicts could continue receiving drugs to maintain their drug habits and avoid the pains of withdrawal. Most of these clinics, however, were short-lived, as the Narcotic Division of the Prohibition Unit, led by Levi G. Nutt, deemed these clinics illegal, and ordered them to be shut down. By 1923, all of the narcotic clinics in the country were closed.

The first narcotic clinic established by a government entity in the United States came before the federal government became involved in the question of narcotics control and addiction treatment. Dr. Charles E. Terry, the City Health Officer of Jacksonville, established a narcotic clinic so addicts could receive free narcotic prescriptions in 1912. The main reason Terry created the clinic was to institute tighter control over the flow of opiates, as many pharmacists complained that a good number of addicts who they served were too poor to go to a doctor for a prescription. In addition, the public clinics forced addicts to go to a government clinic, where they would receive help in their struggle against addiction, instead of to private physicians who could have prescribed drugs indefinitely, thus feeding, instead of curing, addiction. After the clinic opened in August of 1912, 646 addicts began receiving services there. The early success of his clinic made Terry a strong proponent of getting public health services, and not just police departments, involved in the addiction problem, since clinics provided a way to both treat and keep track of addicts and their drug-taking.

After the passage of the Harrison Narcotics Act, many local officials began to fear that the sudden lack of availability of opiates could cause a public health crisis if large numbers of addicts suddenly started having withdrawal symptoms. Some in the federal government also recognized the difficult situation that the Harrison Act put addicts in, and in July of 1915 it issued recommendations for the temporary supply of narcotics to addicts until they could kick the habit. The federal government also advised revenue officials to work with local authorities to assure that the abrupt withdrawal of drugs would not lead to a public health crisis. For a brief while, federal officials permitted certain physicians in some regions to continue prescribing maintenance doses, while in other places, the municipal government established narcotic clinics—between eighty and ninety of them operated throughout the country. In some cities, federal officials allowed Health Departments and police stations to continue providing maintenance treatments to addicts. Even after the 1919 Supreme Court rulings in the *Webb* and *Doremus* cases outlawed maintenance prescriptions by private practitioners, many of these public institutions dispensed narcotics, and many municipalities set up new narcotic dispensaries to provide legal supplies of opiates to addicts.

The situation changed, however, in 1920, after Levi G. Nutt became the head of the Narcotic Division of the Prohibition Unit. To decide if maintenance treatment was medically necessary, the Revenue Bureau charged with enforcing the Harrison Act sent out questionnaires to leading physicians and scientists to solicit their opinion on the outpatient maintenance treatment of addicts. Most of the medical authorities surveyed opposed the maintenance treatments given in clinics, instead advocating for addicts to undergo detoxification treatments in inpatient settings. In 1920, the American Medical Association introduced a resolution opposing the maintenance clinics. Further research by the Narcotic Division showed that the clinics were not effective in curing addiction, and that many dispensed narcotics with no intention of weaning addicts off of opiates until they were drug-free. Taking these factors into account, Nutt decided to close the narcotics clinics, and oppose

maintenance treatments in all cases except those involving the elderly or incurable patients. Believing that there was no valid medical treatment for addiction other than withdrawal of drugs, the Narcotic Division reasoned that there was no need for clinics to distribute narcotics to the addicted, and began ordering them to be shut down. By 1923, the last of the major narcotic clinics, located in Shreveport, Louisiana, was closed.

The closure of the narcotic clinics, together with the Supreme Court decisions in the *Doremus* and *Webb* cases, left many addicts with little choice but to quit or to turn to the black market for supplies. Not surprisingly, increasing numbers of them wound up in the criminal justice system, and federal prisons were flooded with individuals convicted of narcotic-related offenses in the mid-1920s. By 1928, almost one-third of the inmates in federal penitentiaries were incarcerated for violating the Harrison Act, and there were more people behind bars for breaking drug laws than there were individuals incarcerated for violating the prohibition of liquor. Eventually, the high numbers of addicts in federal prisons led the federal government to create special institutions that were both prisons and hospitals—the Public Health Service Narcotic Hospitals—for addict offenders in the 1930s.

(See also **Harrison Narcotics Act**; **Nutt, Levi G.**; **Public Health Service Narcotic Hospitals**; *United States v. Doremus* and *Webb et al. v. United States*)

References

Belenko, Steven R., ed. 2000. *Drugs and Drug Policy in America: A Documentary History*. Westport, CT: Greenwood Press.

Courtwright, David T. 2001. *Dark Paradise: A History of Opiate Addiction in America.* Cambridge, MA: Harvard University Press.

Musto, David F. 1987. *The American Disease: Origins of Narcotic Control.* Expanded Edition. New York: Oxford University Press.

NARCOTIC CONTROL ACT

The Narcotic Control Act was a piece of legislation that became law in 1956, and severely stiffened penalties for drug trafficking and dealing in the United States. The Act toughened the already harsh penalties that were established just five years earlier in the Boggs Act, and also introduced the ultimate penalty—death —for certain drug offenses. In addition, the Act also had provisions to facilitate the surveillance and apprehension of drug users and traffickers.

The Narcotic Control Act was an outgrowth of the Boggs Act, which created federal mandatory minimum sentences for drug-law offenders. The legal and medical professions were highly critical of the Boggs Act, and the Federal Bureau of Narcotics (FBN), in turn, vigorously defended the new law as an effective deterrent for would-be drug dealers and users. In spite of the FBN's counteroffensive, Texas Senator Price Daniel introduced a resolution for the Senate Judiciary Committee to review the nation's drug laws and consider drafting new legislation. In hearings held in eight cities, the committee listened to testimonies concerning the nation's drug laws and took suggestions for changes to narcotics control statutes. The committee was concerned by what it heard about drug trafficking, and concluded that rates of drug addiction had

tripled in the decade after World War II ended. Propaganda, often coordinated by the FBN, linking the rise in drug addiction to organized crime and conspiracies out of Communist China also heightened the sense of alarm in the mid-1950s. Thus even though Senator Daniel had been open to suggestions for new treatment options for addicts, the scope and scale of the problem led the committee to suggest more stringent measures to crack down on drug trafficking and cut down on drug supplies, rather than institute treatment measures to address the question of demand for narcotics.

The legislation that emerged as a result of the Senate Committee's investigations—the Narcotic Control Act of 1956—toughened the amendments to the Narcotic Import and Export Act that had taken effect with the 1951 Boggs Act. The Narcotic Control Act increased both the minimum and maximum sentences for trafficking and illegal possession of opiates, cocaine, and cannabis. First offenses were now punishable by between five and ten years imprisonment, while sentences for second offenses were increased to ten to twenty years. Smuggling and dealing were targets of particularly harsh punishments, as the minimum for illicitly importing narcotics was raised to five years in prison, with a maximum of twenty years incarceration. The penalties for repeat offenders were also raised, to a minimum of ten years and a maximum of forty behind bars. The legislation also raised the maximum financial penalty for individuals found guilty of violations from $2,000 to $20,000. To help the FBN enforce the law, the Act authorized narcotic agents to carry guns and arrest suspected violators of drug laws without a warrant.

To facilitate the surveillance of likely drug smugglers, the Act also had a provision requiring addicts, drug users, and those who had drug-related offenses on their criminal record to register and get a Treasury Department certificate before they left the country. In addition, it allowed for the FBN to share intelligence gathered on addicts with state and local governments, and also for the FBN to train state and local narcotics enforcement agents. The Act targeted heroin in particular, as it allowed, at the discretion of juries, for adults caught selling heroin to minors to be sentenced to death. It also stipulated that all heroin—even that which was within the bounds of previous laws—had to be surrendered to the federal authorities, and banned its use for any reason.

While officials in the FBN and other supporters of tougher treatment of drug traffickers supported the Narcotic Control Act, the legislation also drew its share of criticism. The *New York Times*, for example, published an editorial stating that tougher enforcement alone could not solve the drug problem. Addiction experts, such as Lawrence Kolb, also criticized the new draconian measures. Thus even though it toughened the government's stances on how addicts and dealers should be treated, the Narcotic Control Act also had the unintended consequence of creating resistance to the law-and-order approach to narcotics control. While it marked an apex in the development of the federal government's tough approach to the drug problem, the Act also spawned resistance that would ultimately lead to the demise of the law-and-order paradigm in the 1960s and 1970s.

(See also **Boggs Act**; **Federal Bureau of Narcotics (FBN)**; **Kolb, Lawrence**)

References

Belenko, Steven R., ed. 2000. *Drugs and Drug Policy in America: A Documentary History.* Westport, CT: Greenwood Press.

Davenport-Hines, Richard. 2001. *The Pursuit of Oblivion: A Global History of Narcotics, 1500–2000.* London: Weidenfeld & Nicolson.

Musto, David F. 1987. *The American Disease: Origins of Narcotic Control.* Expanded Edition. New York: Oxford University Press.

NARCOTIC DRUGS IMPORT AND EXPORT ACT

The Narcotic Drugs Import and Export Act, sometimes referred to as the Jones-Miller Act, was a piece of 1922 legislation in the United States that governed the international commerce in controlled substances. Though it was originally created to address concerns about drug smuggling into China, the law also broadened the scale and scope of narcotics control in the United States.

The Narcotic Drugs Import and Export Act was the result of a concerted effort to restrict narcotic exports out of the United States that began in the autumn of 1920, when Representative John Miller and Senator Homer Jones met with members of the China Club, a Seattle-based organization interested in improving trade with China. Earlier that year, China Club members had discovered that foreign morphine was being smuggled through the United States and Japan for use in China, and feared that the drug trafficking could endanger American economic interests in China. To address these concerns, Miller and

Jones drafted a piece of legislation. The original proposal would have amended the Harrison Narcotics Act to include a ban on all exports of narcotics out of the United States, and given the Surgeon General the power to decide if crude opium or coca leaves could be imported.

At hearings held on the bill in the winter of 1920–1921, witnesses revealed that the smuggling of opiates and cocaine out of the United States affected not only China, but Canada as well. They also testified that most of the illicit drugs in the United States were probably manufactured domestically, legally exported, and then smuggled back in to the United States illegally. Restricting narcotic exports, therefore, held the promise of not only helping other countries address their drug problems, but also of helping domestic narcotic law enforcement efforts by cutting off the cycle of exporting and importing that fed the illicit drug market within the United States. The fact that the legislation could help domestic control efforts was enough to convince drug manufacturers, who otherwise would have opposed the limitation of exports, to support it.

In February of 1921, Representative Henry T. Rainey introduced a revised version of the bill that Jones and Miller had proposed. Rainey's proposal was less ambitious, as it allowed for the export of narcotics, but only with the approval of the Secretary of State, the Secretary of the Treasury, the Secretary of Commerce, and only if there was assurance that the nation receiving the exports would monitor the distribution and use of the drugs. Exporting drugs that were not believed to have any medicinal use, namely opium that was prepared for smoking, was also prohibited. The law placed tight restrictions on the importation of narcotics, stipulating that they could not be brought into the United States unless deemed necessary for use in medicine. When it became law as the Narcotic Drugs Import and Export Act in May of 1922, it created a new organization—the Federal Narcotics Control Board—to determine if drug exports were legal and if drug imports were necessary under the provisions of the law. The administration of the law was left to the discretion of the Treasury Department's Narcotic Division, which oversaw domestic narcotic control efforts as well. The penalties for breaking the Narcotic Drugs Import and Export Act were stiff, as violators could face fines of up to $5,000 and up to ten years in prison. If foreigners were caught breaking the law, the Act allowed for them to be deported.

In comparison to the Harrison Act of 1914, the Narcotic Drugs Import and Export Act was particularly harsh, as it provided for double the prison time and more than double the fine for individuals caught up in drug smuggling. Together with the Supreme Court decisions in *Webb et al. v. United States* and *United States v. Doremus*, the Narcotic Drugs Import and Export Act contributed to the sharp rise in the number of individuals who were incarcerated for violating the nation's drug laws. The Federal Narcotics Control Board was dissolved with the formation of the Federal Bureau of Narcotics in 1930.

(See also **Federal Bureau of Narcotics (FBN)**; **Harrison Narcotics Act**; *United States v. Doremus* and *Webb et al. v. United States*)

References

Belenko, Steven R., ed. 2000. *Drugs and Drug Policy in America: A Documentary History*. Westport, CT: Greenwood Press.

Davenport-Hines, Richard. 2001. *The Pursuit of Oblivion: A Global History of Narcotics, 1500–2000*. London: Weidenfeld & Nicolson.

Musto, David F. 1987. *The American Disease: Origins of Narcotic Control*. Expanded Edition. New York: Oxford University Press.

NARCOTICS ANONYMOUS (NA)

Narcotics Anonymous (NA) is a twelve-step program for narcotic addicts that is adapted from the Alcoholics Anonymous (AA) model. NA differs from AA in its stance that alcoholism is too narrow a term for what ails its members; instead, NA targets addiction writ large, which it designates a disease. NA emerged out meetings held in Kentucky in 1947, developed in New York City, and officially started in Southern California in 1953. The creation of a World Service Office in Los Angeles in 1972 gave NA greater organizational coherence, and following the 1983 publication of its "Basic Text," NA quickly expanded into an international organization with 43,000 weekly meetings across 127 countries.

The origins of NA can be traced back to an AA member who, as part of AA's Twelfth Step—which encourages carrying the organization's message to others with drinking problems—brought into the AA fold an alcoholic who also used morphine as a means of combating his hangovers. The sponsor, who was referred to as "Houston" in a *Saturday Evening Post* article recounting NA's early history, continued to work with the alcohol/morphine abuser, whom Houston dubbed his "Pigeon," and who was committed to the U.S. Public Health Service Hospital in Lexington, Kentucky.

In conversation with the hospital's director, Dr. V. H. Vogel, Houston argued that AA's Twelve Steps, which were useful in dealing with Pigeon's alcoholism, could be adapted to combat the patient's morphine addiction, which AA—which strictly focused on alcohol—did not address. Dr. Vogel agreed to allow Houston to start such a group for drug-addicted patients in the Lexington hospital, and the first meeting took place on February 16, 1947.

A particularly enthusiastic member of the Lexington group, an addict referred to as "Dan," became clean and started, in New York City in 1948, the first group outside of the Lexington hospital, which he called NA. Despite contacting everyone he knew from Lexington, Dan got only three people to attend these weekly meetings, which took place at a local Salvation Army building. Although the meetings of the nascent NA owed much to AA, the protocol for adapting the Twelve Steps to deal with narcotics addiction was hardly well established. For example, early meetings were marked by debates over how best to work through drug withdrawals, with the group eventually determining that it would encourage members to do so within institutional care.

NA spread slowly and somewhat erratically across the United States, with the first official meeting taking place in Southern California in July 1953. Local fellowships throughout the country held weekly meetings, but rising membership numbers were difficult to sustain in the early years of the loosely grouped organization, in part because of a lack of centralized leadership, and in part because the group was still hammering out its core principles and approaches to combating drug abuse. Thus, one of NA's first publications, a self-titled pamphlet that appeared in 1962 and came to be known among members as *The White Booklet*, attempted to give greater coherence to the organization by defining itself as a nonprofit fellowship or society of people for whom drugs had become a major problem. Like AA, NA articulated a program of regular meetings to help members stay clean, but unlike AA, NA declared that it was unconcerned with what particular substance was being abused by the addict. As such, when NA adapted AA's First Step, which involves members acknowledging their powerlessness over alcohol, the word "alcohol" was removed and, in its place, the term "addiction" was inserted. This seemingly small change actually represented a significant modification, for it announced that as indebted as NA was to the path laid out by AA, it held a different belief about the fundamental nature of addiction. By stressing that addiction—and not the particular substance, be it alcohol or heroin or any other drug, to which the user is addicted —is the problem, NA's revision of AA's First Step reflects the "disease concept" of addiction.

Beyond this conceptual difference about the nature of addiction, NA generally resembles AA in how it operates and works to promote sobriety. As is the case with AA, the bedrock of NA is the meeting of local fellowships, at which addicts join together to provide mutual support in their quest to lead clean lives. These gatherings are open to addicts of all religious, social, racial, and ethnic backgrounds, and members often find therapeutic value in working closely with other addicts, discussing their struggles, and pledging assistance to one another's quests to lead drug-free lives. Weekly

meetings usually take place in buildings run by public, religious, or civic organizations, and they generally consist of individual members who function as meeting leaders guiding other members to take part by sharing their own trials and tribulations in recovering from drug addiction.

NA meetings also resemble those of AA in that they are guided by the principles contained in the Twelve Steps and Twelve Traditions, which are a series of ideas and protocols borrowed from AA that aim to promote recovery from addiction. Among the most important steps are those that involve addicts admitting their problem, believing in a higher power capable of restoring normalcy in their lives, undergoing a searching self-examination, making amends to persons harmed as a result of their addiction, and trying to carry the message of NA to other addicts in need. The most contentious of these principles are those involving a belief in a God or higher power, as NA emphasizes the centrality of spirituality to recovery from addiction. NA maintains that it is, like AA, a nonreligious organization, and members are encouraged to define this God/higher power in their own terms so as to better achieve the spiritual awakening deemed vital to recovery from addiction.

The similarities between the two organizations are such that AA has an official policy of cooperation, though not affiliation, with NA. In fact, NA has no affiliations with treatment centers or correctional facilities of any kind. Similarly, NA employs no professional counselors or therapists in its quest to help narcotics addicts maintain abstinence from all drugs, including alcohol.

Beyond the goings-on at local, weekly meetings, NA exists as a larger institution.

Since 1972, with the founding of the World Service Organization that year, NA has had a central body, and this Los Angeles-based office has proven instrumental in retaining members and growing the fellowship as a whole. In addition to the headquarters and the local meetings, NA maintains a Web site, http://www .na.org, that contains information for prospective and active members, has electronic versions of its periodicals and newsletters, and features a store selling NA books and other literature.

(See also **Alcoholics Anonymous (AA)**; **Public Health Service Narcotic Hospitals**)

References

Carson-Dewitt, Rosalyn, ed. 2001. *Encyclopedia of Drugs, Alcohol & Addictive Behavior. Second Edition.* New York: Macmillan Reference USA.

Narcotics Anonymous. "Facts About NA." [Online information retrieved 05/22/09] http://www.na.org/?ID=Home-basicinfo.

Narcotics Anonymous. 1991. *White Booklet.* Center City, Minnesota: Hazelden Publishing and Educational Services.

NATION, CARRY

Carry Nation was a member of the Kansas Woman's Christian Temperance Union (WCTU) who gained national fame and notoriety, as well as a band of female disciples, as a result of her violent attacks on saloons. She fared less well, however, when she took her prohibitionist message to states in which alcohol remained legal. In the cities of the East, her middle-American, anti-alcohol stance convinced few people that alcohol was evil, but it did lead to Carry Nation becoming the national face of fanatic prohibitionism.

A native of Garrard County, Kentucky, Carry A. Nation (1846–1911) began her career as a prohibitionist after moving to Medicine Lodge, Kansas in 1898 with her second husband. Kansas had a prohibition amendment to its constitution on the books since 1880, but the law was not universally enforced, and many saloons and drugstores openly continued the sale of alcohol. Often, local politicians and law enforcement figures reaped a portion of the profits from alcohol sales via bribes and sporadic fines for tavern owners. In order to fight these conditions, and perhaps animated by the memory of her first husband, who was a heavy drinker, Nation helped found, and became president of, the Medicine Lodge chapter of the Kansas WCTU.

Under her stewardship, Nation's local WCTU branch altered its approach to promoting temperance. Instead of classroom education, which was a hallmark of the WCTU's earlier campaigns, Nation preached reformation at the doors of Medicine Lodge's saloons. With an organ in hand and a seemingly unbreakable determination to disrupt drinkers with her loudly sung temperance songs, Nation set a model for many women in the prohibition movement. Numbers of temperance women emulated her by camping out in front of their neighborhoods' saloons, but not all of them followed her lead when she adopted more violent methods in hopes of eliminating the presence of alcohol in Kansas. In fact, the overwhelming majority of women within the WCTU remained committed to the union's highly systematic and orderly reform efforts.

In 1900, Nation traveled some twenty-five miles from Medicine Lodge to Kiowa, Kansas to smash up a liquor store there with bricks, stones, and pieces of wood and metal. In subsequent attacks, Nation used a hatchet, the weapon that became the trademark of her campaign against alcohol. For these incidents of "hatchetation," Nation was both frequently jailed and eagerly followed by the nation's press. Hatchetation, and the publicity it generated, helped convince Kansans to more dutifully enforce existing anti-alcohol legislation, and to pass a 1901 law that made it easier to prosecute saloon owners.

Hatchetation also generated great media interest in Nation beyond Kansas. Newspaper reporters from across the country followed her attacks on Kansas saloons, and before long, Nation was invited to speak about her violent opposition to alcohol throughout America. There is little evidence to suggest that Nation's speeches had a significant impact in changing attitudes towards alcohol outside of Kansas, and it seems that in some cases, her appearances were actually welcomed by saloon keepers for the publicity it brought their establishments. On occasion, barkeepers would allow Nation's speech to culminate in the hatchetation of their saloons, with the expectation that the publicity brought about by Nation's attack would in turn generate additional business once they reopened. As such, many of her appearances throughout the country came across as theatrical performances, with audiences more interested in witnessing the spectacle of a hachetation than actually hearing Nation's anti-alcohol message.

Towards the end of her life, Nation translated her hatchet-wielding image into financial success. Building off of her saloon-smashing performances, she appeared on vaudeville stages and in performances of *Ten Nights in a Barroom*. She also published two newspapers, *The Smasher's Mail* and *The Hatchet*, as well as an autobiography, *The Use and Need of the Life of Carry A. Nation*. Nation earned additional income from selling autographed pictures of herself, and she even sold tiny souvenir hatchets that could be worn as lapel pins. Nation used much of this income to purchase a home in Kansas City, Kansas that she transformed into a school and shelter for homeless women and the widows and wives of drunkards. Carry Nation died in 1911 in Leavenworth, Kansas.

(See also **Woman's Christian Temperance Union (WCTU)**)

References

Burns, Eric. 2004. *The Spirits of America: A Social History of America*. Philadelphia: Temple University Press.

Lender, Mark Edward. 1984. *Dictionary of American Temperance Biography: From Temperance Reform to Alcohol Research, the 1600s to the 1980s*. Westport, CT: Greenwood Press.

Mendelson, Jack H. and Nancy K. Mello. 1985. *Alcohol: Use and Abuse in America*. Boston: Little, Brown and Company.

NATIONAL COUNCIL ON ALCOHOLISM AND DRUG DEPENDENCE (NCAAD)

The National Council on Alcoholism and Drug Dependence (NCAAD) is the largest public health advocacy group in the United States on alcoholism and drug-related problems. The NCAAD was born out of the desire to better educate Americans about alcohol and alcoholism, and it was founded, initially under the name of the National Committee for Education on Alcoholism (NCEA), in 1944 by

Marty Mann, the first woman to recover from alcoholism through Alcoholics Anonymous (AA). Over the decades since its founding, the NCAAD established, among other things, the first research society dedicated to alcoholism and the first public education campaign promoting the disease concept of alcoholism.

The NCAAD began as the NCEA in 1944 as a result of the work of Marty Mann, who envisioned a public health organization—along the lines of those already in existence dedicated to the medical conditions of tuberculosis, cancer and heart disease—geared towards changing America's perception of alcoholism and alcohol. Mann's initial efforts were supported by a number of prominent Americans, chief among them perhaps being E. Morton Jellinek, one of the nation's most influential proponents of the disease conception of alcoholism. An associate editor of the *Quarterly Journal of Studies on Alcohol* and a creator of the Yale Plan Clinics—which were the first American outpatient clinics for the treatment of alcoholics—Jellinek saw Mann as a natural partner in promoting the idea of alcoholism as a disease, and he offered for Yale to sponsor the nascent organization.

Starting with an annual budget of $13,000 and a small office in New York City staffed merely by a lone secretary and herself, Mann grew the NCEA out of its Yale beginnings and into a national organization with local branches across the country. Spurring this growth was the NCEA's five-point program, which, firstly, aimed to educate local communities about alcoholism. Secondly, it worked to create alcohol information and referral centers in those communities. Thirdly, it pushed for the involvement of community hospitals, rather than jails, in the detoxification of alcoholics. Fourthly, it worked to create clinics for diagnosing and treating alcoholism, and, fifthly, it helped establish rest centers that offered long-term care for alcoholics. Volunteers were responsible for running the local NCEA chapters, and many of the unpaid staffers were recovered alcoholics and members of their families. In support of these local branches and their work on various alcohol-related fronts, the NCEA also promulgated five ideas nationally. First, the NCEA argued that alcoholism is a disease. Consequently, its second point was that alcoholics are sick people. Their third idea was that alcoholics could be helped; the fourth, and related, notion was that alcoholics were worth helping. The fifth and final idea was that because alcohol is a public health issue, it was the public's responsibility to address it.

After a decade of NCEA advocacy, public health campaigns, and work on behalf of alcoholics, Americans proved receptive to the organization's ideas and programs, and many began to view alcoholics not as criminals, but as diseased individuals. Ten years after its founding, the NCEA had grown to include fifty communities spread across twenty-seven states. Helping spur this development were state governments, which began allocating tax dollars to develop alcoholism treatment programs rather than taking punitive measures against alcoholics. By 1953, some 3,000 hospitals offered care for acute cases of alcoholism; by contrast, fewer than 100 hospitals did so when Mann founded the NCEA. Similarly evidencing the sea change in Americans' views on alcoholism, a 1957 Roper poll showed that 58% of the nation viewed alcoholism as a disease; a mere

6% felt that way in 1943, the year before the NCEA's founding. Reflecting these remarkable developments, the NCEA itself underwent a transformation. It amicably separated from Yale and underwent an organizational name change, becoming the National Committee on Alcoholism (NCA).

The organization's development over many of those years had much to do with R. Brinkley Smithers, a recovering alcoholic and philanthropist who was elected to the organization's board of directors in 1954. Under his stewardship, the NCA was able to add a dozen staff members, expand the board of directors to sixty volunteers, establish a direct service program for New York City, and found the earliest reference library of its kind on alcoholism. The NCA also did consulting work with companies worried about the impact of alcoholism on their business, and it entered into working relationships with a variety of labor, health, clergy, and women's organizations. Brinkley's philanthropy likewise enabled the NCA to appoint to its staff Dr. Ruth Fox, who would lead the organization into the medical and research field. The government took note of the NCA's importance as a public health organization, and the Secretary of Health, Education, and Welfare dubbed it America's agency for alcoholism. Federal funding for research projects followed, and in 1966, President Johnson appointed Marty Mann to the first national advisory commission on alcoholism. Now a fixture in Washington, D.C., the NCA successfully advocated for the passage of the 1970 Hughes Act, which established the National Institute on Alcohol Abuse and Alcoholism. In addition to its successes in Washington, D.C., the NCA also developed a number of prominent

educational campaigns intended to destigmatize alcoholism. The organization's messages were worked into the storylines of television sitcoms and dramas, and more overtly, the NCA arranged professional education and training events. For example, its prominent 1976 event, "Operation Understanding," featured fifty-two famous Americans announcing their recovery from alcoholism.

After Marty Mann's death in 1980, the NCA entered a period of flux on multiple fronts. For one, Mann's passing deprived the organization of its key figure, a woman who, even after stepping down as the head of the NCA in 1967, continued to be its biggest advocate through years of public speaking. Without the founder's presence, the NCA also experienced significant financial difficulties that necessitated the philanthropic intervention of R. Brinkley Smithers' foundation. The NCA's name also underwent yet another change, with the organization that was initially called the NCEA becoming the National Council on Alcoholism and Drug Dependence (NCADD) in 1990. The name change reflected the increasing number of alcoholics who were addicted to more than one substance, and it was generated by the growing dissonance between the national organization and its affiliates, whose treatment programs for such patients became far larger than their public education and policy work. The strained relationship between the NCAAD and its affiliates led to the number of local affiliates dropping, in 2000, below ninety after a high of over 230 in the early 1980s.

In recent years, the NCAAD has emphasized the importance of rebuilding its relationship with affiliates. The NCAAD has also renewed its commitment to leading public education campaigns, and as such, it has a leading role in promoting Alcohol Awareness Month and National Recovery Month. Likewise, the NCAAD and its messages continue to be a part of public consciousness through cable television programming, newsletters, and its Web site, http://www.ncaad.org.

(See also **Alcoholics Anonymous (AA)**; **National Institute on Alcohol Abuse and Alcoholism (NIAAA)**; **Jellinek, E. Morton**)

References

Blocker, Jr., Jack S., David M. Fahey, and Ian R. Tyrrell, eds. 2003. *Alcohol and Temperance in Modern History: An International Encyclopedia*. Santa Barbara, CA: ABC-CLIO.

Carson-Dewitt, Rosalyn, ed. 2001. *Encyclopedia of Drugs, Alcohol & Addictive Behavior. Second Edition*. New York: Macmillan Reference USA.

Lender, Mark Edward and James Kirby Martin. 1982. *Drinking in America: A History*. New York: The Free Press.

National Council on Alcholism and Drug Dependence. "NCADD History and Mission." [Online article retrieved 05/20/09] http://www.ncadd.org/history/index.html.

NATIONAL COUNCIL ON PROBLEM GAMING (NCPG)

The National Council on Problem Gaming (NCPG) is an organization that works to call attention to the problem of compulsive gambling within the United States. Its two main goals are: one, to be the advocate for problem gamblers and their families, and, two, to take no position for or against legalized gambling. Following these guidelines, the NCPG has grown from the first professional group dedicated to the issue of problem gaming into an organization with thirty-five state affiliates.

The NCPG emerged out of the initiative of another organization dedicated to helping compulsive gamblers, Gamblers Anonymous (GA). GA started to take shape after the January 1957 meeting, in Reno, Nevada, of two Alcoholics Anonymous (AA) members who also had gambling problems. The two men met regularly, avoided gambling, and determined that a twelve-step approach like the one used by AA to promote alcohol abstinence could be applied to individuals with gambling problems. They resolved to hold such a meeting when they returned to Los Angeles, and the first official GA meeting took place in that city on September 13, 1957. The organization grew significantly over the next decade and a half, as did its members' sense that the time was right for the creation of another organization dedicated to calling national attention to the issue of compulsive gambling. GA itself could not establish such an organization and still remain true to its code of anonymity.

As a result, the Board of Trustees of GA in the New York City area took the step of asking their Spiritual Advisor, Monsignor Joseph A. Dunne, to create a Council on Compulsive Gambling. The goal of the Council on Compulsive Gambling, which would become the NCPG, was to lead a public education campaign that framed compulsive gambling as a treatable illness. In a sense, then, the NCPG's aim somewhat paralleled those of the National Council on Alcoholism and Drug Dependency (NCADD), which became the nation's largest public health advocacy group on alcoholism and drug-related problems. And just as the

NCAAD was instrumental in promoting, and gaining broad public acceptance of, the disease conception of alcoholism, so too would the NCPG strive to convince Americans that compulsive gambling was a disease. With this as the nascent organization's charge, Dunne, along with the pioneering Dr. Robert Custer and a number of other individuals and foundations, founded the NCPG in 1972.

While Dunne spearheaded the NCPG's public education efforts, Custer worked to establish treatment programs for compulsive gamblers. Custer's connection to the treatment of compulsive gambling began when members of GA and Gam-Anon, a group modeled after Al-Anon that assists relatives and loved ones of compulsive gamblers, visited him at the Veterans Administration Hospital in Brecksville, Ohio, where he agreed to extend alcohol treatment programs to include individuals who were also compulsive gamblers. Custer's work led him to posit a definition of compulsive gambling that, in 1980, would be adopted by the American Psychiatric Association in the Diagnostic Statistical Manual III under the title of "pathological gambling."

In the midst of the NCPG's growth, it officially incorporated itself as a nonprofit organization in 1975. Connected with its new status, the NCPG increased its national prominence by producing nationwide media programs that included the distribution of a quarterly newsletter. The NCPG also played a more significant role in politics, helping convince Maryland's state legislature to pass House Bill 1311, which made Maryland the first state to legally recognize its obligation to provide a treatment program for compulsive gamblers. The bill consequently helped fund the first treatment center for compulsive gamblers in association with Johns Hopkins University Hospital. In May of 1981, Connecticut passed similar legislation. In October of the same year, New York also passed a law recognizing compulsive gambling as a treatable illness, and the bill furthermore funded the Office of Mental Health for education, prevention, treatment, training, and research. The relationship between the NCPG and states further developed when, in 1983, New Jersey approved funding for a Council on Compulsive Gambling within the state. As a state affiliate of the National Council, it trained health providers, educators, and the criminal justice system within the state to work with compulsive gamblers. Over the years, the NCPG developed state affiliates across the country, with the number of such affiliates currently standing at thirty-five.

On a national level the NCPG continues to direct a number of programs. For one, it operates the National Problem Gambling Helpline Network, which serves as a single national access point to local resources. The NCPG also distributes literature on problem gambling treatment, research, and recovery, and it additionally administers the National Certified Gambling Counselor credential. Furthermore, the NCPG both holds the annual National Conference on the Prevention, Treatment, Research and Recovery of Problem Gaming and organizes National Problem Gambling Awareness Week. It also maintains a Web site, http://www.ncpgambling.org.

(See also **Al-Anon**; **Alcoholics Anonymous (AA)**; **Custer, Robert L.**; **Gamblers Anonymous (GA)**; **National Council on Alcoholism and Drug Dependence (NCAAD)**))

References

Carson-Dewitt, Rosalyn, ed. 2001. *Encyclopedia of Drugs, Alcohol & Addictive Behavior. Second Edition.* New York: Macmillan Reference USA.

Dunne, Joseph A. 1985. "Increasing Public Awareness of Pathological Gambling Behavior: A History of the National Council on Compulsive Gaming." *Journal of Gambling Behavior.* 1, no. 1: 8–16.

National Council on Problem Gaming. "About NCPG." [Online information retrieved 05/21/09] http://www.ncpgambling.org/i4a/pages/index.cfm?pageid=3285.

THE NATIONAL INSTITUTE ON ALCOHOL ABUSE AND ALCOHOLISM (NIAAA)

The National Institute on Alcohol Abuse and Alcoholism (NIAAA), which was formed in 1970 under President Richard Nixon, serves as the nation's primary institute and source of funding for alcohol-related research. It is the first U.S. federal agency dedicated exclusively to alcohol since the Prohibition Bureau, and it is guided by the idea that alcoholics deserve medical treatment as opposed to social rejection or moral censure.

The origins of the NIAAA are located in the history of efforts to reframe alcoholism as a medical condition instead of a moral failing. With the founding of Alcoholics Anonymous (AA) in 1935, the nation became more appreciative of an approach to alcoholism based on the idea of aiding alcoholics in their recoveries instead of simply judging them as morally suspect. Similarly, the research and publications coming from the Yale Center on Alcohol Studies beginning in the mid-1930s helped shift the nation's focus onto alcoholism as a disease that warranted scientific research along the lines of other sicknesses. In the following decades, the disease conception of alcohol was further institutionalized with the founding of the National Committee for Education on Alcoholism, which was later renamed the National Council on Alcoholism and Drug Dependence, and the American Medical Association's 1955 statement that alcoholism was a treatable disease. In the 1960s, the American Psychiatric Association and the American Public Health Association also declared alcoholism an illness.

With growing momentum behind the idea of alcoholism as a treatable illness, in 1970, President Richard Nixon signed the Comprehensive Alcohol Abuse and Alcoholism Prevention, Treatment, and Rehabilitation Act, generally known as the Hughes Act. The law took the name of Senator Harold E. Hughes of Iowa, the first admitted recovering alcoholic to serve in Congress. The Hughes Act recognized alcohol abuse and alcoholism as major public health issues. Consequently, the bill created the NIAAA to deal with these problems.

The Hughes Act defined the NIAAA's mission as one of researching, developing, and conducting programs aimed at preventing and treating alcoholism and helping rehabilitate alcoholics. Additionally, the Hughes Act, among other things, required that alcoholism programs be made available to federal civilian employees, prohibited discrimination with regard to the hiring and firing of recovered alcoholics in nonsecurity jobs, and authorized the distribution of federal funds to states and researchers for a variety of alcohol-related projects across the country. In particular, the NIAAA funded projects geared towards developing prevention and treatment programs for specific groups, such as Native Americans, drunk drivers, women, employed individuals, the poor, the homeless, and young people.

In 1981, the NIAAA was overhauled under the Reagan administration. These changes came in the wake of criticisms over the NIAAA's lobbying efforts, the way the group distributed its funds, and its advocacy of responsible drinking, which was seen by some as an indirect endorsement of alcohol consumption. The new NIAAA was decentralized and ultimately moved within the National Institutes of Health, along with sister organizations like the Alcohol, Drug Abuse, and Mental Health Administration and the National Institute on Drug Abuse. These moves also forced the NIAAA into a near-exclusive focus on science and research with a biomedical orientation.

One of the NIAAA's most important research endeavors has been Project MATCH, an eight-year, nationwide clinical study geared towards determining the efficacy of various treatment approaches through patient responses. Launched in 1989 and monitoring 1,726 patients in over thirty alcohol-related institutions and agencies, the study compared the approaches and results of three major alcohol-abuse treatments. Project MATCH studied the twelve-step facilitation therapy connected to AA, the cognitive-behavioral therapy approach to alcohol treatment that focuses on coping skills to prevent relapses, and motivational enhancement therapies that were designed to increase drinkers' commitments to behavioral change.

Interestingly, this large clinical trial concluded that there were no significant differences in levels of success from the three therapies.

The NIAAA has also, in recent years, focused on research involving the genetics of alcoholism and the efficacy of intervention methods of treating alcohol abuse. With regard to the latter, the NIAAA has aided trials surrounding the pharmacological treatment of alcohol dependence, particularly the use of naltrexone, an opioid-receptor antagonist, and acamprosate, a drug that scientists believe may restore the chemical balance in the brain that is disturbed by alcoholism.

In addition, the NIAAA has widely supported research involving underage drinking. Especially in the 1990s, the NIAAA focused its efforts on the issue of college drinking by developing the Task Force on College Drinking. Similarly, the NIAAA has involved itself in studying interventions for reducing drinking and driving and the accidents associated with it.

Information on these research endeavors and many other projects undertaken by the NIAAA are available at the group's Web site, http://www.NIAAA.nih.gov. A great deal of this material can be easily downloaded, but much of the NIAAA's findings are also published as part of a congressional mandate to summarize the state of the nation's alcohol-related problems and researchers' efforts to deal with them. This publication is the *Alcohol and Health Report*, and the NIAAA also produces the journal, *Alcohol Research and Health*, which has appeared since 1973.

(See also **Alcoholics Anonymous (AA)**; **Naltrexone**; **National Council on Alcoholism and Drug Dependence (NCAAD)**, **National Institute on Drug Abuse (NIDA)**)

References

Blocker, Jr., Jack S., David M. Fahey, and Ian R. Tyrrell, eds. 2003. *Alcohol and Temperance in Modern History: An International Encyclopedia*. Santa Barbara, CA: ABC-CLIO.

Mendelson, Jack H. and Nancy K. Mello. 1985. *Alcohol: Use and Abuse in America*. Boston: Little, Brown and Company.

National Institute on Alcohol Abuse and Alcoholism. "About NIAA." [Online information retrieved 11/12/2008.] http://www.niaaa.nih.gov/AboutNIAAA/.

NATIONAL INSTITUTE ON DRUG ABUSE (NIDA)

The National Institute on Drug Abuse (NIDA) is the federal agency that serves as the government's center for research on drug abuse and addiction. NIDA's mission is to advance scientific research on addiction, and the organization addresses the most fundamental and essential questions about drug abuse. It focuses on understanding how drugs work in the brain and body, developing and testing new treatment and prevention approaches, and detecting and responding to emerging drug abuse trends.

Before the 1970s, the center of government research into addiction was located at the Addiction Research Center at the U.S. Public Health Service Narcotic Hospital in Lexington, Kentucky. The structure of the federal government's anti-addiction efforts underwent an overhaul in the early 1970s, however, with the closure of the Narcotic Hospitals as community treatment for addiction became more prevalent. Further changes were made with the dismantling of the Federal Bureau of Narcotics, the creation of the Drug Enforcement Administration, and the passage of the 1970 Comprehensive Drug Abuse Prevention and Control Act. In 1972, the Drug Abuse Office and Treatment Act was part of these broader changes, as Congress sought to strike a balance between taking a punitive, enforcement-centered approach, and the recognition that drug abuse was also a social and public health problem. The Drug Abuse Office and Treatment Act had several provisions designed to address the health concerns associated with addiction. It created a Special Action Office for Drug Abuse Prevention within the White House, provided guidelines for giving grants to states so they could develop and evaluate prevention services, and authorized the creation of NIDA as part of the National Institute on Mental Health. NIDA's charge under the law was to develop and conduct comprehensive health, education, training, research, and planning programs for drug abuse prevention and treatment, and also to oversee programs for the rehabilitation of drug users. Its first director was Robert L. DuPont, who served in the post until 1978. When it began operating in 1974, the Addiction Research Center at Lexington became the center of NIDA's research program.

Soon after its formation, NIDA began two of its most enduring programs—the Monitoring the Future Survey, and the Research Monograph Series—in 1975. The Monitoring the Future Survey is a survey of high school seniors that measures levels of nonmedical drug use and attitudes towards it. While useful as a research tool, the Monitoring the Future Survey has sometimes been used for political ends as well, as was the case in the 1980s when politicians supporting the harsh provisions of the Anti-Drug Abuse Acts used it to scare the public about trends in cocaine and crack abuse among youths. In 1991, NIDA expanded the Monitoring the Future survey to include eighth graders and tenth graders as well. The Research Monograph Series is the set of publications NIDA uses to disseminate scientific information concerning addiction, with scientific papers that cover subjects concerning drug abuse treatment and prevention. In 1976, NIDA began the Community Epidemiology Work Group, which allowed for local and state representatives to meet with NIDA staff to discuss drug abuse trends in their communities and identify populations at risk for developing addiction problems. In 1979, NIDA moved its clinical research program from Lexington to Baltimore.

When Congress and the Reagan Administration recognized the connection between intravenous drug use and the HIV/AIDS epidemic, NIDA saw its budget quadruple so it could conduct further research into both diseases. In the 1980s, NIDA also began its monthly newsletter, *NIDA Notes*, and set up its Drug Abuse Information and Treatment Referral hotline. NIDA has also achieved some major breakthroughs in the study of addiction and its treatment, as it received FDA approval for medications for the treatment of opioid dependence, and NIDA researchers successfully cloned the dopamine transporter, which plays a key role in many psychoactive drugs' actions in the brain. Recent years have also seen NIDA expand the gamut of its research and prevention efforts beyond illicit substances, as in 1999 it created the Transdisciplinary Tobacco Use Research Centers to study tobacco

addiction and find new ways to combat it, and it has since expanded its research efforts to study behavioral addictions as well. NIDA has also continued to expand its public education and prevention efforts, launching the "NIDA Goes to School" initiative to provide middle school students with information on how drugs affect the brain, as well as programs designed to provide drug education to elementary school students.

In 1992, NIDA was transferred to the National Institutes of Health. Today, NIDA has eleven main divisions and offices. The Office of the Director leads the Institute by setting research and programmatic priorities. The Division of Epidemiology, Services, and Prevention Research plans, develops and supports research on the nature and consequences of drug use, gathers data to better support prevention and early intervention services, conducts addiction prevention research, studies the consequences of drug abuse, and researches treatment programs. The Division of Basic Neuroscience and Behavioral Research supports outside research in the biomedical and behavioral sciences that look at addiction as a public health problem, while the Division of Clinical Neuroscience and Behavioral Research focuses on the study of addiction as it relates to brain functioning and individual behavior. The Center for the Clinical Trials Network supports a network of sixteen regional training centers and over 200 community treatment programs in hopes of bridging the gap between the latest science on addiction treatment and its practice in real-world settings. The Division of Pharmacotherapies and Medical Consequences of Drug Abuse plans and directs studies in order to identify, develop, and obtain FDA approval for medications that can assist in the treatment of addiction. The Intramural Research Program, based in Baltimore, conducts research on the biological and behavioral mechanisms that cause drug abuse and addiction. The Office of Science Policy and Communications coordinates NIDA's research programs, and develops policy options based on the Institute's latest research. The Office of Extramural Affairs provides scientific analyses of NIDA's external research activities, while the Office of Planning and Resources Management provides administrative and management support services for the organization.

NIDA's current director is Nora D. Volkow, a doctor who pioneered the use of brain imaging techniques to investigate the toxic and addictive properties of psychoactive drugs. She has served as the director of NIDA since 2003.

(See also **Anti-Drug Abuse Acts**; **Crack Epidemic**; **Primary Source Documents**; **Public Health Service Narcotic Hospitals**; **Reference Essay**)

References

Belenko, Steven R., ed. 2000. *Drugs and Drug Policy in America: A Documentary History.* Westport, CT: Greenwood Press.

Chepesiuk, Ron. 1999. *The War on Drugs: An International Encyclopedia.* Santa Barbara, CA: ABC-CLIO.

National Institute of Health. "The NIH Almanac." [Online article retrieved 04/28/09] http://www.nih.gov/about/almanac/organization/NIDA.htm.

National Institute on Drug Abuse. "Important Events in NIDA History." [Online article retrieved 04/28/09] http://www.nih.gov/about/almanac/archive/1999/organization/nida/history.html.

NATIONAL MINIMUM DRINKING AGE ACT

The 1984 National Minimum Drinking Age Act is the piece of federal legislation that effectively made the age at which one can legally drink in the United States twenty-one years old. Though it does not directly mandate that alcohol cannot be consumed by anyone under the age of twenty-one, the law requires that states have such laws on the books if they are to receive federal funding for highway construction. According to studies, the Act has accomplished its main goal—to decrease fatalities caused by drunk driving.

At the beginning of the twentieth century, several laws prohibiting the sale of alcohol to minors were implemented as part of the broader trend towards temperance, which culminated with the passage of the Volstead Act in 1919. When alcohol prohibition was repealed in 1933, each state implemented a legal minimum drinking age for the purchase and consumption of alcohol, and most set that age at twenty-one. In the following decades, the question of the drinking age received little public attention, though states began to lower their drinking ages in the mid-1970s after the voting age was dropped from twenty-one to eighteen. Between 1970 and 1975, twenty-nine states lowered their drinking ages to either eighteen or nineteen, and around the same time, studies began to show that there were increased rates of teenagers being involved in car accidents. In response, some states—beginning with Maine in 1977—began to raise their drinking ages back up. Research showed that in states that had raised their drinking age, there were declines in the number of car accidents involving young drivers. Soon, advocacy groups, led by Mothers Against Drunk Driving, began pushing states to raise their drinking ages, and between 1976 and 1983, many did. Some states resisted, however, since they believed that by raising the drinking age, they would simply encourage youths to cross state lines to drink—not discourage them from engaging in the practice. In response to the states that did not make the changes they were hoping for, advocates for a higher drinking age began pushing for federal legislation to raise the minimum drinking age across the country.

The resulting legislation, the 1984 National Minimum Drinking Age Act, did not directly legislate that the nation's minimum drinking age had to be twenty-one. Instead, it used funding leverage to cajole states to change their laws, stipulating that if a state did not have a minimum drinking age of twenty-one by 1986, it would lose 10% of its federal funding for highway construction. Threatened with losing a major source of federal dollars, the states that had not yet raised their drinking age did so in short order, and by 1988 all states had made their minimum drinking age twenty-one years old. Studies conducted in the 1980s showed that the Minimum Drinking Age Act had its desired effect, as rates of car accidents involving youths dropped dramatically. Overall, it was estimated that by raising the drinking age to twenty-one, states have decreased the number of night-time, single-vehicle crashes among youths by 13%. According to the National Highway Traffic Safety Administration, having the minimum drinking age at twenty-one saves over 1,000 lives per year. Other studies

also found that by raising the drinking age, states were able to reduce rates of vandalism and suicide among youths.

In spite of the law, it is estimated that over half of high school seniors drink alcohol, and nearly a third of them drink heavily.

(See also **Mothers Against Drunk Driving (MADD)**; **Volstead Act (18th Amendment)**))

References

American Medical Association. "Facts About Youth and Alcohol." [Online article retrieved 05/11/09] http://www.ama-assn.org/ama/pub/physician-resources/public-health/promoting-healthy-lifestyles/alcohol-other-drug-abuse/facts-about-youth-alcohol/minimum-legal-drinking-age.shtml.

Carson-Dewitt, Rosalyn, ed. 2001. *Encyclopedia of Drugs, Alcohol & Addictive Behavior. Second Edition*. New York: Macmillan Reference USA.

Hanson, David J. "The National Minimum Drinking Age Act of 1984." [Online article retrieved 05/11/09] http://www2.potsdam.edu/hansondj/youthissues/1092767630.html.

U.S. Government. "Title 23—United States Code: Highways." [Online information retrieved 05/11/09] http://epw.senate.gov/title23.pdf.

NATIONAL ORGANIZATION FOR THE REFORM OF MARIJUANA LAWS (NORML)

The National Organization for the Reform of Marijuana Laws (NORML) is a nonprofit advocacy group that lobbies to change the legal status of marijuana in the United States. It is the oldest and largest organization advocating for the reform of the nation's marijuana laws.

NORML was founded in 1970 by Keith Stroup, and was initially funded by Hugh Hefner, the founder and publisher of *Playboy* magazine. By its second year, it had assembled an eclectic group ranging from drug-using hippies to lawyers who used marijuana recreationally and civic leaders who believed that the nation's marijuana laws were too strict. NORML seemed to have achieved a major victory in 1972, when President Richard Nixon's National Commission on Marihuana and Drug Abuse conducted an exhaustive study of the drug, and found that the drug was largely harmless and recommended reductions in sentencing for marijuana-related offenses. Nixon, however, did not agree with the Commission's findings, and marijuana remained a Schedule I drug under the Comprehensive Drug Abuse Prevention and Control Act of 1970. Unsuccessful on the national legislative front, NORML turned to the states, where it helped garner publicity for the issue and advised state legislators on what strategies and expert witnesses would be most effective, sometimes paying expenses so outside witnesses could travel to states to testify. Within a few years NORML's advocacy bore legislative fruit, as in 1973 Oregon ended criminal penalties for smoking the drug, and by 1975, Alaska, California, Maine, Colorado, and Ohio had followed suit. NORML also began an extensive legal program, providing aid to individual defendants and court challenges against the constitutionality of federal anti-marijuana laws and the government's ban on the use of the marijuana for medical purposes. It seemed that NORML was gaining momentum at the federal level as well in 1976, when Jimmy Carter endorsed the decriminalization of marijuana early in his campaign. Once he was elected president, however, Carter backed off his earlier support of marijuana law reform. NORML faced new challenges with the rise of conservatism in the late 1970s, and President Reagan's tough stance on illegal drugs in the 1980s. Nonetheless, NORML had an extremely productive first decade, as all told, it led successful efforts to decriminalize marijuana offenses in eleven states, and significantly lower penalties for marijuana offenses in many others.

Today, NORML continues to advocate for marijuana law reform at both the state and federal level, pushing for voter initiatives concerning marijuana laws and for legislative reform. It is active in the media, working to provide a different perspective on marijuana-related issues. NORML also serves as an umbrella group for a national network of citizens who want to end marijuana prohibition and legalize the use of the drug, and it has a network of lawyers in every state that can help individuals who run into trouble for violating federal marijuana laws. NORML does not, however, advocate for marijuana use, nor does it believe it should be completely unregulated. Instead, it focuses on removing criminal penalties for private possession and responsible use of the drug by adults, and wants the law to allow for its cultivation for personal use and casual nonprofit transfers of small amounts of the drug. It believes that like there is for alcohol, there should be a controlled market for marijuana, where consumers could purchase it from safe, legal, and regulated sources.

And, as is the case with alcohol, the organization does not advocate its use by children, nor driving while under the influence of the drug. Another major area of concern for NORML is the use of marijuana as a medicine for the relief of pain caused by nerve diseases, nausea, spasticity, glaucoma, and movement disorders, and also its use as an appetite stimulant for patients suffering from HIV-AIDS. On this front, NORML has the support of more than sixty United States and international health organizations, though according to federal law, the drug is still not allowed for medical use. In the 1990s, NORML unsuccessfully brought legal action against the Drug Enforcement Administration in hopes of altering federal laws concerning the medical use of marijuana. In addition, the group actively works to support the right of farmers to cultivate the nonpsychoactive strain of cannabis, hemp, for industrial uses such as food and fiber production.

More information on NORML and its current activities is available at the group's Web site: http://norml.org/index.cfm?Group_ID=3374.

(See also **Comprehensive Drug Abuse Prevention and Control Act**; **Marihuana Commission**; **Reagan, Ronald and Nancy**; **State Drug and Alcohol Control Laws**)

References

Anderson, Patrick. 1981. *High in America: The True Story Behind NORML and the Politics of Marijuana.* New York: Viking Press.

Chepesiuk, Ron. 1999. *The War on Drugs: An International Encyclopedia.* Santa Barbara, CA: ABC-CLIO.

National Organization for the Reform of Marijuana Laws. "FAQ's." [Online article retrieved 05/02/09] http://norml.org/index.cfm?Group_ID=3418.

National Organization for the Reform of Marijuana Laws. "Introduction." [Online article retrieved 05/02/09] http://norml.org/index.cfm?Group_ID=5493.

National Organization for the Reform of Marijuana Laws. "Medical Use." [Online article retrieved 05/02/09] http://www.norml.org/index.cfm?Group_ID=5441.

NUTT, LEVI G.

Levi G. Nutt was a pharmacist who rose to prominence as a drug law enforcement official when he became the head of the Narcotic Division of the Prohibition Unit in the 1920s. He was a key player in the move against maintenance treatment of addicts, and legal crackdowns on violations of the Harrison Narcotics Act.

Levi G. Nutt was born in 1866 and began his career as a pharmacist in Ohio. He started working for the Bureau of Internal Revenue in 1901, and later he worked for the federal unit responsible for the enforcement of the Harrison Act. From there, Nutt was appointed head of the Prohibition Unit's Narcotic Division.

When he assumed control over the Narcotic Division in 1920, Nutt had more resources than his predecessors who tried to enforce the provisions of the Harrison Act, as the Division's budget nearly doubled, providing for the employment of 170 agents devoted to narcotics control. In March of 1920, Nutt made a tour of the country to visit narcotic clinics to evaluate maintenance treatments given in these institutions, and he generally found them ineffective. Nutt believed that the danger of death from withdrawal was exaggerated, and that the narcotic clinics were part of the drug problem since they provided places where addicts could get their drugs, thus feeding the habit instead of compelling drug users to seek out a cure. Nutt reasoned that efforts at maintenance treatment were pointless anyway, since he believed that most addicts were either mentally deficient or psychopaths, and prone to relapse no matter what care they received. The 1919 cases *United States v. Doremus* and *Webb et al. v. United States*, in which the Supreme Court ruled that maintenance treatment of addiction violated the Harrison Act, gave legal backing to Nutt's approach. Under Nutt's leadership, the Narcotic Division decided to close narcotic clinics that gave drugs to addicts sometime in late 1919 or early 1920, and the Division also opposed the maintenance treatment of almost all addicts. By 1923, Nutt's campaign against the narcotic clinics was complete, as the last of narcotic clinics, in Shreveport, Louisiana, was shut down.

By the mid-1920s, Nutt had established a law-and-order approach to the drug problem, sending large numbers of drug-law violators to federal penitentiaries, and he claimed that this approach kept the scourge of narcotic drug addiction from spreading. In particular, he maintained that levels of addiction that did not have medical origins were decreasing. Surveys conducted by the Narcotic Division confirmed this thesis, showing that the estimated number of addicts in the country dropped from 106,025 in 1924 to 91,245 in 1926. Strict enforcement under Nutt led to compliance with the nation's drug control regime, as doctors became aware of the dangers of giving maintenance treatments to addicts, and fearful of running afoul of the law if they prescribed opiates. In this respect, the Narcotic Division under Nutt achieved its main goal—to cut down on the number of addicts in the United States. Under his leadership, federal appropriations for narcotics control grew substantially, increasing from $1 million in 1920 to $1.6 million by 1930. Nutt also advocated for the creation of the Public Health Service Narcotic Hospitals in the late 1920s, maintaining that the only way to further reduce the spread of drug addiction was to isolate addicts in institutions. Consequently, he supported the legislation that created public institutions for addiction treatment, but not because he believed addicts could be cured—instead, he believed that isolating them was the most effective way to keep addiction from spreading.

Nutt remained the head of the Narcotic Division until early 1930, when links between his family and notorious gangster (and drug trafficker) Arnold Rothstein led to his removal. Nutt was replaced by Harry J. Anslinger, then the Assistant Commissioner of the Prohibition Bureau, and the enforcement of narcotics laws was transferred to a new unit, the Federal Bureau of Narcotics. Nutt was transferred to become a field supervisor of alcohol prohibition agents, and then the head of the Alcohol Tax Unit in Syracuse, New York, until he retired. He passed away in 1938.

(See also **Anslinger, Harry J.**; **Narcotic Clinics**; **Prohibition Unit**; **Public Health Service Narcotic Hospitals**; *United States v. Doremus* **and** *Webb et al. v. United States*)

References

Belenko, Steven R., ed. 2000. *Drugs and Drug Policy in America: A Documentary History*. Westport, CT: Greenwood Press.

Courtwright, David T. 2001. *Dark Paradise: A History of Opiate Addiction in America.* Cambridge, MA: Harvard University Press.

Musto, David F. 1987. *The American Disease: Origins of Narcotics Control.* Expanded Edition. New York: Oxford University Press.

NYSWANDER, MARIE

Dr. Marie Nyswander was a psychiatrist and psychoanalyst who, with her husband Vincent Dole, developed methadone maintenance for the management of opiate addiction in the 1960s. In addition, she was a strong advocate for viewing opiate addiction as a medical problem, opposing the federal government's stance that drug addiction was above all a criminal issue.

Marie Nyswander was born in Reno, Nevada, on March 13, 1919, and she graduated from Sarah Lawrence College in 1941, and then from Cornell Medical College in 1944. In 1945, she began working for the Public Health Service, and did her residency working with drug addicts at the Public Health Service Narcotic Hospital in Lexington, Kentucky. Though she still believed that drug addiction was a condition rooted in psychology, Nyswander was dismayed by the brutal detoxification regimens she saw addicts undergo at Lexington, and soon began campaigning for the authorities to treat addiction as a disease instead of a crime. This ran against the prevailing trends at the federal level, as the Federal Bureau of Narcotics instead advocated handling the drug problem with tighter enforcement of drug laws and stricter punishment of drug law violators, rather than with expanded treatment. In 1956, she advanced her views

on addiction treatment with her book, *The Drug Addict as Patient.* Much like Alfred R. Lindesmith would do nine years later in his book *The Addict and the Law*, Nyswander began her argument in *The Drug Addict as Patient* by outlining the history of narcotic control in the United States, telling the story of how the federal government's interpretation of the Harrison Narcotics Act led to the arrest, prosecution, and intimidation of physicians who prescribed drugs to addicts, and consequently to the neglect of care for addicts. By cutting off all means of legal supplies of narcotics, Nyswander pointed out, the government transformed addicts, even those who were otherwise respectable members of the community, into criminals by virtue of their drug-taking behavior. Instead of using a punitive method, Nyswander endorsed adopting a system similar to the British, who allowed for maintenance prescriptions to addicts who needed them in order to function. To treat addicts, Nyswander endorsed the use of methadone, a synthetic narcotic that was longer-acting than heroin, meaning that its use was less likely to provoke withdrawal symptoms, making it less painful than other withdrawal methods. Nyswander argued that once addicts were stabilized on methadone, psychotherapy was important for their rehabilitation, and she also recommended ambulatory hospitalization treatment, a therapeutic setup where recovering addicts would have lived in hospitals, but gradually been allowed to slowly reintegrate into the community during the day.

In the 1950s, Nyswander ran a private practice, where she was one of few private physicians in the country to provide treatment for opiate addicts outside of the Public Health Services Narcotic Hospitals. In the 1960s, she opened a storefront clinic in Harlem, New York City, where she treated addicts as well. In 1964, Dr. Vincent Dole, a physician at Rockefeller Hospital in New York, invited Nyswander to join a research group he led to study the biology of addiction. Nyswander recruited addicts to participate in studies of drugs to help wean addicts off of heroin during her time working with Dole, and the research she helped lead found that methadone yielded positive results in efforts to cure addicts. Instead of trying to wean addicts off of methadone, Nyswander and Dole maintained some patients on high, nondiminishing doses of the drug. In 1965, Nyswander and Dole got married.

Nyswander also worked at Beth Israel Hospital in New York, where she began conducting clinical work with methadone. She also served on several advisory boards, including the Liaison Task Panel of the President's Commission on Mental Health under Jimmy Carter. Thanks to her pioneering work, Nyswander, along with Dole, received the first annual award from the National Drug Abuse Conference in 1978, and the New York Urban Coalition created an award in her honor, the Nyswander-Dole Award, in 1982. Nyswander passed away in 1986, at the age of 67, from cancer.

(See also **Dole, Vincent**; **Lindesmith, Alfred R.**; **Methadone**; **Public Health Service Narcotic Hospitals**)

References

Acker, Caroline Jean. 2002. *Creating the American Junkie: Addiction Research in the Classic Era of Narcotic Control*. Baltimore: Johns Hopkins University Press.

Kolbert, Elizabeth. 1986. "Dr. Marie Nyswander Dies at 67; Expert in Treating Drug Addicts." *The New York Times*. (April 21): B8.

Kosten, Thomas R. 1998. "Images in Psychiatry: Marie Nyswander, 1919–1986." *American Journal of Psychiatry*. 155: 1766.

Nyswander, Marie. 1956. *The Drug Addict as a Patient*. New York: Grune and Stratton.

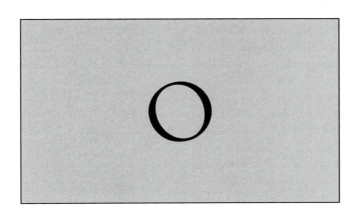

OFFICE OF NATIONAL DRUG CONTROL POLICY (ONDCP)

The Office of National Drug Control Policy (ONDCP) is the organization assigned with coordinating federal, state, and local efforts to control illegal drug abuse, and formulating national strategies to carry out the government's anti-drug activities. In total, the ONDCP is responsible for overseeing and coordinating the activities of over fifty federal agencies and programs.

The ONDCP was established by the 1988 Anti-Drug Abuse Act to coordinate federal anti-drug efforts. To reduce illicit drug use, manufacturing, and trafficking, as well as drug-related problems such as crime and dangers to public health, the Director of the ONDCP is empowered to create a National Drug Control Strategy, which directs the federal government's anti-drug efforts by establishing a program, budget, and guidelines for cooperation among federal, state, and local

entities. The Director of the ONDCP also evaluates, coordinates, and oversees domestic and international drug control efforts, and ensures that they support and complement local anti-drug initiatives. The Director advises the President on changes in the organization, management, budgeting, and personnel of other federal agencies that could affect the federal strategy for tackling the drug problem.

The first head of the ONDCP, commonly referred to as the "drug czar," was William J. Bennett, who was appointed by President George H. W. Bush to serve in the role from 1989 until 1991. Bennett took a tough stance against illicit drugs, pushing for tighter enforcement of the nation's drug laws and calling for tougher penalties for drug law violators, even calling for drug dealers to receive the death penalty. He strongly opposed calls from groups such as the National Organization for the Reform of Marijuana Laws to legalize or decriminalize certain drugs. Bennett's reign marked a continuation of the tough talk and action on drugs that had begun under President Ronald Reagan, and Bennett claimed that drug use decreased during his tenure. Since Bennett, the ONDCP has been led by Bob Martinez, Lee P. Brown, General Barry McCaffery, and more recently, John P. Walters. In 2002, President George W. Bush established an ambitious goal for the ONDCP, aiming to reduce drug use amongst youths by 10% within two years, and 25% within five years. According to the ONDCP, this program has been relatively successful, as the organization claims it achieved an 11% reduction in drug use by 2004 and a 23% reduction by 2007. The ONDCP is limited in how much it can advocate reform, since part of the Act that reauthorized it in 1998 stipulated that the head of the organization has to oppose any attempts to legalize currently illicit drugs.

Today the ONDCP has three major priorities. The first is prevention, as the organization is active in supporting prevention and early intervention programs that reduce drug use, and backing efforts to highlight the negative health and social consequences that can stem from using illicit drugs. Secondly, it focuses on improving access to quality treatment for addicts, so they can obtain the care they need to achieve a lasting recovery from the problems caused by substance abuse. Finally, it focuses on market disruption, working with the Drug Enforcement Administration and other law enforcement bodies to keep illicit drugs off of America's streets.

More information on the ONDCP and its activities is available at its Web site: http://www.whitehousedrugpolicy .gov/index.html.

(See also **Drug Addiction and Public Policy**; **Anti-Drug Abuse Acts**; **Reagan, Ronald and Nancy**)

References

Chepesiuk, Ron. 1999. *The War on Drugs: An International Encyclopedia*. Santa Barbara, CA: ABC-CLIO.

Office of National Drug Control Policy. "About." [Online article retrieved 05/03/09] http://www.whitehousedrugpolicy.gov/about/index.html.

Office of National Drug Control Policy. "Reauthorization Act of 1998." [Online article retrieved 05/03/09] http://www .whitehousedrugpolicy.gov/about/98 reauthorization.html.

Office of National Drug Control Policy. "The President's National Drug Control Strategy, January 2009." [Online article retrieved 05/03/09] http://www.white housedrugpolicy.gov/publications/policy/ ndcs09/index.html.

ON-LINE GAMERS ANONYMOUS AND THE DAEDALUS PROJECT

Video-game addiction, though not a clinically diagnosed condition, is increasingly understood as a real phenomenon with real consequences, and On-Line Gamers Anonymous (OLGA) is a fellowship for problem gamers and their loved ones that utilizes a twelve-step approach to recovery. Video-game addiction has also been the focus of the Daedalus Project, which conducted tens of thousands of surveys to better assess the psychology of gamers, including those who developed unhealthy attachments to their video games. Utilizing Daedalus Project data, recent scholarship has argued that 8.5% of video-game players exhibit pathological patterns of play.

OLGA is a mutual aid support group for addicted gamers and their families. It was founded in May 2002 by Elizabeth

Woolley, whose son, Shawn, committed suicide in 2001 while logged on to the massively multiplayer online role-playing game (MMORPG) EverQuest. She has attributed her son's death to what has been called excessive game playing, video-game addiction, or pathological video-game use. She accused Sony Online Entertainment, the producer of EverQuest, of creating an addictive and dangerous game, but the most lasting response to her loss has been the creation of a self-help fellowship for recovering gamers (as well as their family members and friends) in which members help one another recover from the problems caused by their attachment to video games.

Sometimes referred to as OLG-Anon, OLGA takes the form of a twelve-step program. It can thus be likened to organizations such as Narcotics Anonymous, Gamblers Anonymous (GA), or Debtors Anonymous, which have all patterned themselves after Alcoholics Anonymous (AA) in their approach to recovering from their particular addictions. What differentiates OLGA from these AA-inspired organizations, however, is the fact that the vast majority of OLGA members get together at online meetings instead of at a physical gathering. Group discussions, then, take place on message boards on their Web site, http://www.olganon.org. Face-to-face meetings of OLGA were begun in London, Ontario, but have recently been suspended due to lack of attendance.

OLGA's Web site and discussion boards are thus the crux of the fellowship, with members able to anonymously log on and work towards recovering from their gaming problems. As part of this process, OLGA offers a (self-admittedly) nondiagnostic screening tool for gamers to determine if their relationship to video games is pathological. Consisting of forty-six questions, it is reminiscent of the questionnaire put together by GA that served for many years as a professional means of diagnosing gambling addiction, but there is no particular number of "yes" answers to OLGA's questions that determines if an individual has a problem with gaming. Instead, OLGA states that it is up to each respondent to determine if excessive gaming is a problem.

OLGA is also concerned with the danger that particular games or gaming formats may or may not pose. It does not believe that all games are inherently bad or evil, but it claims that some games are manufactured with the knowledge that many of its players will develop an addictive relationship to them. OLGA thus professes, in a stance that goes beyond the more narrow fellowship focus of AA, a desire to one day work closely with game manufacturers to promote what it calls responsible game play. In the meantime, however, the organization's Web site features online discussions about games that have been reported to be addictive, with MMORPGs generally believed by OLGA members to be the most addictive in nature. Though other formats, such as console games, are deemed to have addictive qualities, MMORPGs are singled out because they never end and game players' success is dependent upon time spent playing. MMORPGs are also considered highly addictive in nature because they encourage a level of social interaction that can replace, or provide an escape from, real-life social activity, with online friends becoming more important than real friends. Many discussion boards are thus dedicated to OLGA members sharing stories of their pathological MMORPG experiences, thereby finding a fellowship that is helpful in their recovery from excessive gaming.

The Daedalus Project is another Web site dealing with MMORPG experiences. Founded by Nick Yee, the Daedalus Project revolves around the survey data he has collected from tens of thousands of MMORPG players. The Web site features analysis of this large amount of information in the form of, among other things, an online journal whose first issue dates back to January 10, 2003. The last issue came out on March 9, 2009, and the Daedalus Project is currently in hibernation, meaning that the surveys and findings are not being updated, though all of the information collected over the six years of its activity remains available.

Yee used this mass of information to better understand the psychology of MMORPG players, including MMORPG addiction, which he concluded was a very real phenomenon. Quantifying his data, Yee reported that, regardless of age group, over 40% of MMORPG players who responded to his survey considered themselves addicted to the particular game they played. Similarly, 30% of females aged twelve to seventeen reported having unsuccessfully tried to quit their game of choice, whereas this figure dropped to 4.8% amongst women older than thirty-five years of age. Almost 19% of boys aged twelve to seventeen reported having unsuccessfully tried to quit their game of choice, but this figure was just 6.4% amongst men older than thirty-five years of age. From the data he gathered, Yee determined that the phenomena of dependence and withdrawal that are associated with substance addiction also factor in the lives of some MMORPG players. Other scholars have utilized Yee's data and findings in their own work, and Yee himself has become an academic whose research centers on other aspects of online gaming.

(See also **Alcoholics Anonymous (AA)**; **Gamblers Anonymous (GA)**; **Narcotics Anonymous (NA)**; **Reference Essay**; **Young, Kimberly S.**)

References

"The Daedalus Project: The Psychology of MMORPGs." [Online information retrieved 05/24/09] http://www.nickyee.com/daedalus/.

Gentile, Douglas. 2009. "Pathological Video-Game Use Among Youth Ages 8 to 18: A National Study." *Psychological Science*. 20, no. 5: 594–602.

On-Line Gamers Anonymous. "About OLGA & OLG-Anon." [Online information retrieved 05/24/09] http://www.olganon.org.

Yee, Nick. 2002. "Ariadne—Understanding MMORPG Addiction" [Online article retrieved 05//24/09] http://www.nickyee.com/hub/addiction/home.html.

P. LORILLARD

P. Lorillard is the oldest tobacco company in the United States. Founded in the eighteenth century and later controlled by American Tobacco Company, P. Lorillard was central to the industry's move towards filtered cigarettes in the 1950s with the introduction of a "micronite" filter on its new brand, Kent. Also referred to as simply "Lorillard," the tobacco company agreed to the Master Settlement Agreement (MSA) in 1998.

P. Lorillard's history as a tobacco company dates back to the eighteenth century, when French immigrant Pierre Lorillard founded a tobacco processing plant in New York City in 1760. Later a part of American Tobacco Company, it became independent again in 1911 when the government broke up the tobacco monopoly under antitrust laws. On its own, P. Lorillard was one of the nation's smaller tobacco companies, but through clever advertising worked its way up the industry's ladder. In 1919, P. Lorillard was the first tobacco company to produce an advertisement featuring a woman holding a cigarette. The company was extremely successful in its campaign for its cigarette brand, Old Gold. In addition to being the first to use comic strips in national advertising, Lorillard's Old Gold campaign featured innovations such as blindfold tests, double cellophane wrapping, and a remarkably successful prize contest that elevated sales by more than 70% in 1937. As a result, Lorillard became the fourth tobacco company in what had previously been the Big Three of American Tobacco, R. J. Reynolds, and Liggett & Myers.

In the early 1950s, the Big Four became worried about the impact that reports such as *Reader's Digests'* 1952 article "Cancer by the Carton"—which brought recent scientific findings linking smoking to cancer to a popular audience —would have on their industry. New awareness of tobacco's dangers generated a significant drop in the nation's level of cigarette consumption, and Lorillard joined forces with the other major tobacco companies to form, in

1954, the Tobacco Industry Research Committee (TIRC). The TIRC was devised by the country's premier public relations firm, Hill & Knowlton, and led by noted geneticist Clarence Cook "C.C." Little in order to present the tobacco industry as an ally of science and public health. With this endeavor, Lorillard and the other major tobacco companies were successful in stymieing —for about a decade—what was a growing scientific consensus about the serious health hazards of smoking, and helped rekindle sales of cigarettes.

Beyond being a part of the tobacco industry's joint response to public concerns about cigarette smoke's health effects, Lorillard made its own attempt to allay smokers' worries by introducing a new, and allegedly healthier, cigarette line, which they named "Kent." Sensing an economic opportunity amidst the serious threat that 1950s medical findings posed to their bottom line, Lorillard responded to the medical backlash against cigarettes by placing a filter on the tip of their Kents. This micronite filter was originally made out of crocidolite, a form of asbestos, so its addition was hardly good for smokers' health. Still, Kent proved a popular new product, as smokers who were concerned about their health felt reassured by the filter and generally believed they were consuming a less dangerous product. Kent's success led to other tobacco companies producing their own lines of filtered cigarettes, spawning the so-called "tar derby," in which each cigarette brand claimed that their products were smoother or milder than the competition's. These adjectives were used in order to evoke the idea that consumers were purchasing a "safe" cigarette, and the American public clearly bought into the idea of filtered

cigarettes. By 1954, filtered cigarettes comprised about 10% of the cigarette market, and they doubled their market share by the following year. Filter-tipped cigarettes accounted for half of all cigarettes sold in the United States in 1957, and by the 1970s, that figure would rise to almost 90%, signaling the public's increasing awareness of smoking's health effects, but also its belief that smoking a filtered cigarette afforded them a greater measure of protection from smoking-related illnesses and diseases.

The tar derby that Lorillard helped set off with Kent was not as beneficial to consumers' health as many smokers imagined. Though filters may have appeared to make cigarettes safer, the reality was that they did not bring about much of a change to the levels of tar and nicotine that smokers consumed. Lorillard was one of the first manufacturers to understand this phenomenon, as it seems its micronite filter was a bit too effective for smokers' tastes. Kent customers began complaining that they were not experiencing the same "kick" that unfiltered cigarettes had provided them with, so Lorillard swapped out the micronite filter for a looser fitting filter tip that allowed more tar and nicotine to get through. Similarly, cigarette manufacturers upped levels of tar and nicotine in their new products in order to counteract the effects of filtration. Some studies have also shown that smokers of filtered cigarettes sometimes altered their manner of inhalation in order to increase the levels of tar and nicotine they consumed, thereby negating whatever health benefits a filter tip may have afforded them while all along feeling reassured by the illusion of safer smoking.

Lorillard's knowledge of the true health hazards of its products became public as a result of *Cipollone v. Liggett Group, Inc. et al.*, a landmark 1980s lawsuit that signaled a turning point in the history of litigation against the tobacco industry. Rose Cipollone, who smoked for about forty years and ultimately died from lung cancer, switched to Lorillard's True cigarettes in 1974, reportedly at the behest of her doctor. True, which billed itself as being low in tar and nicotine, was suggested by the doctor, who reasoned that if Cipollone intended to continue smoking, it would be the healthiest brand for her. In the course of the lawsuit that Cipollone's family brought against Lorillard, Philip Morris, and Liggett & Myers, attorney Marc Edell uncovered internal industry documents that revealed Lorillard was concerned about smoking's link to cancer as far back as the mid-1940s. Other industry papers documented the role that Lorillard, as well as other tobacco companies, played in distorting and suppressing the dangers of smoking through the TIRC. And despite overwhelming evidence to the contrary, Lorillard continued to deny the carcinogenic nature of cigarettes well into the 1990s. In a deposition connected to the *Broin v. Philip Morris* trial, which revolved around the danger of second-hand smoke, Lorillard chairman and CEO Andrew H. Tisch stated that he did not believe the warning labels that appear on cigarette packs to be accurate or true.

The actions of Lorillard and other tobacco manufacturers were fully exposed with the 1998 MSA. In addition to requiring Lorillard to pay billions of dollars to states in compensation for the healthcare costs of dealing with smoking-related illnesses, the MSA included the stipulation that industry documents be placed on an easily navigable and publicly accessible Web site.

Lorillard's documents are available at http:// lorillarddocs.com.

(See also ***Cipollone v. Liggett Group, Inc. et al.***; **Master Settlement Agreement (MSA)**; **Tobacco Industry Research Committee (TIRC)**; **Tobacco Institute**)

References

Brandt, Allan M. 2007. *The Cigarette Century: The Rise, Fall, and Deadly Persistence of the Product That Defined America.* New York: Basic Books.

Burns, Eric. 2007. *The Smoke of the Gods: A Social History of Tobacco.* Philadelphia: Temple University Press.

Cordry, Harold V. 2001. *Tobacco: A Reference Handbook.* Santa Barbara, CA: ABC-CLIO.

Goodman, Jordan, ed. 2005. *Tobacco in History and Culture: An Encyclopedia.* Detroit: Thomson Gale.

Parker-Pope, Tara. 2001. *Cigarettes: Anatomy of an Industry from Seed to Smoke.* New York: The New Press.

PARTNERSHIP FOR A DRUG-FREE AMERICA

The Partnership for a Drug-Free America (PDFA) is a nonprofit coalition of professionals in the communications industry dedicated to using the media to reduce the demand for illicit drugs in the United States. Though its work supports the federal government's anti-drug education efforts, the organization receives no government funding, as it is financed entirely through donations from corporations, agencies, and private foundations.

The PDFA began in 1986, when Phil Jaonou, the chairman of the advertising agency Daley & Associates, introduced the idea of creating an organization to combat the glorification of drug use in the mainstream media. In the mid-1980s, the problems caused by illicit drug use had become prominent in the news, and the government, led by Ronald Reagan, identified it as a major social and public health problem. In this environment, Jaonou found a receptive audience for his idea to create an advertising campaign dedicated to making youths more aware of the dangers that illicit drugs posed. His work began with a $300,000 grant from the American Association of Advertising Agencies to launch what was originally planned to be a temporary, three-year effort that would spend $1.5 billion to spread anti-drug messages though the media. Shortly thereafter, the PDFA set up offices in New York City and hired Dick Reilly to be its first Chief Officer. The first PDFA advertisement aired on April 13, 1987.

Though it fell short of its $1.5 billion goal, the PDFA generated about $150 million worth of advertising in its first three years. Using all major media outlets, including television, radio, the Internet, and print advertisements, the PDFA has, thanks in large part to pro-bono help from many leading advertising agencies, been able to reach the public on both the local and national level for the last twenty years. The PDFA became more ambitious over time, setting itself a goal of disseminating $1 million worth of advertising every day. By 1998, the PDFA became the second-largest advertiser in the United States, spending about five times as much on its messages as Coca-Cola, and trailing only McDonalds in its annual production of advertisements. The stated goal of this media blitz was to ensure that every single American would receive at least one anti-drug message per day.

The PDFA has three major goals—to reduce demand for drugs by changing attitudes through the media, to track changes in attitudes towards illegal drugs, and to evaluate the impact that PDFA messages have on them. Towards these ends, the PDFA receives corporate contributions and advertising time, and then a twenty-five-member creative review board reviews submissions for campaign ideas. In order to create content that they think will be effective, the PDFA has chosen to reject government funding, since it would likely place limits on what sort of advertisements it could produce and run. This has allowed the group to run some shocking, but very effective advertisements, most famously one from the 1980s that showed how drugs can "fry" peoples' brains. In this spot, an egg is shown with the audio caption, "This is your brain." Then the egg is cracked and fried, at which point the narrator says, "This is your brain on drugs. Any questions?"

As with the "this is your brain on drugs" advertisement, the PDFA uses modern marketing techniques in order to ensure that its messages are powerful and impact their target audiences. Over a hundred advertising agencies lend their expertise to the PDFA to assist in their efforts, which target eight primary groups—children, teens, adults, parents, Hispanics, Blacks, healthcare providers, and employers. In addition to traditional advertising, the PDFA has also used more innovative advertising techniques, placing inserts into movies and cartoons, putting advertisements on cereal boxes and milk cartons, placing bumper stickers on toy cars, airing ads at gas stations, and taking out advertising space in telephone books.

Though many applaud the PDFA's efforts, the organization also has its critics. Many accuse the group of spreading falsehoods about drug use in its advertisements, and others claim that it focuses more on fear-mongering rather than education in the messages it disseminates to the public. In addition, by portraying drug users in such a negative light, some scholars have claimed that the organization hardens public attitudes and makes viewers less likely to support drug-treatment initiatives. Furthermore, the alcohol and tobacco industries were heavy contributors to the organization when it began its work. This led to charges that the PDFA was, by emphasizing the dangers of illicit drugs, neglecting to highlight the equally dangerous character of legal drugs such as alcohol and tobacco. Today, the PDFA also focuses on highlighting the dangers of alcohol use. Though it stopped accepting funding from alcohol and tobacco companies in 1994, the organization continues to take in donations from the pharmaceutical industry, which also pushes some drugs that have as much harmful potential as illicit substances. Since 9/11, the PDFA has run spots making direct links between drug use and terrorism, a connection that, while containing grains of truth to it since terrorist organizations do engage in drug trafficking, was considered an exaggeration by many critics.

(See also **Anti-Drug Abuse Acts**; **Reagan, Ronald and Nancy**)

References

Buchanan, David R. and Lawrence Walleck. 1998. "This Is the Partnership for a Drug-Free America: Any Questions?" *Journal of Drug Issues*. 98, no. 2: 329–356.

Partnership for a Drug-Free America. "20 Years of Partnering with Families." [Online article retrieved 05/03/09] http://www.drugfree.org/General/Articles/Article.aspx?id=cfd5a031-7fc8-43c5-8a22-9b36eddbf72a&IsPreviewMode=true&UVer=c659fb1a-3757-488a-8b8a-9d46c9ce4ba6.

Partnership for a Drug-Free America. "About." [Online article retrieved 05/03/09] http://www.drugfree.org/Portal/About/.

Trudeau, Christine. 2005. "Partnership for a Drug-Free America and Corporate Drug Wars." [Online article retrieved 05/03/09] http://www.cannabisculture.com/articles/4258.html.

PATENT MEDICINES

Patent medicines were formulas, tonics, and other concoctions that were sold as medicines, both in the United States, and elsewhere, until the early-twentieth century. These preparations often included habit-forming drugs, and historians speculate that they may have led countless numbers of people to ingest harmful chemicals, or become addicted to the substances in these preparations, without even knowing it. It was not until the passage of the Pure Food and Drug Act in 1906 that the contents of patent medicines had to be revealed to the public.

The poor, and people who lived in rural areas, often did not have access to health care in the nineteenth century, and many never saw a doctor unless they had a serious medical problem. Instead of professional medical treatment, they used traditional healing methods and folk remedies to soothe their everyday aches, pains, and worries. People often turned to these remedies for relief from chronic illnesses like asthma and arthritis, psychological problems like depression and alcoholism, and even for more serious infectious diseases like cholera and malaria. Druggists, mail-order services, traveling salesmen, and even pharmaceutical companies sold these medicines to gullible or desperate buyers, claiming that they had found a secret formula that could cure whatever ailed them. The packages for these medicines were almost always unmarked, and rarely had a list of ingredients that permitted buyers to ascertain what they were actually consuming. These tonics were sold as "patent medicines," even though in fact, the inventors never actually patented the concoctions they sold. Often, this was because the "secret formula" was little more than a mixture of opium derivatives mixed with alcohol and other sedatives, along with spices or other chemicals to disguise the taste.

Even though they contained potentially addictive substances, these medicines were often marketed to people who should not have been taking such dangerous drugs. Many patent medicines were marketed as "soothing syrups," and used to calm irritated babies and help them go to sleep. Others were advertised as cures for addiction, but actually contained the drugs they claimed to counteract. Formulas like Opacura and Denarco, for example, were sold to addicts who, desperate for a cure, believed that these medicines would help them kick their habits. Only after taking the medicines for years did many unfortunate addicts realize that the drugs they had been taking to get over their morphine habits actually *contained* morphine as their main ingredients. At times, it was not until somebody investigated these secret formulas that their actual contents would become public knowledge. Even though the inventors of patent medicines would be publicly disgraced and embarrassed once their dirty secrets were made known to the public, it would not be until after they had sold their concoctions to thousands of unwitting customers.

It was not until the first decade of the twentieth century that this situation began to change. Reformers and muckrakers—journalists who wrote stories exposing the misdeeds of crooked politicians and big corporations—began agitating for better consumer protection in a variety of areas, including the sale of medicines. Eventually, their work led to the 1906 passage of the Pure Food and Drug Act, which required that the contents of preparations containing alcohol, opium, or opium derivatives be listed on the medicine's packaging or labeling.

(See also **Pure Food and Drug Act**; **Wiley, Harvey Washington**)

References

Courtwright, David T. 2001. *Dark Paradise: A History of Opiate Addiction in America*. Cambridge, MA: Harvard University Press.

Morgan, H. Wayne. 1974. *Yesterday's Addicts: American Society and Drug Abuse, 1865–1920*. Norman, OK: University of Oklahoma Press.

Musto, David F. 1987. *The American Disease: Origins of Narcotics Control*. Expanded Edition. New York: Oxford University Press.

THE PHILIPPINES

The roots of narcotics control in the United States, and internationally, were largely intertwined with the story of the United States and its opium policy in the Philippines, an island chain off of the eastern coast of Asia.

In the 1890s, the United States was working to become an international power and stretch its influence across the globe like many European countries (Britain, France, Germany, and Holland in particular) had done in their colonial exploits throughout the nineteenth century. In particular, the United States wanted to expand its influence over Cuba, and in 1898 it declared war on Spain, which had control over the island nation. The conflict, which came to be known as the Spanish-American War, lasted four months, and as part of the settlement, the United States gained control over not only Cuba, but also other Spanish colonial holdings in Puerto Rico, Guam, and the Philippines. The war with Spain, and the tremendous territorial gains the United States made as a result, fed feelings of patriotism in the United States, and many back in Washington saw the conflict as part of a larger American project to help spread American freedom and civilization to foreign peoples. In addition, the Philippines gave the United States its first territory in Asia, and the country wanted to use the island chain as a base to expand its financial interests in the region.

While the United States hoped to use the Philippines as a launching pad for its expansion of influence into Asia, the Filipinos themselves had different ideas. Though the United States was instrumental in getting the Spanish out of the Philippines, Filipino nationalists also played a key role in the defeat of Spain, having fought courageously alongside U.S. forces in a war that they hoped would eventually lead to their independence. Despite the hopes of the Filipino fighters, the United States was not willing to grant the Philippines independence. Officials in Washington wanted to maintain their newfound influence in Asia, and they also feared other that countries

(specifically Germany) would invade if the country was not protected by the United States. As it became clear that the United States had no intentions of leaving, a rebellion erupted, and a group of insurrectionists continued to fight the occupying forces until 1902.

While military strength allowed the United States to withstand attacks from the Filipino rebels, the United States also realized that it could not rule by force alone. To show that they were not just another colonial power looking to exploit the Philippines and its people the way that the Spanish had done, the U.S. government sought ways to show that it was there to help—and not oppress—the Filipino people. One way they did this was to undertake policies to help or, in the opinion of the U.S. occupiers, "enlighten" the Filipinos. By building schools, hospitals, and churches, the United States hoped to show that their intentions there were good. A key component of this plan was the goal of spreading Christianity, a religion that, according to the racist and ethnocentric theories that many in the United States believed at the time, was "superior" to the traditional ways of non-Western peoples. In 1902, a Canadian-born churchman who had been living in Boston, Charles Henry Brent, became the first Episcopal Bishop for the territory, and began working to spread Christianity among the Filipinos.

Both the government and Brent thought that a good way to show that the United States wanted to help the people of the Philippines was by assisting them with their opium problem. When the Philippines were under Spanish rule, the opium habit was widespread, as the Spanish colonial government operated a monopoly in which they sold the drug and made money off of it by putting high taxes on it. Once the Spanish were kicked out, the drug became even more widespread since it was no longer subject to such high taxes. At first, the United States planned to curb the habit by reinstituting a monopoly system like the Spanish had used, but reformers in Washington thought it would be immoral for the U.S. government to make profits by selling the drug the way the Spanish had. To come up with a better solution, Philippine Governor (and future president) William Howard Taft appointed a committee to study the issue, and in its final report, the committee recommended phasing out the availability of the drug until it was banned except for medicinal purposes. People back in Washington wanted to take a stricter approach, and by 1908, recreational opium use was banned throughout the Philippines. By taking decisive action to help Filipinos overcome what seemed to be a widespread opium problem, government officials both in Washington and in the Philippines believed that they were acting in the best interests of the Filipino people, and hoped to gain their support as a result.

The problem, however, was that despite the U.S. policy in the Philippines, the drug was still widely available because it could so easily be smuggled from China and other places in Asia. Brent and other anti-opium reformers maintained that for the prohibition on recreational opium use in the Philippines to be effective, the drug's availability needed to be restricted throughout the region, and control needed to be international. In 1906, the United States proposed having an international conference to discuss the issue. In 1909, the first international conference concerning opium control met in Shanghai, followed by a series of meetings at The Hague in the years leading up to World War I. According to Brent, Hamilton Wright, and other representatives of the United States at these conferences, it was important for the United States to practice what it preached, and have domestic controls over opium that were in line with the international laws the United States was advocating. As a result, reformers at home began pushing for national laws restricting opium use, eventually leading to the passage of the Opium Smoking Exclusion Act in 1909, and the Harrison Narcotics Act in 1914. Consequently, within a generation of the United States gaining control over the Philippines, concerns over opium there led the United States to make changes, both at home and abroad, that would institute the narcotics control regime that remained in place throughout the first half of the twentieth century.

(See also **Brent, Charles Henry**; **Hague Convention**; **Shanghai Commission**; **Wright, Hamilton**)

References

Bewley-Taylor, David R. 1999. *The United States and International Drug Control, 1909–1997*. London: Pinter.

Davenport-Hines, Richard. 2001. *The Pursuit of Oblivion: A Global History of Narcotics, 1500–2000*. London: Weidenfeld & Nicolson.

McAllister, William B. 2000. *Drug Diplomacy in the Twentieth Century*. London: Routledge.

Musto, David F. 1987. *The American Disease: Origins of Narcotics Control*. Expanded Edition. New York: Oxford University Press.

PORTER, STEPHEN G.

Stephen G. Porter was a Republican Congressman from Pennsylvania who became active in the arena of narcotics control in the late 1920s. Though he believed that narcotics control could be made more effective by enacting tougher international controls over drugs, Porter was unsuccessful in his efforts to influence the League of Nations' drug control efforts. He did, however, succeed in making significant changes in the administration of narcotics control efforts at home, and he was a key player in the creation of public institutions to house and treat addicts.

Stephen Geyer Porter was born in Ohio on May 18, 1869, and his family moved to Pennsylvania when he was eight years old. He studied medicine for two years before entering law school and eventually passing the bar exam in 1893, when he began practicing law in Pittsburgh. He worked as the city solicitor of Alleghany and chairman of the Republican State convention before being elected to Congress, where he served from 1911 until his death in 1930.

After Representative Henry T. Rainey, who had been one of the leading proponents of tighter narcotics control in Congress, failed in his re-election campaign in 1920, Porter assumed congressional leadership in questions pertaining to narcotics. Through his involvement with community organizations, Porter was able to garner political support for more stringent controls over controlled substances. Porter believed that the root of America's drug problem lay not at home, but rather overseas, and that tighter international control over narcotics would help curb narcotic use domestically by cutting down on the availability of drugs that could be smuggled into the United States. In particular, Porter believed that the Hague Treaty, which governed international narcotics control, needed to have a provision that limited the production of raw opium and coca leaves across the world. Without limitations on the raw materials used to make narcotics, Porter believed, any attempts at narcotics control, even with domestic legislation such as the Harrison Narcotics Act, would fail. To create a system of international control over raw opium and coca leaves, Porter believed that the United States needed to begin by showing the international community that it strongly supported tighter international control measures. In 1923, he took a first step to this end by authoring a House Joint Resolution calling for Britain, Persia, Turkey, Peru, Bolivia, Java, and the Netherlands to restrict their production of raw opium and coca leaves. Later that year, Porter was part of the U.S. delegation to the League of Nations Advisory Committee on Traffic in Opium and Other Dangerous Drugs, where he continued to argue that controls on production were necessary to tackle the problem of drug abuse. The League adopted Porter's resolution that December, putting the United States in the odd position of leading the League's campaign against narcotics even though it was not a member of the organization.

To show that America's drug control intentions were sincere, Porter became active on the domestic front, working in Congress to ban heroin and put forth a congressional resolution that would make the American position clear when countries reconvened in Geneva to consider the next step in international narcotics control. He proposed a bill to ban heroin in April of 1924, and testimony in deliberations on his bill highlighted the dangers that the drug posed, especially to American youth. The resulting legislation amended the 1909 Smoking

Opium Exclusion Act to prohibit the manufacture of crude opium for the creation of heroin, thus effectively outlawing its production and use in the United States. Porter hoped that by prohibiting heroin, the United States would not only cut down on use at home, but also set an example that would convince other nations to follow suit, thus cutting down on the production of heroin worldwide and making it less likely that foreign heroin could be smuggled onto American shores.

Having helped establish solid domestic controls that he hoped would serve as a model for international legislation, Porter led the U.S. delegation to the Second Geneva Conference in 1924. With support from Congress, Porter was uncompromising in his desire to place international limitations on the production of both raw and manufactured opiates. Other nations, however, were unwilling to comply with Porter's demands. Many opium-producing countries were reticent to place limitations on their domestic production of the drug, and member nations did not agree to ban the manufacture of heroin as the United States had done. Much to the chagrin of European representatives at the conference, Porter and the American delegation walked out of the negotiations in February of 1925, refusing to sign an agreement that did not meet their demands. Many Americans supported Porter's decision to boycott the convention, and Porter's strong reputation in Congress enabled him to dissuade the State Department from supporting the 1925 Geneva Convention.

Though unable to achieve his goals for a more comprehensive international narcotic control regime, Porter proved effective in advancing drug control legislation on the home front. Porter believed that addicts were victims of a disease, and had long advocated for the creation of publicly funded institutions to help cure drug addiction. In 1929, one of his proposals became law, and authorized the creation of two Public Health Service Narcotic Hospitals to detain and cure addicts. Porter also worked to increase the efficiency of America's drug control efforts, both at home and abroad, by creating a government agency to enforce the Harrison Act and represent the United States at subsequent international narcotics control conferences. The Narcotic Division under the Prohibition Unit of the Treasury Department had become subject to charges of corruption under the leadership of Levi G. Nutt, and the Federal Narcotic Control Board, which was created by the Narcotic Drugs Import and Export Act of 1922, had proven ineffective. By uniting domestic and international control under one agency, Porter reasoned, the United States could better coordinate its campaign for more effective drug control both at home and abroad. In addition, by administratively separating narcotics control from the Treasury Department's apparatus assigned with enforcing liquor prohibition, Porter believed that drug control would benefit, since alcohol prohibition was becoming both difficult to enforce and widely unpopular. In the spring of 1930, Porter's vision was realized with the creation of the Federal Bureau of Narcotics (FBN) under the leadership of Harry J. Anslinger.

Before the FBN could begin its work however, Porter passed away in Pittsburgh in June of 1930.

(See also **Federal Bureau of Narcotics (FBN)**; **League of Nations**; **Public Health Service Narcotic Hospitals**)

References

Darst, Joseph M. 1950. *Biographical - Directory of the American Congress, 1774–1949*. Washington, D.C.: U.S. Government Printing Office.

Courtwright, David T. 2001. *Dark Paradise: A History of Opiate Addiction in America*. Cambridge, MA: Harvard University Press.

Musto. David F. 1987. *The American Disease: Origins of Narcotic Control*. Expanded Edition. New York: Oxford University Press.

PROHIBITION PARTY

The Prohibition Party is a national temperance party originally organized by temperance advocates disenchanted with the anti-alcohol efforts of the Republicans and Democrats. When it was founded in the nineteenth century, the Prohibition Party thus represented a heightened politicization of the temperance movement, and its political ambitions went far beyond those of previous temperance groups such as the Washingtonians. At the turn of the century, however, the Anti-Saloon League of America (ASL) overtook the Prohibition Party as the political lead in the prohibitionist cause. Despite its decline, however, the Prohibition Party is still in existence today.

The Prohibition Party was founded in 1869, but it emerged as an offshoot of the Good Templars, a temperance organization founded in 1859 on principles derived from the Washingtonian movement. Over the course of the 1860s, the Good Templars' membership grew dramatically, leading it to venture beyond the apolitical, individual focus of the Washingtonians, and move towards a greater politicization of the temperance cause. This new temperance position was articulated most prominently by James Black, a former Washingtonian and the founder of the Pennsylvania Republican Party, who began calling for a new political party dedicated to making alcohol prohibition the law of the land.

This move towards establishing a prohibitionist party emerged from a Spring 1869 proposal from the Grand Lodge of the Good Templars. Assembling later that year in Chicago, the convention members argued that none of the existing political parties were willing to adopt a strong policy stance on the question of prohibition. The Republican Party, in particular, was singled out for its moral failures in combating alcohol. Perceived by many to be the nation's moral party for its stance against slavery, the Republican Party appeared morally exhausted and thus unable to properly take up the cause of prohibition. Attendees of the Chicago convention also argued that Republican politicians played a critical role in weakening or removing anti-liquor legislation in some northern states, thus making them unreliable allies in the crusade against alcohol. Hence, on September 1, 1869 in Chicago's Farwell Hall, the (National) Prohibition Party was born.

The newly founded Prohibition Party did not attract huge membership numbers right off the bat. Reconstruction in the South after the Civil War remained the dominant issue in American politics in the 1870s, leaving little room for major policy discussions about alcohol. The party started to gain support in the 1880s, as more Americans became convinced by the argument that the Republicans were not reliable allies in the battle against alcohol. The new prominence of the Prohibition Party was especially visible with the 1884 presidential election, in which they garnered 150,000 votes—up from a mere 10,000 votes four years earlier. The Prohibition Party received 250,000 votes in the next election (1888), and in the following election (1892), they topped out at 271,000 votes. These numbers, however, never represented more than 2.2% of the total votes cast.

The reasons for the party's electoral success in the 1884 and 1888 elections also contain an explanation for their meager gains in 1892. In the 1884 vote, the Prohibition Party was greatly aided by the Woman's Christian Temperance Union, and emboldened by increased membership, it was able to advance a more comprehensive national platform and campaign. Prohibition Party leaders thus went beyond sectarian and local concerns, and put forth a party platform based on broad national issues—prohibition being but one of them. The Prohibition Party also took positions on women's suffrage, poverty, public health, and political corruption, and it sought out allies across the board by appealing to groups ranging from southern Whites to Blacks. In 1892, the party continued to broaden its platform, but it began to tackle so many issues that had nothing to do with prohibition (corporate regulation, monetary policy, land ownership policy, lynching, and equal pay for men and women) that it became unclear what the party's main goals were. After this ambitiously broad platform disappointingly generated a mere 21,000 additional votes for the party in that year's election, the Prohibition Party effectively split into two wings. By the 1896 election, the party existed in two fairly distinct blocs—a reformist camp that wanted to expand the range of issues the party would campaign on, and a conservative one that wanted to stick to the question of alcohol. This internal split hurt the Prohibition Party tremendously, and it effectively marked the end of its run as a major player in national politics.

In the wake of the Prohibition Party's split, the mantle of prohibitionist political activity shifted primarily to the ASL. The ASL constituted itself not as a national party along the lines of the Prohibition Party, but rather as a nonpartisan pressure group that was far more successful than the Prohibition Party in affecting anti-liquor laws. Despite the rise of the ASL, the Prohibition Party remained in existence, even through Prohibition and its repeal. The Prohibition Party saw the Eighteenth Amendment as an insufficient measure as long as it lacked the support of a prohibitionist political party to guarantee its enforcement. The Twenty-First Amendment, which repealed prohibition, merely confirmed the Prohibition Party's views, so its passage, too, did not spell the end of the party. The Prohibition Party remains in existence today, but with many decades passed since prohibition and its repeal, it is no longer a significant player in national politics.

(See also **Anti-Saloon League (ASL)**; **Washingtonians**; **Woman's Christian Temperance Union (WCTU)**))

References

Blocker, Jr., Jack S., David M. Fahey, and Ian R. Tyrrell, eds. 2003. *Alcohol and Temperance in Modern History: An International Encyclopedia.* Santa Barbara, CA: ABC-CLIO.

Mendelson, Jack H. and Nancy K. Mello. 1985. *Alcohol: Use and Abuse in America.* Boston: Little, Brown and Company.

Pegram, Thomas P. 1998. *Battling Demon Rum: The Struggle for a Dry America, 1800–1933.* Chicago: Ivan R. Dee.

PROHIBITION UNIT

The Prohibition Unit, which was later renamed the Prohibition Bureau, was the federal agency in charge of enforcing national prohibition until 1933, as well as the Harrison Narcotics Act until 1930. Plagued by local and state resistance, understaffing, lack of funding, and corruption, the Prohibition Unit struggled mightily in its efforts to police illegal alcohol, though its Narcotic Division did have some success in enforcing the nation's drug laws.

The Prohibition Unit (renamed the Prohibition Bureau in 1927) was established in December of 1919 as a part of the Treasury Department in order to enforce the Volstead Act. It was authorized to seize and sell any vehicles used in the transporting of illegal liquor. It could also close, for up to a year, any place used to manufacture or sell illegal drink, and it could fine first-offense bootleggers up to $1,000 and jail them for six months. Bootleggers who violated the Volstead Act on multiple occasions faced steeper punishments from the Prohibition Unit. It was also empowered to enforce the Harrison Act, as its Narcotic Division cracked down on drug dealers and users, as well as physicians who continued to prescribe opiates in violation of federal policy.

Throughout its troubled existence, the Prohibition Unit faced problems when it came to enforcing the nation's alcohol laws. As national prohibition went into effect in 1920, many advocates of the alcohol ban were realistic about the difficulties involved in garnering immediate and full compliance with the new law. They expected numerous early violations of the Volstead Act, but they also believed that, over time, Americans would comply as they realized the benefits that would come with the nation's move away from alcohol. Many even believed it would take a generation before true prohibition became a reality, with it perhaps taking that long before Scientific Temperance Instruction—a public school temperance education program driven by the Woman's Christian Temperance Union—paid its dividends with a new generation of abstinent young adults. Similarly, temperance advocates argued that compliance would ultimately come because Americans unhappy with prohibition would eventually realize that their duty to follow the U.S. Constitution was greater than their desire for a drink. Ultimately, it seemed logical to conclude that enforcement would not be an enormous task because, after all, enough Americans supported national prohibition to pass a constitutional amendment. Thus no large-scale enforcement program was launched, in large part because it was not thought necessary. Instead, it was optimistically thought that the modestly endowed Prohibition Unit would be sufficient to police the liquor ban.

The Prohibition Unit was thus poorly equipped to the point of being unable to enforce national prohibition. Some of its shortcomings as an enforcement agency can be traced to the influence of the Anti-Saloon League of America's (ASL) Wayne Wheeler, who wielded great power in Washington and was the true author of the Volstead Act. Wheeler put the overworked Internal Revenue Service/Treasury Department, as opposed to the Justice Department, in charge of enforcing his Volstead Act since he believed this would allow the ASL to have a greater influence over the government's prohibition efforts.

Wheeler also exempted Prohibition Unit agents from civil service requirements so that he would be able to pick and choose who would work for the agency, but the end result was a unit filled with agents of dubious quality. For example, within the first six years of prohibition, one out of every twelve agents of the Prohibition Unit was fired for acts of corruption such as taking bribes or conspiring to sell illegal liquor. The Prohibition Unit was consequently overhauled in 1927 so its agents had to fulfill civil service requirements, and although it was renamed the Prohibition Bureau as a result, little else changed with regard to its ability to effectively enforce the Volstead Act. Regardless of name, it had deeper difficulties.

One major problem was budgetary. Congress allocated the Prohibition Unit an initial yearly budget of $6,750,000, which only allowed for the deployment of 1,526 agents—one for every 71,000 Americans. This inadequate budget increased slightly over the years, but not enough to prevent lowly paid agents from being tempted by the lucrative bribes being offered by bootleggers. Likewise, congressional funds were not sufficient to police the nation's thousands of miles of unguarded borders from extensive and sophisticated smuggling efforts such as Bill McCoy's "Rum Row" of alcohol-carrying ships just off the American shore in international waters. Nor did meager congressional funds enable the Prohibition Unit to shut down a sizeable portion of the illegal stills and speakeasies within the country. The underfinanced and understaffed Prohibition Unit admitted that in 1925 it had stopped just 5% of the liquor being smuggled into the United States. The Narcotic Division was more successful at enforcing drug laws than the rest of the Prohibition Unit was at carrying out alcohol prohibition, as its squad of about 200 agents was better equipped to handle the relatively manageable challenge of enforcing laws concerning opiates and cocaine. By 1928, almost one-third of the prisoners in federal penitentiaries were there for Harrison Act violations, a sign of the Narcotic Division's capacity to prosecute and convict large numbers of drug law violators. Even though violations of alcohol prohibition were much more widespread than infractions of the Harrison Act, there were significantly more drug cases successfully prosecuted. The high number of drug law prisoners led to prison overcrowding, which in part fueled the push for the creation of Public Health Service Narcotic Hospitals in 1928.

The problems with alcohol prohibition enforcement revealed that Prohibition Unit leader John Kramer was ill-equipped to carry out the task of enforcing liquor laws. Kramer had confidently predicted that the law would be obeyed in cities of all sizes and that alcohol would in all ways cease being manufactured, sold, or distributed. Two years later, Kramer admitted that such a promise could not be kept without the greater participation of local and state officials, who were routinely more than willing to let the Prohibition Unit try and do the work of enforcement—and foot the bill for it. In fact, as prohibition continued, local and state officials became less committed to enforcing the liquor ban, and this extended beyond their minimal financial contributions. Sheriffs, councilmen, and mayors alike often did not want to risk their political livelihoods by angering their constituents who opposed prohibition, especially when the

Prohibition Bureau was only minimally successful in its efforts. Popular opinion, too, played a significant role in the local and federal failures to enforce prohibition, as juries frequently refused to convict obvious violators of the Volstead Act. In New York, for instance, there were approximately 7,000 arrests for violations of the Volstead Act between 1921 and 1923, but only twenty-seven of these resulted in convictions. As a result, in 1924, New York City effectively abandoned its enforcement of prohibition. On the narcotics front, the Prohibition Unit was more successful, but scandals at the highest levels—especially indications that Narcotic Division head Levi G. Nutt had family links to notorious gangster and drug trafficker Arnold Rothstein—led to organizational upheaval. In 1930, Nutt was replaced as head of the Narcotic Division, and in 1930 the task of enforcing federal drug laws was given to a new federal agency, the Federal Bureau of Narcotics.

When it came to alcohol prohibition, the Prohibition Bureau's organizational overhaul and changes in leadership failed to stop widespread violations of the Eighteenth Amendment and the Volstead Act. A growing national movement to repeal prohibition, too, signaled that the country was moving in a direction that would make the Prohibition Bureau increasingly irrelevant and ultimately obsolete. The Twenty-First Amendment repealed national prohibition in 1933 and spelled the end of the Prohibition Bureau.

(See also **Anti-Saloon League (ASL)**; **Harrison Narcotics Act**; **McCoy, Bill**; **Nutt, Levi G.**; **Speakeasies**; **Volstead Act (18th Amendment)**; **Woman's Christian Temperance Union (WCTU)**)

References

Clark, Norman H. 1976. *Deliver Us from Evil: An Interpretation of American Prohibition.* New York: W. W. Norton Company.

Kyvig, David E. 2000. *Repealing National Prohibition.* 2nd ed. Kent, OH: Kent State University Press.

Lender, Mark Edward and James Kirby Martin. 1982. *Drinking in America: A History.* New York: The Free Press.

Musto, David F. 1987. *The American Disease: Origins of Narcotic Control.* Expanded Edition. New York: Oxford University Press.

Pegram, Thomas P. 1998. *Battling Demon Rum: The Struggle for a Dry America, 1800–1933.* Chicago: Ivan R. Dee.

PUBLIC HEALTH SERVICE NARCOTIC HOSPITALS

The Public Health Service (PHS) Narcotic Hospitals were institutions that the federal government designed to house, imprison, treat, and try to cure addicts from 1935 through 1974. These two institutions—one just outside of Fort Worth, Texas, the other just outside of Lexington, Kentucky—represented the U.S. government's first efforts to treat addiction and come up with a cure for it, even though the institutions resembled prisons as much as they did hospitals. Until community treatment of addiction became widespread in the late 1960s, the PHS Narcotic Hospitals were among the only institutions that offered treatment for addicts in the United States.

The PHS Narcotic Hospitals originated as attempts to fix some of the problems that tight enforcement of drug laws had created. Tougher application of the Harrison Narcotics Act in the 1920s filled federal prisons in the United States with drug-law violators. By 1928, approximately 1,600 out of the 7,598 individuals in federal prisons were addicted to opiates, and there were more violators of the Harrison Act in prison than any other class of offender. Wardens at these prisons argued that their institutions were not prepared to handle addict inmates, as many smuggled drugs into prison, caused problems with nonaddicted inmates, and relapsed as soon as they regained their freedom. Officials in the Justice Department were also unhappy with the number of addict offenders who wound up in prison, and sought a sentencing alternative for addicts that would be less harsh than prison. In late 1927, members of Congress began making recommendations for alternative ways to detain convicted addicts, and Pennsylvania Republican representative Stephen G. Porter introduced one that became law in 1929. The "Porter Narcotic Farm Bill," as it was called, authorized the establishment of two U.S. Public Health Service Narcotic Hospitals, which were referred to as "narcotic farms" for the confinement and treatment of drug addicts. It took six years for the law to take effect, as the first narcotic farm opened five miles west of Lexington, Kentucky in 1935, and the second opened seven miles southeast of Fort Worth, Texas in 1938. The institution near Lexington generally housed addicts from areas east of the Mississippi River, while the one near Fort Worth held addicts from areas west of

it. In 1936, these institutions were dubbed "narcotic hospitals" instead of "narcotic farms."

When they opened, the PHS Narcotic Hospitals were blends of psychiatric institutions and minimum-security prisons. The stated goals of the institutions were rehabilitative. They aimed to minimize the number of relapses among inmates by evaluating them when they first entered the facilities, assigning them to specialized wards and behavioral regimens, and providing social workers to help guide inmates back into society when they were released. Both institutions had farms and dairies (hence the term "narcotic farm") since it was believed that pastoral work was therapeutic for individuals suffering from mental disorders such as addiction. Beyond just soothing the physical pains of addicts in withdrawal, staff at the narcotic hospitals sought to treat the mental and emotional problems that accompanied addiction and withdrawal as well. By the late 1930s, treatment in the hospitals was generally broken down into four distinct elements: First came the stage of drug withdrawal, which usually lasted less than two weeks. Second, addicts were moved to a drug-free environment for recovery, and given several months to adjust to life without drugs. Third, addicts were given psychotherapy in order to encourage and persuade them to stay drug-free. Fourth, addicts were assigned to work either on the farms, in maintenance, or in shops. Addicts who broke the rules of the federal narcotic hospitals were given disciplinary action, which usually consisted of losing privileges or extended sentences. Overall, the recommended duration of treatment at the PHS Narcotic Hospitals was between four and six months. In spite of this therapeutic program, studies as late as the 1960s still concluded that life in the PHS Narcotic Hospitals was more like internment in a prison than it was a stay in a hospital or rehabilitation program.

In the 1930s and 1940s, the PHS Narcotic Hospitals were among the only treatment resources available to addicts in the United States since many physicians and hospitals refused to treat addicts. Consequently, admissions to the two institutions grew steadily during these years, from just 823 in 1935 to 3,875 in 1949. What is more, many addicts came to the PHS Narcotic Hospitals voluntarily in hopes of being cured before they ran afoul of the law, though since they could not be compelled to complete the program, most of them left the institutions before they were cured. When rates of heroin addiction rose sharply in the early 1950s, so did the number of admissions to the PHS Narcotic Hospitals, as an average of 4,218 individuals entered them annually during the 1950s. In the 1960s, admissions began to decrease, largely due to the creation of state and local treatment programs that provided treatment alternatives to the PHS Narcotic Hospitals. Admissions rose slightly once again with the implementation of the Narcotic Addict Rehabilitation Act in 1966, though funding issues ultimately led to a decrease in the number of admissions until the hospitals were closed in 1974.

In addition to providing treatment for addicts, the hospital at Lexington also became a center for addiction research, led by its first medical director, Dr. Lawrence Kolb. In the 1930s, cures for addiction, and potential morphine substitutes, were tested on inmates at

Lexington. Clinical observations at Lexington in the 1940s confirmed Kolb's belief that most addicts had personality problems, and in the late 1940s, experiments there first showed the potential that methadone had as a substitution treatment for opiate addicts. In 1948, the research division at Lexington was administratively separated from the hospital wing, and became the National Institute of Mental Health's Addiction Research Center. Among the major projects carried out at the Addiction Research Center were a series of experiments on rats that helped scientists better understand relapse and opioid-seeking behavior, and a study that showed the potential that narcotic antagonists could have on individuals suffering from protracted withdrawal symptoms. In addition to research carried out at the Addiction Research Center, the programs at both Lexington and Fort Worth studied the effectiveness of community agencies and halfway houses in reintegrating ex-addicts into society during the late 1950s and early 1960s.

By the late 1960s, the Narcotic Addict Rehabilitation Act had begun to fund state and local services for the treatment of drug users, and community treatment continued to expand with the passage of the Community Mental Health Services Act. The hospital at Fort Worth closed in October of 1971, and was transformed into a federal prison. The hospital at Lexington, on the other hand, was remodeled and modernized so that all of the bars, grilles, and other trappings that made it seem like a prison were removed. The number of staff at Lexington was increased, while the patient population was reduced, leading to more intense therapeutic interactions between staff and patients. However, by the early 1970s, the growth of community addiction treatment reduced the number of addicts who came to Lexington, and funding was gradually redirected from Lexington to local programs as well. In 1974, the hospital at Lexington closed, and like the institution at Fort Worth, it was converted into a federal prison.

(See also **Harrison Narcotics Act**; **Kolb, Lawrence**; **Methadone**; **Narcotic Addict Rehabilitation Act**; **Porter, Stephen G.**)

References

Acker, Caroline Jean. 2002. *Creating the American Junkie: Addiction Research in the Classic Era of Narcotic Control*. Baltimore: Johns Hopkins University Press.

Courtwright, David T. 2001. *Dark Paradise: A History of Opiate Addiction in America*. Cambridge, MA: Harvard University Press.

Kosten, Thomas R. and David A. Gorelick. 2002. "The Lexington Narcotic Farm." *American Journal of Psychiatry*. 159, no. 1: 22.

Martin, William R. and Harris Isbell, eds. 1978. *Drug Addiction and the U.S. Public Health Service*. Rockville, MD: National Institute on Drug Abuse.

Musto, David F. 1987. *The American Disease: Origins of Narcotic Control*. Expanded Edition. New York: Oxford University Press.

PURE FOOD AND DRUG ACT

The Pure Food and Drug Act of 1906 marked the first time that vendors in the United States were required to place labels on food, medicines, and other consumer products that were sold to the general public.

At the turn of the twentieth century, the most recent federal law governing the sale of drugs had been passed in 1848. Yet by 1900, changes in science, technology, and industry had made this law outdated. Developments in science allowed for the creation of synthetic medicines and processed foods, and the makers of these products learned how to use chemistry to adulterate their products and defraud customers. The makers of patent medicines, for example, would sell unlabelled concoctions that actually contained poisons or habit-forming drugs, but they figured out ways to add ingredients that could mask the taste and smell of the poisons in the formulas they sold. Food producers were also creative with their use of science, using chemicals to transform low-quality ingredients into products that they could sell. With the development of factories and a nationwide transportation network in the late 1800s, it became easier for companies to produce and transport these adulterated products cheaply. The result was that consumers often had no idea what they were actually buying and ingesting. Consequently, the people who purchased these products could become sick, while the businessmen who oversaw these operations became rich. Both public health and morality, it seemed, were put at risk by the freedom manufacturers had to sell products without properly labeling them. Journalistic exposés, like Upton Sinclair's *The Jungle*, which detailed the misdeeds of the meatpacking industry, and Samuel Hopkins Adam's "Great American Fraud" series on the dangers of patent medicines in *Collier's*, helped spread awareness of the problems that could arise when corporations and manufacturers could sell products without being obligated to tell the public what they were selling or how it was made. People concerned with corporations taking advantage of public ignorance and defrauding them began advocating for stricter rules over the labeling of consumer products. Harvey Washington Wiley, a chemist with the Department of Agriculture, and the American Medical Association were particularly concerned with the dangers of unlabelled patent medicines.

In 1905, President Theodore Roosevelt began pushing Congress to enact a bill to regulate the trade in food and drugs, and in June of 1906, it finally passed as the Pure Food and Drug Act. The law made it illegal to transport adulterated or mislabeled foods or drugs across state lines, and offenders could have their products seized, or be fined and jailed themselves. Drugs now had to follow purity standards laid out in the U.S. pharmacopoeia and national formulary; substituting ingredients that were not on the label was no longer allowed, and making false or misleading claims about a food or drug became an offense. Federal scientists from the Public Health Service were also empowered to inspect and certify that medicines were being properly labeled before being sold to the public. The Act also gave officials with the Bureau of Chemistry—the federal agency that would later become the Food and Drug Administration—new regulatory powers.

Though it did not make it illegal to sell preparations that contained narcotics or alcohol, the Pure Food and Drug Act did mark a significant shift in the sale and distribution of these drugs. By stipulating that patent medicines had to state on their labels if they included alcohol, opium, opium derivatives, cocaine, or other potentially habit-forming drugs, the law made it impossible for the makers of these formulas to deceive consumers as they had before. Also, many people who may have been unaware that they were consuming habit-forming drugs when they took patent medicines would now know what they were taking. As a result, many consumers stopped purchasing patent medicines that contained these drugs, and the manufacturers of many patent medicines changed their formulas so they no longer included alcohol or narcotics. Thus even before the passage of the Harrison Narcotics Act that placed limits on the availability of narcotics in 1914, and the Volstead Act that prohibited alcohol took effect in 1920, people in the United States began consuming less narcotics and alcohol in 1906.

(See also **Food and Drug Administration (FDA)**; **Harrison Narcotics Act**; **Patent Medicines**; **Wiley, Harvey Washington**)

References

Courtwright, David T. 2001. *Dark Paradise: A History of Opiate Addiction in America.* Cambridge, MA: Harvard University Press.

Hilts, Philip J. 2003. *Protecting America's Health: The FDA, Business, and One Hundred Years of Regulation.* New York: Alfred A. Knopf.

Morgan, H. Wayne. 1974. *Yesterday's Addicts: American Society and Drug Abuse, 1865–1920.* Norman, OK: University of Oklahoma Press.

Musto, David F. 1987. *The American Disease: Origins of Narcotics Control. Expanded Edition.* New York: Oxford University Press.

Swann, John P. "History of the FDA." [Online article retrieved 05/22/09] http://www.fda.gov/oc/history/historyoffda/default.htm.

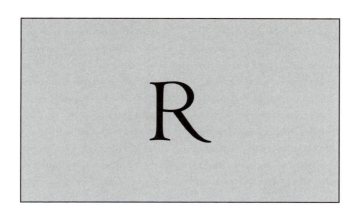

REAGAN, RONALD AND NANCY

More than any other presidency in U.S. history, the tenure of Ronald Reagan (and his wife Nancy) in the White House marked a high point in presidential enthusiasm in the war against drugs. Both enthusiastic in his desire to eradicate the drug problem, and shrewd enough to use the drug problem as an issue that he could capitalize on for political gain, Reagan brought the U.S. campaign against illicit drugs to new heights.

Before Reagan entered the White House in 1980, the United States had already been waging a campaign against illicit drug use for nearly a century. As far back as 1914, when the Harrison Narcotics Act first placed federal restrictions on the transfer and use of opiates and cocaine, the federal government had sought to limit drug use and trafficking, and pieces of legislation such as the 1951 Boggs Act, the 1956 Narcotic Control Act, and the 1970 Comprehensive

Drug Abuse Prevention and Control Act created a progressively tougher, more thorough drug control regime in the United States. In spite of these measures, rates of drug use grew from the 1960s through the 1980s, particularly with the rise of amphetamine, cocaine, and crack use. From the beginning of his presidency, Reagan sought to tackle the drug problem head-on, with a focus on cutting off illicit supplies of narcotics through international efforts abroad and tougher penalties for drug-related offenses at home. Reagan believed that illicit drugs represented one of the gravest dangers facing the nation, and promised to establish a policy to crack down on illicit drug production and trafficking. In the early 1980s, he announced a plan to hire 900 new drug law enforcement agents and 200 more federal prosecutors, to establish drug task forces in major cities, and to build $150 million worth of new prisons to house drug-law offenders. In particular, Reagan targeted the growing drug trade in the Miami area, creating a new task force led by

Vice President George H. W. Bush to address the problem in 1982. Reagan sent a slew of federal law enforcement agents to South Florida, bolstering the presence of the FBI, the Customs Service, the Bureau of Alcohol, Tobacco and Firearms, and the Internal Revenue Service in order to investigate drug-related crimes, stop the proliferation of weapons in the drug trade, and crack down on money laundering operations. By 1985, the government had seized twenty-five tons of cocaine and 750 tons of marijuana in South Florida, though it is questionable how successful the task force was, since the street price of cocaine in the region dropped dramatically at the same time the government was carrying out its intensive operations there.

To help better coordinate the nation's drug control efforts, Reagan put the FBI in charge of drug enforcement and investigations, giving it authority over the Drug Enforcement Administration. In 1981, he authorized intelligence agencies to investigate and take an active role in breaking up international drug rings. He also issued an executive order in 1982 that strengthened the Office of Policy Development to help the president oversee prevention, treatment, and rehabilitation programs. To further enhance drug law enforcement, Reagan also convinced Congress to amend the law so the Department of Defense could provide military training, intelligence, and equipment to law enforcement agencies when they went after drug traffickers, and he also enabled members of the Army, Navy, Air Force, and Marines to operate military equipment for civilian law enforcement agencies carrying out drug-related operations. In 1982, these arrangements were codified by law with the passage of the Department of

Defense Authorization Act. The 1984 Comprehensive Crime Control Act strengthened the interdiction efforts of drug law enforcement authorities, and the Controlled Substances Registration Protection Act of that same year increased penalties for stealing drugs regulated by the Comprehensive Drug Abuse Control and Prevention Act from pharmacies. The 1984 Bail Reform Act made it more difficult for individuals accused of breaking drug laws to get out on bail. Reagan also increased the budgets for drug control dramatically, as funding for drug-law related programs nearly doubled between 1981 and 1986. Most importantly, the Reagan administration saw the passage of the Anti-Drug Abuse Acts of 1986 and 1988, providing billions of additional dollars to fight drug abuse and trafficking, and stiffening penalties for drug-law offenses. According to the Reagan administration, these measures increased the prices of controlled substances on the black market, a sign that they were becoming increasingly difficult to procure illegally. These domestic measures were bolstered by increased international efforts to crack down on drug production and smuggling, particularly in Latin America. Despite these efforts, however, drug abuse remained a prevalent social problem in the 1980s, and seeing that some of Reagan's initiatives were not as effective as planned, many intellectuals began advocating for the legalization and decriminalization of controlled substances.

To complement the supply-reduction efforts of her husband, First Lady Nancy Reagan also became an outspoken leader in the battle against addiction during her time in the White House, most notably with her "Just Say No" public health campaign. The idea behind the campaign was that by teaching children to say "no" to drugs from the start, the government could decrease interest in illegal drugs, and thus cut down on demand, over time. Inspired by Reagan's campaigning, thousands of "Just Say No" clubs and organizations were established across America. Though its supporters say the campaign has been good since it spread awareness of the dangers of drugs, critics claimed that it had little impact on rates of drug use, and that it simplified what are the often complex issues surrounding drug addiction.

Overall, the presidency of Ronald Reagan saw the "war on drugs" reach new heights, as the government toughened laws and increased expenditures in order to crack down on the drug traffic. Though he saw pieces of legislation that expanded treatment options for addicts go through Congress during his presidency, Reagan's term was one marked by a tough, law-and-order approach to the drug problem that harkened back to the federal government's strategies in the 1950s. These efforts to address the drug problem with increased law enforcement ultimately yielded mixed, if not ineffective, results, as did the campaign led by Reagan's wife to discourage youths from experimenting with controlled substances.

(See also **Anti-Drug Abuse Acts**; **Drug Addiction and Public Policy**; **Drug Enforcement Administration (DEA)**; **Drug Smuggling**)

References

Belenko, Steven R., ed. 2000. *Drugs and Drug Policy in America: A Documentary History*. Westport, CT: Greenwood Press.

Chepesiuk, Ron. 1999. *The War on Drugs: An International Encyclopedia*. Santa Barbara, CA: ABC-CLIO.

Davenport-Hines, Richard. 2001. *The Pursuit of Oblivion: A Global History of Narcotics, 1500–2000*. London: Weidenfeld & Nicolson.

Musto, David F., ed. 2002. *Drugs in America: A Documentary History*. New York: New York University Press.

RECOVERY CIRCLES

Native American recovery circles represented the first temperance movements in North America. Likely emerging independently of Non-Native American temperance efforts, Native American efforts to curb alcohol use began in the eighteenth century and linked temperance and abstinence to Native revitalization and spiritual revival. Nineteenth-century Native American alcohol-abuse recovery programs were marked by an incorporation of Christian elements, while twentieth-century efforts have, to a large extent, built off the Alcoholics Anonymous (AA) model.

Predating the first temperance movements among European immigrant communities, reports of a Native American "seer" preaching against the use of alcohol among the Shawnee and Onondaga exist from as early as 1737. By the end of that decade, numerous Native American preachers in the Northeast and Great Lakes region were singling out alcohol use as a key factor in the decline of Native traditions. Building upon this linkage between alcohol use and cultural decline, six Delaware Prophets, each of whom utilized their own tales of recovery from alcohol abuse, fashioned recovery circles, or abstinence-based cultural revitalization movements, which began in the mid-1740s and lasted until the mid-1760s. The most famous of the Delaware

Prophets, Neolin, called for abstinence from alcohol as a means of personal purification and cultural unity amongst Native Americans. In fact, in his plea for abstinence, Neolin saw sobriety as a means of freeing Native peoples from the pernicious influence of Whites. Once freed from the oppressive and exploitative grip of alcohol, which Neolin saw as a colonial tool of domination, he believed that Native Americans of the region could recapture a lost unity and forge a kind of pan-Indian identity. Recovery circles of the eighteenth century thus explicitly linked cultural revitalization to a rejection of foreign influences, with alcohol representing the most dangerous import.

In the nineteenth century, though, abstinence-based, Native American revitalization movements integrated elements of Christianity into their programs for cultural revitalization via abstinence. For instance, the Handsome Lake Code was preached by an alcoholic Seneca named Handsome Lake who nearly drank himself to death. After miraculously recovering from what, according to the reports of the time, appeared to be his death on June 15, 1799, an alive and sober Handsome Lake extolled a Code that, among other significant features, centered upon his people's resurrection and revitalization through sobriety. Unlike the recovery circles started by the Delaware Prophets, however, the Handsome Lake Code, which incorporated a number of Christian elements, such as the tale of his resurrection, became institutionalized and enjoyed a life well beyond that of its founder. The Code, also known as the Longhouse Religion, was organized into a formal church, and by 1845 started utilizing a standardized approach to dealing

with alcohol abuse recovery and prevention, as well as mechanisms for preserving its culture.

The Native American Church represented another nineteenth-century effort to combat alcohol abuse and preserve Native American cultural traditions via the co-opting of Christian traditions. Started by a Comanche known as Quanah Parker, the Native American Church advocated the use of peyote in recovery from alcohol abuse. Like Handsome Lake, Parker was an alcoholic who quit drinking as a result of a near-death experience. Unlike Handsome Lake, however, Parker's revelation came while under the influence of peyote, and the vision he received was of Jesus Christ instructing him to abstain from alcohol and to encourage his people to use peyote. Parker thus took what had been a practice of the north Mexican tribes, infused it with Christian components, and spread the gospel of peyote-induced, direct experiences of Jesus through a group of itinerant roadmen. Though the use of a controlled substance like peyote may seem a questionable route to sobriety, studies have documented alcoholics successfully abstaining from drink after becoming members of the Native American Church. Peyote is used sparingly within the Native American Church, so members' ability to quit drinking may well result from the traditional practices and cultural activities in which individuals within the Church are expected to participate.

A different twentieth-century approach to combating alcohol abuse in Native American communities comes from AA. From its first meeting—the encounter of two alcoholics in 1935—until today, AA has been centered on members standing in front of the group to make personal declarations or tell their life stories. Over time, AA developed a Twelve-Step Program and Twelve Traditions as guiding components, and these texts reflect, to a certain degree, AA's Protestant origins. Likely as a result of significant differences between Protestant elements in AA's makeup and Native American religions and traditions, Native Americans generally did not find traditional AA activities as helpful in their quest for sobriety as other members did. To meet the needs of Native American alcoholics, AA has crafted a Native American version of its Twelve-Step Program that seems to better fit the contours of Native American life and culture, particularly in highly acculturated urban centers. In general, this version of AA incorporates Native American symbols and practices of a pan-Indian nature, and some of AA's Steps and Traditions are reworded to better reflect Native American religious ideas and motifs. Changes are also made to the typical AA meeting structure in order to better mesh with Native American cultural practices.

A more recent development in Native American sobriety programs has been the Wellbriety Movement. Championed and developed by the nonprofit organization White Bison, Wellbriety incorporates the Red Road concept of all Native Americans traveling upon a balanced and harmonious path as a symbol of a clean and detoxified people. In general, Wellbriety and White Bison employ pan-Indian imagery and ideas in working towards community development and traditional well-being via increased Native American sobriety.

(See also **Alcoholics Anonymous (AA)**)

References

Blocker, Jr., Jack S., David M. Fahey, and Ian R. Tyrrell, eds. 2003. *Alcohol and Temperance in Modern History: An International Encyclopedia.* Santa Barbara, CA: ABC-CLIO.

Coyhis, Don L. and William L. White. 2006. *Alcohol Problems in Native America: The Untold Story of Resistance and Recovery.* Colorado Springs, CO: White Bison, Inc.

O'Brien, Suzanne J. Crawford, ed. 2008. *Religion and Healing in Native America: Pathways for Renewal.* Westport, CT: Praeger.

RIBBON REFORM CLUBS

The Ribbon Reform Clubs were a group of abstinence-based societies that provided mutual aid for men who were heavy drinkers. They constituted a major part of the Gospel Temperance Movement of the late-nineteenth century, and members of groups like the Blue Ribbon Movement and the Red Ribbon Reform Club were identifiable by their colored lapel ribbons, which designated their pledge of abstinence from alcohol. Ribbon Reform Clubs could boast of millions taking the pledge by the mid-1880s, but by the end of the decade they were overtaken within the temperance movement by prohibitionist forces.

The Blue Ribbon Reform Club began in New England in the early 1870s under the leadership of reformed drinker Joshua Knox Osgood, who underwent a religious conversion experience, ceased drinking, and subsequently persuaded eight of his drinking companions to join him in signing a pledge of abstinence from alcohol. As more men in the group pledged abstinence and mutual support for one another in achieving this goal, members began donning blue ribbons on their lapels to designate their commitment to an alcohol-free lifestyle. As a result of the group's iconic symbol, they came to be known as "the temperance reform club and blue ribbon movement."

This group blossomed into the Blue Ribbon Movement only after leadership passed from Osgood to Francis Murphy, a hard-drinking, Irish Catholic-born hotel keeper living in Portland, Maine who found himself in jail in 1870 for violating liquor sales laws. While behind bars, Murphy, like Osgood, underwent a religious conversion that led him to Protestantism and sobriety. Shortly after his release, Murphy began delivering evangelically infused speeches across New England on the virtues of abstinence and quickly convinced throngs of drinking men to take the pledge. He held days-long meetings in public halls that featured personal testimonies from reformed drinkers and, of course, Murphy's own moving oratory. Inspired men who took the pledge at these revivalist events formed the bases of local Blue Ribbon clubs, so named because Murphy's followers wore the same symbolic blue lapel ribbon that Osgood had originally introduced. By the 1880s, the Blue Ribbon Movement had grown into hundreds of local chapters spread across twenty-eight states. This remarkable expansion had much to do with Murphy's nonconfrontational approach within the temperance movement. Guided by the movement's motto of "with malice toward none and charity for all," Murphy differed from prohibitionists within the movement by refusing to chastise saloon owners or ostracize drunks. Instead, Murphy emphasized the importance of moral suasion, identification with the plight of the drunkard, Christian salvation, and mutual aid.

As an alcohol mutual aid society, Blue Ribbon clubs operated in a similar fashion to the Washingtonians, who, in the middle of the eighteenth century, democratized the temperance movement by appealing to, and identifying with, lower and middle class drinkers. Just as the Washingtonians employed moral example, testimonials, and support groups, Blue Ribbon club meetings served as a kind of therapeutic replacement for the saloon and the male camaraderie it provided. And similarly to the Washingtonian model, members of the Blue Ribbon movement found that providing mutual aid and support to drinkers helped keep themselves abstinent.

The Blue Ribbon Movement's success can also be attributed to its connections to another prominent temperance group, the Woman's Christian Temperance Union (WCTU). After being invited to Chicago in 1874 by Frances Willard, the WCTU's president at the time, Murphy made such an impact in the city that eleven new reform clubs sprang up in the city upon his departure. Similarly, within ten weeks after a speech he delivered on November 26, 1876 in Pittsburgh, forty thousand residents of the city signed a pledge of abstinence and became members of the Blue Ribbon Movement. However, the Blue Ribbon Movement's most significant expansion took place not in big cities like Chicago and Pittsburgh, but rather in midsized towns and in the West, where the temperance movement previously had little success. While Murphy was able to garner an impressive number of followers after his speeches, the Blue Ribbon Movement had a tougher time keeping its members within the fold, as by the late 1880s, prohibitionism became preeminent within the temperance movement.

Another prominent Ribbon Reform Club was the Red Ribbon Reform Club, which, like the Blue Ribbon Movement, was led by a reformed drinker who inspired new members to take a pledge of abstinence. The Red Ribbon Reform Club was founded by Henry A. Reynolds, a physician and surgeon who lost his medical practice as a result of his drinking problem. After signing a pledge of abstinence at a temperance meeting in 1874, Reynolds began speaking about his history with alcohol and launched a reform club of his own in Bangor, Maine, either in 1874 or 1875. With the motto of "dare to do right," Reynolds' club held meetings that resembled those of Blue Ribbon clubs in their emphasis on mutual support, a male camaraderie to replace the saloon experience, and the importance of Christianity in remaining sober. And Reynolds' clubs, again like Murphy's movement, soon expanded as a result of its collaboration with the WCTU, which began in 1876. Club meetings would typically take place on weeknights, with public WCTU meetings held on weekends. In the same year that Reynolds partnered with the WCTU, he adopted a red lapel ribbon as the club's symbol of membership and abstinence. As the Red Ribbon Reform Club, Reynolds' movement spread to the Midwest, and it did so with the support of the YMCA, as well as Methodist, Congregationalist, and Baptist churches. Reynolds did not, however, team up with prohibitionist elements within the temperance movement, and perhaps as a result, the Red Ribbon Reform Club faded in significance by the late 1880s.

Ribbon Reform clubs such as the Blue Ribbon Reform Movement and the Red Ribbon Reform Club began as small clubs in the 1870s and blossomed into alcohol mutual aid societies with millions of members pledged to abstinence within a decade. By the end of the 1880s, however, Ribbon Reform Clubs were overtaken within the temperance movement by prohibitionist forces, in particular the Anti-Saloon League of America.

(See also **Alcohol Mutual Aid Societies**; **Anti-Saloon League (ASL)**; **Woman's Christian Temperance Union (WCTU)**)

References

Blocker, Jr., Jack S., David M. Fahey, and Ian R. Tyrrell, eds. 2003. *Alcohol and Temperance in Modern History: An International Encyclopedia*. Santa Barbara, CA: ABC-CLIO.

Lender, Mark Edward and James Kirby Martin. 1982. *Drinking in America: A History*. New York: The Free Press.

RUSH, BENJAMIN

Signatory to the Declaration of Independence, delegate to the First Continental Congress, and co-founder of Philadelphia Bible College and Dickinson College, Benjamin Rush drew upon his medical background as a doctor and psychiatrist to become one of the first Americans to argue that excessive alcohol use could constitute a major danger to the future success of the fledgling democracy. His influential *An Inquiry into the Effects of Ardent Spirits on the Human Mind and Body* (1784) was one of the earliest attempts to understand the mental and physical dangers that came with alcohol abuse, and it generally concluded, on medical and moral grounds, that drunkenness generated unpatriotic, or "anti-republican," attitudes and behavior that thus threatened to undermine all that had been achieved with the

Revolutionary War. This argument, though it did not amount to a call for the prohibition of alcohol, helped pave the way for the emergence of the temperance movement.

Born on December 24, 1746 in Philadelphia, Benjamin Rush received his Bachelor of Arts degree from Princeton and his M.D. from the University of Edinburgh. The latter diploma put Rush among the 10% of colonial American doctors who actually possessed a medical degree, and as a result of his successful practice, he became known as the Hippocrates of Pennsylvania. He was the nation's first professor of chemistry, served as surgeon general during the Revolutionary War, and acted as the physician to prominent American families like the Adamses and the Hancocks. When Rush wrote of the ills of alcohol, then, he did so with a medical background and credibility that few in America possessed.

His stance against the consumption of liquor can be traced back to his time as surgeon general, when he attempted to eliminate soldiers' daily rum ration on the grounds that far from being salubrious, spirits actually caused "fluxes" and fevers. He argued against hard alcohol from a medical standpoint in a 1772 pamphlet entitled "Sermons to Gentlemen Upon Temperance and Exercise," but his views reached a far broader audience in 1784 with the publication of *An Inquiry into the Effects of Ardent Spirits on the Human Mind and Body*. In greater psychological and scientific detail, this document, which sold over 170,000 copies by 1850, laid out his theories on the disastrous consequences of Americans' continued consumption of liquor.

In this seminal text, Rush argued that drunkenness results from a loss of willpower. Initially, drinking is entirely a matter of choice, he claimed, but it becomes a habit and then a necessity. What begins as a decision to drink alcohol can thus become a dependency, and Rush connected this notion to the future of Americans' liberty by asserting that a nation corrupted by alcohol is one that can never be free. Rush wrote that alcohol generated vices that would lead to the dishonoring and enslavement of the country, and he worried that drunkenness would lead America towards impoverishment, criminality, and civil disorder. Similarly, Rush feared an American government elected by voters who were intemperate and corrupted by their consumption of alcohol. As a result, Rush highlighted the unpatriotic or, in Rush's terms, "anti-republican" and "anti-federal," consequences of inebriety.

Medically, too, the consumption of alcoholic spirits represented a threat to Americans' well-being in Rush's eyes. Thus, in addition to the unpatriotic behavior and moral corruption caused by drinking hard alcohol, inebriates were liable to contract conditions such as gout, jaundice, and epilepsy as a result of their imbibing. Alternatively, Rush claimed, physical and mental health and vitality resulted from drinking nonalcoholic beverages. Rush's ideal, then, was abstinence from hard alcohol, but he conceded that fermented beverages, such as cider, beer, and wine, had their proper place within the American diet and lifestyle. The moderate consumption of these beverages during meals would give an individual strength, nourishment, and cheerfulness, he argued. In fact, Rush admitted that even distilled alcohol had two positive, medicinal applications: it worked as a means of thwarting fainting spells, and it could be used to ward off fevers and chills. Later editions of

An Inquiry into the Effects of Ardent Spirits on the Human Mind and Body even included a "Moral and Physical Thermometer," which depicted his correlations between different beverages and their effects upon the drinker.

Since spirits, aside from those two medicinal applications, were the dangerous component in the equation, Rush advocated that drinkers wean themselves off of hard alcohol by gradually moving to less potent and harmful drinks like wine and beer. If this proved too difficult a transition to make for devotees of spirits, he similarly suggested the consumption of a weak rum punch that could be gradually diluted over time to the point that the beverage became alcohol-free. Towards this end, Rush put forward a drink he called the "switchel," which was a combination of water, sugar, and vinegar; it does not seem to have caught on. Rush even envisioned that by the twentieth century, the consumption of spirits would be as rare in families as a drink made of a solution of arsenic or a concoction of hemlock. Rush also developed a treatment system to change the drinking habits of severe inebriates. His basic therapy consisted of cold baths and total abstinence in such cases, but when he found that such an approach was not very successful as a result of being unable to control the drinkers' environment, Rush proposed the creation of detoxification asylums. These "sober houses" would serve as sites wherein habitual drinkers could be removed from everyday, social situations in which alcohol proved too alluring to resist. Patients would thus be housed until cured of their desire for drink.

In general, Rush drew upon his medical background to argue for personal moderation rather than legal prohibition as the means of altering Americans'

relationship to alcohol. Despite not calling for total abstinence, his message was latched onto by temperance organizations which, over time, moved away from Rush's call for moderation. Though he paved the way for temperance groups such as the American Temperance Society, Rush more directly influenced secular temperance groups who appropriated his notion of hard-alcohol abuse as an anti-federal act that imperiled American democracy. After an impactful life, Rush passed away on April 19, 1813 in his hometown of Philadelphia.

(See also **American Temperance Society (ATS)**; **Primary Source Documents**; **Woman's Christian Temperance Union (WCTU)**)

References

Blocker, Jr., Jack S., David M. Fahey, and Ian R. Tyrrell, eds. 2003. *Alcohol and Temperance in Modern History: An International Encyclopedia*. Santa Barbara, CA: ABC-CLIO.

Burns, Eric. 2004. *The Spirits of America: A Social History of America*. Philadelphia: Temple University Press.

Lender, Mark Edward and James Kirby Martin. 1982. *Drinking in America: A History*. New York: The Free Press.

Lender, Mark Edward. 1984. *Dictionary of American Temperance Biography: From Temperance Reform to Alcohol Research, the 1600s to the 1980s*. Westport, CT: Greenwood Press.

Murdock, Catherine Gilbert. 1998. *Domesticating Drink: Women, Men, and Alcohol in America, 1870–1940*. Baltimore: The Johns Hopkins University Press.

Sournia, Jean-Charles. 1990. *A History of Alcoholism*. Trans. by Nick Hindley and Gareth Stanton. Oxford: Basil Blackwell.

SECONDHAND SMOKE

Secondhand smoke, or environmental tobacco smoke (ETS), is the smoke inhaled by individuals who themselves are not actively smoking, and for this reason it is also sometimes referred to as passive smoking. Though secondhand smoke has existed since smoking began, it was not until the 1970s, when scientific research began to discover the health hazards it poses, that it became a serious matter of public policy. With a growing recognition of the dangers of ETS, numerous smoking restrictions, such as the Clean Indoor Air Act, have been passed in order to protect the nonsmoking public from inhaling secondhand smoke.

Until the 1950s, few Americans viewed smoking cigarettes as a major health threat, and consequently, even fewer considered secondhand smoke a hazard. In the early 1950s, however, a wave of scientific reports, including *Reader's Digest*'s 1952 blockbuster, "Cancer by the Carton," which linked smoking to lung cancer, reached a popular audience and created a major shift in American attitudes towards tobacco. In the wake of these reports, some 40% of Americans believed that smoking caused lung cancer. Public fears were temporarily allayed by the public relations efforts of the Tobacco Industry Research Committee (TIRC), a tobacco industry-financed entity that worked to create uncertainty and doubt as to whether cigarettes were carcinogenic by distorting, discrediting, or suppressing findings that concluded that smoking represented a serious health threat. But with the Surgeon General's 1964 report, which concluded that smoking causes serious disease, the true dangers of lighting up were quite evident.

With the Surgeon General's report irreversibly establishing the act of smoking a cigarette as a major health risk, a few science reporters in the late 1960s took the next logical step and reasoned that if tobacco smoke was so dangerous to a smokers' health, it might also represent a considerable health threat to individuals breathing in the vicinity of smokers. Testing this hypothesis proved to be a difficult and time-consuming endeavor, though, and the studies that would confirm the serious health effects of inhaling secondhand smoke were not published until after a grassroots movement to curb smoking in public places had emerged in the early 1970s.

The first groups to argue for smoke-free air as a nonsmokers' right drew upon the civil rights, antiwar, and environmental movements as inspirations. They enlisted volunteer activists and formed organizations like Americans for Non-Smokers' Rights, which was based in Berkeley, California, and Group Against Smoking and Pollution (GASP), which was founded by Clara Gouin in 1971 and had fifty-six local chapters spread across several states by 1974. GASP's newsletter, *Ventilator*, advanced the notion that nonsmokers had a right to breathe smoke-free air. Each chapter of the organization aggressively pushed for the passage of local and state ordinances that would regulate smoking in places of public accommodation like restaurants and office buildings. Beyond their legislative efforts, GASP members went directly to restaurant owners, and numbers of them agreed to create nonsmoking sections in their businesses well before the passage of any laws mandating such areas. In some cases, restaurant owners even expanded these sections upon discovering how popular they were with nonsmoking customers.

These local-level developments led to more far-reaching restrictions on secondhand smoke, particularly after the 1972 Surgeon General's report on smoking identified ETS as a potential health hazard to nonsmokers. Though the Surgeon General did not yet define the precise nature of the threat that secondhand smoke posed to nonsmokers, there was enough momentum for the Civil

Aeronautics Boards to require, in 1973, the creation of a nonsmoking section on all U.S. airlines. 1973 also marked the passage of the first state law restricting smoking in public places. Following two years of grassroots organizing and campaigning from Arizonans Concerned About Smoking, Arizona banned smoking in buses, theaters, elevators, museums, and libraries. The state further legislated the creation of designated smoking areas in public spaces like government buildings and hospitals. Minnesota soon followed Arizona's lead by becoming, in 1975, the first state to pass a comprehensive Clean Indoor Air Act. In large part the result of work by the Twin Cities' local chapter of the Association for Non-Smokers' Rights, Minnesota's act forbade smoking in all public places unless specifically allowed, and it stipulated that at least 30% of restaurant seating needed to be reserved for nonsmokers. By 1981, thirty-six states had smoking restrictions of some form, and by the mid-1980s, almost all states had some restrictions on public smoking. As such, around 80% of the nation's population lived in areas that were covered by these laws, and by 1988, all domestic flights had become nonsmoking.

The tobacco industry did not passively accept these tremendous changes to the place of smoking in public life, and their fight against nonsmokers' rights took place on two fronts. On one level, the tobacco industry attempted to cast secondhand smoke as an issue of manners, rather than one of health. Though their efforts were, for the most part, unable to prevent the passage of most smoking restrictions, the tobacco industry argued that legislative regulation on behalf of nonsmokers' rights amounted to an un-American violation of smokers' rights. To counter what they argued was an undue governmental intrusion into an individual smoker's personal life, Philip Morris even went so far as to offer a Bill of Rights for smoking. It also helped fund the National Smokers' Alliance as a counter-organization to grassroots groups like GASP. On a second level, the tobacco industry put its considerable resources behind a push to discredit the scientific link between secondhand smoke and cancer or other serious illnesses. After the Tobacco Institute's 1978 survey confirmed a fairly widespread public support for bans on smoking in public places, the tobacco companies decided to create an institution along the lines of the TIRC (which had by then been renamed the Council for Tobacco Research) that would fund scientific research into indoor air quality so as to suggest that other elements in the air supply were responsible for the diseases and illnesses being linked to secondhand smoke. The Center for Indoor Air Research (CIAR) was thus founded in March 1988 to create uncertainty about the risk ETS posed to nonsmokers, and the reports it produced consistently trumpeted the line that there was insufficient evidence to conclude that secondhand smoke posed any health risk.

Despite the CIAR's undertakings, the tobacco industry was unable to convince many people of ETS's harmlessness, especially after two major studies on secondhand smoke appeared in 1986. One came from the National Academy of Sciences (NAS), which reported that children of smokers were twice as likely to suffer from respiratory illnesses as children with nonsmoking parents. The Surgeon General's report from the same year was even more damaging to the

CIAR's efforts, as it concluded that the best way to protect nonsmokers from the dangers of ETS would be to establish entirely smoke-free work sites, and not just nonsmoking areas. The two reports even put a number on the amount of lung cancer deaths in the United States attributable to the secondhand smoke, with the Surgeon General claiming it be around 3,000, while the NAS estimated the figure to somewhere between 2,500 and 8,400. These arresting estimations were further buttressed by a 1992 report by the Environmental Protection Agency, which found tobacco smoke to be a Class A human lung carcinogen—putting it in the same category as asbestos and benzene. The report also suggested that 20% of lung cancer cases among nonsmokers resulted from secondhand smoke. Subsequent studies have concluded that secondhand smoke is even more dangerous than previously thought, with some research indicating that as many as 50,000 Americans die each year as a result of ETS-related illnesses.

Reports about ETS such as these were central to the legal difficulties the tobacco industry experienced in the 1990s. The most salient example is *Broin v. Philip Morris*, a class-action lawsuit filed on behalf of Norma Broin, an American Airlines flight attendant who had never smoked but still contracted lung cancer at an early age, and approximately 60,000 other nonsmoking flight attendants who sought roughly $5 billion in redress from big tobacco as a result of illnesses and injuries suffered as a result of their exposure to secondhand smoke. Facing a difficult case, the tobacco companies avoided admitting to secondhand smoke's health risks to nonsmokers by agreeing, out of court, to a $349 million settlement. ETS's health hazards were thus, by the late-twentieth century, firmly established, even if the tobacco industry was reluctant to publicly admit it.

In recent years, secondhand smoke regulation has been extended, in many places, to traditional bastions of public smoking such as bars. Many cities have also banned smoking at sports stadiums, beaches and parks as a result of ETS health effects. California has been one of the most vigorous states in its restriction of smoking on behalf of nonsmokers, with recently passed legislation banning the act of smoking in a vehicle that contains minors. Some communities within the state have even recently taken the controversial step of restricting smoking within private residences, such as apartment buildings, in order to shield neighboring nonsmokers from the hazards of secondhand smoke.

(See also **Smokers' Rights**; **Tobacco Industry Research Committee (TIRC)**; **Tobacco Institute**)

References

Brandt, Allan M. 2007. *The Cigarette Century: The Rise, Fall, and Deadly Persistence of the Product That Defined America.* New York: Basic Books.

Cordry, Harold V. 2001. *Tobacco: A Reference Handbook.* Santa Barbara, CA: ABC-CLIO.

Goodman, Jordan, ed. 2005. *Tobacco in History and Culture: An Encyclopedia.* Detroit: Thomson Gale.

Parker-Pope, Tara. 2001. *Cigarettes: Anatomy of an Industry from Seed to Smoke.* New York: The New Press.

SHANGHAI COMMISSION

The Shanghai Commission was an international meeting that convened in 1909 to explore the possibility of instituting a global system to place controls over the production, consumption, and trade of opiates. Though the meeting accomplished little in the way of formal policy decisions, it was a landmark nonetheless since it established the role that the international community would play in narcotics control from that point on.

The main issue that brought diplomats to Shanghai was the opium problem in East Asia, particularly among populations in China and in other territories throughout the region. A major reason earlier efforts at reducing rates of opium use in Asia failed was that the international community did not cooperate. European colonial powers such as Britain, France, and Holland all had extensive opium businesses in their Asian possessions, and had instituted systems where the authorities were in charge of growing and selling the drug. Thus there was a tension between, on the one hand, the public health efforts to limit opium use, and on the other hand, European financial interests, with fiscal concerns usually winning out over sanitary or moral ones. In the late-nineteenth century, however, European powers, with some encouragement from the United States, began to change their attitude towards the opium trade. Organizations opposed to the shipping of opium into China emerged in Holland and Britain, and by the turn of the twentieth century, they began to turn public opinion in these countries against their governments' policies of enriching the colonies by pushing opium onto Asian populations. In addition, a new power in the region—the United States—was eager to put tighter controls on the Asian opium trade to help make its opium policy in the Philippines more effective. The United States was also eager to help China in its struggle against opium so that the Chinese would support the United States' financial interests in the region, and open up business opportunities for U.S. businesses on the Chinese mainland. In 1903, the Chinese made agreements with the United States and Britain to limit shipments of opiates into the country, and later in the decade, the British agreed to cut opium imports into China by 10% every year. In 1909, several of the world's leading opium producing powers agreed to meet at a conference convened by the United States in Shanghai to consider further measures that could be taken to help limit the levels of opium abuse in East Asia.

Delegates from Britain, France, Japan, Russia, Germany, Portugal, Holland, Austria-Hungary, Italy, Persia, China, Siam, and the United States showed up for the conference in Shanghai in February of 1909. Even though they attended, many countries were reluctant to participate if the conference would result in a treaty that forced them to make significant cuts to their drug businesses. Two major drug-producing countries—Turkey (which grew opium) and Switzerland (which was a major manufacturer of synthetic drugs)—refused invitations to the conference. Once the conference began, no countries were willing to commit to any reductions in opium production or changes in opium policy that could do harm to their domestic drug industries or colonial opium businesses. Nonetheless, the nations present at the Shanghai Commission—with the exception of Portugal—agreed on nine resolutions concerning the necessity of an international effort to help China suppress the opium habit. More important for the future of participating countries' domestic drug laws was the Commission's call for each nation at the conference to institute tighter internal controls on the circulation and use of opiates. The signatory powers agreed that their governments should take measures to reduce the prevalence of opium smoking in their territories, that each country's opium regulations should become increasingly stringent, and that each nation should take steps to regulate not only opium, but also its potentially addictive derivatives (such as morphine). The Commission also agreed with the United States' call for the control of opiate exports not just to Asian territories, but to any country that had laws regulating them, thus establishing the principle that drug control was to be an international undertaking.

Despite the agreements struck at Shanghai, the Commission's resolutions were only of an advisory nature, and they set out no specific legislative or administrative steps that signatory powers should take. Consequently, few of the nations that signed the Shanghai accord acted to bring their domestic policies in line with the recommendations made in the meeting. Frustrated with the lack of concrete action that resulted from the meeting, the United States began calling for a second international opium conference to meet and make stronger commitments to the cause of international opium control. This conference, which met at The Hague under the leadership of U.S. diplomat Hamilton Wright in 1911, marked the next major step towards international drug control. Yet despite the Shanghai conference's shortcomings, it was nonetheless significant since it set the world on a path towards instituting a global narcotics control regime, one that, despite changes over time, has remained in place for nearly a century.

(See also **Brent, Charles Henry**; **China and the Chinese**; **Hague Convention**; **Wright, Hamilton**)

References

Bewley-Taylor, David R. 1999. *The United States and International Drug Control, 1909–1997*. London: Pinter.

Davenport-Hines, Richard. 2001. *The Pursuit of Oblivion: A Global History of Narcotics, 1500–2000*. London: Weidenfeld & Nicolson.

McAllister, William B. 2000. *Drug Diplomacy in the Twentieth Century*. London: Routledge.

Report of the International Opium Commission, Shanghai China, February 1 to February 26 1909. 1909. London: P.S. King & Son.

SMOKERS' RIGHTS

The notion of "smokers' rights" emerged in response to a nonsmokers' rights movement that began in the early 1970s. With grassroots nonsmoking organizations successfully generating local and statewide smoking restrictions to protect the public from the health hazards of secondhand smoke, an embattled tobacco industry claimed that smokers' rights were being violated. Casting smoking as a basic liberties issue, tobacco companies attempted to foster a countervailing smokers' organization that ultimately failed, despite public relations moves like the promulgation of a Bill of Rights for smoking, to generate a genuine smokers' rights movement.

The tobacco industry's campaign on behalf of smokers' rights came in response to a nonsmokers' rights movement that began on a grassroots level in the early 1970s. The first groups to argue for smoke-free air as a nonsmokers' right drew upon the civil rights, antiwar, and environmental movements as inspirations. Comprised of volunteer activists, organizations like Americans for Non-Smokers' Rights and Group Against Smoking and Pollution (GASP) advanced the notion that nonsmokers had a right to breathe smoke-free air. On the local level, these groups aggressively pushed for the passage of local and state ordinances that would regulate smoking in places of public accommodation like restaurants and office buildings. Beyond their legislative efforts, GASP members went directly to restaurant owners, and numbers of them agreed to create nonsmoking sections in their businesses well before the passage of any laws mandating such areas.

Despite the fact that science had yet to conclusively prove the serious health hazards of secondhand smoke, the nonsmokers' rights movement helped enact a number of public smoking restrictions across the country and in the nation's skies. By 1973, nonsmoking sections existed on all airlines, and in that same year, Arizona became the first state to ban smoking in buses, theaters, elevators, museums, and libraries. Two years later, in large part as a result of the Twin Cities chapter of the Association for Non-Smokers' Rights, Minnesota passed the first statewide Clean Indoor Air Act, which, among other things, forbade smoking in all public places unless specifically allowed. The number of similar smoking restrictions multiplied in subsequent years, so that 80% of the nation's population lived in areas that were covered by these laws by the mid-1980s.

The tobacco industry did not passively accept these tremendous changes to the place of smoking in public life, and one of their tactics to combat the non-smokers' rights movement was to help foster a countermovement in support of what was dubbed "smokers' rights." This mimicking went beyond a similarity in names, as the tobacco industry explicitly linked their movement, as had nonsmokers' rights groups, to the civil rights movement. Similarly, in response to the American Cancer Society's Great American Smokeout, which encouraged smokers to quit, Philip Morris distributed a Great American Smoker's Kit, a pamphlet that encouraged smokers to convince nonsmokers that smoking was a basic right. Further casting smoking as an American freedom imperiled by the zealotry of the nonsmokers' rights movement, Philip Morris went so far as to distribute a Bill of Rights for smoking to its customers. Among the rights afforded to smokers according to this document were the right to accommodation in the workplace and public places and the right to freedom from undue government intrusion. And in order to help transform these ideas into an organization and movement capable of rivaling the non-smokers' rights drive, the tobacco companies helped fund the National Smokers' Alliance (NSA). This allegedly grassroots organization, which claimed around 3 million members, was in fact industry-led and created with the assistance of a public relations firm. Largely seen for what it truly was, the NSA was unable to develop a movement on par with the nonsmokers' cause.

When these efforts largely failed, the tobacco industry attempted to shift the terms of the nonsmokers' rights debate by stressing the need for accommodation. The Accommodation Program, launched by Philip Morris in the early 1990s, stressed that the best way to resolve the increasingly contentious issue of public smoking was not through legislating smoking restrictions, but rather via mutual respect between smokers and nonsmokers. Still casting smoking bans as an unwarranted government intrusion in the personal lives of smokers, Philip Morris claimed that tolerance and accommodation could prevent the supersession of either group's rights. If hotels, restaurants, and bars voluntarily set aside public spaces for smokers, as Philip Morris' pamphlets suggested, the rights of both groups would be protected and increased legislation would be unnecessary.

The 1990s nonetheless marked an expansion of smoking restrictions in public places across the country, and the accomplishments of the smokers' rights movement paled in comparison to the achievements of the nonsmokers' rights movement. Smokers' rights campaigns and a policy of encouraging accommodation proved insufficient to halt a growing number of smoking bans that emerged to protect nonsmokers from secondhand smoke. Ultimately, once science confirmed the serious health hazards posed by secondhand smoke, the public and government determined that nonsmokers' access to clean air effectively trumped smokers' traditional freedom to smoke in public places.

(See also **Secondhand Smoke**)

References

Brandt, Allan M. 2007. *The Cigarette Century: The Rise, Fall, and Deadly Persistence of the Product That Defined America*. New York: Basic Books.

Cordry, Harold V. 2001. *Tobacco: A Reference Handbook*. Santa Barbara, CA: ABC-CLIO.

Goodman, Jordan, ed. 2005. *Tobacco in History and Culture: An Encyclopedia*. Detroit: Thomson Gale.

SMOKING OPIUM EXCLUSION ACT

The Smoking Opium Exclusion Act of 1909 was the first federal law targeting the importation of narcotics into the United States. Its impact, however, was limited, since it was hastily crafted for political reasons, and its provisions soon became unnecessary with the passage of the Harrison Narcotics Act of 1914. Nonetheless, the legislation did mark a new step in the federal government's campaign against recreational drug use.

As the habit of smoking opium became more prominent among non-Chinese populations in the 1870s, many local municipalities and state governments throughout the Western United States began passing laws banning the practice. These laws had limited impact, however, and many reformers believed that federal legislation that would make it either too expensive or risky to smoke opium would be the most effective way to curb the practice. The problem, however, was that many believed the federal government did not have the authority to pass legislation on social problems like drug use—such powers were thought to be reserved for the states.

In the early 1880s, some members of Congress introduced legislation that would have increased the import duties on opium that was prepared for smoking, taxed its domestic manufacture at a higher rate, or even banned its importation altogether. None of these measures passed. By the early 1900s, however, the push to institute tighter domestic controls over opium smoking in the United States began gaining momentum. The renewed push for opium control came not so much from a growing opium problem at home as it did from international concerns. As the United States prepared for the first international opium conference at Shanghai in 1909, the U.S. delegation led by Hamilton Wright wanted the United States to have a model law in place to show that its desire to institute a global drug control regime was sincere. If the United States began pushing for international controls without having any effective drug laws on the books at home, they feared, the United States would be open to charges of hypocrisy, and the conference would fail.

Though Wright would have preferred a piece of comprehensive drug control legislation (like the Harrison Act he eventually helped become law in 1914), it would have been too complicated and controversial to pass such sweeping legislation before the conference began. Instead of aiming to control all narcotics, Wright and Secretary of State Elihu Root pushed for more modest legislation by proposing a bill that would have prohibited the importation and use of opium that was already prepared for smoking. By narrowly tailoring the legislation to avoid affecting the commerce in morphine, heroin, or other preparations, Root and Wright maximized the likelihood that the law would pass; unlike manufactured opiates and medicinal preparation that included opium, there was no major industry or lobby behind smoking opium, meaning that opposition to such a law would be relatively weak. The act was proposed as a bill in January of 1909, and became law that February, less than a week before the meeting at Shanghai began. For Wright and others in the U.S. delegation, the law passed just in time for them to show the world that the United States was taking action to curb drug use at home, and to allow them to argue that other countries should do the same.

Aside from bolstering the case of the U.S. delegation at Shanghai, the Smoking Opium Exclusion Act was a watershed in the history of U.S. drug policy. It was the first nationwide policy aimed specifically at recreational drugs (the Pure Food and Drugs Act of 1906 concerned medicines). It banned the importation of opium that was prepared for smoking, and inflicted punishments of up to $5,000 or 2 years in prison for violations. Even more importantly, it made the opium habit a more expensive and dangerous one to maintain. The import ban made smoking opium increasingly scarce in the United States, and as a result, it became extremely expensive. Though this may have discouraged some from smoking the drug, it also created incentive for smugglers and illicit dealers to start doing business in the drug since it could be very profitable. Also, many people who had been smoking opium began switching to other, more potent derivatives of opium, like morphine and heroin, which were not covered by the ban. It would not be until 1914, when the more comprehensive Harrison Act took effect, that these other substances would become subject to equally stringent government controls.

(See also **Harrison Narcotics Act**; **Pure Food and Drug Act**; **Primary Source Documents**; **Shanghai Commission**; **Wright, Hamilton**)

References

Belenko, Steven R., ed. 2000. *Drugs and Drug Policy in America: A Documentary History*. Westport, CT: Greenwood Press.

Courtwright, David T. 2001. *Dark Paradise: A History of Opiate Addiction in America*. Cambridge, MA: Harvard University Press.

Musto, David F. 1987. *The American Disease: Origins of Narcotics Control*. Expanded Edition. New York: Oxford University Press.

SPEAKEASIES

With the passage of the Eighteenth Amendment and its supporting Volstead Act, alcohol consumption was driven out of the saloon and into a new site for illicit communal drinking during the era of prohibition—speakeasies. Generally expensive and often glamorous, speakeasies became a lasting symbol of drinkers' opposition to national prohibition. The speakeasy's emergence in 1920 signaled the end of saloons, which did not reappear once prohibition was repealed in 1933. Furthermore, the drinking styles fostered by speakeasies, including the consumption of hard alcohol and mixed drinks, continued as features of post-prohibition bars and cocktail lounges.

The Eighteenth Amendment and the accompanying Volstead Act brought about national prohibition, but they did not make alcohol disappear from American life. In fact, despite these major laws, consuming alcohol remained a legal act; under prohibition, technically only manufacturing and selling alcohol were illegal activities. This allowed for the legal production of cider via home brewing, and it spurred the growth of legitimate home winemaking as well. Outside of the home, however, hard alcohol was also available to drinkers—particularly urban ones—as a result of the extensive efforts of bootleggers and smugglers. These illegal beverages could be clandestinely bought in places like drugstores, barbershops, and hotels, but the most popular place to purchase and consume this alcohol was the speakeasy.

The speakeasy differed from its pre-prohibition predecessors, the tavern and the saloon. While the speakeasy lived a kind of underground existence, the colonial era and early American tavern was an open fixture of society. Taverns were important sites of communal gatherings and discussions, and they served as social and business centers. With the burgeoning of the Industrial Revolution during the middle of the nineteenth century, taverns gave way to saloons as the primary site of drinking in America. Saloons featured greater class and gender separation than taverns did, but they also became the focus of temperance activities. From the "hatchetations" of Carry Nation to the more systematic opposition of groups such as the Woman's Christian Temperance Union or the Anti-Saloon League of America, the saloon became the symbolic target of the growing prohibition movement.

National prohibition's arrival in 1920 spelled the end of the saloon era and ushered in the speakeasy as the new locale for communal drinking. Consumption within the home, to be sure, was an important consequence of prohibition, which, instead of ending drinking, had the unintended effect of driving it into the home. But for those who desired a more social ambiance when drinking, the illegal speakeasy emerged as the best substitute for the saloon experience. Speakeasies may have derived their name from the need of drinkers to speak quietly within the building lest they arouse the suspicions of policemen on the street, or the term "speakeasy" may simply have been related to the Irish term for an illegal drinking spot. Regardless of the term's origin, the speakeasy flourished during prohibition, particularly in urban areas. While some speakeasies were oriented towards working class drinkers, the most successful and famous ones catered to those affluent members of society who longed for a drink despite the illegality of it. As a result, these speakeasies were typified by an often luxurious atmosphere, fine dining, or live musical accompaniment that lent an air of respectability and class to what was, in reality, the breaking of federal law. Thus, despite their illegality, speakeasies were more inviting to women than saloons had been. Women frequented speakeasies far more than they did saloons, and speakeasies generally catered to both sexes. In addition to serving a different clientele, speakeasies also served drinks that would not have been found in saloons. Cocktails, in particular, became features of the speakeasy experience. Prohibition generally had the unintended consequence of elevating consumption rates for hard alcohol, and drinking cocktails became a marker of sophistication, elegance, and being hip. As a result, diners at speakeasies generally consumed cocktails, instead of wine, before or after dinner.

Speakeasies flourished, particularly in places like New York City, which effectively abandoned its enforcement of prohibition after 1924. In 1929, Police

Commissioner Grover Whalen estimated that there were 32,000 speakeasies operating within the city. Such a figure was over twice as high as the number of legal drinking establishments that existed there before prohibition. Even New York City's mayor, Jimmy Walker, was often sighted openly flouting prohibition in the city's speakeasies.

Following prohibition's repeal in 1933, many speakeasies became legitimate houses of alcohol once again. They did not, however, revert to being saloon-like establishments. Modern American bars often remain very open to female drinkers, and they feature cocktails that, in many cases, gained their popularity during the era of speakeasies. Still, the majority of alcohol in America is consumed within the home, attesting to the lasting impact prohibition had on American drinking patterns beyond the popularity of speakeasies.

(See also **Anti-Saloon League (ASL)**; **Nation, Carry**; **Volstead Act (18th Amendment)**; **Woman's Christian Temperance Union (WCTU)**)

References

Barr, Andrew. 1999. *Drink: A Social History of America*. New York: Carroll & Graf Publishers, Inc.

Blocker, Jr., Jack S., David M. Fahey, and Ian R. Tyrrell, eds. 2003. *Alcohol and Temperance in Modern History: An International Encyclopedia*. Santa Barbara, CA: ABC-CLIO.

Burns, Eric. 2004. *The Spirits of America: A Social History of America*. Philadelphia: Temple University Press.

Mendelson, Jack H. and Nancy K. Mello. 1985. *Alcohol: Use and Abuse in America*. Boston: Little, Brown and Company.

Murdock, Catherine Gilbert. 1998. *Domesticating Drink: Women, Men, and Alcohol in America, 1870–1940*. Baltimore: Johns Hopkins University Press.

SPECIAL NARCOTIC COMMITTEE

The Special Narcotic Committee (SNC) was a committee formed by the Treasury Department to study narcotics control and recommend changes in the law and its administration in 1918 and 1919. Ultimately, the SNC influenced the federal stance towards narcotics and drug control by authoring a bill that strengthened the provisions of the Harrison Narcotics Act, and also by conducting research that advanced the federal government's assertion that narcotic drug use was actually increasing, not decreasing, after the passage of the Harrison Act in 1914.

The SNC was formed in the spring of 1918, when Commissioner of Internal Revenue Daniel C. Roper proposed the creation of a committee to examine narcotics control more closely. Treasury Secretary William McAdoo appointed the committee on March 25, 1918, in hopes that it could help overturn the Supreme Court's decision in *Jin Fuey Moy v. United States*—which established that possession of narcotics was not a punishable offense under the Harrison Act— and advance arguments against the maintenance treatment of addiction. The committee was chaired by Representative Henry T. Rainey (Democrat, Illinois), and also included former chief of pharmacology for the U.S. Public Health Service Reid Hunt, A. G. DuMez, also of the Public Health Service, and Deputy Commissioner of the Internal Revenue Bureau B. C. Keith.

One of the SNC's first accomplishments was the tightening of restrictions over narcotics under the Harrison Act. Through provisions Rainey added to the Tax Act of 1918, the SNC was able to close many of the loopholes in the Harrison Act that had become clear in the *Jin Fuey Moy* Supreme Court case. For one, Rainey's legislation instituted a tax of one cent per ounce of narcotics, thus establishing that the Harrison Act was indeed a revenue measure. What this meant was that any individual in possession of a package containing narcotics that did not have a tax stamp could be brought up on charges of illegal possession unless they could produce a prescription from a physician to prove that they had the drugs for medical purposes.

The more important accomplishment of the SNC was the June 1919 release of its final report, titled *Traffic in Narcotic Drugs*. The report was based largely on a questionnaire survey given to the 173,000 physicians and pharmacists who had registered with the federal government under the Harrison Act. The response rate to the survey was relatively low, between 30% and 40%, so the SNC extrapolated numbers from those who responded to come up with the rough estimate that there were 250,000 addicts in treatment in the United States. Assuming that only a minority of addicts ever sought out treatment, the SNC concluded that there were over 1 million addicts in the country, and that per capita consumption of opium was higher in the United States than in any other industrialized nation. As historian David F. Musto points out, the numbers reported by the SNC in the report were probably gross exaggerations, but they were still cited as evidence that the drug problem was growing. (Musto, 1987, 138) *Traffic in Narcotic Drugs* also predicted that the number of addicts would continue to grow, since alcohol prohibition would lead many drinkers to turn to narcotics. It also warned of the growing size and scope of the black market for drugs, and the development of increasingly organized drug rings that smuggled narcotics across the Canadian and Mexican borders.

Traffic in Narcotic Drugs also addressed the question of addiction and maintenance treatment. With the Supreme Court's anti-maintenance decisions in the *Doremus* and *Webb* cases in 1919, the report predicted that many addicts would become desperate for narcotics, and it recommended that both the federal and local governments provide medical care for them as they underwent detoxification. However, the SNC did not endorse any form of medical treatment for addiction, and warned that the likely result of limited availability could be that addicts would become violent. Addiction, therefore, became more than just a medical problem that afflicted addicts; given the high numbers of addicts estimated in the SNC report, and the belief that they could become violent if denied their drugs, it also became a potential menace to public safety.

Even though it was only in existence for little more than a year, the SNC had a lasting impact on the trajectory of narcotic drug policy in the United States. By closing loopholes in the Harrison Act, and spreading fear about the spread of narcotics addiction, the work of the SNC contributed to the hardening of attitudes towards both drug users and traffickers in the 1920s.

(See also **Harrison Narcotics Act**; ***Jin Fuey Moy v. United States***; ***United***

States v. Doremus and *Webb et al. v. United States*)

References

Acker, Caroline Jean. 2002. *Creating the American Junkie: Addiction Research in the Classic Era of Narcotic Control.* Baltimore: Johns Hopkins University Press.

"More than 1,000,000 Drug Users in U.S." 1919. *New York Times.* June 13.

Musto, David F. 1987. *The American Disease: Origins of Narcotic Control.* Expanded Edition. New York: Oxford University Press.

STATE DRUG AND ALCOHOL CONTROL LAWS

The federal government became involved in regulating the use of opiates and cocaine in 1914, the use of alcohol in 1919, the use of marijuana in 1937, and the use of other potentially habit-forming substances after World War II. Yet before these controls were instituted nationwide, several states and localities instituted their own controls over these substances.

The first major substance to become subject to state controls was alcohol. The colony of Georgia tried to ban alcohol in 1735, but the law proved ineffective, and was repealed in 1742. Beginning with the work of Benjamin Rush in the late-eighteenth century, however, modern conceptions of alcoholism began to develop in the United States. Temperance societies and other groups that advocated for the prohibition of alcohol became increasingly powerful over the course of the nineteenth century, as over 5,000 of them emerged nationwide by

the 1830s, and they had well over a million members. Though many of these groups originally focused on convincing citizens to voluntarily limit their alcohol consumption, they became more militant as they grew in numbers, first preaching abstinence from alcohol, and then moving on to advocate for legal prohibition of the substance when they found that voluntary pledges to stop using alcohol excessively did not keep people from developing drinking problems. By the middle of the nineteenth century, many politicians joined the cause, leading to four distinct waves of state prohibition laws. The first wave began with Maine's 1851 law banning the manufacture of intoxicating liquor, allowing only municipal agents to sell it, and limiting its use to industrial and medicinal purposes. Police in Maine were empowered by the law to search and seize illicit alcohol, and individuals who violated the statute were heavily fined, and jailed if they were repeat offenders. The Maine law served as a model for advocates of prohibition elsewhere, and by 1855 fifteen other states had passed similar laws. Resistance from ethnic groups and the liquor industry ultimately led to the repeal of many of these statutes. The second wave of state prohibition laws came in the 1880s and 1890s, as groups such as the Woman's Christian Temperance Union and the Prohibition Party began to gain influence. Political pressure led seventeen states, beginning with Kansas in 1880, to hold referenda on alcohol prohibition, though only four of them wound up instituting it. At the beginning of the twentieth century, groups such as the Anti-Saloon League of America resumed pressuring states to pass laws banning alcohol. Many of the state laws that were passed in the early-twentieth century banned the use of alcohol, though some of them allowed for the importation and production of liquor, thus limiting their effectiveness. By 1917, two years before Congress passed the Volstead Act, thirty-one states had some form of alcohol prohibition. After the passage of the Eighteenth Amendment, a fourth wave of state prohibition laws took hold, as states sought to modify their laws to be in harmony with the national prohibition regime. By 1933, when prohibition was repealed, every state except for Maryland had passed a prohibition law at some point in the previous century. When national prohibition was repealed, many states repealed their bans on alcohol, though some persisted for a long time. Oklahoma, for example, did not repeal its prohibition law until 1959, and the last state prohibition statute to be taken off the books was Mississippi's law, which was rescinded in 1966.

While other substances were not as widely controlled by state laws in the late-nineteenth and early-twentieth centuries, many states did have statutes controlling their use for non-medicinal purposes. Pennsylvania was the first state to regulate morphine with an 1860 law that controlled the drug with its anti-poisons law. In the late-nineteenth century, several states, such as Ohio and Nevada, passed laws banning opium smoking, and limiting to druggists the right to sell opium. In 1897, Illinois became the first state to take action against cocaine, banning its sale or transfer except with a doctor's prescription. Anticipating the sweeping federal legislation that was to come with the Harrison Narcotics Act in 1914, some states, such as West Virginia, New York, and Indiana, passed more comprehensive laws in the

first decade of the twentieth century, stipulating that cocaine and opiates could only be sold and used for medicinal purposes. In 1913, Tennessee passed a narcotics control act that allowed addicts to receive prescriptions for opiates legally, in hopes of cutting off the illicit market for the drugs. In 1914, months before the passage of the Harrison Act, New York passed the Boylan Act, which was the first piece of state legislation that allowed for the civil commitment of drug addicts.

The Boylan Act, however, was the exception, as most state laws were looser, with most of them merely stipulating that narcotics could only be dispensed with a prescription, and that narcotic prescriptions could not be refilled. The sanctions for violating many state laws were light, inflicting only fines or short prison terms on individuals convicted of breaking them. This became worrisome for enforcement officials with the Federal Bureau of Narcotics (FBN), since they wanted the help of state and local police in cracking down on offenses related to drug use and drug dealing not covered under the Harrison Act, and also with the enforcement of federal rules governing drug possession, use, and dealing. In 1932, most states took a major step towards filling in gaps in federal drug control policy and enforcement by adopting the model law issued by the Uniform State Narcotic Act, thus harmonizing state drug laws so that they buttressed the Harrison Act, and giving states a share of the responsibility for enforcing the nation's drug laws. The four states that did not adopt the Uniform State Narcotic Act, though they did not have identical legislation, had very similar laws governing the sale and use of narcotics. In the 1950s, after the Boggs Act stiffened federal penalties for drug-law violators, the FBN again pushed for states to adopt equally tough laws. When the Comprehensive Drug Abuse Prevention and Control Act reclassified drugs in 1970, it once again became important for states to make their anti-drug laws consistent with the federal scheme for controlling them, leading to the issuing of another uniform state drug law act. With the passage of the Anti-Drug Abuse Act of 1988, yet another model state drug law was issued, this time recommending not only uniform enforcement measures, but also suggesting prevention, treatment, and rehabilitation laws for both alcoholics and drug users. In spite of these moves to harmonize state drug laws, there are still some discrepancies between state and federal narcotic control laws today, particularly when it comes to penalties for marijuana possession and the questions surrounding medical marijuana. In these cases, federal law technically trumps state law, though sometimes the federal laws are not enforced as strictly as state laws.

(See also **Anti-Saloon League (ASL)**; **Boylan Act**; **Federal Bureau of Narcotics (FBN)**; **Volstead Act (18th Amendment)**; **Webb-Kenyon Act**; **Woman's Christian Temperance Union (WCTU)**)

References

Belenko, Steven R., ed. 2000. *Drugs and Drug Policy in America: A Documentary History*. Westport, CT: Greenwood Press.

Blocker Jr., Jack, David M. Fahey, and Ian R. Tyrrell, eds. 2003. *Alcohol and Temperance in Modern History: An International Encyclopedia*. Santa Barbara, CA: ABC-CLIO.

Burns, Eric. 2004. *The Spirits of America: A Social History of Alcohol*. Philadelphia: Temple University Press.

Carson-Dewitt, Rosalyn, ed. 2001. *Encyclopedia of Drugs, Alcohol & Addictive Behavior. Second Edition*. New York: Macmillan Reference USA.

Earlywine, Mitch. 2002. *Understanding Marijuana: A New Look at the Scientific Evidence*. Oxford: Oxford University Press.

Musto, David F. 1987. *The American Disease: Origins of Narcotic Control. Expanded Edition*. New York: Oxford University Press.

STEROIDS AND SPORTS

More properly designated as anabolic-androgenic steroids (AAS) because of their bodybuilding (anabolic) and masculinizing (androgenic) effects, steroids are synthetic versions of the male sex hormone testosterone that are illicitly used by, amongst others, athletes in order to enhance their physical performance and appearance. Though they have been banned by the International Olympic Committee since 1975 and prohibited by nearly every sporting organization, they are nonetheless taken by a significant, though ultimately unknown, number of athletes in a variety of sports, with weightlifting, cycling, football, and baseball being among the most prominent. Athletes who take steroids tend to use AAS in stacks and cycles, going well beyond the level of steroids that might be medically prescribed. This practice leads some steroid users to have many problems, including psychological addiction, physiological withdrawal issues, and a bevy of adverse side effects.

AAS were created in the mid-1930s, shortly after testosterone was first isolated by scientists. It is unclear when the illicit use of steroids truly began, but the first reports of such usage date back to 1954 and describe male and female Russian athletes, and weightlifters particularly, taking AAS in order to increase their weight and muscle strength. Steroid use amongst American athletes also first took place within the world of weightlifting, with the York Barbell Club in York, Pennsylvania emerging as the site of much experimentation in the late 1950s and early 1960s. Hoping to help Americans fare better against their steroid-using, Russian competitors, Dr. John Ziegler developed Dianabol—a steroid designed to be less androgenic than other AAS—and administered it, along with amphetamines, to American Olympic weightlifters.

Competitive weightlifters' use of AAS was hardly the only example of the Cold War being reflected in international athletics, as American Olympians in a variety of sports took steroids in the 1950s. Many of the athletes on steroids in this era felt that AAS were a kind of wonder-drug, while others likely took them because they felt they simply could not compete with athletes who were on steroids. In response to this phenomenon, the International Olympic Committee began to ban drug use among athletes in 1968. The prohibition covered some twenty stimulants and narcotics, but steroids were not among the banned substances. The omission of AAS from the list was not an indication that steroid use was minor amongst Olympians, for steroid use by American athletes was fairly widespread at the 1968 Mexico City Games. Instead, the International Olympic Committee did not ban steroids because no reliable test for AAS existed at that point. In addition, science was as

yet unsure of the precise amounts and ratios of steroids that naturally occur in the body, thus making AAS detection even more difficult.

It is probably safe to assume that AAS use factored significantly in Olympic competitions up until the mid-1970s, when the detection of exogenous testosterone in urine became scientifically possible. The International Olympic Committee consequently banned AAS in 1975. The 1976 Olympic Games in Montreal were the first to feature athletes being tested for steroids, and numerous competitors were disqualified from it and subsequent Olympiads or stripped of the medals they unfairly won. In what is perhaps the most famous case of this, Canadian sprinter Ben Johnson had his gold medal taken away after testing positive for an AAS at the 1988 Summer Olympic Games in Seoul, South Korea. Despite catching Johnson, the International Olympic Committee was widely seen as insufficiently policing its athletes' use of steroids. A decade later, it agreed to implement the anti-doping rules and regulations of the independent World Anti-Doping Agency, which was created in the aftermath of a 1998 drug-use scandal that rocked the Tour de France.

The Olympics are hardly the only athletic competition to have been tainted by the illicit use of steroids. AAS use had become an institutionalized staple in professional football by 1963, when the San Diego Chargers distributed oral steroids for players to take at their team meals. The origin of this practice may be traced to the team's strength coach, Alvin Roy, who had been affiliated with United States' weightlifting team. Baseball, too, has a checkered history with AAS, and it is generally believed that steroids made their way into the game some time in the mid- to late 1960s. Steroids became a far more significant element on the diamond in the last two decades, and it is now common to refer to a "steroid age" in baseball's history. Discussion of AAS in baseball came to the forefront when sluggers Mark McGwire and Sammy Sosa both surpassed the game's long-standing, single-season home run record. In the course of their much publicized pursuit of the record, McGwire admitted to using androstenedione, a muscle-building supplement that was legal at the time but has subsequently been banned by Major League Baseball, the World Anti-Doping Agency, and other sports organizations. In 2003, baseball banned steroid use and began testing for it, and 5.77% of 1,438 anonymous urine samples tested positive for AAS. In 2005, Congress held hearings investigating the use of AAS amongst baseball players, and McGwire stated that the game had a steroid problem, though he refused to answer questions about his own drug use. In the wake of these hearings, Major League Baseball Commissioner Bud Selig hired, in March 2006, former Maine Senator George Mitchell to launch an independent investigation into steroid use in the sport. The resulting Mitchell Report, which was released on December 13, 2007, implicated eighty-six players.

In addition to the aforementioned Congressional hearings, the government became involved in the issue of steroids and sports as a result of its investigation of the Bay Area Laboratory Co-Operative (BALCO), which begun in August 2002 and focused on the alleged money laundering and illegal distribution of steroids and other performance-enhancing drugs by BALCO's founder, Victor Conte. IRS

agents subsequently linked BALCO to a number of high-profile athletes, including baseball home-run king Barry Bonds and Olympic sprinter Marion Jones. Such high-profile cases seem to have done little to diminish the athletic world's interest in AAS, however, as athletes in a variety of sports continue searching for an illicit medical edge.

(See also **Food and Drug Administration (FDA)**; **Primary Source Documents**; **Reference Essay**)

References

Rosen, Daniel M. 2008. *Dope: A History of Performance Enhancement in Sports from the Nineteenth Century to Today.* Praeger. Westport, Connecticut: Praeger.

Taylor, William N. 1991. *Macho Medicine: A History of the Anabolic Steroid Epidemic.* Jefferson, North Carolina: McFarland & Company, Inc.

Taylor, William N. 2002. *Anabolic Steroids and the Athlete.* Jefferson, North Carolina: McFarland & Company, Inc.

Wadler, Gary I. and Brian Hainline. 1989. *Drugs and the Athlete.* Philadelphia: F.A. Davis Company.

Westreich, Laurence M. 2008. "Anabolic Androgenic Steroid Use: Pharmacology, Prevalence, and Psychiatric Aspects." *Psychiatric Times.* 25, no. 1: 47–53.

Yesalis, Charles E., ed. 1993. *Anabolic Steroids in Sport and Exercise.* Champaign, Illiniois: Human Kinetics Publishers.

STUDENTS AGAINST DESTRUCTIVE DECISIONS (SADD)

Students Against Destructive Decisions (SADD, originally known as Students Against Driving Drunk) began in 1981 after the alcohol-related deaths of two teens in separate crashes in the span of one week in Wayland, Massachusetts. Central to this community-based advocate group is a signed contract between young people and their parental figures that pledges youths to making safe decisions, particularly with regard to avoiding the perils of drinking and driving. SADD currently has approximately 10,000 chapters across the nation's middle schools, high schools, and colleges.

SADD began its organizational life as Students Against Drunk Driving in response to the death of two high school hockey players in Wayland, Massachusetts. Wayland High School hockey coach and Health instructor Robert Anastas teamed up with fifteen students to create a student-based, anti-drunk driving organization. Initially limited to Wayland High School's juniors and seniors, SADD quickly grew beyond its small beginnings, and by the following year it had developed into a national organization with chapters in Massachusetts, Arizona, North Carolina, Connecticut, New York, New Jersey, Florida, Pennsylvania, and Maine. Currently, SADD has chapters in all fifty states and in Canada, and some 350,000 active members participate in these chapters.

The focal point of SADD is the Contract for Life, a document designed by Anastas and his students that, once signed by a young person and his or her parents (or another adult/parental figure), commits the student to making safe and sound decisions. In particular, a student agrees to call home for advice and/or transportation, at any hour and from any place, in the event that he or she has been drinking or their friend or date who is driving has been drinking. For their part, parents in turn pledge to either retrieve, with no questions asked at the time, their child from any place and at any hour, or pay for a taxi to bring their child home. Parents additionally promise to themselves seek safe and sober transportation home when they have had too much to drink. According to SADD, by 1990, more than 5 million such contracts had been signed. The original Contract for Life has since been amended, with the document now additionally including declarations, on the student's part, to do his or her best to abstain from alcohol and drugs. The student furthermore agrees to always wear a seat belt.

These alterations reflect SADD's 1997 decision to rename itself Students Against Destructive Decisions and thus dedicate itself to helping teens protect themselves against more than just drunk driving. As part of SADD's enlarged mission to help students facing a variety of destructive decisions, the organization developed educational materials on issues such as HIV and AIDS, smoking, teen violence, depression, and suicide. In addition, SADD has taken the somewhat controversial stand of not endorsing or condoning certain programs or activities that may, or at least intend to, reduce teenage drunk driving. For example, SADD rejects Safe Ride or Designated Driver programs for young people out of the belief that they encourage and enable the use of alcohol by underage youths.

To spread its message on campus and throughout communities, SADD holds peer-led classes, theme-focused forums, teen workshops, conferences, and rallies. SADD also engages in legislative work, actively lobbying for anti-drunk driving laws. Information regarding SADD's various activities is available from their Web site, http://www.sadd.org, and through *Decisions*, a newsletter published by SADD's national office.

(See also **Mothers Against Drunk Driving (MADD)**)

References

Blocker, Jr., Jack S., David M. Fahey, and Ian R. Tyrrell, eds. 2003. *Alcohol and Temperance in Modern History: An International Encyclopedia.* Santa Barbara, CA: ABC-CLIO.

Jacobs, James B. 1992. *Drunk Driving: An American Dilemma.* Chicago: University of Chicago Press.

Ross, H. Laurence. 1992. *Confronting Drunk Driving: A Social Policy for Saving Lives.* New Haven, CT: Yale University Press.

Students Against Destructive Decisions. "History of SADD." [Online article retrieved 05/21/09] http://www.sadd.org/history.htm.

Students Against Destructive Decisions. "SADD's Mission." [Online article retrieved 05/21/09] http://www.sadd.org/mission.htm.

SUBSTANCE ABUSE AND MENTAL HEALTH SERVICES ADMINISTRATION (SAMHSA)

The Substance Abuse and Mental Health Services Administration (SAMHSA) is an agency under the U.S. Department of Health and Human Services devoted to helping individuals with mental health and substance abuse problems lead fulfilling lives. SAMHSA aims to do this by supporting research into mental health and substance abuse problems, and by funding programs that aim to identify at-risk individuals, prevent the development of mental health and substance abuse disorders, and provide support for individuals suffering from mental illness and addiction.

SAMHSA was established on October 1, 1992 when the federal government's mental health and substance abuse agencies were overhauled. The Alcohol, Drug Abuse, and Mental Health Administration, which had been established in 1974, was dismantled, and the research components of the National Institute on Alcohol Abuse and Alcoholism, the National Institute on Drug Abuse, and the National Institute of Mental Health were subsumed under the National Institute of Health. The service components of these agencies were united under a new organization—SAMHSA. The agency's mission is to ensure that all individuals with mental illness and substance abuse problems have the opportunity to lead a fulfilling life that includes an education, a job, a home, meaningful personal relationships, and a family.

Through its centers and offices, SAMHSA administers grant programs and contracts to support state and local efforts to expand and enhance programs that can provide early intervention for individuals at risk for developing mental health or substance abuse problems. The organization aims to increase the availability and range of substance abuse treatment and mental health recovery programs that serve Americans in their communities. SAMHSA has four main programs. Its Center for Mental Health Services works to ensure that scientifically backed methods for preventing and treating mental illness are practiced throughout the country, and aims to improve access to mental health care by removing barriers that keep people with mental illness from receiving the services they need. The Center for Mental Health Services also aims to improve mental health throughout the country, and it tries to facilitate the effective rehabilitation of people with mental illness. Its Center for Substance Abuse Prevention provides national leadership in the development of policies, programs, and services that aim to prevent the abuse of illicit drugs, alcohol, and tobacco. To do this, the Center for Substance Abuse Prevention disseminates information on best practices in substance abuse prevention, and works with state and local authorities, as well as community organizations, to help them apply these practices effectively. The Center for Substance Abuse Treatment aims to bring effective alcohol and drug treatment programs to every community in the country by expanding the availability of effective treatment and recovery services for individuals suffering from alcohol and drug problems, and it also works to reduce the barriers that keep addicts from getting the services they need. Its fourth major division, the Office of Applied Studies, collects, analyzes, and disseminates data on mental health and drug-related problems. Among its major programs are the National Survey on Drug Use and Health, the Drug Abuse Warning Network, and the Drug and Alcohol Services Information System.

Today, SAMHSA has several priority program areas. They include programs that focus on treating co-occurring disorders (for people who have mental illness and addictions), increasing the nation's substance abuse treatment capacity, transforming the public mental health system, instituting more effective suicide prevention programs, working to prevent homelessness, and checking the spread of diseases such as HIV/AIDS and hepatitis, which are often related to substance abuse disorders.

More information on SAMHSA and its activities is available at its Web site: http://www.samhsa.gov.

(See also **National Institute on Alcohol Abuse and Alcoholism (NIAAA)**; **National Institute on Drug Abuse (NIDA)**)

References

National Institute of Mental Health. "Important Events in NIMH History." [Online information retrieved 05/04/09] http://www.nih.gov/about/almanac/archive/1998/organization/nimh/history.html.

Substance Abuse and Mental Health Services Administration. "About." [Online information retrieved 05/04/09] http://www.hhs.gov/samhsa/about/1336.html.

Substance Abuse and Mental Health Services Administration. "About Us." [Online information retrieved 05/04/09] http://www.samhsa.gov/About/background.aspx.

SURGEON GENERAL'S REPORTS ON TOBACCO

Appearing on an almost annual basis after the inaugural report in 1964, the Surgeon General's reports on tobacco have scientifically established the many health hazards of smoking. The first Surgeon General's report on tobacco, which appeared when almost half of American adults smoked, was a groundbreaking document that culled years of research and concluded, among other things, that smoking was a cause of lung and laryngeal cancer. Similarly repercussive was the 1988 report on nicotine addiction, which concluded that cigarettes were addicting, nicotine was the drug that causes addiction, and the pharmacologic and behavioral processes at work in nicotine addiction were similar to those determining addiction to drugs like heroin or cocaine.

The first Surgeon General's report on smoking was born out of a committee that started to come together in 1962. In that year, President Kennedy's Surgeon General, Luther Terry, announced that he would be forming a committee to investigate the impact of smoking upon health, and the group he judiciously convened consisted of five smokers and five nonsmokers. The committee was not opposed by the tobacco industry's pseudo-scientific institution, the Tobacco Industry Research Committee (TIRC), thereby making it all the more difficult for the conclusions the committee eventually reached to be called into question by big tobacco. The committee's groundbreaking findings, which were based upon a review of more than 7,000 articles about smoking, health, and disease, were published on January 11, 1964 under the title, *Smoking and Health*. Cognizant of the potential impact of the committee's findings, Terry scheduled the news conference surrounding the report's release on a Saturday so as to avert any panic that might arise on Wall Street. Similarly, Terry made sure that information as potent as that contained in the report made its way into the hands of as few people as possible before the news conference. As such, the White House received a copy of *Smoking and Health* only two hours before its official release.

The historic report constituted both the most authoritative and direst assessment of the health effects of tobacco use up that point. It concluded that cigarette smoking was a cause of both lung and laryngeal cancer in men; in the case of women, cigarette smoking was described as a probable cause. Chronic bronchitis and emphysema were found to be far more common in smokers than nonsmokers, and the report also determined that the rates of coronary artery disease were 70% higher among smokers. Additionally alarming to a nation of some 70 million regular smokers was the report's conclusion that the fatality rate from lung cancer was 1,000% higher among smoking men than nonsmoking men. In response to these findings, the committee stated that smoking represented a health hazard of such a degree as to warrant appropriate remedial action, though they left such an action undefined.

These conclusions represented a tremendous blow to the tobacco industry, which had successfully weathered the first wave of reports linking cigarette smoking to cancer and other diseases in the early 1950s by hiring the public relations firm, Hill & Knowlton, which helped form the TIRC and was behind the publication, in hundreds of newspapers across the country in 1954, of "A Frank Statement to Cigarette Smokers." That letter-form advertisement had alleviated growing concern over the health effects of smoking by claiming that there was no proof that cigarette smoke was a cause of lung cancer, but *Smoking and Health* made such a stance no longer scientifically tenable. The TIRC tried to regain some of the legitimacy it lost in the wake of the report by changing its name to the Council for Tobacco Research, but the superficiality of this move highlighted that the tobacco industry could have no significant answer to *Smoking and Health*.

American smokers, too, were hit hard by the committee's conclusions, and in January and February of 1964 many smokers tried to quit in what was called "The Great Forswearing." In March, however, even the knowledge of smoking's dangers was not enough to prevent what soon came to be known as "The Great Relapse." The continued smoking of cigarettes surprised Terry, who believed that *Smoking and Health* would be enough to convince Americans to quit an extremely hazardous practice, and he suggested that the addictiveness of cigarettes was stronger than had been indicated the conclusions of the first Surgeon General's report on smoking.

Additional Surgeon General's reports on various aspects of smoking appeared almost annually after the groundbreaking *Smoking and Health*, and in 1988, the Surgeon General released a report focusing on the addictiveness of smoking. The topic had been previously discussed, as the 1964 report committee's pharmacology expert believed that smoking was habit-forming and that smokers could undergo withdrawal. He was, however, unwilling to go so far as to conclude that smoking was addictive by the standard definitions of the time. The Surgeon General in the 1980s, C. Everett Koop, had no such reservations, and the report he released in May 1988 was based upon a significant amount of new research. *The Health Consequences of Smoking—Nicotine Addiction: A Report of the Surgeon General* concluded that cigarettes were addicting and that nicotine was the drug causing addiction. It additionally determined that the pharmacologic and behavioral processes at work in nicotine addiction were similar to those determining addiction to drugs like heroin or cocaine. Koop even explicitly explained that his document overturned the 1964 report's conclusion that cigarette smoking was habituating instead of addicting.

Koop's report was yet another blow to the tobacco industry, which by then had been denying the addictiveness of cigarettes in important lawsuits such as *Cipollone v. Liggett Group Inc. et al.* Internal industry documents, however, revealed big tobacco's longstanding knowledge of nicotine's addictiveness, and whistleblower Jeffrey Wigand provided further confirmation of this. Food and Drug Administration (FDA) head David Kessler would later utilize the conclusions reached by Surgeon General's reports like those from 1964 and 1988 when he declared, in 1996, that cigarettes were essentially nicotine-delivery devices and should thus be brought under the regulatory authority of the FDA.

(See also ***Cipollone v. Liggett Group, Inc. et al.***; **Food and Drug Administration (FDA)**; **Hill & Knowlton**; **Kessler, David**; **Primary Source Documents**; **Tobacco Industry Research Committee (TIRC)**; **Wigand, Jeffrey**)

References

Brandt, Allan M. 2007. *The Cigarette Century: The Rise, Fall, and Deadly Persistence of the Product That Defined America*. New York: Basic Books.

Cordry, Harold V. 2001. *Tobacco: A Reference Handbook*. Santa Barbara, CA: ABC-CLIO.

U.S. Public Health Services. Office of the Surgeon General. 1988. *The Health Consequences of Smoking—Nicotine Addiction: A Report of the Surgeon General*. [Online article retrieved 05/24/09] http://profiles.nlm.nih.gov/NN/B/B/Z/D/_/nnbbzd.pdf.

U.S. Surgeon General's Advisory Committee on Smoking and Health. 1964. *Smoking and Health: Report of the Advisory Committee to the Surgeon General of the Public Health Service*. [Online article retrieved 05/24/09] http://profiles.nlm.nih.gov/NN/B/B/M/Q/_/nnbbmq.pdf.

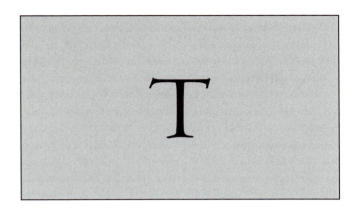

TERRY, CHARLES E.

Charles E. Terry was one of the leading addiction researchers in the opening decades of the twentieth century. Throughout his career, he advocated for the maintenance treatment of addicts, both in his personal medical practice and as a matter of principle.

Terry was born in Connecticut in 1878, and earned his medical degree from the University of Maryland in 1903. Seven years later, he became the first full-time health officer of the city of Jacksonville, where he established one of the nation's first narcotic clinics for the treatment of addicts. He served as the editor of *Delineator* magazine, and he published many articles in the *Journal of the American Public Health Association* in the 1910s and 1920s. He also worked as the Executive Director of the Bureau of Hygiene. In 1921, he was appointed the executive secretary of the Committee on Drug Addictions, a position he held until the late 1920s. Most notable of Terry's accomplishments

during his work with the Committee on Drug Addictions was the 1928 publication of a voluminous work on opiate addiction, *The Opium Problem*, which he co-authored with his wife, Mildred Pellens.

Terry became a prominent figure in national debates about addiction during his tenure as the health officer in Jacksonville. In 1912 Terry became sympathetic to the plight of opiate users, and helped push through an ordinance that established a city clinic where addicts could receive free narcotic prescriptions. Terry's initiative was not simply driven by a desire to help addicts procure drugs more easily; it was also designed to serve as a control over where addicts received their drugs. Before the establishment of the Jacksonville Narcotic Clinic, attempts by Florida's State Pharmaceutical Association to bring cases against physicians who dispensed narcotics to addicts too liberally resulted in no convictions. Terry's ordinance allowed for the state to track doctors who wrote unusually large prescriptions of habit-forming drugs by requiring druggists to keep drug prescriptions in ledgers that health inspectors could check. In the event that an individual was indeed addicted, Terry's ordinance allowed for addicts to receive free prescriptions, thus eliminating an excuse that many druggists who dispensed dangerous drugs liberally had been using—that they sold drugs without prescriptions because their patrons were too poor to go to a doctor for a prescription. More importantly, it brought addicts into contact with the Jacksonville Health Department, which would register them and provide them with the prescriptions they needed. Within a year of the ordinance's enactment in 1912, 646 habitual users registered with Terry's clinic. Terry's Jacksonville ordinance also had a repressive side, as it stipulated that possession of habit-forming drugs without a prescription constituted a misdemeanor. Based on his experience treating addicts in Jacksonville, Terry concluded that the majority of opiate addiction had its roots in the excessive prescription of narcotics by physicians, and he called for both physicians and pharmacists to become more prudent in their dispensation of narcotics. He also became sympathetic to the plight of addicts during his work in Jacksonville, and began to argue that addicts were not criminals, but rather sick and desperate individuals worthy of treatment.

After the passage of the Harrison Narcotics Act in 1914 made it more difficult for addicts to procure the drugs they needed to survive, Terry continued his public campaign to try to convince both the public and the medical profession that addiction was a disease, not a form of deviancy. As the Narcotic Division of the Prohibition Unit began cracking down on narcotic clinics, Terry remained one of their staunchest defenders, though his efforts fell short as all of the nation's narcotic clinics were shut down by 1923.

In 1919, Terry lent his support to the creation of a new organization—The Committee on Drug Addictions—that was eventually formed in 1921. Terry was active in the Committee's activities throughout the 1920s. In the middle of the decade, Terry conducted a series of surveys of physicians and pharmacists in the United States to determine how much opiates were necessary for medical practice in the country in order to contribute data to the League of Nations, which was trying to create a worldwide international opium control regime and limit opium production to the world's medicinal needs. His other major work in the 1920s was the co-authorship, along with his future wife Mildred Pellens, of *The Opium Problem* in 1928. *The Opium Problem* was an enormous work, spanning over 1,000 pages and drawing from over 4,000 different sources from Europe and the United States. The main theses of the work were that addiction was a disease and should be treated as such, that the implementation of the Harrison Act and the ban on maintenance treatment in the United States worsened the plight of the addicted, and that bans on the sale of opiates created a widespread, and well-organized, black market for narcotics. Terry and Pellens argued that maintenance treatment was preferable since addicts were, in their opinion, essentially normal individuals who became addicted to drugs due to circumstances that were beyond their control, and he was sympathetic towards the plight of addicts who had to go to the black market for drugs when legal supplies became scarce with tighter enforcement of the Harrison Act. Besides excessive law enforcement, the work also pointed a guilty finger at the medical profession, blaming it for facilitating addiction by prescribing opiates too liberally, and for stigmatizing the condition of addiction by refusing to treat it as a medical problem. Physicians' reluctance to treat addiction left addicts in an unenviable situation, Terry and Pellens argued, as it forced them to frantically hunt for the few doctors who would prescribe them drugs, but gave them little hope of ever being cured. The law-and-order approach towards treating addiction that became prominent in the United States in the 1910s and 1920s was particularly problematic, they maintained, because it discouraged addicts from seeking medical treatment, thus denying researchers opportunities to learn about addiction by studying addict patients in the course of medical practice. Terry and Pellens' outspoken criticism of U.S. drug policy led some members of the Committee on Drug Addictions to oppose the public release of *The Opium Problem*, though it eventually was published in 1928.

In the late 1920s, the Committee on Drug Addictions came under the sway of individuals such as Katharine Benet Davis and Lawrence B. Dunham, who advocated the anti-maintenance, law-and-order, and supply-control approaches to the addiction problem. This isolated Terry, who in 1931 began criticizing federal drug control policy and advocating for the creation of maintenance clinics once again. He retired from the Committee on Drug Addictions in the early 1930s. He then moved on to work at the Harlem Valley Hospital in New York, and due to failing eyesight, he retired to his native Connecticut, where he lived until his death in 1945. Though he was marginalized from the field of drug policy

in the 1930s, Terry's work remained influential, as it inspired the work of later critics of federal drug policy, such as Alfred Lindesmith, in the 1960s.

(See also **Committee on Drug Addictions**; **Harrison Narcotics Act**; **Lindesmith, Alfred R.**; **Narcotic Clinics**)

References

Acker, Caroline Jean. 2002. *Creating the American Junkie: Addiction Research in the Classic Era of Narcotic Control*. Baltimore: Johns Hopkins University Press.

Courtwright, David T. 2001. *Dark Paradise: A History of Opiate Addiction in America*. Cambridge, MA: Harvard University Press.

Musto, David F. 1987. *The American Disease: Origins of Narcotic Control*. Expanded Edition. New York: Oxford University Press.

Terry, Charles E. and Mildred Pellens. 1928. *The Opium Problem*. New York: Bureau of Social Hygiene.

TOBACCO INDUSTRY RESEARCH COMMITTEE (TIRC)

The Tobacco Industry Research Committee (TIRC), created in 1954, was the brainchild of Hill & Knowlton, a public relations firm hired by the CEOs of the tobacco companies to improve the image of cigarettes at a time when a number of scientific reports began linking smoking to cancer. Led by biologist Clarence Cook "C.C." Little, the TIRC was a tobacco industry-financed entity that worked to create uncertainty and doubt as to whether cigarettes were carcinogenic by distorting, discrediting, or suppressing findings that concluded that smoking represented a serious health threat. Initially quite successful, the TIRC (which was renamed the Council for Tobacco Research in 1964) was eventually disbanded as part of the 1998 Master Settlement Agreement.

The TIRC emerged out of a rare meeting of top executives from the major tobacco companies that took place at the Plaza Hotel in New York City on December 14, 1953. Big tobacco's CEOs convened there in order to craft a coordinated, long-term response to widely read and repercussive reports such as *Reader's Digest*'s December 1952 piece entitled "Cancer by the Carton," which brought recent scientific findings linking smoking and cancer to a mainstream audience. Similar articles soon followed in a variety of popular publications, generating a significant drop in the nation's level of cigarette consumption and leading to roughly 40% of the public believing that smoking caused lung cancer. Recognizing that a new approach was needed in order to ensure the survival of the cigarette industry, the tobacco companies at this New York meeting agreed to hire the renowned public relations firm Hill & Knowlton to stem the scientific and popular tide against smoking.

John W. Hill, the president of Hill & Knowlton, launched the TIRC in 1954 after toying with a couple of other potential titles for this new group. The tobacco industry initially floated names such as "The Committee of Public Information" and "The Cigarette Information Committee," but Hill argued that "Research" needed to be in the name in order to lend the institution a greater air of scientific legitimacy. The concept of "research" was central to Hill's game plan, as he saw the TIRC chiefly as an entity to co-opt science, which in the 1950s threatened to fundamentally reorient the public's relationship to cigarettes. By casting the TIRC as a legitimate research agency, rather than the industry-financed entity it truly was, big tobacco could air its views with a seemingly scientific respectability. With the TIRC discrediting and distorting reports that linked smoking to cancer and simultaneously publishing its own (biased, but cleverly disguised) findings that suggested otherwise, what appeared to be a growing consensus that smoking cigarettes constituted a serious health threat was transformed, within the span of the decade, into a debate over whether cigarettes were carcinogenic.

The TIRC was able to achieve this dramatic transformation of public opinion via a multifaceted campaign that began with a full-page advertisement announcing the organization's creation. Appearing in 448 newspapers in 258 cities, "A Frank Statement to Cigarette Smokers," introduced an estimated 43 million readers to the TIRC, which was described as an institution dedicated to supporting scientific research into tobacco's health effects. The advertisement, which took the form of a letter from big tobacco to the general public, included the statement that the tobacco industry accepted people's health as a basic responsibility, which it claimed was paramount to any other business consideration. The tobacco industry further stated that it believed its products were not harmful to one's health, and it claimed an ongoing cooperation with scientists and public health officials. The TIRC thus came across as a public service institution allied with science, despite the fact that it was actually formed in order distort, undermine, and discredit the growing chorus of scientific reports that linked smoking to cancer and other illnesses.

To give a face of respectability to what was fundamentally an industry-supported and industry-supporting entity, renowned geneticist Clarence Cook "C.C." Little was chosen to serve as the TIRC's scientific director. Little was an avowed skeptic of the link between smoking and cancer, and he consistently promoted the notion that such a connection was controversial and far from certain. As such, many of the studies that Little promoted while at the helm of the TIRC stressed the role of heredity in cancer, thereby articulating a potential uncertainty regarding smoking as carcinogenic. And in general, Little's TIRC consistently advanced the position that there were many possible causes of cancer, thus making it shortsighted to conclude that cigarettes are carcinogenic. This stance was promoted through the TIRC's periodical *Tobacco and Health*, which was distributed, free of charge, to, among other influential professions, doctors and dentists. With a circulation of over 500,000, the TIRC's claims influenced untold numbers of doctors and patients. While many doctors and scientists felt the findings published by Little to be essentially compromised, the TIRC was nonetheless generally successful in its efforts to change what was a growing scientific consensus about cigarettes' pernicious health effects in 1953 into a fairly broad public and scientific debate by 1960. The public relations coup that the TIRC brought about thus amounted to effectively transforming science, which represented a grave threat to big tobacco's future success, into an industry tool that could convince concerned consumers to continue, or even begin, smoking.

On an operations level, the TIRC consisted of a Scientific Advisory Board (SAB), which was initially made up of seven respected scientists who were chosen by the tobacco industry, and an administrative staff, which largely directed the work that the seemingly independent SAB conducted so that the TIRC's findings did not harm the interests of big tobacco. Most of the projects sponsored by the TIRC actually had little to do with smoking, and instead focused on immunology, pharmacology, and virology in order to argue that other causes—not cigarettes—were responsible for increases in public health problems. When the TIRC did undertake a study of cancer, its research generally focused on genetic factors so that any conclusions the scientists might reach would not jeopardize the tobacco industry's basic claim that cigarettes were not carcinogenic. In this way, the TIRC simultaneously satisfied both SAB members' interest in pursuing scientific research and the tobacco industry's aim of funding science that appeared related to smoking but which would not undercut their claim that cigarettes were safe to smoke.

In 1964, the TIRC was renamed the Council for Tobacco Research (CTR), in part because of growing concerns about the agency's purported scientific objectivity. By the 1970s, it was clear to most that the TIRC/CTR was little more than a public relations enterprise. The TIRC/CTR's oft repeated claim that science had yet to discover what caused lung cancer came across as a tired explanation that stood in stark contrast to the findings of a growing number of scientists, including some of the tobacco industry's own researchers (though their work and conclusions would not be made public for many years), that smoking cigarettes was clearly a cause of cancer. As a result, in 1968, Hill & Knowlton ended their partnership with the tobacco industry, and the Tobacco Institute overtook the CTR as the public relations arm of big tobacco. A less powerful and influential CTR existed until the 1998 Master Settlement Agreement, under the terms of which the CTR was forced to disband.

(See also **Hill & Knowlton**; **Master Settlement Agreement (MSA)**; **Tobacco Institute**)

References

Brandt, Allan M. 2007. *The Cigarette Century: The Rise, Fall, and Deadly Persistence of the Product That Defined America*. New York: Basic Books.

Cordry, Harold V. 2001. *Tobacco: A Reference Handbook*. Santa Barbara, CA: ABC-CLIO.

Goodman, Jordan, ed. 2005. *Tobacco in History and Culture: An Encyclopedia*. Detroit: Thomson Gale.

Parker-Pope, Tara. 2001. *Cigarettes: Anatomy of an Industry from Seed to Smoke*. New York: The New Press.

TOBACCO INSTITUTE

The Washington-based Tobacco Institute was the tobacco industry's trade group and lobbying organization. Founded in 1958 with the help of the public relations firm Hill & Knowlton, the Tobacco Institute worked alongside, and eventually overtook, the Tobacco Industry Research Committee (TIRC) as the unified voice and public relations arm of the nation's cigarette manufacturers. The Tobacco Institute, which for forty years directed its resources toward shifting public policy and popular attitudes regarding smoking and its health effects, was disbanded under the terms of the 1998 Master Settlement Agreement.

The Tobacco Institute was founded by the tobacco industry in 1958 after consultations with Hill & Knowlton, its public relations firm at the time. The tobacco companies began their partnership with the renowned firm in 1953 as a result of a growing wave of scientific reports that linked smoking to cancer. With publications in periodicals like *Reader's Digest*, *Ladies Home Journal*, *The New Republic*, *Consumer Reports*, and *The Nation* leading to roughly 40% of the public holding the belief that smoking caused cancer and consequently generating a significant drop in the nation's level of cigarette consumption, the tobacco companies turned to Hill & Knowlton in order to stem the scientific and popular tide.

With the recognition that a new approach was necessary in order to ensure the survival of the cigarette industry, Hill & Knowlton quickly established the TIRC the following year, and the Tobacco Institute about five years later. These two industry-led agencies worked towards the same goal—to create favorable public policy and popular attitudes regarding smoking in the face of growing scientific evidence of smoking's dangers —but took slightly different approaches. The TIRC immediately announced itself as an institution dedicated to supporting scientific research into tobacco's health effects, though in reality it was designed, and functioned, as an entity that distorted, undermined, and discredited the growing chorus of scientific reports that linked smoking to cancer and other illnesses by co-opting the mantle of objective science. Alongside the influential TIRC (which was renamed the Council for Tobacco Research in 1964), Hill & Knowlton created the Tobacco Institute in order to help maintain the TIRC-generated uncertainty and controversy over the health effects of cigarettes. If it was the TIRC's design to sponsor deceptive science, it was the Tobacco Institute's job to help popularize its misleading findings. The Tobacco Institute was able to do this in large part because of Hill & Knowlton's extensive media contacts, which enabled them to shape the ways various media outlets discussed and reported the science of smoking and its health effects. In at least one case, the Tobacco Institute manipulated public opinion via secretly paying for an ostensibly objective magazine article to promote the tobacco industry's views. A less disingenuous but no less effective technique of the Tobacco Institute was to keep files on scientific experts, from laboratory researchers up to the Surgeon General, in order to be able to quickly launch attacks on the credibility of their conclusions. By promptly publishing "white papers" that rebutted damaging scientific findings, the Tobacco Institute was able to advance the notion that science's link between smoking and cancer was both debatable and deserving of "balanced" coverage. In effect, the Tobacco Institute popularized a controversy over smoking's health effects when, in actuality, science had essentially reached a consensus about smoking constituting a serious health hazard.

The Tobacco Institute was even able to create this debate regarding smoking and health within the medical profession. One means of achieving this was their distribution of the periodical, *Tobacco and Health*, at no cost to doctors and dentists. With a circulation of over 500,000 and its basic message that the link between smoking and cancer was uncertain, *Tobacco and Health* helped prevent the medical establishment from universally concluding that smoking was bad for their patients' health.

The Tobacco Institute was most active, however, in the arena of lobbying. By 1978, it had seventy lobbyists on its payroll, and by the late 1980s, the Tobacco Institute operated on a budget believed to be greater than $20 million. Its lobbyists, in Washington and elsewhere, repeatedly pushed the notion that the tobacco industry's financial well-being was an important element of the nation's economy. They made this central point through two annual publications, *Tax Burden on Tobacco* and *Tobacco Industry Profile*. Beyond lobbying efforts to resist increases in federal cigarette taxes, the Tobacco Institute actively labored to fight David Kessler's attempt to bring tobacco under the regulatory authority of the Food and Drug Administration in the mid-1990s.

By that time, however, Hill & Knowlton was no longer affiliated with Tobacco Institute. The influential public relations firm that had created the Tobacco Institute and directed its efforts ended its partnership with the tobacco companies in 1968 when the industry's legal concerns took priority over public relations. The Tobacco Institute continued to lobby on behalf of big tobacco up until the Master Settlement Agreement (MSA). That historic 1998 accord between forty-six states and the tobacco industry included an arrangement to dissolve the Tobacco Institute. After forty years of shaping and manipulating public policy and popular opinions about the place of tobacco in American life, the Tobacco Institute closed on January 29, 1999. The Tobacco Institute has not entirely disappeared, however, as the MSA stipulated that the

Tobacco Institute's documents, which detail decades of the industry's internal machinations, be placed on an easily navigable and publicly accessible Web site. These documents are available at http://www.tobaccoinstitute.com.

(See also **Food and Drug Administration (FDA)**; **Hill & Knowlton**; **Kessler, David**; **Master Settlement Agreement (MSA)**; **Smokers' Rights**; **Tobacco Industry Research Committee (TIRC)**)

References

Brandt, Allan M. 2007. *The Cigarette Century: The Rise, Fall, and Deadly Persistence of the Product That Defined America*. New York: Basic Books.

Burns, Eric. 2007. *The Smoke of the Gods: A Social History of Tobacco*. Philadelphia: Temple University Press.

Cordry, Harold V. 2001. *Tobacco: A Reference Handbook*. Santa Barbara, CA: ABC-CLIO.

Goodman, Jordan, ed. 2005. *Tobacco in History and Culture: An Encyclopedia*. Detroit: Thomson Gale.

TOWNS, CHARLES B.

Charles B. Towns was one of the leading figures in addiction treatment in the first two decades of the twentieth century, even though his cure for addiction was later debunked by scientists. He was also active in early narcotics control efforts, and was a staunch advocate of the view that all addictions were diseases that needed to be cured. He remained a leading figure in the field of addiction through the 1930s.

Charles B. Towns was born in La Grange, Georgia on January 12, 1862. He began his career as an insurance salesman in Georgia, and moved to New York City in 1901 to work in the stock market. After a failure working for a brokerage firm, Towns began claiming that he had devised a cure for drug habits, and he placed advertisements in the newspaper to convince people to try it out. Even though he had no medical training, Towns was confident that he could perfect a lasting cure for drug addiction. Experimenting on unsuspecting addicts whom he sometimes physically restrained, Towns claimed to have perfected a "cure" for addiction—a concoction that consisted of bark, hyoscyamus, and belladonna—that he gave to addicts every thirty minutes. He would provide addicts with this mixture, combined with a regimen of strychnine and laxatives, to sedate them while purging their system of drugs, and he would also administer progressively diminishing doses of opiates over the course of three days. By the end of the treatment, Towns claimed, addicts would feel better, and no longer want to use opiates. At first, many in the medical profession were skeptical about Towns' methods, and claimed that it did little but induce discomfort and diarrhea. But within a few years, he was able to convince Dr. Alexander Lambert of Cornell University that his formula worked, and soon it gained the approval of the scientific community when it was published in the *Journal of the American Medical Association*. Soon Towns founded the Towns Hospital, where he started a business giving his "Towns-Lambert" addiction cures to addicts. Towns boasted that he was able to cure 75 to 90% of the addicts who entered his program within five days. This claim, however, was most certainly an exaggeration; if an individual did not return to his clinic, Towns assumed that they had been "cured," and he did not account for the possibility that they may have relapsed or found his methods too painful to endure again.

Lambert, who was also President Theodore Roosevelt's personal physician, arranged for Towns to market his cure overseas, and by 1908, Towns claimed to have treated 4,000 opium addicts in China. He soon expanded his method to include the treatment of alcoholism and tobacco addiction as well, and in 1915 he published a work to spread word of his cure—*Habits That Handicap: The Menace of Opium, Alcohol, and Tobacco, and the Remedy*. The apparent success of Towns' methods was used not only to medical ends, but also political ones; the promise his cure held made it seem possible that any addict could be cured, and that by extension, it would not be cruel to legally force them to quit using narcotics. He did not hesitate to use his prestige to influence policy, as he advocated for tighter federal controls over narcotics. He was particularly active in the anti-narcotics campaign in his adopted home state of New York. In 1913, he drafted an anti-narcotic law for New York State, which was eventually presented in the legislature and passed as the Boylan Act in 1914. He also spoke out publicly against what he deemed the shortcomings of the Harrison Narcotics Act, claiming that the government needed to crack down on smuggling, and close up potential loopholes in the legislation.

By the 1920s, many in the medical community began to question the efficacy of Towns' cure, but many hospitals continued similar methods in their treatment of addiction, and Towns himself continued to treat addicts through the 1930s. Towns used his skills as a salesman to continue attracting patients, claiming that his cure worked not only for opiates, but also addiction to alcohol, tobacco, coffee and tea, all of which he claimed were potentially dangerous. One of the more prominent individuals attracted to his cure was Bill Wilson, the future founder of Alcoholics Anonymous, and Towns' view of alcoholism as a treatable disease helped inspire Wilson as he wrote *The Big Book of Alcoholics Anonymous*. Towns' fame began to wane in the 1930s, and he passed away in 1947.

(See also **Alcoholics Anonymous (AA)**; **Boylan Act**; **Harrison Narcotics Act**)

References

Acker, Caroline Jean. 2002. *Creating the American Junkie: Addiction Research in the Classic Era of Narcotic Control*. Baltimore: Johns Hopkins University Press.

Belenko, Steven R., ed. 2000. *Drugs and Drug Policy in America: A Documentary History*. Westport, CT: Greenwood Press.

Lobdell, Jared C. 2004. *This Strange Illness: Alcoholism and Bill W..* New York: Aldine de Gruyter.

Musto, David F., ed. 2002. *Drugs in America: A Documentary History*. New York: New York University Press.

Musto, David F. 1987. *The American Disease: Origins of Narcotic Control*. Expanded Edition. New York: Oxford University Press.

"Obituary." 1947. *New York Times* (February 22): 13.

UNITED NATIONS

The United Nations is an intergovernmental organization that succeeded the League of Nations after World War II, with the aim of facilitating cooperation between governments in the fields of international law, international security, economic development, social progress, human rights, and world peace. As the global organization charged with addressing the most serious threats to international peace, stability, and health, the United Nations today helps orchestrate and enforce the global drug control regime, and also leads research into how states can best address the problems posed by addiction.

The United Nations was founded in 1945, as the successor to the League of Nations after World War II. Before the conflict, international agreements struck at Shanghai, The Hague, and Geneva had set up an international drug control regime administered by the League of Nations, but the outbreak of war in 1939 disrupted coordinated international drug control efforts. Nonetheless, the illicit drug traffic was interrupted during World War II, as disruptions to international trade hampered drug smuggling operations. However, the drug trade had potential to explode when hostilities ended. Political unrest in opium-producing countries such as China and Yugoslavia threatened to bring about a boom in uncontrolled narcotics production, and the development of new synthetic substances during the war could have created a new wave of addiction to substances other than opiates and cocaine. Soon after the United Nations was founded, the new organization began to pick up the work of drug control that had been left off by the League of Nations. In 1946, the drug control powers previously held by the League of Nations were given to the United Nations, and the organization established its Commission on Narcotic Drugs to set its drug policy agenda. In 1948, its Synthetic Narcotics Protocol required member nations to inform the body's Secretary General of any drugs used, or capable of being used, for medical or scientific purposes, in order to track the development of new synthetic drugs, so that the World Health Organization (WHO)—the United Nations' body in charge of public health—could decide if they were habit-forming and recommend international controls if necessary. A Drug Supervisory Board (DSB) was charged with overseeing the trade in synthetic narcotics. Though synthetic drugs were quickly brought under control, opium and coca production increased in the years following World War II, as nations in Latin America continued to produce coca and many of the countries in Southeast Asia that gained independence following the conflict were not subject to the opium control treaties that had been administered by the League of Nations. To address the potential problem of unregulated opium production, the United Nations initially considered establishing an international opium monopoly, but fears that opium-producing countries would exploit the system, as well as disagreements between countries that grew the drug and those that synthesized it for use, doomed the proposal. Instead, the United Nations adopted an Opium Protocol in 1953, which aimed to limit opium production by only allowing for the drug to be cultivated for medical and scientific purposes. The 1953 Protocol allowed just seven countries to grow opium for export, and required that other countries limit their opium production to their own domestic needs. The DSB was given the responsibility of determining how much opium each country would be allowed to grow, and a Permanent Central Opium Board (PCOB) was empowered to supervise international efforts to control opium production, investigate cases where

countries produced more than their annual allotment, and call for an embargo of opium imports and exports to punish noncompliant countries. The protocol required three of the seven states allowed to export opium to sign the treaty in order to be ratified—something that did not happen until Greece signed the agreement in 1963. Several important opium-producing states, notably Bulgaria, the Soviet Union, and Yugoslavia, did not sign the 1953 Protocol, thus limiting its impact, and opium production and processing accelerated in Southeast Asia. The agreement was significant, however, in setting the stage for subsequent treaties, and the DSB and PCOB occasionally uncovered violations of the international control regime by drug growers and traffickers. Opium, however, was the only drug subject to such tight controls under the 1953 Protocol, and other drugs began to proliferate; coca production flourished in Latin America, while industrialized countries began to manufacture increasing amounts of barbiturates, tranquilizers, and amphetamines in spite of the 1948 Synthetic Narcotics Protocol.

In 1961, the United Nations convened a conference to draft a new treaty, and seventy-three nations—including all of the major world powers other than China, major drug manufacturing states, and many countries that were key producers of opium, coca, and cannabis—attended. Countries from Asia and Latin America that grew opium, coca, and cannabis came to the negotiations hoping for looser restrictions on the raw materials that went into narcotics, arguing that manufactured drugs should be regulated just as strictly. These countries also sought to weaken the authority of the international control bodies to require reports on drug production and carry out inspections. Switzerland, West Germany, the Netherlands, Italy, Britain, and Japan, all of whom were heavily involved in the manufacture of synthetic drugs, came to the conference hoping to continue to regulate raw opium, coca, and cannabis, but did not want to see more stringent controls placed on the psychotropic drugs they produced. The treaty that came out of the conference—the Single Convention of 1961—wound up placing tighter controls over both raw materials used to make narcotics and manufactured drugs by requiring signatory nations to adjust their domestic legislation to institute tighter controls over psychoactive substances. The Single Convention united previous international treaties concerning drug control by setting up different control regimes for different drugs, depending on their effects. The Convention called for Schedule I drugs, including coca, opiates that had medical uses such as morphine, and some extracts of cannabis, to be produced, manufactured, imported, exported, distributed, and traded only if they were going to be used for medical and scientific uses. Schedule II drugs were subject to similar regulations, except when it came to the retail trade. As had been the case in prior agreements, countries were required to limit their production of these drugs to their medical and scientific needs. Schedule III drugs were subject to less restrictions, while Schedule IV drugs, including heroin, were considered particularly dangerous, and signatory countries were allowed, if they deemed it necessary, to ban their production and use. New drugs could be added to the Schedules without amendments to the Convention, through the WHO and the United Nations' Commission on Narcotic Drugs. Regulations governing opium, coca, and cannabis, however, were written into the text of the legislation—not simply as parts of the scheduling system—so they could not be deregulated without significant changes to the treaty. In 1968, an International Narcotics Control Board was created to regulate the production of, international trade in, and dispensation of, controlled substances, and also advise countries on how to crack down on the illicit traffic. In 1971, the Convention on Psychotropic Substances supplemented the 1961 Single Convention by adding LSD, MDMA, and other psychoactive drugs to the list of controlled substances, and the 1988 Convention Against Illicit Traffic in Narcotic Drugs and Psychoactive Substances called for signatory nations to strengthen provisions against money laundering and other offenses related to drug trafficking. Today, more than 95% of the member states of the United Nations are parties to the 1961, 1971, and 1988 conventions.

In 1997, the United Nations merged its Drug Control Program and its Center for International Crime Prevention to create a new organization, the United Nations Office on Drugs and Crime (UNODC), which assists member states in their fights against the drug traffic, organized crime, and terrorism. The UNODC operates in all regions of the world through a network of field offices, and relies on voluntary contributions from governments for 90% of its budget. To address the public health side of the drug problem, the WHO works on the problem of addiction—both to controlled and noncontrolled substances. The WHO assists countries in their efforts to prevent and reduce the negative effects of substance abuse, reduce rates of nonmedical use of psychoactive drugs, and it also assesses the potential that psychoactive drugs have for abuse, in order to advise the United Nations on how they should be regulated.

(See also **Drug Addiction and Public Policy**; **Hague Convention**; **League of Nations**; **Shanghai Commission**)

References

Carson-Dewitt, Rosalyn, ed. 2001. *Encyclopedia of Drugs, Alcohol & Behavior Second Edition*. New York: Macmillan Reference USA.

International Narcotics Control Board. "Mandate and Functions." [Online article retrieved 05/09/09] http://www.incb.org/incb/en/mandate.html.

McAllister, William B. 2000. *Drug Diplomacy in the Twentieth Century: An International History*. London: Routledge.

Sun Wyler, Liana. 2008. "CRS Report for Congress: International Drug Control Policy." [Online article retrieved 05/09/09] http://www.csdp.org/research/RL34543_20080623.pdf.

United Nations. "Convention on Psychotropic Substances, 1971." [Online article retrieved 05/09/09] http://www.unodc.org/pdf/convention_1971_en.pdf.

United Nations Office on Drugs and Crime. "About UNODC." [Online article retrieved 05/09/09] http://www.unodc.org/unodc/en/about-unodc/index.html.

United Nations. "Single Convention on Narcotic Drugs, 1961: As Amended by the 1972 Protocol Amending The Single Convention on Narcotic Drugs." [Online article retrieved 05/09/09] http://www.unodc.org/pdf/convention_1961_en.pdf.

United Nations. "United Nations Convention Against Illicit Traffic in Narcotic Drugs and Psychotropic Substances, 1988." [Online article retrieved 05/09/09] http://www.unodc.org/pdf/convention_1988_en.pdf.

Waddell, Ian G. 1970. "International Narcotics Control." *The American Journal of International Law*. 64, no. 2: 310–323.

World Health Organization. "Management of Substance Abuse." [Online article retrieved 05/09/09] http://www.who.int/substance_abuse/en/index.html.

UNITED STATES INTERNATIONAL DRUG CONTROL EFFORTS

To assist in its campaign to keep illicit drugs from reaching the United States, the Drug Enforcement Administration (DEA) undertakes a rigorous campaign to eliminate the crops that are grown in order to produce illicit drugs, and to intercept drugs as they come into the United States in order to prevent them from reaching local drug dealers. These efforts, however, only capture a small amount of the drugs that come into the United States illegally, as the DEA estimates that it is able to capture just $1 billion of the $65 billion worth of drugs that are illegally imported into, and transferred within, the United States each year.

Before the formation of the DEA in 1973, the Federal Bureau of Narcotics and U.S. customs worked to track and intercept illegal shipments of drugs coming into the country. After World War II, Federal Bureau of Narcotics agents were sent to Asia and Europe to work in tandem with criminal investigative branches attached to the U.S. military to assure that drug smuggling did not emerge in areas that had been under Japanese and German control. In subsequent decades, the Bureau sent agents across the world, working with informants and pressuring local police and governments to do more to crack down on the drug traffic.

To disrupt smuggling across U.S. borders, the government created Operation Intercept, which allowed for searches of all individuals crossing into the United States from Mexico. When the border searches came to an end, Operation Co-operation—which allowed for U.S. agents to be stationed in Mexico—began, thus further increasing American drug enforcement agents' presence outside of the United States. In 1972, U.S. drug agents, together with French police, broke up the "French Connection," an organized crime syndicate that had been smuggling large amounts of heroin into the United States—a success that showed how effective international efforts at drug control could be. With the formation of the DEA, American law enforcement became much more involved in international efforts to curtail the drug trade.

In the 1970s and 1980s, the United States stepped up its international efforts to curtail illicit drug production and trafficking. In 1975, the Mexican government began a crop eradication program, flying over and destroying fields of poppies used to make heroin, in Operation Condor. In 1976, it began Operation Trizo, which allowed for Mexican nationals to fly U.S. State Department planes to spray herbicides over poppy fields, thereby destroying crops that were used to make some of the heroin that was smuggled into the United States. The large number of arrests that accompanied Operation Trizo caused an economic crisis in the poppy-growing regions of Mexico, so to reduce the potential for social upheaval, the Mexican government asked the United States to call off the operation in 1978. In 1975, another international operation, Operation Stopgap, was created to crack down on drug

supplies coming to the United States from Colombia. The DEA flew up and down the Colombian coastline, and reported suspicious watercraft back to the United States; Coast Guard vessels were then put on alert, and Navy satellites were used to track the vessels as they moved towards the United States. This operation led to the seizure of over 1 million pounds of marijuana. In 1977, the DEA began working with the FBI, and achieved a major success in Operation Banco, which broke up a major drug smuggling ring based in Miami. In 1979, the DEA and Customs teamed up on Operation Boomer/Falcon, which focused on drug smuggling in the Turks and Caicos Islands, and led to the seizure of record quantities of illicit drugs.

In the 1980s, the DEA continued to carry out both domestic and international operations to cut of the illicit drug traffic. In the early 1980s, Operations Grouper and Tiburon targeted marijuana being smuggled from Colombia; in 1980, Operation Swordfish cracked down on the drug trade in Miami, while operations in New York and Detroit led to the arrest of a smuggling operation that brought Asian heroin into the country via Italy; and in 1983, a National Narcotics Border Interdiction System (NNBIS) was created to coordinate the work of federal agencies assigned to cut off drug supplies by air, sea, and land. The NNBIS launched Operation Blue Lightning in the early 1980s to crack down on drug smuggling in the area around the Bahamas. The DEA also worked internationally to capture individuals responsible for harming DEA agents, as it did in 1985 with Operation Leyenda, which led the organization to step up activities in Mexico and Costa Rica. In the late 1980s, the DEA worked with the

Colombian government to seize the assets of major traffickers, and at the end of the decade, Operation Snowcap led the DEA to carry out operations in twelve Latin American countries to suppress the growth and smuggling of cocaine into the United States. In 1988, the United States launched its first anti-drug operation that was directed from overseas, with Operation Blast Furnace, which aimed to reduce drug-growing and -processing operations in Bolivia. Most notably, in 1989 the United States was able to convict former Panamanian leader Manuel Noriega for working with international drug cartels. In the 1980s, the United States also supported crop-eradication programs in Colombia, Belize, Myanmar, Thailand, and Jamaica. In the 1990s, the DEA continued its operations, seizing drug assets of major traffickers in Britain, arresting leaders of the Cali drug cartel from four countries in Operation Green Ice, and also carrying out major operations in Asia, Latin America, and Africa. In addition, the United States has supported programs that substitute other crops that can be harvested as alternatives to opium in Pakistan, Thailand, and Turkey, and similar programs to displace coca production in Peru and Bolivia. Since 1990, the United States has shifted its international drug control efforts away from crop eradication, and increased its focus on keeping drugs from coming into the country and targeting major trafficking organizations.

U.S. agents' high level of involvement in international affairs, while deemed necessary if the United States is to effectively suppress the global drug traffic according to some, is seen by others as a troubling side-effect of the United States' war on drugs. Costing large sums of money and affecting lives across the globe, the United States' expansion of drug control beyond its own borders has, some critics would argue, escalated the war on drugs while doing relatively little to actually cut down on the amount of illicit drugs that reach American streets.

(See also **Drug Addiction and Public Policy**; **Drug Enforcement Administration (DEA)**; **Federal Bureau of Narcotics (FBN)**; **Drug Smuggling**)

References

Carson-Dewitt, Rosalyn, ed. 2001. *Encyclopedia of Drugs, Alcohol & Addictive Behavior. Second Edition.* New York: Macmillan Reference USA.

Chepesiuk, Ron. 1999. *The War on Drugs: An International Encyclopedia.* Santa Barbara, CA: ABC-CLIO.

Drug Enforcement Administration. 2008. "DEA History in Depth." [Online article retrieved 04/18/09] http://www.usdoj.gov/dea/history.htm.

Huggins, Laura E., ed. 2005. *Drug War Deadlock: The Policy Battle Continues.* Stanford, CA: Hoover Institution Press.

Nadelmann, Ethan. 1993. *Cop Across Borders: The Internationalization of U.S. Criminal Law Enforcement.* University Park, PA: Pennsylvania State University Press.

UNITED STATES V. BEHRMAN AND LINDER V. UNITED STATES

In the 1920s, there were two major Supreme Court cases involving the Harrison Narcotics Act, and in particular the question of whether or not doctors were allowed to prescribe maintenance treatments of opiates to addicts. In the two cases *United States v. Behrman* and *Linder v. United States*, the Supreme Court came to seemingly contradictory conclusions on this question, though ultimately the anti-maintenance interpretation of the law continued to have the most powerful influence on both law enforcement officials and medical practitioners.

Though the Court had already addressed these issues in the 1919 court case *Webb et al. v. United States*, legal questions remained in the 1920s. While it had already been established that doctors could not prescribe opiates just to relieve withdrawal symptoms, at what point could it be established that a doctor was indeed facilitating addiction? A step toward establishing this was made in 1922, with *United States v. Behrman*. The case involved a New York physician, Morris Behrman, who gave Willie King, a patient whom he knew was addicted to morphine, heroin, and cocaine, huge prescriptions for these drugs—enough to create 3,000 doses of them for non-addicts. King did not have any disease that necessitated the use of narcotics, so the authorities arrested Behrman for giving an addict drugs for self-administration. Behrman claimed in defense that he was indeed treating a disease—King's drug addiction. In a 6-3 decision, the Supreme Court ruled against Behrman, arguing that given the huge amount of drugs he had prescribed, and the fact that Behrman knew King was an addict, the doctor's prescriptions were not written for legal purposes. The only reasons that Behrman would have given such large prescriptions, the Court concluded, would have been either to facilitate King's addiction, or to give King enough drugs that he could sell or give them to others—both of which would have been violations of the

Harrison Act and the *Webb* decision. Some justices, notably Justice Oliver Wendell Holmes, dissented, arguing that doctors should be able to prescribe according to their professional judgment. But in spite of these objections, the court ruled against Behrman. The case established the precedent that even if doctors claimed they were prescribing controlled substances for medical reasons, there were limits to the amounts they could legally dole out to their patients. The case also gave footing to the principles established in the *Webb* ruling, as it further supported the idea that doctors could not legally prescribe drugs to addicts, and that narcotic prescriptions could be ruled illegal regardless of the physician's intent. Addicts, therefore, were left in the precarious position of having no legal sources for the drugs that they needed to avoid withdrawal symptoms. Doctors were also affected by the decision, as it emboldened officials in the Narcotic Division of the Prohibition Unit to crack down on physicians who prescribed narcotics to addicts, and many medical professionals were sent to prison in subsequent cases built upon the principles established in the *Behrman* decision.

In 1925, the Supreme Court heard a case involving Charles Linder, a Spokane, Washington physician who sold morphine and cocaine to an addict who was working as an informer for the Treasury Department. Instead of issuing a ruling that supported the *Webb* and *Behrman* decisions, however, the Court unanimously ruled in favor of Linder in this case. Given the small amounts of drugs involved, the Court found that Linder had not intentionally violated the law and that there was no reason to suspect that the recipient of the drugs had intention to sell them since she had received such small amounts—much less than were involved in the *Webb* and *Behrman* cases. In addition, the Court asserted that such prosecutions fell outside of the purview of the Harrison Act since it was a revenue measure designed to regulate commerce, not medical practice. The main significance of the case, however, was that it established the principle that doctors could prescribe small amounts of drugs to addicts, as long as it was done in good faith and as part of their medical practice, even if it was to relieve the suffering addicts experienced when forced to endure withdrawal. Implicit in the decision was the belief that addiction was indeed a disease, and that its treatment with small amounts of narcotics was acceptable medical practice. Though the case opened a potential loophole for physicians to provide maintenance prescriptions to addicts, the ruling had few ramifications outside of the courtroom. Officials in the Narcotic Division continued to carry out raids on physicians who prescribed drugs to addicts, scaring many doctors away from prescribing narcotics as the Court stipulated they could. In addition, lower federal courts were reluctant to follow the logic used in the *Linder* case, since popular opinion and sectors of the medical profession were at best indifferent, and sometimes hostile, towards addicts at this time. Consequently, even though the *Linder* case opened a legal window of opportunity for advocates of maintenance treatment, there were few real-world changes that emerged from the ruling. Nonetheless, the Treasury Department, fearing that the Harrison Act could be overturned as a result of the *Linder* decision, pushed for amendments to be made to the Harrison Act to fill the loopholes opened by the case. No such amendments were ever made,

though the Treasury Department's fears that the Harrison Act was in danger were allayed when the Supreme Court reaffirmed its constitutionality in the 1928 case *Nigro v. United States*.

(See also **Harrison Narcotics Act**; *United States v. Doremus* **and** *Webb et al. v. United States*)

References

Belenko, Steven R., ed. 2000. *Drugs and Drug Policy in America: A Documentary History*. Westport, CT: Greenwood Press.

Lindesmith, Alfred R. 1965. *The Addict and the Law*. Bloomington, IN: Indiana University Press.

Musto, David F. 1987. *The American Disease: Origins of Narcotic Control*. Expanded Edition. New York: Oxford University Press.

UNITED STATES. V. DOREMUS AND WEBB ET AL. V. UNITED STATES

United States v. Doremus and *Webb et al. v. United States* were two landmark 1919 Supreme Court cases that upheld the constitutionality of the 1914 Harrison Narcotics Act. These cases gave the federal government the latitude it needed to prosecute both doctors who dispensed narcotics for questionable medical purposes, and also addicts themselves.

According to the Harrison Act, people needed to have a stamp issued by the government if they were going to have narcotics in their possession. One exception, however, was for patients who received the drugs after getting a prescription from their physician. The law stipulated that these medical professionals could only prescribe narcotics "in good faith" and "in the course of...professional practice"—wording that was designed to prevent them from giving out prescriptions to recreational users or addicts. In a 1916 Supreme Court ruling, *United States. v. Jin Fuey Moy*, however, the government suffered a setback in its efforts to enforce the law as the Court found that a doctor who had prescribed morphine to an addict was not in violation of the act's provisions.

In the years immediately following *Jin Fuey Moy*, however, attitudes towards narcotics and addiction became more severe. After the United States entered World War I, many began to fear that a number of soldiers coming home from the battlefields of Europe would return with drug addictions that began when they took morphine as a painkiller. In addition, the movement towards alcohol prohibition was gaining momentum, and there was concern that alcoholics, when denied access to liquor, would switch over to narcotics. Fear of communism, which gripped the United States in the aftermath of the Bolshevik Revolution in Russia, also played a role in increased anxiety over drugs, as alarmists feared that drug habits could lead to degeneration and make the United States more vulnerable to a communist conspiracy. The fact that rates of addiction among the wealthy and middle classes declined thanks to the Pure Food and Drug Act of 1906 and the Harrison Act fed these fears, as the addict population shifted towards the social margins by the end of World War I. All of these factors converged to harden attitudes towards addiction and drug users. The consequences of these changes became clear in 1919, when the Supreme Court made two landmark decisions in the *Doremus* and *Webb* cases.

United States v. Doremus involved the prosecution of Charles T. Doremus, a San Antonio physician who, in March of 1915, provided 500 tablets of heroin to Ameris, an addict who was not suffering from any disease other than addiction, and Doremus did so without filling out the proper forms required by the Harrison Act. Beyond not keeping proper records and providing narcotics simply to feed addiction, Doremus could have been feeding the black market, since he provided Ameris with such a large amount of drugs that he could not only use them, but also sell them to others illegally. When Doremus was charged, the District Court found him innocent, claiming that the Harrison Act was unconstitutional since it was being used as more than just a revenue measure. According to the lower court, this use of the Harrison Act constituted an unjust encroachment of federal police powers into states' jurisdictions, since Doremus' actions did not significantly compromise the federal government's ability to collect tax revenue. The Supreme Court, however, disagreed. In its ruling, issued in March of 1919, the Court found that the Harrison Act indeed allowed the federal government to punish those who dispensed narcotics without a revenue stamp, and also that it could stipulate under what circumstances physicians could provide narcotics to patients. The Court supported the Treasury Department's claim that physicians could only give out prescriptions for controlled drugs in the course of their "professional practice." According to the ruling, providing narcotics to a patient without a prescription was illegal, and Doremus was found guilty. The constitutionality of the Harrison Act on these grounds, therefore, was upheld.

Webb et al. v. United States involved the case of two individuals in Memphis —a doctor (Webb) and a druggist (Goldbaum). The government claimed that Webb prescribed morphine to addict patients too freely—not to alleviate pain from a disease or to provide them with small amounts of morphine so they could wean themselves off of the drug, but rather in amounts large enough that they could continue to use the drug as much as they pleased. Even though Webb was writing prescriptions as a physician, he was doing so in a manner that, according to authorities, facilitated addiction instead of curing it. Goldbaum, the druggist, filled prescriptions written by Webb, even though he knew that many of Webb's scripts were being used to feed addicts' drug habits. The issue for both Webb and Godlbaum was whether or not prescribing and dispensing narcotics to known addicts just to maintain their addiction was within the bounds of the law. Evidence that the two were knowingly giving drugs to addicts was convincing, as Webb wrote prescriptions for over 4,000 individuals to receive morphine, and Goldbaum filled 6,500 of them in an eleven-month period. Even though Webb wrote prescriptions in accordance with the law, and Goldbaum possessed the revenue stamps required by the Harrison Act, the District Court found them guilty of conspiracy to violate the law since they were dispensing such a large amount of narcotics to such a large number of people. When Webb and Goldbaum took their case to Washington, D.C., the Supreme Court heard the case, and upheld the conviction. Some members of the Court believed that Webb and Goldbaum should have been innocent because they followed the letter of the law. The majority, however, held

that Webb and Goldbaum were not acting in good faith to cure addiction, but rather facilitating it by prescribing and dispensing narcotics so liberally. The majority opinion held that the actions of Webb and Goldbaum went not against the letter of the Harrison Act, but against its intention, which was to eliminate addiction and drug use—not legally facilitate it.

After the *Doremus* and *Webb* decisions, many of the doctors who had prescribed narcotics to addicts became more prudent in their prescription habits, and many of the narcotic clinics that had sprung up after the Harrison Act took effect closed. In the 1920s, the *Webb* ruling was upheld in *United States v. Behrman*, and though the Supreme Court opened a window for a different understanding of the Harrison Act in *Linder v. United States*, the interpretation of the Harrison Act in the *Webb* decision remained the law of the land. Consequently, many addicts, now without any legal channels to obtain their drugs, turned to the black market for narcotics, which grew substantially in the 1920s.

(See also **Degeneration Theory**; **Harrison Narcotics Act**; *Jin Fuey Moy v. United States*; *United States v. Behrman* **and** *Linder v. United States*)

References

Courtwright, David T. 2001. *Dark Paradise: A History of Opiate Addiction in America.* Cambridge, MA: Harvard University Press.

Musto, David F. 1987. *The American Disease Origins of Narcotics Control.* New York: Oxford University Press.

United States v. Doremus. 249 U.S. 86 (1919).

Webb et al. v. United States. 249 U.S. 96 (1919).

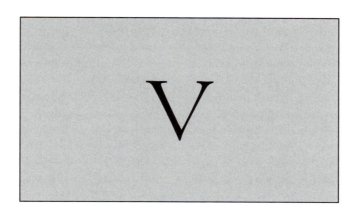

VOLSTEAD ACT (18TH AMENDMENT)

The Eighteenth Amendment to the U.S. Constitution ushered in national alcohol prohibition, but it was not until the passage of the Volstead Act that the new ban on the sale or commercial manufacture of alcoholic beverages was officially implemented as federal law in 1920. The Volstead Act was passed by Congress under the title of the National Prohibition Act, but it was popularly known as the Volstead Act because of the support and sponsorship given to the bill in the House of Representatives by Minnesota Congressman Andrew Volstead.

The name of the act is a bit of a misnomer, however, as its chief author was not Volstead, but rather Wayne B. Wheeler, the General Counsel and chief Washington lobbyist for the Anti-Saloon League of America (ASL). The ASL was a highly professional and organized lobby dedicated to the single issue of temperance, and the nonpartisan political pressure it applied translated into a broad base of power that extended to the point of being able to draft national prohibition legislation. The Volstead Act prohibited the sale or commercial manufacture of alcoholic beverages, and it enabled the enforcement of national prohibition, with the Bureau of Internal Revenue taking the lead. The law empowered the Bureau of Internal Revenue, which became the Internal Revenue Service in the 1950s, to fine brewers or distillers $1,000 for a first offense, or jail them for six months. Second offenses carried punishments of $10,000 and five years of jail time. The Volstead Act was not supported by President Woodrow Wilson, who vetoed the bill when it first came to his desk in 1919. His veto was based upon a general opposition to altering the U.S. Constitution. If Americans were unhappy with alcohol, he believed, it should have been the responsibility of state and local authorities—not the federal government—to institute tighter controls over its sale and consumption. Wilson's argument and opposition became a moot point, however, as

Congress overrode his veto by a 176 to 55 vote, thus making the Volstead Act, and thereby national prohibition, federal law on January 20, 1920.

However, with the passage of the Volstead Act, all alcohol did not instantly become illegal. The Act permitted Americans to retain all alcohol purchased before July 1, 1919, though these beverages could only be consumed in the home. As a result, many people rushed to purchase as much alcohol as they could before the summer of 1919, and hoard it so they could continue drinking after prohibition took effect. In addition, the Volstead Act also allowed men and women to manufacture their own wine and hard ciders, as long as these drinks were consumed in the home by members of the family. The law permitted an adult to produce 200 gallons of such drinks each year. So-called "near beer" (a brew that contained less than 0.5%, compared to 3 to 5% in regular beer) was also permissible under the law. Additionally, alcohol could still legally be produced by factories for medicinal purposes. Sacramental wines remained legal, too, with the Volstead Act authorizing, for example, each Jewish family to have one gallon of wine per year per adult.

Some of these exceptions were seized upon by those who still enjoyed drinking alcohol. Since up to 200 gallons of wine or hard cider per year could be produced within the home, many Americans transformed their places of residence into houses of alcohol production. The Volstead Act thus had the unintended consequence of driving many Americans not to sobriety, but rather to drinking at home. In a more marked defiance of the Volstead Act, speakeasies offered the experience of drinking in a bar or club for those who illicitly wanted to imbibe alcohol outside of the home. By 1925, New York City alone had anywhere between 30,000 and 100,000 speakeasies. Despite these infractions, the Volstead Act was somewhat effective, as levels of alcohol consumption did decrease overall during prohibition.

However, the Volstead Act's prohibitions on sales or commercial manufacturing of alcoholic beverages were transgressed so often that the court system became jammed with cases. Reports from the time noted that 22,000 persons were convicted of violating the Volstead Act in the first eighteen months after its passage. By 1926, the number of such cases increased to 37,000. In general, as Prohibition continued, there were growing rates of violation of the Volstead Act. Nationally, 44% of cases brought against U.S. citizens between 1920 and 1933 involved violations of the Eighteenth Amendment and the Volstead Act. In North Carolina, West Virginia, Minnesota, and Arkansas, the figure was 50% or greater. In southern Alabama, the center of moonshine production, the figure was as high as 90%. In 1928 and 1929, the Justice Department reported that prohibition cases accounted for almost two-thirds of all federal district court criminal cases and over half of all civil suits against the government. In order to try and combat the growing lawlessness that Prohibition had generated, the Volstead Act was modified in 1929 by stiffening penalties for infractions against it, but this failed to increase the effectiveness of the law.

The Volstead Act's days were numbered when Franklin Delano Roosevelt became the Democratic Party's candidate for president in 1932. The Association

Against the Prohibition Amendment had by that point convinced the Democrats to make repealing the Eighteenth Amendment a part of the party's platform. Just over a week into his presidency, Roosevelt asked the Senate to modify the Volstead Act so as to allow the manufacture and sale of beer and light wines. Two days later, on March 16, 1933, the Senate followed through with Roosevelt's request, effectively killing the Volstead Act. Prohibition was fully overturned with the final ratification of the Twenty-First Amendment on December 5, 1933, making legal once again the manufacture and sale of hard alcohol.

(See also **Anti-Saloon League (ASL)**; **Association Against the Prohibition Amendment (AAPA)**; **McCoy, Bill**; **Prohibition Unit**; **Speakeasies**)

References

Burns, Eric. 2004. *The Spirits of America: A Social History of America*. Philadelphia: Temple University Press.

Clark, Norman H. 1976. *Deliver Us from Evil: An Interpretation of American Prohibition*. New York: W. W. Norton Company.

Lender, Mark Edward and James Kirby Martin. 1982. *Drinking in America: A History*. New York: The Free Press.

Pegram, Thomas P. 1998. *Battling Demon Rum: The Struggle for a Dry America, 1800–1933*. Chicago: Ivan R. Dee.

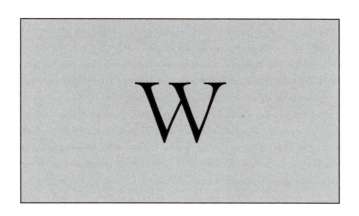

WASHINGTONIANS

The Washingtonians (or, as they are sometimes referred to, the Washingtonian revival or the Washingtonian movement) were one of the most significant temperance organizations of the mid-nineteenth century. The Washingtonians democratized the temperance movement and diversified its methods, for in addition to the existing use of evangelism and political activity within America to bring about temperance, the Washingtonians advanced the cause of alcohol reform through moral example, testimonials, and support groups. In this regard, the Washingtonian revival can be seen as an early example of "therapeutic temperance," a tradition that continued with groups such as Alcoholics Anonymous.

The Washingtonian movement began in 1840 with a decision made by six Baltimore drinkers. The story has it that while imbibing in Chase's Tavern one evening, the group's barroom discussion turned to the pernicious impact alcohol consumption was having upon their lives. Ignorant of, but intrigued by, what transpired at temperance meetings, the drinking crew decided to send a member of its group to attend a nearby temperance lecture and report back. Inspired by the lecture, the attendee convinced the other members of the group to pledge abstinence, and the drinking friends decided to form a new society dedicated to the reform of other drunkards. They named themselves the Washington Temperance Society, reportedly because they likened their struggle to gain freedom from alcohol to George Washington's revolutionary struggle against the British in colonial times.

With astonishing rapidity, the Washingtonians gained members who pledged to abstain from drink. Their success in gaining new adherents can perhaps be best understood as resulting from their novel appeal to lower-middle and working class alcoholics. Before the Washingtonians, the cause of temperance reform was largely led by teetotalers, elites, and religious individuals within established reform societies. While the ranks of the Washingtonians certainly included some elites, evangelicals, and abstainers, the movement was primarily one of artisans, workers, and small employers who sought to better their personal and economic lives by refusing alcohol. Women, too, joined the Washingtonian cause by launching auxiliaries called Martha Washington Societies. The diverse make-up of the Washingtonians constituted a democratization of the temperance movement.

The Washingtonians were also successful in gaining members because of their emphasis on saving individual alcoholics, as opposed to other temperance groups that advocated greater social reform and pushed for tighter legal restrictions on alcohol. In focusing on saving the individual drinker from his or her drinking problem—and not advocating prohibition—the Washingtonians likely appealed to drinkers who may otherwise have resisted more political or religious temperance organizations. Similarly, because many other temperance societies had bypassed drunkards by deeming them hopeless and irredeemable, heavy drinkers saw in the Washingtonian revival a movement comprised of individuals very much like themselves. As such, in 1842, Abraham Lincoln recognized the Washingtonians—themselves a group of recovering drinkers—as particularly well positioned to help other drinkers by being able to see the good in alcoholics whom others would write off as lost causes or simply bad people.

With this benevolent approach to reforming inebriates, the Washingtonian revival quickly spread from Baltimore to New York City and Boston, where Washingtonian speakers were invited to address drinkers at public meetings. These extremely successful rallies resulted in thousands of drunkards signing their names as a pledge of abstinence. But beyond the impressive spectacle of large rallies and powerful orators, however, the Washingtonians were influential because of their continued emphasis upon the individual drinker. Washingtonians stressed that for drinking habits to change it was necessary for the drinker to change his or her lifestyle. As a result, local Washingtonian societies gathered for weekly meetings for the purposes of support, encouragement, advice, and solidarity. Members often told sobering tales about the harmful effects that alcohol had on their lives, the benefits of their newfound sobriety, and the importance of remaining free of drink. When members relapsed into drinking, other members would rally around in support, providing the emotional, financial, and medical support to help them through the crisis. In this regard, Washingtonian methods prefigured the techniques that would later be employed by Alcoholics Anonymous. The Washingtonians also employed tactics that would become central to the mission of groups such as the Woman's Christian Temperance Union (WCTU). Anticipating the so-called "environmental approach" of the WCTU, Washingtonians labored to provide reformed drunkards with social alternatives to drinking. As an alternative to the lure of social life in the bar, Washingtonians created free reading rooms with newspapers and (temperance) literature, and they rented or built halls for group singing or mounting theatrical productions. These endeavors were central to the Washingtonian notion that successfully changing drinking habits depended upon altering the drinker's lifestyle.

The Washingtonian movement counted over a million members within its ranks by 1843. For a group that had been founded just three years prior, this seems an implausible figure, but accounts from the time indicate that 100,000 drunkards and half a million temperate drinkers were persuaded by the Washingtonians to sign a pledge of complete abstinence. One year later, however, the Washingtonian revival was waning, and by 1847, almost every local society had ceased meeting. The precipitous decline was in large part due to the loss of support from church and other temperance organizations, which had initially been supportive of the Washingtonian movement. As the 1840s progressed, these groups chafed at the notion of continuing to open their meeting places to a group that, with its emphasis on rehabilitating the individual drunkard, did not pay enough attention to broader religious and prohibitionist concerns. As a result, clergy and older temperance societies withdrew their support of the Washingtonians, and decided that their agendas would be better served by reinvesting energies in the cause of prohibition. The fact that many members of Washingtonian groups were ultimately unable to remain abstinent seemingly supported the conclusion that only way to truly defeat alcohol was to prohibit it. Over the course of the late 1840s and through the 1850s, many Washingtonians drifted into other temperance societies and fraternal orders, such as the Sons of Temperance and the Order of Good Templars. The Washingtonian revival's more long-lasting impact and legacy can be seen in contemporary groups such as Alcoholics Anonymous, which resembles the Washingtonians in its use of therapeutic temperance.

(See also **Alcoholics Anonymous (AA)**; **Woman's Christian Temperance Union (WCTU)**)

References

Blocker, Jr., Jack S., David M. Fahey, and Ian R. Tyrrell, eds. 2003. *Alcohol and Temperance in Modern History: An International Encyclopedia*. Santa Barbara, CA: ABC-CLIO.

Lender, Mark Edward and James Kirby Martin. 1982. *Drinking in America: A History*. New York: The Free Press.

Mendelson, Jack H. and Nancy K. Mello. 1985. *Alcohol: Use and Abuse in America*. Boston: Little, Brown and Company.

WEBB-KENYON ACT

The 1913 Webb-Kenyon Act was an important milestone in the early-twentieth-century antiliquor campaign that both secured prohibition laws previously passed at the local and state level, and also helped pave the way for national prohibition in 1920.

The Webb-Kenyon Act's passage in 1913 was presaged by decades of antiliquor activity and legislation. Perhaps most important in the lead-up to the passage of the Webb-Kenyon Act were the temperance activities of the Anti-Saloon League of America (ASL) and the Woman's Christian Temperance Union, which resulted in the creation of many local-option ordinances across the country. The ASL, in particular, focused on pushing for local-option elections, by means of which voters could determine whether saloons in their districts should be granted or denied licenses to sell alcohol. Focusing on various local-option elections—as opposed to larger, all-or-nothing state and federal campaigns—gave temperance advocates the flexibility to concentrate their efforts on winnable elections, and in this way they were able to effectively extend prohibition, piece by piece, to parts of states that had, as a whole, resisted going dry. By additionally working to elect local and state politicians sympathetic to prohibition, they built a coalition of politicians and voters willing to extend local prohibition laws. As a result of these advances on the local and state level, antiliquor forces were successful in getting nine states to pass state-wide prohibition laws by 1913.

Despite these local-option successes, prohibition advocates were frustrated by the continued presence of alcohol in areas that, by law, should have been alcohol-free. Though prohibition was in place, liquor dealers in wet states found exporting their alcohol into dry states to be extremely lucrative business. Dry states became prime target areas for expanding alcohol sales, thus jeopardizing prohibitionist gains that had been made via local-option elections. In order to prevent the influx of alcohol into dry states, the ASL went beyond their local- and state-level success and focused on federal law. Since the federal government regulated interstate commerce—the recently passed, anti-prostitution Mann Act of 1910 clearly evidenced this—antiliquor advocates extended their fight against booze by attacking the transportation of intoxicating beverages on a federal level with the Webb-Kenyon Act. The Act made it a federal crime with serious penalties to transport alcohol from wet states into states where booze was legally prohibited. Such a law was necessary to cement existing state prohibition laws because enforcement officers in dry states had no power over interstate commerce, and as such were essentially impotent when it came to stopping shipments of alcohol that were legally manufactured elsewhere across state lines.

On a certain level, the Webb-Kenyon Act's passage was a result of effectively casting it as a state's rights bill. By stating that the bill would bar the entry of liquor into any state if the alcohol was to be used in a way that violated state law, the ASL presented the Webb-Kenyon Act in a manner palatable to wets who resented federal control. This framing suggested that the nature of the bill was merely to allow state prohibition laws to operate without the interference of the federal government. As a result, Southern wets who were resentful of federal raids on moonshiners did not vehemently oppose the bill. The Webb-Kenyon Act thus figured simultaneously as agreeable federal legislation and an important strengthening of existing state prohibition laws.

The primary architect of this adroitly framed act was Senator William Squire Kenyon of Iowa, who personally abstained from drink and believed that temperance legislation was in the nation's best interests. The Webb-Kenyon Act's other namesake sponsor was Edwin Webb, a dry Congressman from North Carolina who pushed it through the U.S. House of Representatives. At first, the bill that the two men helped pass was summarily vetoed upon reaching the desk of President William Howard Taft, who was a vocal opponent of legal prohibitionism. Senator Newell Sanders of Tennessee, however, promptly got enough members of both houses of Congress to override Taft's veto, making the Webb-Kenyon Act federal law in 1913. The Webb-Kenyon Act's status as federal law was not truly solidified, however, until Wayne Wheeler, the powerful national attorney of the ASL and true author behind the Volstead Act, successfully defended the constitutionality of the Webb-Kenyon Act in front of the Supreme Court in a 1917 test case.

Emboldened and encouraged by the Webb-Kenyon Act, whose passage ultimately could not be stopped despite even a presidential veto, the ASL sponsored a "Jubilee Convention" later in 1913 in which the antiliquor movement declared that it would thereafter work towards a constitutional amendment for national prohibition. Five states passed state prohibition laws against alcohol in 1914, five more followed suit the next year, and four more states did the same in 1916. Twenty-six states had state-wide prohibition laws by the time the nation began fighting in World War I. The Eighteenth Amendment was ratified in January 1919, and national prohibition became effective the following year.

(See also **Anti-Saloon League (ASL)**; **Prohibition Party**; **State Drug and Alcohol Control Laws**; **Volstead Act (18th Amendment)**; **Woman's Christian Temperance Union (WCTU)**)

References

Lender, Mark Edward. 1984. *Dictionary of American Temperance Biography: From Temperance Reform to Alcohol Research, the 1600s to the 1980s*. Westport, CT: Greenwood Press.

Mendelson, Jack. H. and Nancy K. Mello. 1985. *Alcohol: Use and Abuse in America*. Boston: Little, Brown and Company.

Murdock, Catherine Gilbert. 1998. *Domesticating Drink: Women, Men, and Alcohol in America, 1870–1940*. Baltimore: Johns Hopkins University Press.

Pegram, Thomas P. 1998. *Battling Demon Rum: The Struggle for a Dry America, 1800–1933*. Chicago: Ivan R. Dee.

Rose, Kenneth D. 1996. *American Women and the Repeal of Prohibition*. New York: New York University Press.

WHISKEY REBELLION

The Whiskey Rebellion, which took place in 1794, was a violent uprising, primarily in Pennsylvania, of Americans angry with Secretary of the Treasury Alexander Hamilton's 1791 decision to levy a federal tax on whiskey distillers. Only after President George Washington assembled a force of 15,000 militiamen to put down the rebellion was the tax reluctantly paid. The suppressed rebellion evidenced the authority of the federal government to tax whiskey production, but it also marked the beginning of a tradition of underground whiskey production, often referred to as moonshining.

The Whiskey Rebellion's origins can be traced back to Congress' 1791 decision to levy a seven-and-a-half cent tax for each gallon of whiskey that was distilled from American grain. The tax soon increased to nine cents, and if the alcohol was produced from an imported product, such as molasses, the tax could reach eleven cents per gallon. Hamilton's measure also included a fee of sixty cents per year for each gallon of capacity in a farmer's still. It is likely that Hamilton viewed these taxes as a key component of the nation's health, both fiscally and physically, as historians have argued that Hamilton's measure may have been motivated by the need to finance the nation's continuing conflict with Native Americans, by the aim to bring equality to a marketplace in which molasses and rum were already taxed, and by the desire to curb America's level of alcohol consumption. At Hamilton's request, the federal government had assumed the states' debts from the Revolutionary War, and the federal government was also saddled with the costs of defending the country against attacks from Native Americans. Hamilton thought that a tax on spirit distillation would thus help the United States cope with its debts and operating costs. Additionally, Hamilton, who drank infrequently, possibly envisioned the tax as having a positive impact on the nation's well-being, as he believed that the extreme consumption of ardent spirits had a deleterious impact upon the physical, moral, and economic health of communities.

Hamilton's views were not universally held, however. Thomas Jefferson considered the tax a mistake, and farmers opposed its imposition on the grounds that it represented both an unfair financial burden on poor farmers and an unacceptable violation of their rights. With tax collectors effectively empowered by the federal government to inspect farms for hidden or untaxed spirits, farmers felt the federal government was, like the dreaded British, overstepping its bounds. Farmers were also troubled by this new federal tax because, should they wish to challenge a tax collector's assessment, they would have to leave their farm and travel to a distant federal court. The popular resistance to the tax was most vociferous in southwestern Pennsylvania, where, it has been estimated, 25% of America's stills were located. Farmers there announced that they had no intention of paying the tax, and that if tax collectors wanted to avoid a violent confrontation, government agents should stay away. When government revenue agents did try to enforce the law, they were often met with strong resistance. In Allegheny County, there were accounts of a federal marshal being attacked, and of a mob setting fire to a regional tax inspector's home. Numerous other fires, beatings, and attacks took place in the region, and a very common tactic of the angry farmers was to tar and feather tax collectors. Attacks were not focused exclusively on outsiders who attempted to enforce the tax, however, as farmers who cooperated with federal authorities and paid taxes on their distilled spirits are known to have been attacked by their rebel neighbors. Their crops and animals were stolen or slaughtered, and their homes and barns were broken into and damaged by mobs. In Washington County, one man was even attacked at knifepoint for allowing a building he owned to be used as a tax office.

Though focused in Pennsylvania, acts of violence were not relegated to that state's southwestern corner. Unhappiness with the tax extended west, as frontier farmers felt the tax was a challenge to their way of life, which, in many cases, involved using whiskey as a local currency for barter exchange. As a result, protesters from North and South Carolina, Virginia, and Kentucky joined Pennsylvanians in physically opposing the tax's implementation, often invoking the analogy of the Stamp Act of 1765, a British tax viewed by colonial Americans as unreasonably harsh and which helped spark the Revolutionary War. By 1794, the Whiskey Rebellion had reached new heights of violence and organization. In July of that year, 500 to 700 members of the Mingo Creek (PA) militia clashed with soldiers from Fort Pitt, who were headed by Major James Kirkpatrick. In the bloody fight, which took the lives of combatants from both sides, the most significant casualty was James McFarlane, the militia's commander.

Undeterred by his death, on August 2nd some 7,000 rural protesters marched on Pittsburgh in a show of continued defiance to Hamilton's tax.

In response, President Washington amassed a force of 13,000 to 15,000 militiamen from eastern Pennsylvania, Maryland, Virginia, and New Jersey. Under the leadership of Revolutionary War general and Virginia governor Henry Lee, and with Washington and Hamilton accompanying, this immense army overwhelmed the insurgents. Washington's three peace negotiators, who were sent ahead of the army to meet with representatives of the rebellion, secured an end to the Whiskey Rebellion before the army reached Pittsburgh. The rebels scattered in advance of the army's arrival, and the federal government contented itself with capturing twenty men for trial in Philadelphia. Two of them, John Mitchell and Philip Vigol, were convicted of treason and sentenced to death, though Washington eventually pardoned them both. By that point, the federal government had quashed resistance, enforced the unpopular tax, and effectively demonstrated its authority. The government's power was not absolute, however, as moonshiners began to covertly produce whiskey in response. Thus, the failure of the Whiskey Rebellion marked the beginning of both federal control over, and a tradition of underground production of, whiskey.

(See also **Alcohol Bootlegging and Smuggling**; **Volstead Act (18th Amendment)**))

References

Barr, Andrew. 1999. *Drink: A Social History of America*. New York: Carroll & Graf Publishers, Inc.

Burns, Eric. 2004. *The Spirits of America: A Social History of America*. Philadelphia: Temple University Press.

Rorabaugh, William J. 1979. *The Alcoholic Republic: An American Tradition*. New York: Oxford University Press.

WIGAND, JEFFREY

Jeffrey Wigand was in charge of research at the tobacco company Brown and Williamson from December 1980 to March 1993, heading projects to develop a "safer" cigarette. He was fired in 1993 as a result of his vocal claims about the hazards of smoking, and in 1995 he became the nation's most famous whistleblower as a result of his appearance on *60 Minutes* and the deposition he gave in a Mississippi case against big tobacco. In 1999, his story was turned into the critically acclaimed motion picture *The Insider*, with Russell Crowe playing Jeffrey Wigand.

Jeffrey Wigand was born in 1943 in New York City, the oldest of five children in a strictly Catholic household that eventually moved upstate near Poughkeepsie. He enrolled in classes at Duchess Community College but dropped out, in 1961, in order to join the Air Force, which sent him to an air base in Misawa, Japan. While in the country, he managed a hospital operating room, became fluent in Japanese, and learned martial arts, and after briefly going to Vietnam in 1963, he returned to the United States and earned a bachelor's degree in chemistry from the State University of New York in Buffalo. From the same university he also earned a master's degree and doctorate, both in biochemistry. After working in the medical field for a number of companies, including Pfizer and Union Carbide, a headhunter eventually connected him with the position of senior vice president of scientific research for Brown & Williamson in Louisville, Kentucky. It was a curious job placement, as Wigand had spent years working in the health industry, did not smoke, believed that cigarettes were carcinogenic and addictive, and was a committed scientist. A $300,000 a year paycheck and research budget in the millions of dollars likely allayed whatever concerns he may have had, and he later explained that he thought the job would give him the opportunity to develop a safer cigarette and thus make a difference. What he found upon beginning his employment, however, was that Brown & Williamson's research facilities were extremely antiquated and poorly staffed. In his quest to produce both a low-tar cigarette and a cigarette that would burn at a lower temperature and thus theoretically reduce smoking's fire risk, he hired a physicist, toxicologist, and an analytical chemist, but before either of these project got terribly far, Wigand realized that the company was not eager to see these plans succeed.

One indication of this was an environment that did not support open scientific inquiry. An example of this was a meeting of company researchers in Vancouver to discuss the possibility of developing an artificial substitute for nicotine, one that would mimic nicotine's pleasurable effects upon the central nervous system but lack its adverse cardiovascular effects. While the meeting itself seemed to support scientific investigation into creating a safer cigarette, Wigand later testified that the meeting's notes were highly redacted by Brown & Williamson's corporate counsel, the law office of J. Kendrik Wells, out of fear that the documents, if ever publicly released, would open the tobacco company to a liability suit. Wigand was also concerned by the issue of tobacco additives. By law, Brown & Williamson was required to submit a list of additives found in their products to the Department of Health and Human Services; however, the list remained, under agreement, unpublished so as to protect what was claimed to be proprietary information. As a result, a potentially carcinogenic additive such as coumarin, which gave tobacco a vanilla-like flavor, but had been banned in U.S. foods, could avoid government regulation and make its way into Brown & Williamson's pipe tobacco. When Wigand argued that coumarin should be removed to protect public safety, he claimed the company was reluctant to tinker with their product and possibly affect sales. Wigand was also disturbed by Brown & Williamson's general reluctance to support or promote a safer cigarette. After years of work on developing such a product, he concluded that the tobacco company would not promote a safer cigarette, since this would be tantamount to admitting that traditional cigarettes were dangerous to a smoker's health. Beyond the lawsuits that might follow such a move, making a health claim about their product would bring cigarettes under the regulatory control of the Food and Drug Administration (FDA). In Wigand's 1995 deposition, he stated the company had told him that if science affected sales, science would be of secondary importance.

Brown & Williamson CEO Thomas Sandefur, who later denied this claim, fired Wigand on March 24, 1993. Concerned about Wigand going public with inside information about the tobacco industry, Sandefur had Wigand sign a confidentiality agreement, under the terms of which he received a severance package that included health insurance for a daughter of his who required costly medical treatment on a daily basis for her spina bifida. Unable to find work, Wigand somewhat riskily agreed to help Lowell Bergman, a veteran CBS producer for *60 Minutes* who was seeking expert advice on a story he was doing on Philip Morris' abandoned project to develop fire-safe cigarettes. Wigand felt that such work would not violate the terms of his confidentiality agreement because the story dealt with Philip Morris, rather than his former employer. When he subsequently advised the FDA about how the tobacco industry knew cigarettes were addictive and how they manipulated nicotine levels to keep smokers hooked, Wigand received phone calls threatening his life, was followed, had his lawyers' offices broken into, and had his compensation package from Brown & Williamson cancelled. The loss of health insurance was particularly damaging to Wigand, as it greatly hampered his ability to pay for his ill daughter's medical care. Wigand then received FBI protection, and he continued meeting with FDA head David Kessler.

Wigand also agreed to a filmed interview with Bergmann, with it conditional on CBS legally protecting him if he were sued for breaking his confidentiality agreement with Brown & Williamson. Wigand taped the interview, but the segment was not shown during its scheduled debut in the fall of 1995. The interview— in which Wigand stated that cigarettes were nicotine-delivery devices, said that coumarin remained in pipe tobacco, and asserted that tobacco executives had committed perjury by swearing, under oath, that nicotine was not addictive—

was not aired because of CBS' concern about legal repercussions, particularly in the wake of ABC having paid $15 million in legal costs to settle a case brought against it by the tobacco industry. An additional factor may have been a fear of jeopardizing Westinghouse's impending purchase of CBS, which was chaired by Laurence Tisch, the son of Lorillard's chairman, Andrew Tisch. A transcript of the interview was nonetheless leaked to the *New York Daily News*, and Brown & Williamson subsequently sued Wigand for breach of his confidentiality agreement. With the transcript of Wigand's damaging interview now public, the tobacco industry launched a smear campaign that would paint him as an unreliable witness. They accused him of shoplifting, failure to pay child support, and spousal abuse, and the scrutiny likely contributed to Wigand's divorce from his second wife. Still, after a February 1996 article about Wigand's claims ran in the *Wall Street Journal*, CBS decided it was safe to finally air the *60 Minutes* interview. By then, Wigand had already given a major deposition in a Mississippi case against the tobacco industry, and Wigand's testimony was a central piece of Ron Motley's successful litigation against big tobacco. Up against a wall, Brown & Williamson dropped their suit against Wigand as part of the Master Settlement Agreement of 1998.

Already well known for being a whistleblower, Wigand became even more famous after his story was made into the major motion picture, *The Insider*, with Russell Crowe portraying Wigand. Wigand spent three years teaching Japanese and science at DuPont Manual High School in Louisville, earning the Sallie Mae First Class Teacher of the Year award in 1996. He is the founder of the nonprofit group Smoke-Free Kids and was appointed special advisor to Canada's Minister of Health.

(See also **Food and Drug Administration (FDA)**; **Master Settlement Agreement (MSA)**; **Tobacco Industry Research Committee (TIRC)**)

References

Cordry, Harold V. 2001. *Tobacco: A Reference Handbook*. Santa Barbara, CA: ABC-CLIO.

Newsmakers 2000. Issue 4. Gale Group, 2000.

Pringle, Peter. 1998. *Cornered: Big Tobacco at the Bar of Justice*. New York: Henry Holt and Company, Inc.

Zegart, Dan. 2000. *Civil Warriors: The Legal Siege on the Tobacco Industry*. New York: Delacorte Press.

WILEY, HARVEY WASHINGTON

Harvey Washington Wiley, as head of the federal Department of Agriculture, became famous as the father of the 1906 Pure Food and Drug Act, which aimed to regulate dangerous substances, including alcohol and narcotics. Upon leaving his government post in 1912, Wiley became a powerful advocate of prohibition as a high-ranking member of the Anti-Saloon League.

Harvey Washington Wiley was born on October 18, 1844 in Kent, Indiana and graduated from Hanover College. He also received diplomas from Indiana Medical College and Harvard University. His education came in the fields of chemistry and medicine, and Wiley built upon this training by spending the first decade of his professional career as a professor of chemistry at Purdue University and as Indiana's state chemist. From being the top chemist in his native Indiana, Wiley went a step further and became chief chemist in the federal Department of Agriculture in 1883. In the nearly thirty years that he spent in nation's Department of Agriculture, Wiley overhauled its operations and ambitions. A department that employed six people when he arrived developed into one of the federal government's most effective agencies, and its staff grew to over 500 employees under Wiley. However, Wiley's most famous accomplishment as head of the Department of Agriculture was his campaigning for the 1906 passage of the Pure Food and Drug Act, which marked one of the most significant developments of the Progressive era.

The Pure Food and Drug Act forbade the transportation across state lines of adulterated or mislabeled food and drugs, and established that drugs had to follow purity standards set by the U.S. pharmacopoeia and national formulary. Items containing alcohol or narcotics remained legal, but by stipulating that ingredients such as alcohol, opium, opium derivatives, cocaine, or other potentially habit-forming drugs must be listed on labels, consumers gained a far greater awareness of what they, up until the passage of the Act, had been consuming blindly. As a result of this increased transparency, Americans began consuming less alcohol and narcotics. For his labor on behalf of this important bill's passage, Wiley became known as the "Father of the Pure Food and Drug Act." Wiley and his Pure Food and Drugs Act also had a bearing on the long-contentious definition of whiskey in the United States. Though the 1906 act only loosely defined whiskey, Wiley used his post to enforce the law. For example, Wiley blocked the importation of Canadian Club whiskey because it was not labeled a blend. Wiley's stance on whiskey's proper labeling was ultimately overrun in 1909 when President William Howard Taft, as a result of the liquor industry's prodding, decided that the centuries-old popular definition of whiskey—any liquor distilled from grain—would remain in effect.

Linked to Wiley's broader aim of protecting the nation's health via the regulation of harmful substances and chemicals in Americans' diet, he eventually concluded that alcohol and narcotics were also dangerous. When it came to alcohol, Wiley did not start out as a prohibitionist, but over time, he came to consider all forms of alcohol an unmitigated evil. Hence, when he left the post of chief chemist of the Federal Department of Agriculture in 1912, Wiley backed national prohibition. He even suggested worldwide prohibition as a means of combating the pernicious effects of alcohol. He also advocated for tighter controls over narcotics, and proposed an amendment to the Pure Food and Drug Act that would have banned interstate commerce in patent medicines that contained habit-forming drugs such as opium, though this change in the law never came to fruition. Nonetheless, he was a strong advocate for tighter controls on the trade in narcotics.

When his career in the Department of Agriculture ended, Wiley worked as a crusader against what he saw as a worldwide alcohol problem, joining the Anti-Saloon League in 1925, and serving as the vice president of its District of Columbia chapter. He fervently championed the Volstead Act and the Eighteenth Amendment, and his dedication to the antiliquor cause did not waver despite widespread popular resentment of, and opposition to, prohibition in the years leading up to its constitutional repeal. Wiley died on June 30, 1930 in Washington, D.C., three years before the repeal of national prohibition.

(See also **Anti-Saloon League (ASL)**; **Pure Food and Drug Act**; **Volstead Act (18th Amendment)**)

References

Blocker, Jr., Jack S., David M. Fahey, and Ian R. Tyrrell, eds. 2003. *Alcohol and Temperance in Modern History: An International Encyclopedia*. Santa Barbara, CA: ABC-CLIO.

Lender, Mark Edward. 1984. *Dictionary of American Temperance Biography: From Temperance Reform to Alcohol Research, the 1600s to the 1980s*. Westport, CT: Greenwood Press.

Musto, David F. 1987. *The American Disease: Origins of Narcotics Control*. Expanded Edition. New York: Oxford University Press.

WOMAN'S CHRISTIAN TEMPERANCE UNION (WCTU)

The Woman's Christian Temperance Union (WCTU) was the nineteenth century's most important temperance organization. In addition to its extensive anti-alcohol campaigns, the WCTU engaged in a variety of reform efforts, including women's suffrage, making it the first mass movement of women in American history.

The women's crusade against alcohol began in the 1870s with somewhat spontaneous challenges by women to saloon keepers, initially in Hillsboro, Ohio, but also across the country. This loose movement of women gained greater organizational coherence with the founding of the WCTU in Fredonia, New York in 1873. Under the leadership of its second president, Frances Elizabeth Willard (1829–1898), the WCTU played an important role in both the women's suffrage and temperance movements. Willard's stewardship, which began in 1879, transformed the WCTU from a fairly conservative group into a politically powerful organization with broad reform ambitions. Willard effectively expanded the WCTU's initial mission of temperance into a multifaceted platform that attracted a much wider female membership base, with around 150,000 to 200,000 members and 10,000 local units at its height.

Much of the WCTU's success as a major union was the result of Willard's leadership. A devout Methodist from Wisconsin, Willard rose to prominence as the first woman in the United States to become president of an institution of higher learning. After three years as dean of women at Northwestern University, Willard devoted herself full time to temperance and suffrage work, helping put together the WCTU's first national convention, which took place in Cleveland, Ohio in 1874, and featured the union's distinctive white ribbon emblem. In Willard's WCTU, women labored hard on the local and state levels by sponsoring temperance speeches, organizing petitions, distributing prohibition ballots, and raising money for shelters. "Hatchetation," the violent technique of physically attacking saloons carried out by more radical members like Carry Nation, represented only a short-lived aberration

from the union's highly systematic and orderly reform efforts. One of Willard's most significant actions was to advance a "Do Everything" policy for the WCTU in 1881. This mission effectively linked the temperance movement to a multitude of other causes, and the WCTU created between thirty-five and forty-five separate "reform departments" to work on the various issues now a part of its expanded platform. The "Do Everything" WCTU featured departments that, among other things, pursued women's suffrage, disseminated information on tobacco and narcotics, worked towards world peace, advocated prison reform, called for higher wages for workers, aided prostitutes, opposed gambling, worked to suppress the desecration of the Sabbath, called for grape juice to replace sacramental wine, fought against bigamy, and worked to assimilate immigrants, Blacks, and Native Americans into mainstream society. Willard herself worked as the director of the Social Purity Department, which lobbied for laws against rape, prostitution, and sexual intercourse with women under the age of eighteen. With this much-broadened platform, the WCTU attracted a far wider membership base than they might have been able to if they remained focused on the single issue of temperance.

Perhaps the most important and successful reform department within the WCTU was the Department of Scientific Temperance Instruction, which promoted temperance education within the nation's public school system. The literature that the WCTU produced for temperance curricula asserted that alcohol was a poison, and that people should never drink. Towards this end, the WCTU solicited the support, though it was sometimes only reluctantly given, of scientists. For instance, the prominent medical researcher Thomas D. Crothers developed Scientific Temperance Instruction materials for the WCTU to distribute in public schools. But his partnership with the WCTU was not exactly a perfect union, as Crothers was reluctant to accept a prohibitionist platform. Regardless, these efforts were successful in getting Congress to pass a law that made temperance education compulsory in all schools under federal control.

Most of the WCTU's efforts revolved around the notion of "home protection," which stressed that alcohol was a women's issue because liquor had a major impact upon goings on within the home. Since the home was traditionally the woman's domain, it was only sensible, the WCTU argued, that women politically involve themselves in temperance activities that, by eliminating drunkenness, would help improve family life. As a result of the theme of "home protection," the WCTU was effectively able to link the temperance and women's suffrage movements in a way that was highly attractive to thousands of women who were previously politically uninvolved.

Despite significant political influence on the local and state levels, Willard was less effective in making the WCTU a national political power. Willard's attempts to make the WCTU a political force for national prohibition revolved around the union's 1884 endorsement of the Prohibition Party, which was founded in 1869 as a national temperance party by advocates who had grown frustrated with the ineffectual anti-alcohol efforts of the Republicans and Democrats. However, this temporary political alliance between the WCTU and the Prohibition Party led to the defection of many Republican women from the WCTU and the subsequent founding of a splinter, nonpartisan branch of the WCTU. The 1890s thus saw the diminution of the WCTU as a player in national politics. The WCTU fared even worse toward the turn of the century. In 1898, Willard died, and the WCTU would not find a leader as capable of mobilizing the group's base like she had done. At the same time, financial woes for the WCTU compounded the difficulties generated by Willard's passing. As a result, the Anti-Saloon League of America (ASL) was primed to take over the lead of the temperance movement in the twentieth century. Dominated by men, nonpartisan in its approach, and dedicated to the single political goal of national prohibition, the ASL effectively displaced the WCTU from the position of the nation's most important temperance organization.

The WCTU did not disappear, however, and the union exists to this day. It became a charter member of the United Nation's Non-Governmental Organizations, and the union's chief publication, *The Union Signal*, lives on as a quarterly journal. The WCTU maintains a Web site (http://www.WCTU.org), and it continues to oppose alcohol, tobacco, narcotics, and pornography, primarily through a variety of classroom education projects, including annual essay contests.

(See also **Anti-Saloon League (ASL)**; **Crothers, Thomas Davison**; **Nation, Carry**; **Prohibition Party**; **Woman's Christian Temperance Union (WCTU)**))

References

Blocker, Jr., Jack S., David M. Fahey, and Ian R. Tyrrell, eds. 2003. *Alcohol and*

Temperance in Modern History: An International Encyclopedia. Santa Barbara, CA: ABC-CLIO.

Burns, Eric. 2004. *The Spirits of America: A Social History of America.* Philadelphia: Temple University Press.

Lender, Mark Edward and James Kirby Martin. 1982. *Drinking in America: A History.* New York: The Free Press.

Mendelson, Jack H. and Nancy K. Mello. 1985. *Alcohol: Use and Abuse in America.* Boston: Little, Brown and Company.

Murdock, Catherine Gilbert. 1998. *Domesticating Drink: Women, Men, and Alcohol in America, 1870–1940.* Baltimore: The Johns Hopkins University Press.

Pegram, Thomas P. 1998. *Battling Demon Rum: The Struggle for a Dry America, 1800–1933.* Chicago: Ivan R. Dee.

Szymanski, Ann-Marie E. 2003. *Pathways to Prohibition: Radicals, Moderates, and Social Movement Outcomes.* Durham, NC: Duke University Press.

Woman's Christian Temperance Union. 2008. "Issues of Concern." [Online information retrieved 11/12/2008] http://www.wctu .org/issues.html.

WOMEN'S ORGANIZATION FOR NATIONAL PROHIBITION REFORM (WONPR)

The Women's Organization for National Prohibition Reform (WONPR) was a major national organization that worked towards repealing national prohibition. It was founded in 1929 and headed by Pauline Morton Sabin, a wealthy and politically connected socialite who initially supported prohibition but changed her stance as a result of what she saw as a lack of respect for the Constitution that an unpopular ban on alcohol produced. Sabin's WONPR thus represented a marked departure from the Woman's Christian Temperance Union (WCTU), and it challenged the widely held belief that American women were strong supporters of prohibition.

Prior to the creation of the WONPR, women were generally considered to be strongly on the side of prohibition. The association of women with temperance activity was based upon prominent figures like Frances Willard, who headed the WCTU during the height of its powers, and Carry Nation, whose radical use of her characteristic hatchet to fight liquor made her the face of antiliquor crusading to millions of Americans. Furthermore, Willard's WCTU emphasized the notion of "home protection," which stressed that alcohol was a women's issue because liquor had a major impact upon the goings on within the home. Since the home was traditionally the woman's domain, it was only sensible, the WCTU argued, that women politically involve themselves in temperance activities that would better help them maintain their homes and the families within them. One of the WCTU's great achievements, then, was to effectively cast prohibition as a women's cause. The WONPR's emergence challenged this notion and altered the prevailing view that women stood united behind prohibition.

Many of the founding members of the WONPR were wealthy women whose husbands were active in the Association Against the Prohibition Amendment (AAPA), leading to the accusation that WONPR efforts were in reality the doings of the AAPA. Scholars have demonstrated, however, that the WONPR was a self-supporting and independent organization that truly represented the views of American women who were worried about the disregard for the Constitution that national prohibition seemed to be engendering. As such, the WONPR attracted more than 10,000 members across much of the United States within a year of its founding. The WONPR even claimed to have as many as 1.5 million members by 1939. Though the figure cannot be verified, scholars nonetheless believe that the WONPR constituted the country's largest anti-prohibition association by a large margin. And as WONPR founder Pauline Sabin put it, women joined the anti-prohibition organization "because they don't want their babies to grow up in the hip-flask, speakeasy atmosphere that has polluted their own youth." (Barr 1999, 152) Alcohol thus remained a women's issue, though now it was prohibition that threatened the fabric of family and society.

The WONPR was an important contributor to the success of the repeal movement in large part because of its symbolic, numerical, and political challenge to the WCTU as the organization that was most representative of women's views on alcohol. The modern, sophisticated, and fashionable image of the WONPR's largely middle- and upper-class members contrasted with the stereotypically staid and traditional WCTU member. Once it surpassed the WCTU in number of members, the rise of the WONPR began to signal that a changing of the guard had taken place. And since it had more members than the WCTU, the WONPR was able to place greater and more effective pressure on politicians.

The WONPR was a presence at both national political conventions in 1932, with its leaders addressing both Democrats and Republicans.

The WONPR sided with the former party after the Democrats made repealing prohibition a part of the party platform, and it endorsed Franklin D. Roosevelt in his presidential bid. Once he was elected, the WONPR wielded its lobbying power and applied political pressure on Congress to pass the amendment that repealed prohibition. Similarly, the WONPR was an important force in state contests that ratified the Twenty-First Amendment. The WONPR dissolved itself at a celebratory dinner two days after prohibition was repealed in 1933.

(See also **Prohibition Unit**; **Nation, Carry**; **Woman's Christian Temperance Union (WCTU)**)

References

Barr, Andrew. 1999. *Drink: A Social History of America*. New York: Carroll & Graf Publishers, Inc.

Blocker, Jr., Jack S., David M. Fahey, and Ian R. Tyrrell, eds. 2003. *Alcohol and Temperance in Modern History: An International Encyclopedia*. Santa Barbara, CA: ABC-CLIO.

Clark, Norman H. 1976. *Deliver Us from Evil: An Interpretation of American Prohibition*. New York: W. W. Norton Company.

Kyvig, David E. 2000. *Repealing National Prohibition*. 2nd ed. Kent, OH: Kent State University Press.

Murdock, Catherine Gilbert. 1998. *Domesticating Drink: Women, Men, and Alcohol in America, 1870–1940*. Baltimore: Johns Hopkins University Press.

Pegram, Thomas P. 1998. *Battling Demon Rum: The Struggle for a Dry America, 1800–1933*. Chicago: Ivan R. Dee.

Rose, Kenneth D. 1996. *American Women and the Repeal of Prohibition*. New York: New York University Press.

WRIGHT, HAMILTON

Hamilton Wright was a physician who became one of the staunchest advocates of narcotics control in the early-twentieth century, and was considered by some to be the father of American narcotics control. Through personal stubbornness and political skill, he became one of the architects of both global and domestic drug policies when they first took shape in the years before World War I, and he remained one of the most outspoken leaders of the campaign against narcotics—opium in particular—until his death in 1917.

Hamilton Kemp Wright was born in 1867, and began his career as a medical researcher specializing in the study of tropical diseases. He became involved in public health policy after he married a woman from a family with strong political connections in 1899. When the U.S. government began looking at the international opium problem more closely, President Theodore Roosevelt appointed Wright a member of a committee devoted to the study of the opium problem in 1908. Soon after his appointment to the opium committee, Wright enthusiastically worked to become a leading expert on the drug, its effects, and what steps should be taken to solve the opium problem both in Asia and at home. In addition to reading what others wrote about the opium problem abroad, Wright also conducted a national survey to estimate the prevalence of opium use in the United States, gathering information from prisons, police departments, local health and pharmacy authorities, and manufacturers. He also toured the country to see how the drug was used and controlled in U.S. cities. In the course of his research, Wright became alarmed by what he considered the widespread and problematic use of opium, its derivatives, and other drugs such as cocaine throughout the United States. Soon, he began pushing for the United States to institute a strict set of laws controlling access to these drugs and making them illegal except for medical use. As the first international conference to consider the opium problem prepared to meet at Shanghai in 1909, Wright pushed for national legislation that could be presented to the international meeting as an example of what good drug control legislation would look like. Together with Secretary of State Elihu Root, Wright advocated for new national laws, and in February of 1909, he succeeded with the passage of the Smoking Opium Exclusion Act.

After serving as one of the U.S. delegates at Shanghai, Wright remained a key player in the development of both international and domestic drug policy in the 1910s. In 1911, when officials from Britain, Germany, and Holland tried to delay the next international drug control conference at The Hague, Wright pressured representatives from these countries to come together and meet sooner rather than later. He then served as the chief U.S. delegate to The Hague conference that met in 1911. At times, Wright's insistence and self-righteousness irritated the representatives of other nations, as he came across as overly moralistic, irritating, and brazen in his demands that other nations adhere to the United States' agenda for international drug control. At one point, others who were advocates of a tighter international control system asked Wright to quit the anti-narcotics campaign since he tended to anger his opponents instead of convincing them to agree with his agenda. Steadfast in his belief that he was an essential part of the crusade against narcotics, however, Wright refused to quit, and he remained an influential leader in the move towards international narcotics control until the outbreak of World War I.

Even more importantly, however, Wright continued to push for tight federal narcotics laws at home. When he returned from the Shanghai conference, Wright warned that the opium habit was more widespread in the United States than in any other industrialized country, that drug habits were growing at an alarming rate, and that addiction would become a grave social problem if the federal government did not take swift and decisive action. Many of Wright's arguments had racist overtones, as he tried to convince lawmakers that opium was particularly problematic because of its association with Chinese minorities, and that cocaine was especially threatening because it made African Americans behave dangerously. According to Wright, even more disconcerting was that the opium habit was seemingly spreading beyond minority circles, and becoming a major epidemic among the White population as well.

Beyond trying to scare lawmakers into taking action, Wright also furthered the cause of drug control by writing model laws that he wanted legislators to introduce in Congress. In 1909, he drafted a piece of legislation that would have controlled the sale and purchase of drugs through taxation, requiring sellers to register with the government, record all of their drug transactions, and most importantly, have a special stamp issued by the federal government. He also wanted heavy punishments for anyone who was caught in possession of narcotics without this government stamp. First, he tried to persuade Illinois Congressman James R. Mann to introduce the bill, but Mann refused. Later, he convinced Vermont Congressman David Foster to introduce a bill that would have put new controls over opiates, cocaine, chloral, and cannabis, which eventually was defeated in 1911 because of opposition from the pharmaceutical industry. A few years later he had greater success, working with New York Democrat Francis Burton Harrison to draft, and eventually get Congress to enact, the Harrison Narcotics Act in 1914.

After his death in 1917, Wright's widow continued his work, and served as an American assessor of the League of Nations Advisory Committee on Opium until 1925.

(See also **Harrison Narcotics Act**; **Hague Convention**; **Shanghai Commission**)

References

McAllister, William B. 2000. *Drug Diplomacy in the Twentieth Century.* London: Routledge.

Davenport-Hines, Richard. 2001. *The Pursuit of Oblivion: A Global History of Narcotics, 1500–2000.* London: Weidenfeld & Nicolson.

Musto, David F. 1987. *The American Disease: Origins of Narcotics Control.* Expanded Edition. New York: Oxford University Press.

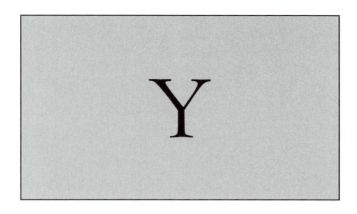

YOUNG, KIMBERLY S.

Kimberly S. Young is a psychologist and one of the pioneers of the study of Internet addiction. As both a practitioner and a researcher, Young has brought attention to the previously unknown problem of Internet addiction.

Kimberly S. Young earned her bachelor's degree from the State University of New York, at Buffalo, before getting her master's degree in clinical psychology and earning a Psy.D. from Indiana University of Pennsylvania. She then worked performing psychological assessments in the departments of neurology and psychiatry at Strong Memorial Hospital, in Rochester, New York, and she is currently a professor of Management Sciences at St. Bonaventure University's School of Business in New York. In 1995, Young founded the Center for Internet Addiction Recovery, and she has served as its director since its inception.

Young's interest in Internet addiction was spawned as the Internet was proliferating in the early 1990s, and, more pointedly, when she received a call from a friend whose husband was going online obsessively. At the time, many in the mainstream media were beginning to describe people who spent large amounts of time on the Internet as "online addicts," but there were few studies that had actually examined the phenomenon in detail. Struck by how her friend's husband's behavior was similar to many of the signs of gambling addiction, Young devised a questionnaire for Internet users to see what their online behaviors had in common with the actions of compulsive gamblers and alcoholics. In November 1994, she posted her questionnaire in chatrooms. She asked users if they found themselves becoming preoccupied with the Internet, if they needed to go online for increasing amounts of time to feel satisfaction, if they had tried to cut back but were unable to, if they experienced moodiness or depression when they had to go without the Internet, if they jeopardized jobs or relationships with their Internet use, if they lied to others about their Internet use, and if they used the Internet as a way to escape unpleasant feelings. Within a day after posting her questionnaire, Young had received forty responses from people all over the world, many of them answering yes to her questions. As she continued her study, Young found that approximately 80% of nearly 500 responses met the criteria for addiction as a result of their Internet use. Soon, the mainstream media took notice of Young's research, and began reporting on the spread of a new disorder—Internet addiction. In 1996, Young presented the first paper on Internet addiction at the meeting of the American Psychological Association. Thanks in large part to her work, clinics to treat Internet addiction were launched in Illinois and in Massachusetts, while some universities began offering counseling programs for Internet addicts. In 1995, Young launched her own Web site, the Center for Internet Addiction Recovery, to serve as a national resource on Internet addiction. In 1998, Young published *Caught in the Net: How to Recognize Internet Addiction—and a Winning Strategy for Recovery* to explain what Internet addiction looks like, why it happens, and what individuals suffering from the disorder can do about it.

Young has continued her work on Internet addiction, expanding her studies to look at the phenomena of excessive Internet use in the workplace, sex addiction and the Internet, online gambling addiction, and the treatment and evaluation of Internet addiction disorders. At the Center for Internet Addiction and Recovery, Young continues to offer assessment tools for individuals to determine if they have an Internet addiction problem, while she also serves as an expert witness in court cases in which Internet addiction and related disorders may play a role.

(See also **On-Line Gamers Anonymous and the Daedalus Project; Reference Essay**)

References

Center for Internet Addiction Recovery. "Dr. Kimberly Young's Bio." [Online information retreived 05/10/09] http://www.netaddiction.com/bio/bio.htm.

St. Bonaventure University. "About SBU: Young, Kimberly." [Online information retrieved 05/10/09] http://www.sbu.edu/About_SBU.aspx?id=11334.

Young, Kimberly S. 1998. *Caught in the Net: How to Recognize Internet Addiction—and a Winning Strategy for Recovery.* New York: Wiley.

PRIMARY SOURCE DOCUMENTS

DOCUMENTS 1–3:
DISCOVERING THE DANGERS OF ADDICTION

In the eighteenth and nineteenth centuries, medical researchers became aware of addiction as it is currently understood. Before this time, compulsive use of psychoactive substances was considered a habit, or a sin, as there was little understanding of addiction as a disease. This began to change in the late-eighteenth century with Benjamin Rush's work on alcoholism (Document 1). Rush was the first to describe compulsive drinking as a progressive disease, and though the term "alcoholism" would not become common until the late-nineteenth century, he did recognize the condition as an "addiction" that needed to be treated as a disorder and cured. If left untreated, he warned, the condition would lead to disease, madness, and destitution. Much of Rush's thought would influence the way that alcoholism would be viewed well into the twentieth century. In the mid-nineteenth century, European researchers discovered that other psychoactive substances—opiates and cocaine—could also become extremely habit-forming. In the United States, one of the leading medical researchers who spread the idea that these drugs could be addictive was Thomas D. Crothers. In Document 2, Crothers described the development of morphine addiction, which at the time was referred to as "morphinism" or "morphinomania." Document 3 describes a lecture Crothers gave at the New York School of Medicine, detailing how cocaine could become habit-forming and evolve into a social menace.

Document I

Benjamin Rush, *An Inquiry into the Effects of Ardent Spirits upon the Human Body and Mind.* Sixth Edition. New York, 1811: 1–36.

The effects of ardent spirits divide themselves into such as are of a prompt, and such as are of a chronic nature. The former discover themselves in drunkenness, and the latter, in a numerous train of diseases and vices of the body and mind. . . .

This odious disease (for by that name it should be called) appears with more or less of the following symptoms, and most commonly in the order in which I shall enumerate them.

1. Unusual garrulity.

2. Unusual silence.

3. Captiousness, and a disposition to quarrel.

4. Uncommon good humour, and an insipid simpering, or laugh.

5. Profane swearing, and cursing.

7. [sic] A disclosure of their own, or other people's secrets.

8. A rude disposition to tell those persons in company whom they know, their faults.

9. Certain immodest actions . . . .

10. A clipping of words.

11. Fighting . . . .

12. Certain extravagant acts which indicate a temporary fit of madness. These are singing, hallooing, roaring, imitating the noises of brute animals, jumping, tearing off clothes, dancing naked, breaking glasses and china, and dashing other articles of household furniture upon the ground, or floor. After a while the paroxysm of drunkenness is completely formed. The face now becomes flushed, the eyes project, and are somewhat watery, winking is less frequent than is natural; the under lip is protruded-the head inclines a little to one shoulder—the jaw falls—belchings and hiccup take place—the limbs totter—the whole body staggers.

The unfortunate subject of this history next falls on his seat, he looks around him with a vacant countenance, and mutters inarticulate sounds to himself. He attempts to rise and walk. In this attempt, he falls upon his side, from which he gradually turns upon his back. He now closes his eyes, and falls into a profound sleep, frequently attended with snoring, and profuse sweats. . . .

It belongs to the history of drunkenness to remark that, its paroxysms occur, like the paroxysms of many diseases, at certain periods, and after longer or shorter intervals. They often begin with annual, and gradually increase in their frequency, until they appear in quarterly, monthly, weekly, and quotidian or daily periods. Finally, they afford scarcely any marks of remission either during the day or the night. . . .

It is further remarkable, that drunkenness resembles certain hereditary, family, and contagious diseases. I have once known it to descend from a father to four out of five of his children. I have seen three, and once four, brothers who were born of sober ancestors, affected by it, and I have heard of it spreading through a whole family composed of members not originally related to each other. . . .

Let us next attend to the chronic effects of ardent spirits upon the body and mind. In the body, they dispose to every form of acute disease, they moreover *excite* fevers in persons predisposed to them, from other causes. . . . Hard drinkers seldom escape, and rarely recover from them. The following diseases are the usual consequences of the habitual use of ardent spirits. . . .

1. A decay of appetite, sickness at stomach. . . .
2. Obstructions of the liver. . . .
3. Jaundice and dropsy of the belly and limps, and finally of every cavity in the body. . . .
4. Hoarseness, and a husky cough, which often terminate in consumption, and sometimes in an acute and fatal disease of the lungs.
5. Diabetes. . . .
6. Redness. . . . .
7. A fetid breath composed of every thing that is offensive in putrid animal matter. . . .
8. Frequent and disgusting belchings. . . .
9. Epilepsy. . . .
10. Gout. . . .
11. Madness. . . . .

Most of the diseases which have been enumerated are of a mortal nature. They are more certainly induced, and terminate more speedily in death, when spirits are taken in such quantities, and at such times, as to produce frequent intoxication. . . .

Not less destructive are the effects of ardent spirits upon the human mind. They impair the memory, debilitate the understanding, and pervert the moral faculties. . . .

A more affecting spectacle cannot be exhibited than a person into whom this infernal spirit, generated by habits of intemperance, has entered. It is more or less affecting according to the station the person fills in a family, or in society who is possessed by it. Is he a husband? How deep the anguish which rends the bosom of his wife! Is she a wife? Who can measure the shame and aversion which she excites in her husband? Is he the father, or is she the mother of a family of children? See their averted looks from their children, and their blushing looks at each other! Is he a magistrate? Or has he been chosen to fill a high and respectable station in the councils of his country? What humiliating fears of corruption in the administration of the laws, and of the subversion of public order and happiness, appear in the countenances of all who see him! Is he a minister of the gospel? Here language fails me—if angels weep—it is at such a sight.

In pointing out the evils produced by ardent spirits, let us not pass by their effects upon the estates of the persons who are addicted to them. Are they inhabitants of cities? Behold! Their houses stripped gradually of their furniture, and pawned, or sold by a constable, to pay tavern debt. See! Their names upon record in the dockets of every court, and whole pages of newspapers filled with advertisements of their estates for public sale. Are they inhabitants of country places? Behold! Their houses with shattered windows, their barns with leaky roofs—their gardens overrun with weeds—their fields with broken fences, their hogs without yokes, their sheep without wool—their cattle and horses without fat—and their children filthy and half clad, without manners, principles, and morals. This picture of agricultural wretchedness is seldom of long duration. The farms and property thus neglected, and depreciated, are seized and sold for the benefit of a group of creditors. . . .

Thus we see poverty and misery, crimes and infamy, diseases and death, are all the natural and usual consequences of the intemperate use of ardent spirits. . . .

The remedies which are proper to prevent the recurrence of fits of drunkenness, and to destroy the desire for ardent spirits, are religious, metaphysical and medical. I shall briefly mention them.

1. Many hundred drunkards have been cured of their desire for ardent spirits, by a practical belief in the doctrines of the Christian religion. . . .

2. A sudden sense of the guilt contracted by drunkenness, and of its punishment in a future world. . . .

3. A sudden sense of shame. . . .

4. The association of the idea of ardent spirits, with a painful or disagreeable impression upon some part of the body has sometimes cured the love of strong drink. I once tempted a negro man, who was habitually fond of ardent spirits, to drink some rum (which I placed in his way) and in which I had put a few grains of tartar emetic. The tartar sickened and puked him to such a degree, that he supposed himself to be poisoned. I was much gratified by observing he could not bear the sight, nor smell of spirits, for two years afterwards. . . .Some men drink only in the morning, some at noon, and some at night. Some drink only on a market day, some at one tavern only, and some only in one kind of company. Now by finding a new and interesting employment, or subject of conversation for drunkards at the usual times in which they have been accustomed to drink, and by restraining them by the same means from those places and companions, which suggested to them the idea of ardent spirits, their habits of intemperance may be completely destroyed.

5. The love of ardent spirits has sometimes been subdued by exciting a counter passion in the mind. . . .

6. A diet consisting wholly of vegetables. . . .

7. Blisters to the ankles. . . .

8. A violent attack of an acute disease. . . .

9. A salivation. . . .

10. I have known an oath taken before a magistrate, to drink no more spirits, produce a perfect cure of drunkenness.

11. An advantage would probably arise from frequent representations being made to drunkards, not only of the certainty, but of the *suddenness* of death, from habits of intemperance.

12. It has been said, that the disuse of spirits should be gradual, but my observations authorize me to say, that persons who have been addicted to them, should abstain from them *suddenly* and *entirely*. "Taste not, handle not, touch not," should be inscribed upon every vessel that contains spirits in the house of a man, who wishes to be cured of habits of intemperance. To obviate for a while, the debility which arises from the sudden abstraction of the stimulus of spirits, laudanum, or bitters infused in water, should be taken, and perhaps a larger quantity of beer or wine, than is consistent with the strict rules of temperate living. By the temporary use of these substitutes for spirits, I have never known the transition to sober habits, to be attended with any bad effects but often with permanent health of body, and peace of mind.

Document 2

Thomas D. Crothers, *Morphinism and Narcomanias from Other Drugs.* Philadelphia: W.B. Saunders & Company, 1902: 42–51.

The term "morphinism" describes a condition following the prolonged use of morphin either by the needle under the skin or in solution by the mouth.

Morphinomania is a term used to designate the condition of persons in whom the impulse to use morphin is of the nature of a mania, possessing the mind and dominating every thought, leaving but one supreme desire—to procure morphin and experience the pleasures it gives. Such a person insists on relief at once, and is not contented with anything less.

Usually morphin is taken by the needle, and, like a dipsomaniac among the alcoholics, the impulse of the sufferer to procure narcotism and rest is a veritable mania. Such persons exhibit intermittent nerve storms or periods of great excitement, nervous discomfort, and psychic pain, which may pass away and return again after an interval.

The morphinist is a temporizer. If he cannot procure morphin, he will use spirits or any other narcotic until he secures drug rest. Unlike the morphinist, the morphinomaniac will not be satisfied with anything but the one drug, and that must be had at once. If he cannot procure morphin, opium in any form will be used. The morphinomaniac is often a psychopath from heredity, with a defective neurotic organization, while the morphinist may simply have a poisoned, exhausted organism. The morphinomaniac seldom uses cocain, chloroform, or ether, but the morphinist turns readily to these drugs. The morphinist not infrequently becomes a morphinomaniac. His former secretiveness disappears, and delirium and delusional states appear, often ending in insanity or in death from acute inflammations.

These two classes are not always marked. They frequently merge into each other, making it difficult to distinguish between them. When they can be separated, the prognosis and treatment are more certain.

These forms of morphinism are not confined to one class, but appear in persons of all social ranks. Morphinism is often noted in the prosperous classes, while morphinomaniacs are seen lower down, among the tramps, criminals, and degenerates. The latter class appear frequently in public hospitals and dispensaries, where their addiction is associated with chronic diseases. The use of morphin is considered by most hospital physicians as a moral disorder, hence it is of minor interest to them and rarely excites much attention.

Morphinism is one of the most serious addictions among active brain-workers, professional and business men, teachers, and persons having large cares and responsibilities. There is something very fascinating in the physiologic action of morphin which enables the judge who is nervous and confused, after the use of a single dose to regain his former clearness and self-possession; or for the tired physician suffering from unsteadiness and exhaustion to become strong again.

In this way business and professional men, scholars, teachers, and others, are able to overcome difficulties and to go on with more confidence and clearness after the use of morphin than before. The large army of invalids who suffer from nameless real and imaginary ills find in it a most pleasing nepenthe. The idlers who suffer from ennui and are tired with the monotony of life have a new world opened to them by this drug. No wonder the degenerate, starved, and depressed pauper turns to it for a solace which no other drug can bring.

The relief and temporary narcotism are delusive, from the fact that the latter produces a pathologic condition demanding a repetition of the dose until the disease impulse for more is finally uncontrollable. The morphin hunger is more persistent and difficult to overcome than the desire for alcohol, and far worse in its effect upon the physical and mental organization. The higher the brain culture and development, the more certain and persistent are the disastrous defects produced by it. In all this the concealed degeneration makes it more delusive. The early use of morphin, and sometimes its continued use for years, may exhibit little physical impairment, but in all cases the will and moral forces suffer from the beginning. . . .

In many cases the first use of morphin is followed by great depression, with disturbance of the stomach and general irritation. These unpleasant effects often are easily overcome, and with repeated doses grow less and less and then disappear altogether. . . .

Where morphin acts as a pleasing sedative from the start, there is undoubtedly some peculiarity in the constitution favoring its use. Where it acts as an irritant and stimulant, some repelling power exists, which may be finally overcome by the continuance of the drug. The fact of early sensitiveness to its use is very important in the study and treatment. . . .

The narcotism of morphin is a temporary suspension of brain forces, with defects of cell and nerve energy; degeneration and changes of both functional and organic activity follow. Morphinism is a form of insanity, and the use of the drug leads slowly or rapidly to disease of both the brain and nervous system. The constant narcotism of the higher brain-centers soon impairs their integrity and destroys their normal condition. When the craving for morphin becomes serious and imperative from the withdrawal, the indications are unmistakable of serious and possibly permanent impairment.

In a very large number of cases morphinism may be divided into three stages. . . .

The first stage is that in which the drug is taken for some specific purpose, such as colic . . . . the effects of the drug are often satisfactory, and the relief which follows is complete, with no unpleasant after-effects. The recurrence of these or off similar conditions at intervals is followed by the same pleasing results. . . . It is but a step from its use for relief of physical pain to that for mental and psychic troubles . . . This is the first stage, and may last from a few weeks to several years, during which morphin may be considered only as an excellent remedy to be taken for pain and suffering . . . .

The second stage begins at a point where morphin is used for days and weeks for some specific physical derangement; then for imaginary pains, with the same satisfactory results. Later the increasing dependence upon this drug for the relief of all forms of suffering and pain leads to its continued use, until its abandonment becomes difficult and painful, and often causes much discomfort and distress. The mind during this second stage becomes profoundly convinced of its value. Even when the effort to discontinue it is followed by suffering, the impressions of its value still remain.

Then comes the third stage, in which morphin is used continuously and the attempt to give it up is abandoned because it is accompanied by so much discomfort and suffering. The second stage, like the first, may extend over a long period, but the third stage is unlimited except by treatment.

Document 3
"The Curse of the Cocaine Habit." *The San Francisco Call*
May 5, 1901: 10.

In a lecture before the New York School of Clinical Medicine, Dr. Thomas D. Crothers . . . characterized cocainism as one of the three great scourges of the world, alcoholism and morphinism being the other two.

Custom-house reports, the lecturer said, show an enormous increase recently in the importation of this drug, and not more than one sixtieth part of what is now sold is used for legitimate purposes. The vice of cocainism is spreading alarmingly among the poor as well as the rich, as the drug is becoming cheaper all the time. A one-ounce package, which less than five years ago cost $6, can now be purchased for 75 cents.

One result of this cheapening is that the cocaine habit is becoming common among tramps and paupers as well as business and professional men. It is no longer an aristocratic vice, if it ever was. In New Orleans and other parts of the South and West, the drug is freely bought in 5-cent packages.

Dr. Crothers regards the use of the drug, even as a local anesthetic for surgical purposes, as exceedingly dangerous, especially in cases where the subsequent reaction is characterized by headache, lassitude, and depression. Yet its use in surgery is becoming very common. The lecturer also deprecated the fact that many popular proprietary remedies contain cocaine in large quantities.

It is almost a specific for catarrhal troubles, and though using it as a remedial agent unconsciously many persons, charmed with its speedy and delightful results, become addicted to it habitually, and finally become slaves to its use.

Its first effects in small doses are to create a feeling of elation, of greatly increased mental and physical superiority, and of freedom from care and anxiety. The morphinist finds in it a substitute to relieve the sense of depression following the use of the narcotic. The hard-drinker is charmed with its effects, as his depression yields to a sense of elation and abnormal exaltation.

But in the use of cocaine there follows a sure reaction. In short time there are developed characteristic symptoms of the habitual cocainist. If he be a lawyer, a writer or a clergyman he shows marvelous fluency and prolixity of speech. He has a rare fecundity of words, but they betray a tendency toward circumlocution and irrelevancy. In letter writing he betrays his secret vice by his diffuseness without directness.

"There are novels, which are highly popular to-day," said the lecturer, "which show almost conclusive evidence of having been written under the influence of cocaine, and several poems characterized by marvelous rhythm and smoothness, have had their inspiration in this drug.

"Habitual use of it impaired the judgment and results in the grandiose ideas often associated with paretic disease. One's sense of right and wrong becomes impaired. A man formerly open and frank becomes secretive, selfish and dishonest. A Wall Street authority told me that he knew of three of the most reckless operators of recent years whose losses of fortunes are directly due to impairment of their judgment through the use of cocaine.

"After the abnormal sense of elation and power come delusions. The victim fears sudden attack. He sits up at night watching for burglars. He is fearful of accident and abnormally suspicious of imaginary persecutors. Most victims in this stage carry revolvers.

"One of them came to me in this condition. He was a physician, who had lost his wife and family in the Johnstown flood, and had taken to cocaine to soothe him in his great affliction. He had two revolvers when he told me of the secret. He was rational enough in most matters, but thought he had hidden enemies. I finally persuaded him to surrender his firearms, and the first night he compromised on a stout baseball bat under his pillow. He finally conquered the appetite, but it required years of hard struggling."

Dr. Crothers narrated many similar instances, especially among brain workers. He recommended as the best curative method complete abstinence from the drug, combined with Turkish and electric baths, mineral waters and tonics, judicious restraint, careful and abstemious diet and a long rest. He knows of no specific cure of the habit.

DOCUMENTS 4–6:
THE SPREAD OF ADDICTION AND THE CALL
TO ACTION IN THE LATE-NINETEENTH
AND EARLY-TWENTIETH CENTURIES

As both scientists and the general public became aware of the dangers posed by addictive substances, many began to warn of the spread of addiction and called for the government to take action to check it. In Document 4, Representative White of Kentucky urged Congress to pass a law prohibiting alcohol in Washington, D.C. Reflecting the temperance sentiment of the time, White put forth the argument that alcohol use was widespread, and causing major social harm to increasing numbers of Americans. White framed the call for prohibition in the nation's capital as part of a larger nation-wide trend towards prohibition, saying that it was a serious moral issue, akin to that of abolishing slavery before the Civil War. Citing legislation that certain states and counties across the country had passed prohibiting alcohol, he warned his colleagues that if they did not take similar action, they would be voted out of office. In Documents 5 and 6, journalists described the spread of opium and cocaine use in different parts of the country, warning of the ever-increasing prevalence of the use of these drugs. Anticipating the calls for restrictive legislation against these drugs that would come with the passage of the Harrison Narcotics Act in 1914, these pieces also hint that government intervention to control these substances would be an effective way to combat the spread of addiction.

Document 4
Representative White on Alcoholism
in Washington, D.C. (15 Congressional Record 4225–4227).
Friday, May 16, 1884.

Last year there were 15,607 arrests in the District of Columbia, of which number there were 11,387 arrested for offenses against the person. . . . . For intoxication alone there were 3,752 arrested, and for disorderly conduct 529. . . .

The population of the District of Columbia in 1870 was . . . total 160,744.

It is sad to think that here at the capital of the nation, during the last fiscal year, for every ten persons in the District of Columbia there was one person arrested, and that more than one fourth of the number arrested were under the influence of intoxicating liquor. . . .

When we know, as every intelligent man must know, that the injurious effects from the use as a beverage of intoxicating liquors are universally admitted, and that spirituous liquors are powerful instruments for evil and corruption in our elections, and that the unbridled traffic in spirituous liquors promotes contentions, riots, ignorance, and poverty, and that the iniquity of alcoholism is visited through the parent "upon the third and fourth generations," and that the effects of alcoholism are filling our prisons, houses of correction, and institutions of charity with criminals and sufferers and covering the land with woe and misery, I confess that a feeling of mortification comes over me when I think of the cool manner in which my amendment, offered a few moments ago, to prohibit the manufacture and sale of intoxicating liquors in the District of Columbia, was ruled out on a point of order, and a chuckle of delight was heard to echo through the Hall of this House in the Capitol of the nation.

Mr. Chairman, do you not know that during the last ten years this country has produced the enormous quantity of 740,000,000 gallons of distilled spirits alone, and that all but 70,000,000 gallons of that quantity have been consumed in the United States? Is it any wonder that Hon. William T. Price, in House Report No. 1107, after a most careful investigation of the alcoholic liquor traffic, is led to the following conclusions: . . .

"It is computed that the cost to the consumers of the liquors sold by the 176,776 retail liquor dealers the last fiscal year was about $850,000,000. In an able article in the New York Tribune, September 27 1882, the sum is put down at $800,000,000. The writer says: 'It does no good to sneer at the agitation in regard to the liquor traffic.

The subject is too important to be laughed down.

Aside from the law-defying it has elicited, aside from all its moral and religious aspects, the question, considered purely as one of dollars and cents in its effects upon the national prosperity and wealth, is one of the most important that can be named.

Directly and indirectly this country spends in the liquor traffic every year a sum exceeding half the national debt. The cost to the country of this traffic, direct and indirect, is greater than the profile of all its capital not invested in real estate. It costs every year more than our whole civil service, our Army, our Navy, our Congress, including the river and harbor and the pension bills, our wasteful local governments, and all national, state, county, and local debts, besides all the schools in the country. In fact, this country pays more for liquors than for every function of every kind of government.

How is that question to be put aside with a sneer?'

'There is certainly paid for drink more than $800,000,000 and the entire sum raised by taxes of all kinds. . . .

Among the petitioners for the passage of this bill (for a commission on the alcoholic liquor traffic) the belief is entertained that this enormous traffic is detrimental to the public welfare; that large is the amount of revenue paid to the national Government by the distillers, brewers, and liquor dealers, and the loss is infinitely greater to the tax-payers of this country from the expenditures occasioned by the liquor traffic.

That it is the cause of at least 90 per cent of all the crime existing.

That it is the cause of three-fourths of all the pauperism in the country.

That it causes the existence of 600,000 drunkards.

That 100,000 annually die from the effects.

That 9,338 are annually made insane from the use of intoxicants.

That the number of days' work lost to the country annually by reason of their traffic, at $1 per day, is not less than a quarter of a million of dollars.

That by the laws of heredity the cases of insanity are increasing with terrible rapidity.

That it creates 120,000 widows and orphans annually.

That it causes 50,000 murders annually . . . .

That 100,000 are annually sent to jail for drunkenness.

Are all these charges true?

If you admit their truth, you can not deny that some remedy should be applied, if you desire to see this a happy people or a prosperous nation." . . .

The country looks to Congress to begin reform in the District of Columbia: 350,000 voters in Ohio have taken a firm stand, and the politicians of that State have learned that a Republican candidate for governor can not carry water on both shoulders.

Iowa has taken the lead and shown to the world that the Republican party in that State has gained more strength since it declared for "free homes" against "free saloons," and enforces laws to the effect that "no person shall manufacture, sell, or keep for sale as a beverage any intoxicating liquor whatever, including ale, wine, and beer." . . .

Be it said to the honor of the grand old Commonwealth of Kentucky that before the adjournment of the 12th instant of the General Assembly of that State, by special acts it became "unlawful for any person to sell, directly or indirectly, and spirituous, vinous, or malt liquors, ale, wine, or beer, or a mixture thereof, of either," in Laurel, Rock Castle, Jackson, Owsley, Clay, besides nine other counties in Southeastern Kentucky. . . .

We owe it to the 56,000,000 of people of the United States to have as good government in the District of Columbia as there is in the State of Iowa. We can only do so by closing up the saloons here. . . .

This question, like that of slavery in 1856, is in politics and it is not to be sneered away. It is a live issue. If any man doubts it he will be permitted to become a converted Thomas in the November election. There are no less than 1,000,000 voters in the United States who believe in the principles involved in the prohibition victory in Iowa. They are so distributed from Maine to California, from North Carolina to Oregon, as to make themselves felt in the fall elections, and you may be assured that they are not sleeping.

Document 5

"The Opium Habit: Some Extraordinary Stories of the Extravagant Use of the Drug in Virginia—Correspondence of the Cincinnati Enquirer." *The New York Times*, March 2, 1878: 2.

The opium-eating in this vicinity still goes on; and as some cities and some sections have a reputation for the number of drunkards they generate, so Staunton has the name of being the great opium city of this part of the country. And it is deplorable to observe how the evil has increased. At a conference of druggists, held day before yesterday, it was reported that the increase in 1877 over 1876 was 95 per cent; that 1876 over the preceding year was 64 per cent, and that 1875 over the preceding year was 50 per cent.

The evil is like an epidemic. It is in the atmosphere. It seizes a person, never to let loose. A man sees another using the terrible drug, and before he is aware of it he is eating opium himself. When I telegraphed, three weeks ago, about the sensation that was created here by certain developments, not half had been told. It is true that there have been no deaths equal to that of the lady who dropped dead from disappointment because she could not get her opium but the young man who swalled 15 grains of morphine at a drugstore counter, three or four weeks ago, and lived, took 20 grains at one pop since, and died. He was a young Jew, and had only been a victim to the vice a few years. As I intimated before, the asylums here—the lunatic, inebriate, and others—consume a great deal of morphine in a legitimate way, but what they use is a drop in the bucket.

Nearly 100 pounds of opium a week. That is what the druggists reported, which is pretty heavy for a city of 8,000 or 10,000. A large quantity of the truck sold in Staunton is bought by country people, for the craving for it all down the valley is as strong, if not stronger, than it is in the city. Your correspondent has just visited all of the apothecaries here, and the tales that they tell are fearful. "See that handsomely-dressed English lady passing on the other side of the street?" "Yes." "Well, she is one of our best customers. She commenced to take morphine about two years ago. She used to send a servant for quarter-grain doses; now she uses four grain doses." "Have you many such customers as she is?" asked the writer. "Oh yes. Let me see . . . we have 15 regular lady customers that I think of at this moment, who take over two grains of morphine at a time, and 12 men who take between two and six grain doses at a time." "You think the evil here is on the increase?" "My goodness! Yes." Your correspondent found Mr. Tyree waiting on a bevy of dashing girls. There were four of them, and they seemed to be "sweet sixteens." When they left the store Mr. Tyree said: "There they go; they are some of your opium-eaters." "What! Those pretty things?" "Why yes; they commenced to use the dangerous stuff only a few months ago; now they each spend $6 a week for it. It is sad," he continued, "but there is no stopping them after they once begin it." As Mr. John Benner's I was informed that two of the eight leading ministers of the city used opium; that one of them took it in the shape of laudanum. But the most startling statement made by any of the apothecaries was by on (he requested me not to mention his name) who looked at his prescription list of last year, and found that he had sold 79,593 doses of morphine during the year.

Mr. Forman said to the writer, "You have no idea what means many ladies use to get opium without their families knowing it." "Are most of your opium customers ladies?" I asked. "Yes; I have about 40 regular lady customers, and about 20 or 25 male customers. I have seen married women come to the door and send a servant in with the money; they wouldn't come in themselves for fear they would meet some one who would tell. Sometimes they buy enough at once to last for two or three months. I found one lady buying so much opium that I thought it would be an act of charity to tell her husband. I did tell him, and he said "I know she uses it, but let her have all she wants; I can't stop her." Mr. Forman continued: "I collected a bill of $125 of a prominent citizen a few days ago. It was for opium sold to his wife, who died a month or two ago. I was afraid he would refuse to pay it, but he didn't say a word. He settled without grumbling." The prescription clerk at Wayt & Brother's said that one of their customers was a young lawyer who drank a quart of laudanum a week.

Another was a book-keeper who drank a gallon of laudanum in three weeks. I called upon Dr. B. P. Reese at his office. He is . . . one of our leading physicians. He told me that he had been trying to get some legislation passed on opium for over a year. The member from this district had promised to prepare a bill for the House of Delegates, levying a heavy tax on opium, but he had not yet presented it. Dr. Reese thought the druggists were wrong to sell opium. He said he never prescribed it except in very exceptional cases. Dr. Murphy thought the bell-punch used in bar-rooms, which levies a tax of 2½ cents a drink, had driven many poor people to use opium. Dr. Dilkes attributed the spread of the opium evil to the fact that all of the pulmonic remedies contain a large share of opium.

Dr. Taylor agreed with the druggist that the evil was on the increase not only in Staunton, but all along the valley. He thought the preachers ought to preach against it. "But then," he observed, "one of the parsons himself uses opium to excess." All the junk-dealers and pawnbrokers have much to tell. "I believe she would sell the last rag off'n her back," said old Lloyd, "but what she would have opium." This remark was addressed to a small, ragged child who had just brought the junk-dealer a nice shawl. It seems that the girl was a frequent visitor at Lloyd's, and came to sell things for a lady who was once wealthy, but who had been reduced to penury by her extravagant craving for opium. The junk-dealer said that she used to send silk dresses to the pawnbrokers, but now she had come down to selling things the pawnbrokers would not take. Isaac Harris, a pawnbroker, told the writer that most of his watches had been left by young gentlemen who were well-known opium-eaters.

"Something must be done," said Mr. Markland, an elder of the church. "The evil is one of the saddest I ever beheld. The church doesn't seem to be any safeguard, for I believe that half of the church members in town are addicted to the deplorable habit in question." At the meeting of citizens held some days a go a resolution was passed requiring druggists not to sell opium unless on a doctor's prescription, but the druggists said they would have to sell it unless there was some law passed against it.

Harrisonburg is a small city down the valley. The evil is as great in proportion to the size of the place as it is here. Mr. Baker, one of the druggists of the town, was in Staunton a day or two ago, and in conversation with the writer remarked: "I don't believe there are 20 people in Harrisonburg who are free from the use of opium. Harrisonburg used to be a great place for bar-rooms, but now I believe the apothecaries beat them." The reports from Woodstock, a town in the valley, 50 miles from Staunton, give similar accounts. Dr. Hanson, a well-known M.D., says that he believes there is something in the morphine of the Shenandoah Valley that creates the craving for the evil drug. Mr. Albert Rogers, who lives at Winchester, says that the farmers in his vicinity have recently become terribly addicted to opium eating. He says there were three Yankees who removed to the Winchester neighborhood. About a year ago they went to farming. Neither of them had ever tasted opium. Now they each eat a pound a month. There is no telling when this evil will end. The general feeling seems to be that the only way to stop it is to force legislation. Opium ought not to be allowed to come into the valley. But the trouble is that so many people use it that it will be a hard matter to find enough with clean skirts to carry public sentiment against it.

Document 6

"Negro Cocaine Fiends: The Use of the Drug Has Now Spread to the Cotton Plantations." *Richmond Dispatch,* November 16, 1902: 14.

It has been learned that cocaine, as well as whiskey, was peddled by whiskey pirate-ship Hazel, whose skipper, Captain Hull, was recently arrested on the Mississippi River, charged with shooting the Sheriff and other citizens of Chicot County, Ark. In his defense, Hull explains that he did not introduce cocaine among the negroes of the Yazoo Delta, but merely did what a great many planters are doing—supplied the demand for it.

The cocaine habit began among the negro roustabouts of New Orleans, who found that the drug enabled them to perform more easily the extraordinarily severe work of loading and unloading steamboats at which, perhaps, for seventy hours at a stretch, they have to work, without sleep or rest, in rain, in cold, and in heat. The pay is high ... but the work is impossible without a stimulant.

Whiskey, while protecting the negro against the rain and cold, did not give him the endurance against fatigue that was needed. Cocaine proved to be the very stimulant needed.

Under its influence the strength and vigor of the laborer is temporarily increased, and he becomes impervious to the extremes of heat and cold. But cocaine is filling the insane asylums with wrecks.

From the roustabouts the cocaine habit spreads to the levee camps along the Mississippi, where the work is hard and the conditions of life and work unfavorable. Finally it reaches the plantation hand and here it got the same footing.

While the work on the cotton plantation is not so hard as levee building or loading steamboats, still at the cotton-picking season it calls for extraordinarily long hours. As there is never enough labor to pick all the cotton it is to the interest of the planters to have the negroes work as much extra time as possible.

The planters, therefore, hold out every encouragement to the negro hands to put in a big day's work. The negroes found that the drug enabled them to work longer and make more money, and so they took it.

Its use has grown steadily. On many of the Yazoo plantations this year the negroes refused to work unless they could be assured that there was some place in the neighborhood where they could get cocaine and one big planter is reported to keep the drug in stock among the plantation supplies and issue regular rations of cocaine just as he was accustomed in the past to issue rations of whiskey.

Cocaine has not been in use on the river plantations long enough to do the harm it has done in New Orleans, but the problem is looming up as an important one. In the mean while the efforts to prevent the spread of the cocaine habit in New Orleans and other southern cities have been quite successful. It has been found impossible to cure the cocaine fiends who are fast drifting to the insane asylums, killing themselves, or being killed, but it has been found possible to stop the future sale of cocaine in the drugstores and to keep the younger negroes from taking up the habit.

The negroes themselves have been very active in this movement, and the police have shown so much energy that the public sale of the drug has almost ceased in New Orleans.

A crusade against the use of the drug has begun in most of the towns, but as yet no effort has been made to prevent its sale in the country districts.

DOCUMENT 7:
PROVING COCA-COLA IS HARMLESS

Before the passage of the Pure Food and Drug Act in 1906, fears of alcohol and drugs being ingredients in medicines and beverages were prevalent. One new popular beverage, Coca-Cola, had originally contained cocaine as an ingredient, though by 1905 it had been removed from its formula, thus making it a true "soft drink." In Document 7, the Adair County News *of Columbia, Kentucky ran a piece that assured the public Coca-Cola contained neither alcohol nor cocaine, and that it was a good, temperance-friendly alternative to alcoholic beverages. The fact that such a piece was published highlights the public's desire to know what contained harmful substances and what did not, even before the passage of the Pure Food and Drug Act.*

Document 7
"Coca-Cola Is Harmless: Results of an Investigation Made by Authorities, A Harmless Beverage." *The Adair County News* (Columbia, KY) September 27, 1905: 2.

The past few years have seen a remarkable growth in temperance convictions in all parts of the United States. There has also been a remarkable diminution in the consumption of spirituous liquors. While these two facts are related to each other, in other words, the growth of temperance accounts in part for the diminution of the liquor traffic, there has been a powerful auxiliary to temperance in the very refreshing beverages that have experienced such wide popularity in recent years. None of them has become so famous as Coca-Cola, which was manufactured originally in Atlanta, Ga., but is now made by the same parent company, not only in Atlanta, but in Philadelphia, Chicago, Dallas, and Los Angeles. . . . Largely on account of the increasing use of Coca-Cola, a perfectly harmless beverage, the soda fountain has supplanted the saloon in many places. But let us see what these analyses of authorized and disinterested experts reveal as to the merits and alleged demerits of Coca-Cola. Here they are:

First is a letter . . . by the chief of the U.S. Government Bureau of Chemistry, in the Department of Agriculture, which is in response to an inquiry as to whether Coca-Cola contains cocaine or any other harmful ingredients. Mr. Wiley, the chief, replied that while he had never examined Coca-Cola, it had been the subject of analysis by different Food Commissioners, and according to their reports, they were, none of them, able to demonstrate the presence of cocaine. . . . The Food Commission to which Chief Wiley refers are those appointed by the several States to guard the people against injurious food and drinks. Every report that has been made by these commissions so far as we can learn, has been highly favorable to Coca-Cola. A characteristic one is that from the State of Georgia, which is given herewith, because Georgia is the original home of this preparation:

John M. McCandles, State Chemist . . . "Gentlemen: Referring to your recent inquiry. . . . In the matter of Coca-Cola, there was a bill introduced in the last Legislature imposing a tax upon all the soda-water syrups, and I believe it was amended to put a still higher tax upon Coca-Cola than upon any other syrup, because of its supposed injurious character. I analyzed a sample of Coca-Cola I bought in the open market, and tested carefully for cocaine, and also for morphine, neither of which were present. I found 1.37 grains of caffeine per fluid ounce of the Coca-Cola syrup, and calculated that this amount was considerably less than would be found in a cup of coffee. . . . My final judgment about the matter was that there was nothing more injurious in Coca-Cola than would be found in tea or coffee."

Quite as conclusive as the report of the State Commissions is that of Dr. Louis Shaefer, President of the Shaefer Alkaloid Works . . . . large manufacturers of cocaine, caffeine, strychnine, and other alkaloids: "I made . . . a thorough analysis of the obtained syrup, using the best knowledge of my long experience in the chemistry of Alkaloids, to isolate the Alkaloids of the sample. I found that the sample contained a small percentage of Caffeine, which is the Alkaloid of Cola Nuts, and which also exists in large quantities in tea leaves and coffee beans. Outside of Caffeine, I could not isolate any other Alkaloids. . . . I especially directed my efforts to the detection of Cocaine. For this purpose I made repeated fractional examinations of the Total Aklaloid obtained from the syrup. I narrowed the fractions which should contain all the Cocaine of the sample, if there were any present, repeatedly down, to find in each case, that not a trace of Cocaine, which has been pronounced characteristic, could be detected. The above experiments prove to me conclusively that the Coca-Cola Syrup, as sold by the Coca-Cola Company, does not contain a trace of Cocaine." . . .

In view of the many false and perhaps malicious reports that were current concerning the presence of Cocaine in Coca-Cola, Dr. B.H. Warren, the Dairy and Food Commissioner of the State, caused an analysis to be made of the syrup by chemists appointed by the authority of law, to perform such duties for the dairy and food commissions . . . obtained a sample of Coca-Cola . . . and reported as a result of careful analysis: "No cocaine detected. . . . "

Finally, to answer every question which might be inspired by ignorance, prejudice, or malice, we might ask: Is Coca-Cola intoxicating? It positively is not. Does Coca-Cola contain alcohol? It certainly does not. Does Coca-Cola contain cocaine? It certainly does not. In view of the above facts, supported incontestably by an expert analysis and testimony, the makers of Coca-Cola cordially recommend it to the pubic who wish a delightful, invigorating, refreshing beverage, and who wish to see that beverage supplant the harmful, intoxicating, inebriating liquors that contribute so much to the world's misery. It is in view of the above that such reputable papers as the

"Saturday Evening Post," the "Christian Herald" and "The Ram's Horn" and many others which are notably strict in respect to their advertising columns, have given large publicity to Coca-Cola, believing that in so doing they are not only benefiting themselves in a business way, but are benefiting the public decidedly by helping to introduce a beverage in place of wine, beer, and whiskey, which is scarcely less stimulating, but is far more beneficial.

DOCUMENT 8:
SMUGGLING DRUGS AFTER THE SMOKING OPIUM EXCLUSION ACT

In 1909, Congress enacted the Smoking Opium Exclusion Act, prohibiting the importation of opium that was prepared for smoking. Legislation did not, however, curb demand, and within months of the law taking hold, opium smuggling from China to the West Coast of the United States became common. As Document 8, an article from The San Francisco Call, *shows, the illicit traffic in narcotics became increasingly organized, and at times violent, shortly after the Smoking Opium Exclusion Act took effect. Thus, even before the Harrison Narcotics Act of 1914 and the Volstead Act, it became apparent that legislation designed to limit the use and transport of psychoactive substances would create new, unintended challenges—a growing black market for the drugs that legislation was designed to control.*

Document 8
Lindsay Campbell, "Foiling the Opium Smugglers."
The San Francisco Call, January 23, 1910: 3.

A five tael tin of opium is about the same size and shape as a deck of playing cards. The difference between its cost in Shanghai and its selling value in San Francisco is about $20. It can be bought in Shanghai as easily as a bunch of flowers can be purchased in San Francisco and may be sold here, at the aforementioned profit, as easily as it can be bought in Shanghai. A deck of cards, or even two or three decks, may be so disposed about the person that its bulk will attract no attention, even if the person whose attention is undesirable may be specially detailed by the government of the United States to detect and investigate all irregular bumps and knolls in the raiment of those who pass before him. What is true of cards is true of opium, and with the additional incentive of that $20 profit, the operation of stowing contraband becomes an art.

It is because it seems so easy and is so profitable that the smuggling of opium into this country from the orient has developed into a steady business in which there are so many engaged that the total amount brought in is large, even if the efforts of the individual smugglers are limited to a few tins at a time.

Opium was never worth so much in this country as it is now, and the price here is steadily soaring. The cost in Shanghai remains about the same. Every advance here means that much more profit for the smuggler. Increased profit incites the smuggler to greater effort and calls for extra vigilance on the part of customs officials.

The United States recently joined with other powers in an effort to wipe out the practice of smoking opium. America's contribution to this international program of reform was the passage of a law forbidding the importation into this country of opium prepared for smoking. To make the law effective Congress provided severe penalties for those found guilty of breaking it, and further to aid in the work of suppression decreed that the mere having smuggled opium in one's possession should constitute a felony.

There was a large quantity of opium here in bond and more on the way to this country when the law was passed, and as laws may not work backward the importers were allowed to pay the duty and take the drug. This stock of legally imported opium is rapidly diminishing. Every pipe of it that is converted into dreams increases the value of the unsmoked residue, as, when it is gone, nobody may legally have any more. The only opium then on the market will be smuggled opium, and as handling that will be as risky an undertaking for the man who sells as for the man who buys, hitting the pipe in a few months is going to be an expensive luxury.

Theoretically, there will be no more opium. The opium smoker, however, values his dreams more than either money or liberty, and as long as that is the case there will be men prepared, at a price, to let him dream again.

In the past there have been rings well organized that handled contraband opium on a large scale. In those days, however, there was no law against its importation in the regular way, and large quantities could be placed on the market without attracting too much attention. In those days, moreover, opium factories were running full blast in British Columbia. There was plenty of it, and the means of getting it here were innumerable.

Now, however, the only opium manufactured is turned out in the orient, British Columbia having closed down its factories in accordance with an agreement made at the International opium conference. This narrows the channel by which the forbidden drug can reach this country, and in a measure simplifies the task of preventing its importation. Clever as the old coast smugglers were, and daring, they were children and bunglers compared with the oriental innocents upon whom the higher up smugglers now depend almost entirely for their supply of contraband.

All the liners running between here and the orient carry Asiatic crews. Of every 100 of these Chinese firemen, sailors and cabin boys 99 are natural born traders, who have taken the job at a fraction of a white man's wage largely for what they can make on the side. Some of them run gambling games, by means of which they acquire a large percentage of their shipmates' wages and with which they not seldom pluck a sportive passenger who is tempted to buck the almond eyed tiger because it looks so easy. Others execute commissions on both sides of the Pacific for clients on the opposite shore and practically every one of them carries on a steady traffic in opium to provide the capital for carrying on his other enterprise.

This is how the game is worked today. The head smuggler is usually a white man possessed of means and sufficient political influence to help him out of any scrape into which his illicit business may lead him. His aids he finds in the ranks of the stevedores and others whose work gives them the liberty of the oriental liners' gangways. There are, of course, many stevedores whose respect for the law would not allow them to lend themselves to this kind of industry, but there are others, and enough of them to carry out the head smuggler's scheme, who are more than willing to take a little risk for the sake of making a little easy money. Furthermore, many of them look upon smuggling as an almost legitimate form of sport, and there are men on the Pacific Mail wharf today who could be trusted with uncounted gold, but who think no more of hiding a tin of opium in their shirt bosom and bringing it ashore than they do of quitting work when the 12 o'clock whistle blows.

The Chinese on the ships, although willing enough to engage in the opium traffic, are not prepared to use their own money. The head smuggler must pay cash in advance, and with his money, received in San Francisco, the Chinese buys the opium in Shanghai. If anything goes wrong, and there are more slips between the factory in Shanghai and the pipe in Chinatown than between the cup and the lip, the loss falls on the man here who advanced the money.

Very few of the Chinese members of the steamship crews are allowed ashore at this port, and as the head smuggler does not dare to make himself too conspicuous, he intrusts [sic] his money to his allies among the stevedores, who, in the course of their work, find ample opportunity to turn it over to Ah Fat or Bum Gee or any other Celestial.

There are nearly 200 of these Chinese on some of the big ships. No one of them is asked to bring more than a few tins, as, by dividing the transaction among many, the chance of a total loss is materially reduced.

When the ship returns each stevedore looks up the Celestial to whom he intrusted [sic] the smuggler's gold. If the customs searchers have not found the heathen's cache the slant eyed trader watches his opportunities and slips the opium, perhaps only a tin a day, to the white confederate, who tucks it away about his person, where it will be least conspicuous. When quitting time comes the longshoreman leave ship and wharf, and before they return the dope has all been assembled in custody of the head smuggler, who has ways of his own for getting the drug into Chinatown, where he receives gold for it.

To search every man who leaves a big liner in the course of a day would be impracticable. During the stay in port between the hours of 7 o'clock in the morning and 5 o'clock in the afternoon there is a steady stream of hustling humanity passing up and down a dozen gangways. Inspectors are so stationed that they command a view of every gangway and every man whose dress or demeanor excites the least suspicion is halted and searched. An experienced smuggler, however, takes mighty good care that his dress tells no tales and that his demeanor, if it expresses anything, speaks the utmost indifference for the eagle eyes that he knows are scanning his face and searching the lines of his raiment.

The offshore side of the steamer is also carefully watched day and night, but the greatest reliance in the task of preventing the illegal landing of opium is placed upon the government searching force, made up of picked officers, men familiar with every nook and corner of the big liners and experienced in the curves, both physical and psychological, of the smuggling game.

The work of these searchers begins when the liner anchors in quarantine and does not finish until the gangway is hauled down on sailing day. One or more of the searchers are always among the last to leave the ship.

Searching a liner is one of the most disagreeable tasks that falls to the lot of a customs officer, and one to which only experienced men are detailed. It is dirty work and dangerous, for, although no inspector has ever lost his life while so engaged, attempts to maim or kill them have been frequently made, and that they were unsuccessful has been due largely to their own vigilance.

Clad in overalls and armed with a long steel probe, a bullseye lantern or an electric torch, according to the part of the ship to be explored, the searchers tackle their job while the ship is still anchored in quarantine. They always work in pairs for reasons that will appear later. When a new liner is placed in commission the searchers are among the first to get copies of the ship's plans, a study of which is a help in revealing possible hiding places for opium or other contraband. . . .

The search extends to all parts of the ship. The captain's cabin is no more exempt than is the inside of the planoia. Down in the bilges where Stygian darkness hides the liquid source of evil odors is a favorite place for hiding the precious five tael tins of poppy product and packages of it have been found in the crow's nest. The lifeboats, tightly laced in their canvas covers, are always under suspicion. In each boat is a locker in which is stored the food that the law requires to be carried for use in case of emergency. By throwing the canned goods and hard tack overboard the smugglers makes room in one of these lockers for quite a stock of opium. On a big liner there are many boats and each boat contains half a dozen possible hiding places for dope.

The steam laundry of a modern liner is a veritable maze of hiding places, but does not offer anything like the obstacles to a search that are encountered in the engine room, fireroom or forecastles.

John Chinaman must have his joss with him at sea as on land and each watch, both firemen and sailors, on a China liner maintains its little temple. This means four shrines, in each which sits an ugly little god. Before each god burns an oil lamp, to replenish which at every change of the watch is the religiously observed duty of the No. 1 man. Sacreligious custom house searchers make regular raids on these shrines and more than once the wooden god has been found to owe an apparent increase in stature to a temporary base of opium.

The entrance to many of the dark places below decks is merely a manhole. Three searchers squeezed their way through one of these a few years ago to search a generous space that the plans showed to exist next to the skin of the ship. Suddenly they detected the odor of ammonia. They managed to get out and found that somebody had opened a vent in one of the ammonia pipes near the manhole. They later found opium in that place and they concluded that the ammonia episode was not an accident and ever after the searchers work in pairs and when one squeezes himself into one of these dark places the other stands guard at the entrance.

Searchers working below have found heavy weights mysteriously falling from above in their vicinity. Steam has been turned on at awkward times. A searcher was once shut up in an ice chest for half an hour and another almost started across the

Pacific a prisoner in the specie room, the door of which had been slammed and locked while he was inside searching for opium.

To add to the difficulties of preventing smuggling by the searching process the enemy is flitting back and forth all the time the inspectors work. These slant eyed conspirators take careful note of what places are searched, and when the searchers double on their own tracks, as they frequently do, they sometimes find opium in a corner that was empty perhaps the day before.

Only a few months ago the oil cans on one of the China liners were found to be filled with opium. To the vent inside the can a pipe extending to the bottom of the can had been soldered. This pipe was filled with oil. The body of the can was filled with opium, which was done by cutting off the bottom and soldering it on again. When the searcher hefted these cans he found them apparently full. To make sure that the contents was oil he unscrewed the cap and inserted his probe. It went to the bottom of the pipe, and an examination of the probe showed that the can contained oil from top to bottom. If one of the Inspectors had not accidentally kicked a can and found the resistance suspiciously solid for a liquid opium might still be coming across the Pacific in Standard oil packages.

Two inspectors were scuffling one day at the saloon entrance on one of the Oriental and Oceanic liners. One of the men fell and struck with his head against what should have been a solid mahogany newel post. The post gave forth a sound like a drum, and the investigation that followed showed that the post had been hollowed out. For what purpose was evident from the fact that a dozen tins of opium were found in the interior.

On one steamer that has done its share of smuggling was found a space between the back of the coal bunkers and the outside skin of the ship. In the side of the ship was a small port that was never used for legitimate purposes. As this port showed on the plan the searchers decided to look it up. They had to excavate a drift over the top of the coal, but it was worth the labor, for in the cavity they found a big consignment of opium and the gear used in getting it ashore.

To land opium via this port it was necessary to have a confederate in a small boat under the wharf. At night time the port was opened and a thin line lowered into the water. The man in the boat carried this line under the wharf and, when he had moored his boat, signaled and then hauled away. To the light line was attached a heavier one and in a few minutes there was rigged a regular life line, over which, by means of some sort of breeches buoy attachment, the opium was trolleyed from the ship to the small boat. They were never caught at this, but the gear found with the opium told the story with graphic eloquence.

Two Chinese recently walked ashore from one of the big Maru liners. One of them carried a suitcase that appeared to be heavy. A customs inspector was on the wharf and when he attempted to search the Celestials the one who had no suitcase protested. The protest was overruled. When it came the turn of the man with the suitcase he submitted with a smile. In his case the search was perfunctory, intentionally so for the benefit of the one who had protested, and further to impress the reluctant Chinese the inspector waved his hand and said "That's all right," when the willing one bent down as if to open the suitcase.

Ten minutes later these two Celestials met a member of the searching force about half a mile from the dock. He halted the pair and made them open the suitcase.

It was filled with five talel tins of opium which they were taking to Chinatown to convert into $20 gold pieces. . . .

When the Korea was last in port the customs searching force swooped down on the Pacific Mail wharf and searched every stevedore as he left the wharf at the end of his day's work. Only one was found who had opium concealed about him, but as he was closely related to a man whose interest in smuggling is suspected of being more than platonic the cache was considered important. The opium was in a stocking which was tied around his thigh. When it was taken away from him he boasted that at the noon hour he had succeeded in taking off two tins.

The efforts of the searchers were richly rewarded a few days ago on the liner Siberia, where opium was found in the piano, in the siren, in the walls of the sand locker, hidden among the holy stones in the chain locker, substituted for cork in the life preservers and in the cook's grease can. It was found under the seats in the smoking room and a card table in the dining saloon yielded six tins. In two days the inspectors found on board the Siberia more than $6,000 worth of dope.

DOCUMENTS 9–10:
THE FEDERAL GOVERNMENT ACTS AGAINST
ALCOHOL AND NARCOTICS

In the 1910s, the advocates who pushed for the federal government to take action against drug and alcohol use got their wish. In 1914, the federal government passed the Harrison Narcotics Act, which severely limited the availability of opiates and cocaine. Later in the decade, the Volstead Act ushered in the era of alcohol prohibition. Though alcohol prohibition was short-lived, lasting only until 1933, the drug control mechanisms set up by the Harrison Act endured until the 1970s, when the nation's drug control legislation was overhauled. In Document 9, a reporter described some of the evidence seen by the Ways and Means Committee as it deliberated the legislation that would eventually become the Harrison Act. It is worth noting that the testimony heard by the committee played upon racial fears—linking opium use with Chinese minorities, and drug use in general with crimes committed by Blacks. In Document 10, Congressman Melville-Clyde Kelly of Pennsylvania framed the fight against alcohol as a patriotic one for the health and well-being of the nation.

Document 9
"See an Opium Outfit: Payne's Committee Hears Arguments against Narcotics." *The New York Tribune*, December 15, 1910: 4.

Such staid and circumspect members of the Ways and Means Committee as Sereno E. Payne, John Dalzell, Joseph W. Fordney and Oscar W. Underwood learned all the intricacies of "hitting the pipe," viewed an opium outfit and all the accessories of the "dope fiend" at close range today. Not that Mr. Payne and his distinguished associates took a trip to Chinatown, but that Chinatown, figuratively speaking, was brought to the dignified atmosphere of the Ways and Means Committee room.

Dr. Christopher Koch, of Philadelphia, vice-president of the Pennsylvania Board of Pharmacy, who wants the importation of opium and other narcotics restricted, appeared before the committee and gave its members a first hand view of the workings of an opium outfit.

Messrs. Payne, Delzell, and the others viewed Dr. Koch's exhibit with much interest, but no one expressed any desire to take a puff from the "dope pipe." Mr. Payne seemed especially wary.

Dr. Koch brought to the hearing samples of almost every drug that ever induced man to dream. He talked a while and then drove his points home with a practical demonstration of just how opium and other narcotics are sold and used. He declared that the cocaine habit is an essentially American vice, and that almost 50 per cent of the criminal classes are addicted to its use. The majority of the criminal assaults in the South, he said, could be traced to the use of drugs by negroes. The drug habit, he declared, is on the increase and is extending to the professions, especially to doctors, lawyers, and trained nurses. Thirty-five per cent of the Chinese of this country, he added, smoke opium, and the yearly importations amount to 400,000 pounds. He urged legislation that would virtually prohibit the traffic.

Dr. William J. Shieffels, of New York, representing the National Association of Retail Druggists, urged an amendment to the proposed law which would confine the punishment of dealers to those who "knowingly" sell the forbidden narcotics.

Document 10
"Representative Kelly on Alcohol Prohibition."
(58 Congressional Record 2457). Friday, July 11, 1919.

Mr. Chairman, this fight has been going on for generations. It began at the very birth of the Republic, when Dr. Benjamin Rush, chairman of the Committee on Independence in the Continental Congress, published his book on "The Evil Effects of Alcohol." For 143 years the war has raged. Defeated times without number, the forces of sobriety and efficiency and morality have returned to the attack against the liquor traffic.

Every year has seen new recruits added to the forces fighting against that traffic. Scorned and ridiculed at first, these fighters for a sober America at last marshaled an invincible army. They knew that no question is ever finally settled until it is settled right. Little by little they advanced their standards. Where the vanguard rested today the rear camped on the morrow.

During this long struggle the liquor traffic fought without regard to the laws of man or God. It defied its foes with the brazen impudence born of long success. It undertook to control government. It named its own candidates for office. It made cowards of public men. It manipulated the ballot and robbed the ballot box. It purchased newspapers to deceive the people. It sent out paid lecturers to misrepresent the fact. It threatened business men with ruin and boycotted those who had the courage of their convictions. It stepped forward to fight by the side of every commercialized vice which was under fire from an indignant citizenship. It allied itself with the Prussian foe against which America fought in a death grapple.

Then the end came. The people of the United States issued their sovereign decree that the liquor traffic be outlawed. They determined that no compromise was possible. They determined a fundamental solution for a fundamental evil.

By a two-thirds majority of Congress, backed by the ratification of 45 out of 48 States, they spoke their will. They insisted upon putting the liquor business out of Government, the Government out of the liquor business, and the liquor business out of business. (Applause)

Does anyone here mean to say that the people of America did not mean that? Such talk is folly. The people demanded the banishment of the liquor traffic—root and branch. With all their power they said that very thing, and they expect Congress to obey their command.

And still, in the very face of these facts, we are expected to listen to these "constitutional" arguments so volubly expressed on this floor. When I hear these arguments I thank God that I am not a constitutional lawyer. When all other pleas fall, the Constitution is the last refuge of these experts in keeping people from securing what they desire. It is curious to note, also, that they always use the Constitution to shield the robbers, never the robbed: always the exploiters, never the people who are being exploited.

My friends, there is one fundamental principle in the Constitution which these experts overlook. It is that the people's will is the supreme law. . . .

Mr. Chairman, all these camouflage arguments made by advocates of the liquor traffic are useless. The war is won. The liquor traffic was brought to the bar of the American conscience, was given a fair trial, and declared guilty.

The very few days of trial, even under unfavorable conditions, abundantly prove the claims of those who favored the overthrow of King Alcohol. . . .

The last figures that I compiled show that every year in America the sum of $1,373,000,000 for the operation of our machinery to deal with criminals and crime . . . it is easy to see how that immense sum may be cut down to a fraction of its size by the elimination of the evil which makes necessary such expenditures. The fact is that the liquor traffic never has been a revenue producer. It is the most ruinous tax collector Uncle Sam ever had, and thinking Americans have acted on that knowledge.

DOCUMENTS 11–12:
CALLS FOR ADDICTION TO BE TREATED AS A DISEASE

Though alcohol prohibition grew weaker as it wore on, the government's policies against drug use became tougher over time, especially after 1919, when the Supreme

Court ruled that maintenance prescriptions of narcotics were not permissible under the Harrison Narcotics Act. In Document 11, Dr. Ernest S. Bishop argued that addiction should be treated as a disease, and not just as a law-and-order problem. In spite of calls for change, federal drug policy became even tougher after World War II, particularly with the passage of the Boggs Act in 1951 and the Narcotic Control Act of 1956. These moves elicited a good amount of criticism, as many began to question the wisdom of treating addiction more as a crime and less as a disease. Document 12, an excerpt from Indiana University sociologist Alfred Lindesmith's writings, illustrates some of the arguments against the tough law-and-order approaches that were taken by Congress and officials in the Federal Bureau of Narcotics.

Document 11
Ernest S. Bishop, "Narcotic Drug Addiction: A Public Health Problem." *American Journal of Public Health* 9 (7), July 1919: 481–488.

... Education concerning the material physical facts of addiction-disease is the fundamental essential in arresting further unnecessary spread of narcotic drug addiction, and in repairing as far as possible, the damage already done. ...

Delay in the accomplishment of this education is responsible for much of what seemed to be erroneous and unfortunate in legislation and administration, and has left us today after years of effort along with other lines, with practically no competent nor adequate facilities for instruction or treatment, nor common ground of authoritatively established and generally appreciated fact as a basis for competent and intelligent procedure.

As a definite clinical entity of physical disease, addiction is practically untaught in the schools and unappreciated by the average medical man. The medical profession has as a whole ignored the subject as a clinical study or laboratory investigation. ... Very little is widely disseminated of fundamental physiology, pathology, symptomatology, and physical phenomena in this disease of narcotic addiction. ...

It is unfortunate that the attention of the public and even of the scientific professions, has been distracted by and focused upon spectacular manifestations and irresponsible actions exhibited by some of those who are addicted to narcotics, and in whom in most cases the irresponsibility antedated the addiction or was simply a coincident result of environment and circumstances of life and not a characteristic manifestation of narcotic drug use.

Irresponsibility, degeneracy and deterioration are not essential or even characteristic attributes of the narcotic drug addict. They are entirely absent in very large numbers if not a majority of those afflicted with this disease, many of whom, forced to conceal their affliction because of popular conception of this condition and lack of available competent handling of it, occupy positions of highest responsibility, great personal achievement, honor and respect. Some of our greatest and finest and best men and women are unsuspected sufferers from addiction-disease, constantly seeking relief and understanding help, praying for the day when enlightenment shall come, and they if revealed as addicted, shall not be stigmatized as "dope-fiends" and classed with criminals and degenerates to their social, personal, and economic disgrace and detriment. . . .

Lack of knowledge of the disease facts of narcotic addiction is also responsible for the practical absence of widespread provision for humane and intelligent handling, for much of the jeopardy and fear of the medical practitioner towards these cases, and for the existence of conditions resulting in the rapid growth and increase of the worst evils of the present situation.

The worst evils of the narcotic situation are not, as is widely taught, rooted in the inherent depravity and moral weakness of those addicted. They find their origin in opportunity, created by ignorance and neglect and fear, for commercial and other exploitation of the physical suffering resulting from denial of narcotic drugs to one addicted. The many widely advertised and intrinsically unworthy "drug cures" derive their prosperity from the desperate desire of the narcotic addict to be cured of the condition which may at any time cause him intense physical suffering. The worst evil of the narcotic situation in the past few years, and especially since enforcement of restrictive legislation without provisions for education and adequate treatment, is the rapid increase and spread of criminal and underworld and illicit traffic in narcotic drugs. This exists because conditions have been created which make smuggling and street peddling and criminal and illicit traffic tremendously profitable, and it would not exist otherwise. It is simply and plainly the exploitation of human suffering by the supplying to desperate and diseased individuals at any price which may be demanded, one of the necessities of their immediate existence.

Such exploitation would become unprofitable if adequate and humane provisions were available for treatment, and if the average practitioner of medicine was familiar with and knew how to handle addiction-disease, and was encouraged to admit cases to his practice, instead of being in constant uncertainty as to the meaning and possible interpretations and administrations of the laws.

The financial possibilities of commercial exploitation of the sufferings of addiction disease are responsible for the tremendous increase of late of narcotic addiction, of non-medical or non-therapeutic origin, among the youth. . . .

It is this class of youthful addicts that has so alarmingly increased since the enforcement of the various narcotic laws. For this increase, however, the laws themselves are not so much to be blamed as is the totally inadequate meeting of the clinical and therapeutic and educational needs of the situation. There has been practically no organized scientific, medical or public health activity . . . . directed towards the clinical and therapeutic and educational needs of the situation. . . . . .

The bureaus and departments of public health are the best equipped for immediate and competent work of this sort. It is the most useful health education movement and activity today, and as organized effort hitherto the most neglected. In it, and in it alone, lies the foundation for control and remedy of the narcotic drug problem.

Document 12
Alfred Lindesmith, *The Addict and the Law*. Bloomington: Indiana University Press, 1965: vii–x, 17–18, and 269–271.

During the 1930's, the police conception of addiction was relatively rarely challenged and there was little research on matters that pertained to policy. . . . The Federal Bureau of Narcotics felt, at that time, that it had both the drug problem and critics of the Bureau's policies under reasonably effective control. The number of addicts was said to be diminishing steadily, dope rings were being broken up with satisfactory regularity, and there were few complaints about excessive leniency on the part of judges. . . . after the war ended, it appeared to officials that the narcotic problem had dwindled to an almost irreducible minimum. Then came the explosion in the form of rapidly rising arrest rates and a greatly increased involvement of young persons.

The postwar period has been one of bitter controversy as established ways of viewing addiction and handling addicts have been increasingly questioned and sharply challenged on the basis of enlarged experience, increased knowledge, and new conceptions of the problem. The usual spontaneous reaction of ordinary people and of legislators to a deteriorating crime situation is to call for increased punishment. This occurred with respect to narcotics in the United States, with the result that from about 1950 into the 1960's penalties for narcotics offenses at both federal and state levels were increased to an extraordinary extent. These increases were ordinarily asked for by the police and passed by huge majorities in most legislatures. This was generally applauded by the press.

At the same time that penalties were being increased, a dissident movement began to gather strength and to raise fundamental questions challenging the basic conceptions of the program. In increasing numbers, Americans, traveling to Great Britain and other countries where addicts are handled as patients rather than criminals, returned to write articles and books. Comparisons began to be made between alcoholics and opiate addicts; leading magazines and newspapers criticized the police conception of the addict; the image of the addict in television programs and stage productions became that of an unfortunate victim to be pitied and helped rather than prosecuted and imprisoned. . . .

While the use of marihuana is illegal, the use of alcohol is not, even though alcohol produces physical dependence and is addicting in the same sense that heroin is, while marihuana is not an addicting drug. The reader might well ponder what the effects would be if alcohol were handled as heroin is and if all alcoholics were subjected to the treatment accorded opiate addicts. He should also consider how far he would like to have his government authorized to interfere with the obnoxious or undesirable personal habits of its citizens and where the line ought to be drawn dividing matters of public concern from those that are merely personal. How, for example, should cigarette smoking be dealt with? Or barbiturate addiction? Or the excessive use of tranquilizers and amphetamines?

Opiate-type drugs do not directly incite to crime or to irresponsible behavior as alcohol does, for example. They have a sedative, tranquilizing effect and if all other things were equal would probably inhibit rather than encourage crime. The crimes of drug users are overwhelmingly crimes against property committed to secure the means of obtaining drugs. Some addicts are criminals first and drug addicts second, and others are criminals primarily because they are addicts. Both types must, in the United States, almost necessarily raise money by illegal means when they use drugs.

It is difficult to understand the concern of officials and courts to prevent doctors from keeping addicts "comfortable" as though there were something inherently reprehensible in this. The same officials and courts know that drug-using informers working for the government are kept "comfortable" and that addiction is used as leverage to compel addicts to act in the interests of the police. This use of addicts as informers is sometimes called a "dirty business," involving as it does the exploitation of disease, but it is nevertheless sanctioned or at least tolerated by the courts. When the police see to it that an informer is provided with drugs they are not concerned with effecting a cure nor with the addict's welfare. The doctor, on the other hand, finds that the operation of the law prevents him from acting in the interests of an addict patient. It is generally thought to be one of the noble functions of medicine to relieve unnecessary suffering and to keep patients in comfort, and yet the medical man who seeks to apply these principles to drug users is threatened with criminal prosecution.

The withdrawal distress that develops several hours after an addict is deprived of drugs is often a severe and prolonged ordeal that harms the addict's health and sometimes even results in death or in suicide. When the courts tacitly approve of present police practices which cause addicts repeatedly to undergo this experience without medical attention they in effect set up the narcotics detective as a judge and as an executioner, and invite the drug peddler to substitute for the doctor in ministering to the addict. The drug peddler is perhaps the most despised criminal in the United States today, but as the law is presently enforced, he is the only person to whom the addict can go to secure relief from his suffering. The courts appear to have been indifferent to this fact.

Reform of present methods of handling addiction ought to take into consideration a number of objectives concerning which there should be relatively little controversy. . . . The goal of all drug control measures is, in a general way, the enhancement of the common or social good. When we say this, we should keep in mind that the drug addict is a member of society and that drug control measures ought to take his welfare into account.

Concerning the addiction problem as a whole, the following aims would probably be agreed upon as desirable by all parties in the current controversy:

1. Prevention of the spread of addiction and a resultant progressive reduction in the number of addicts.
2. Curing current addicts of their habits insofar as this can be achieved by present techniques or by new ones which may be devised.
3. Elimination of the exploitation of addicts for mercenary gain by smugglers or by anyone else.

4. Reduction to a minimum the crime committed by drug users as a consequence of their habits.

5. Reducing to a minimum the availability of dangerous addicting drugs to all nonaddicts except when needed for medical purposes.

6. Fair and just treatment of addicts in accordance with established legal and ethical precepts taking into account the special peculiarities of their behavior and at the same time preserving their individual dignity and self respect.

Other aims and principles of an effective program which are of a more controversial nature but which are implied by the above are the following:

7. Antinarcotic laws should be so written that addicts do not have to violate them solely because they are addicts.

8. Drug users are admittedly handicapped by their habits but they should nevertheless be encouraged to engage in productive labor even when they are using drugs.

9. Cures should not be imposed upon narcotics victims by force but should be voluntary.

10. Police officers should be prevented from exploiting drug addicts as stool pigeons solely because they are addicts.

11. Heroin and morphine addicts should be handled according to the same principles and moral precepts applied to barbiturate and alcohol addicts because these three forms of addiction are basically the same.

The most effective program for achieving these ends in Western nations seems to be one which gives the drug user regulated access to the medical profession with the physician determining the mode of treatment in accordance with the circumstances of the particular case. Characteristically, this type of program almost invariably involves, wherever it is used, some sort of supervision and regulation of medical practice with regard to addicts by public health officials. Police measures enter the picture only infrequently when medical controls fail . . .

DOCUMENTS 13–15:
THE AMERICAN GOVERNMENT REPORTS ON,
AND ATTEMPTS TO ACT AGAINST,
THE HEALTH HAZARDS OF TOBACCO

In the early 1950s, a number of scientific reports about the health effects of smoking generated substantial concern, both among the American public, which became anxious about its well-being, and amidst the tobacco industry, which worried about the impact to its bottom line. Hill & Knowlton, the famous public relations firm hired by the tobacco companies, was temporarily successful in co-opting the mantle of objective science and quelling Americans' fears about cigarettes through the work of the pseudo-scientific institution it established, the Tobacco Industry Research Committee. Legitimate scientific inquiry into tobacco continued, however, and the Surgeon General's report on smoking and health in 1964 (Document 13) was a landmark publication that consolidated many years of research findings. The report concluded, among other things, that cigarette smoking was a cause of lung and laryngeal cancer in men, a probable cause of lung cancer in women, and the single most important cause of chronic bronchitis. It recommended remedial action, and the following year, Congress mandated that warning labels appear on cigarette packages. Document 14 represents another condensation of decades of science, as Surgeon General C. Everett Koop's 1988 report on nicotine concluded that cigarettes were addicting, that nicotine was a drug that causes addiction, and that the pharmacologic and behavioral processes at work in nicotine addiction were similar to those determining addiction to drugs like heroin or cocaine. Building upon the Surgeon General's findings about nicotine addiction and whistleblower Jeffrey Wigand's revelations about the tobacco industry's manipulation of nicotine levels in cigarettes, the head of the Food and Drug Administration (FDA), David Kessler, boldly announced, in 1996, that his agency would regulate tobacco, since it believed cigarettes were essentially drug-delivery devices. In March 2000, however, the Supreme Court ruled that only Congress— not the FDA—could establish jurisdiction over tobacco. Document 15 reveals a continued interest in granting the FDA regulatory authority over tobacco, a power that may finally be granted in 2009.

Document 13
Advisory Committee to the Surgeon General of the Public Health Services, "Smoking and Health." [Online article retrieved 05/20/09] http://profiles.nlm.nih.gov/NN/B/B/M/Q/_/nnbbmq.pdf.

THE EFFECTS OF SMOKING: PRINCIPAL FINDINGS
Cigarette smoking is associated with a 70 percent increase in the age-specific death rates of males, and to a lesser extent with increased death rates of females. The total number of excess deaths causally related to cigarette smoking in the U.S. population cannot be accurately estimated. In view of the continuing and mounting evidence from many sources, it is the judgment of the Committee that cigarette smoking contributes substantially to mortality from certain specific diseases and to the overall death rate.

LUNG CANCER
Cigarette smoking is causally related to lung cancer in men; the magnitude of the effect of cigarette smoking far outweighs all other factors. The data for women, though less extensive, point in the same direction.

The risk of developing lung cancer increases with duration of smoking and the number of cigarettes smoked per day, and is diminished by discontinuing smoking. In comparison with non-smokers, average male smokers of cigarettes have approximately a 9- to 10-fold risk of developing lung cancer and heavy smokers at least a 20-fold risk.

The risk of developing cancer of the lung for the combined group of pipe smokers, cigar smokers, and pipe and cigar smokers is greater than for non-smokers, but much less than for cigarette smokers.

Cigarette smoking is much more important than occupational exposures in the causation of lung cancer in the general population.

CHRONIC BRONCHITIS AND EMPHYSEMA

Cigarette smoking is the most important of the causes of chronic bronchitis in the United States, and increases the risk of dying from chronic bronchitis and emphysema. A relationship exists between cigarette smoking and emphysema but it has not been established that the relationship is causal. Studies demonstrate that fatalities from this disease are infrequent among non-smokers.

For the bulk of the population of the United States, the relative importance of cigarette smoking as a cause of chronic broncho-pulmonary disease is much greater than atmospheric pollution or occupational exposures.

CARDIOVASCULAR DISEASES

It is established that male cigarette smokers have a higher death rate from coronary artery disease than non-smoking males. Although the causative role of cigarette smoking in deaths from coronary disease is not proven, the Committee considers it more prudent from the public health viewpoint to assume that the established association has causative meaning than to suspend judgment until no uncertainty remains.

Although a causal relationship has not been established, higher mortality of cigarette smokers is associated with many other cardiovascular diseases, including miscellaneous circulatory diseases, other heart diseases, hypertensive heart disease, and general arteriosclerosis.

OTHER CANCER SITES

Pipe smoking appears to be causally related to lip cancer. Cigarette smoking is a significant factor in the causation of cancer of the larynx. The evidence supports the belief that an association exists between tobacco use and cancer of the esophagus, and between cigarette smoking and cancer of the urinary bladder in men, but the data are not adequate to decide whether these relationships are causal. Data on an association between smoking and cancer of the stomach are contradictory and incomplete.

THE TOBACCO HABIT AND NICOTINE

The habitual use of tobacco is related primarily to psychological and social drives, reinforced and perpetuated by the pharmacological actions of nicotine.

Social stimulation appears to play a major role in a young person's early and first experiments with smoking. No scientific evidence supports the popular hypothesis that smoking among adolescents is an expression of rebellion against authority. Individual stress appears to be associated more with fluctuations in the amount of smoking than with the prevalence of smoking. The overwhelming evidence indicates that smoking—its beginning, habituation, and occasional discontinuation—is to a very large extent psychologically and socially determined.

Nicotine is rapidly changed in the body to relatively inactive substances with low toxicity. The chronic toxicity of small doses of nicotine is low in experimental animals. These two facts, when taken in conjunction with the low mortality ratios of pipe and cigar smokers, indicate that the chronic toxicity of nicotine in quantities absorbed from smoking and other methods of tobacco use is very low and probably does not represent an important health hazard.

The significant beneficial effects of smoking occur primarily in the area of mental health, and the habit originates in a search for contentment. Since no means of measuring the quantity of these benefits is apparent, the Committee finds no basis for a judgment which would weigh benefits against hazards of smoking as it may apply to the general population.

THE COMMITTEE'S JUDGMENT IN BRIEF
On the basis of prolonged study and evaluation of many lines of converging evidence, the Committee makes the following judgment: Cigarette smoking is a health hazard of sufficient importance in the United States to warrant appropriate remedial action.

Document 14
Surgeon General, "The Health Consequences of Nicotine Addiction: A Report of the Surgeon General" (1988)
[Online article retrieved 05/20/09] http://profiles.nlm.nih.gov/ NN/B/B/Z/D/_/nnbbzd.pdf.

This Report explores in great detail another specific topic: nicotine addiction. Careful examination of the data makes it clear that cigarettes and other forms of tobacco are addicting. An extensive body of research has shown that nicotine is the drug in tobacco that causes addiction. Moreover, the processes that determine tobacco addiction are similar to those that determine addiction to drugs such as heroin and cocaine.

ACTIONS OF NICOTINE
All tobacco products contain substantial amounts of nicotine. Nicotine is absorbed readily from tobacco smoke in the lungs and from smokeless tobacco in the mouth or nose. Levels of nicotine in the blood are similar in magnitude in people using different forms of tobacco. Once in the blood stream, nicotine is rapidly distributed throughout the body.

Nicotine is a powerful pharmacologic agent that acts in a variety of ways at different sites in the body. After reaching the blood stream, nicotine enters the brain, interacts with specific receptors in brain tissue. and initiates metabolic and electrical activity in the brain. In addition, nicotine causes skeletal muscle relaxation and has cardiovascular and endocrine (i.e., hormonal) effects.

Human and animal studies have shown that nicotine is the agent in tobacco that leads to addiction. The diversity and strength of its actions on the body are consistent with its role in causing addiction.

TOBACCO USE AS AN ADDICTION

Standard definitions of drug addiction have been adopted by various organizations including the World Health Organization and the American Psychiatric Association. Although these definitions are not identical, they have in common several criteria for establishing a drug as addicting.

The central element among all forms of drug addiction is that the user's behavior is largely controlled by a psychoactive substance (i.e., a substance that produces transient alterations in mood that are primarily mediated by effects in the brain). There is often compulsive use of the drug despite damage to the individual or to society, and drug-seeking behavior can take precedence over other important priorities. The drug is "reinforcing"—that is, the pharmacologic activity of the drug is sufficiently rewarding to maintain self-administration. "Tolerance" is another aspect of drug addiction whereby a given dose of a drug produces less effect or increasing doses are required to achieve a specified intensity of response. Physical dependence on the drug can also occur, and is characterized by a withdrawal syndrome that usually accompanies drug abstinence.

After cessation of drug use, there is a strong tendency to relapse.

This Report demonstrates in detail that tobacco use and nicotine in particular meet all these criteria. The evidence for these findings is derived from animal studies as well as human observations. Leading national and international organizations, including the World Health Organization and the American Psychiatric Association, have recognized chronic tobacco use as a drug addiction.

Some people may have difficulty in accepting the notion that tobacco is addicting because it is a legal product. The word "addiction" is strongly associated with illegal drugs such as cocaine and heroin. However, as this Report shows, the processes that determine tobacco addiction are similar to those that determine addiction to other drugs, including illegal drugs.

In addition, some smokers may not believe that tobacco is addicting because of a reluctance to admit that one's behavior is largely controlled by a drug. On the other hand, most smokers admit that they would like to quit but have been unable to do so. Smokers who have repeatedly failed in their attempts to quit probably realize that smoking is more than just a simple habit.

Many smokers have quit on their own ("spontaneous remission") and some smokers smoke only occasionally. However, spontaneous remission and occasional use also occur with the illicit drugs of addiction, and in no way disqualify a drug from being classified as addicting. Most narcotics users, for example, never progress beyond occasional use, and of those who do, approximately 30 percent spontaneously remit. Moreover, it seems plausible that spontaneous remitters are largely those who have either learned to deliver effective treatments to themselves or for whom environmental circumstances have fortuitously changed in such a way as to support drug cessation and abstinence.

TREATMENT

Like other addictions, tobacco use can be effectively treated. A wide variety of behavioral interventions have been used for many years, including aversion procedures (e.g., satiation, rapid smoking), relaxation training, coping skills training, stimulus control, and nicotine fading. In recognition of the important role that nicotine plays in maintaining tobacco use, nicotine replacement therapy is now available. Nicotine polacrilex gum has been shown in controlled trials to relieve withdrawal symptoms. In addition, some (but not all) studies have shown that nicotine gum, as an adjunct to behavioral interventions, increases smoking abstinence rates. In recent years, multicomponent interventions have been applied successfully to the treatment of tobacco addiction.

PUBLIC HEALTH STRATEGIES

The conclusion that cigarettes and other forms of tobacco are addicting has important implications for health professionals, educators, and policy-makers. In treating the tobacco user, health professionals must address the tenacious hold that nicotine has on the body. More effective interventions must be developed to counteract both the psychological and pharmacologic addictions that accompany tobacco use. More research is needed to evaluate how best to treat those with the strongest dependence on the drug. Treatment of tobacco addiction should be more widely available and should be considered at least as favorably by third-party payors as treatment of alcoholism and illicit drug addiction.

The challenge to health professionals is complicated by the array of new nicotine delivery systems that are being developed and introduced in the marketplace. Some of these products are produced by tobacco manufacturers; others may be marketed as devices to aid in smoking cessation. These new products may be more toxic and more addicting than the products currently on the market. New nicotine delivery systems should be evaluated for their toxic and addictive effects; products intended for use in smoking cessation also should be evaluated for efficacy.

Public information campaigns should be developed to increase community awareness of the addictive nature of tobacco use. A health warning on addiction should be rotated with the other warnings now required on cigarette and smokeless tobacco packages and advertisements. Prevention of tobacco use should be included along with prevention of illicit drug use in comprehensive school health education curricula. Many children and adolescents who are experimenting with cigarettes and other forms of tobacco state that they do not intend to use tobacco in later years. They are unaware of, or underestimate, the strength of tobacco addiction. Because this addiction almost always begins during childhood or adolescence, children need to be warned as early as possible, and repeatedly warned through their teenage years, about the dangers of exposing themselves to nicotine.

This Report shows conclusively that cigarettes and other forms of tobacco are addicting in the same sense as are drugs such as heroin and cocaine. Most adults view illegal drugs with scorn and express disapproval (if not outrage) at their sale and use. This Nation has mobilized enormous resources to wage a war on drugs—illicit drugs. We should also give priority to the one addiction that is killing more than 300,000 Americans each year.

We as citizens, in concert with our elected officials, civic leaders, and public health officers, should establish appropriate public policies for how tobacco products are sold and distributed in our society. With the evidence that tobacco is addicting, is it appropriate for tobacco products to be sold through vending machines, which are easily accessible to children? Is it appropriate for free samples of tobacco products to be sent through the mail or distributed on public property, where verification of age is difficult if not impossible? Should the sale of tobacco be treated less seriously than the sale of alcoholic beverages, for which a specific license is required (and revoked for repeated sales to minors)?

In the face of overwhelming evidence that tobacco is addicting, policy-makers should address these questions without delay. To achieve our goal of a smoke-free society, we must give this problem the serious attention it deserves.

Document 15

U.S. Senate, "Hearing 110–100. The Need for FDA Regulation of Tobacco: Hearing of the Committee on Health, Education, Labor, and Pensions" (2007) [Online article accessed 05/20/09] http:// frwebgate.access.gpo.gov/cgi-bin/getdoc.cgi?dbname= 110_senate_hearings&docid=f:33769.pdf.

This hearing focuses on the need for FDA regulation of tobacco products, the most lethal of all consumer products. Used as intended by the companies that manufacture and market them, cigarettes will kill one out of every three smokers. Yet the Federal agency most responsible for protecting the public health is currently powerless to deal with the enormous risks of tobacco use.

Public health experts overwhelmingly believe the passage of S. 625, bipartisan legislation that will at long last give the FDA authority to regulate tobacco products, is the most important action that Congress can take to protect children from this deadly addiction.

If Congress fails to act and smoking continues at its current rate, more than 6 million of today's children will ultimately die from tobacco-induced disease.

Smoking is the No. 1 preventable cause of death in America. Nationally, cigarettes kill well over 400,000 people each year. That's more lives lost than from automobile accidents, alcohol abuse, illegal drugs, AIDS, murders, and suicides combined and Congress cannot continue to ignore a public health crisis of this magnitude.

Giving FDA authority over tobacco products will not make the tragic toll of tobacco use disappear overnight. More than 40 million people are hooked on this highly addictive product and many of them have been unable to quit, despite repeated attempts. However, FDA action can play a major role in breaking the gruesome cycle that seduces millions of teenagers into a lifetime of addiction and premature death.

What can FDA regulation accomplish? It can reduce youth smoking by preventing tobacco advertising that targets children. It can help prevent the sale of tobacco products to minors. It can stop the tobacco industry from continuing to mislead the public about the dangers of smoking. It can help smokers overcome their addiction. It can make tobacco products less toxic and less addictive for those who continue to use them. And, it can prohibit unsubstantiated health claims about supposedly "reduced risk" products.

Regulating the conduct of tobacco companies is as necessary today as it has been in the years past. The facts presented in the Federal Government's landmark lawsuit against the tobacco industry conclusively demonstrate that the misconduct is substantial and ongoing. The decision of the Court states:

> "The evidence in this case clearly establishes that Defendants have not ceased in engaging in unlawful activity . . . Defendants continue to engage in conduct that is materially indistinguishable from their previous actions, activities that continue to this day."

Only strong FDA regulation can force the necessary change in their corporate behavior.

We must deal firmly with tobacco company marketing practices that target children and mislead the public. The tobacco industry currently spends over $15 billion each year to promote its products. Much of that money is spent on ways designed to tempt children to start smoking before they are mature enough to appreciate the enormity of the health risk. The industry knows that nearly 90 percent of smokers begin as children and are addicted by the time they reach adulthood.

If we are serious about reducing youth smoking, the FDA must have the power to prevent industry advertising designed to appeal to children wherever it will be seen by children. This legislation will give FDA the authority to stop tobacco advertising that glamorizes smoking to kids. The FDA's authority must extend to the sale of tobacco products as well to ensure that children under 18 are not able to buy cigarettes.

The tobacco industry has a long dishonorable history of providing misleading information about the health consequences of smoking. The FDA must have clear and unambiguous authority to prevent such misrepresentations in the future. The largest dis-information campaign in the history of the corporate world must end.

The nicotine in cigarettes is highly addictive. Medical experts say that it is as addictive as heroin or cocaine. Yet for decades, while tobacco companies were publicly denying the addictiveness of their products, they were actually chemically manipulating the nicotine in them to make it even more addictive. A newly released analysis by the Harvard School of Public Health demonstrates that cigarette manufacturers are still manipulating nicotine levels. Between 1998 and 2005, they significantly increased the nicotine yield for major brand cigarettes.

FDA must have the power to take the necessary steps to help addicted smokers overcome their addiction and to make the product less toxic for smokers who are unable or unwilling to stop.

This legislation will require manufacturers to submit "reduced risk" products to the FDA for analysis before they can be marketed. No health-related claims will be permitted until they have been verified to the FDA's satisfaction. These safeguards are essential to prevent deceptive industry marketing campaigns, which could lull the public into a false sense of health safety.

Enacting this bill this year is the right thing to do for America's children. They are depending on us. By passing this legislation, we can help them live longer, healthier lives.

DOCUMENT 16:
THE GOVERNMENT TACKLES STEROIDS

Anabolic-androgenic steroids, which had long been used by athletes, became an issue of greater concern in the late 1980s. Canadian sprinter Ben Johnson was famously stripped of his Olympic gold medal in 1988, and in a survey from that same year, 6.6% of American high school seniors admitted to trying steroids. These revelations led Congress, in 1991, to add steroids to the list of Schedule III drugs. The use of performance-enhancing drugs did not disappear, however, and some athletes, such as baseball slugger Mark McGwire, admitted taking muscle-building supplements like androstenedione, which have steroid-like effects on the body but were not covered by the Anabolic Steroid Act of 1990. In an attempt to prevent the use of these "steroid precursors," Congress passed the Anabolic Steroid Control Act of 2004 (Document 16). Despite the passage of this act, performance-enhancing drugs remain a serious issue in the arenas of professional and youth sports.

Document 16

U.S. House of Representatives, "H.R. 3866–U.S. House of Representatives: Anabolic Steroid Control Act of 2004" [Online article accessed 05/20/09] http://frwebgate.access.gpo.gov/cgi-bin/ getdoc.cgi?dbname=108_cong_reports&docid=f:hr461p1.108.pdf.

H.R. 3866, the "Anabolic Steroid Control Act of 2004," will help to prevent the abuse of steroids by professional athletes. It will also address the widespread use of steroids and steroid precursors by college, high school, and even middle school students. Steroid use has been banned in the United States since the passage of the Anabolic Steroids Control Act of 1990. Many athletic organizations conduct testing for steroids, but the illegal use of these substances continues to be a problem among professional athletes.

Additionally, since the ban of these particular products, some individuals have developed new substances that have the same effects on the body as anabolic steroids but are not banned substances. These "steroid precursors" are as dangerous to the body as those banned under the original act. Many health organizations as well as several athletic organizations believe that the list of banned substances should be updated to include such substances.

The legislation would add several new substances to the list of banned substances and provide increased penalties (up to twice the current maximum term of imprisonment, maximum fine, or maximum term of supervised release) for any individual who traffics in steroids within 1,000 feet of an athletic facility. Additionally, the legislation was amended by the Subcommittee on Crime, Terrorism, and Homeland Security to include a requirement that the Department of Health and Human Services and the Department of Justice report to the House and Senate Committees on the Judiciary within 2 years regarding the need to add additional dangerous substances to the list.

BACKGROUND AND NEED FOR THE LEGISLATION
Anabolic-androgenic steroids are man-made substances related to male sex hormones. "Anabolic" refers to muscle-building, and "androgenic" refers to increased masculine characteristics. "Steroids" refers to the class of drugs. There are more than 100 types of these drugs, which are legally available only by prescription, to treat conditions that occur when the body produces abnormally low amounts of testosterone, such as delayed puberty and some types of impotence. They are also prescribed to treat body wasting in patients with AIDS and other diseases that result in the loss of lean muscle mass. Abuse of anabolic steroids, however, can lead to serious health problems, some of which are irreversible. This bill adds steroid precursors to the list of controlled substances based on medical evidence that, once ingested, these products have the same effect on the body as many of the steroids that are currently prohibited for use without a prescription.

Today, athletes and others abuse anabolic steroids to enhance performance and also to improve physical appearance. Anabolic steroids are taken orally or injected, typically in cycles of weeks or months (referred to as "cycling"), rather than continuously. Cycling involves taking multiple doses of steroids over a specific period of time, stopping for a period, and starting again. In addition, users often combine several different types of steroids to maximize their effectiveness while minimizing negative effects (referred to as "stacking").

Some of the consequences of long-term use of steroids include aggression, extreme mood swings, liver tumors, liver cancer, kidney tumors, jaundice, heart attacks, high blood pressure, high cholesterol, severe acne, and trembling. Other side effects may be gender specific such as breast development in men, reduced sperm count, infertility, increased risk of prostate cancer, male-pattern baldness in women, changes in, or cessation of, the menstrual cycle, facial hair growth or deepening of the voice in women. In addition, those who inject steroids, as opposed to oral ingestion or topical use, run the risk of contracting or transmitting HIV or hepatitis.

In a recent high profile case, the United States Department of Justice charged four individuals in the San Francisco area with conspiring to distribute anabolic steroids and other performance enhancing drugs to dozens of athletes from Major League Baseball, the National Football League, and track and field. The criminals are getting smarter about how to evade the law either by marketing prohibited steroids as "nutritional supplements," manufacturing steroids in clandestine labs, or developing new products that have the effects of steroids but are currently not on the list of controlled substances.

Even more problematic than the use of these substances among professional athletes is the message their use sends to our young athletes, particularly adolescent males.

In addition to the other effects outlined above, adolescents who take steroids may face premature skeletal maturation and accelerated puberty changes which may result in stunted growth. The National Institute on Drug Abuse at the National Institute of Health annually assesses drug use among the nation's 8th, 10th, and 12th grade students. Rates for anabolic steroid use in the past year remained stable at under 1.5 percent for students in 8th, 10th, and 12th grades in the early 1990s, then started to rise.

Peak rates of past year use occurred in 2002 for 12th-graders (2.5 percent), in 2000 and 2002 for 10th-graders (2.2 percent), and in 1999 and 2000 for 8th-graders (1.7 percent). In 2003, steroid use by 10th-graders declined significantly to 1.7 percent. The rate among 12th-graders, 2.1 percent, was also down from 2002, but not significantly. Among 8th-graders, 1.4 percent reported steroid use in the past year. Although these numbers show a decline, they are still above the rates of use in the 1990s. Most anabolic steroids users are male, and among male students, past year use of these substances was reported by 1.8 percent of 8th-graders, 2.3 percent of 10th-graders, and 3.2 percent of 12th-graders in 2003.

H.R. 3866, the "Anabolic Steroid Control Act of 2004," was introduced by Representatives Sensenbrenner, Conyers, Sweeney, Osborne, and Berman on March 1, 2004. The bill serves as the House counterpart to S. 2195, bipartisan legislation introduced by Senators Biden and Hatch and endorsed by a broad cross-section of groups representing the medical and sports communities, including the National Football League, Major League Baseball, the U.S. Anti-Doping Agency, the American Medical Association, and the Major League Baseball Players Association.

Many of these same groups have weighed in on H.R. 3866 as well. In fact, in describing their position on this issue, the Major League Baseball Players Association has stated, " ... if Congress chooses to expand the definition of Schedule III anabolic steroids in order to cover certain steroid precursors, we would not only support such a decision but also would automatically expand our testing program, jointly administered with the clubs, to cover such substances."

DOCUMENTS 17–18:
BEYOND SUBSTANCE: BEGINNING TO RECOGNIZE BEHAVIORAL ADDICTIONS

Documents 17 and 18 highlight the move since the 1980s to recognize non-substance-based compulsive behaviors as addictions. In Document 17, researcher Durand F. Jacobs put forth a general theory of addictive behaviors, highlighting how people who are addicted to both psychoactive substances and behaviors experience a common "dissociative state" when indulging in their addictive behaviors. In Document 18, National Institute of Drug Abuse director Nora D. Volkow pointed to affinities between substance abuse and food addiction, and put forth the hope that research into the mechanisms of these behaviors can help scientists better understand not only addiction to psychoactive substances, but also food addiction and obesity.

Document 17

Durand F. Jacobs, "A General Theory of Addictions; Rationale for and Evidence Supporting a New Approach for Understanding and Treating Addictive Behaviors." In Howard J. Shaffer, Sharon A. Stein, Blase Gambino, and Thomas N. Cummings, *Compulsive Gambling: Theory, Research, and Practice.* 1989. Lexington Books: Lexington, MA: 35–36 and 60.

A general theory of addictions is proposed, using the compulsive/pathological gambler as the prototype subject. Addiction is defined as a dependent state acquired over time by a predisposed person in an attempt to relieve a chronic stress condition. Two interacting sets of factors are said to predispose persons to addictions: an abnormal physiological resting state, either hypertensive or hypotensive, and childhood experiences that have produced a deep sense of personal inadequacy and rejection. All addictions are hypothesized to follow a similar three-stage course, (that is, discovery, resistance to change, and exhaustion). After finding support for these propositions in an exploratory study of compulsive gamblers, a matrix design was applied to collect similar information from different kinds of addicts and normals.

As predicted by the general theory, a common dissociative-like state was found to prevail among compulsive gamblers, alcoholics, and compulsive overeaters while indulging in their respective additive behaviors that significantly differentiated them from normative samples of youth and adults who also indulged in the same activities and substances. This condition has been termed an "altered state of identity." A major objective of this line of theory-directed investigation is to develop a screening instrument that will identify high-risk youth so that early intervention may prevent the development of addictive patterns of behavior. . . . These findings may broaden understanding of the motives that drive addictions and thereby supplement current models for diagnosing and treating this general class of behaviors. Optimally, the work reported here will stimulate further research to explore whether dissociative-like reactions are to be found in still more forms of addictive behavior and, if so, how these phenomena seem to be related to other dimensions in this area of study. . . .

One may confidently conclude from this study that addicts of markedly disparate types share a common dissociative-like state that clearly sets them apart from normal groups of adolescents and adults who also indulge in the same types of substances or activities. The findings that addicts reported a significantly higher frequency for experiencing dissociative-like reactions when indulging than did normals may have clinical as well as forensic utility for differentiating addicts from nonaddicts (that is, other excessive indulgers or abusers) who present themselves or are referred by families, employers, or the courts to health professionals for evaluation and treatment.

Further research undoubtedly will explore the incidence and prevalence of dissociative-like reactions among still other types of addicts. These might include assessing the relationships between dissociative reactions and stage or course of an addictive career . . . age and sex distributions among different addict groups . . . sensation seeking . . . . arousal level changes when indulging . . . . a neurological substrata . . . . reducer/augmenter correlates among different kinds of addicts . . . . scores on Twenty Question inventories constructed by self-help groups such as Gamblers Anonymous . . . Alcoholics Anonymous, Narcotics Anonymous, Sex Anonymous, Overeaters Anonymous, and so on.

Meanwhile, the type and extent of dissociative-like experiences associated with a given form of indulgence may serve as clinical "hard signs" for early identification of high-risk adolescents and adults before they become emeshed in an addictive pattern of behavior. The ultimate goal . . . is to augment and encourage systematization of the knowledge base about addictions, so that one day timely interventions can be designed to prevent them.

Document 18
Nora D. Volkow, "NIDA Will Contribute to Obesity Research." NIDA Notes, Volume 21, Number 4 (October 2007) [Online article accessed 04/09/09] http://www.nida.nih.gov/NIDA_notes/NNvol21N4/DirRepVol21N4.html.

The United States has a serious weight problem. Two-thirds of our adults are overweight or obese. The prevalence of overweight among our children has nearly tripled since 1970. The consequences for the Nation's health and economy are grave. Obesity has been shown to decrease overall life expectancy and to increase the risk for cardiovascular disease, type 2 diabetes, and other chronic conditions. Annually, it costs an estimated $117 billion or more in lost productivity and future earnings. To identify new strategies for prevention and treatment, the National Institutes of Health (NIH) has established an Agency-wide obesity task force and research plan NIDA's assignment on the 25-Institute task force represents a natural extension of the Institute's research agenda. Addiction and compulsive eating both involve impaired impulse control and distorted valuation of the rewards to be derived from a certain behavior—i.e., drug-taking or eating. The two conditions have roots in some of the same brain areas and circuits, including the hypothalamus, prefrontal cortex, and limbic system. The knowledge NIDA-funded scientists have developed of how those areas function normally and in the context of drug abuse undoubtedly will have great application to understanding the other compulsive behavior . . . . The hormone orexin appears to foster cravings for both food and drugs . . . Several other NIDA-supported studies are investigating compounds found to be effective in suppressing appetite and food intake. Some of the most promising produce their effects by blocking the brain's cannabinoid receptors, which are targeted by THC, the active ingredient in marijuana (cannabis), a drug with marked effects on appetite. Researchers hope to translate this knowledge into medications for weight control, drug abuse treatment, or both.

FURTHER READING

Acker, Caroline Jean. 2002. *Creating the American Junkie: Addiction Research in the Classic Era of Narcotic Control*. Baltimore: Johns Hopkins University Press.

Acker, Caroline Jean and Sarah W. Tracy, eds. 2004. *Altering American Consciousness: The History of Alcohol and Drug Use in the United States, 1800–2000*. Amherst, MA: University of Massachusetts Press.

Barr, Andrew. 1999. *Drink: A Social History of America*. New York: Carroll & Graf Publishers, Inc.

Belenko, Steven R., ed. 2000. *Drugs and Drug Policy in America: A Documentary History*. Westport, CT: Greenwood Press.

Bennett, E. Gerald and Donna Woolf, eds. 1991. *Substance Abuse: Pharmacologic, Developmental, and Clinical Perspectives*. Albany, NY: Delmar Publishers.

Bewley-Taylor, David R. 1999. *The United States and International Drug Control, 1909–1997*. London: Pinter.

Bickel, Warren K. and Richard J. DeGrandpre, eds. 1996. *Drug Policy and Human Nature: Psychological Perspectives on the Prevention, Management, and Treatment of Illicit Drug Abuse*. New York: Plenum Press.

Blocker, Jr., Jack S., David M. Fahey, and Ian R. Tyrrell, eds. 2003. *Alcohol and Temperance in Modern History: An International Encyclopedia*. Santa Barbara, CA: ABC-CLIO.

Boon, Marcus. 2002. *The Road of Excess: A History of Writers on Drugs*. Cambridge, MA: Harvard University Press.

Booth, Martin. 1996. *Opium: A History*. New York: St. Martin's Griffin.

Brandt, Allan M. 2007. *The Cigarette Century: The Rise, Fall, and Deadly Persistence of the Product That Defined America*. New York: Basic Books.

Burnham, John C. 1993. *Bad Habits: Drinking, Smoking, Taking Drugs, Gambling, Sexual Misbehavior, and Swearing in American History*. New York: New York University Press.

Burns, Eric. 2004. *The Spirits of America: A Social History of America*. Philadelphia: Temple University Press.

Buxton, Julia. 2006. *The Political Economy of Narcotics: Production, Consumption, & Global Markets*. Nova Scotia, Canada: Fernwood Publishing.

Burns, Eric. 2007. *The Smoke of the Gods: A Social History of Tobacco*. Philadelphia: Temple University Press.

Carson-DeWitt, Rosalyn, ed. 2001. *Encyclopedia of Drugs, Alcohol & Addictive Behavior*. New York: Macmillan Reference USA.

Chepesiuk, Ron. 1999. *The War on Drugs: An International Encyclopedia*. Santa Barbara, CA: ABC-CLIO.

Coombs, Robert Holman, ed. 2004. *Handbook of Addictive Disorders: A Practical Guide to Diagnosis and Treatment*. Hoboken, NJ: John Wiley & Sons, Inc.

Cordry, Harold V. 2001. *Tobacco: A Reference Handbook*. Santa Barbara, California: ABC-CLIO.

Courtwright, David T. 2001. *Dark Paradise: A History of Opiate Addiction in America*. Cambridge, MA: Harvard University Press.

Crothers, Thomas D. 1902. *Morphinism and Narcomanias from Other Drugs*. Philadelphia: W.B. Saunders & Company.

Davenport-Hines, Richard. 2001. *The Pursuit of Oblivion: A Global History of Narcotics, 1500–2000*. London: Weidenfeld & Nicolson.

Drug Enforcement Administration. 2008. "DEA History in Depth." http://www.usdoj.gov/dea/history.htm.

Earlywine, Mitch. 2002. *Understanding Marijuana: A New Look at the Scientific Evidence*. Oxford: Oxford University Press.

Edwards, Griffith. 2000. *Alcohol: The Ambiguous Molecule*. London: Penguin Books.

Erickson, Patricia G., Edward M. Adlaf, Reginald G. Smart, and Glenn F. Murray, eds. 1994. *The Steel Drug: Cocaine and Crack in Perspective*. New York: Lexington Books.

Fish, Jefferson M., ed. 2006. *Drugs and Society: U.S. Public Policy*. Lanham, MD: Rowman & Littlefield Publishers, Inc.

Frances, Richard J., Sheldon I. Miller, and Avram H. Mack, eds. 2005. *Clinical Textbook of Addictive Disorders*. New York: Guilford Press.

Goodman, Jordan, ed. 2005. *Tobacco in History and Culture: An Encyclopedia*. Detroit: Thomson Gale.

Gwinnell, Esther and Christine Adamec. 2006. *The Encyclopedia of Addictions and Addictive Behaviors*. New York Facts on File.

Huggins, Laura E., ed. 2005. *Drug War Deadlock: The Policy Battle Continues*. Stanford, CA: Hoover Institution Press.

Inaba, Darryl S. and William E. Cohen. 2000. *Uppers, Downers, All Arounders: Physical and Mental Effects of Psychoactive Drugs*. Medford, OR: CNS Publications.

King, Rufus. 1972. *The Drug Hang-Up: America's Fifty-Year Folly*. Springfield, IL: Bannerstone House.

Klieman, Mark A. R. 1992. *Against Excess: Drug Policy for Results*. United States: Basic Books.

Kranzler, Henry R. and Domenic A. Ciraulo, eds. 2005. *Clinical Manual of Addiction Psychopharmacology*. Washington, D.C.: American Psychiatric Publishing, Inc.

Lender, Mark Edward and James Kirby Martin. 1982. *Drinking in America: A History*. New York: The Free Press.

MacCoun, Robert J. and Peter Reuter. 2001. *Drug War Heresies: Learning from Other Vices, Times & Places*. Cambridge: Cambridge University Press.

Martin, William R. and Harris Isbell, eds. 1978. *Drug Addiction and the U.S. Public Health Service*. Rockville, MD: National Institute on Drug Abuse.

McAllister, William B. 2000. *Drug Diplomacy in the Twentieth Century*. London: Routledge.

Morgan, H. Wayne. 1974. *Yesterday's Addicts: American Society and Drug Abuse, 1865–1920*. Norman, OK: University of Oklahoma Press.

Murdock, Catherine Gilbert. 1998. *Domesticating Drink: Women, Men, and Alcohol in America, 1870–1940*. Baltimore: Johns Hopkins University Press.

Musto, David F., ed. 2002. *Drugs in America: A Documentary History*. New York: New York University Press.

Musto, David F. 1987. *The American Disease: Origins of Narcotic Control*. New York: Oxford University Press.

Parker-Pope, Tara. 2001. *Cigarettes: Anatomy of an Industry from Seed to Smoke*. New York: The New Press.

Parrot, Andrew, Alun Morinan, Mark Moss, and Andrew Scholey. 2004. *Understanding Drugs and Behaviour*. West Sussex, United Kingdom: John Wiley & Sons, Ltd.

Pegram, Thomas P. 1998. *Battling Demon Rum: The Struggle for a Dry America, 1800–1933*. Chicago: Ivan R. Dee.

Rasmussen, Nicolas. 2008. *On Speed: The Many Lives of Amphetamine*. New York: New York University Press.

Ray, Oakley and Charles Ksir. 1993. *Drugs, Society & Human Behavior*. St. Louis: Mosby.

Schuckit, Marc Alan. 2006. *Drug Abuse and Alcohol Abuse: A Clinical Guide to Diagnosis and Treatment*. New York: Springer.

Shaffer, Howard J., Sharon A. Stein, Blase Gambino, and Thomas N. Cummings, eds. 1989. *Compulsive Gambling: Theory, Research, and Practice*. Lexington, MA: Lexington Books.

Sournia, Jean-Charles. 1990. *A History of Alcoholism*. Trans. Nick Hindley and Gareth Stanton. Oxford: Basil Blackwell.

Spillane, Joseph E. 2000. *Cocaine: From Medical Marvel to Modern Menace in the United States*. Baltimore: Johns Hopkins University Press.

Swann, John P. "History of the FDA." [Online article retrieved 05/22/09] http://www.fda.gov/ oc/history/historyoffda/default.htm.

Thombs, Dennis L. 2006. *Introduction to Addictive Behaviors*. Third Edition. New York, Guilford Press.

Thompson, William N. 2001. *Gambling in America: An Encyclopedia of History, Issues, and Society*. Santa Barbara: ABC-CLIO.

Volpicelli, Joseph and Maia Szalavitz. 2000. *Recovery Options: The Complete Guide*. New York: John Wiley & Sons.

Weil, Andrew T. and Winifred Rosen. 1993. *From Chocolate to Morphine: Everything You Need to Know About Mind-Altering Drugs*. Boston: Houghton Mifflin Company.

White, William L. 1998. *Slaying the Dragon: The History of Addiction Treatment and Recovery in America*. Bloomington, IL: Chestnut Health Systems.

Young, Kimberly S. 1998. *Caught In The Net: How to Recognize Internet Addiction—and a Winning Strategy For Recovery*. New York: Wiley.

Zegart, Dan. 2000. *Civil Warriors: The Legal Siege on the Tobacco Industry*. New York: Delacorte Press.

Index

About the Authors

HOWARD PADWA, Ph.D., studied at the University of Delaware, the London School of Economics, and the *Ecole des Hautes Etudes en Sciences Sociales* in Paris before completing his Ph.D. at the University of California, Los Angeles. He currently lives in Los Angeles, where he conducts research on public mental health policy.

JACOB CUNNINGHAM, M.A., studied at the University of California, Santa Cruz, and did his graduate work at the University of California, Los Angeles. He currently resides in Los Angeles, where he teaches history at Hebrew Union College.